Nelson

By the Same Author

Portraits of His Majesty's Ships, *Agamemnon,
Captain, Vanguard, Elephant* and *Victory.*
(21″ × 14″.)

Painted by Nicolas Pocock, 1808, for Messrs. Clarke and
M'Arthur's "Life and Services of Admiral Lord Nelson,"
in which an engraving by James Fittler was reproduced with
the following inscription—" Mr. Pocock has happily succeeded
in giving very accurate likenesses of the several ships in which
Nelson distinguished himself, as Captain, Commodore and
Admiral, and he has grouped them at anchor at Spithead,
having their sails loose to dry. In the background there is
a distant view of Portsmouth."

*Reproduced from the original oil-painting at the National Maritime
Museum, Greenwich, by kind permission of the Trustees, the
National Maritime Museum, Greenwich.*

Nelson

by

CAROLA OMAN

New Introduction
by Stephen Howarth

NAVAL INSTITUTE PRESS
Annapolis, Maryland

Publishing History
Nelson was first published in the USA in 1946 (Doubleday) and in
Great Britain in 1947 (Hodder and Stoughton). The original British
edition is now reproduced complete and unabridged, with the
addition of a new Introduction by Stephen Howarth.

Printed and bound in Great Britain

INTRODUCTION

Carola Oman was born on 11 May 1897. Her father, Sir Charles Oman KBE, was a distinguished historian, author of (among many other books) a seven-volume study of the Peninsular War. As can happen when a parent who enjoys history also has the knack of passing on that pleasure, Carola followed a similar path. In the course of her long life – she died aged 81 years and one month, on 11 June 1978 – she wrote nearly thirty books. Her range was wide: modern novels, historical novels, a volume of poetry, books for children, biographies and an autobiography. But of all those works, this is probably the best.

Carola Oman's *Nelson* first appeared in 1946, in the United States. In contemporary Britain a continuing post-war shortage of woodpulp meant that paper was still severely rationed, and publication there was delayed until 1947. When it finally appeared, it was far from being the first life of Nelson. Pamphlet pen-portraits of the admiral had appeared in his lifetime, followed immediately after his death in 1805 by a flood of 'complete', 'accurate' or 'authentic' biographies, many of which displayed none of those qualities.

The first really authoritative account, by James Clarke and John M'Arthur, came in 1809. Clarke was a royal chaplain; M'Arthur, as former secretary to Admiral Hood, had known Nelson professionally. Using all their many connections and working 'From His Lordship's Manuscripts', they produced a two-volume work – a great book, magisterial and fundamental. Even so, it was limited. It could hardly have been otherwise. In part this was because they were deeply conscious of the sensitivities of Nelson's surviving immediate relatives, and did not wish to give offence. More generally, as happens in every age, they themselves were constrained by the mores and morals of their time. Aspects of Nelson's life which upset other people upset them too. So – although Nelson's passionate affair with Lady Hamilton had been absolutely notorious – when they came to describing the last years of his life, Clarke and M'Arthur practised a form of self-censorship and simply avoided writing about his greatest human love.

The next important Nelson biography came in 1813 from a man

who had no pretensions at all as an historian, naval or otherwise – but Robert Southey was a wonderful poet. In that same year he became Poet Laureate, and though he compounded Clarke and M'Arthur's deliberate errors with some accidental ones of his own, his life of Nelson was not only one of the best written but also one of the most widely read.

Numerous other biographies followed at intervals throughout the nineteenth century. Only a few of these were at all important. Probably the three most beneficial works were the seven-volume *Dispatches and Letters ... with Notes* (compiled by Sir Nicholas Harris Nicolas and published in 1844–46); Sir John Laughton's *Nelson Memorial* of 1896, which made it clear that the Royal Navy of Nelson's generation had contained an unusually large number of other officers with extraordinary talent; and lastly, in 1897, the two-volume *Life of Nelson: The Embodiment of the Sea Power of Great Britain* by the eminent American historian and naval officer Alfred Thayer Mahan.

However, these were by no means all the Nelson biographies written, and in the late 1940s Carola Oman's work could have been seen as only the latest in a line (a long one even then) of volumes about Britain's most famous sea-officer. But *Nelson* was very soon recognised as a biography of prime importance. Reviewing it in *The Daily Telegraph*, Harold Nicolson wrote: 'The proportions of her book are so excellent, her persuasiveness so compelling, that the final portrait emerges, cleaned of the gilt and varnish of legend, but undoubtedly superb. It is a fine book to have written and a fine book to read.' In the *Illustrated London News*, Sir John Squire was equally enthusiastic: 'I can do nothing but admire this colossal work. Miss Oman can write, and she has new material. Hers must be the standard biography to date.' In confirmation of these critics' views, Oman's *Nelson* was awarded the *Sunday Times'* annual prize for English literature in 1948, and it has remained a bedrock account ever since. No one who wants to know about Nelson's life should ignore it, and every subsequent biographer of the admiral is indebted to it.

The biographical line has not ended: every few years, we see another new description of his outstanding life. If other books related to him (catalogues, poems, pamphlets, essays – and they are not all in English) are counted in the calculation, then a current listing by Michael Nash, an expert Nelsonian bibliographer, includes 'well over a thousand titles' on Nelson.

Though most are out of print, nevertheless this startling statistic raises several questions. Why on earth has so much been written about Nelson? Why do people still like to write about him, and to read and talk about him? And (perhaps the most pertinent question here) why, when versions of his life are so abundant, is this facsimile of Oman's original *Nelson* a valuable book?

The answers are actually not hard to find. Taking first the quantity of writing about Nelson, and its continuance – this is not just because Nelson was an outstanding commander, strategist and tactician; so was Wellington, but not half as much has been written about him. Nor is it just that the elements of Nelson's life – drama, endurance, burning love and betrayal, humble beginnings, and death at the moment of supreme victory – present such a perfectly formed story. All those are important, and (as long as the love affair was left out) for the Victorian age they were often enough. But the Victorians' near-idolatry of Nelson and their cult of 'the Hero' now seem grotesque.

Although they were closer to him in time, we can know him better than they did, and can like him for better reasons, more akin to the feelings of his contemporaries. Throughout the fleet the news of his death was greeted with an astonishing, spontaneous outburst of sorrow, and the night before his funeral, his chaplain, the Reverend Doctor Alexander Scott, wrote: 'When I think, setting aside his heroism, what an affectionate, fascinating little fellow he was ... I become stupid with grief for what I have lost.' So did everyone who knew him, whether naval or civilian, as well as an incalculably huge number of people who never met him at all; and strange to say, he still has that effect. Sooner or later, everyone who learns about Nelson succumbs to the unique charm and supreme professionalism of the little admiral, and (if they are frank, as the Navy unashamedly was then) they feel the truth of the chaplain's verdict and the reality of his loss.

Turning to the other question – the value, among so many other biographies, of this facsimile – its answer is simple: the entire canon of Nelson historiography is either pre- or post-Oman. Nor is it hard to justify such a sweeping statement. In brief, Carola Oman had more and better material than anyone who went before her; and she used it so brilliantly that everyone who came after her was bound to be influenced by her work.

In 1905, when she was a little girl of eight, the centenary of Trafalgar was celebrated and Nelson's death commemorated with services and other ceremonies of remembrance throughout the British Empire. The whole of Britain (and especially England) was awash with Nelson memorabilia; but though at least one important past biography was re-issued for the occasion, no significant new one was attempted. Some of the nineteenth-century biographies of Nelson had been such towering achievements that it seemed they could scarcely be improved upon. In particular, Mahan's study took proper profit from its predecessors, and, as the first written by a senior naval officer, was especially perceptive. It was also quite recent; its first edition was (like Carola) only eight years old at the time, and a single-volume second edition was only six years old. Thus, for the very good reason that there appeared to be little new to say about Nelson's life overall, most Nelsonian writers of the next generation (1900–1945) turned their attentions away from his life as a whole and focused instead either on aspects of it (most notably in Sir Julian Corbett's 1910 study of Trafalgar) or on collateral subjects.

The latter category became a varied and valuable one. Two of its most helpful components were a pair of sensitive biographies about the women closest to Nelson's heart: Walter Sichel's *Emma, Lady Hamilton* (1905) and E.M. Keate's *Nelson's Wife* (1939). Among other collateral publications of the period there were *Nelsonian Reminiscences* (1843, re-issued 1905) and *East Anglian Heroes* (1905), the Byam Martin papers (1903) and the Hotham papers (1909), *Coke of Norfolk* (1912), *Nelson in England* (1913), the 3-volume *Wynne Diaries* (1935–40) and *The Admirals Hood* (1941). Whether based on personal knowledge of Nelson or research, all these and others made available much material which nineteenth-century biographers either had not seen or had chosen not to use. Nelson might not be in the spotlight, but for the intelligent student of his career there were many sidelights to be found here.

When Carola Oman began work on this book at the age of forty-five, she had, all told, an unprecedented set of resources to draw upon. She read and absorbed them all. To begin with, of course she had the major nineteenth-century Nelson biographies: Clarke and M'Arthur, Southey, Nicolas, Pettigrew, Jeaffreson, Morrison, Laughton, Mahan. She had the minor biographies too, including the haphazard, the scurrilous, the contentious and the tendentious, and sorted the few grains of wheat from the chaff. Moreover, unlike all these Nelsonian authors, major or minor, she also had the works on collateral subjects which appeared in the first decades of the twentieth century. All of these, though, were published secondary works, available to anyone; if there had been nothing more to it, anyone could have written *Nelson*. But there was more.

Carola Oman had in addition the enviable right of access to many primary sources (particularly Nelson's letters in autograph) which either had never been published or had been editorially abused. The opportunity to go back to the originals – to go mining in the motherlode, so to speak – gave her the chance to check, correct and develop much of what had gone before. Quantities of fool's gold were identified and discarded, and the real thing assessed and assayed. And again, there was more. Although any other equally fortunate and dedicated researcher could have uncovered the same material, it would not follow that they too could have turned their discoveries into a work of art. Lastly, therefore, but by no means least in importance, Carola Oman was not just a miner in the archives; she was also by then an experienced author with considerable artistic skill. Putting all these factors together, she could hardly have failed to produce a masterpiece.

It may be, too, that one further element was influential – one which is so obvious, it is easily overlooked. With the publication of *Nelson*, Carola Oman's status in the canon was at once so firmly established that an elementary fact about her has rarely, if ever before, been taken into consideration. Before her, only two other women, Hilda Gamlin and Clemence Dane, had published anything of significance about Nelson; and neither had written his biography.

Hilda Gamlin wrote five books, including *Emma, Lady Hamilton* (1891) and *Nelson's Friendships* (1899); but she refused to believe that there was anything sexual in the relationship between Nelson and Emma Hamilton, going to extraordinary (and in the absence of any other evidence, very persuasive) lengths to prove that they were 'just good friends'. Clemence Dane, for her part, produced three Nelson works during World War II: a long poem, an anthology of letters derived mainly from Nicolas's edition of a hundred years earlier, and a novel, all three being designed to boost British morale. Under her real name, Winifred Ashton, she wrote many other novels on various subjects, but no biographies.

In short, out of all the great biographers of Nelson, Carola Oman was (and currently still is) the only woman. Though it is impossible to say exactly what effect her feminity had on her approach to the subject, it is equally impossible to suppose it had none; and it is noticeable that Lady Nelson and Lady Hamilton are brought to life by her in a wholly exceptional way. Oman treated both the rivals in love more fairly, with more engagement, more compassion and more understanding, than had any of her predecessors; and if there had been no other value in her work, that in itself would have been a substantial bequest to her successors.

Until she wrote this book, there was no major twentieth-century biography of Nelson. In her foreword she paid tribute to the best of the previous century's biographers – especially to Sir Harris Nicolas, whose work she called 'the Bible of the Nelson student'. Yet after reading *Nelson*, it seemed to some that she had been too modest. Nicolas had not written 'the Bible' entire, but only the Old Testament; and Oman had written the New.

*

The foregoing alone is ample justification for this facsimile of Oman's original. But as with the creation of the work itself, there is something more. Since its first publication, *Nelson* has often been reprinted; yet by no means always in its original form. Given the opportunity for a masterwork, Carola Oman took it in full, and (unlike most subsequent editions of her book) the original contained complete source notes. A doubting or a curious reader could check them for himself or herself; and so can we. Furthermore, the present facsimile text is enhanced by a bound-in page (rather than the original risky and awkward fold-out) of the Nelson family tree, and by a similar page of errata. Oman's original *Nelson* was utterly brilliant, but – she was the first to admit – not perfect, and later editions contained some corrections. Here we have the best of both worlds, and for most of us it is the nearest that we can or need approach to mining the motherlode for ourselves.

Stephen Howarth
Shelton, Nottinghamshire
1996

PREFACE

Nelson Monuments, with the exception of a few, spontaneously erected close upon the news of Trafalgar, were not much liked by his contemporaries, and are to-day revered rather for the man than the manner of commemoration. When, at last, Trafalgar Square was pronounced complete, the result was condemned by Londoners : the gentlest critics complained of sensations of disappointment, and "unworthiness". The Neo-Gothic tower dominating the Calton Hill, Edinburgh, has been several times threatened with demolition.

Something of the same fate has attended the efforts of authors. "The bibliography of Nelson", wrote Sir J. K. Laughton, in 1894, "is enormous, but comparatively little of it has any real value." The first biography of Nelson was published during his life-time, after the battles of the Nile and Copenhagen, and before Trafalgar ; but John Charnock, an enthusiastic naval volunteer, who had a rich source in Captain William Locker, Nelson's old sea-daddy, "improved" original letters and contrived to produce a work of outstanding dullness. A number of ephemeral memoirs of no authority were rushed into print to meet the popular demand upon the death of a hero. In 1809 came something solid. The Rev. James Clarke, Librarian and Chaplain to the Prince of Wales, and John M'Arthur, who had been Secretary to Lord Hood and Sir Hyde Parker, had collaborated before, in the monthly "Naval Chronicle". Both had been afloat in the Royal Service, and M'Arthur, when Purser of the Victory, had often encountered Nelson. They had been generously supplied with material, particularly by the Nelson family. Their list of "Orders received prior to publication", printed in the first of their two handsomely-produced, weighty, illustrated, calf-bound quarto volumes, contains

the names of all who had known Nelson best. As a book
of reference their work falls into the " difficult " category,
as it is unprovided with an index; but no reviewer drew
attention to this in 1809, or to a more serious omission.
The biographers announced that for the last four years
of their hero's life, they had preferred to devote themselves
exclusively to " his more splendid public character". The
authors of " The Life and Services of Horatio, Viscount
Nelson, from his Lordship's MSS." had also to contend
with one more disadvantage than is inevitable in a biography composed with a strict eye to the susceptibilities
of survivors.

The public of their own day accepted the semi-official
biography with docility. Proofs were sent to the widowed
Lady Nelson, to Earl Nelson and his sisters, and, upon her
own request, to Lady Hamilton. A special copy, upon
vellum, was acquired by the British Museum. A second
edition (still un-indexed), in three volumes, followed in 1840.
At a date when no Englishman's home of any pretensions
was complete without a library, it was expected that every
library should contain a copy of the standard life of a national
hero.

Meanwhile, an author who could write had unblush-
ingly " lifted " the undigested material of Messrs. Clarke
and M'Arthur into English literature. The Poet Laureate,
in 1813, added scarcely any information of value, and some
mistakes, but " Southey's Nelson " is one of the tales that
hold children from play and old men from the chimney
corner. (An edition published in 1922, with notes by Sir
Geoffrey Callender, saves the modern reader from accepting
the inaccuracies of 1813.) Another contemporary, James
Harrison, stands, by general consent, lowest in esteem of
Nelson biographers. He was a man of dreadful calling,
a hireling, and his duty, as he understood it, was to produce,
against time, a two-volume biography of Nelson, designed
at all costs to exalt the claims of Lady Hamilton to a Government pension. The result, published in 1806, has been

described by David Hannay, a severe critic, as " one of the most nauseous of known books ", and it has always been so much resented for its insincerity that the fact that it contains a little information obtainable nowhere else is usually overlooked.

In 1814, having stolen the originals from a patroness who had no more to give, Harrison printed, anonymously, "The Letters of Lord Nelson to Lady Hamilton", which had a succès de scandale, was denounced as a forgery by many of the hero's admirers, and gave a tottering woman the last shove towards a premature grave. The stolen originals have never come to light, but they certainly passed en bloc into the possession of Dr. James Pettigrew, and were used by him in 1849 for yet another two-volume biography. As Pettigrew offered no explanation of his ownership of these startling documents, in a book otherwise " distressful bread ", he was discredited and much abused. Other letters from the collection which he made have drifted into the market at intervals, the most important being the lot bought by Mr. Alfred Morrison at Sotheby's in 1888, privately printed in 1894, and generally known as " The Morrison MS." The whereabouts and correct text of the " Harrison" letters remain a source of speculation. There should, somewhere, be sixty-two of them, all in the unmistakable, foursquare, toppling, hasty but highly-legible, left-handed writing of Nelson's later years. They have not been quoted from sight since Pettigrew used them. They may have been destroyed.

They were sought for in vain by Sir Harris Nicolas, who completed in 1846 his seven-volume collection of " The Letters and Despatches of Vice-Admiral Lord Viscount Nelson", the work which remains to-day the Bible of the Nelson student. Nicolas had full access to the essential MSS. which were inherited by Nelson's niece, Lady Bridport, and bought from her son in 1895, by a special grant of Parliament, for the Nation. The ninety-two volumes in the British Museum are catalogued as Add. MSS. 34,902–92,

" Nelson Papers ", and 35,191, " Bridport Papers ". Sir Harris was unlucky in that the relicts of Messrs. Clarke and M'Arthur refused permission for him to inspect the material lent to these authors. He was obliged to do as he had done in the case of the " Harrison " letters, print from what had been already published, and he did so unhappily, as he had reason to believe that the collaborators had disregarded the first principles of editorship.

Much that Sir Harris Nicolas longed to see is now available, and has been consulted for the present biography. Inspection of the manuscripts collected by the late Lady Llangattock, foundress of the Nelson Museum, Monmouth, disclosed five bound volumes, labelled " Nelson Papers ". Of these, the first three contain the originals of letters from Nelson to his wife, opening with his proposal of marriage following a verbal declaration, and ending with his last note before the stormy home-coming which resulted in a separation. All the letters quoted by Clarke and M'Arthur are there, and comparison of what they printed with the originals shows that they not only cut, and ran several letters into one ; they altered the wording, giving false evidence which has been repeated by every succeeding Nelson biographer. There are, in addition, in these three volumes, upwards of a hundred and twenty letters in the hand of Nelson which have never been printed; and the biographers of 1809 principally eschewed not the trivial or repetitive, but the intimate. The remaining two volumes of " Nelson Papers " in the Llangattock collection, one labelled " Holog. Coresp." and four portfolios, include Nelson family correspondence, the " recollections " supplied by Lady Nelson to M'Arthur, Nelson's own Journals of his Calvi and Bastia campaigns, and his actions at St. Vincent, eight well-known letters to Lord St. Vincent, Lady Hamilton and Horatia (from Pettigrew's collection), many to Lord Hood (mostly printed by Nicolas from Clarke and M'Arthur's transcripts), and a large assortment of miscellaneous letters, documents, pamphlets and bills, formerly the property of Lady Nelson.

Five " Letter-books " contain copies of Nelson's official correspondence from 1796–1804, and there are also five Logs—those of H.M.S. Vanguard, Foudroyant *and* Samuel and Jane, *dating from 1798–1800, and those of H.M.S.* Victory *from May, 1803–July 25, 1805.*

Amongst the considerable collections at the National Maritime Museum, Greenwich, are to be seen those of Nelson's daughter (Nelson-Ward MS.), over two hundred letters to Lady Hamilton from Nelson's brothers, sisters and nieces, and three series from Lady Hamilton (one to Horatia, one to her nurse and one to Nelson's friend Alexander Davison).

Harvard University Library possesses the collections bequeathed by Miss Amy Lowell, Mr. Joseph Husband and an anonymous donor. The Husband collection includes a log of the Victory *(Dec. 30, 1792–April 26, 1794) an autograph copy of the " Order of Battle " issued by Nelson before Trafalgar, and dated October 10, 1805, an autograph copy of Nelson's Calvi Journal (7 pp.) and more than two hundred letters, including four from Lady Hamilton to Nelson, three of which came from the scattered Morrison MS. A signed copy of Nelson's Memorandum of October 9, 1805, was a gift to Harvard University Library in memory of the late Lionel de Jersey Harvard. " Harvard Library Notes ", Number 22, May 1929, contains an article by Mr. James P. Baxter, " The Nelson Manuscripts in the Harvard College Library ".*

The authorities, published and unpublished, on which the following text is founded are stated in notes grouped at the end of the book, under reference numerals which correspond to those in the margins of the text. As Add. MSS. 34902–92 (British Museum) have been unavailable during the War years, it has not always been possible to give folio numbers for quotations from " The Nelson Papers " : in such cases reference has been made to the transcripts of Mr. T. Foley and Sir Harris Nicolas.

The author wishes firstly to record her debt of gratitude

to the late Sir Geoffrey Callender, Director of the National Maritime Museum, Greenwich, for assistance and advice extending over four years; she would also thank the Council of the Borough of Monmouth for permission to inspect and make transcripts from the Llangattock MS. in the Nelson Museum, Monmouth; John Eyre-Matcham, Esq. and Messrs. John Lane (publishers of " The Nelsons of Burnham Thorpe ", by the late Miss Eyre-Matcham) for permission to quote from the Matcham MS.; the Hon. Mrs. Fremantle for permission to quote from " The Wynne Diaries ", edited by Anne Fremantle; Brigadier Sir H. Floyd, Bart., for the loan of the Polar Journals of Thomas Floyd, R.N. (1751–78); T. A. Thorpe, Esq., for the loan of the letters of George Thorpe, R.N. (1790–97) (and the Editor of " Blackwood's Magazine " for permission to quote from Mr. T. A. Thorpe's article in Vol. 1535 " Blackwood's Magazine "); the Rev. Hugh Nelson-Ward for information kindly communicated on the subject of his grandmother, Horatia; Kenneth Pridie, Esq., for advice on the subject of Nelson's amputation; the Rector of Burnham Thorpe for local information; Miss Henrietta Tayler for the revision of proofs; and James Ross, Esq., City Librarian at the Central Municipal Library, Bristol, for bringing together many volumes.

C. O.

Flax Bourton, Bristol.
April 1942–April 1947.

CONTENTS

MAPS AND PLANS

ILLUSTRATIONS

Corrections by Carola Oman to the First Edition of *Nelson*

The Nelson Family

Edmund
1750

Horatio
1751

Maurice
1753–1801

Susanna
1755–1813
m.
Thomas Bolton
1752–1834

Rev. William,
1st Earl Nelson,
1757–1835
m.
Sarah Yonge (1)
1749–1828
m.
Hilaire Barlow (2)
1801–1858

Rev. Edmund Nelson
1722–1802
m.
Catherine Suckling
1725–1767

Vice-Admiral Horatio,
Viscount Nelson,
1758–1805
m.
Frances Herbert Woolward,
Viscountess Nelson,
1758–1831
widow of
Dr. Josiah Nisbet
1747–1781

Anne
1760–1783

Edmund
1762–1789

Rev. Suckling
1764–1799

George
1765–1766

Catherine
1767–1842
m.
George Matcham
1753–1833

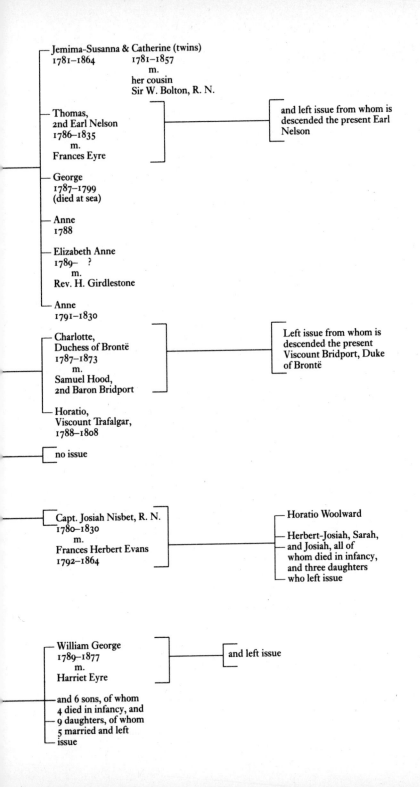

Jemima-Susanna & Catherine (twins)
1781–1864   1781–1857
                   m.
                   her cousin
                   Sir W. Bolton, R. N.

Thomas,
2nd Earl Nelson
1786–1835
   m.
Frances Eyre

and left issue from whom is
descended the present Earl
Nelson

George
1787–1799
(died at sea)

Anne
1788

Elizabeth Anne
1789– ?
   m.
Rev. H. Girdlestone

Anne
1791–1830

Charlotte,
Duchess of Brontë
1787–1873
   m.
Samuel Hood,
2nd Baron Bridport

Left issue from whom is
descended the present
Viscount Bridport, Duke
of Brontë

Horatio,
Viscount Trafalgar,
1788–1808

no issue

Capt. Josiah Nisbet, R. N.
1780–1830
   m.
Frances Herbert Evans
1792–1864

Horatio Woolward

Herbert-Josiah, Sarah,
and Josiah, all of
whom died in infancy,
and three daughters
who left issue

William George
1789–1877
   m.
Harriet Eyre

and left issue

and 6 sons, of whom
4 died in infancy, and
9 daughters, of whom
5 married and left
issue

CHAPTER I

1758–1778
(*ætat* 0–20)

"NEPHEW TO CAPTAIN SUCKLING"

I

ON Friday, September 29, 1758, a fine day in an autumn described as very fair, the wife of the Rector of Burnham Thorpe, Burnham St.-Albert-with-Alp and Burnham Norton, Norfolk, gave birth to a son.

The curtain rises upon a placid scene. The auspices were propitious. The birthplace was lavishly picturesque. Burnham Thorpe Parsonage House was surrounded by gardens in which the Rector devotedly, but not always successfully, cultivated " lay-locks ", syringas, hyacinths and particularly roses : " Burgundy rose plants, a cluster rose, a Hundred leaf rose, moss roses and rose *de Meaux* ". In September, according to him, " the air from our light gravell soil, impregnated with the sweet *Farinæ* of the field, is as healthy as any spott whatever ". The child was welcome, as children are apt to be where first efforts to raise a family have been attended by tragedy. He was a sixth child and fifth son, but his two eldest brothers had died in infancy. The parents were well-matched in every respect. Both came of good stock; the lady's ancestry being slightly though unmistakably more lustrous than that of her husband, a fact which the Rector, least worldly of men, gratefully recognised. (On the death of the third Earl of Orford, in 1791, the Rev. Edmund Nelson put his household into mourning, and instructed a married daughter, " You may with great propriety do the same. If any ask why? you may say that the late Lord's grandfather, Sir R. Walpole, and your great grandmother, were sister and brother. So stands the consanguinity.")

The name Horatio had entered the Walpole family in 1678. It was disliked by its second bearer, who wrote from Strawberry Hill that he preferred to sign himself " Horace—an English name for an Englishman ". Horatio, first Baron Walpole of Wolterton, had been sponsor and had given his name to the second of the Rev. Edmund Nelson's short-lived children. His son and successor was asked to perform the same duties on November 15, 1758. The parish register shows that Horatio Nelson had already been privately baptised on October 9, but this entry need not be taken to suggest delicacy. The same had been done eighteen months before in the case of his brother William, whose health was robust for seventy-eight years.

The public christenings of the Rector's children took place in the parish church of All Saints, Burnham Thorpe, less than a mile, as the crow flies, from the Parsonage House. The fields and hedgerows on the route were bright in summer with poppies, daisies, cornflowers, musk thistles and mulleins. Hawthorns, chestnuts and much yew shadowed the holy ground. The simple and dignified little church has suffered restoration, but stands essentially as it did on the day that Horatio Nelson received the name which he was to bear for less than forty-eight years. Its nave is supported by round pillars dating from the middle of the thirteenth century. In the chancel, a knight who died on Christmas Eve, 1420, lies with his mailed feet on his house-dog, and the collar of the SS. on his steel corselet. A worn font of Purbeck marble, at which children of the village are still baptised, now has for company a great rood and a lectern made of wood from H.M.S. *Victory*.

The other sponsors for Horatio Nelson were " Dr. Hammond ", a second cousin of Mrs. Nelson, Rector of the Walpole living of Great Massingham, and " Mrs. Joyce Pyle ", who here makes her sole appearance in history.

2

Nelson's birthplace was pulled down three years before his death, but contemporary demand produced many likenesses, of which one of the most attractive is a sketch, painted from memory, by a member of the neighbouring family of Crowe.

The Old Parsonage House was a two-storied, *L*-shaped building, composed of a couple of small houses, or big cottages, of different dates and sizes. The larger and taller half contained the tall, hooded front door and six square windows, and upon an end wall, which was a sun-trap, climbing fruit-trees were trained. The smaller half boasted two sash, two casement and two dormer windows, and the steep roof of both portions was covered by the red, fluted tiles still noticeable in the district. In the foreground of this sketch, close by a white-painted wicket-gate, sheep graze, apparently upon the front lawn; but from the Rector's letters it may be gathered that the amenities of his garden included a ha-ha. A son-in-law, whose activity in garden-planning was so great that the Rector nicknamed him " Capability " Matcham, saw to it that the natural stream, running through the pleasure-grounds " bordered with Cresses, Thyme and Vervain ", took up a more fashionable pose, and there is evidence that Captain Nelson himself, during a period of unemployment, was a painstaking gardener of the destructive order.

His thirty acres were a continual source of alternate solace and dismay to the Rector, who delighted in chronicling the growth of his corn, turnips, pease and beans, and in walking forth upon his " charming openn lawns and fields ", (" there Nature will meet you smiling "), but could not, in his less resilient moments, imagine how a farmer ever contrived to make a living.

Within the house there is mention of a little dressing-room with adjoining bedroom, " somewhat like a Bath lodging ", and a guest-chamber which Captain Nelson and his lady, fresh from the West Indies, were brought to confess was the coldest they had ever inhabited. There were domestic quarters to which the Rector sent a present of hot punch on the birthday of his absent sailor son; the parlour was lit by candles in girandoles, and for a family that rose early and dined at 4 p.m., nine o'clock was bed-time.

That Horatio Nelson was the son of a clergyman is a state-ment which needs amplification. Both his grandfathers were East Anglian clergy; two of his great-uncles, eight cousins and two of his brothers took holy orders.

The Nelsons' nearest neighbours at Burnham Thorpe were the Crowes at the Hall, distant cousins but close friends, and the seven daughters and one son of Sir Mordaunt Martin, Baronet, " of a very ancient and Knightly family ", once Marshal of the Vice-Admiralty Court in Jamaica, but now settled at Burnham Westgate. Bird names haunted the Nelsons, for after the Crowes and Martins followed a troop of Ravens, old-established attorneys. With the Cokes of Holkham, where everything was done " in Stile, with some ceremonious splendour ", there was, during the youth of Horatio Nelson, no intimacy. There is record of a single business interview in 1783 between Captain Nelson and " Coke of Norfolk ", a man six years his senior, but twenty years later the Earl of Leicester proudly exhibited the chair in which the Victor of Trafalgar had sat, and an upper chamber was adorned with a portrait of the Admiral and christened " Nelson's room ". Rolfe cousins from Hilborough Rectory and Canon Poyntz of North Creake were constant guests, and when Countess Spencer, mother of Georgiana, Duchess of Devonshire (and, what was more important to a sea-officer, presently mother of the First Lord of the Admiralty), visited her brother the canon, this ideal dowager was " as usual, extremely polite ".   Further afield lay " your titled relations ", the genial Durrants of Scottow Hall, the Townshends at Raynham, the Walpoles of Wolterton, " very good people ", and the Walpoles at Houghton.

The children of Burnham Thorpe Rectory were enthusiastically East Anglian, fully alive to the charms of a county rich in romance and mellifluous place-names—Cressingham, Blakeney, Costessey—rich, also, in old manor houses, ruined abbeys and castles, in bowling-greens, where nut-brown ale was drunk, and in clear-bedded lagoons, haunts of the heron and kingfisher, where windmills and wherries drowsed beneath immense quick-changing skies, and atmospheric effects were often of unearthly beauty.   To have been born " a Norfolk woman " at once recommended a stranger to them.   In nursery days the sturdy William was noted for always getting " the largest Norfolk dumpling ".   When a married daughter went to Sussex, she found that no hare tasted so well as a Norfolk hare.   They could even make merry over the " eynd ", the characteristic mist that sometimes and suddenly creeps up like battle-smoke over eastern Norfolk, and of " being arrested by the Bailiff of Marshland ", the fever and ague of the Fen district.

Their immediate background in a county of which two-thirds is bounded by tidal water, was of rolling fields and wooded hills, but within four miles of the Rectory came a low, flat coastline of muted colour, of sand and salt-marsh, and a streak of light, shifting and bright as fish scales, on which far sails moved slowly.   There was always a salt tang in the air blowing in at the oddly assorted windows of the Old Parsonage House, and on early mornings of silver frost, gulls stood on the lawns.   On wild winter nights a distant roar was eternally audible, on wide summer days a ceaseless murmur.   Of course such a district had produced naval heroes.   Cockthorpe, in the adjacent hundred of North Greenhoe, was the birthplace of three Admirals—Myngs, Narbrough and Cloudsley Shovell.   Local legends told of villages engulfed since the Conquest, whence mariners heard church bells ringing on holy days, and at Brancaster Bay, famous for its submarine forests, fishermen still dragged ashore the tusks of mammoths. The grave little churches of the north-west marshes, mostly flint-walled, guarded recumbent effigies and brasses of naïve beauty.

It could not be denied that, owing to their exposed position, the Burnhams were in winter and early spring colder than the rest of the county. On a Christmas evening the Rector returned thanks that he had been able to make his way, through deep snow, to perform his duty at two parishes without injury; on a March day the beeches seemed to him to be making languid efforts. When his youngest daughter settled awhile at Barton Hall, in that part of the county to which the quiet rivers, broadening out into shallow meres, have given the name of Broadland, her active pen drew warmer pictures, reminiscent of Dutch masters—" The women weeding in the field; the water lilies flowering on the broad; the laylocks fading; birds singing concealed in trees and shrubs in the heat of noon; the cows seeking the shade, while horses feed exposed . . . the fishermen with their eel-spears in pursuit of their prey; the common spread with the various domestics of the tenants, cows, pigs, ducks, geese . . . a picture of plenty and enjoyment."

The towns which loomed largest in the lives of the young Nelsons were Norwich, Lynn and Aylsham. There is cheerful mention of the Sessions Ball at Norwich, the Lynn Feast, the Aylsham Assembly. As they grew up, stage-coach, diligence, post-chaise, chariot and farm cart were setting down in these places gentry in velvet and powder, bagmen, abigails, rustics in hoods and smocks—all the types of Constable, Gainsborough, Downman, Wheatley and Morland. It was the date of " Farmer George ", " Who'll Buy my Sweet Lavender ? " and " Heart of Oak are our Ships ".

3

The New Year of 1768, bleakest season amongst the parishes of the north marshes, found Burnham Thorpe Parsonage a house of mourning. The Rector's wife had died on the day after Christmas, and her mother five days later. The Rector performed both funeral services, entered both burials in the registers, and then, repairing heavily to his darkened home, faced the fact that it had fallen to his lot to be in future " double parent " to eight children, the youngest ten months old. No spinster or widowed sister on either side of the family was available to help him. He believed that he had never mixed enough in the great world to be an entertaining or valuable companion. He only hoped that if he should, hereafter, fall short in care and affection, his children would excuse him, and consider with compassion that his task had been too hard. " Insipid ", " whimsical and very unfitt for society " were his unsparing descriptions of himself. He was six-and-forty, a tall man, with loosely-hung limbs, long irregular features, dark brows, and shoulder-long, prematurely white hair. He never considered remarriage, and more than a quarter of a century later remembered the anniversary of " this day your poor Mother was laid in the peacefull grave ". His father, although the younger son of a younger son, had been educated at Eton, and Emmanuel College, Cambridge. He, too, had been a Cambridge man; only delicacy had prevented his being sent to a public school. He foresaw now that the day of small things had come to the Parsonage House. Until eight children were settled in the world his anxieties would not cease. And, indeed, until Captain Nelson began to send home prize money from the Mediterranean, they did not cease.

The children of Burnham Thorpe Parsonage were brought up by a father whose notions of discipline were so strict that he deemed it an indulgence for a back to touch the back of a chair, and held that weak eyes were no excuse for using glasses. His staff included four characters who sound Shakespearian—" Will, indoors " and " Peter, without ", " Tom Stocking " and " Nurse Blackett ", who, when her duties were accomplished, retired to become the spouse of Mr. High, landlord of the " Old Ship " Inn, Brancaster Bay. A succession of Dollys and Mollys from the village were glad to enter service at the Parsonage, where the children were many, and the master was absent-minded, but capable, when roused, of seizing a house-breaker by the collar and throwing him out of doors. Their fare was frugal. " Palisades of roast beef, or canals of Soup or rich Ragou " were not amongst the fortifications provided by a parent who pronounced " Air, Exercise, Warmth and Cleanliness " the first essentials for infant welfare, and " a Liberall Education the only antidote against Selfish cunning, a passion few are exempt from ".

Horatio Nelson was nine years old when he lost his mother. She died at the age of forty-two, having borne eleven children in seventeen years. Her figure is shadowy; a portrait by a lesser artist shows a formal, upright lady in the costume of the days when the Young Pretender was hourly expected in London.

But the theory that the mothers of heroes are women of spirit seems in this case to find some support. Her eldest daughter explained, in maturity, " Somehow, the Navy must always be interesting to me. I may say I suck'd it with my mother's milk, for she was quite a heroine for the sailors." Her sailor son's only recorded memory of her was that " she hated the French ". She came of blood that had done the State some service.

The 21st day of October was always kept as a festival at Burnham Thorpe Parsonage House. On that day, in the year 1759, the *Dreadnought* (Captain Maurice Suckling), together with two other 60-gun ships, had engaged a vastly superior French squadron in West Indian waters. Captain Suckling, of Woodton Hall, Norfolk, brother of Mrs. Edmund Nelson, had used, on this occasion, the sword of his great-uncle and godparent, Captain Galfridus Walpole. On May 26, 1711, Captain Walpole, serving under Sir John Norris, affectionately known in the Mediterranean Fleet as " Foul-weather Jack ", had lost his right arm in an action against the French in Vado Bay. Captain Walpole, who had ended life as Treasurer of the new hospital for disabled seamen at Greenwich, had been brother of Sir Robert Walpole and the famous beauty, Dorothy, Lady Townshend, the spectral " Brown Lady " of Raynham, and uncle of Admiral George Townshend.

Further back, the pedigree of Horatio Nelson's mother showed names deeply rooted in the East Anglian soil—Sheltons, who bore the symbol of the escallop shell, in token of their presence at the siege of Adrianople, four hundred years before the Norman Conquest ; Bullens of moated Hever Castle and the Manor of Blickling, whence Henry VIII had taken an ill-fated queen ; Wodehouses of Kimberley, who had sent a standard-bearer to fall on Musselburgh Field ; Jermyns of Deepden, who had given a portly Chamberlain to Henrietta Maria. The augmentation of a sprig of honey-suckle to the Suckling coat-of-arms had been bestowed by Elizabeth Tudor, after a Norfolk progress. Sir John Suckling had ridden north to welcome her Scots successor to England, and been rewarded in the fullness of time with the office of Secretary of State. His poet son had bartered Barsham Old Hall to an uncle for the price of a troop of horse, raised to serve the Martyr King. The name Maurice, borne by the eldest brother of Horatio Nelson, had begun to appear in the family when Maurice of Nassau, the first soldier in Europe, was the hero of every Protestant household.

Maurice Nelson was the first of the children of Burnham

Thorpe Parsonage House to leave home. The Sucklings had rallied to the aid of the Rector. Mr. William Suckling of Kentish Town, an official in the Customs and Navy Office, had promised to find an opening for one nephew; Captain Suckling would take another to sea. Maurice, according to his father's record, left *9* home in the year of his mother's death, to become a clerk in London, at " the Auditor's office in the Excise, under Mr. John Fowle ". He was fifteen. Boys were " brought forward " early in the eighteenth century. Even the Rector of Burnham Thorpe uses this expression, which strikes coldly on the modern ear. Writing at a later date of a midshipman grandson who had died at sea, he stoically adds, " There is another boy whom I have desired to be kept at school two years longer, and then brought forward." The ages of these boys were fourteen and ten.

Anecdotes of the young Horatio Nelson are in plentiful supply, *10* and cannot be disregarded, as the source was his own family. Unfortunately, the Chaplain to the Prince of Wales, to whom they were entrusted as official biographer, had an ear for the histrionic. The result has been that posterity has received a chilling impression, not at all confirmed upon reference to original letters or the accounts of contemporaries who did not " improve " upon conversations or incidents.

The first story belongs to the period of tender infancy. When upon a visit to his widowed grandmother at Hilborough, he went bird-nesting in company with a cow-herd. Dinner-hour passed without his return, and alarm was felt lest a child so fair and fragile might have been carried off by gipsies. He was found, after long search, exhausted but composed, seated by the side of an impassable stream. To his grandmother's remark that she wondered fear and hunger had not driven him home, he replied, " I never saw Fear. What is it ? " ; or, in another version, " Fear never came near me." On a spring morning when he was seven, his bed was discovered untenanted. He had spent the hours of darkness sleeping at the foot of a tree which he had identified, just before he was forcibly removed to bed, as containing the nest of a rare bird. On a midwinter night, as proof that he had made his way through the dark silence of country fields to the church-yard, he brought back a spray from the giant yew which shaded the south-west corner of the church. Church-meadow, Burnham *11* Thorpe, even in daylight, was a ghostly spot, for the grassy mounds which diversified its surface were all that remained of a former village, wiped out by mediæval plague. . . .

His education began at the Royal Grammar School, Norwich, a town in which a great-aunt, Mrs. Henley, and a cousin, Mrs. Berney, were ready to nourish small boys on half-holiday. Before he passed on, aged eleven, with his brother William, one year older, to Sir John Paston's School, North Walsham, he was once allowed to attend his father at the marriage of a village couple. He signed himself as witness " Horace " Nelson, but the Rector corrected the signature for a ceremonial occasion to " Horatio ".

At North Walsham a headmaster of the flogging tradition awaited him, and an elderly French master, known by young tormentors as " Jemmy Moisson ". Horace Nelson, lowered by sheets from a dormitory window, appropriated his Welsh pedagogue's pears, and distributed them amongst his mates, but did not himself partake. ("I only took them because every other boy was afraid.") Five guineas were offered for the name of the culprit, but were offered in vain.

A Hamburg merchant, an Olympian of North Walsham days, writing to the victor of the Nile and Copenhagen in the year 1802 to ask for a consul's appointment, was unctuously reminiscent.

> " Your lordship, though in the second class when I was in the first, was five years my junior, or four at least, and at that period of life such a difference in point of age is considerable. I well remember where you sat in the schoolroom. Your station was against the wall, between the parlour door and the chimney; the latter to the right."

What Nelson minor learnt from " Classic Jones " and the thin marbled volumes of a rather small establishment can only be deduced from internal evidence. It would appear that certain Shakespeare plays were either included in the curriculum or available at home. From the instruction of M. Moisson a young patriot emerged entirely unscathed, to his subsequent discomfiture, but when the Commander-in-Chief of the Mediterranean Fleet quoted Cato, Jones's pupil recognised the note.

His brother is the authority for the last glimpses of the schoolboy. On a winter's morning, when the roads were becoming blocked by snow, William and Horace returned gleefully to tell their father that there was little possibility of their reaching North Walsham for the opening of term. The Rector said that they must make one more effort. He depended upon his sons not to give up the attempt unless they were convinced it was impossible. They set out again, and William presently thought that the time had come for retreat, but Horace insisted that they must persevere : " Remember, brother, it was left to our honour."

During the Christmas holidays of 1770–71, while their father was taking his annual " recruit " at Bath, William and Horace read in a local newspaper that the *Raisonnable*, of 64 guns, was being recommissioned in view of war with Spain. She had been captured from the French twelve years past, and, like most captured ships taken into the English service, had retained her old name. The appointment of her Captain was presented as likely to be of interest to Norfolk readers—Captain Maurice Suckling of Woodton. Their naval uncle was the most romantic figure in the boys' world. He had no heir, for his long-wooed cousin, a daughter of the first Lord Walpole, had faded and died within two years of a fashionable wedding at St. George's Church, Hanover Square. That the Mayfair house prepared by Captain Suckling for his bride, and sold abruptly by him after her loss, suggested to his younger nephew all that was elegant and desirable is evident from the fact that when he himself was looking for a London home, at the height of his celebrity, he sent word from Palermo that, if possible, he would like " the house in Park St. which had been Captain Suckling's ".

To read in a newspaper that their uncle, who had been on half-pay for some time, was going to sea again, and with a prospect of active service, was naturally of intense interest to the boys of Burnham Thorpe Parsonage. To Horace the paragraph suggested something further : " Do, brother William, write to my father at Bath, and tell him I should like to go with my uncle Maurice to sea." William obediently wrote, and the Rector, who was in weak health and still had seven children to place, passed on the request, and in due time came a hearty answer from a surprised sea-officer : " What has poor Horace done, who is so weak, that he above all the rest should be sent to rough it out at sea ? But let him come ; and the first time we go into action, a cannon-ball may knock off his head, and provide for him at once." 13

Horatio Nelson was rated on the books of the *Raisonnable* as midshipman, from January 1, 1771. He was twelve years and three months old. But he had not been " brought forward ". He had brought himself forward. An anticlimax followed when it appeared that the boy would have to go back to school as usual next term. The *Raisonnable*, captured in the year of his birth, was not yet ready for sea. His elder brother well remembered the dark and cold March morning when the eagerly awaited summons came, and Mr. Nelson's servant, Peter, arrived at Sir John Paston's Grammar School to escort Horatio Nelson to the Lynn diligence. Here the Rector, who regarded London as the place where "every man pays by the inch", and was not a little terrified at the prospect of a London inn, met his sailor son, and together they embarked for the capital. Fortunately there was no need for the ingenuous couple to go to a London inn. They went to Mr. William Suckling's handsome mansion in Kentish Town, which was built of brilliant new Georgian red-brick, and had fourteen very wide stone steps leading up to the entrance door, and in the ornamental grounds of about five acres a very fine avenue of elms. Within, Mr. Suckling's house exhibited equally fine furniture and *bibelots*, many oil-portraits and wax medallions depicting Pelhams, Walpoles and Townshends, and a black butler named Price. In these reassuring surroundings father and son presently parted, and the aspirant was forwarded alone on the last lap of his journey. He was put on the stage-coach for Chatham : the *Raisonnable* was lying in the Medway. (So, as it happened, was the *Victory*, ordered in the year of his birth.) At Chatham his troubles began. He was set down with the other passengers : nobody was present to meet him. He had difficulty in finding the *Raisonnable*, and when he had identified her, could not discover anyone who would take him out to her. At length an unknown officer questioned the straying child, recognised the name of Captain Suckling, and offered the chilled and forlorn figure "some refreshment" at his own house. This Good Samaritan then presumably saw to it that his guest got on board the *Raisonnable* before nightfall, for the Captain's nephew remembered pacing her decks for the remainder of that endless first day of his naval career, in solitary state and silence. Captain Suckling was not in his ship, and not expected for some days. His nephew Horatio Nelson was not expected at any date by anyone. It was not until the following day that "somebody" took compassion on him and spoke to him.

The rigours of the midshipman's berth in the eighteenth century have been often described, and there is no reason to think that Captain Suckling's nephew escaped the common lot. He never himself mentioned early miseries, but another boy, thirty years later, noticed an illuminating flash. The scene was the dinner-table of the Commander-in-Chief in the Mediterranean on the anniversary of the Battle of Cape St. Vincent, and Mr. Midshipman Parsons, much to his alarm, found himself, as the youngest guest present, set on the right side of a withered Admiral with one eye and one arm, " in all the brilliancy of stars and medals ", in a state-room filled with Mediterranean sunshine and presentation silver.   He was too shy to look up during the meal; when it was over, and the cloth was removed, Lord Nelson offered the customary greeting, " A glass of wine with you, Mr. Parsons ", and opened conversation with the words, " You entered the Service at a very early age to have been in the action off St. Vincent."   Parsons replied, " Eleven years, my lord."   The Admiral's smile vanished, and the boy heard him mutter, " Much too young."

14

4

The *Raisonnable* did not see action against Spain.   In 1767 France had ceded the Falkland Islands to Spain, but two years previously Commodore Byron had taken formal possession for Great Britain, on the grounds of prior discovery, and formed an English settlement at Fort Egmont, on the small island of Saunders.   The Spanish and English settlers had remained in official ignorance of each other's existence until 1770, when Spain attacked, but finding France at present unlikely to support her, presently withdrew her claims.   In 1771 she yielded the islands to Great Britain by convention.   The alarm of war died down in England, the *Raisonnable* was paid off, and Captain Suckling was given command of the *Triumph*, of 74 guns, stationed as guardship in the Thames.   He considered the problem of the boy, Horace, who had served as midshipman in the *Raisonnable* for five months and one day, and the result of his reflections was something irregular but decidedly sage.

On an early summer day of this year, an inconspicuous merchant vessel, belonging to the house of Messrs. Hibbert, Purrier and Norton, slipped down the Thames and spread her sails west.   She was bound for an archipelago stretching from Florida and Yucatan to Venezuela; for the Bahamas and Greater and Lesser Antilles; for the tropics, and islands where a boy who had seen nothing but three Norfolk towns, and London from a stage-coach, might behold sugar and tobacco plantations, and reptiles and armadillos, and orchids and humming-birds, and forests of palm and Xanthoxylon, the admired and valuable satin-wood of commerce.   After a long spell of hearing no noises but those familiar to the crew of a small boat in mid-Atlantic, he would hear negroes singing, and the patter of mules' hooves and the chatter of parakeets. Captain Suckling had kept his nephew's name on the muster-book of the *Triumph*, altered his rating to " Captain's servant ", and commended him to Mr. John Rathbone, now in the employ of a West-India trading house, but once master's mate in the *Dreadnought*. Mr. Rathbone, an excellent seaman, could teach a sharp lad much more of mathematics, navigation and hydrographical charts than he would learn in a guardship lying in the Thames estuary, and the regulations of the Royal Navy allowed no youngster, unless he was the son of an officer, to go to sea until he was thirteen. Fourteen months later Captain Suckling again altered his nephew's rating, this time to midshipman of the *Triumph*. The boy Horace was back at Chatham again. He had returned from his first cruise improved in physique, and if not much more of a scholar, in his own opinion, at least, " a practical seaman ". He had suffered another sea-change, of which his uncle may not have been aware. He had returned from his year in a trader filled with generous admiration for the men of the Merchant Service, and with a better balanced view of their place in the body politic. If the defence of sea-borne commerce brought the officers of the Royal Navy most honour, the King's Service, nevertheless, still depended for work aloft on recruitment from Merchant Service personnel. Meanwhile every ship-of-the-line had attendant craft, and the ardent midshipman who desired to be a good seaman was told that if he studied his navigation conscientiously, he might be allowed to handle the cutter of the *Triumph* (used for the transport of stores from land, and of liberty men to sea) and even the decked long-boat. During the winter of 1772 he learnt to be " a good pilot ", in scenes familiar to every lover of London's river-side, and doubly picturesque at this date. He got to know the Thames thoroughly, from the Pool and Tower, " Guardian of the City of London ", to the difficult submerged delta. From Chatham he studied the Swin, chief avenue for traffic leading to the open sea, the North Sea and the Kentish coast, past Whitstable, Herne Bay and Margate sands to North Foreland. Only " by degrees ", according to his own account, did he learn to become " confident of myself amongst rocks and sands, which has many times been of great comfort to me ".

15

His trip to the West Indies had been arranged for him by his uncle; his next adventure was, like his choice of a profession, his own idea. The Honourable Daines Barrington, lawyer, naturalist and antiquary, brother of Captain Samuel Barrington of the Royal Navy, and author of an unsatisfactory translation of King Alfred's version of *Orosius*, had become fascinated by the subject of Arctic exploration.   He had studied the records of previous explorers, interrogated the masters of whalers, and finally induced the Royal Society to approach Lord Sandwich, First Lord of the Admiralty.   Early in 1773, England learnt that the Government was commissioning two ships, under the command of a naval captain, eldest son and heir of an Irish peer, ordered to report on the possibilities of a North-East Passage into the South Seas.   More than a century and a half had passed since the first epoch of English Arctic adventure had been brought to a close by the pronouncement of William Baffin that the North-West Passage to India was not a practicable proposition.   The expedition of 1773 was avowedly undertaken primarily in the interests of science, but of course there was much talk throughout the country, in newspapers, magazines, at the dinner-table and in the parlour, of so romantic a project as a new voyage of discovery to the frozen regions, mentioned by Homer as having midnight sun at midsummer and no sun in midwinter, and believed by the Elizabethan heroes to contain " north of Boreas ", a happy land of perpetual light.   More professional interest was taken by the midshipmen of the *Triumph* guardship, lying at Blackstakes, many of whom had joined the Navy at a date of expansion owing to an alarm of war, and realised that the prospects of active service were not at present promising, and those of promotion in time of peace much less so.

The North Pole expedition became a fact, and the names of the two vessels being provisioned and strengthened against ice, at Deptford, became known.   They were the *Racehorse* and *Carcass*, sloops, mounting bombardment guns, mortars and weapons of the howitzer class; ketch-rigged, mainmast and mizzen, to allow room for the guns in the bows.   Captain Constantine Phipps, leader of the expedition, was going in the *Racehorse*, and Captain Skeffington Lutwidge, second-in-command, in the *Carcass*.   Two masters of Greenland-men had been engaged for each ship, as pilots, and Dr. Irvine, who had installed an ingenious apparatus for distilling fresh from salt water, and understood dietetics, had advised that extra stores of butter and rice should be carried.   The First Lord himself was going to pay a visit to the ships before they sailed; special clothing, suitable for Arctic weather, was being provided by the Navy Board— flannel jackets, waistcoats and breeches, and stockings and mitts of lamb's wool. Unfortunately for the young gentlemen of the midshipmen's berth, " no boys " was the order of the day. Their places were to be filled by effective men. Boys on such an expedition would be " no use ". The decision sounded final, yet a loophole in the regulations existed. The captain of a man-of-war might select some personal attendants without consulting the Navy Board. When the expedition sailed from the Nore, on His Majesty's birthday, June 4, both Captains Phipps and Lutwidge took with them " persons under age ". Horatio Nelson had used " every interest ", after an introduction to Captain Lutwidge, to obtain the post of cockswain of the Captain's gig. Philip d'Auvergne, a member of the large Jersey branch of that family, claiming descent from a cadet of the house of the last reigning Duc de Bouillon, had successfully approached Captain Phipps. Thomas Floyd, another midshipman of the *Racehorse*, had already begun to keep a journal destined to show posterity Nelson's Arctic expedition from a boy's point of view.

On June 27, their fellow-travellers, the gulls, who had accompanied the explorers in great numbers from the Shetlands, suddenly deserted and a flock of strange birds took their place. Next day the ships came in sight of a wedge-shaped island, possessed of many pudding-shaped hills and long, branching fjords, and, towards the north, bold, snow-covered peaks silhouetted against a cloudy sky. Since they had arrived in the summer, the polar willow, the only tree known on west Spitsbergen, was in flower, and some shrubs of lowly habit, sorrel, ranunculi, saxifrages and scurvy grass, were visible above melting snow. Dr. Irvine went ashore, and the boys saw him striding up a hill accompanied by a large black dog. A great many seals approached the ships, holding up their heads and swimming like a pack of foxhounds, and in the distance four whales were descried.

A week later the ships were among thick ice in slow, uneasy motion. The heat of the sun greatly decreased, and fog descended. The *Racehorse*, with both pilots at the masthead, fired signals every quarter of an hour to apprise the *Carcass* of her position. Unseen ice could be heard breaking with a noise like thunder. By July 30 the explorers were becalmed in a large bay, with three visible openings between the islands which formed it, all apparently ice-blocked. Next morning the ice was fast closing in upon them : they got out their ice-anchors and moored along-side an ice-field. Captain Lutwidge and Mr. Cran, Master of the *Carcass*, who had gone ashore in a four-oared boat, returned after two hours to announce that they had ascended a height which commanded a wide view, and been rewarded by the spectacle of ten or twelve leagues of smooth, unbroken ice, bounded only by the horizon. Their homeward journey had been difficult, and they had several times been obliged to haul their boat over young ice. Both ships cast off, having a light breeze to the eastward, and tried to force a passage, but by noon were obliged to anchor again. During the afternoon the ice closed in, and the *Racehorse* and *Carcass* presently lay within two lengths of one another, moored to the same field. There was now no water to be seen except a single hole, or lake, of about a mile-and-a-half in circumference.

The weather was exhilarating, and the ships' companies, as cheerful as hounds released from kennel, filled their casks with astonishingly soft, pure ice-water from the lake, and afterwards enjoyed winter sports on the ice in the Christmas scenes which they had been led to expect. Mr. Floyd noted that snowflakes, up here, were of two varieties, some shaped like icicles, others like stars. With nightfall, the clouds which had filled the skies by day miraculously disappeared, and two eighteenth-century bomb-ketches, with snow frozen on the rigging, were silhouetted against the translucent green skies of summer Arctic night.

Their captains meanwhile were not so carefree. The Greenland pilots, who had never been so far north before, were beginning to show signs of anxiety, and pointed out that the short summer season of these regions was already well advanced. They could only suggest that parties should be set to saw an exit to the westward for the imprisoned ships. Captain Phipps's best hope was for a strong E. or N.E. wind, but the ships had driven into shoal water, and must, if they or the field to which they were moored took the ground, be inevitably lost, and probably overset. Captain Phipps, M.P., who was, as his midshipmen proudly related, "an orator", sent for the officers of both ships and warned them of his intention of making ready the boats in preparation for quitting the ships, a business which would occupy some days. He made an experimental trip himself, in his launch, a week later, and got about two miles, with rather greater ease than he had dared to expect. His crew hauled the launch over the ice with a good will, and on his return to the *Racehorse*, in time for dinner, he was glad to notice that *morale* was high. Everyone in both vessels appeared to repose entire confidence in their officers and suffered no vain regrets at the prospect of having to abandon ship. Spirits, indeed, in the *Carcass* were presently too high for the peace of mind of that excellent man, Captain Lutwidge.

Between three and four o'clock of a misty morning, Captain Lutwidge observed, to his mingled wrath and dismay, a couple of small, uniformed figures on the ice a considerable distance from the ship, separated only by a chasm from a large and menacing bear. Two of the " persons under age " who had used every interest to be allowed to join the Government expedition to the frozen North had taken advantage of thick fog during the middle watch to depart on a private hunting expedition. Signal for their return was instantly made, and one figure wavered. The other defiantly proceeded to discharge a musket at " the bruin ". The weapon failed to fire, but the boy stood firm, apparently intent upon getting to closer quarters and stunning his seven-foot adversary with the butt of his useless piece. A bold and timely shot, fired by order of the infuriated Captain of the *Carcass*, had the desired effect of dismissing the bear and bringing both boys back to the ship. The chief offender was young Nelson, and when asked at an awful interview to explain conduct so unworthy of his office, he answered frankly, " Sir, I wished to kill the bear, that I might carry its skin to my father." Captain Lutwidge, who had not in his inward eye any picture of the dazzling effect that would be produced by a white polar-bear skin on the stone-cold floor of a study at " dear, dear Burnham ", noticed idly that when this lad was agitated, the only visible sign was a thrusting-out of mobile lips. In after-years Admiral Lutwidge told his bear story with good humour, and Lord Nelson's brother-in-law entered it in a privately printed memoir, designed to amuse nieces and nephews of the hero.

One more well-attested anecdote of Nelson came back with the Polar explorers of 1773. Nelson, to his great satisfaction, was given command of a four-oared cutter with twelve men. By skilful navigation he was the means of saving the crew of a boat belonging to the *Racehorse*. At 6 a.m. on July 29 some officers of the *Racehorse* fired at, and wounded, a walrus. These "sea-horses", as he called them, were, according to Mr. Floyd, as large as bullocks, as big as the bottom of a small boat, and owing to their protruding ivory tusks, of extremely diverting appearance. The one attacked by an officer of his ship dived, to reappear surrounded by many companions who made an attack upon the boat. The monsters had seized an oar from one man, and the boat was in danger of being overturned, when the launch of the *Carcass* arrived to the rescue.

By evening on August 7 Captain Phipps calculated that the boats could not be got to the water's edge in less than a week, and if by that time, in spite of every effort, the situation of the ships was unaltered, he would not be justified in staying by them any longer. Meanwhile, he ordered that both attempts should be carried on.

On the night of the 8th orders were given for every man to hold himself in readiness to go away with the boats at 4 a.m. No extra clothing was to be carried, but every man was provided with a musket, ammunition and a bag containing thirty pounds of bread. Mr. Floyd, having attired himself in " two shirts, two waistcoats, two pairs of breeches, four pairs of socks, and my best hat ", and stuck into his belt a pistol, a comb, a razor, a woollen nightcap and his precious journal, fell peacefully asleep on deck. Shortly before midnight he was awakened by a great noise. " The wind had shifted in our favour. Everyone was hard at work. Everything, as if by magick, wore a better form."

During the following afternoon the hampering fog which had persisted for days vanished, and the explorers perceived that they had been driven much further to the westward than they had realised, and, what was more encouraging, that the ice had driven even further. Before dawn they had got past their boats and taken them on board. Next day wind sprang up to the N.N.E., all sail was set, and they made their way, though not without damage, through heavy ice to the open sea. They anchored on August 11 in Smeerenberg Harbour, New Friesland, and reached Orfordness on September 25. The ships were paid off on October 15.

Captain Phipps's *Voyage towards the North Pole*, with engravings from sketches by Philip d'Auvergne and others, published in the following year, tells the official story of an expedition that was stopped by ice north of Hakluyt Headland, reached the Seven Islands, and discovered Walden Island. It is not a tale of success, and until the Napoleonic Wars came to an end, no further schemes of Polar research were undertaken by England.

19

5

Eleven days after the *Carcass* was paid off, a Mr. Bentham of the Navy Office presented his compliments to a Mr. Kee, whom he believed to be agent to Mr. Surridge, Master of the *Seahorse* frigate,

and begged Mr. Kee to give a letter of introduction to the bearer,
" Horatio Nelson, a young lad, nephew to Captain Suckling,
who is going in that ship ". He rightly supposed " the Master
is a necessary man for a young lad to be introduced to ".

A squadron, under Commodore Sir Edward Hughes, was
fitting out for the East Indies, and Captain Suckling's nephew,
who had spent the summer months in the Arctic, was keen enough
on his profession not to wish to lose the chance of such a voyage.

Mr. Kee had no reason to regret his letter, for the Master
of the *Seahorse*, finding during the next eighteen months that
Captain Suckling's nephew was extremely attentive to his duties
when stationed in the foretop at watch and ward, recommended
him to Captain George Farmer, who rated him midshipman.

The *Seahorse* visited almost every part of the East Indies,
from Bengal to Basra, but only tantalising glimpses of the
young Nelson in the gorgeous East are available. He thought
Trincomalee " the finest harbour in the world ". Ten years
later, hearing that Commodore Cornwallis was going out to India
with a convoy, he wrote advising him that under Mr. Surridge
the midshipmen of the *Seahorse* had constantly taken lunar
observations, and since her master had been a very clever man, he
believed her log-book to be almost if not the best in the Navy
Office. " We went the outward passage, and made the islands
of St. Paul and Amsterdam before we haul'd to the northward."
The only precaution which must be taken in approaching the
peninsula was to be assured one was well to the eastward, for
from April to June currents set so strong that ships, fancying
themselves far to the eastward and northward of Ceylon, had
been known to haul up westerly and get foul of the Moldives.

In his forties, amidst gay scenes in Naples, he confided to the
spinster daughter of a deceased Admiral that once, when he was
seventeen, he had sat one evening with a convivial East Indian
party to the gaming-table. He had risen from the green cloth a
winner, to the tune of £300. Reflecting next morning what
would have been his situation had he lost instead of winning this
sum, he had made a resolution never to play again.

At length, almost inevitably, the midshipman who had been
noted by Mr. Surridge as a fine physical specimen went down with
fever. In the East Indies at this date a lingering illness was
something unusual, but to hear of the illness, death and burial of
a friend within forty-eight hours was quite normal. Nelson's
" malignant disorder ", which produced temporary paralysis and

" nearly baffled the power of medicine ", all but terminated his career. It banished for ever the glowing colouring and tendency to outgrow his uniform, remarked with approval by Mr. Surridge. No one henceforward ever described him as anything but " light-haired ". Dr. Perry, Chief Surgeon of the *Salisbury*, on being summoned to report on the case, said that a passage home was the only hope, and a patient who was to suffer from the after-effects most of his life, assisted by re-infection whenever he returned to tropical countries, was carried on board a home-bound frigate, physically a mere object of compassion. Captain James Pigot showed every kindness to a midshipman with a ghastly air, " almost a skeleton ", who did not seem likely to last many days, and the *Dolphin* sailed on a passage likely to occupy six months. Gradually, and in his own opinion entirely due to the care of Captain Pigot, the boy entered upon a protracted convalescence.

At some date between March and August 1776, as he lay in his cot, listlessly conscious of nothing but ship-noises and sunset, in a 20-gun frigate bound from the mouth of the Ganges for Portsmouth, this austerely bred son of a Norfolk parsonage who had entered His Majesty's Service at the age of twelve underwent an experience which he deemed extraordinary. Struggling back to life on a broken wing, barely re-harnessed to the body, he considered his chances in this transitory life, and particularly his hopes of rising in his profession—" the difficulties I had to surmount, and the little influence I possessed ". To his dismay, he began to know depression of a poignancy that had never troubled him before. He foresaw, with the cold and penetrating eye of one just returned from the Valley of the Shadow, that according to all reasonable expectation he must end a failure : the daunting arguments seemed unanswerable. The meagre figure, lying in his obscure sick-bed, " almost wished myself overboard ". In later years Captain Hardy was perfectly familiar with talk of " the radiant orb " which his Admiral believed to beckon him on in his career. Its first appearance was at this moment. In the rise of spirits which followed the young Nelson's hour of darkness and desertion, " a sudden glow of patriotism was kindled within me, and presented by King and Country as my patron. My mind exulted in the idea. ' Well, then,' I exclaimed. ' I will be a hero, and confiding in Providence, I will brave every danger.' "

It seems clear that the story of the boy ended on that day.

6

He returned to find that his "influence" was better than he had known. During his absence, Captain Suckling had succeeded Sir Hugh Palliser as Comptroller of the Navy. This post was most important at a date when the Admiralty left all business of shipbuilding and repairs, and the mustering of men, to the Navy Board. The head of the Navy Office was at least as influential a person as the First Lord of the Admiralty. The Comptroller's nephew was immediately appointed by Admiral Sir James Douglas to act as Fourth Lieutenant of the *Worcester*, of 64 guns, just about to sail with a convoy for Gibraltar.

The diary of Captain Mark Robinson of the *Worcester* shows that on October 8 Mr. Horatio Nelson (whose appointment dated from September 24, the very day on which the *Dolphin* was paid off at Woolwich) joined his ship at Portsmouth, and " brought letters from his uncle ". On the following day Captain Robinson introduced Mr. Nelson to Sir James Douglas, and wrote a letter to Captain Suckling. Next evening, after a very busy twenty-four hours "getting live-stock on board, and getting the Ship ready for sea ", the Captain of the *Worcester* entertained two guests at dinner—the Mayor of Portsmouth and the Comptroller's nephew. To the Mayor, the Comptroller's nephew was not a negligible figure, for the Comptroller was likely to become Member of Parliament for Portsmouth. Next day, and again within the week, Captain Robinson, taking Mr. Nelson with him, dined with the Mayor, and when the *Worcester* came in sight of an un-mistakable landmark in the second week of the New Year, Acting Lieutenant Nelson was sent ashore at Gibraltar with the Captain's letters for the British Consul at Cadiz. Captain Robinson, a lucky man to have found a Comptroller's nephew whom he might favour with a clear conscience, gave the Acting Lieutenant charge of a Watch, and said, more than once, that he felt as easy when Mr. Nelson was upon deck, as any officer in his ship. The Comptroller's nephew, who knew that he was young for such a responsibility, was very pleased. He was at sea in the *Worcester* with convoys throughout a winter of very bad weather, but when she returned to Portsmouth to be paid off, early in April, the Captain was the person to be left in a sick-bed. Mr. Nelson sent word into Norfolk of his arrival in England, and hastened to London by a road with which he was to become very

familiar.   He hoped for a family reunion at Kentish Town, but
first he had to face an ordeal.

On Wednesday, April 9, 1777, bearing with him the necessary
proofs that he had gone to sea more than six years, together with
the journals kept by him in H.M.S. *Raisonnable*, *Triumph*, *Carcass*,
Seahorse, *Dolphin* and *Worcester*, Mr. Horatio Nelson presented
himself for his examination as Lieutenant.   His certificates
further deposed that he appeared to be more than twenty years
of age, but if this was so, the appearance was deceptive, for he
was still five months short of his nineteenth birthday.   The
signatures of Captains Suckling, Lutwidge, Farmer, Pigot and
Robinson testified " to his diligence, etcetera, and that he can
splice, knot, reef a sail etcetera, and is qualified to do his duty
as an Able Seaman and Midshipman ".   The syllabus included a
viva voce examination.

When the candidate was shown into the room where officers of
the Navy Board awaited him, " he at first appeared somewhat
alarmed ".   The Comptroller, who by virtue of his office occupied
the seat of honour, gave no sign of recognition.   The Captains
began to fire their questions, and the candidate, called upon to
talk of business he understood, gradually gained confidence.   By
the time that the Captains had done with him, it was clear that
here was one of the cases in which there could be no doubt.   But
not until that moment did the Comptroller rise from his place,
and assuming the grand manner, beg leave to introduce his
nephew.   Several officers present expressed " their surprise at
his not having informed them of this before ", to which the
Comptroller complacently replied, " No, I did not wish the
younker to be favoured.   I felt convinced he would pass a good
examination, and you see, gentlemen, I have not been disappointed."   *23*

Next day the young Nelson received his commission as Second
Lieutenant of the *Lowestoffe* frigate, and two days later his
father arrived in town.   Two sisters, " Sukey and Nancy ",
aged twenty-one and sixteen, were already at Kentish Town on a
visit, and Maurice, not yet four-and-twenty, was entering his
ninth year at a desk in the Auditor's office.   It was in a cheerful
humour that a young sailor in a hurry wrote from the solemn
precincts of the Navy Office on the following Monday, to his
brother William, aged twenty, undergraduate at Christ College,
Cambridge, and destined for holy orders.

" If it is not too troublesome, turn over," suggested the

newly appointed Lieutenant at the bottom of his first sheet, which briefly recounted the arrival of the family in London, and his commission " for a fine Frigate ". " So I am now left in World to shift for myself, which I hope I shall do, so as to bring Credit to myself and Friends." He was well able to picture the domestic amenities of his new situation—the larboard cabin in the gun-room, eight feet by six, furnished by a cot of canvas on an oaken frame swinging from hooks, presenting the view of a flap-table purchased from a bum-boat or the last occupant, a latten candlestick, a sea-chest on a well-worn strip of matting, and a couple of metal rings enclosing a ewer and basin. . . . He told Brother William that he was due to leave London within forty-eight hours for an unknown destination. Wherever he might go he would keep on writing, and if William chose to answer, Maurice or Mr. Suckling would always know where to forward a letter. In a postscript he sent best respects to a school-friend of North Walsham days, his cousin, Horace Hammond, son of another Norfolk rectory.

This early Nelson letter, written in an hour of high spirits, on an April day, contrasts sadly with many of later date. The script is a small neat " fine Italian ", and the signature of " Your Affectionate brother, Horatio Nelson " is not innocent of flourishes. He signed himself " Horatio ", though in the family circle he was always " Horace ", and his father, when abbreviating with more than usual passion, would allude to " yr bro: Hor: ".

7

The *Lowestoffe* was fitting out at Sheerness for Jamaica station. She did not sail for another month, and her Second Lieutenant found time to sacrifice to the conventions. He called upon Mr. John Francis Rigaud, R.A., a native of Geneva settled at 74, Great Titchfield St., and ordered his portrait in uniform. He gave some sittings, but not enough. The likeness was unfinished when he sailed, and waited thus, in the studio of an academician accustomed to a naval *clientèle*, for another four years. A less agreeable occupation, resulting in illness, had claimed the sitter. As the First Lieutenant of the *Lowestoffe* was on leave, an unpleasant duty had fallen to his lot. The lamentable, but as it was then held inevitable, business of pressing men for service in a newly commissioned frigate was in progress. No guardship lying in the estuary was available to receive the future ship's company of the *Lowestoffe*, so a *rendezvous* was opened near the Tower of London, at which genuine volunteers might enlist, and deserters, gaol-birds, vagabonds and such "able-bodied persons" as were liable to be pressed for service in the fleet might be retained. On a chilly spring night, while engaged on this distressing and sordid business on the banks of the Thames, Nelson began to feel very ill, and presently became inarticulate. A stalwart and resourceful midshipman called Bromwich arrived at the *rendezvous* bearing his ardent but frail senior on his broad shoulders. That this attack was due to a recurrence of his malaria, and that he was returning to the very worst climate for a person predisposed to this disease, was fortunately not recognised by Nelson or any other officer of the *Lowestoffe*. As usual, sea-air set him up again, and he was in good health and spirits by the time that the frigate dropped anchor in Carlisle Bay, Barbados, early in July. He had found in her Captain a character, in the fullest sense of the word, who was to become a lifelong friend. Captain William Locker (as his portraits by Gilbert Stuart, preserved amongst those of the Governors of Greenwich Hospital, bear witness) was a cheerful-looking person, with a weather-beaten countenance, apple cheeks, a benevolent brow from which powdered hair was thinning and a penetrating eye. At the date when Nelson first met him, he was six-and-thirty, limped slightly—result of boarding a French privateer under heavy fire off Alicante, in the year before Nelson's birth—and was a devoted exponent of the methods and practices of that great sea-officer and exemplary though peremptory man, Admiral Lord Hawke. Captain Locker, who came of a naval family and had married into a naval family, took a scholar's interest in naval history, and a human interest in his young officers, to whom he confided such pithy advice as "Always lay a Frenchman close, and you will beat him". There was hope of opportunities to do so, for already American privateers, and French privateers flying American colours, were dealing destruction to British trade in West Indian waters. The *Lowestoffe*, with her convoy of eighteen sail of merchantmen, arrived in Port Royal in mid-July. She took an American sloop with a rice cargo a month later, and on her second cruise from Jamaica, in foul November weather, overhauled an American letter of marque, between Cape Maize and Cape Nicola Mola. A heavy sea was running, and the First Lieutenant of the *Lowestoffe* failed to board the prize. Captain Locker came on deck, and seeing a boat still lying alongside and likely to be swamped, bawled, "Have I no officer in this ship who can board the prize?" Upon

Horatio Nelson, *aetat* 18½, Second Lieutenant, H.M.S. *Lowestoffe.*

By *John Francis Rigaud, R.A. (1742–1810).* (49″ × 42″.)

Nelson gave sittings for this portrait before sailing for Jamaica station, in 1777, but left it unfinished in the artist's studio until his return to England, when, in 1781, he presented it to Captain William Locker, R.N., with the words, " It will not be the least like what I am now, that is certain; but you may tell Mr. Rigaud to add beauty to it." Rigaud labelled it, when completed, " Captain Horatio Nelson, 1781," and Locker lent it to R. Shipster of Woolwich when the printsellers began to demand the portrait of an Admiral of growing reputation. Shipster's small stipple engraving, published August 14, 1797, was labelled, " Horatio Nelson, Esq., now Sir Horatio Nelson, K.B., Rear-Admiral of the Blue Squadron."

Reproduced by kind permission of Earl Nelson, from the collection at Trafalgar House.

this, the Master of the *Lowestoffe* ran to the gangway, but found himself forestalled by the Second Lieutenant, who shouted, " It is my turn now, and if I come back it is yours." The prize had been carrying a heavy press of sail in hopes of escape, and was by this time almost water-logged. The *Lowestoffe's* boat went in on the decks of the American, and out again with the scud. Nelson very nearly did not come back. He succeeded in getting on board the prize, but after doing so was so long separated from the *Lowestoffe* that her Captain began to be anxious.

Captain Locker was not the man to deter a promising beginner. When the *Lowestoffe* sailed for her third cruise from Port Royal he gave Nelson command of a schooner—another prize, but re-named by the Captain, who was a proud parent. Mrs. Locker, heiress of Admiral Parry, had been christened " Lucy ", and her first-born, now six years old, was her name-child. In the *Little Lucy*, Nelson, who had found that " even a frigate was not sufficiently active for my mind ", but who was young enough to be " much obliged " for a gift of sweetmeats, made himself " complete pilot for all the passages through the Islands situated on the north side Hispaniola ". He remained at sea when the *Lowestoffe* returned to Port Royal on the last day of the Old Year to heave down and new-sheath her bottom, and he took another prize in the small hours of February 9, 1778, off the West Corcos.

With early spring came changes. Sir Peter and Lady Parker arrived from New York station. Sir Peter had been appointed to succeed Admiral Gayton. Locker, who had been inter-mittently unwell since August, recommended his Second Lieutenant most warmly to the new Commander-in-Chief, and Sir Peter took the Comptroller's nephew into his own flagship, the *Bristol*, as Third Lieutenant. By September, Nelson had risen to be First. The two West Indies stations, even in times of peace, offered good prospects of promotion, and war with France had now begun. Two friends succeeded Nelson— Lieutenant Cuthbert Collingwood in the *Lowestoffe* and Lieutenant James Macnamara as Third Lieutenant in the *Bristol*.

Mid-October, the anniversary of Captain Maurice Suckling's celebrated engagement in 1759, found his nephew cruising off Cape Francis Viego, the very scene. He had heard from England in April that his uncle was not well. On his return to Port Royal on October 24, after a cruise which he wrote down as " pretty successful ", he learnt that his wealthy and childless patron had

died in July.   The Comptroller had left a Will, intended to be
temporary, drawn up two months after his marriage, in which
blanks had been left for the names of his sister's children.   Every
nephew got five hundred pounds legacy and every niece a thousand
pounds.   His last words to his brother-in-law before a paralytic
seizure had been an assurance that the Rector would live to see
Horace an Admiral.   There were various small legacies to Walpole
kin. Mr. William Suckling of Kentish Town inherited the
residue of the estate, together with all lands, and was going to
give the dress sword of Captain Galfridus Walpole to " poor
Horace ".   " Poor Horace " wrote to his father that he should
always remember with gratitude that his dear good uncle had not
forgotten him, even in his last illness.   The Comptroller had
most kindly taken the trouble to mention his name to Sir Peter
Parker.   To Mr. William Suckling, he wrote :

> " I trust I shall prove myself, by my actions, worthy of supplying
> that place in the service of my country which my dear uncle left me. . . .
> I feel myself to my country, his heir.   I feel . . . had I been near him
> when he was removed, he would have said, ' My boy, I leave you to my
> country ; serve her well, and she'll never desert, but will ultimately
> reward you.' "

But even at twenty, the Comptroller's nephew realised that
he had lost far more than a wise and kind uncle.   He told his
father to be of good cheer ; all his children would do well in the
world yet.   But twice, between calm words, the word " uneasy "
obtruded itself.   He was " very uneasy ", " so uneasy that at
present I cannot write ".   27

CHAPTER II

1778–1783
(*ætat* 20–24)

POST-CAPTAIN

I

SIR PETER PARKER, who had intended to promote the Comptroller's nephew, held to his purpose after the Comptroller's death. The young man to whom his attention had been directed by interest retained it by merit. Moreover, Lady Parker approved of Nelson, and this Admiral's lady was one of those redoubtable naval wives, reminiscent of the figurehead of an eighteenth-century ship-of-the-line, and regarded by her husband's officers with something of the mixture of awe and proprietary admiration reserved for such ornaments.

Nelson found himself, in December 1778, appointed a Commander to the *Badger* brig, and ordered to protect the settlers of the Mosquito shore and Bay of Honduras against American privateers. His first attempt to deal with people on shore was a success. " They unanimously voted me their thanks, and expressed their regret on my leaving them." A deputation waited upon him to ask him to explain to Sir Peter Parker and Governor Dalling what would be their situation should Spain declare war—a very necessary precaution, as within twelve months she did so. He was next detailed to protect the north side of Jamaica, where he captured *La Prudente* of 80 tons—and had to wait two days until the papers of this French prize were discovered, stuffed in an old shoe. He was in his twenty-first year, and rising in the Service with record speed. A new note enters his letters. " The men you mentioned, I should be very happy to have with me, as the one is very assiduous, the other, you know, one of my favourites. . . . I wish I could give a good character of Mr. Capper; he is a drunkard; I need say no more. We shall part." " I know of no remonstrances—I never allow inferiors to dictate." When the master of a Cork merchant-man came on board the brig and was very abusive at having five of his crew pressed for service in the *Badger*, Nelson, who had not meant to take any men from a homebound vessel, but knew that the *Amity Hall* was sheltering two deserters from the *Badger*,

27

performed a judgment of Solomon. " I can't say but I was warm to be talked to in such a manner." He returned two men and a neutral, but told the master that he should keep the other two " for his impertinent behaviour ". Next day, the master, who had retreated saying that he would have the law of Commander Nelson, returned to beg pardon. " And we parted very good friends—though I believe all he told me was false."

" Always at sea, but not with much success " was his bulletin to his father this month. He had not heard from Burnham for nearly a year. However, a few days later he had an opportunity of distinguishing himself, and witnessed a scene which he never forgot. While the *Badger* was lying in Montego Bay, on a June afternoon, the *Glasgow*, of 20 guns, came in and anchored. Two and a half hours later, smoke, closely followed by flames, was observed to be streaming towards the sunset skies. A steward, stealing rum out of the after-hold of the *Glasgow*, had upset a light amongst casks of liquor. Her crew were saved, mainly owing to the prompt action of the *Badger*. Nelson came up with his boats and ordered them to cast their powder overboard, and point their guns skyward, before leaping into the water. They were taken into the brig, causing overcrowding in a ship already troubled by the fever that came with the rains, and Nelson found Captain Lloyd " very melancholy indeed ", as he well might be, and the First Lieutenant, whom he commended by letter to Locker, " a very good young man, I believe, and has not saved a rag but what was on his back ".

The candid and helpful Locker had at last resigned his command, and was going home " to peace and plenty ", in search of health. For many weeks his pupil hoped for a farewell meeting. " If you come on the North Side, and I hear of it, I will come in. . . . I lose my best friend by your going. . . . I shall always write to you." This promise, fortunately for biographers, was most faithfully kept.

On June 11, the pressing anxiety for his future which had haunted Nelson since hearing of his naval uncle's death was finally removed. He was promoted Post-Captain, and appointed to the *Hinchingbrooke*, a 28-gun frigate, formerly an enemy merchantman, re-named in honour of the First Lord's ancestral home. Further promotion could come by seniority only; no junior officer could now be passed over his head. He realised how much luck had to do with such moments in a career. " I got my rank by a shot killing a Post-Captain, and I most sincerely hope I shall, when I go, go out of World the same way."

2

When the important tidings penetrated to Burnham Thorpe, the Rector sent to the silversmiths a case of tea-caddies, once the property of his wife. An inscription that they were a gift to Captain Nelson was engraved, but many months were to pass before the caddies could be put into the daily use suggested by their donor.

The *Hinchingbrooke* was away on a cruise, and as weeks passed without her return, rumour reported her capture, but meanwhile her new Captain was very much employed. The victorious Comte D'Estaing had arrived in Hayti with his armada and troops from Martinique. Jamaica, expecting invasion every day, was " turned upside down ". Her military and naval commanders chose Captain Nelson to take charge of the battery of Fort Charles, Port Royal—key to the harbour, to Kingston and Spanish Town, " the most important post in the whole Island ". The British residents of Jamaica displayed desirable spirit, even considering that they were deeply interested. Mr. Hercules Ross, another friend of Locker, offered all his vessels to Sir Peter Parker, and his negroes to Governor Dalling, to serve in the batteries. " Very public-spirited," commented Nelson, who believed that he was amongst a defending force of 7,000 opposed to invaders numbering 25,000. (" I leave you in England to judge what stand we shall make.") The only possibility which depressed him was that of having to learn the French language as a prisoner of war.

In England, the Spanish Ambassador was packing, the Dutch Ambassador was beginning to look gloomy, and His Majesty had sent a son into the Navy. Prince William Henry, wrote his father to the Commissioner, Portsmouth Dockyard, would arrive between one and two, next Monday, bringing a hair trunk, two chests and two cots, done up in a mat. Not the slightest notice was to be taken of him on arrival; he was to be treated exactly as any other midshipman. He was not yet fourteen, but had begun Geometry, and his father flattered himself that Sir Samuel Hood would be pleased with the appearance of the boy.

While the *Prince George,* with Prince William Henry on board, took part in the August cruise of the Channel Fleet, Captain Nelson waited in Jamaican heat, in a small white fort, attended by redcoats and negroes, sweeping with his glass the bluer waters beyond a landlocked harbour, for its size the most perfect he had seen, and at present crowded with shipping. But the French Admiral sailed on, to Savannah, to meet with a repulse, after which he returned to France, and in September the *Hinchingbrooke* arrived in Port Royal, safe and sound. Her Captain gladly departed in her for a cruise, and took prizes which brought him a share of about £800. Had he stayed in the *Lowestoffe*, he would by now have found himself much richer, and have taken part in an engagement, for in the capture of a fort in the Bay of Honduras she was lucky enough to find Spanish treasure-ships lying in the harbour. Nelson, who was beginning to feel the usual effects of having been thirty months on Jamaica station—he only realised that he was " never well in Port " there—sent a casualty list to the absent Locker. Not all the deaths reported by him had taken place in action. " Poor Hill ", after recovering from his wounds, including the loss of a hand, had succumbed to fever, and ten days ago, " that worthy good man, Captain Deane ", had followed suit. Nelson, who believed without question that another unfortunate officer, whose ship had been captured by the French, had died of no other disease than " a broken heart ", had attended Deane's funeral at Green Bay. As usual out here, it had taken place within twenty-four hours of death, " amidst the tears of his officers, his Ship's company and his many friends. . . . Our mess is broken up. Captain Cornwallis and myself live together. I hope I have made a friend of him." This officer was the Captain of the *Lion*, a younger son of the first Earl Cornwallis, thirty-six years old, of middle height, but stout, and so red in the face that amongst seamen he was known as " Billy-go-tight ". His complexion was an affliction, not an indication, for he was strictly temperate. He was also known as " Blue Billy ", " Coachee " and " Mr. Whip ". When a man has so many nicknames he is not generally unlovable, and Nelson's hopes were well-founded. A quarter of a century later he gratefully recalled that amongst the " sentiments which have greatly assisted me in my naval career ", introduced to his notice by this single-hearted officer, were—" that you can always beat a Frenchman if you fight him long enough ", " that the difficulty of getting at them is sometimes more fancy than fact ", " that people never know what they can do until they have tried ", and finally that, " when in doubt, to fight is always to err on the right side ".

2

Dr. Benjamin Moseley was a fair example of what happens when an exiled professional man allows himself to become too much interested in native life. He held the post of Surgeon-General at Kingston for fifteen years, and when he had become inured to the custom of his patients to die of tetanus after his successful operations, he occupied his spare time with enquiries into negro superstitions. Some results of these, some anecdotes of the behaviour of sharks, and an account of the ill-fated San Juan expedition of 1780 were incorporated by him in his *Treatise on Tropical Diseases, and on the Climate of the West Indies*; and when his work attained a fourth edition in 1803, Lord Nelson contributed a note. Dr. Moseley did not himself accompany Captain (Brevet-Major) Polson and Captain Nelson to Nicaragua. A younger man, Dr. Thomas Dancer, who was interested in botany and held advanced views on sanitation, sailed from Port Royal on February 3, 1780, with the joint military and naval force bound for the Mosquito coast. He also afterwards reported in print on the expedition.

The force ordered on a particular service consisted of about two hundred regulars, of the 60th and 79th Regiments, one hundred of Major Dalrymple's Loyal Irish, two hundred Jamaican volunteers and a few marines. Their object was more impressive than their numbers. They were to obtain command of Lake Nicaragua, " which for the present may in some degree be looked upon as the inland Gibraltar of Spanish America ", and after " that first conquest ", and the capture of the rich cities of Grenada and Leon, were to force a passage to the Pacific, " thus cutting off all communication between the north and south ". The scheme had originated in the brain of Governor Dalling, at Port Royal, but in London Lord George Germain, Secretary of State for the Colonies, was enthusiastic, and " the more sanguine part of the English began to dream of acquiring an empire in one part of America, more extensive than that which they were on the point of losing in another ". The opening paragraph of Governor Dalling's plan of operations concluded with the words " by these different movements, I do not see how we can fail to bring about that grand object, a communication between sea and sea ". Nelson's comment was, " How it will turn out, God knows." He added that he did not expect to return before the end of June, and that after " this trip ", if he did not feel better, he should apply for home leave. Sir Peter had promised him command of the first frigate in which a vacancy should occur, and Captain Glover of the *Janus* had just sailed on a cruise which he seemed unlikely to survive. But if it came to that, Nelson had himself been twice "given over" by the physicians of Jamaica since Locker had last seen him.

The military destined for San Juan were disembarked in Honduras at Cape Gracias à Dios, and encamped upon a swamp to await the arrival of a reinforcement from the 79th Regiment. When this detachment of veterans from Black River appeared, it was soon evident that they should have been in hospital instead of preparing for active service. Another setback was caused by the fact that the natives, who were needed to supply craft and act as guides and pilots up the river, disappeared inland as soon as the *Hinchingbrooke* and transports came in view. The Indians of the Mosquito coast believed that the English came for no other reason than to carry them slaves to Jamaica. The troops were all re-embarked, and Captains Nelson and Polson took the action which appeared to them necessary, though they were far from assured of support from headquarters when it became known that they had obliged unwilling natives of the Mosquito shore to join them. "A light-haired boy came to me in a little frigate," recollected Captain Polson. "In two or three days he displayed himself, and afterwards he directed all the operations." ⁶ They anchored at several places down the coast until they had collected sufficient Indians, and arrived at Greytown, at the mouth of the San Juan river, towards the end of the month. Here, Nelson's instructions ended. He had convoyed the troops successfully to the Spanish main, and was at liberty to return to Port Royal. But he had discovered that not a man amongst those whom he would be leaving had ever been up a river "which none but Spaniards since the time of the buccaneers had ever ascended", and no one had any idea of the positions of the enemy forts. About two hundred men, with ammunition and siege-train, were embarked in Mosquito shore craft, and two of the *Hinchingbrooke's* boats and Nelson went with them.

The story from this point becomes fully as nightmarish as the tropical vegetation described by Dr. Moseley. The banks of the San Juan, according to him, were at this time of year entirely composed either of unwholesome mud, submerged during the rainy season, from which, after sunset, arose death-dealing miasma, or of decaying leaves and vegetables which had never seen the full light of the sun. For overhead, in some stretches, trees grew so thickly that the scene, even at midday, was suffused by no more than an uncanny greenish light. The principal cape above Greytown was named Monkey Point for good reason. No sound but the chatter of these beasts, and the stirring of a heavy leaf as the lizard or snake slipped by, were heard by the sweating and pig-tailed marines, seamen and redcoats, as they penetrated through chequered green twilight towards unknown fortresses. Another enemy, as yet unsuspected, was already at work amongst them. "Yellow Jack", a disease peculiarly rife all round the Caribbean, was choosing his victims. It was a lamentable fact that the expedition planned at Government House, Port Royal, and approved in a stately chamber in London, had been sent three months too late. The invaders had arrived at the end of the dry season, and the river contained very little water in its lower reaches, and many shoals and sandbars over which boats had to be dragged. Men who got wet through three and four times a day complained of headache from the glare arising from the white sand of the district. Further up, currents and rapids awaited them. That they persevered, and reached a fortified island called San Bartholomew by the 9th of April, was, in the opinion of Dr. Dancer, chiefly due to the exertions of Captain Nelson's men from the *Hinchingbrooke* and the Indians. Most of the soldiers, either from ignorance or indolence, seemed dis-inclined to make much effort. Nelson, whose language on land operations was still that of the sea, was the first to "board" the enemy outpost. He led an attack on the fort, at the head of a small party of his men, supported by a Captain Despard. The Spanish garrison, taken by surprise, fled without offering opposition. Only sixteen miles now lay between the expedi-tionary force and Fort San Juan, which Dr. Dancer invariably, and Nelson sometimes, referred to as "the castle". Stores and ammunition were landed a few miles below the fort, and on their march through swamp and forest towards it, Dr. Dancer was unpleasantly surprised by an evidence of the potency of the local reptile. A soldier who was bitten under the eye by a snake dangling from a tree fell out, exclaiming of intense pain. By the time that a stretcher-party had returned for him, his body was putrefying. When they came in sight of "the castle", the sea-officer was all for another bold assault, but the military preferred to lay siege, a business which entailed eleven days' preparation. Simultaneously the dry season, having presented every encum-brance, came to an end; torrential rains set in, and amongst those to be smitten by the prevalent sickness was Nelson: never-theless, he continued on duty—"made batteries, and fought them". A small further reinforcement of troops appeared on

D

the scene.   They had been brought to Bluefields by the corvette
Victor, and amongst the letters which she had carried from Port
Royal was one from Sir Peter Parker.   Captain Glover had died.
Captain Nelson was recalled to take command of the *Janus*.

Fort San Juan surrendered on April 24, but Nelson just
missed hearing the news in Nicaragua.   He sailed from Bluefields on the 23rd, and found on board the *Victor* an old companion
who tended him zealously.   Mr. Tyson had been his purser in
the *Badger*.

The story of the San Juan expedition, as far as Nelson was
concerned, was over.   It was a failure, and the narrative continued
by Dr. Dancer, until he too fell ill, shows that it was a ghastly
failure.   The Indians deserted after the capture of the fort.
The " castle ", so much desired, proved destitute of the hoped-
for provisions and " worse than any prison ".   Dr. Dancer was
ashamed to give the name " hospital " to the noisome sheds,
surrounded by mired offal and the hides of slaughtered cattle,
in which he was obliged to bestow his sick.   Colonel Kemble,
who had arrived to take over the command from Captain Polson,
gave orders for the erection of a more sanitary building, but no
labour was obtainable.   Soon there were not sufficient fit men
left to act as orderlies, or even to dig trenches in which the dead
might be decently buried.   Corpses were flung into the river by
men whose reason seemed permanently affected.   Dr. Moseley
believed that some fell victims to tigers and to the " gallinazo ",
the carrion crow of Nicaragua, who does not wait for death to
begin his meal.   The expedition had not been stinted of medical
and surgical equipment, but most of this lay down at Greytown
awaiting transport up a now turbulent river : ammunition had
been given priority.   A few men struggled on to the lake, but in
October, lashed by thunderstorms of the tropical variety, nearly
all that remained of the San Juan expedition stumbled into Bluefields.   Only a small garrison was left in the sinister " castle ",
" to await orders ", until death, or the Spaniard, came for them.
Nelson learned at length that of the *Hinchingbrooke's* two hundred
men, not more than ten survived.   He had himself seen eighty-
seven report sick in a single night, and a hundred and forty-five
buried.   Yet, neither soon after the event, nor later, did he
condemn the whole project as futile and ill-judged.   He always
thought that if only the expedition had been sent at the proper
season (in which case it might have encamped in the healthy
Grenada and Leon country, and a road for stores from Bluefields

might have been constructed), the end of the story would have been different. Sickness, not Spanish arms, had defeated a sterling body of men sent on a great adventure. He had taken part in a tragedy, not a failure.

8

When he arrived at Port Royal, he had to be carried ashore in his cot. " Cuba Cornwallis ", to whose lodging-house he was first taken, had nursed him before. This negress, who had adopted the surname of the noble Captain who had obtained her freedom from slavery, was famous in the island for having saved the lives of many naval officers. Before Nelson moved to the country house of the hospitable Parkers (where he had a relapse), he saw Governor Dalling " several times ", and succeeded in writing a long letter to Polson, congratulating him on his capture of Fort San Juan before the arrival of a superior officer, and telling him that there would be " no more heard " about their taking Indians from the shore upon the expedition. He sent messages, and good wishes for their recovery, to a long list of sick friends : he assured Polson that the Governor would be with them before July. His behaviour on his first expedition did not pass unremarked. Polson in due time reported officially to headquarters, " I want words to express the obligation I owe to that gentleman. He was the first on every service, whether by night or day. There was scarcely a gun but what was pointed by him or Lieut. Despard." Governor Dalling, for his part, wrote privately to Lord George Germain, hoping that His Majesty might be graciously pleased to manifest a satisfaction of Captain Nelson's conduct.

The Admiral's lady and her housekeeper took turns in sitting up with the fever-patient. Mrs. Yates, questioned years afterwards, distinctly remembered Captain Nelson as a most amiable sufferer. But presently the lady of the house had to depart from " Admiral's Mountain " for her town house on the humid coast, and a native staff, accustomed to having an eagle eye kept upon them, when they discovered that the English women were safely gone, took no further notice of the sick sea-officer lying abed. They became as invisible as the Indians of the Mosquito shore. " Oh ! Mr. Ross ! " wrote Captain Nelson from the mountains on a June day, " what would I give to be at Port Royal. Lady P. not here, and the servants letting me lay as if a log." He also sent word home that he was ill again, and his family must not be surprised to see him. His brother Maurice, who had his own troubles, and who had seen the records of invalided Post-Captains of no private means, wrote to his brother William that he hoped Horace would manage to stay where he was. The *Janus*, of 44 guns, was a fine frigate, quite new. Maurice, who had, much to his relief, got transferred to the Navy Office shortly before the death of the Comptroller, was well-informed as to his naval brother's movements and prospects. Jamaica, to one seated at a desk in Seething Lane, sounded so desirable.

Nelson took up his duties on board the *Janus* and had another and more serious relapse. Many visits to the medical fraternity followed, and so strong was the impression produced by the agreeable personality of the Surgeon-General, that in 1797, when suffering agonies after the amputation of his right arm, Sir Horatio insisted on calling in Dr. Moseley ; and in 1803 concerned friends felt themselves obliged to point out to Vice-Admiral Viscount Nelson that old Moseley, who had attended him in Jamaica in 1780, was not an eye-specialist. The inevitable end of this chapter in the history of Nelson took place on August 30, when he signed a note, addressed, " To Sir Peter Parker, Knight, Vice-Admiral of the Blue, and Commander-in-Chief at Jamaica," opening, " Sir, Having been in very bad state of health for these several months past," and ending with the miserable words, " I am therefore to request that you will be pleased to permit me to go to England."

He sailed from Port Royal five days later, as a passenger in the *Lion*, and for the second time within four years believed that he owed his life to the kindness and attention shown to a helpless patient by the captain of a British frigate. This time the officer was a friend—William Cornwallis. As before, removal from an inimical climate produced immediate improvement. The *Lion* arrived at Spithead on November 24, and in London the invalid was well enough to enjoy meetings with Locker. But even Kentish Town in midwinter was not the place for a sea-officer whose first object was re-employment, and with the New Year, the accepted date for the Rector of Burnham Thorpe's annual " recruit ", his son joined him at Bath.

3

Number 2, Pierrepont Street, was a neat house built of the local golden-grey stone, facing west, almost on the corner of the fashionable North Parade. From the corner of the street could be seen a typical Bath prospect, including the Abbey tower and the promenade called Orange Grove. The name commemorated the visit of a Dutch prince, but Captain Nelson, walking the streets of Bath on mild days of west wind and bright sun, hearing of cold weather elsewhere, was reminded of the West Indies. " This is like Jamaica to any other part of England."

In mid-January he had spoken of the possibility of having to move to other lodgings. Mr. Spry, apothecary, had not a single room unbooked for the season. If Locker should come from London, after his boys went back to school, he would have to be accommodated elsewhere. But Locker could not be persuaded that his was a Bath case. He forwarded a copy of the latest Navy List and stayed cooped-up in Gray's Inn. The gentle Rector of Burnham Thorpe, having unconsciously selected the comfortable Bath lodging in which he was to die in 1802, turned home. He had seen his son safely through an alarming illness, " carried to and from bed with the most excruciating tortures ". Time, a Bath physician and surgeon, a full course of physick, the waters and the baths, had once more worked the boasted cure. Nelson pronounced his inside, at any rate, " a new man ". He was not perfectly happy as yet about his left arm, which had a disconcerting habit of going quite dead and white from shoulder to finger-tips and coming back to life red, swollen and intensely painful : however, the inspiring Dr. Woodward seemed to view this train of symptoms with equanimity. The awkward moment had passed when a very sickly and slightly shabby officer, standing in a shadowy consulting-room, exclaiming at the smallness of a Bath physician's charge, had received an answer so much after his own heart that he treasured the stately cadences for the ear of a future wife. " Pray, Captain Nelson, allow me to follow what I consider my professional duty. Your illness, sir, was brought on by serving your King and Country, and believe me, I love both too well to be able to receive any more."

The convalescent liked Bath, which appeared, to one who had not as yet a large acquaintance in London, to possess many of the attractions without the disadvantages of the capital. The London papers arrived within ten or eleven hours of publication. At street corners, flooded with sunshine on winter days, the visitor met whole parties of unexpected West India friends. But the truth was that he did not " set very easy " under the hands of physicians and surgeons, and by March, striding the echoing grey streets at a good pace, " near perfectly restored ", he was beginning to notice with regret that the wind hung so much westerboard. It must hinder the sailing of the Grand Fleet.

He left Bath in the London coach on an April day, travelling with Captain Kirke and family—a melancholy journey, for Mrs. Kirke, poor woman, had just been told by the medical men that they could do nothing for her. Nelson, who had been so glad when Kirke's sailor servant arrived at his lodgings to say that the master and family were come down, had recommended his own physician and surgeon. "Mrs. Kirke's case is *incurable*." The word looked dreadful, underlined in his letter to Locker. At Newbury he left the Kirkes. He had an invitation to stay with Captain Robert Kingsmill, at Sidmonton Place, Kingsclere, and here, "thirty miles on the other side London", he hoped to meet his "sea-daddy". He had promised Locker, who collected the likenesses of naval friends, the three-quarter-length portrait of Lieutenant Nelson ordered from Mr. Rigaud in 1777, and, to the best of his belief, still in the artist's studio. He did not think that, whatever it was like, it could in the least resemble him now.

¹¹

4

On May 6, 1781, he passed from Whitehall through a small courtyard, masked from the street by an elegant stone screen designed by the brothers Adam, and hobbled into a solemn building well known to every sea-officer, the scene of many hopes, fulfilled and frustrated. He was scarcely able to get about, but the news from America was bad. At the Admiralty, a personage who was, outside its walls, one of the most detested characters in London, a personage of somewhat ghastly countenance, possessed of great charm of manner, was short but not discouraging. Lord Sandwich could fix no time when Captain Nelson should be employed. He promised to employ him at the first opportunity. Another man might have felt relief, for there was no doubt that he was not yet fit for service. He had, it seemed, after all, left the country too soon. The symptoms which Dr. Woodward had hoped would pass off had returned, and in an aggravated form, involving his left thigh and leg, as well as his arm. He had consulted an eminent London surgeon of valuable connections, and Mr. Adair, brother-in-law of Lord Albemarle and Admiral Keppel, agreed with Dr. Woodward that further care and treatment should totally banish Captain Nelson's disorder. The unwilling patient relaxed again in his uncle's comfortable home at Kentish Town. As soon as possible he took the road down to Norfolk; here problems awaited him.

¹²

The Rev. Edmund Nelson, who was nothing if not methodical,

began in the year of his naval son's return to keep " A Family
13 Historical Register ", to which he added as events occurred.
The entry under the name of his eldest daughter showed that he
had made an experiment very unusual at the date.

> " *Susanna* had a good school education, but as I could not give her
> a fortune equal to an independency, I thought it most for her advantage
> to be placed out to some female trade.   Accordingly, at the age of
> eighteen, she was bound as an apprentice for three years to Messrs
> Walters, reputable milliners at Bath, where she acquitted herself with
> much credit and propriety.   At the expiration of that term she went
> assistant into a shop at Bath.   In the year 1777, she had a legacy of
> £500 left her by John Morris Esq, our good, faithful and generous friend,
> and after the death of her uncle she gave up the thoughts of following
> her trade, being possessed of £2,000."

Susanna, after a few months at home, had bestowed herself,
in her twenty-sixth year, upon a young merchant, carefully
mentioned by her father as having been of good birth, " and in a
prosperous way of trade in corn, malt, coals, etc."   She was
now, after the custom of the day, " Mrs. Bolton ", even to her
nearest and dearest, and happily settled in her bridegroom's small
native town of Wells-next-the-Sea, surrounded by a large and
sometimes noisily jovial circle of friends and relations, all very
glad to see Captain Nelson, and mostly hoping that if he should
ever touch at any of the wine countries, he would not forget them.

William, who was now a curate, " The Rev. Mr. Nelson,
junior ", also extended a hearty welcome to a man of the world.
To his brother's dismay he had become fired with the idea of
being appointed chaplain of a man-of-war.   He was sure that
Horace could see the right people to get him into so desirable a
situation.   In vain Horace pointed out that " fifty pounds,
where you are, is much more than equal to what you can get at
sea ", and that if William had the bad luck to get with a disagreeable captain and inferior officers, he would find the life
intolerable.

His two younger brothers were equally unsettled.   Edmund,
who had been placed with the Ravens to learn the profession of
attorney, had gone off to Ostend to act as an assistant in his
brother-in-law Bolton's accounting house.   Suckling, aged sixteen,
at present bound apprentice to Mr. Blavers, linen-draper at
Beccles, was looking forward to spending a year in London, as
journeyman.   Mrs. Bolton, who had been old enough to notice
her mother's decline, who was now expecting to become a mother
herself, and whose taste for speaking her mind had been increased

by marriage to a " downright " partner, said quite openly that
her poor mother had " bred herself to death ". There seemed no
doubt that as the family had increased in numbers, it had, so far
as the sons were concerned, deteriorated in physique and ability.
Nor was the returned officer perfectly happy about his younger
sisters. " *Anne,*" according to her father's record, " from the
time of leaving school, to the age of nineteen, lived in London, at
a Capital Lace warehouse, Ludgate St, for which I gave a premium
of £100. . . . She is, I apprehend, a Free-woman of the City of
London, as her indentures are enrolled in the Chamberlain's
Office." But upon receiving her uncle's legacy, Anne, like her
elder sister, had without hesitation obtained her release and
settled gratefully to the life of daughter at home. She was now
twenty. Even Kate, youngest of the family, for whom the
Comptroller's bounty had come in time to save her from a " female
trade ", was now in her fifteenth year. Their travelled brother
sadly felt that they lacked scope. " Although I am very fond of
Mrs. Bolton, yet I own I should not like to see my little Kate
fixed in a Wells society."

In good time the best of news recalled him to London. He had
been appointed to commission the *Albemarle*. The sympathetic
and knowledgeable Maurice accompanied him when he went
down to Woolwich on August 23 to pay his respects to the
Commissioner of the Dockyard and perform, for the first time
under English skies, the old and handsome ceremony of hoisting
his pendant. The *Albemarle* was a French merchantman, *La
Ménagère,* captured in 1780, and a glance at her would have
told a cynical officer why she was being converted into a
28-gun frigate in the autumn of 1781, and why a young and
insistent captain with a poor health record was being employed
so promptly. When Locker set eyes upon her, he said damaging
things. On the outbreak of war, the number of seaworthy ships
in the British Navy had been startlingly inadequate, and now the
war was not going well. Nelson, however, saw her with the eye
of a lover. He was, he said, " perfectly satisfied with her as a
28-gun frigate. She is in dock alongside the *Enterprise*, and in
some respects, I think, excells her. She has a bold entrance and
clean run." He could not deny that although she had the same
beam as the *Enterprise*, she was four inches narrower on the gun
deck, and between decks very low indeed. She was having her
under-water timbers resheathed with copper, and would not be
out of dock for a fortnight at least. The Admiralty was being

very civil to him, allowing him to choose all his own officers, and the faithful Bromwich was to be one of his lieutenants.

A fortnight later his quarter-deck was filled, much to his satisfaction. He had got an exceeding good master, and good warrant officers, and most of the volunteers, who were beginning to come in, were seamen. The *Albemarle* became as busy as a hive, and smelt strongly of tar. The last of her rigging had been set up, her decks had been sanded and blacking had begun. "Not a man or officer in her I would wish to change." He sent full details of her progress to William (who was now deeply interested) and promised that if he should call at Yarmouth and find their influential relative Lord Walpole there, he would certainly entertain him. By Sunday, October 14, the *Albemarle* went down the river to the Nore. She sailed better than her Captain had dared to hope. "I think we go full as well as the *Enterprise*." But he was feeling so sick that he could hardly refrain from taking to his bed.

5

Since the story of the *Albemarle* is rather a sad one, it is best briefly told. She was never a good sailer, except going directly before the wind, and eventually her disillusioned Captain supposed that her first owners, the French, must have taught her the habit of running away. Being a brute to handle, she was also an unlucky ship, but the worst disaster to befall her was sheer ill-luck.

The winter of 1781-2 was one of persistent foul weather, and Nelson, who had spent the last three years, ailing, in the tropics, ruefully suggested that he was now being frozen for a season, to test his powers of survival. The *Albemarle*, with the *Argus* and *Enterprise*, reached Elsinore early in November, and there was obliged to wait for over a month, while two hundred and sixty sail of merchantmen, "laden with cargoes of the utmost National importance", gradually assembled for convoy. Their homeward passage was marked by disappointing incidents. A privateer got amongst the fleet, and the *Albemarle* chased her for an hour without success. She proved to be the *Cutter* of Folkestone, commanded by the notorious "Fall, the Pirate", who, under French colours, had fired upon several Scottish coastal towns. The convoy "behaved as all convoys that ever I did see, shamefully ill, parting company every day". Only a hundred and ten sail arrived in Yarmouth roads with the escorting frigates on December 17, and were there detained another three weeks by adverse winds. Undeterred by the spectacle of "a coast full of wrecks", Mr. William Nelson, still fascinated by the idea of becoming a naval chaplain, came up to Yarmouth to spend the last Sunday of the Old Year on board his brother's ship. He very nearly had to go to the Downs in her, as on the day following his call it was not possible to send a boat ashore. Unfortunately, waking to find that the *Albemarle* and convoy, which had been the leading feature of the seascape for so long, had vanished overnight as if by magic, only increased William's belief in the romance of a sea-faring life. His brother was enduring the reality. After "driving from one end of the Downs to the other" for nearly a month, and twice parting from her anchors, the *Albemarle* was ordered round to Portsmouth to take in eight months' provisions. Her Captain, whose considered opinion of the North Sea in the festive season was now one which many subsequent officers have endorsed, considered this order with pleasure. He had feared the Admiralty asleep, and the Downs station, "a horrid bad one", his inescapable fate. Eight months' provisions were a sure sign of a long cruise, and he knew that a squadron under Sir Richard Bickerton, whose acquaintance he had cultivated last year, was fitting out to reinforce the East India fleet. "Alas! how short-sighted are the best of us!" At 8 a.m. on the dark and stormy morning of January 26, a large East India store-ship, the *Brilliant*, driven from her anchor in the Downs, fouled the bows of the *Albemarle*. The *Albemarle*, lightly constructed, suffered heavy damage. Her Captain's first reaction was philosophic. "All done in five minutes! We ought to be thankful we did not founder. Such are the blessings of a sea life!" Only to Locker did he add to a terse account of the accident the bitter words, "I was ordered for Foreign service." He believed that the *Albemarle*, "poor *Albemarle*" henceforward, was so much changed for the worse that she would probably be paid off. "What is to become of us now, I know not." But he had not seen figures available at the Navy Office. While he waited at Spithead for a wind to bring him into harbour, "Mr. White, the builder of Portsmouth Dockyard", a character who sent best respects to Captain Locker, came on board to take a preliminary survey of damage, which he presently estimated as reparable in three months. "Old England at this time of need" was not going to send to the knacker's yard any frigate which could possibly be made serviceable. The accident had been sufficiently dramatic to interest reporters, and Lord and Lady Walpole of Wolterton sent civil enquiries to Burnham Thorpe Parsonage House for the safety of Captain Nelson. His lordship's godson thought it would have been more to the point had they provided a Rectory for his brother William. Meanwhile, Sir Richard Bickerton sailed, in time to take part in the last of the five pitched battles between Sir Edward Hughes and Admiral Suffren. Not until the middle of April was her Captain able to get the " old *Albemarle* " out of Portsmouth, upon what he described as " a damned voyage ". He had been ordered to join the *Dædalus* (Captain Pringle) at Cork, and escort another convoy, this time across the Atlantic. What was worse, he believed that he might have to winter in the Americas. Friends whose opinion was valuable, " my Navy friends ", urged him to apply to Admiral Keppel for an exchange, which he would certainly get. His surgeon, the eminent Mr. Adair, brother-in-law to the new First Lord, might be prevailed upon to drop a hint. He decided, however, that it would not be advisable to ask the new First Lord to cancel orders given by a violently inimical predecessor. He had been introduced to Admiral Barrington, who had twice refused the command of the Channel Fleet, who had gone to sea at ten, and who, despite his bowed shoulders and white locks, " gets amongst all the youngsters here, and leaves out the old boys ". The Admiral, brother to Mr. Daines Barrington, progenitor of the Phipps Arctic Expedition, had looked interested when he heard Captain Nelson's name. Given time, Nelson believed that, from that quarter, he could easily have obtained a better station and a better ship. But he decided to obey orders, and hope for a happy return in the autumn.

While he waited for a wind at Portsmouth, an officer one year his senior, who had been very lucky at last, made a happy return attended by considerable popular enthusiasm. Charles Pole, of the *Success*, another of the young men marked down by Locker as promising, and represented in his portrait-gallery of pupils with a future, had captured the *Santa Catalina*, the largest frigate afloat, after an action off Cape Spartel, in which his seamanship had been, by general consent, as conspicuous as his daring. But both, wrote his contemporary to Locker, were surpassed by the young officer's modesty, when called upon to give an account of the affair to Portsmouth audiences.

6

The *Albemarle* had a tedious passage of ten days from Spithead to Cork Cove, where her consort, the *Dædalus*, arrived the same morning. With their convoy of between thirty and forty vessels, they sailed on April 26, 1782, with a fair wind, for the New World. Eleven days later, at night, in a hard gale and thick weather, some 300 leagues to the westward of Cape Clear, the *Albemarle* parted from the *Dædalus*, and had not seen her or most of the convoy again when she anchored on May 27, in sight of a bleak and barren coast, with walls of brown rock, broken at frequent intervals by deep fjords and large bays. Nelson, whose view of Britain's senior colony did not extend to the interior, was not complimentary. "The entrance of this harbour is so narrow that you cannot sail unless the wind blows right out." Tantalising rumours of an action fought between Rodney's and De Grasse's fleets in West Indian waters well known to him had reached Newfoundland. He dismissed St. John's as "a disagreeable place", and fretted at being kept there without news of Pringle, whose orders had been to go upon Newfoundland station after seeing the *Albemarle* and convoy to the mouth of the St. Lawrence. However, he hoped that Pringle had gone on to the westward; and with all in his own ship he was more than satisfied. "They are all good. Indeed, I am very well off." A couple of days later he got news overland that Pringle and the rest of the fleet were in Capelin Bay, where he joined them, and on July 2 the *Albemarle* arrived safely at the Isle of Bec, in the St. Lawrence. Nelson had only forty-eight hours in which to gain a pleasant first impression of a picturesque upper and lower town of predominantly French attractions, before sailing on a cruise that lasted until late September. During these months, on a station renowned for possibilities of prize-money, he was lucky in taking several prizes, but unlucky in that not a single one reached port. One romantic and one thrilling incident took place while he cruised off Cape Cod and Boston.

On July 14 the *Albemarle* captured an American fishing schooner, whose owner was almost home, with a cargo which represented nearly all his worldly possessions. Nelson, who "imagined we are just getting into the Gulf Stream, by its being so very squally", and who had no officer on board acquainted with the shoals of Boston Bay, ordered Mr. Nathaniel Carver, Master of the *Harmony* of Plymouth, Massachusetts, to come on board the *Albemarle* and undertake the duties of pilot. The American obeyed with speed and skill, and without a change of countenance. When his task was completed, Nelson made him a short speech, announcing that it was not the custom of English seamen to be ungrateful. " I return your schooner, and with her this certificate of your good conduct." This certificate, signed " Horatio Nelson ", was duly framed and long a treasured exhibit of a Boston home. A month later, when the *Albemarle* was again in Boston Bay, the coastal fog of a high summer morning parted to display, within gunshot, four French sail-of-the-line and the *Iris* frigate—" part of M. Vaudreuil's squadron, who gave us a pretty dance for between nine or ten hours ". As all beat " poor *Albemarle* " in sailing, Nelson threw off the large ships by running boldly amongst the shoals of St. George's Bank. The *Iris* still followed, but when the *Albemarle* shortened sail, and hove-to in defiance, out of sight of the line-of-battle ships, the French frigate prudently retired and was seen no more.

By mid-September a new danger was threatening the *Albemarle*. Ship's company and officers alike began to be conscious of muscular pains, spongy gums, bodily lassitude and corresponding mental depression. The symptoms of scurvy were too familiar to the experienced sailor of the eighteenth century, and Nelson resignedly gave the order to stand away for Quebec. Since he had sailed again from the St. Lawrence within two days of his arrival there, without re-provisioning, his men had enjoyed their last fresh meal at Portsmouth on April 7, and for the last eight weeks he and his officers had been subsisting on salt beef. At this propitious moment, the fearless Carver, of Plymouth, Massachusetts, made an unexpected reappearance alongside. Determined not to be outdone in generosity by the English captain, he had brought off, at considerable personal risk, a present of four sheep, several crates of fowls and a large quantity of fresh greens. A contest of courtesy took place before the New Englander would consent to accept any payment from an officer who had learnt a lesson in dietetics, which he was ever afterwards careful to impress on juniors. No subsequent letter of Nelson records that he ever again contracted scurvy.

After he had seen his men into hospital there, he was obliged to linger a month in the neighbourhood of Quebec. The season was the loveliest of the North American calendar, and much to his surprise, the bracing and inspiring climate of " Fair Canada " suited him perfectly. He wrote home that he had never before known what " Health, that greatest of blessings ", could mean. Although he knew that his expectation and wish were to return as soon as he could to England, he gave himself up whole-heartedly to the entertainment offered by an exhilarating community.

Quebec had, since 1764, rejoiced in an organ of public opinion— a chronicle of daily events, fashion and city gossip. At the Freemasons' Hall, a vast old stone building near the head of Mountain Hill (formerly the *Chien d'Or*, residence of Pierre Philibert), Captain Miles Prentice " hung out with good cheer the olive branch of Freemasonry, and of loyalty to his sovereign ". The *belles* of the balls at the Freemasons' Hall were Captain Prentice's daughter and her cousin, Mary, daughter of " Sandy " or " Saunders " Simpson, Provost-Marshal of the Garrison.   Miss Simpson, hymned by the poetasters of the *Quebec Gazette* as " Diana " on account of " her noble and majestic air ", was sixteen, of " heavenly charm ", and to be lovelier yet.   Her home, Bandon Lodge, was just inside the old St. Louis Gate of the city.   Nelson became " violently attached ".

He made other great new friends amongst " Quebecers of note ", not " Navy friends "—the Lymburners, the Davisons. . . . Alexander Davison was, like "Saunders" Simpson, a gentleman of Scottish ancestry, but he came from Northumberland.   He was a bachelor, aged thirty-three, a merchant and shipowner in the Canada trade, cultured, a man of parts and affairs.   At a house within view of the harbour, he offered much hospitality to officers from home.   The season, the scene and " Diana " were combining to complete Nelson's conquest, when the voice of duty called. Suddenly, " arrives the *Drake* Sloop and *Cockatrice* cutter, with orders for the Transports to be fitted for the reception of Troops, and to be sent to New York; in consequence thereof, old Worth has given me orders to carry the Fleet to New York—a very *pretty job* at this late season of the year, for our sails are at this moment frozen to the yards."   The remainder of this story has, hitherto, in biographies of Nelson, rested upon a single testimony.   15

On October 14, when the *Albemarle* had gone down the river from Orleans Island, ready for sea, Alexander Davison, walking on the beach, noticed her Captain returning to the harbour.   He greeted his young friend at the landing-stage, and asked, with some anxiety, the reason for his reappearance.   A brief and heated conversation followed, against a background of wooded heights in flaming autumn colours, dazzling skies and frosted shipping. Nelson divulged that after having made his farewells in Quebec,

he had found himself irresistibly compelled to fly back to lay his
heart and fortune at the feet of the lady who, for him, epitomised
the charms of her country. Davison, in sharp alarm, used the
strongest arguments he could against this sudden resolution.
If the lady accepted Nelson's heart and fortune, it must mean
the close of a promising career. The acquaintance was, as far
as time was concerned, very slight. The Provost-Marshal's
daughter, famed for her "accomplishments" and aloof bearing,
was but sixteen. Nelson sadly listened to reason, and, accompanied by Davison, returned to the *Albemarle* in Bec roads,
whence he sailed for New York six days later.

He dropped anchor near Sandy Hook lighthouse, twenty
miles south of the south end of Manhattan Island, on November 11,
"with all my Fleet safe", a fortunate record for the season. A
single letter from him dated "New York" exists, and his
comments on the English society of the station were not flattering.
"Money is the great object here, nothing else is attended to."
From the moment that he set eyes upon a squadron of the West
India fleet lying in New York harbour, his mind was made up.
This detachment of twelve sail-of-the-line had taken part in
Rodney's action of April 12—the Battle of the Saints—had
followed a division of the vanquished French fleet which had gone
to refit in Boston, and would shortly be returning to the Antilles.
The battle-scarred veterans from the south, riding at anchor off
Sandy Hook, were under the command of Lord Hood.

7

On a mid-November day of 1782, when Lord Hood's flagship,
the *Barfleur*, was lying in the narrows off Staten Island, the
midshipman who had the watch on deck saw a barge from
Admiral Digby's fleet come alongside. A moment later he
perceived "the meerest boy of a captain I ever beheld". The
visitor's dress also made him stare. For his call upon Lord Hood,
the Captain of the *Albemarle* had attired himself in a full-laced
uniform, and a waistcoat with flaps, of surprisingly old-fashioned
cut. His lank fair hair was unpowdered, and his stiff Hessian
pigtail was of extraordinary length. The midshipman, who had
never before had the pleasure of encountering such a combination
of youth and antiquity, could not imagine who this officer was,
nor on what business he came. His curiosity was satisfied when
the Admiral presently introduced him to Captain Nelson, whose
pleasant manner and the enthusiasm which he displayed when

speaking on professional subjects soon showed that here was
" no common being "; nor did Captain Nelson neglect, on this
auspicious occasion, to turn a correct phrase on his loyal attachment to the midshipman's august father.   For if the name and
bearing of Nelson had suggested nothing to Prince William
Henry, Nelson, from the moment that he met the stare of those
protuberant light-blue eyes, set in that slightly cod-like but
bronzed countenance of heavy features, had very little doubt
as to the identity of the midshipman.   Prince William Henry,
whose father was justifiably pleased with his look in the uniform
of a Service described by His Majesty as " noble and most
glorious ", was, at the age of seventeen, unmistakably a son of
the House of Hanover, and a very fine lad.   He had not yet
begun to put on weight, although he had already displayed the
propensity for making long-winded unnecessary speeches which
was an outstanding characteristic of the Duke of Clarence and
William IV.   He was not to prove an intelligent man, or valuable
officer.   His early zeal for the Service, which Nelson remarked
with so much pleasure, deteriorated, in the opinion of later
critics, into " morbid official activity ", while Nelson's prophecy
that he would be " a disciplinarian, and a strong one " was so
lamentably fulfilled that lieutenants of spirit went to almost
any length to avoid serving under His Royal Highness.   But
everyone who met the Sailor Prince as midshipman was delighted
with him, and Nelson's enthusiasm never waned.   To the
Prince's credit it must be noted that he appreciated Nelson long
before he was a man of mark, kept all his letters and told him
so, and at a period when Nelson was unemployed and not smiled
upon at the Admiralty, wrote to him, " Never be alarmed, I will
always stand your friend."   Every appearance of William IV in   16
connection with Nelson brings out his best side, from that first
meeting on board the *Barfleur*, when he recognised " no common   17
being ", to the pompous funeral service of 1806, when spectators
beheld the portly Duke of Clarence reeling, blinded with tears,
against a massive pillar of St. Paul's.   He fades from the story
of Nelson in a glow of amiability, arising in a fashionable concert-
chamber, with great *empressement*, to lead from the room, upon
his arm, Mrs. Matcham, youngest sister of his long-departed
friend.   He had discovered that the band was about to strike up
" The Death of Nelson ".   18

8

The result of Nelson's call upon Lord Hood was of importance in his career, and there is evidence that he realised this. He had taken the bold step of coming to ask an Admiral whom he had met once, a few days previously, for something which he had long desired—" a better ship and a better station ".

On his arrival at Sandy Hook, Admiral Digby, Commander-in-Chief, had greeted him with the words, " You are come on a fine station for making prize-money ", to meet the startling reply, " Yes, sir, but the West Indies is the station for honour." To return without delay to that " grand theatre of Actions " was Nelson's object, and Lord Hood's squadron was likely to sail within the week. Fortunately, he had not mistaken his moment or his man. He presented himself with all the vigour and address he could muster, as " a candidate for a Line-of-Battle Ship ", and the keen-faced, hook-nosed, self-reliant Admiral to whom he made this request did not suggest that he was being asked something impossible. He said, without hesitation, that he would write to Admiral Digby and ask for Captain Nelson and the *Albemarle*. Before parting he promised the meagre but alert young officer of four-and-twenty, who preferred action to prize-money, " his friendship ". Nelson's antecedents were not unknown to him. He had been well acquainted with the late Captain Suckling, both in the Service and as Member of Parliament for the borough of which Lady Hood's father had been Mayor. He must, also, have made his enquiries, for he presently told Prince William Henry that if he wished to ask any questions about naval tactics, the Captain of the *Albemarle* could give him as much information as any officer in the fleet—a surprising statement, since Nelson's only experience of action had been on the Nicaraguan expedition, and he had never yet served with a fleet.

Events then moved quickly, as they must. Admiral Digby was persuaded to part with an inferior frigate and a strange young officer who looked as if he needed prize-money but said he did not, and on November 22 the *Albemarle* sailed with Lord Hood's squadron. On the 21st Lieutenant Bromwich was sent for by Captain Knight of the *Barfleur*, and put through a regular inquisition regarding the Bahama shoals. The reason averred was that Lord Hood expected the enemy to attempt some of the passages between them. The reason why Mr. Bromwich had been summoned by the Admiral's Flag-Captain was not made

E

known to him until he had been dismissed, and got into conversation with lesser officers of the *Barfleur*. He then learned that Lord Hood had said to Captain Nelson, " I suppose, sir, from the length of time you were cruising amongst the Bahama Keys that you must be a good pilot there ", to which Nelson had replied, " My Lord, I am well acquainted with them, but my Second Lieutenant is far my superior in that respect."

Nelson did not see the service for which he had hoped under Hood's flag. While the Admiral cruised off the west end of Hayti, ready to attack De Vaudreuil, the enemy went through the Mona passage between San Domingo and Puerto Rico, and to Nelson's disgust was next heard of off Curaçao. " Where they are, God knows. We are all in the dark in this part of the world whether it is Peace or War." The war was indeed almost finished. Spain and America were ready for peace. In France grim internal troubles were threatening. One last chance of action was seized by Nelson. On a March morning, when she was a few leagues to the windward of Monte Christi, the *Albemarle* fell in with H.M.S. *Resistance*, whose Captain reported that the French had taken Turk's Island in the Bahamas, three weeks previously, with a hundred and fifty regular troops and three warships. " I determined to look what situation the French were in, and if possible retake it. The *Tartar*, who joined company a few hours later, I ordered to put herself under my command, which, with the *Resistance* and *La Coquette*, a French Ship-of-War, prize to the *Resistance*, made a tolerable outward show." On the following night the *Albemarle* (having collected one more frigate, the *Drake*) anchored at Turk's Island, and Nelson sent in a flag of truce, calling upon the enemy to surrender. To this, the French Commander replied complacently that he should defend himself. During the night the *Tartar* vanished, but with daylight Nelson landed one hundred and sixty-seven seamen and marines under the command of the Captain of the *Drake*, and on the appearance of another frigate, the *Admiral Barrington*, ordered her and the *Drake* to go off the town and bombard it. Upon their getting within gunshot, he was surprised and disappointed to see an enemy battery open upon them. However, the *Drake* and *Admiral Barrington* " were both brought to an anchor opposite the battery, in a masterly manner ", and for upwards of an hour returned the enemy's steady constant fire. The master of the *Drake* and the boatswain and six men of the *Admiral Barrington* were wounded, when further batteries opened fire, and enemy troops with cannon were reported waiting upon a post concealed behind a hill. " With such a force, and their strong situation, I did not think anything farther could be attempted." Nelson's spirited project had not been a success, but since he called off his men in time, it was not a costly failure.

One more adventure awaited the *Albemarle* before the West Indies learned that peace preliminaries had been signed. While cruising under French colours in search of De Vaudreuil off Curaçao, the French-built frigate captured a Spanish launch, which, being hailed in French, came unsuspectingly alongside, and answered every necessary question as to the number and force of the squadron in Puerto Cabello. The surprise of her crew at finding themselves prisoners was equalled by that of Nelson when he found that his prize was filled with illustrious *savants*, engaged upon a scientific tour of exploration. Without discovering the identity of the leader of the party (who was travelling under the name of the Comte de Deux Ponts), Nelson, after offering them the best meal he could raise, permitted them to resume their harmless occupation. On his return to Port Royal he found Lord Hood's fleet under orders for home. Prince William was to pay a visit to Havana, *en route*, and Nelson, as a suitable officer acceptable to the young royalty, was detailed to attend him.

The *Albemarle*, with a fine present of rum and cigars for Locker on board, which her Captain hoped that the Customs House would not seize, came into Portsmouth harbour on June 26, 1783. " After all my tossing about in various climates, here at last am I arrived, safe and sound. I found orders for the *Albemarle* to be paid off at this place. On Monday next I hope to be rid of her." On July 3 he saw the last of her, and a touching scene took place after he had made his farewells. " The whole Ship's company offered, if I could get a Ship, to enter for her immediately. . . ." The scene was remarkable, as well as touching, because at Spithead the crews of several ships, being paid off in consequence of the peace, were proving mutinous. Nelson proceeded to London, and for the first time took lodgings in the capital, where for a further three weeks he was fully employed on business connected with the officers and men of his unlamented frigate.

" My time, ever since I arrived in Town, has been taken up in attempting to get the wages due to my good fellows for various Ships they have served in the war. The disgust of Seamen to the Navy is all owing to the infernal plan of turning them over from Ship to Ship, so that men cannot be attached to their officers or the officers care twopence about them."

The case of "poor Bromwich" was still troubling him a month later. Try as he would, he could not get this deserving character confirmed as a lieutenant.   19

Lord Hood in London did not forget a young officer of vivid quality whom he had fancied at Sandy Hook. On July 11 he took Nelson to a *levée* at St. James's, and presented him to his sovereign, who had a very kind word for a friend of Prince William, followed by a command for Captain Nelson to come to Windsor to take leave of the Sailor Prince, who was about to embark upon an educative Continental tour.

Fresh from his first attendance at Court, still in the full-dress uniform of his rank, Nelson went to dine with a friend in Lincoln's Inn. Alexander Davison, back from Quebec, was as comfortably lodged in London as he had been on the banks of the St. Lawrence. While the traffic of London at peace, on a late summer's day of 1783, sounded afar, Nelson began to consider with his most interesting friend outside the Service the problem of the future. Davison had political aspirations, and money. Nelson knew that he had closed the war without a fortune; he trusted that he had closed it without a speck on his character. After his very satisfactory reception at Court this morning, he believed that this must be so.

But before he could relax, he had to beg leave to shed his "iron-bound" full-dress uniform coat. Davison produced a dressing-gown. They then talked until the sun went down.   20

CHAPTER III

1783–1787

(*ætat* 24–28)

"SENTIMENTAL JOURNEY"

I

IN 1749, shortly after the Peace of Aix-la-Chapelle, William Hogarth, innocently and patriotically engaged in sketching the English royal coat-of-arms still visible on the principal gate of Calais, found himself arrested as a spy and hauled before the Commandant of the town. No explanations that he was an artist by profession prevailed. After an ennervating period under close guard, he was ignominiously escorted on board a boat bound for England. Never a Francophile, he took his revenge by producing one of his most lively crowd-pictures. In " Calais Gate ", the gluttonous friars, leathern-faced fishwives and ragged and tawdry soldiery of France were savagely pilloried.

Horatio Nelson, landing at Calais at 10.30 a.m. on Thursday, October 23, 1783, after an easy passage of three and a half hours from Dover, was amused to discover that Monsieur Grandsire, at whose inn he breakfasted, was the son of Hogarth's landlady. The young sea-officer was, like most young men of his day, familiar with engravings of " Calais Gate ", and with Sterne's *Sentimental Journey*. Indeed, in his first long descriptive letter to Locker he compared his experiences with those of Sterne, though he had as yet no incidents at all sentimental to report.

The English, justly famous for their insatiable desire for travel, and with appetites whetted by several seasons' confinement, were pouring into the Continent this autumn, as they always did after the conclusion of a peace treaty. At Florence they found Prince Charles Edward Stuart in a very melancholy state since the flight of his young wife. At Naples the English Ambassador's house was closed. Sir William Hamilton had taken advantage of the peace to enjoy a year's leave. At the Royal Military School, Brienne, a scowling shabby boy of fourteen, who spoke French very badly, had, after all, been reserved for a career in the Artillery. Last year's visiting inspector had recommended that, since the cadet Buonaparte seemed to possess the necessary firmness of character, he should be sent into the Navy. This year's inspector thought differently.

53

Nelson had spent an agreeable summer, based upon his lodgings, Number 3, Salisbury Street, Strand. He had borne his London brother, Maurice, with him for a visit to Norfolk; he had paid his duty call upon the Parkers, now returned from Jamaica, and with the riches accumulated there, and all their old zest, busy pulling down a mediæval mansion in Essex and building a new one. He had not passed through an English summer without contracting one of his heavy colds. Nevertheless, the north of France was his choice for the winter. He had heard too much of the tiresome scenes that took place when one of His Majesty's ships commanded by an officer who knew no language but his own captured a prize. ("Boatswain's mate, pass the word for any man who can speak French to come aft on the quarter-deck.") It was even worse when the papers of a foreign vessel needed examination, for a seaman who had picked up some French or Spanish very likely could not read it. Besides, French was an accomplishment expected in high society.

His first application to their Lordships, for six months' leave of absence to go into France "on my private occasions", mentioned the town of Lisle as his goal. Mr. Stephens, Secretary to the Admiralty, who was receiving many similar letters, failed to reply, and Nelson, after a week's wait, wrote again, having during the interval made his arrangements. When the desired permission came he had nothing left to do except pick up his travelling companion. James Macnamara, messmate of days in Sir Peter Parker's flagship, recommended St. Omer. "Mac", who had the advantage of his friend in that he could make himself understood by French natives, said darkly that if an Englishman settled in a town where there were English, he might find life very difficult, but Nelson had heard that St. Omer was "a dirty, nasty town"—a thing which he could well believe after his first whiff of Calais. After performing a perfunctory tour of that historic city, and dining, they ordered a post-chaise, and prepared to embark for the interior. When the post-chaise arrived, with a flourish, at Monsieur Grandsire's doors, Nelson had another wary smile at French taste. The little postillions, in their large jack-boots, cut most ridiculous figures; the horses which they drove with so much imprecation seemed to a quiet English eye to resemble rats. The officers entered their equipage, and immediately made two discoveries which, taken in conjunction, were serious. Chaises in France possessed no springs, and roads were "generally paved, like London streets". The

young gentlemen were "pretty well shook together" by the
time that they had covered two posts and a half, and by no
means inclined to push on to Montreuil-en-Mer, another forty-five
miles, at a pace which they calculated not to exceed four miles an
hour. "Marquees" had an elegant sound. They decided to
spend the night there, and presently drew up at the solitary inn
of a small village, situated in dumb, dark country, of salt-laden
airs, notably remote and melancholy on an early autumn evening.
"'Inn' they called it—I should have called it a pig-stye. We were
shown into a room with two straw beds, and, with great difficulty,
they mustered up clean sheets, and gave us two pigeons for
supper, upon a dirty cloth and wooden-handled knives. O what
a transition from happy England!" But being both five-and-
twenty, on holiday, and determined not to be upset by trifles,
they enjoyed a good laugh, and, going to bed, slept very soundly.
Next morning, Marquise having no charms to detain them, they
set out with first daylight for Boulogne, which they found packed
with English, but mostly of a type with whom other English
would not wish to make closer acquaintance. Nelson thought
that the excellence and cheapness of the wine with which he
was served at breakfast might account for the presence of most
of these countrymen.

After breakfast, France began to look better. "The roads
mostly are planted with trees, which make as fine an avenue as
to any gentleman's country seat . . . you drive in almost a
continued avenue." The travellers put up at "the same inn,
with the same jolly landlord that recommended La Fleur to
Sterne", and were so much taken with the plains of Picardy that
they would gladly have "fixed" in Montreuil. But it soon
appeared that the difficulties were insurmountable. Sixty noblemen's families, owners of the surrounding "finest country for
game that ever was", abode in haughty privacy in the many
handsome houses which the young English gentlemen had
remarked on their arrival. The remaining residents, being
"very poor indeed", dwelt meekly in hovels. They were
actually waiting for the French Revolution, and when an English
Ambassador traversed this road, bent on peace negotiations, in
October 1796, he saw nothing but fallen pillars and grass-covered
drives to mark the entrances to *châteaux* represented by heaps of
blackened stones. Nelson in 1783 only realised that in Montreuil
there was "no middling class of people", and that "amidst such
plenty, they are poor indeed". Suitable lodgings and tutors for

English officers being obviously unobtainable, next day, with real regret, they left a deceptively attractive-looking small town where partridges cost only 2½d. a brace, and pheasants and wood-cock were proportionately cheap. Their entry into Abbeville, after dark, was at an unlucky moment. Two other travelling English, " Lord Kingsland and Mr. Bullock ", had decamped that Saturday afternoon, after an enjoyable and prolonged stay. Not much edified by the spectacle of provincial French in the throes of realising financial loss, and appreciating that English were likely for some time to be unpopular in Abbeville, Nelson consented " to steer for St. Omer ".

A week later, safely " fixed " in the place which " Mac " had always favoured, he bought Chambaud's *Grammar of the French Tongue*, on the title-page of which he wrote neatly, " Horatio Nelson began to learn the French Language on the first of November, 1783 ". He never succeeded.

2

By late December, he was softly humming—

> " But when a lady's in the case,
> All other things, they must give place."

His address, as he had instructed Locker, was " *Monsieur Nelson, chez Madame Lamourie, St. Omer-en-Artois* ", and St. Omer was all and more than " Mac " had promised. It had many old houses, inclining heavily above harbour and canal, but also plenty of well-paved, well-lighted streets of good shops, in which a number of cheerful English were visible, and even two sea-officers, to whom he took the violent instinctive dislike characteristic of travelling English for unintroduced compatriots. Captains Ball and Shephard (for he knew their names, although they had not troubled to call) had adopted the effeminate French addition of *épaulettes* to their uniform, a thing which made him think (quite mistakenly as events proved) that he should dislike them very much if he did get to know them. To find good lodgings with a pleasant French family had been quite easy, and the Mesdemoiselles La Mourie, one of whom made the lodgers' breakfast and the other their tea, were always ready to play a game of cards in the evening, after the officers' dinner had been sent in by the *traiteur*. But until Nelson learnt to address them in their own tongue, his acquaintance with these sirens must be confined to nods and becks and wreathed smiles, for they showed

not the slightest intention of ever understanding English. Reinforced in his resolution " I must learn French ", he restricted
his English visiting list to two names. Mr. Massingberd was
brother of an officer whom he had known in the *Lowestoffe*. Mr.
Andrews, a clergyman, was blessed with the large number of
olive-branches usual for a person of his period and means. After
several visits, Nelson was still hazy as to how many children of
what sexes there were in the *maison* Andrews. He was clear
about three only—a naval son, George, and two grown-up
daughters, " about twenty years of age ", who played and sang
whenever he was invited to dine. These young ladies had " such
accomplishments " that Nelson felt sure that had he been a
millionaire he would instantly have offered for the elder, who was,
besides, a beauty. " I must take care of my heart, I assure you."
However, as she could have no fortune, and his income was at
present " by far too small to think of marriage ", such dreams
were vain. He was " very happy in the acquaintance ", and
there the matter must end. Soon, French, in spite of perseverance
and patience (of which he feared he had a small stock), went on
but slowly, and as the winter days shortened, and frost set in,
his thoughts and steps tended with dusk to turn more and more
often towards an English parlour in a French provincial town,
where the exile was sure of a warm fire and a welcome. The
clergyman parent, the naval brother, the young ladies seated at
the instrument all spoke to him of home, and he presently got
sad news from home. His sister Anne had died—" at Bath, after
a nine days' illness. It was occasioned by coming out of the
ballroom immediately after dancing ", he told Locker, adding
that his sister had been in her twenty-first year. She had, in
fact, been twenty-three, but Nelson was always polite where a
lady's age was concerned. " Nanny ", " neat and taciturn ",
who had lost her bloom in a Capital Lace warehouse in Ludgate
Street, had left him a little seal, with the cipher A.N., which, alternatively with a much larger one, displaying the head of Neptune,
he used until armorial bearings were assigned to Sir Horatio
Nelson, K.B.

While his friend, whose French was now fluent, sallied forth
to take part in " a very elegant ball ", Nelson stayed in his
lodgings with Chambaud's *Grammar* for companion. " My mind
is too taken up with the recent account of my dear sister's death,
to partake of any amusements." It worried him that he had
received no word since the tragedy from his father, or of his

father from Mr. Suckling. His fancy ranged over a future in
which the Rector died of grief for the loss of Anne and his remaining spinster sister was left alone in a hard world. He would
then have to retire from the Service, pick up what job he could,
and " fix in some place that might be most to poor Kitty's
advantage. . . . She shall never want a protector and a sincere
friend while I exist." In such circumstances it was clearly
madness to think further of Miss Andrews. He considered
cutting short his French trip and returning at once to England,
or accepting " a most polite invitation " to go to Paris. This
came from " the officer whom I detained off Puerto Caballo ".
Not until he had settled in France had Nelson discovered that
the courteous *savant* whom he had surprised in time of war,
collecting Natural History specimens off the Venezuelan coast,
was " a much greater man than I suspected ". The gentleman
" who went by the name of the Count de Deux Ponts " and
expressed great appreciation " of the attention paid to him when
on board my ship " was to become much greater than even he
suspected. He was to die King of Bavaria. The date was a
fascinating one for a visit to the French capital, and there is no
doubt that a Prince of the Empire, who was in addition a General
of the French Army and a Knight of the Grand Order of St. Louis,
could have shown a young guest also Versailles, and the last of a
world of furious luxury and frivolity, already doomed. But
thanks to the charms of Miss Andrews, Nelson's French was still
unequal to such an ordeal, and, in any case, he had come abroad
to economise. He toyed with the idea of accepting the invitation
in the spring on his road to the south of France. Christmas saw
him still at St. Omer. On January 14 he addressed a long letter
to Uncle Suckling, beginning :

" There arrives in general a time in a man's life (that has friends)
that either they place him in life in a situation that makes his application
for anything further unnecessary, or give him help in a pecuniary way
if they can afford it, and he deserves it. That critical moment in my
life has now arrived." [He had discovered that Miss Andrews was not
absolutely penniless : she had a small fortune] ". . . £1,000 I understand.
The whole income I possess does not exceed £130 per annum. Now I
must come to the point. Will you, if I should marry, allow me a hundred
a year, until my income is increased to that sum either by employment
or any other way ? A very few years will, I hope, turn something up,
if my friends will but exert themselves. If you will not give me the
above sum annually, to make me happy for life, will you exert yourself
either with Lord North or Mr. Jenkinson, for to get me a guardship,
or some appointment in a public office, where the attendance of the

principal is not necessary, and of which they must have a number to dispose of?

"If nothing is done for me, I know not what I have to trust to. Life is not worth living without happiness, and I care not where I may linger out a miserable existence.

"I am prepared to hear your refusal, and have fixed my resolution if that should happen; but in every situation I shall be a well wisher to you and to all your family, and pray that they nor you may never know the pangs which at this instant tear my heart.

"God bless you, and assure yourself that I am your most affectionate and dutiful nephew, Horatio Nelson."

Mr. Suckling noted his compliance on the back of this letter, but by the time it reached him, Nelson was already in London. Such a sudden change of plans demands some explanation.

3

The General Election of 1784 has not been much mentioned in biographies of Nelson. He was under orders for the Leeward Islands by the time that polling took place, and already by the end of January hotly announced in a letter to his brother William that he "had done with politics". But there is no doubt that for a few hectic days in the middle of this month he was bitten with the idea of standing for Parliament. Nor was his interest in politics suddenly conceived, or as easily killed as he declared in his first disappointment. Eleven years later he was sufficiently attracted by a tentative approach from some political luminary to suggest that H.M.S. *Agamemnon* should be summoned home, in order that he might present himself as a candidate. But by that time he had learnt much. His account of his public services did not lack colour. His list of sponsors was impressive, and strictly *en règle*—as far as family went, the Duke of Portland, *via* his kinsman Lord Walpole; professionally, Lord Hood, Admiral Cornwallis, Lord Hugh Conway. Conversations with Sir Gilbert Elliot had seemed to show him the principal patriotic characters rearranged. In 1795 he was certain that he must stand in "the real Whig interest". In 1784, Mr. Pitt, exactly and rousingly, expressed his political opinions, and Mr. Pitt was said to be throwing his net wide. Nothing came of either project.

When he arrived suddenly in London, he gave correspondents several reasons for his return. He told Locker, "some little matters in my Accounts obliged me to come over". To his brother William he wrote that he needed the advice of good London physicians. He also presented himself in the unexpected guise of man-about-town. " My time has been so much taken up by running at the ring of pleasure. . . . London has so many charms that a man's time is wholly taken up." But in the first week of January, seated in his St. Omer lodgings wrestling with the problem of Miss Andrews, he had realised that Parliament might be dissolved at any moment. " I hope it will, that the people may have an opportunity of sending men that will support their interests." Acting on the idea that " out of sight, out of mind " may work conversely, he had come over to pursue a possibility which cannot have been entirely illusory. He caught a violent cold on arrival, and made it worse attending a *levée* at St. James's. He " danced attendance " in other influential circles. He applied for an interview with the First Lord, who asked him whether he wished to be employed, to which he could only answer " yes ". Lord Hood, who was himself thinking of standing, in the event of a dissolution, was much more encouraging. He at once invited the young aspirant with a feverish cold to dine at 12, Wimpole Street, and after that first dinner said " that his house was always open to me, and that the oftener I came the happier it would make him ". Soon " Brother William " and Locker came to hear more, to receive daily bulletins (" to-night the ministry will try their strength. I shall not conclude my letter till late, as perhaps I may hear how matters are likely to go "), very warm opinions on Mr. Fox and " a turbulent faction that are striving to ruin their Country ", and eulogies of Mr. Pitt, together with instructions to William to vote for him at Cambridge. Nelson and his young friends hoped " to unkennel Fox at Westminster ", in which they were disappointed. Who these friends were, except that they talked good rank party stuff, and that he met them at the houses of Lord Hood (for whom they were already canvassing, " although not openly ") and Captain Kingsmill (who was " looking out for a Seat "), is not disclosed. Captain Kingsmill, born Brice, who had taken the name of his lady when she inherited the estates of her grand-father, found a seat. Unfortunately for Nelson, all his family connections, in this heyday of nepotism, were Walpole—" the merest set of Cyphers—in Public affairs, I mean. . . . As to your having enlisted under the banners of the Walpoles," he told William, who was still hoping for a Walpole living, " you might as well have enlisted under those of my grandmother."

By the last day of January, Nelson's pretensions had received their quietus. " Let who will get in, I shall be left out." He left town as abruptly as he had arrived, and spoke of spending the winter in Norfolk, where " poor little Kate is learning to ride, that she may be no trouble to us ". He was waiting for a fair wind for the Lesser Antilles by the time that the results of the Westminster Election convulsed London, and Lord Hood, who had also been the son of a simple country clergyman, was returned at the head of the poll. But the political connections of " the greatest sea-officer I ever knew " had always been valuable. He had entered life under the patronage of the Grenvilles, the Lyttletons and the Pitts. However, if his friends would not get Nelson a seat, they could get him a ship. He was appointed to the *Boreas*, another 28-gun frigate, on March 18. During the interval he had found himself " pulled down most astonishingly ". He had considered returning to France, " to many charming women, but no charming woman will return with me ". This sounds as if a refusal from Miss Andrews may have been the chief reason for his flight from St. Omer, but it is as likely that he left her full of hope, and gave up dreams of matrimony and a political career together. He took her younger brother George to sea with him in the *Boreas*, so he must have been in friendly communication with the family after his departure.

Whatever the circumstances of his double disappointment, he prepared to sail for the Leeward Isles in an unusually bitter mood. Even William had been surprised at his getting a ship when so many officers were unemployed. " You ask," wrote Horatio crushingly, " by what interest did I get a Ship? I answer, having served with credit was my recommendation to Lord Howe, First Lord at the Admiralty. Anything in reason that I can ask, I am sure of getting from his justice." He was having to take William with him. He had tried every polite expedient to avoid this— pointed out that William had just, at last, attained a Rectory, that their father's health was most uncertain, and that the old gentleman needed companionship so soon after his loss. William was still set upon becoming a chaplain in a man-of-war. His brother could not satisfy that ambition, but he could, if he must, take his clergyman brother with him, in his own frigate, as a guest, and invite him upon suitable occasions to hold a service. His last note on the subject told William, " Come when you please, I shall be ready to receive you. Bring your canonicals and sermons. Do not bring any Burnham servants." He was, as he expressed it, to be " pretty well filled with *lumber* " on this voyage. " I am asked to carry out Lady Hughes and her family—

a very modest request, I think; but I cannot refuse, so I must put up with the inconvenience and expense." Also the ship was " full of young midshipmen, and everybody is asking me to take someone or other ". He could not refuse to take Lady Hughes, because she was the wife of the Admiral commanding at the Leeward Islands. Her expenses, which he discovered that he was to pay, were likely to come to nearly two hundred pounds, which sounded staggering to an officer who had recently contemplated matrimony on two hundred and thirty per annum. But he did not fail to ask Locker if he had any " young gentleman " to add to his *ménagerie*. " I shall have great pleasure in paying every attention in my power to him."

The *Boreas*, said to be a very fine frigate, well-officered and manned, was lying in Long Reach, ready to sail, when he went down to take possession of her. His troubles began at once.

> " On Monday, April 12th, we sailed at daylight, just after high water. The d——d Pilot—it makes me swear to think of it—ran the Ship aground, where she lay with so little water that the people could walk round her till next high water. That night, and part of the next day, we lay below the Nore with a hard gale of wind and snow; Tuesday I got into the Downs; on Wednesday I got into a quarrel with a Dutch Indiaman who had Englishmen on board, which we settled, after some difficulty. The Dutchman has made a complaint against me; but the Admiralty, fortunately have approved my conduct in the business, a thing they are not very guilty of where there is a likelihood of a scrape."

On Sunday the 18th he reported from Spithead to Mr. Stephens at the Admiralty, " Sir, I have the honour to acquaint you that His Majesty's Ship under my command, arrived at this place yesterday, and enclosed is her state and condition."

Lady Hughes and party joined the ship from Portsmouth, and Nelson, crossed in love and done with politics, found that in addition to a large and rustic elder brother, over thirty mothers' darlings, or rejects, and an Admiral's lady who never stopped talking, he was to take charge of a sugary *débutante*. For Lady Hughes had a daughter, and it instantly became sufficiently obvious that the poor " Rosy " was being taken to the Leeward Islands for no other object than to find a husband. The Captain of the *Boreas* came first on Lady Hughes's list, but if he would not offer, almost any other gentleman, even his parson brother, would serve. The methods of Lady Hughes were crude, but she was not blind to the agonising fact that an adored child brought scarcely anything except youth to market. Nelson saw that " the mother will be the handsomer in a few years ". His methods also were crude. After his first terrifying vision of the amorphous " Rosy " he hastened to Portsmouth, hired steeds and invited another young lady for an expedition on Portsea Common. Retribution came swiftly and painfully. The " black-guard horse " bolted, and " carried me round all the Works into Portsmouth, by the London gates, through the Town out at the gate that leads to Common, where there was a waggon in the road ". Nelson flung himself from his steed, " unluckily upon hard stones ", and " to crown all ", the young lady, whose horse had emulated his, was saved by a total stranger " from the destruction she could not have avoided ".

Three weeks later Locker received a letter, franked by Kings-mill, now Member for Tregony, who had scribbled on the back, " Nelson's last, I imagine ; he sailed to-day. He is a very good young man and I wish him every enjoyment of life." But as yet the very good young man was not enjoying life at all. As the *Boreas* pursued, in increasingly pleasant weather, that slow course towards sunlit isles of which Lady Hughes nourished such high hopes, the poor lady became increasingly proprietary. She felt proprietary in a frigate which her husband had commanded in '63 ; she maddened Nelson by calling his ship " *dear Boreas* ". On a sheet of paper, headed " Walking the *Boreas* quarter-deck on the 30th May, 1784 at 7 in the evening ", he jotted down a list of her passengers and officers : " Lady Hughes, Miss Hughes, Captain Nelson, Lieutenants Wallace and Dent " (he spelt Wallis, who was a stranger, wrongly), " James Jameson, Master, Reverend Mr. Nelson, Masters Mates, Bromwich and Powers. . . ." (" Poor Bromwich ", he had told Locker, within a week of his appoint-ment, " must go out as Master's Mate with me ; he cannot get confirmed.")

Cupid's darts, so anxiously awaited by Lady Hughes, began to fly about, but not in the right direction. Before the voyage was done it was apparent, even to her austere Captain, that both Lieutenants of the *Boreas* and her Scottish Surgeon were paying great attention to the purser's wife. But for her attendant " specimen of English beauty ", he would not have disliked Lady Hughes. He saw that the couple really were " very pleasant good people ". They were not sea-sick and they were delighted with his ship. Lady Hughes, for her part, long after she had given up hopes of such a relationship, continued to feel maternal affection for a young man obviously designed by nature to be a good husband and father, and years later, following a

meeting with a brother-in-law of the hero at Bath, she felt
impelled to send Mr. Matcham a line on the subject of Captain
Nelson's "infinite kindness and goodness of heart displayed in
his management of his many young midshipmen. He every day
went into the schoolroom, and saw them do their nautical business,
and at twelve o'clock he was always the first on deck, with his
quadrant." Naturally, not all the thirty "younkers" were bold
boys.

"The timid, he never rebuked, but always wished to show them
he desired nothing of them that he would not instantly do himself; and
I have known him say, 'Well, sir, I am going a race to the mast-head,
and beg I may meet you there.' No denial could be given to such a
wish; and the poor fellow instantly began his march. Captain Nelson
never took the least notice with what alacrity it was done, but when
they met in the top, instantly began speaking in the most cheerful
manner, and saying how much a person was to be pitied that could
fancy there was any danger, or even any thing disagreeable in the
attempt. After this excellent example, I have seen the timid youth lead
another, and rehearse his captain's words."

10

The thirty midshipmen included, as well as her own son, a
Maurice Suckling, a distant cousin of the Captain, and she little
knew that while she beamingly noted the stiff young bachelor's
astute and humane treatment of "the young gentlemen who
have the happiness of being on his quarter-deck", he was
gloomily recording that he could not as yet make much of either
Maurice William or the Admiral's son.

On June 1 the *Boreas* arrived off Madeira, and found H.M.S.
Resource and a Dutch East-Indiaman lying at anchor in Funchal
Bay. Next morning betimes a state barge came alongside. The
Governor had sent the major of his guards to convey Lady
Hughes and *suite* to view the beauties of Prospero's isle. This
offer was politely declined, and at 10.30, having breakfasted,
Lady and Miss Hughes, attended by Captain Nelson, Lieutenants
Wallis and Dent, the Reverend Mr. Nelson, Mr. Lane, Lieutenant
of Marines, and ten midshipmen, went into the barge of the *Boreas*.
The frigate, completely manned, fired a salute of eleven guns,
followed by three cheers, when her barge had attained a suitable
distance, to which the barge replied. "Nothing could have a
more imposing appearance." The party proceeded to call upon
the Governor and the Consul, and since the Consul omitted to
return their call, pleading that the Government allowed him no boat
for such a purpose, Captain Nelson marked Mr. Murray's inatten-
tion to etiquette by failing to include him in invitations for Friday,

June 4. On this date, His Majesty's birthday, H.M.S. *Boreas* and *Resource* and the Dutch East-Indiaman fired a salute of twenty-one guns, which was returned by the two forts of Funchal, and after a dinner-party on board the *Boreas* " the healths of the king, queen and their thirteen children were drank in as many bumpers ". Sunday's engagements opened with Divine Service, attended by the English merchants of Funchal, who afterwards thanked the Rev. William Nelson for an excellent sermon. To her Captain's relief, the *Boreas* got under sail on Tuesday, at 8 p.m. Lady Hughes was eager to greet her husband. Nelson, having contracted successfully with Higgins of Funchal for a quarter of a cask of Madeira for Locker, and four casks for the Governor of Dominica (who was going to help him in the matter of Locker's Dominica estates), had no desire to linger. During the evening of the 14th " the usual pastimes on Crossing the Line were observed: Old Neptune came on board and received the customary fine ", and the Captain seized the opportunity to give a straight talk to his officers and men on the inevitable results of failing to pay due respect to diet and hygiene in the tropics. Twelve days later the *Boreas* anchored in Carlisle Bay, Barbados, and Nelson found himself Senior Captain and Second-in-Command on the station. Lady Hughes's last memory of him as host was happy. " The day we landed at Barbados, we were to dine at the Governor's. Our dear Captain said, ' You must permit me, Lady Hughes, to carry one of my Aide-de-camps with me.' " This character, of course, proved to be one of his " younkers ", and he presented the young gentleman to the Governor with the words, " Your Excellency must excuse me for bringing one of my midshipmen, as I make it a rule to introduce them to all the good company I can, as they have few to look up to besides myself during the time they are at Sea."

4

He was not at first sight favourably impressed by the Leeward Islands, and in his present mood was inclined to be ruthless in comment and act. He reported to the Commander-in-Chief, and found Sir Richard Hughes (whose chosen instrument was the violin) " tolerable, but I do not like him, he bows and scrapes too much for me ". Sir Richard, at five-and-fifty, was not a figure for whom it was possible to indulge hero-worship. He had lost the sight of an eye, but not in action. The disability was the result of an accident with a table-fork, when attempting

11

F

to kill a cockroach. He lived in a boarding-house in Barbados
" not much in the style of a British Admiral ". He was a
baronet; his father and grandfather had both, for many
years, been Commissioner at Portsmouth; his lady had been
a great-niece of the celebrated Sir Hans Sloane. Nelson, who
had taken great pains on the voyage that the Admiral's lady
should appear in due state, felt miserably that the Hugheses
failed to present themselves with the prestige suitable to their
position. The unavoidable sequel to such behaviour was
apparent to his critical eye. Between them, the Hugheses,
the climate and the piping days of peace were producing dire
effects upon an unpopular station. " The Squadron is cursedly
out of tune."

The Rev. William Nelson was the first victim of the climate.
Three months of the Leeward Islands sufficed for him. He sailed
for home in September, leaving his brother without a confidant,
but the biographer with a second rich source of long, intimate
letters. Both the Collingwood brothers were on the station, but
Cuthbert, the only officer for whom Nelson could feel both
affection and regard, was at the moment of his arrival away at
Grenada. Another old messmate, little Charles Sandys, whom
he had known and liked as a merry, laughing lieutenant, had
developed a failing not uncommon in exiles. " I am sorry to say
that he goes through a regular course of claret every day." Soon
poor Sandys, enamoured of a young lady of Antigua, whose
beauty struck him speechless, but who had the sense to refuse
him consistently, was " between Bacchus and Venus, scarcely
ever thoroughly in his senses. . . . I am very sorry for him, for
his heart is good, but he is not fit to command a Man-of-War."
Dismissing Sandys (with the expectation that the next hurricane
months would carry him off) and the remainder of his fellow   12
officers as " geese " and " a sad set ", Nelson turned to the one
bright spot in his existence. " Was it not for Mrs. Moutray,
who is *very very* good to me, I should almost hang myself at
this infernal hole." The lady who bore this unmelodious name
was the wife of the Commissioner at Antigua. She was much
younger than her husband; her family consisted of a single
son, aged eleven, destined for the Service. She had leisure,
accomplishments and the most distinguished manners ever
observed by an impressionable officer who had at present " nobody
I can make a confidant of ". She did not disturb his lacerated
heart by any resemblance to Miss Andrews, who had been a

beauty, but, as he realised now, an *ingénue*. The Commissioner
and lady offered Nelson hospitality at "Windsor" while the
Boreas was painting. He at once conceived for Mrs. Moutray
one of those perfectly hopeless, desperately respectful passions,
as common amongst young exiles as the habit contracted by
Sandys. "Her equal I never saw in any country or in any
situation." And this sentimental journey had amongst its
fascinations for the young romantic the fact that it was doomed
from the first. Commissioner Moutray's health was weak.
Sooner or later he must go home. "I really am an April day,
happy on her account, but truly grieved if I only consider myself."
Mrs. Moutray very sweetly and soothingly promised to make
herself known to Captain Nelson's little sister, if the Rector of
Burnham Thorpe should carry "dear Kate" to Bath next
winter. ("What an acquisition to any female to be acquainted
with, what an example to take pattern from!" groaned her
worshipper.) This sentimental journey lasted eight months.
She sailed, eventually, in March, and in May he revisited the
house on the hill above English Harbour where he had spent his
"happiest days in this world", and indulged the pathetic fallacy:
"E'en the trees drooped their heads." A certain tamarind,
hallowed by some lofty memory, had possessed sufficient sensibility
to die. "All was melancholy; the road is covered with thistles;
let them grow. I shall never pull one of them up. By this
time I hope she is safe in old England. Heaven's choicest
blessings go with her."

It may be guessed that after the exit of Mrs. Moutray the
stage was set for the entry of Mrs. Horatio Nelson, and that
almost any lady of reasonable discretion and attractions might
hope to play that part. She had made her first apologetic
appearance within a few days of his saying farewell, "with a
heavy heart", to her predecessor, and it was hard upon her that
she must begin to play with a partner preoccupied by professional
trouble, and against a noise of distant but furious dispute, which
13   gave the tropical scene an additionally uneasy, headachey air.

5

About the time that Horatio Nelson decided that "the
Admiral and all about him are great ninnies", Sir Richard Hughes
began to be certain that in his new Senior Captain he had a
trouble-maker. There was a whiff of trouble when the *Boreas*
was not properly saluted on beating into Fort Royal Bay,

Martinique. Nelson wrote at once to the Governor, who proved his respect for the British flag by ordering the arrest of his neglectful subordinate. The French Governor proceeded to be so attentive to the officers of the *Boreas* during their stay that Nelson himself pleaded successfully for the release of the captive. On his arrival in English Harbour, Antigua, on February 5, 1785, he received a second and worse shock. The *Latona* was lying there with a broad pendant hoisted.

> " As her Captain was junior to me, I sent to know the reason for her wearing it. Her Captain came on board, who I asked the following questions :
>
> " ' Have you any order from Sir Richard Hughes to wear a Broad Pendant ? '
>
> " Answer : ' No.'
>
> " ' For what reason do you then wear it, in the presence of a Senior Officer ? '
>
> " Answer : ' I hoisted it by order of Commissioner Moutray.'
>
> " ' Have you seen by what authority Commissioner Moutray was empowered to give you orders ? '
>
> " Answer : ' No.'
>
> " ' Sir, you have acted wrong, to obey any man who you do not know is authorised to command you.'
>
> " Answer : ' I feel I have acted wrong; but being a young Captain, did not think proper to interfere in this matter, as there were you and other older Officers upon this Station.' "

Little Sandys then gladly departed, and Nelson addressed himself to Commissioner Moutray, who proved to possess a memorandum from Sir Richard, authorising him to act as Commander-in-Chief on the station during the absence of a senior officer. " Until you are in commission I cannot obey any order I receive from you ", said Nelson. " I know of no superior officers beside the lords commissioned of the Admiralty, and my seniors on the post list." He wrote to Sir Richard twice, and to the Secretary to the Admiralty. He felt himself on firm ground, as an officer must retire from the active list and be placed on half-pay before he could be appointed Commissioner of a Dockyard. Sir Richard also wrote home, and the result of this skirmish was that their Lordships informed Captain Nelson, " he ought to have submitted his doubts to the Commander-in-Chief on the station, instead of having taken upon himself to controll the exercise of the functions of his Appointment ". Their Lordships were clearly supporting a senior officer. That the note was a reprimand must be obvious to the thickest skinned, and Nelson's skin, as far as reprimands from Headquarters went, was never thick. To the end, an unpleasant note from their Lordships cost him a disturbed night. But he was six-and-twenty, and sick of a slack station.

His next difference with his Commander-in-Chief (which, since an answer from home took three months, overlapped his first) was far more serious. It had, indeed, been brewing from the moment of his arrival. Correspondence on the subject had begun with the New Year, and it was to embroil him with every authority in the islands. Sir Richard had been induced to waive the Navigation Laws in respect to vessels of the United States trading in the islands. "His easy temper", said Nelson politely, "had made him the dupe of some artful people." The Admiral's compliance suited nearly every prominent planter, merchant and Customs House official on the station, but not, as Nelson pointed out, "the interests of Great Britain". Sir Richard behaved in character throughout this weary business. When first approached by Nelson and Cuthbert Collingwood, he hedged. He had no instructions from home. Nelson told him that this was "very odd, as every captain of a man-of-war was furnished with the Statutes of the Admiralty, in which was the Navigations Act. . . . He said he had never seen the Book." On being presented with a copy, he "seemed convinced". He had "never seen or noticed" the Act before, but would now issue an order that the Navigation Laws should be enforced. "In December, to my astonishment," Nelson received contrary instructions. Sir Richard, after nearly two months' release from the company of his emphatic Senior Captain, had taken "good advice". After mature consideration, he required his officers not to hinder what was going on. "Let the residents of the various Islands decide the various cases." On finding that Nelson was not prepared to do this, indeed was going to defy such instructions, he sourly washed his hands of him, with a nervous reminder that he would get himself "into a scrape". Nelson stated his views at length, on paper, to Sir Richard, to the Admiralty, again and again, and to Lord Sydney, Secretary of State. ("My name most probably is unknown to your lordship, but my character as a man, I trust will bear the strictest investigation. I stand for myself, no great connexion to support me if inclined to fall.") He also wrote anxiously, for professional advice, to Uncle Suckling, "a person that has been in the Customs House since a boy". In the last resort, when his situation did begin, as Sir Richard had prophesied, to look very ugly, he addressed a humble memorial to the King's Most Excellent Majesty. "I had no alternative to save myself from being ruined."

The news of what he was about soon spread, and he found himself ostracised by the society of the islands. Supported by

Cuthbert Collingwood, he visited the Governor, who began by explaining that he was all for suppressing the illegal trade, but his difficulties were many. Americans putting into port would produce wonderful excuses, swear, " even as the sea-phrase is, ' through a nine inch plank ' that their vessel leaked, or had sprung a mast. Then the Customs grant a permit to land a part or whole of their cargo to pay expenses, under which permits they land innumerable cargoes." Governor Shirley, relishing the probable results of Captain Nelson's action as little as his Admiral, said at some moment during their interview that " Old Generals were not in the habit of taking advice from young gentlemen ", to which Nelson replied, " I have the honour, sir, of being as old as the Prime Minister of England, and think myself as capable of commanding one of His Majesty's Ships as that Minister is of governing the State." (Mr. Pitt was still his idol.) As he expected, he was able to deal with Governor Shirley, but the abuse continued. It was at this point in the struggle that, being upon a cruise to St. Kitts and Nevis, he, and Wilfred Collingwood acting under his orders, turned back every American in sight, and having given four vessels lying in Nevis roads forty-eight hours' warning to hoist their proper colours and depart, seized them. The fat was then in the fire. Sir Richard regretfully gave up the idea of sending another captain to supersede Nelson and court-martialling his disobedient junior. He " stood neuter ". " I am sure of casting my gentlemen ", said Nelson calmly, and he was right. But a new danger awaited him. When the American masters went on shore they were met by an attorney primed by the furious inhabitants of Nevis, who had clubbed together and raised a sufficient sum for the ships' owners to sue Nelson for assault and imprisonment. Forty thousand pounds was mentioned as the sum claimed for damages. A marine had been on sentry duty at the cabin door while their evidence was taken; he was represented as " a man with a drawn sword ", who had put them in terror of their lives. To avoid arrest, Nelson was obliged to stay in the *Boreas* for eight weeks, until the trial came on. Attempts to serve writs on him were frustrated by Lieutenant Wallis. The end of the story came three months later, when orders arrived from England that the costs of Captain Nelson's defence were to be paid by the Treasury. By the same packet came congratulations to Sir Richard Hughes and the officers under his command for their activity and zeal in protecting the commerce of Great Britain.

"Don't let me forget," added Nelson, detailing the saga to Locker, "the President of Nevis offered, in Court, to become my bail for £10,000 if I chose to suffer the arrest. He told them I had only done my duty, and although he suffered more in proportion than any of them, he could not blame me." In the last paragraph of a letter which covers four and a half pages of close print, he tantalisingly mentions, "I think I have found a woman who will make me happy."

15

6

Mr. John Richardson Herbert, President of the Council of the Island of Nevis, generally referred to by his family as "the President", or "Mr. H.", and by his acquaintance as "the Governor" or "Governor Herbert", was a character ripe for the pen of Sir Walter Scott, Miss Austen, Mr. Thackeray and, in his more despotic moments, even Miss Barrett of Wimpole Street.

He was a man of birth. His grandfather had been the Honourable James Herbert, son of Philip, fourth Earl of Pembroke and first Earl of Montgomery; nephew and namesake of Sir Philip Sidney; favourite of James I, but not of Charles I. Since the fourth Earl of Pembroke had received from his infatuated Sovereign grants of West India islands, and from his first wife ten surviving children, it was natural that one of his younger sons should settle in Nevis, loveliest of the Caribbean Leeward Isles, and christened by Columbus at the same time that the discoverer gave his own Christian name to its nearest neighbour, St. Kitts.

Nevis, viewed from the sea, resembled a highly-coloured illustration of a treasure-island in a child's picture-book. It was almost circular, and its lower slopes displayed the sharp green of the sugar-cane, fringed by groves of cocoanut. Its conical summit, of a much darker blue than the surrounding waters, was continually capped by the snow-white clouds which had reminded Columbus of the Mountains of Nieves, in Spain. To complete its exotic attractions, it was evidently of volcanic origin, and annually subject to tornadoes. James Herbert built in Nevis a house which he called Pembroke Lodge, and erected his coat-of-arms, in stone, above the gateway of entrance. His grandson also built something palatial in the style of his day. Montpelier, a large white house, guarded by pillars without, and within closely shuttered against West Indian glare, furnished by an owner to whom expense was no object, at a date when fashion expressed itself in terms of much gilding, crystal, floral brocade and polish, was the finest residence in an island measuring only eight miles by six and a quarter, but unequalled in products of the luxury trade.

Nelson, who first visited the President in January 1785, was naturally impressed. " Herbert is very rich and very proud. . . . Although his income is immense, yet his expenses must be great, as his house is open to all strangers and he entertains most hospitably." Mr. Herbert's generosity, indeed, included making gifts to people whom he had never seen. He thought that Captain Nelson's parson brother, who had desired to become chaplain in a man-of-war, sounded a good fellow, and he mentioned intentions of sending him " a cask of remarkably fine rum, double-proof ", to be enjoyed with a fat Norfolk Christmas turkey. " I can't give you an idea of his wealth, for I don't believe he knows it himself ", said Nelson. This was correct. Mr. Herbert, who " must live like myself ", did possess, in addition to his salary as President, considerable wealth not easily realisable. The stock of negroes and cattle upon his estate—which Nelson, like most of " Mr. H's " guests, coupled in this manner—were valued at £60,000. For the past seven years Montpelier had exported to England an average of five hundred casks of sugar. Many other plantations and houses in Nevis, at a time when their value was rapidly diminishing, were mortgaged to him. Nelson knew how soon a West India house might fall into decay. He had, after many enquiries by letter and word of mouth, gone out of his way to make a personal tour of inspection to the Dominica estate left to Locker's wife by her father, Admiral Parry. The fair and pale young sea-officer, escorted by native guides, had toiled with great difficulty through trackless woods above St. Rupert's Bay, towards a deserted house into which mulattoes had crept after the English Admiral had left. . . . He could hardly believe his eyes when his guide had, at last, halted and pointed in silence at a site entirely choken by tropical undergrowth. He could see nothing but a thicket. Not a stone was visible. In the West Indies Nature hurried to fill a vacuum.

The President of Nevis was a widower. He was not at present on good terms with his only child, Martha, who intended to marry Mr. Andrew Hamilton of the island. His household included, in addition to innumerable faithful blacks, a fluctuating number of nieces (who " came out " upon long visits and generally married), and an invalid sister, " Miss Sarah ". Nelson

brought one of the nieces with him on his second trip to Nevis—
Miss Parry Herbert, also niece to the Governor of Barbados,
David Parry. ("They trust any young lady with me, being an
old-fashioned fellow.") There was also a permanent niece who
at the time of his first two visits was absent, staying with friends
in St. Kitts. "Dear Fanny", whom the President mentioned
portentously as being "as dear to him as a child, perhaps dearer,"
kept house for a man "who must have his own way in
everything"—no easy task. She was a young widow, and a
particularly fine little boy of five, who occupied the echoing
nurseries of Montpelier, was her property. Nelson heard of her,
and she also heard of Nelson. For that species of white magic
which sometimes informs a female that she has met the future
partner of a beloved relative, caused yet another of the nieces to
include the following paragraphs in a letter to Mrs. Nisbet:

> "We have at last seen the Captain of the *Boreas*, of whom so much
> has been said.
>
> "He came up, just before dinner, much heated, and was very silent;
> yet seemed, according to the old adage, to think the more. He declined
> drinking any wine; but after dinner, when the President, as usual, gave
> the following toasts, 'the King', 'the Queen and Royal Family', and
> 'Lord Hood', this strange man regularly filled his glass, and observed
> that those were always bumper toasts with him; which having drank,
> he uniformly passed the bottle, and relapsed into his former taciturnity.
>
> "It was impossible, during this visit, for any of us to make out his
> real character; there was such a reserve and sternness in his behaviour,
> with occasional sallies, though very transient, of a superior mind. Being
> placed by him, I endeavoured to rouse his attention by showing him all
> the civilities in my power; but I drew out little more than 'Yes' and
> 'No'.
>
> "If you, Fanny, had been there, we think you would have made
> something of him; for you have been in the habit of attending to these
> odd sort of people."

16

Two months passed before Nelson's frigate was again to be
seen in Charlestown harbour, and again by a chance he missed
Mrs. Nisbet. He arrived too early on the morning of March 11.
In the character of chaperon to the lively Miss Parry Herbert, he
had hastened his charge up from H.M.S. *Boreas* to the shelter of
her uncle's roof. The travellers arrived to find a West India
house still asleep. While the new niece from home ran upstairs
to announce herself, Nelson waited in a room next to that prepared
for breakfast. Children, as well as sea-officers, stir early. He
presently found himself regarded by a very bright pair of dark
eyes. "Good God!" ejaculated the President to his household,

when he appeared late at the breakfast-table, having completed a toilet interrupted by the necessity of descending to greet an early caller, " Good God ! If I did not find that great little man of whom everybody is so afraid, playing in the next room, under the dining-table, with Mrs. Nisbet's child."

A few days later the Captain of the *Boreas* came to dine, and the elusive wraith who acted as hostess for her uncle was able to thank him, with that mixture of pride and apology so becoming to a young mother, " for the great partiality he had shown to her little boy ". She could not know that she reminded him instantly of Mrs. Moutray, and at a moment when his heart was bleeding for the loss of that paragon. The ladies' points in common were obvious, and where there was a difference, it was distinctly in favour of the younger. Mrs. Nisbet had, like her predecessor, leisure, accomplishments and a single fine son; but no middle-aged husband loomed behind her, making chaste romance impossible. She displayed the same type of elaborate manners which Nelson had so much admired in the Commissioner's drawing-room (" Her manners are Mrs. Moutray's "), but the ceaseless entertainments over which Mrs. Nisbet diffidently presided much exceeded in scope and size those of the lady of Antigua. She was fluent in the French tongue, an exquisite needlewoman, and according to rumour (which lied) her musical talents were beyond the ordinary. As hostess of the principal house in a treasure-island, and dear as a child to a man who did not know his own wealth, she was highly elegant. The *fichu* gowns of muslin and sash in which she flitted about the groves and drooped in the saloons of Montpelier were inspired by those in which the Queen of France was playing at being a shepherdess or a milkmaid at the Little Trianon. Her features were fine, her eyes dark grey ; of her dark curls a lover could not judge, for in 1785 all ladies were in powder by dinner-hour. Most important of all, Mrs. Nisbet's " English complexion " was the pride of the island. Nelson fell in love swiftly, as usual. He saw her first on some day between the 13th and 15th of March, " a few days after " March 11. On the 13th of March he said farewell to Mrs. Moutray, who sailed on the 20th, and in the first week of May, fresh from his valedictory pilgrimage to the shrine of the Commissioner's lady, he repaired to Nevis, to call, not upon the President, but upon " Miss Parry Herbert and a young widow ". By June 28 he was confiding to Brother William, " *Entre nous.* Do not be surprised to hear I am a *Benedict*, for if at all, it will be before a month. Do not tell." However, he himself had already said too much. Grave Captain Collingwood had congratulated Mrs. Nisbet on a bloodless conquest. Before he sailed for Barbados in mid-August, Nelson " spoke ", and followed up his verbal proposal by a letter.

" My dear Mrs. Nisbit [sic],

" To say how anxious I have been, and am, to receive a line from Mr. Herbert, would be far beyond the descriptive powers of my pen. Most fervently do I hope his answer will be of such a tendency as to convey real pleasure, not only to myself, but also to you. For most sincerely do I love you, and I think that my affection is not only founded upon the principles of reason but also upon the basis of mutual attachment. Indeed, My charming Fanny, did I possess a Million, my greatest pride and pleasure would be to share it with you ; and as to living in a Cottage with you, I should esteem it superior to living in a palace with any other I have yet met with.

" My age is enough to make me seriously reflect upon what I have offered, and commonsense tells me what a Good choice I have made. The more I weigh you in my mind, the more reason I find to admire both your head and heart. But come, don't say, ' What a vain young Man is this ! 'tis a modest way of telling me I have given a proof of my sense by accepting him.' No ! To Your heart do I own myself most indebted, yet I trust you approved of me for this obvious reason—' He esteems me, therefore he is the person I ought to expect most happiness from, by a return of affection. . . .'

" My temper you know as well as myself, for by longer acquaintance you will find I possess not the Art of concealing it. My situation and family I have not endeavoured to concial [sic].

" Don't think me rude by this entering into a correspondence with you. Consider that separation from the objects we esteem loses some of its stings by a mutual unreserved correspondence."

17

The President answered, after an interval, in kindly noncommittal vein. " My dear boy," said Nelson ruefully to Collingwood, " I want some prize-money." But the President's delay and vagueness were pardonable. Miss Sarah Herbert had died.

Nelson's second love-letter was a model for a young gentleman addressing his future bride on the death of a maiden aunt.

" I partake in all the sorrows you experience ; and I comfort myself that however great your grief may be, at losing a person who was so deservedly dear to you as your good Aunt, yet, when reason takes place, you must rather have pleasure in knowing she is released from those torments she has undergone for months past. Time ever has, and in the present instance I trust may have, a tendency to soften grief into a pleasing remembrance; and her unspotted character must afford you real comfort. Call Religion to your aid; and it will convince you that her conduct in this world was such as insures everlasting happiness in that which is to come."   18

"Dear Fanny", as she was to be henceforward, had not written to her "H.N.", but she had never in the course of a rather unsuccessful love-scene given any promise to correspond. He suggested in a postscript, "Do I ask too much, when I venture to hope for a line? Otherwise," he feared, "I may suppose my letters may be looked on as troublesome."

November found him engaged upon the inevitable letter to Uncle Suckling. "I open a business which perhaps you will smile at, in the first instance, and say, 'This Horatio is for ever in love'." He had obtained an interview with Mr. Herbert, an interview at which the President had evidently been majestic. "I have told him I am as poor as Job; but he tells me he likes me, and I am descended from a good family, which his pride likes." The trouble was that Mrs. Nisbet (most surprisingly when one came to think of it) turned out to be without a fortune. For the moment, at any rate, anything which she could bring towards a match must depend entirely upon the generosity of Mr. Herbert, who could not, he declared, "do much in my lifetime. When I die, she shall have twenty thousand pounds; and if my daughter dies before me, she shall possess the major part of my property." Nelson believed that the President might be persuaded to give his niece an annual allowance of two or three hundred a year, but he would much prefer that "whatever he may do at her marriage, may flow spontaneously". Finally, and most agonisingly for an ardent suitor, Mr. Herbert intended retiring in about eighteen months' time, and did not wish to lose his housekeeper before then. But meanwhile he had no objections to Captain Nelson paying his addresses.

Nelson's two letters to his uncle on this subject, both full of misstatements, show how headlong had been his wooing and how   19
inaccurate the information he had culled about Mrs. Nisbet. To Nelson, an acquaintance of eight months might perhaps fairly be presented as "of pretty long standing", and chivalry, or sheer ignorance, may have led him to subtract five years from her age; but he cannot have heard, either from her or Mr. Herbert, that she had been an orphan since she was two, and that her husband had died eighteen months after their marriage, in Nevis. It is even doubtful whether she can have told him that her husband

had " died insane ". The facts were quite different. Frances
Herbert Woolward, born in the early half of 1758, and baptised
at Nevis in May 1761, was a few months older than Nelson. Her
father was William Woolward, Senior Judge of Nevis, and her
mother, who died during Fanny's infancy, Mary, " Molly ", one
of the three sisters of President Herbert. Fanny's father survived
until she was nearly one-and-twenty, and she married, within
four months, the physician who had attended him. Although
she was an only child, and William Woolward had been a partner
with his brothers-in-law in the firm of Herbert, Morton and
Woolward, she had no income. Dr. Josiah Nisbet was descended
from the ancient and honourable Scottish house of Nisbet of
Nisbet in Ayrshire, and his paternal grandmother had been
Emilia Douglas, granddaughter of the seventh Earl of Moray.
The Nisbet family had been settled for two generations in Nevis,
at an estate called Mount Pleasant, but Josiah was a second son.
He graduated as M.D. at Edinburgh, at the age of twenty-one,
and returning to Nevis, practised there. President Herbert
promised his niece a dowry of £2,000, but this had not yet been
paid when the honeymoon couple sailed for England. Their
reason for leaving the West Indies was that Dr. Nisbet was
suffering from sun-stroke. The oppressed couple performed their
long journey " home ", and a child, named Josiah, was born,
eleven months after the marriage, in England. For a further
seventeen months Mrs. Nisbet attended her invalid physician,
who then died at a house in the Cathedral Close at Salisbury. He
was buried at Stratford-sub-castle, and " his affectionate wife "
erected to his memory a tablet, surmounted by the Nisbet coat-
of-arms. For the second time in her life she was left unprovided for, and this time she was in a strange land and with
an infant child. She took the only possible course. She appealed
to her Uncle Herbert, who provided her with an invitation
to Montpelier and a settled home. She had been a widow for
over four years when Nelson first met her, for though her
attractions were highly marketable from the contemporary point
of view, she had, in the Anglo-Saxon phrase, " seen a wolf ", and
her wolf was the wolf at the door. Her features, her wits, her
eye had been sharpened. She never outgrew the bird-like
nervousness engendered by her early experiences, and was
abnormally sensitive on the subject of money. When she was
forty-three she wrote to Nelson at Naples, complaining that
payment of the legacy left to her son by the President was more

than twelve months overdue, but without her husband's support
she hesitated to approach her cousins. " I have seen such
dreadful quarrells about money in my own family, that I dread
to say a word."   It is possible that the President, misunderstand- 22
ing the origin of distressing symptoms which he had observed,
told Nelson that Fanny's first husband had died insane.   She
herself must either have confirmed this impression, or never
alluded to a period in which she had suffered severe shock; for
Nelson, as an experienced West India captain, was well aware of
the difference between being what he called " struck with the
sun " and insane.   Before leaving the depressing subject of her 23
finances it may be stated that the two or three hundred a year
which Nelson had believed that the President would give her on
her second marriage, and the legacy of £20,000, eventually took
the shape of an annual allowance of £100 and a legacy of £4,000.
Nor, although the President's only daughter died without issue,
did his niece ever inherit anything further.   Mr. Herbert, very
naturally, left his property in Nevis to a sister's son resident
in the island, instead of to a sister's daughter, wife of a sea-
officer resident in Norfolk.   Magnus Morton received the
Montpelier estate on the condition of his taking the name of
Herbert.   24

Nelson believed at the time of his engagement that Mrs.
Nisbet's " little fellow " would in time receive sufficient from his
father's and grandfather's estates to make him " totally independent ".   The President mentioned a legacy of £1,000 and
intentions of putting Josiah in the way of making his own living.
Josiah's legacy was £500, to be paid when he was twenty-one.   He
was twelve when Uncle Herbert died, and his stepfather had just
been appointed to commission a ship-of-the-line.   Uncle Suckling,
grimly commenting that the legacy was more than he had
expected, offered to advance the first £100, and Nelson, with the
words " My objection to the Navy now he is certain of a small
fortune, is in some measure done away ", took the boy to sea with
him.

7

Captain Nelson and Mrs. Nisbet settled down to the eighteen
months' engagement dictated by expediency.   He spent the
hurricane season of 1785 in Nevis, and was back there again by
New Year's Day of 1786, " as merry as I wish . . . sitting by the
woman who will be my wife. . . . Every day am I more than

ever convinced of the propriety of my choice." In March he sailed for a three months' cruise, and letters came to Montpelier from "off the Island of Deseada", "Carlisle Bay" and "Barbarous Island". They should have been reassuring to the most tremulous widow pledged to remarriage.

> "Separated from my dearest, what pleasure can I feel? none, be assured; all my happiness is centred with thee; and where thou art not, there am I not happy. With my heart filled with the purest and most tender affection do I write this. . . . Fortune, that is money, is the only thing I regret the want of, and that only for the sake of my affectionate Fanny. But the Almighty who brings us together, will, I doubt not, take ample care of us, and prosper all our undertakings. No dangers shall deter me from pursuing every honourable means of providing handsomely for you and yours; and again let me repeat, that my dear Josiah shall ever be considered by me as one of my own."

He had written home to announce his engagement. William was told:

> "The dear object you must like. Her sense, polite manners, and to you I may say, beauty, you will much admire; and although at present we may not be a rich couple, yet I have not the least doubt but that we shall be a happy pair :—the fault must be mine if we are not."

Mr. Suckling learnt:

> "Her heart is equal to her head. . . . Her mental accomplishments are superior to most persons of either sex; and we shall come together as two persons most sincerely attached to each other from friendship. . . . My affection for her is fixed upon that solid basis of esteem and regard that I trust can only increase by a longer knowledge of her."

"In due course" a bunch of congratulatory replies arrived. William, led astray, as he might well be, by his brother's original mention of marriage within the month, concluded Horace a husband by now, and desired his love to Mrs. Nelson. "I am not married yet", Horatio had to confess. "In England you think these matters done in a moment"; and to Mr. Suckling, "I have not an idea of being married till nearly the time of our sailing for England." Suddenly, he had hopes of return that year. Sir Richard Hughes was ordered home, but nobody in the squadron had the least idea whether he was to be replaced, or what was to become of them. "Lord Howe is so close, nothing is to be got out of him." The Admiral sailed alone in June, preceded by

Lady Hughes, proudly escorting a married daughter. A bold major of the 67th Regiment had been the happy man. " O what a taste ! " said the Captain of the *Boreas*, who never could forgive Rosy, even when she was safely Mrs. John Browne. This wedding was the first of a series in his circle. It was closely followed by that of his friend Captain Kelly to Miss Sally Morton, first cousin to Mrs. Nisbet. (Spiteful rumour said that the Admiral had offered Kelly £5,000 and Miss Rosy.) During the next year three announcements from home took Nelson by surprise. William had married, not the Miss Ellen or the Miss Dorothea so often recommended in jest. (" Marry Ellen, and then you are settled for life." . . . " Push for Miss Dorothea, and then you will soon be a Bishop, without any interest but money, which is indeed the strongest of any.") One of these cousins could have brought him a better living, the other, a redoubtable heiress, did see her husband Bishop of Salisbury. But William had, his brother expected, pleased himself. His bride was announced as Miss Sarah Yonge, daughter of the Vicar of Great Torrington, Devon, and sister of Chancellor Yonge of Swaffham. Nobody told that she was eight years William's senior. Captain Nelson begged his best respects. " You will treat her kindly and tenderly, I have no doubt. . . . I believe it is most generally the man's fault if he is not happy."

His sister Kitty's match was a good one from every point of view. His " little Kate ", whom he had resentfully pictured condemned to the " clack " of a small seaport town, or spinsterhood in a country cottage provided by an impecunious naval brother, had reaped, in her first Bath season, the fairy-tale reward due to virtue and beauty. As well as being a charming and talented man, handsome and energetic, Mr. George Matcham, explorer and author, had inherited and augmented an East India fortune.

The third wedding in Nelson's family was the most surprising. Uncle Suckling had answered his nephew's letter of last November very kindly. He had, as usual, no wish that Horace's heart should break for lack of a little temporary pecuniary assistance. He would help, should it be necessary. But something in the letter, a single sentence, perhaps misunderstood, had struck the recipient as chilly—had cut him to the quick. The fact was that Mr. Suckling was thinking of getting married himself, and although he admitted that the children of his deceased sister had claims, he had children of his own to consider before he

25

26 settled. A long-established character well known to the family
27 of Burnham Thorpe as "Madam", subject to the gout, had
vanished from the scene, it is impossible to say how, as although
directly Mr. Suckling married Miss Rumsey of Hampstead,
etiquette obliged his nephews to enquire in every letter for the
health of Mrs. Suckling, "Madam" had never been mentioned,
except *en passant* between the brothers. Horatio, who knew his
uncle thoroughly, told William that he was "truly glad to hear
of this marriage. It will add to his felicity, for had he not done
that, he must have kept a woman, which you will allow would
28 have been very disagreeable."

Mrs. Nisbet's *fiancé* now knew how he stood. The hour had
clearly come when he must make a determined effort to discover
the intentions of her uncle. He suffered pangs of apprehension
after his letter had been sent. He would have preferred to
approach the subject in an interview. But that, at present, was
impossible. Nor, after twelve months' courtship, mainly on
paper, was his "young widow" in the least less coy.

> "I will not begin by scolding you, although you really deserve
> it, for sending me such a letter. Had I not known the warmth of
> your Heart by this time, I might have judged you had never seen
> me. However, I have fixed my resolve of not saying more."

Mrs. Nisbet received from "Barbarous Island" on May 4 her
first hint of what it would mean to be a sailor's bride.

> "Never, never, do I believe shall I get away from this detestable
> spot. Had I taken your advice and not seized any Americans, I should
> now have been with you; but I should have neglected my duty, which
> I think your regard for me is too great for you to have wished me to
> have done. Duty is the great business of a Sea-officer. All private
> considerations must give way to it, however painful it is."

It was sad that their engagement must be clouded by so much
talk of "fortune—that is money", but his Fanny's answers
were gentle and considerate, and after a flying visit in July he
was at once more happy and more miserable. As the hot season
of '86 wore on he began to feel less and less well, and correspondingly impatient.

> "At first I bore absence tolerably, but now it is almost insupportable,
> and by and by, I expect it will be quite so. . . . I am alone, in the Com-
> manding Officer's house, while my Ship is fitting, and from sunrise until
> bedtime, I have not a human creature to speak to; you will feel a

G

little for me, I think. I did not use to be over-fond of sitting alone. The moment old *Boreas* is habitable in my cabin, I shall fly to it, in order to avoid mosquitoes and melancholies."

The mosquitoes also performed their duty, and presently a letter from his lady-love found him stupid with fever, hardly able to read and with only a faint recollection of what he had been about recently. He had to tell her that although his chief complaint was in his chest, he had no pain, and the doctors said there was no fear of a consumption. To Locker he had written quite the reverse, but a lady must be tenderly rallied.

> " As you begin to know something about Sailors, have you not often heard that salt water and absence always wash away love? Now, I am such a heretic as not to believe that Faith. For behold, every morning since my arrival, I have had six pails of salt water at daylight poured upon my head, and instead of finding what the Seamen say to be true, I perceive the contrary effect."

Not until the end of September was he able to announce :

> " On the 9th of October barring something extraordinary, you will certainly see H.N. again, and I need not say, if it be possible, with a stronger affection than when he left you."   *29*

He got his wish for October, but in early November something extraordinary did occur. H.M.S. *Pegasus*, under the command of Prince William Henry, suddenly arrived from Nova Scotia. Sir Richard Bickerton had not yet appeared to succeed Sir Richard Hughes. There was something ironic in the situation, for a society which had cold-shouldered the officer who enforced the Navigation Laws was thrown into a fever of excitement by the prospect of entertaining a Prince of the blood-royal, and every engagement made for the Prince's extended tour of the islands must be passed by his commanding officer and old friend, Captain Nelson.

At the end of seven weeks of hardly any sleep, and much too much full-dress uniform, salutes, strong sun, rich foods and loyal bumpers, the Senior Captain on the Leeward Islands station knew himself no courtier. (" What is it to attend on Princes? Let me attend on you, and I am satisfied. Some are born for attendants on great men. I rather think it is not my particular province.") To add to his trials, after the week's engagements had been somehow accomplished, he had to listen to His Royal Highness's complaints of his officers. Their Lordships had wisely supplied an eager twenty-two-year-old royalty with a scholarly and exact First Lieutenant, aged thirty-four, who had a distinguished West India active-service record. Mr. Schomberg appreciated that he was to " dry-nurse " the Prince, but the Prince by no means appreciated his efforts. Nervous tension was marked by the time that the *Pegasus* arrived at Antigua.

Jogging home over country roads, on the night of January 22, after a good dinner and very fine speeches, Nelson flogged himself to respectful attention while Prince William talked himself into a passion, telling the story of Lieutenants Schomberg and Smollett sending boats ashore without acquainting him. On the following evening, when the Senior Officer the Leeward Islands regained his cabin, he found a formal letter from Lieutenant Schomberg stating that as Prince William Henry had thought fit this morning to accuse him publicly of neglect of duty, he begged for a court-martial. Nelson immediately put Schomberg under arrest, and sent for the Prince; but he was too late. There had been many witnesses of a heated scene in which his Captain had upbraided the First Lieutenant of the *Pegasus* for asking for a court-martial, to which Schomberg had replied that His Royal Highness was grown " so very particular " that no officer could serve under him; that he realised that sooner or later His Royal Highness intended that he should be broke, and that if a court-martial acquitted him, he was going to ask for an exchange out of the *Pegasus*. Nelson's actions pleased nobody. Four days later, having good reason to believe that further officers of the Prince's ship were going to ask for a court-martial, he issued an order directing them not to make such applications on frivolous pretexts at a time when he had not sufficient ships to bring them to trial. He had, in fact, placed Schomberg under arrest because he saw that it was quite impossible for him to continue serving under the Prince. He had a very high opinion of Schomberg. He hoped for the arrival of a Commander-in-Chief, the prevention of a court-martial, and the removal of Schomberg from the *Pegasus*. But no god in the machine arrived, and after many weeks of confinement Schomberg believed himself thoroughly persecuted, while the Prince, who was justly nervous of his august father, and " very uneasy " (" I wish to God it had never happened "), still referred resentfully to his First Lieutenant as " this unhappy and deluded man ", and " miserable object ".

In the end, Nelson sent the *Pegasus* down to Port Royal, with a private note of explanation to Commodore Gardner (" His Royal Highness, I can have no doubt, gave the orders alluded to, although Mr. Schomberg might have misunderstood them "); and on a station where a court-martial could have been held, it was avoided. Their Lordships, furnished with the whole correspondence, said that Captain Nelson had done wrong in sending the *Pegasus* to Nova Scotia by way of Jamaica. Schomberg was superseded, and sent back to England, but a few weeks later was appointed First Lieutenant of the *Barfleur*, carrying Lord Hood's flag, whereupon the Prince, who had not yet learnt his lesson thoroughly, sent a regrettable letter to Lord Hood. The last word was said seven months later, when Nelson wrote to the Prince to thank him for having saved a good officer from appearing before a court-martial,

> " which must ever hurt him. Resentment, I know your Royal Highness never had . . . but, now you are parted, pardon me, my Prince, when I presume to recommend that Schomberg may stand in your Royal Favour as if he had never sailed with you : and that at some future date, you will serve him. . . . In full confidence of your belief of my sincerity, I take the liberty of saying that, having seen a few more years than yourself, I may in some respects know more of mankind. Permit me then to urge a thorough knowledge of those you tell your mind to. Mankind are not always what they seem. . . . Nothing is wanting to make you the darling of the English Nation, but truth. Sorry, I am to say, much to the contrary has been dispersed."   ³⁰

8

The " difficult and disagreeable affair " of Lieutenant Schomberg was much more quickly and satisfactorily settled than that of the peculations by His Majesty's Crown Officials in the Leeward Islands, disclosed by Messrs. Wilkinson and Higgins, merchants of St. John, Antigua. They opened their campaign quite correctly. It was their misfortune that they mistimed their attack. The zealous naval captain and royal prince to whom they addressed themselves were both elsewhere by the time that the result of their actions overtook them. They came to English Harbour on April 13, 1787, and delivered to the Senior Officer the Leeward Islands a letter, the duplicate of one enclosed, addressed to His Royal Highness. The Prince, although enjoying " no peace of mind " (since Lieutenant Schomberg had now been under arrest for ninety days), took instant intelligent interest in what he called " the Frauds ". As he was just about to leave Antigua, he could only relinquish the matter into the hands of Nelson, who he was sure would do all that was proper and right. Nelson set to work with characteristic energy and enthusiasm. He interviewed Messrs. Wilkinson and Higgins repeatedly, and decided that they were very shrewd, sensible men of business. They had been partners with a Mr. Whitehead, Agent to the Royal Naval Hospital, Antigua. " Having separated, they have possessed themselves of all Whitehead's Books and Papers." Of course, they were not disinterested. When His Majesty's Government were convinced, as the result of their disclosures, that vast frauds against the Customs had been committed, they expected a percentage of all sums recovered—15 %. Mr. Wilkinson promised that in the various departments at Antigua he believed the sum in question would amount to £500,000; at St. Lucia £300,000; at Barbados not far short. The result of enquiries at Jamaica (which was not under Nelson's command) he reckoned at upwards of a million. Nelson, who knew himself neither a man of business nor a lawyer, set to work, and found that his informants were prepared to offer him, in proof, only one quarter's accounts—those of the March–June five years past. Still, he argued, the frauds they mentioned had probably been committed : otherwise they had all to lose and nothing to gain. " They are certainly men of strong natural parts, and appear wonderfully expert at the per-centage." Throughout the summer months before he sailed for home, he tussled daily with the Naval Ordnance Storekeeper's accounts which the expert gentlemen had left with him. It was very difficult to discover what had been the current market price of goods supplied. All merchants of St. John agreed that a commod-ity in this part of the world was worth what it would fetch at the moment : all were in the habit or signing half-a-dozen vouchers, unread, before they passed in to dinner. He had himself, when left with the command here, been worried when the Navy Deputy Officer brought him bills to sign for goods received. " I insisted upon having the original Vouchers brought to me, that I might examine if they were really purchased at the market-price, and that Government was not cheated." These he could not obtain, so he had written to the Navy Board, and received an answer " which seemed to imply that the old forms were sufficient "—merely a certificate from the Naval Officer and Master Shipwright that so much money was required. " Since that period I have been less close in my examination."

After many hours of toil upon the limited but extraordinary material for research left to him by Messrs. Wilkinson and Higgins, he thought it unquestionable that a fictitious character, " Cornelius Cole ", masked the identity of Mr. Antony Munton, Naval Ordnance Storekeeper, Antigua, to whose name were

entered all credits due to Mr. Cole. He thought the books had
not been tampered with. It was distressing that Doctor Young,
for whom he had a great regard, " a most humane man ", was
clearly amongst the abettors. " The only emulation I can discover,
is who could cheat most." In the impersonal Italian hand which
he had learnt at Norwich Grammar School, when he was the
boldest pupil, and his haystack of fair hair had been of a livelier
colour, Captain Nelson wrote long letters to Prince William
Henry; to Mr. Pitt (for the Prince said Parliament must know of
it); to the new Comptroller of the Navy (" Sir, As a Fraud is
likely to be discovered in the Naval Department which under
your direction ", etc.); to Viscount Howe, First Lord; to the
Commissioners of the Office for the Sick and Hurt; and to His
Grace the Duke of Richmond, Master General of the Ordnance.
The results, in every direction, were disappointing.

The Comptroller replied at once that he had communicated
with the First Lord, and hoped Captain Nelson would do all in
his power to collect evidence. After another three months the
Comptroller's Department forwarded books for Captain Nelson's
perusal. Fourteen months later they decided that Messrs.
Wilkinson and Higgins had best be summoned home to make
good their charges. The Duke of Richmond's letter from Captain
Nelson lay yellowing on his grace's desk for a year before Captain
Nelson learnt that every proper measure should be taken. The
Board should write to Messrs. Wilkinson and Higgins by the next
packet, and if Captain Nelson (whom the Duke had believed still
abroad) should find himself in London, his grace would be very
glad to see him. " I beg you will not think any introduction
necessary." The First Lord wrote, with equal suavity, that he
had communicated with the Navy Board, and agreed that the
gentlemen of Antigua, if they made good their representations,
were entitled to a liberal reward. The Prime Minister, by the
hand of a secretary, merely acknowledged papers sent, which
had been forwarded to the Departments concerned; but of that
quarter Nelson was obstinately hopeful. " The goodness of the
cause we are engaged in will support itself at all times. More
especially, I dare say, with such an upright character as Mr. Pitt."
The Commissioners of the Office for the Sick and Hurt were not
so amiable. Twelve months passed before they requested
Captain Nelson to favour them with his opinion whether the
charges made by " a Messrs. Higgins and Wilkinson ", in a letter
received from these gentlemen, accusing their officers of fraud,

were likely to be true, as they had no other cause to suspect these officers, and were not willing to institute an enquiry without reasonable cause. His Royal Highness (just arrived at Plymouth from Halifax) commanded Captain Nelson to assure Messrs. Wilkinson and Higgins that were he placed in a situation where he could be of any service to this cause he would, most assuredly, sift it to the bottom. Meanwhile, he could only offer good wishes.

But meanwhile Messrs. Wilkinson and Higgins were suffering the inevitable results of stirring up a hornets' nest. Allegations had been transmitted from the West Indies that they were " bad men, and previous partakers in the Frauds ". After eighteen months, Mr. Wilkinson found himself " by a quirk of the Solicitor-General's " lodged in gaol at Antigua. He could only attribute his situation, and this attack upon him in his private capacity, to his discovery of Whitehead's frauds; Mr. Solicitor-General having favoured that person. He fades from the Nelson correspondence still in durance and receiving sad letters from that officer.

Nelson, on half-pay in England, could only profess himself " most sincerely sorry for your situation ", and express hopes that " the Government will afford you every assistance in bringing to maturity the good work begun under my auspices ". His hopes were not without foundation. Having heard from Mr. Pitt's secretary that the Treasury was amongst the Departments to which the matter had been referred, he had sought and obtained an appointment with the Secretary to the Treasury. When he arrived, he found Mr. George Rose—a personage of massive frame and dignified aspect—quite at a loss as to the identity of Captain Horatio Nelson. He pursued the tactics which had been successful with Lord Hood at Sandy Hook, and within a few minutes had made the impression he desired. He was again lucky in his man, for Mr. Rose, now personal friend of Mr. Pitt, and owner of a famous country house where His Majesty was an annual guest, had been born the son of a needy non-juring clergyman, and had " known what it was to be left on the pavement ". He had also been a midshipman, in the West Indies, before Nelson was born, and had married a lady of Antigua. Mr. Rose, after hearing a brief statement of Captain Nelson's services, and the reason why he was here, said that at the moment he could not stay, but he would much like to see the young officer again—to-morrow, and as early as possible. Nelson presented himself at 6 a.m., and they talked till 9. Nelson stayed to breakfast, took his leave immediately the meal was done, and walked home heartened by the knowledge that Mr. Rose was going to " lay the whole before Mr. Pitt ". He must have had suspicions that no speedy miracle would happen, for he warned Messrs. Wilkinson and Higgins that, although he had been assured that the business would never be dropped, and that all proper rewards and recompenses would be made to them, yet he would have them recollect that Government business may be slow, and " I cannot but lament that your discovery should not have been made to a man of more consequence than myself, for in this Country I am not in Office, and am so much retired from the busy scenes of action that although I have every inclination, I have not the ability to do more than represent your situation."

Actually he had done more than he knew. Years later, the Right Hon. George Rose told a Nelson biographer that as an eventual result of that early morning interview " all Captain Nelson's representations were attended to, and every step he recommended was adopted ". But no interview with Mr. Pitt followed, and the next thing Nelson heard of the unfortunate informers was that during the long interval since he had dealt with them they had fatally " shifted their ground ". After declaring that a government official must be sent out to investigate the frauds on the spot, they discovered, as the spot grew uncomfortably warm, that the only solution was their summons home. They leaped at the Comptroller's suggestion that they should be summoned home. Nelson's letters became harassed. He protested that the gentlemen had always told him that they had no confidence in His Majesty's officials in the Leeward Islands. In November '89 he forwarded Messrs. Wilkinson and Higgins' communication of the previous September to the Comptroller without comment. It was returned to him with the suggestion that if he chose that it should be made public, Captain Nelson should send it to the Navy Board. " High officers " were saying that these Antiguan witnesses seemed " very wavering " and that the business seemed likely to end in smoke.

At last, having informed Messrs. Wilkinson and Higgins that he believed Sir John Laforey was going to be sent out to take command of the station, and would probably be the person empowered to investigate all the frauds in the Dockyard during the late war, Nelson could " only sit down and *think* ". The last character to step on to the stage in this tragi-comedy was the

Frances Herbert Woolward, widow of Dr. Josiah
Nisbet and afterwards Viscountess Nelson
(1758–1831). (18½" × 20".)

This portrait by an unknown artist was sold by General Horatio
Reginald Mends, grandson of Lady Nelson, to Lionel Foster,
Esq., who presented it to the National Maritime Museum,
Greenwich.

*Reproduced by kind permission of the Trustees, the National
Maritime Museum, Greenwich*

Attorney-General, to whom Mr. Dyson, Solicitor to the Navy
Board, submitted all papers for his opinion.

As far as Nelson was concerned, the curtain rang down after
two years and three months with a Delphic utterance from the
Duke of Richmond: " With respect to yourself, I can only renew
the assurances of my perfect conviction of the zeal for His
Majesty's Service which has induced you to stir in this business."

31

9

The Captains of the *Boreas* and the *Pegasus* talked of more
agreeable matters than Lieutenant Schomberg and Messrs.
Wilkinson and Higgins as they sailed in fine weather from
Barbados to Grenada, back to Antigua, and from Montserrat, by
way of Nevis, to St. Kitts and the Virgin Islands. Two youthful
figures in blue-and-white uniforms swept with their telescopes the
headlands of St. Lucia, Grenada and Martinique and, with especial
interest, the small rocky islets called " The Saints " in the channel
between Dominica and Guadeloupe. The elder explained how
the fleets had manœuvred on a December day nine years past;
on a July day of the following year; in the next April, and
particularly on April 12, 1782. Captains Nelson and Prince
William were fighting again the actions of Admirals Barrington,
Byron, Rodney and Hood in the late war. Unluckily, although
he had known these waters both before and after those
stirring days, Nelson had not been present at any of the battles
he described so well.

They also, since they dined with one another on alternate
nights, and were both in their twenties, talked of love—or rather
Prince William did. Like most of the many sons of George III,
he adored Romance. After his first cruise, his brothers, the
Prince of Wales and Duke of York, had shown him the pleasures
of the Town. His royal father, when he heard that the midshipman prince had been carried off by the Watch for brawling at
Vauxhall and Ranelagh, had seen to it that he went to sea again
very soon, but on his first leave he had made a spirited attempt
to contract marriage with a fellow-minor. Since Nelson had last
seen him he had travelled for two years in Germany and Italy,
getting into many scrapes. As soon as he discovered that his
friend was an intending bridegroom—which was very soon—he
made a well-meant but not wholly considerate pronouncement.
Nelson must promise him not to get married without his assistance.
Indeed, he must undertake the *rôle* of Father of the Bride, and

himself give Mrs. Nisbet to his friend. On this occasion, for the first and last time, he would break through his rule of never accepting private invitations. Nelson received the proposal with pleasure and concern. The compliment was great, but the inconvenience equally so. He wrote to tell Fanny that she must prepare to be given away by a prince, though when he could not say, as his movements depended entirely upon those of His Royal Highness, " and when I shall see you, it is not possible for me to guess : so much for marrying a Sailor ". He was also sufficiently ingenuous to tell her that the Prince kept on chaffing him on being such a calm wooer. His Royal Highness was sure that Nelson was already a husband, and was keeping it dark. When Nelson told him, " I certainly am not ", the Prince, tidying his face to match that of his companion, and really interested, was sure then that Nelson must have a great esteem for Mrs. Nisbet— not " the thing which is vulgarly called love ". " No, I won't make use of that word ", remembered Nelson, and told Fanny, " He is right, my love is founded on esteem, the only foundation that can make the passion last." 32

The New Year came, the year in which Mr. Herbert was going home, the year in which it had always been fixed that they should get married, and Nelson seemed as far as ever from choosing his wedding-day. He hoped for a spring date, for the *Boreas* was now so leaky that unless he got her home before the next hurricane season he foresaw a further twelve months in the Leeward Islands. And he did not at all fancy another hurricane season at anchor in English Harbour, encouraging the ship's company to combine in concerts, dances and cudgelling contests, and shepherding the younger officers through the violent passages always provoked by private theatricals. February saw him at Montserrat, bound for Nevis and St. Kitts, but his plans for seeing much of the hostess of Montpelier were frustrated. The Captain of the *Maidstone*, upon whom he had depended to attend the Prince to the other side of the island while he enjoyed some privacy with his Fanny, became indisposed. However, he had been able to display both his devotion and the adaptability of the British seaman. The Captain's steward from the *Boreas* had been up to Montpelier to remove an instrument of which its fair owner was making complaint, and as the Captain sat tussling with a difficult letter he was able to announce—" a man is cracking my head with tuning your pianoforte, but there is nothing I wouldn't bear for my dearest Fanny ". He had succeeded in pinning down Mr. Herbert to another business interview, but not, he considered, a satisfactory one, for the President now nonchalantly suggested to an ardent suitor—" I might be united to you when I thought it most convenient, or let it alone till we got to England. I objected to the latter for many reasons." One of these needed tactful approach. If the *Boreas* sailed for home with her execrated Captain still a bachelor, " the ill-natured part of these islands would say I have only been playing the fool with you ".

33

She had said that she would write every day, but he had only received one letter. (" *Number them* ", mentioned a sea-officer.) On February 28, he was already tired, as he surveyed a programme for the next five days which he justifiably described as " a good deal of fag " : to-night, a dinner with the merchants of Nevis, from whom he expected black looks ; to-morrow, a large party at Nicholas Town ; Friday, an equally large party in the town here ; Saturday, sail for Old Road ; Sunday, dinner on Brimstone Hill ; Monday, St. Kitts' merchants' dinner at the country home of a resident particularly obnoxious to him, followed by a Freemasons' Ball. " Tuesday, please God, we sail." He wrote to Fanny on the Saturday, that the journey up to Nicholas Town in the height of the sun had knocked him up. He had had fever ; however, he was better now. Nobody could have been more considerate than H.R.H. and as they sailed to-day he should have some hours at sea, in which to gather reserves of strength to carry him through to-morrow's and Monday's pleasure exertions. " We shall most likely be at Nevis about the 18th, but keep this to yourself."

Three days later Fanny received a startling intimation, prefaced by the words, " How uncertain are the movements of us Sailors ", and, " I am now feeling most awkwardly ". H.R.H. was now also rather unwell, so their itinerary was altered. Tortola was postponed. They were returning directly from St. Kitts to Nevis. She had five days' notice in which to prepare herself for her wedding. She would then get a week's honeymoon, in the island in which she had been born and bred, before her bridegroom sailed again, for the Virgins, whence, after a call at Antigua, he would attend H.R.H. to Grenada, which should finish his tour. By mid-May Prince William Henry should be under sail again for Halifax, and the *Boreas* fit for a passage home. " Happy shall I be when that time arrives." His last letter to Fanny before their wedding ended, " Heaven bless you, and I need scarcely say

34

how much I am, your affectionate Horatio Nelson."

So, on Sunday, March 11, 1787, Nelson's last sentimental   *35*
journey as a bachelor ended. He was twenty-eight. Nevis,
like most of the Leeward Islands, possessed its small white
church, containing monuments to Service victims of the climate,
and less tersely worded memorials to the lives and deaths of
members of the colonist families; but fashion, at the moment,
prescribed that weddings should take place in private houses, so
the Rev. W. Jones, Rector of Figtree church, St. John, was
summoned to officiate in the principal reception room of
Montpelier. Since his engagement had been protracted, the
ship's company of the *Boreas* were ready with the Captain's
wedding-present—a handsome silver watch, made by James
Smith of Edinburgh. An elegant miniature model, in silver, of a
twenty-eight gun frigate under sail, subsequently used by Nelson
as a table-ornament, may have been the gift of the officers of the
Boreas. He had gone through the awe-inspiring conventional   *36*
preliminaries to eschewing the single state, and looked dreadfully,
thought his Prince—more in need of a nurse than a bride. His
Will, leaving all to his beloved wife, and appointing Uncle Suckling
sole executor, had been witnessed by Mr. Wallis, First Lieutenant,
and Mr. Jameson, Master's Mate of the *Boreas*. Although the
wedding was announced as taking place in a very private manner,
many officers were recorded as present, and there is no reason to
fear that Mr. Herbert, whose supreme happiness was a houseful
of guests, did violence to his natural instincts when playing host
to a prince of the blood.

The background of the scene has not altered in a century and
a half, although the scythe of Time has reaped the rich white   *37*
house, together with its jocose wedding-guests, fine in muslin,
powder, broadcloth and bullion, and their attendant troupe of
chocolate faces enlivened by flashing smiles. The stagey back-
cloth once viewed from drawing-room windows, of panting groves
of cocoanut palms printed against blue skies and seas quivering
in the primitive colours peculiar to the tropics in the height of
the dry season, stays unchanged.

The guests and clergyman assembled; the bridegroom
supported by his blonde and large Hanoverian princeling in full-
dress uniform and high good humour. The curtseys and deep
bows necessitated by the entry of a son of His Majesty were
performed. On the bridegroom's side there was present one
relative—his midshipman cousin, Maurice Suckling; on the
bride's many, including the very fine boy of seven, whom the

confident bridegroom was going to treat just like his own children. The Prince offered his arm to Mrs. Nisbet (decked out in Limerick lace of the first quality), who was tremulously sure that to-day would give her the best of husbands and her dear Josiah the best of fathers. H.R.H. on his previous visit to the island, a few weeks earlier, had spent "many happy hours at Montpelier". He found Mrs. Nisbet "pretty, and a sensible woman, and may have a great deal of money, if her uncle, Mr. Herbert, thinks proper : poor Nelson is over head and ears in love. . . . He is now in for it : I wish him well and happy, and that he may not repent the step he has taken." Personally H.R.H.'s predilection at the moment was for striking *débutantes*, but when the knot was tied, with royal tact he congratulated the bridegroom on "having borne off the principal favourite of the island", a sentiment echoed by many of the blue-and-white uniforms present.

After the happy couple had retired, and the guests began to experience the flatness and slight melancholy generally produced by the disappearance of the principal characters of a Comedy, and the drinking of many toasts at an unfamiliar hour in very hot weather, some of Nelson's brother-officers looked gloomy. An admiring midshipman had heard with apprehension that " Captain Nelson has married a complexion ", combined with " a remarkable absence of intellectual endowment ". Next day, Captain Pringle, a gentleman for whom the bridegroom had a particular regard, was still buttonholing listeners to hear—" The Navy, sir, yesterday lost one of its greatest ornaments, by Nelson's marriage. It is a national loss that such an officer should marry; had it not been for that circumstance, I foresaw Nelson would become the greatest man in the Service."

Another midshipman never forgot his surprise at hearing, a few weeks later, that the Captain of the *Boreas*, whom he remembered dancing a minuet in the Island of Nevis with the widow of a Dr. Nisbet (" a pretty and attractive woman and a general favourite "), had not taken his bride home in his own ship. " Though lately married, he went home in his Frigate and she in a Merchant ship. . . . He was then so ill that it was not expected that he could live to reach England, and he had a puncheon of rum for his body in case he should die during the voyage."

CHAPTER IV

1787–1793

(*ætat* 28–34)

FIVE YEARS ON THE BEACH

I

THE village of Redland, in the latter part of the eighteenth century, bore much the same relation to Bristol that Kentish Town did to London.   Indeed, there was much in the district in which Nelson found himself the guest of the Tobins to remind *1* him of early days under the roof of Uncle Suckling.   His connection with his West India host and hostess was distant. Dr. Nisbet had been a cousin of Mrs. Tobin.   Redland possessed a fine common, peaceful lanes and a village green presided over by a new-built classical chapel.   For some forty years, Bristol merchants had been erecting upon its heights townish-looking houses with spacious lawns shaded by cedars of Lebanon, commanding an unrivalled view of the adjacent city.

It was in these soothing surroundings that a modest couple of visitors, not likely to be mistaken for a honeymoon couple, whiled away a month of early spring in 1788—a sea-officer, bearing upon his arm a lady who carried about with her the slightly forlorn air of the young mother who has just parted with her only son.   " Our little boy " had been sent to school.   The Rev. William Nelson had made the arrangements, and Josiah, aged eight, had been despatched, soon after Christmas, in charge of his stepfather's sailor servant, Frank Lepée, to stay at Hilborough Rectory, *en route* for boarding-school.   Nelson wrote that he was sure William's wife, whom he had not yet met, would show every kindness to the child.   He had instructed Frank to stay at the school for a few days, " till the child becomes reconciled. . . . I wish him at school to have the same weekly allowance as the other boys, and whatever else that may be proper for him."   He added that both he and Mrs. Nelson had been very unwell, and that it was no true kindness to allow Josiah to do as he pleased.   At last the time had come to which he had looked forward yearningly from the Leeward Islands, and for many years before he had met Mrs. Nisbet.   He was alone with his wife, though not yet by his own fireside, which would be the completion of happiness. William had sent particulars of a house at Bodney, which was very cheap considering its size; Locker, who now had a house there, recommended Kensington, but was told that nothing so near London could be considered. " Mrs. Nelson's lungs are so much affected by the smoke of London." When his son had been home for ten months, but had not yet found opportunity to visit Norfolk or his family, the Rector of Burnham Thorpe wrote plaintively to his youngest daughter that perhaps, if she met Horace and his lady in Bath, she might be able to collect their intentions with regard to a settled residence. The Rector had received very polite letters from his new daughter-in-law, complaining of ill-health and the difficulty of making plans. " Hard ", she says, " is the Lot of a Sailor's wife."

Nelson, five months after his marriage, had written to Locker, " I begin to think I am fonder of the sea than ever." The fact was that Mrs. Horatio Nelson, who had been housekeeper to an explosive elderly man, to whom expense was no object, when she found herself the wife of an open-handed, ardent, poor young man, was terrified at the thought of setting up a small establishment. At first there was much to be said in support of her choice of existence in lodgings, eked out by prolonged visits to relations and friends. When the Portsmouth bum-boats bobbed merrily around the *Boreas* on the evening of July 4, 1787, her Captain had no other expectation than that she would be paid off in a few weeks. Nearly two months later he made a flying expedition to London in order to leave his lady there with her relations. The *Roehampton*, a luxurious West Indiaman, had had a slow but safe passage. Mrs. Nelson, " never yet having made the *Boreas* her home " (as the Captain of the *Boreas* somewhat sadly mentioned), was not likely to do so now. The exiles' return, so warmly pictured, had taken place at rather a disturbed moment. As the *Boreas* drew towards Spithead, Wilhelmina, wife of William IV, Prince of Orange, a lady of great spirit, on her way to the Hague from her husband's camp near Amersfoort, had been arrested by Dutch republicans. In the previous year they had desired to abolish the Stadtholdership; a project very welcome to France, but very unwelcome to England. The States General and Estates of Holland now passed a resolution approving of the Princess's arrest. She was released quite shortly, but had meanwhile written to her brother, the King of Prussia, who immediately prepared to march into Holland. France was pledged by treaty to defend Holland if she was invaded. England did not at all wish to see the Stadtholder crushed. There seemed at the date of Nelson's arrival a strong probability that England was going to war with France again.

The weather was equally disturbed, and Nelson at once developed one of his colds. " It is not kind in one's Native air to treat a poor wanderer as it has done me since my arrival. The rain and cold at first gave me a sore throat and its accompaniments : the hot weather has given me a slow fever." He could hardly hold up his head while the tedious and noisy business of victualling the *Boreas* for three months was performed, and naturally a ship's company that had expected release after a three years' cruise was in no cheerful mood. He had to forward to London descriptions of deserters. He wrote to ask Lord Howe for a ship-of-the-line in the event of hostilities, but his orders were to be ready to take the *Boreas* to sea at an instant's warning, with the squadron at Spithead. He did not himself believe that France would give ultimate offence for another year, for although England was in a bad state for going to war, yet, " Thank God, the French are worse ". As England was in a bad state, September found the *Boreas* at the Nore, serving as a slop and receiving ship for pressed men. Even the Rector of Burnham Thorpe realised that now Horace's situation was disagreeable. To Locker, who had been called out of retirement to regulate the impress at Exeter, his pupil wrote, " If the Regulating business is a thing you like, most sincerely do I give you joy of it." He had another trouble with which he did not vex his friends and relations. The Admiralty, on his arrival, had been as ungenial as the weather. Throughout these months of difficult and unpleasant duty he was harassed by correspondence with the various Departments involved in his attempts to enforce the Navigation Laws : and, though this might be no more than chance, every temporary appointment which he had made while Senior Officer on the Leeward Islands station could not, it appeared, for one reason or another, be confirmed. He was sharply reprimanded for sending Prince William's ship to Jamaica. He replied to this by begging Mr. Stephens to inform their Lordships that he had duly observed their instructions, and that they might be assured that in future no consideration should ever induce him to deviate in the smallest degree from their orders. As the autumn wore on, Nelson, who had found himself, at the prospect of " a bustle ", " never better ", and " fit for any quarter of the Globe ", became depressed at " laying seven miles from the land on the Impress service . . . as much separated from my wife as if I were in the East Indies ". The alarm of war, after blowing hot and cold, blew over at last. Prussian troops, commanded by the Duke of Brunswick, had been quickly successful in Holland, and the Prince of Orange had re-entered his capital in triumph.

On November 30 the *Boreas* was paid off, at Sheerness, and the extraordinary and unwieldy collection of impedimenta made by her Captain in a cruise of over three years was hauled to light and dispersed, disclosing some minor tragedies. The dispersal was in itself a business entailing many letters and some private arrangements. Nearly everything had to be sent on by sea to the nearest port to its destination, and for some of his purchases the Captain could not face the enormous duty which the Customs House would demand. Nelson in 1787 wrote quite openly of 4 having to smuggle West India luxury products. He had rum for William and Uncle Suckling, wine, rum and nuts for Kingsmill, wine for Lord Walpole of Wolterton, and a mountain of tropical dessert fruits. Poor Wilfred Collingwood's effects were brought forth, and the shrunk and scanty wardrobe and possessions of a promising young officer, of no private means, who had succumbed to tuberculosis, were put in a boat bound for Newcastle-on-Tyne, accompanied by a feeling note to necessarily harrowed relatives. All the wine chosen for Captain Erasmus Gower, a person whom Nelson scarcely knew, had run out, a most disobliging circumstance. He had to make good the deficiency from his own store. Nor were all recipients grateful when they had unpacked their orders, or gifts. Locker, whose frankness was an endearing characteristic, when he had received his consignment of 36 pounds of tamarinds, a 60-gallon cask of rum, a dozen *Noyeau*, a dozen *Véritable* and half a hogshead of Madeira, wrote that he thought the wine not good. The apologetic purchaser could only say that he had paid a very good price for it. Mistakes took place at the Customs House. On a winter's day, nearly two years later, when Captain Nelson entertained a few cherished friends, the host's face underwent a sudden change. Instead of the Madeira which he had kept for such an occasion, he was sipping as good 5 Port as ever he had tasted.

Mrs. Nelson and her husband, united at last, and on a holiday of unlimited duration, spent their first Christmas together as guests of Mr. Herbert. The President had sailed from Nevis in May, but not before witnessing the marriage of his only child

H

and heiress to the man of her choice, a romance happily concluded
largely owing to the efforts of his niece's unworldly husband.

After his marriage Nelson's view of London was altered.   He
never again haunted the small, old streets off the throbbing
Strand, frequented by impecunious junior officers, and so
convenient for visits to the Admiralty, Whitehall and the Navy
Office, Seething Lane, the Victualling Office, Tower Hill, the Pay
Office and the Sick and Hurt Office, Broad Street, and, last but
not least, the coffee-room of Fladong's Hotel, New Oxford
Street.   The Herbert family revolved around the President's
house, 5, Cavendish Square.   To be near her kin, even when
not actually staying with them, Fanny and her husband
lodged in the side-streets of Mary-le-bonne—at 10, Great Marlborough Street and 6, Princes Street.   He never took to " north
of the Park ", and when he came to order a house in London,
told Davison on no account to choose one " on the other side of
Portman Square.   I detest Baker Street."

They " rather hurried " to Bath, when the sad little flurry of
despatching Josiah to boarding-school was accomplished.   Nelson
must place his ailing wife at a spa before he undertook a bachelor
expedition.   Prince William's ship had arrived at Plymouth from
Nova Scotia, and H.R.H. had written inviting his friend to take
part in the festivities celebrating his safe return.   Nelson went
gladly, and found the west country port *en gala*.   Prince William's
brothers, the Heir Apparent and the Duke of York, who had
come down from London to welcome the Captain of the *Pegasus*,
had just taken their departure in a coach-and-six, amidst loud
applause.   A perpetual crowd thronged Fore Street, where
Prince William abode with a wealthy merchant of the town.   By
day there were formal visits to the Dockyard and Marine Barracks,
which were beautifully illuminated every night, and at one a.m.
the Sailor Prince and his brother officers were still lustily performing country dances in the Long Assembly Rooms.   Nelson found
his Prince " everything I could wish—respected by all ".   Some
people who had known and disliked H.R.H. previously, said that
he was a most altered young man.   The *Pegasus* was allowed by
every competent judge to be one of the best-disciplined ships
that ever came into Plymouth.

At Bath, too, " sea-folks " were " pretty numerous ", but
after a fortnight of drinking the waters, a young couple with no
money to spare tired of a spa.   With spring, a country clergyman's son was longing to get into the country.   A further fort-

night of Bath followed their month near Bristol; they then cut themselves entirely loose from the haunts of rank and fashion. They made holiday in South Devon, and by a lucky chance, in early May, met "in this remote corner" just the type of English spring weather dreamt of by West Indians. From "Exmouth Moor", Nelson wrote to Hercules Ross, the patriotic Jamaican who had sent his slaves to man the batteries of Fort Charles, Port Royal, when Admiral D'Estaing was expected. Ross, too, had recently been "united to an amiable woman, the greatest blessing Heaven can bestow". He, however, had retired. "You", wrote Nelson, "have given up the toils and anxieties of business; whilst I must still buffet the waves—in search of what? That thing called Honour, is now alas! thought of no more. . . . My integrity cannot be mended, I hope, but my fortune, God knows, has grown the worse for the Service." He comforted himself that "a uniform course of honour and integrity seldom fails of bringing a man to the goal of Fame at last", but before the month was out had had enough of sunning himself amongst Devon gorse, and was to be seen entering the courtyard of the Admiralty. His object this time was not to ask for a ship, but, in consideration of his services when left in command of the Leeward Islands station, at least the same allowance usually given to a junior officer at Jamaica. His bills for frequent journeys to St. John had all, so far, been settled out of his own pay as Captain of the *Boreas*. He wanted also to see whether it was his fancy that their Lordships were not favourably impressed by his recent exertions. But after doing himself the honour of calling twice upon the First Lord in order to pay his personal respects, and never being happy enough to find his Lordship disengaged, he was obliged to write a letter recounting these and his previous efforts. He also wrote from Cavendish Square to Prince William Henry. Fanny had thought of a way in which she might aid the family exchequer, not in itself uncongenial, though it must mean much residence in London and separation from her husband. Nelson, who knew himself not very good at asking for favours from the great, managed his request as best he could, in the last paragraph of a longish letter:

"There may be a thing, perhaps, within reach of your Royal Highness; therefore, trusting to your goodness, I shall mention it. The Princess Royal must very soon have a Household appointed her. I believe a word from your Royal Highness would obtain a promise of a

situation in Her Royal Highness's Establishment not unbecoming the
wife of a Captain in the Navy; but I have only ventured to say this
much, and leave the issue to your better judgment."

Prince William's answer is not preserved, but Fanny Nelson
never shared the fate of Fanny Burney. The Princess, it is true,
was now twenty-one, and Mary-le-bonne drawing-rooms may have
accorded her a separate establishment, but only persons entirely
out of touch with Court circles could have imagined that, particularly at this moment, any daughter of the most possessive royal
parents in Europe would have been so indulged. At the age of
thirty this Princess accepted a most unappetising husband of
decidedly inferior rank, with no other object than escape.

Nelson presented himself at Court on the King's birthday,
and beheld His Majesty in a scarlet coat, a fancy waistcoat and
diamond buttons; Her Majesty, small and frigid, in much-
ornamented oyster satin; and the three grown-up Princesses in
the powder, spotted muslin gowns, and ribbons and flowers of
pastel shades in which Gainsborough so often and happily
depicted them while they were still young and hopeful. Although
this was not yet known to the general public, the King's health
had been, since the spring, a source of anxiety to his family and
physicians. He was easily over-tired and worried. It was in
the November of this year, while driving in Windsor Park with
the Princess Royal, that he first displayed lunacy. The Court
left for Weymouth soon after the Birthday, but the Court was
not fashionable, and London did not immediately thin. The
Nelsons were still in Cavendish Square when a Grand Cricket
Match was played " at the ground in Mary-le-bonne " near by,
" between the gentlemen of Hampshire and Kent and All
England ". The leaders of Whig society, the Duchess of Devonshire and her sister, were showing visiting French nobility the
sights of the British capital. *Élégantes* of Versailles, whose
heads were soon to be carried on pikes around the streets of
Paris, were pompously feasted in the City of London. At
Number 32, Cavendish Square, while Nelson was at Number 5,
one of England's first portrait-painters was entering in his diary
of appointments—" Master Temple at 8; Attorney-General at
10; a Dog at 11; Sir Gilbert Elliot at 1; Duke of Marlborough at
¼ to 2; Lady Albemarle's Dogs at 3." Six years had passed
since George Romney's diary had begun to record the sittings of
" a lady " whose almost daily visits, at first anonymous, had
presently been noted as those of Miss, or Mrs., Hart. His best

model had departed for Italy, on a spring morning of 1786. His portraits of " Emma ", in a morning-dress, as a Bacchante and as St. Cecilia, now adorned a palace in Naples. But Nelson, who was to buy the " St. Cecilia ", never met the painter known to modish London as " the man in Cavendish Square ".

Nelson came in sight of his home again with midsummer, and alone. It was not entirely the young couple's fault that they had been so long visiting Burnham Thorpe. When Mrs. Horace had threatened a winter visit, the Rector, who knew what Burnham was like under snow, had commented " Forbid it, Fate ! " He had written nervously to his daughter Kitty, that he would be very glad to see Horace for a few days. As to Horace's lady, who wrote him the most distinguished letters from Cavendish Square, he imagined that she would form a very valuable part of his family connections, but he could not imagine what she could do at little Burnham. He knew that she had been bred in West Indian luxury. She was a " fine " lady, and would wish to bring her personal maid, what in the eighteenth century was called her " woman ". At the thought of Mrs. Horatio Nelson's *suite* scorning his own rustic staff—all strong personalities—the Rector was overcome. Nelson managed the first meeting tactfully. He took his lady upon a tour of his Norfolk relations. They began with the Boltons, a household cheerful, whatever the odds. At present his elder sister was sheltering Edmund, fourth surviving son of the family, who had been a partner with Mr. Bolton, but was now not earning, as he was in a decline. Leaving Fanny at Hilborough, with the William Nelsons, her husband rode over to Burnham Thorpe. In his home thoughts from sea he had most often pictured his birthplace as he found it now—in the weeks of haymaking, the elder-flower and the wild rose.

The Rector's latest additions to his register of family prowess did not make cheerful reading. His youngest son, Suckling, on receiving his legacy under the Comptroller's will, and a liberal benefaction from Uncle William Suckling, had bought the house and stock-in-trade of a grocer and draper at North Elmham. That venture was now at an end, and he seemed willing to take holy orders. The Rector hoped that Suckling might pass " amongst a crowd of undistinguished preachers, and gain some respect in the village of his Residence, from his quiet disposition, his liking for conviviality, and his passion for Greyhounds and Coursing ". But taking orders must entail the expense of a

private tutor, followed by a university course at Cambridge.
And while Suckling had merely lost money, Maurice was in debt.
While he shepherded the Captain of the *Pegasus* round the
Leeward Islands, the Captain of the *Boreas*, in obedience to
letters from home, had not neglected to mention to the Sailor
Prince that he had a brother languishing in the Navy Office.   He
had warned his family, " My interest is but rising ".   The Rector's
account of his eldest brother sent Captain Nelson up to London
again, and by the first week in July he had somehow managed
to " entirely liberate poor Maurice from the galling chain ".   On
his return to Norfolk he collected his wife for a visit to his younger
sister, Kitty.   The Matchams had taken a lease of Barton Hall,   12
near Neatishead, where they lived in what the Rector complacently, but unenviously, described as " ease and affluence ".
Unfortunately, alone of his connections by marriage, Mrs. Horatio
Nelson did not fall an instant victim to the charms of " G.M.".
She thought the admired bridegroom of Kitty Nelson, who had,
it is true, the wealthy man's *penchant* for buying, altering and
then selling properties, the most unsettled man she had ever met.   13

While they stayed at Barton, Nelson read in the *Gazette* that
a new Board of Admiralty was appointed.   Lord Chatham was
become First Lord ; Lord Hood one of the two Naval Lords.   He
wrote at once to assure their Lordships of his readiness to serve
whenever they might think proper to call upon his services,
followed his letter by a personal call upon Lord Hood, and was
able to inform Fanny from London in August that his Lordship
had made many enquiries after her, and been most civil.   " He
assured me that a Ship in peaceable times was not desirable ; but
that should any Hostilities take place, I need not fear having a
good ship."

Nelson on half-pay was receiving eight shillings a day.   Fanny
and he both received annual allowances of £100 from their uncles.
But perpetual holiday is an expensive business, and Nelson was
now thirty.   On October 8, he wrote to Cornwallis, expressing his
desire to serve under him in the East Indies.   " Fame says that
you are going out with a convoy."   Although " set down here
in a country life ", and " happily married ", he was perfectly
ready.   Five days later he sent a repetition of his desire " to
serve under you, and for our Country (although I am as happy
in domestic life as a person can be) ".   The reply was most dis-   14
appointing.   Cornwallis answered that nothing would have given
him more pleasure than to have had Nelson in one of his ships.

He had thought of him, remembering him as an officer with East Indian experience, but knowing that Nelson had recently achieved a fireside of his own, had not dared to make such a suggestion. For the present, his appointments were made. He could only say that if more ships were sent out, nothing would please him more than to see Nelson in one of them.

The Horatio Nelsons had by this time settled, though not by a fireside of their own. The Matchams' chariot had carried the whole party from Barton Hall to the Parsonage House, Burnham Thorpe, the understanding being that they were to " cast their anchor " there for a short while. The Rector, on meeting Fanny, and finding that in spite of her *suite* she was unalarming— in fact, rather painfully alive to her situation as a person of limited means—had tenderly invited the young couple to make their home with him and cheer his declining years. They had been planning to winter in France, so that Horace could make one more assault on the language of that country. His wife was already fluent. She had been accustomed, when acting as hostess for her Uncle Herbert, to entertain all the visiting officers recommended by the Governors of the French Islands. They gave up their French plan without much struggle.

The old walled garden at Burnham Thorpe showed signs of the havoc wrought by Mr. Matcham's suggestion of " turning " the stream through the grounds, and the season was an interesting one in the gardener's year. " The very energetic Captain " set to work at once to urge his father's outdoor servant, Peter Black, " poor, forlorn, 'tho wise as ever ", to lustier effort. Mrs. Nelson began to make acquaintance with a very small home, of low rooms, filled with worn furniture and reflections of greenery, with flagged floors, grateful in warm weather, set down in a landscape two-thirds of which appeared to be occupied by sky. The autumn leaves began to fall, and winds to blow across the steel-grey North Sea. In expectation of promised roses from Barton, Nelson achieved a *parterre*. The boot-and-knife boy, Williamson, helped him to dam the stream, on which he was going to sail a model ship-of-the-line. . . .

In October came an expectation of local gaiety, just the occasion to introduce a new member of the family to a wider circle. The Rector expected the Matchams to stay for the event. Mr. Coke of Holkham (the Great House accessible by a footpath over the Burnham fields), who was wont to say that his nearest neighbour was the King of Denmark, intended revelry on the grand scale. The centenary of the landing of William III was the date chosen by one who was so prominent a Whig that Mr. Styleman of Snettisham always had the politeness, when Mr. Coke dined, to turn his portrait of William Pitt to the wall. To his Grand Fête and Ball, however, the great landowner had decided to invite all neighbours with a claim to his attention, irrespective of their political views. The Heir Apparent had intimated his intention of coming down from London with a party of six, so the illuminations included a gigantic Prince of Wales's feathers. An Italian *virtuoso* was summoned a month before the festal day to superintend the arrangements for the ball, supper and card rooms and the fireworks on the lake. At last the cards went out, and as usual in a country neighbourhood where the host has determined not to draw the line too high, enormous offence was unwittingly given. The records of Holkham contain notes of acceptance and refusal to attend this gala, filed under headings varying from " Friendly ", " Civil, with a reason ", " Civil, but no reason ", " Rather angry ", and " Very angry ". Eventually, none of the Nelson family attended the most important social gathering of East Anglia in 1788. The Rector refused without a reason; the Matchams found themselves detained in London. The Squire of Holkham and his lady, unlike Commodore Cornwallis, either had not heard or had forgotten that the parson's sailor son had taken a wife. Captain Nelson's refusal, penned by an injured female, simply states, " Captain Nelson's Compliments to Mr. and Mrs. Coke, and is sorry it is not in his Power to accept their invitation for November 5th." 17

To a loyal family it can have been small consolation that the Holkham Grand Fête and Ball was marred by the failure of the chief guest. The Prince's carriages were stopped on Newmarket Heath by a message desiring his immediate attendance at Windsor. The King's mental malady had declared itself unmistakably on the morning of the 5th. Miss Coke had to be led out to open the ball by a mere peer.

2

All through their first winter at Burnham Thorpe the West Indians shivered and shook. Fanny heaped more and more woollen garments upon her small frame, and finally retired to bed for days together. Even " the most robust Captain " acknowledged " a rheumatick twinge " after his labours in the garden. Presently the wind dropped, the snows came and gardening was no longer possible. When Burnham was winter-bound, all was, in the Rector's language, " Hush, at High Noon as at Midnight ". Even horse-traffic ceased. Only an occasional hardy village figure plunged past the irregular windows of the small shabby house where the Rector, his naval son and his West India daughter-in-law sat in a brown parlour with a stone floor, under the dim and indifferent portraits of ancestors of higher fortune.

The Rector himself was accustomed to the solitude and climate. Horace was at home, and spent the hours of candle-light with his nautical charts, his model ship-of-the-line, Dampier's *Voyages* (which he thought the most interesting book he had ever read) and his correspondence with their Lordships, etc. Fanny, however, hung heavy upon the Rector's conscience. He wished that some amusement could come her way—" a little society and an instrument, with which she could pass away an hour. She does not openly complain. Her attention to me demands my esteem, and to her Good Husband she is all he can expect." Fanny had her fine needlework, her water-colours and, three times a year, " Master Nisbet for the holidays ". When her brother-in-law Edmund arrived home to die, she included him in her kind attentions. But he was listless—past caring for relations new or old; he seemed to prefer the company of his village nurse, Dame Smith. Spring, as usual, came slowly to Norfolk. When the woods began to bud, and the birds to sing, her husband took Mrs. Horatio Nelson, who found Norfolk not so temperate as Nevis, out on bird-nesting expeditions. He knew that the hedge-mongers commonly visited the old yew hedge in the garden. His eye and ear gave him access to a kingdom of simple delights un-suspected by his partner.

He had no private transport, no money to spare and no call to London. He read the local newspapers thoroughly. They told him that in France the Bastille had fallen, and the royal family had been triumphantly escorted from Versailles, by a vociferous mob, to enforced residence in their capital. England was at peace, and her beloved King recovered. Nelson's " interest " could no longer be termed " rising ". " Not being a man of fortune ", he explained to Locker, who was also unemployed, " is a crime which I cannot get over, and therefore none of the Great care about me. I am now commencing Farmer, though not a very large one, you will conceive, but enough for amusement. Shoot, I cannot, therefore I have not taken out a license; but notwithstanding the neglect I have met with, I am happy, and now I see the propriety of not having built my hopes on such sandy foundations as the friendships of the Great." His princeling had been created Duke of Clarence, but at present the patronage of this royalty was rather a disadvantage than the reverse. The Duke had joined with his brothers in their long, unedifying struggle to establish a Regency, and had delivered himself of some startling speeches.

Half a dozen letters—four concerned with Messrs. Wilkinson and Higgins, two to Locker—confirm Nelson's uninterrupted residence at home in the year 1789, " retired, upwards of 120 miles from London ".

3

The west coast of Vancouver Island is generally precipitous, much broken by bays and inlets. One of these harbours, six miles in width, and sending inland three arms, from sixty to a hundred and twenty fathoms deep, was visited by Captain Cook in 1778. He called it by what he took to be its native name—Nootka—and concluded that Spaniards had never been there, but did not formally take possession. For seven seasons of war, after his call, the north-west coast of America knew no strangers. With peace, English ships began to call again at a remote island of singularly mild airs, slightly reminiscent of Scandinavia in midsummer. The English captains had no means of putting to a commercial use the magnificent timber of its dense forests, but they could, and did, water and provision and buy fish and furs. In the same year that the *Boreas* was paid off, after an alarm of war with France had died, Spain began to take interest in a fine harbour which Perez claimed to have discovered four years before Captain Cook's visit. In 1789 a little confused and angry shouting took place amongst the woods and waters of Nootka Sound, the echoes of which were to rouse Europe. Two Spanish ships, the *Princesa* and the *San Carlos*, had been sent by the Governor of Mexico to take possession of Spanish property. They found two English merchant vessels, of classical name, in the harbour of Nootka, their crews stolidly and quite openly engaged in trading with the natives of the island. The English Cabinet heard the first word of what had followed from the Spanish Ambassador to the Court of St. James's on the second day of February, 1790. His Excellency was able to disclose that the English sailors, after being carried to Mexico as captives, had been released. They had been regarded as members of a friendly nation, probably quite ignorant of Spanish rights. But he was obliged to ask that the persons who had planned the expedition of the *Iphigenia* and *Argonaut* should be punished, in order to deter other nations from settling in Spanish territory. Spain had another thorn in her side. She knew that Russia was invading Alaska. England had at the moment no Ambassador at Madrid. Lord Auckland had come home, and his successor had not yet taken up his duties. Pitt applied himself to the problem with vigour. He answered in his haughtiest vein to the Spanish Ambassador that as yet he knew nothing of the facts except as represented by His Excellency. But as these representations were of an act of violence, all discussion of claims must necessarily be suspended until the seized vessels had been restored and adequate atonement made. The name and story of Nootka Sound penetrated even to the *Norfolk News*. Suddenly it seemed that England might be going to war with Spain, and presently, as the weeks passed into spring, also with France, as ally of Spain—a serious situation. In early May, after a meeting of the National Assembly in Paris, fourteen French sail-of-the-line were ordered to make ready to go to sea.

Nelson was in London by May 8, but owing to an untoward incident, he might have been in France. After many months completely devoid of noteworthy event, the shades of Burnham had been roughly visited. His brother William, his brother-in-law, Mr. Matcham, had been kind enough after their visits to leave a horse in the Parsonage House stables. With the approach of better weather he had decided to buy " a Gallwey, a little pony " at the local fair. On April 26 the Captain arrived home on his purchase, very pleased with the result of his first attempt to deal in horseflesh. Indeed, so great was his satisfaction that not until the pony had been rubbed down and watered and fed did he perceive anything amiss in the atmosphere at home. He had for some time been plagued by letters from solicitors representing clients whose ships he had seized while applying the Navigation Laws in the Leeward Isles. It now transpired that during his absence at the fair two men, " in appearance resembling Bow-Street officers ", had forced their way into his father's house, desired to see his lady, and after making her repeatedly declare that she was the wife of Captain Nelson, presented her with a document, telling her to give it to her husband. The document was the notification of an action to be taken against him by

certain American captains, and they laid their damages at
£20,000.

He had no great reason for anxiety. The Secretary to the
Admiralty had informed him, a month before, in answer to
another letter on the subject, that his communication had been
referred to the Treasury, with recommendations that he should
be defended. But he had much cause for wrath. Fanny had
been frightened. The lady of a sea-officer in His Majesty's
Service had been insulted. " This affront I did not deserve ! "
He wrote, on the spot, to the Admiralty, enclosing a copy of the
notice " this day served by a person from London ". He trusted
to their Lordships' protection, hoping they would only think he
had performed his duty. But in the heat of the hour of insult
he also formed a dramatic resolution. If he did not receive a
favourable answer at the earliest possible moment he would
retire to France. Maurice should bring Fanny over to join him
in eternal exile. A note in his wife's hand tells that " He once
spoke of the Russian service ". On May 4 he was able to cancel
these unhappy plans. Captain Pringle had seen Mr. Rose,
and the Secretary to the Treasury, who had not forgotten a
six a.m. interview two and a half years ago, had calmly mentioned
that Captain Nelson, " a very good officer ", need be under
no apprehension. " He will assuredly be supported by the
Treasury."

4

At the Admiralty on May 8 he was not able to get an interview
with Lord Chatham. That was not surprising, since the situation,
as shown in the newspapers, had called up to Whitehall many
figures so well known to the porters of the stately Admiralty
building that these aloof flunkeys did not trouble to show the
poor devils to the waiting-room. In the company of many
other officers on half-pay, some of whom looked as if they should
get employment and others as if they never would, he wrote a
note explaining that he had come up to town immediately on
hearing of " the bustle ", and was ready to undertake whatever
employment their Lordships thought most proper. He went on   20
to Lord Hood's house, and here found his man. Their interview
was brief, and as a result of it Nelson made no further effort to
see Hood for over two years. The Admiral who had " found "
him could not ask the First Lord for a ship for Captain Nelson.
Staggered by this sudden and wholly unexpected removal of

favour, Nelson asked outright the reason. Lord Hood, who never lacked courage, made a reply never effaced from Nelson's brain. " The King was impressed with an unfavourable opinion of me." This sentence struck Nelson so near to the heart that he asked no more. He left the house in Wimpole Street in staring silence, determined never again to trouble his Lordship for his interest or influence.

To be unemployed for a couple of years in time of peace had been a growing anxiety, but the prospect of remaining unemployed when " nearly the whole Service had been called forth " was unendurable. He had never lost sight of " the radiant orb " beckoning him on to brave every danger with his King and Country as Patron; but he had not, in his least optimistic moments, considered the possibility of being denied the chance of braving dangers. Nor, now, upon reflection, would he believe that his King and Country did not need him. He decided, in this sickening and lonely hour, that he must, like better men before him, have become the victim of some misunderstanding— " a prejudice at the Admiralty, evidently against me, which I can neither guess at, nor in the least account for ". The radiant orb stayed in his heaven. " Neither at sea nor on shore, through the caprice of a Minister, can my attachment to my King be shaken.

²¹ That will never end but with my life."

He achieved again, in very different spirits, the tiring and expensive journey back to rural spring-tide Norfolk, and told his expectant and affectionate circle that he had done all that was proper, and could but wait the event; many other officers were in the same state of uncertainty. The Rector, in whose character the virtues of humility and resignation were strongly developed, quite honestly considered the existence of an upright and benevolent landowner (too wealthy to be obliged to follow any profession) superior in happiness to that of a sea-officer. He noticed that Horace was restless, but was glad that his son seemed reconciled to any available employment. He could not deceive himself that though Horace's merit was great, " Still, without Interest, I fear it may be overlooked, where a Boldness and some parliamentary weight stands forward ". He remembered with uneasiness the day when Maurice " might have

²² catched a gleam of sunshine; it is now clouded ". Fanny, who thought the life of a sailor's wife hard, had, in preparation for becoming a grass-widow, settled upon lodgings in the small town of Swaffham—a sad change from Montpelier. Mr. Matcham, ever

generous, wished to offer his brother-in-law a pipe of wine when
he should have a ship. Outside the family, many acquaintances
who had sons to place, or vacant bins in their cellars, enquired
the name of Captain Nelson's new ship.

Another General Election took place during this summer.
"Noisy nonsense", opined the Rector. Fanny, who appreciated
her husband's political aspirations, was careful, seven years later,
to tell him when there seemed a possibility of a local naval
candidate being adopted at Great Yarmouth : "They don't like
their present member. . . . A Navy man was absolutely
necessary for them. I said Sir J. Jarvis [sic] had offered his
services. It was very true but they wanted a man that the
minister would recommend; else they would not get anything
done." Mr. Lucas had mentioned a house in the constituency
that would soon be offered for sale—Sir Barney Bargrave's. But   23
in 1790, "on the beach", out of luck, Nelson knew that he had
not the slightest chance of what he called "a land-frigate".
Amongst the twelve members elected for Norfolk that year five
were new, but not one, according to the Rector, a cause for much
elation. Nelson offered himself and lady for a visit to his god-
parent at Wolterton, a scheme that caused the Rector to entreat
Mrs. Matcham to choose for his daughter-in-law, in London, a
plain handsome bonnet and a cloak, suitable for dinners, calls, etc.
Nelson wrote also to the Duke of Clarence, making no secret of
his position. "My not being appointed to a Ship is so very
mortifying that I cannot find words to express what I feel on the
occasion." By August, getting desperate, he snatched at any
excuse to address a person of rank who was of his profession.
"The retired situation which I am placed in, affords me seldom
any means of information but through newspapers; in which I
read with sorrow that your Royal Highness was prevented from
being at Windsor on the Prince of Wales's birthday. . . ." The
newspapers had also reported, under the heading, "Torbay",
August 1. "Wind fair at W.N.W." "This morning Lord
Howe's flagship threw out the signal for sailing. Thousands of
spectators watched the departure of the Fleet—thirty-one ships-
of-the-line, nine frigates, two brigs, two cutters, a fire-ship and a
hospital ship. . . ."

On September 26 Nelson tried the First Lord again. "My
wish to be employed is so great, that I trespass on your Lordship's
time with a letter. I am sensible I have no great interest to
recommend me nor have I had conspicuous opportunities of

distinguishing myself, but thus far, without arrogating, I can say that no opportunity has been passed by, and that I have ever been a zealous Officer." Mr. Suckling, in the same week, was mentioning his nephew's name to Lord Hawkesbury. The saintly Rector reserved his outward sympathy for " Poor Mrs. Nelson, still kept in the same harry of spirits and uncertainty as she has been for the last six months ", and pointed out that war had not yet been declared. If " the present negotiation " terminated in peace, Horace would have been fortunate in not being appointed to a ship. " And if War must be entered upon, he is still in good time." The present negotiation did terminate in peace before October was out. Pitt's chosen diplomatist for business which must be handled with caution and much delicacy had not blundered. Sir Gilbert Elliot's younger brother, Hugh Elliot, an old school-friend of the Comte de Mirabeau, had fished successfully in troubled waters. A French Ministry, which had relied upon the old recipe of a popular war as the sovereign antidote for internal dissention, was powerless. Spain, faced by an English ultimatum, and finding to her chagrin that Louis XVI was not able to declare war without the sanction of the National Assembly, temporised in time. On October 28 the Nootka Convention was signed, by which England gained the right to trade and settle on the north-west coast of the Americas, and Spain relinquished for ever her claims to sovereignty of the coast as a result of discovery.

Cold weather settled down upon the Burnhams again, and the Rector, who found that failing sight and strength made his performance of duties in two churches, neither close to his home, increasingly difficult, took the lease of a cottage in Burnham Ulph village, leaving the government of the Parsonage House to his son and daughter-in-law. The result of Nelson's last application to a person of influence arrived after the threat of war had passed. Lord Mulgrave, once the rhetorical Captain Phipps of the Arctic Expedition, wrote in worthy vein. Had the armament continued, he would have had the greatest pleasure in mentioning the respect he entertained for Captain Nelson's professional character, " as well as my very sincere personal regard for you, with your very laudable claim for employment ".

In December Lord and Lady Walpole announced themselves ready to receive guests from Burnham Thorpe, and Captain Nelson and lady set out at last for Wolterton. They stayed for several weeks at a country seat so well furnished with lake and woodland that his lordship's witty relative, Mr. Horace Walpole, had announced, on hearing of the first lord's inheritance, that now at last his uncle and aunt would have something they had long needed—firing to keep them warm, and water to clean themselves. The second lord and his lady were a great improvement on their predecessors, but so prosaic a couple that had they not been a peer and peeress, they might not have been much visited. However, they were kin. Nelson, who had recently had good reason to appreciate the necessity for appearing neither hopeless nor obscure, took care to mention his address to the Duke of Clarence, and thereafter the winter stay of his lordship's naval godson and lady became an annual fixture. Annually, also, Nelson made his spring pilgrimage to London to attend a *levée*. "It must one day come to account." And, though he would not trouble Lord Hood again, he never neglected the courtesy when in town of leaving his name at his lordship's doors.

Not a single letter from Nelson's pen in the year 1791 has come to light. From family letters it appears that he took part in the mild provincial gaieties available. At the Lynn Feast and Aylsham Assembly, as season succeeded season, the Horatio Nelsons noticed awkward schoolgirls become extraordinary fine, tall young women, and dowagers, bent on their shilling whist, increasingly garrulous and depleted of front teeth. Violent events taking place in France did not trouble the *belles* of Aylsham while the fiddles sounded, but even in Norfolk repercussions were noticeable, and Nelson wrote at length on the subject to his Prince, who shared his anxiety lest their country be cast into "the wretched deplorable confusion of France". Nelson's opinions, as expressed to a son of the sovereign, were temperate. He hoped that the justices of Norfolk would find courage to do collectively what not one dared do individually—take away the licences from those of the public-houses that allowed societies calling themselves by such names as "Friends of the People" to hold incendiary meetings. On the other hand, he realised that the poor labourers who flocked eagerly to these meetings were not without reason for desiring a changed world. Part of their wants he supposed unavoidable, but he blamed some landlords for prevailing disaffection, which, however, he did not believe to be as yet very dangerous or widespread. It had been quite easy for the son of a respected country clergyman to penetrate to cottages, asking such homely questions as how much did shoes and cobbler's bills for the family cost *per annum*? His Majesty himself made such expeditions, and though caricaturists repre-

sented cruelly, under the title "Affability", a monarch who
gloried in the name of Briton bawling into the ear of a stone-deaf
and scared husbandman, Nelson found, as he had expected, that
Farmer George was securely seated in the hearts of his people.
Even of the most discontented, he noted, "a want of loyalty is
not amongst their faults; and many of their superiors, in many
instances, might have imitated their conduct with advantage ".
So that no country gentleman should have it in his power to say
that Captain Nelson painted too black a picture, he was careful
to enter in his " Account of Earnings and Expenses of a Labourer
of Norfolk, with a Wife and three Children, supposing that he is not
to be one day kept from labour in the whole year ", such extra
money as might be won by the woman gleaning, or the man
turnip-hoeing at the appointed seasons. The Duke of Clarence
received from his naval friend a document ending, " Not quite
twopence a day, for each, and to drink, nothing but water; for
beer our poor labourers never taste unless they are tempted,
which is too often the case, to go to the Ale-house." (The Duke
never knew that, upon second thoughts, Nelson had deleted from
his accompanying letter the burning phrase, " Hunger is a sharp
thorn, and they are not only in want of food sufficient, but of
25 clothes and firing.")

Coursing had been Nelson's favourite relaxation at home, but
by February 1792 he had decided that the pleasure of the sport
was outweighed by the wet jacket and heavy cold that were
generally the sequel. His world was narrowing, do what he
would. When old Dr. Poyntz called at the Parsonage House he
left an emphatic message for William, regarding walnut trees ánd
red filberts. His host really could not remember the drift of the
old gentleman's long-winded instructions, and feared that his
only comment had been that by the time any trees planted by
Brother William this year were bearing walnuts, William would
not be alive. His thoughts had been elsewhere. But when a
sea-captain sat silent, Norfolk friends were generally sympathetic
and capable of appreciating the picture in his inward eye—the
Mediterranean, perhaps, and crews ordered to bathe on a blazing
day, a top-sail bent over the ship's side into the sea, for the less
venturesome; stout fellows diving off the ship's head or from
her yard-arm ; and the Fleet so still, the sea so calm, that a
scarred 74 seemed overpowered by the heat, and asleep upon
the waters. . . . He had received letters from Commodore
Cornwallis, by the *Swallow*. . . . No hopes from that quarter.

I

If Kingsmill had gone to India he had promised to ask for Nelson. "However, that is over for the present. . . . The Navy is to be reduced to 15,000 men." The Prime Minister had told the House of Commons, "There never was a time when, from the situation of Europe we might more reasonably expect fifteen years of peace."

In September a family party always sallied forth from the Parsonage House for rough shooting upon a glebe of thirty acres. Most of the bloodshed was laid at the door of Tom Bolton. William's fire was remarked to evaporate chiefly in threats. Of Horace, it was remembered that "he once shot a partridge; but the manner in which he carried his gun always cocked, as if he were going to board an enemy, and his custom of firing immediately when any birds appeared, rendered any attendance on him a service of considerable danger". By September 1792, Horace, who pronounced "An Enemy floating game is a better mark", had long been persuaded that he could not shoot. His sixth winter "on the beach" began. On December 15 he wrote to his younger sister that all her family in Norfolk were well. Mr. Matcham had recently built a house on an estate with the charming name of Shepherd's Spring, near Ringwood, in Hampshire, but the couple were at present enjoying London. Nelson told his sister that when she and Mr. Matcham chose to come into Norfolk, Mrs. Nelson would be very happy to receive them at the Parsonage House. He cautiously fancied they would find the spring more pleasant than the winter. "We have had one heavy fall of snow, but it has thawed now."

Eleven days after Nelson watched the thaw from his desk in his Norfolk window, the trial of Louis Capet began in Paris. Once more English newspapers were prophesying war with France—a thing their Prime Minister was most desirous to avoid. But Revolutionaries drunk with power had proceeded to acts intolerable to England. The River Scheldt had been closed to commerce by several treaties. A month before Nelson wrote his Christmas letter to his sister, the Convention suddenly declared the Scheldt open. Three days later the support of France was flamboyantly offered to all nations striving for Freedom. Nelson had written to Lord Chatham in October, asking for a ship, and repeated his request after five weeks had passed without his receiving any answer. Rather to his surprise, his second letter produced a reply. "Sir," wrote the Secretary to the Admiralty, on December 12, "I have received your Letter of the 5th instant, expressing your readiness to serve, and I have read the same to my Lords Commissioners of the Admiralty." No man could have judged from this that the end of his time of waiting had come. But in London the name of Nelson no longer reminded one official only of the sufferings of poor Admiral Hughes; and a whole series of Government officials of endless correspondence with a Post-Captain over vexing discoveries of frauds in their Departments; and a very exalted quarter indeed of a " Memorial " from a young officer who had not done much to prevent Prince William making more of a fool of himself in the West Indies than Nature intended. A capable Post-Captain, well down the list, who had exceeded in zeal, and had been left five years " on the beach ", was likely to be employed again in the present crisis.

Whether Nelson was summoned to London in the first week of January 1793 or took the initiative, in a month renowned for its flooded roads and coach-accidents, does not appear, but by January 7 he knew that he was to get a ship and his first of the line. " *Post nubila Phœbus* ", he quoted in ecstasy to Fanny. " Your son will explain the motto. After clouds come sunshine. The Admiralty so smile upon me that really I am as much surprised as when they frowned. Lord Chatham yesterday made many apologies for not having given me a Ship before this time, and said, that if I chose to take a Sixty-Four to begin with, I should be removed into a Seventy-Four." He had closed with the offer of a Sixty-Four, and when he was offered a Seventy-Four, off Toulon, in the following August, his answer was, " I cannot give up my officers." By January 26 he was " fixed for the *Agamemnon*, at Chatham ", " without exception one of the finest Sixty-Fours in the Service ", and unlike the poor *Boreas*, " with the character of sailing most remarkably well ". His first, mercifully formal, interviews with Lord Hood passed off as well as possible. Lord Hood, who was hoisting his flag in the *Victory*, hinted that the *Agamemnon* might be ordered to join his fleet at Gibraltar. At the Admiralty their Lordships, most flatteringly, agreed to Captain Nelson's request that no bills asking for men for the *Agamemnon* should be put up in London until the name of her Captain could be announced. His bills were already posted throughout Norfolk, where a Lieutenant and four mid-shipmen were scouring every port, with instructions to forward the results to Lynn and Yarmouth. Several men from the seven Burnhams had " offered ", but even when he had got his stiffening of Norfolk volunteers—worth two of other men, in his opinion—he feared that he would still be upwards of a hundred short of complement. This meant having to rely upon the captures of the press-gangs, having to sail undermanned or, worst nightmare of a young officer, being unable to sail. He had written to his Service friends in the north to send what they could lay hands upon to Whitby and Newcastle. . . . Locker's broad pendant was flying on board the *Sandwich*, as Commander-in-Chief at the Nore, and the Commodore was discharging Mr. Maurice Suckling and Mr. George Andrews into the *Agamemnon*, and Joseph King, once boatswain of the *Boreas*, out of the *Valiant*, at the request of the Duke of Clarence. Nelson had no scruples in employing " one of the best boatswains I have seen in His Majesty's service ", who might, but for his representations, have been out of the Service and in the mad-house. He had been able to secure his old servant, Frank. . . .   28

During the fortnight before his commission was signed he paid a brief call at home, where the scene was much changed. The doors of the Parsonage House were continually opening, in hard weather, to admit callers arriving in chariots, on horseback or on foot—all on business. The Rev. Dixon Hoste, once squire of Ingoldisthorpe, and now a tenant of Mr. Coke at Godwick House, had a fragile-looking second son, aged twelve, for his distant kinsman's ship. He and the Rev. Mr. Weatherhead had taken the additional precaution of getting their magnificent neighbour of Holkham to recommend the boys to Captain Nelson. The Rev. Mr. Bolton, Susanna's brother-in-law, produced the third Norfolk clergyman's son for the *Agamemnon*. Everyone seemed to have a little " younker " to offer, when what her Captain needed, in view of active service, was a couple of strong-nerved surgeon's mates. Fanny, in her blacks for Uncle Herbert, was fitting out Josiah, and had promised, after the departure of all she held dear, to " take on a new lease of life ", aided by the small legacy which had come to her on the death of the President of Nevis. Her husband, " never better in health ", and " perfectly indifferent to what quarter of the World we go ", was already with her in body only. He told her that " being united to such a good woman, I look back to as the happiest period of my life ", and, since that sounded too like an eternal farewell, " Never fear, I shall come laughing back one day."   29

On the morning of February 4 two tremulous, black-robed figures waved farewell to an equipage containing three persons in His Majesty's uniform, and high spirits. The Parsonage House was to be "in some measure forsaken". The Rector, who would sadly miss his affectionate caller at Burnham Ulph, and was very grateful for the loan of Horace's pony, was not going to let his house. He was going to put in a labourer and wife as caretakers—"Mrs. N. having no wish to return to Thorpe. There are good reasons against it; but as they please." Her husband had not succeeded in turning Mrs. Horatio Nelson into a Norfolk woman. Her programme was now "visits" and lodgings in Swaffham. She had not even considered the possibility of living on at the Parsonage House, listening to the eternal silence of the countryside, which is never to the country-bred ear any more at rest than one of His Majesty's ships. The small business of still-room, poultry-yard and larder, the knowledgeable prodding of "Peter without", in a garden which her husband had set in high order, but in which he would never dig again, were not for her.

Nelson joined his first ship-of-the-line on February 7, 1793. France did not declare war on England and Holland until February 11, but this war was to last his lifetime and ten years more.

5

Another anxiety which he had not mentioned abroad had clouded his five years of waiting.

His brother William, married four months before him, was now the father of a Charlotte Mary, aged five, and an Horatio, a year younger. His younger sister, whose marriage had taken place a fortnight after his own, had lost one infant son, but had a fine surviving boy and girl; thirteen more children were to follow. His elder sister, married in 1780, had by 1793 completed her family of seven, opening with twin daughters, now at boarding-school, and had only lost one child. As a bachelor, Nelson had been noticeably vulnerable to the solemn wiles of infancy, and outside his own family a pronounced child-fancier had been invited to stand sponsor to several Horatios. He had married, in confident expectation of children, a lady who had been prompt in presenting an heir to his predecessor. From no available source does it appear that Frances Woolward ever became pregnant by her second husband. She ailed persistently, but rheumatism, relaxed throat, chest colds and nervous debility are specifically described. Hope had receded gradually during the five years of Nelson's unemployment. By the end of that time, when he looked at his small, neurotic, thirty-five-years-old wife, happy with her shoulder-high midshipman son, he had realised that she was unlikely to bear again. He alluded openly to his disappointment once only. In the *Sketch of my Life* produced in answer to a request from Lord Hood's secretary, John M'Arthur, after the Battle of the Nile, he mentioned under date 1787, " And in March this year I married Frances Herbert Nisbet, widow of Dr. Nisbet of the Island of Nevis, by whom I have no children."

CHAPTER V

1793–1794
(*ætat* 34–35)

SHIP-OF-THE-LINE

I

ON the warm afternoon of Saturday, June 22, 1793, officers of the six sail-of-the-line from Lord Hood's fleet, ordered to water at Cadiz, were entertained before their departure by the naval authorities of that port. Spain, unfavourably impressed by the march of events in France, was showing herself friendly towards England. The visiting captains had been permitted to see what they pleased of the Naval Arsenal of the Isla de Léon, the defensive works of Cortadura, and the dockyards of the wealthiest port of western Europe, one of the first marine cities of the world, head-quarters of the Spanish treasure fleets. They had obtained every-thing that they needed for their ships, except wine, which they could collect at Gibraltar, and the Captain of the *Agamemnon* had succeeded in getting a cask of the famous sherry of Jerez, which, undeterred by past criticism, he was going to send as a gift to the newly appointed Lieutenant-Governor of the Royal Hospital for disabled British sailors at Greenwich—Captain William Locker.

The Captain of the *Agamemnon*, as he feasted with the Spanish Admiral on board the *Concepcion* of 112 guns, was very well satisfied with all he had seen. There were four first-rates in commission at Cadiz, beautiful ships, not so much undermanned as manned by inexperienced men, without any idea of discipline. He fancied that if the vaunted twenty-one sail-of-the-line which they were to join in the Mediterranean were in no better case, they would not be much use in action, a conclusion which rather pleased him. " The Dons may make fine ships—they cannot, however, make men. . . . Long may they remain in their present state." The Captain of a Spanish frigate explained that it was no wonder his men were sickly, for they had been sixty days at sea. Now, after sixty days at sea, " our Jacks " would have been getting healthy. The *Agamemnon*, at the moment, was remark-ably healthy, and her Captain, delighted at the thought that in a few days' sail they would be up the Mediterranean, was never better. " Indeed, nobody can be ill with my ship's company,

they are so fine a set." Since he spoke no Spanish and few of his
hosts understood English, he had leisure to reflect as he banqueted
in view of a city famed since the days of Ancient Rome for its dinners
and dancing-girls, and the sum of his silent reflections was that he,
and the five other British captains present, with a boarding-
party of no more than their ships' barges, could certainly have
taken this foreign first-rate. Spanish festivities commonly last
late; the waters of Cadiz Bay, the turrets of a white-walled city
of five gates, giving access to quiet streets displaying much Italian
marble, were in colour reminiscent of Spanish gold when the
party broke up, but only, it appeared, to proceed to further
gaiety. The English officers were to be taken to the something
translated as the " Bull-Feast ". They presently disembarked at
a rocky island among the salt marshes which lined the southern
shore of the bay, and after making their way through a noisy
concourse of persons, all bending their steps in the same direction,
were escorted to a prominent position in an amphitheatre, which
they were told would hold 16,000. The audience included many
well-dressed women, and the countenances of some of the handsomest bore witness to the fact that Cadiz had, for five hundred
years, been under Moorish occupation. The Spanish hosts
explained that the better sort of people never missed a Bull-
Feast, and that ladies chose their lovers (" husbands ", wrote
Nelson to Mrs. Nelson) for their dexterity in attacking and killing
these animals. As for the lower classes, they would sooner sell
their jackets or go without victuals than be absent.

Ten bulls were selected for to-day's entertainment, and amidst
violent applause, half a dozen men on foot, attired in spangled
yellow and sky-blue tights and scarlet cloaks, marched into the
sandy arena, followed by three cavaliers. The first bull was
led into the ring : the " Feast " began, and the Captain of the
Agamemnon, who had quite calmly realised the necessity for
providing a ship-of-the-line, likely to see action, with sturdy
surgeon's mates, began almost at once to feel sick. A glance
at the suddenly stolid faces of his brother officers told him that
they shared his feelings. " We felt for the bulls and horses."
The footmen were provided with darts, paper flags, goads and
whips to make a timid beast mad, the horsemen with spears,
capable of penetrating six inches. At first he really did not
think that he would be able to sit the affair out. Had the horses
been killed outright, or even the bulls, it would not have been
intolerable. Some hopelessly gored horses were despatched,

but obviously to get them out of the way, not for humanity's sake : and as soon as a vanquished bull lay down a fresh one was prodded forth.

He did sit the " Feast " out, and he believed it was considered a good one, for five horses were disembowelled and two men very severely wounded.   Had the men also been killed, he supposed that the entertainment would have been regarded as a complete success.   For his own part, as he watched the excited audience, he believed that to have seen some of them tossed by an enraged bull would not much have displeased him.

Afterwards, over a solemn night-cap, the officers of six British sail-of-the-line from Lord Hood's fleet agreed that they had seen their last Bull-Feast, and the Captain of the *Agamemnon* wrote to his lady next morning that how Spanish " Donnas " could sit out, much less applaud, such an exhibition was astonishing.

2

His experiences since driving away from the doors of the Old Parsonage House on the morning of February 4 had included only one hour spiced by the expectation of immediate action (under most disadvantageous circumstances), and that had occurred at dawn, a week past.   " We fell in with a Spanish eighty-gun Ship, ninety mounted : there being very little wind, and we the only Ship near her, and fancying her to be French, we fully expected a trimming ; for we must have been in action near an hour before any Ship could have come to our assistance.   However, as we sail well, that is to come."   Otherwise, although entirely absorbed professionally, his hasty notes had for the most part communicated " nothing new here ".

He had joined his first ship-of-the-line on February 7 in company with his First Lieutenant, Mr. Hinton, and Master, John Wilson, and taking his stand on his quarter-deck and unfolding his papers, read aloud to his standing officers his commission.   The usual business of shaking hands and passing a few words with characters known and unknown had been accomplished in good vein. He had a private word later with the Purser, Mr. Fellowes, one of Locker's recommendations, whom he was very much disposed to like, told Mr. Fellowes this, and also that he would not fail a person called upon to perform many duties necessarily odious, provided that he was very careful.   Mr. Fellowes seemed perfectly to understand his instructions.   " I daresay we shall do very well together."   After his first formal inspection of H.M.S.

Agamemnon, four days passed before tl e ship's company completed from the *Sandwich* guardship began to come on board to be passed in review by the Surgeon, Purser and Boatswain. Mr. Fellowes and his clerk plied their pens; Mr. Roxburgh, the inevitable Scots doctor, made his inspection—not very merciless, since men were hard to come by; Joseph King grimly returned to Mr. Fellowes's slop-store such recruits as he deemed unpresentable in their present attire. Uniform did not exist, but since the old hands knew what was best, keen volunteers were imitative and the purser's slop-store offered no variety, the men of the *Agamemnon* in 1793 presented a uniform appearance. Their costume was check shirts, white or buff trousers (cut short in the leg and loose at the ankle to show coloured stockings) and scarlet or buff waistcoats. Their blue jackets, cut very short in the waist, had no collars : a handkerchief, knotted round the neck, protected the tunic from the grease of the pigtail, until the hour came when it was needed to protect the ear-drums from the reverberations of gun-fire. Their headgear was a straw hat painted with black enamel, or japanned, sometimes turned up at one side to show a coloured lining. The ship's name was painted on the hat ribbon, or stamped on a small copper plate attached to it.

The wooden-walled cabin, which was to be the Captain's home for three years, was a great improvement on those he had occupied in frigates, but even after Frank had unpacked his master's luggage, was demonstrably designed for service, not show. Its furniture consisted of a carpet and curtains, a table and chairs, a rack for sword, pistols and telescope, and a locker covered by a leathern mattress.

The *Agamemnon* did not go down the river until mid-March. The sudden expansion of the Navy on a declaration of war, by a country until recently intent upon economy, and without mobilisation plans, had produced the natural results. Lord Hood's fleet was not nearly ready for service. During the first weeks of waiting, Mrs. Nelson, as yet unaccustomed to the unheralded appearances, and equally unforeseen exits, of a seaofficer, was startled by a flying visit from her husband at Hilborough. He mentioned the possibility of another meeting when he got to Spithead, but made no suggestion that she should come to Sheerness, where the " Three Tuns " was acclaimed by British sea-officers, with a sort of perverted pride, as the Worst Inn in the World. In his month there he never slept a night out of his ship. The *Agamemnon's* progress to the Nore from Blackstakes confirmed hopes already high. " We appear to sail very fast; we went, coming out, nearly as fast, without any sail, as the *Robust* did under her top sails." Mr. Nisbet, aged thirteen, was described by an experienced observer as " a little sea-sick ". Nelson himself had not yet reached the age when he frankly confessed to miserable, repeated and incurable sea-sickness. A week of smart gales followed, and although on her arrival at Spithead he was told to take the *Agamemnon* to sea for a week, " for two days it blew so strong we could not get up our anchors ". He had half expected to find Fanny at Spithead on his return. She had moved on to stay with the Matchams at Ringwood. But Mr. Matcham had decided that an expedition to the coast in such weather was likely to be fruitless. " Blowing weather," agreed Nelson, " but nothing for *Agamemnon* to mind "—stout words somewhat modified by the addition, " Maurice came to me, and it blew so hard I could not land him; he consequently went to sea with us." A few days later, the *Agamemnon*, still awaiting Lord Hood, sailed as one of a division of five of the line under the command of Admiral Hotham. In a letter headed " 12 leagues N.W. of the Island of Guernsey ", her husband told Mrs. Nelson that neutrals from French ports said that Nantes, Bordeaux and L'Orient were packed with English vessels, taken prize by French privateers or frigates—a depressing piece of news, if true, and another obvious result of our unreadiness. He thought he should see Torbay before leaving England. His impatience grew. " What we have been sent out for, is best known to the Great Folks in London; to us it appears only to hum the Nation and make fools of us, for where we have been stationed no Enemy was likely to be met with." His next brief line, " Sixteen leagues from Scilly ", told of such fog and drizzle that although Hotham's division had joined the main body under Hood a fortnight past, the *Agamemnon* had been quite unable to get a boat hoisted out. Their latest delay had been caused by the necessity of keeping the approaches of the Channel open for a home-bound convoy of East Indiamen, which had passed safely on the evening of June 6. .

After this relief events moved quickly. The fleet bore up for the Straits in " the finest weather possible ", and in a letter headed " Off Cape St. Vincent, June 14th ", Nelson was able to say that he had at last, a few days past, been able to have himself rowed across to H.M.S. *Victory* to pay his respects to his

Commander-in-Chief. Lord Hood had been civil. "I daresay we shall be good friends again."

3

On Sunday, July 7, the Captain of the *Agamemnon* "performed Divine Service to the Ship's Company and presented them with a Psalm Book and a Seaman's Monitor". Next morning the promised Spanish fleet joined Lord Hood off Alicante, but did not, to Nelson's amusement, "after several hours' trial, form anything which could be called a Line of Battle ahead", and soon announced the intention of returning to Cartagena to refit, leaving to England, he noticed, the honour of keeping the enemy in order. "I really never expect to see them again." Eleven days later, Lord Hood's fleet of fourteen of the line stood close in to Toulon, and sent in a flag of truce, to propose an exchange of prisoners. Neutrals, spoken off Cape St. Sebastian, had told of nearly thirty French battleships ready for sea at Toulon. There appeared to be seventeen, and five still fitting in the harbour, amongst them the *Commerce de Marseille*, Rear-Admiral Trogoff's flagship. "Seventeen ports on each deck", wrote Nelson. "The *Victory* looks nothing to her." French prisoners said that her sides were so thick no shot could go through them, and that she would, with ease, take the English Commander-in-Chief's flagship. He thought it a pity that a rumour that the enemy were fitting forges, to discharge red-hot cannon-balls, should have got out. As the mischief was done, the only remedy would be to get close enough in action to see that these missiles did no harm. The problem now was how to induce "these red-hot gentlemen" to come out of port and offer battle. After several days of heavy gale the flag of truce returned, bringing "no clear answer". Some theorists believed that nothing but hunger would bring the French out, others that when they had equal numbers ready for sea the Toulonese would drive them out. It might be that they would be tempted to attack a diminished enemy. Lord Hood took his fleet up to Nice, "to show ourselves"; but from the Gulf of Lyons, Nelson reported, "There seem to be no French ships at sea; at least we have seen nothing like one." His relations with "the Lord" who did not spare signals to a fleet which failed, in his opinion, to keep as compact order as was desirable, as yet showed no increase in cordiality. The Commander-in-Chief had written to offer the Captain of the *Agamemnon* a 74-gun ship, to which Nelson had replied to the effect that " As the Admiralty chose to put me into a 64, there I stay ", and, " I cannot give up my officers." His reasons seemed to have been accepted as sufficient. " So far, well." He had only just, since the *Agamemnon* was kept continually on the move, found time to reply to a truly exasperating letter which had reached him after three months, and dealt with a claim six years old. He pointed out to the Joint Secretary to the Treasury:

> " It has been totally out of my power to take any steps to receive the prize money due to the Ship's company under my command, nor is it possible that every poor seaman can go to Nevis, to receive his money from the Collector of Customs. They look up to their Captain as their friend and protector, and it was my intention, if the money was paid me, to advertize the distribution of it in London, when every Officer and Seaman, or their relatives, would be on the spot. . . . I humbly hope their Lordships will be pleased to order the money to England."

Only confused accounts of what was happening in the interior penetrated to the British fleet watching and waiting on the Mediterranean coast of France in trying weather. The coast road was very bad, very little used. Since they saw no French ships, it was difficult to believe that Provence, a district unable to feed herself, was not feeling the pinch. The English grew " heartily sick " of their daily view of blue sky, bluer sea, rocky islets of a golden or reddish tint, inclining conifers and eternal olive-groves, amongst which glimmered a few lowly, white-washed habitations. The guillotine had been set to work in Marseille, and the master of a ship from that port said that there were only two sorts of persons left in his country—the one drunk and mad, the other dying of hunger. Provence was said to be ready to attempt to form a separate Republic with British assistance. Civil war seemed imminent, in which case, Nelson supposed, war with England would not continue. Lord Hood sailed up to Genoa to water, and his appearance convinced the Genoese of the inadvisability of attempting to supply Toulon with corn. Still nothing happened. While he lay, supported by only three other ships, on the look-out, during the Commander-in-Chief's absence, Nelson copied and studied a catalogue of the quiescent enemy fleet. Of the battleship *Le Tonnant*, he noted that the principles of her captain, formerly in command of a fire-ship, were doubtful. The captain of *Le Lys*, formerly a pilot, was a " clubbist ", the captain of *Le Centaure*, formerly a boatswain, " very ignorant ". The company of *Le Destin* were

" doubtful, on shore ". Against the names of but seven of the twenty-two commanding officers had it been possible to enter a record of experience and sound principles. August wore on, and a glance at the date turned his thoughts to Burnham Thorpe, now at high harvest. He wished that he could hear of Fanny as settled somewhere agreeable, or perhaps got to Wolterton, a little earlier than usual, for the annual stay. Unless engaged in ejecting the French from Corsica by then, he might spend a peace Christmas with her. Unfortunately, he would come home no richer than he had left, if things went on as they were at present. " All we get is honour and salt beef." He fretted increasingly that no action was being taken, either to attack disturbed southern France, or to offer her British protection should she proclaim herself royalist. " We have attempted nothing."

Three days after he penned these words, the fruit of the long blockade dropped quietly from the bough. Commissioners from Marseille arrived on board the *Victory* to treat for peace. They expected to meet their opposite numbers from Toulon, who were ready to declare for Louis XVII and alliance with England, but were detained by riots in the town. Incredible though it seemed, the French fleet was never coming out. The Toulonese, apprehensive of sharing the fate meted out to the inhabitants of Marseille by the Republican General Carteaux, wished to place their ships, citadel and the forts of the adjacent coast provisionally at the disposal of Lord Hood. " The old saying ' That hunger will tame a lion '," wrote Nelson, " was never more strongly exemplified." Rear-Admiral Trogoff had retired ; his successor, St. Julien, a tippler, announced that he would dispute the entry of the English fleet, but his men were insubordinate, and when Lord Hood's landing-parties took possession of the forts commanding the roadstead, St. Julien, with five thousand seamen, went ashore, where he presently surrendered to the Spanish commander, De Langara.

The Spanish fleet had made a complacent reappearance as their allies entered " the strongest place in Europe " in triumph, but Nelson was not present to take part in the scene. Lord Hood had chosen the *Agamemnon*, a fast sailer, for a special mission. Her Captain's orders were to proceed, without an instant's delay, carrying despatches for the Vice-Consul at Oneglia (to be forwarded to the British Minister in Turin) and despatches to be delivered personally to the British Envoy and Minister Plenipotentiary to the Court of the Two Sicilies. After watering, he was to rejoin the fleet in Hyères Bay. Nothing could have been less diffuse than Lord Hood's instructions, but at sea, on her passage up to Oneglia, the *Agamemnon* fell in with the *Tartar*, homeward bound with the Commander-in-Chief's despatches, and her Captain, Lord Hugh Conway, sent a hasty line to Nelson. He explained that he had already written to the Envoy at Naples, urging him to ask at the Court of the Two Sicilies for as many Neapolitan troops as possible, to be despatched instantly to assist the Allies to hold Toulon against advancing Republicans. The British and Spanish landing-parties had been barely able to man the essential forts in the Toulon district. "Pray, press Sir W. Hamilton. . . . Will take your commands, if you have any, but in God's name, keep the boat as short a time as possible."

At dawn on September 12, 1793, Nelson completed a long letter, composed in snatches during the last five days : "Begun off the Island of Sardinia, and finished at anchor, off Naples." He had come in sight, with dusk, of the city which mortals are advised to see before they die, and Naples, he was bound to admit, viewed from her bay, at the hour when her windows, from harbour to terraced heights, began to twinkle, did not disappoint. Quickly the operatic scenery took on British national colours, and a lady at Swaffham was told, "We are now in sight of Mount Vesuvius, which shows a fine light to us in Naples Bay, where we are lying-to for the night, and hope to anchor to-morrow." He did not, as he scanned the famous panorama, indulge in any great expectations. "My poor fellows have not had a morsel of fresh meat or vegetables for near nineteen weeks, and in that time I have only had my foot twice on shore, at Cadiz. We are absolutely sick with fatigue. . . . I may have lost an appointment by being sent off ; not that I wish to be employed out of my Ship. . . . I have only to hope I shall succeed with the King of Naples." His full-dress uniform was prepared for the morrow's events, which might, or might not, include an audience with royalty. He remembered to tell Fanny that he had captured a vessel worth about £10,000, bound from Smyrna for Marseille. If she was condemned it might mean prize-money—"add something to our comforts". Since the only kindness he could show to his wife was attention to her son, he had ordered Josiah to go ashore with him to-morrow.

Later, in a moment of solitude, before a day which must bring either a chilling repulse or important response, the beauty of the scene touched him to add a breathless postscript : "We are in the Bay all night, becalmed, and nothing could be finer than the view of Mount Vesuvius."

4

The cool classic splendours of the newly decorated royal *suite* in the Palazzo Sessa were indeed a change after nineteen weeks of Mediterranean glare in the Captain's cabin of the *Agamemnon*. Nelson, who had anchored and gone ashore as soon as possible on Thursday morning, had for two days no opportunity to write home describing a mission which had been an unqualified success. The correspondents to whom he addressed himself from the British Embassy on September 14 were his wife and his Uncle Suckling.

Everything had gone right, from the moment of his arrival in Naples, or, to be exact, before he had set foot there, for the entry of a British warship into their bay had been watched with interest by Neapolitans high and low, and the King, who had been a King since he was a boy, and at the age of forty-two retained much of the boy in his habits and manners, had literally come half-way to meet the English Captain. The news of Lord Hood's "most glorious and great" success had been received with enthusiasm and relief by a community already strongly pro-British, or at least anti-Jacobin, and enough could not be done for the officer who brought such tidings. Several accidental circumstances had combined to make Nelson's mission unexpectedly easy. The Queen (whom he did not mention in his letters home) was a sister of the unhappy Marie Antoinette, soon to be carried from the Conciergerie prison to the scaffold. Since she was also a daughter of the late Empress of Austria, and had been accorded by her marriage treaty a voice in the Neapolitan Councils of State, it went without saying that the influence of Maria Carolina was great. Her husband's Prime Minister, who owed his appointment to her machinations, was an Englishman—Sir John Acton—a fortunate chance for a sea-officer who spoke no language but his own. Lastly, the British Envoy and Minister Plenipotentiary enjoyed closer relations with the Court than any of his predecessors. He attended the sport-loving King on what he called Nimrodical expeditions; his wife was more in the Queen's confidence than any Neapolitan lady, a situation partially explained by the fact that Maria Carolina's notions of benevolent despotism entailed the employment of a secret police, drawn from all classes of society. Few persons in her Court dared trust one another.

Amyly Lyon (*1765?-1815*) afterwards Lady Hamilton, as " Circe ".

By George Romney (*1734-1802*) (94" × 58".)

This picture was painted not later than 1782, when William Hayley, biographer of Romney, received a letter from a friend mentioning the " very powerful impression " made by it upon a party who saw it in the artist's studio, at 32, Cavendish Sq. Sawrey Gilpin, engaged to supply the beasts, never finished them, and the picture was first sold, together with many others from Romney's Hampstead studio, on April 27, 1807, after the artist's death. Its second owner, William Long, surgeon and painter, " supplied the deficiency ", introducing below Circe's wand, an additional wolf, visible in some mezzotints. On Long's death, the picture was bought, on June 28, 1890, by the Hon. H. C. Gibbs, who removed Long's additions. It then passed by inheritance to the present owner.

Reproduced by kind permission of Lord Aldenham, from the collection at Briggens, Ware, Hertfordshire.

Twenty years, even thirteen years ago, Sir William Hamilton, cousin of the Duke of Hamilton, cousin of Lord Abercorn, uncle of the Duchess of Atholl and Earl of Warwick, had dreamt of rising in his profession, of exercising his talents at the Courts of Spain and France. The climate of Naples was relaxing; her ladies were not in the first fashion. At sixty-three, his aquiline features, bronzed by the suns of twenty-nine Neapolitan summers and twenty-two ascents of Vesuvius, were of pronouncedly aristocratic cast, but his expression was more interesting than that of the average man of fashion. Though a recent severe illness had shaken him, he was still elegantly spare, muscular and energetic. He and his heir, Charles Greville, were always " Hamilton " and " Charles " to one another, never " uncle " and " nephew ". But he had almost given up the idea of serving his country dramatically at a Court where opportunities never offered. The Fellow of the Royal Society, the archæologist, the dilettante had begun to predominate in his character, adding to its attractions. He was beginning to be entirely satisfied with his *palazzo* in the city, from which he could enjoy his morning " roll " in the Mediterranean, and drive daily, during the hot weather, to dine at his seaside casino at Posilipo, renamed " Villa Emma " in compliment to his mistress. For evenings when ice glazed the streets of Naples he had his box at the San Carlo Theatre, or, if " sick of masks and lights ", his cabinets of cameos, coins and specimens of volcanic eruptions. (He had once been observed in a picturesque side-street, clad in full Court dress, helping a ragged peasant to carry a basketful of classic vases.) At his " sweet, delightful country house ", sixteen miles from Naples, close to their Majesties' rococo palace of Caserta, he spent the months of spring and autumn. He had no family to consider. His first marriage, at the age of twenty-eight, " somewhat against my inclination ", to Miss Barlow of Laurenny Hall, Pembrokeshire, had assured him of a fortune which he, who had met great fortunes, mentioned merely as " a little independence ". His plain, pious and pathetically adoring wife had died in 1782. Two years past, after consideration, and with the approval of Neapolitan society, he had taken the serious step of marrying a young Englishwoman of obscure birth but far from obscure appearance, who had been his companion at the Embassy for five seasons. She was not only young enough to have been his daughter. Had the only child of his first marriage survived, she would have been several years the senior of the second Lady Hamilton.

K

Miss Hart, who had signed the register at her marriage " Amy Lyon ", but was addressed by her husband as " Emma ", had been presented by him to his circle as a young countrywoman, come to Italy to study music and the arts. She was very generally known to have been relinquished to him by his impecunious nephew and heir, but the establishment at the Palazzo Sessa had always presented a correct *façade*, so much so that long before the wedding ceremony (performed quietly during a short spell of leave in England) native and even English guests had believed their hostess to be secretly Lady Hamilton. A duenna known as Mrs. Cadogan, Miss Hart's mother, resided under Sir William's roof, acting as housekeeper with self-effacing good manners which suggested that she had long acquaintance with the houses of the great. She also saved her employer much money; for he was apt, in rueful moments, to refer to the British Embassy, Naples, as " The King's Arms "—a hostelry that got good custom from travelling English. [6]

The British Envoy and Minister Plenipotentiary, presented late with a chance of distinction in the diplomatic field, prepared to play his part with gusto. After his first meeting with Lord Hood's messenger, he returned to instruct his lady that Captain Nelson was to be their guest, a decision which surprised her, as no visiting sea-officer had previously been shown such attention. When Lady Hamilton was further instructed that the room redecorated for occupation by the sixth son of her sovereign, Prince Augustus Frederick, was to be put at Captain Nelson's disposal, she realised that more than diplomatic considerations were influencing her husband. Two persons hard at work, [7] from wholly creditable motives, to produce a valuable first impression, had been able to like one another sincerely. Sir William had recognised " no common being ". Nelson, who had arrived prepared to act for Lord Hood " with a zeal no one could exceed ", had met a character who represented his picture of the ideal *grand seigneur*. A friendship which was to survive unusual circumstances had been formed at sight.

Lady Hamilton also had her task and her reward. Her duty during the busy days that followed the sudden appearance in the Bay of Naples of H.M.S. *Agamemnon* was to entertain the Captain's midshipman stepson, the awkward boy who, in the language of his day, he always termed, " my son-in-law ". As Lady Hamilton was devotedly grateful to her husband, and naturally good-humoured, she exerted herself, and her efforts

were not unnoticed by a guest who did not mention in his letters
home that the beauty of his hostess made greater demands upon
the attention than he had been able to bestow. " Lady Hamilton ", wrote Nelson to his wife, " has been wonderfully kind and
good to Josiah. She is a young woman of amiable manners, and
who does honour to the station to which she is raised."

5

Nelson, already " knocked-up " when he arrived in Naples,
had little peace during his four days there, though Sir William
and General Acton did all possible to smooth his path. There
was, from the first, no difficulty about his obtaining an audience
with a King who sent for him every day, described the British
Navy as the Saviours of Italy, and of his Dominions in particular,
and promised to provide for Lord Hood, in his own handwriting,
" the handsomest letter that could possibly be ". At a dinner
at the Palazzo Reale, which occupied a sea-frontage of 800 feet,
the visiting English Captain was placed on the King's right hand,
although the Ambassador of his nation was present. What was
more to the point, Sir John Acton, evidently a person of more
ability than his countenance suggested, confidently assured him
that six thousand troops of a nation generally averse from disciplined sudden action should be embarked forthwith to support
Lord Hood. A royal carriage took Nelson five and a half miles
over dusty roads to the palace of Portici, which the King had
appointed as their next place of meeting. Sunday (according
to the ungodly custom of all foreigners, the gayest day of the
week) was fixed for a visit of the King to H.M.S. *Agamemnon*.
The difficulties in the way of returning hospitality in a ship which
had been at anchor but twenty days in the last five months were
great, and Nelson had hoped, in Naples, to rest a ship's company
with a sick list of nearly a hundred. Sir William undertook to
support the prestige of the British Navy from the cellars and
kitchens of the British Embassy.

When Nelson wrote home on Saturday, September 14, he had
scarcely had the chance to learn his way about the house in which
he had slept for two nights after hot days of kaleidoscopic action.
There had been snatched hours, between appointments, in a
noble set of rooms on the second floor, filled with diffused southern
sun and objects of *vertu*. In Sir William's private apartments
his guest had learnt much more of the eminent persons whom
he was to encounter than must meet the light of day. The

Palazzo Sessa was not an official residence. Sir William had taken the lease of a private mansion from the Sessa family, and spent largely on "improvements". Its situation, half-way up the hillside of the Pizzofalcone quarter, gave it an unequalled prospect of one of the most famous scenes in the world. Its exterior, like that of most of its kind, was somewhat forbidding. In a country of strong sun, shuttered windows abounded. Within, furnished by one of the first *virtuosi* of Europe, it was an Aladdin's cave. On the ground floor of the central building and wings were accommodated the results of a lifetime as collector of classical antiques, referred to humorously by Sir William as "my lumber". The "English Room" had been constructed to the designs of Robert Adam. There were also worthy reception-rooms in which Lady Hamilton offered the entertainment known as her "Attitudes". This did not sound enjoyable, as it consisted in her posing, generally in dumb-show, with the aid of such adjuncts as a shawl and a tambourine, to represent the primitive emotions, while Sir William directed lighting effects; but, without exception, everyone who had ever witnessed Lady Hamilton's "Attitudes" agreed that they were remarkable. Her husband proudly claimed that she was "better than anything in the antique". Actually, her features, lit by good health and great vitality, although faultless, were far from reminiscent of cold, classical perfection, and destined to find admirers in every generation.

Sunday's festivities began early, with the arrival on board the *Agamemnon* at 10 a.m. of Sir William and Lady Hamilton, the Bishop of Winchester and family, Lord and Lady Plymouth, Lord Grandison and daughter, besides, as her Captain hurriedly noticed, "other Baronets etc.". "I gave them breakfast; manned ship etc." According to arrangements, the King was to appear at one o'clock, and Nelson was again to dine on shore with His Majesty. Preparations had been made to hoist the Royal Standard of the Two Sicilies as the King came on board and "entertain him with a cannonading". But after the breakfast, and before one o'clock, Nelson received a note from Sir John Acton which caused him to take the decision of asking his guests to depart at once, as he must get to sea as soon as possible. A French man-of-war, and three sail under her convoy, had anchored near Sardinia. Naples boasted seven sail ready for sea and a Spanish frigate of forty guns, but her Prime Minister's message said nothing of employing them. "Unfit as my Ship was, I had nothing left for the honour of our Country, but to sail, which I did in two hours afterwards. It was necessary to show them what an English Man-of-war would do."

Everything lent from the British Embassy was returned, except a butter-pan, which Nelson apologetically recorded in his letter of thanks twelve days later. This letter was the first of a series to pass between him and Sir William during the five years that elapsed before he met again, under even more encouraging circumstances, a host and hostess whose kindness had left an ineffaceable impression on his mind.

6

The French had got either into Leghorn or some Corsican port. The *Agamemnon* saw nothing of them. Nelson determined to go into Leghorn himself, " absolutely to save my poor fellows ". He was too late to save his surgeon's second mate, whose burial at sea took place with the usual ceremonies, off the north end of Corsica. Nothing could have seemed further than the smiling Neapolitan scene as he waited throughout the night of September 27, in a gale and thick weather, watching an enemy frigate of forty guns lying at anchor off Leghorn. She had been ready to weigh as he hove in sight, and was obviously waiting for the first dark moment to get out. Luckily she could scarcely hope to escape in such weather, without running aboard the vigilant English 64. As there seemed no hope of persuading her to quit neutral waters while he was in attendance, he gave up the idea of going in to Leghorn, and stood for Toulon. He arrived there on October 5, at the same moment as the second division of Neapolitan ships bringing the troops promised by Acton. Lord Hood, much pleased with an officer who had acted on his own initiative with success, showed his regard by despatching the *Agamemnon* to sea again, after only three days in Toulon. The sealed orders which Nelson opened when he was off the island of Porquerolles told him to place himself under the direction of Commodore Linzee, at Cagliari, in Sardinia. Further sealed orders, for Linzee, which he carried, told the Commodore to take his squadron on a mission to Tunis.

Off Corsica on October 11 the *Agamemnon* spoke a ship from Gibraltar, and Nelson got his first letters from home since he had left England. Her present host could not disguise the fact that Mrs. Horatio Nelson, who had not yet " fixed " anywhere, was fretting. Nelson wrote to his wife in slightly sterner vein than usual. " My dear Fanny, I received a letter from Mr. Suckling yesterday, and was indeed truly sorry to hear you were not perfectly well. Why should you alarm yourself? I am well, your son is well, and we are as comfortable in every respect as the nature of our service will admit." He went on to say that every day at Toulon, at present, afforded " some brilliant Action " on shore. " I have only been a spectator, but had we remained, I should certainly have desired to land." He mentioned that as he had sat at a court-martial on board a ship in the harbour, shot and shells discharged from a royalist French 74, three frigates and four mortar-boats, firing at a battery held by the enemy, had screamed overhead for four hours. This accompaniment had " made no difference " to the progress of the court-martial.

His first " little brush " with the enemy took place ten days later. At 2 a.m. on the morning of October 22, when running down the island of Sardinia, he came in sight of five sail, which, perceiving themselves observed, altered course. He stood after them, and a couple of hours later got within hail of the hindermost, but was careful not to fire into her, in case she might prove to be a Neapolitan or Sardinian, escorting a convoy. She failed to reply when hailed in French, and made sail, so the *Agamemnon* fired one shot from an 18-pounder ahead of her, and at the same moment opened her lower deck ports. Thereupon the frigate set all her sails. A running fight continued for three hours, the other ships on her weather quarter steering after the *Agamemnon*. With daybreak, the *Melpomene*, of forty guns, hoisted national colours, and began firing stern-chasers. As she was smaller and faster than the *Agamemnon*, she was able to yaw and deliver broadsides while only the *Agamemnon's* bow guns could bear. Also, since he had been obliged to land many sick in Toulon, Nelson had only three hundred and fifty men at quarters. By nine o'clock the *Melpomene*, separated from her consorts, had suffered so severely that, had not the wind failed, she must have surrendered or sunk, but the *Agamemnon's* rigging was badly damaged, and three more French frigates, a corvette and a brig were coming down upon her with all sail set. Nelson summoned his officers, to discuss whether he could possibly close with the *Melpomene*, and, without some small refit, and refreshment for his men, prepare to enter upon further action. The unanimous answer was that he certainly could not, so he ordered that " some of the best men be employed refitting the rigging, and the carpenters getting crows and capstern bars to prevent

our wounded spars coming down ", and, since it might be half
an hour before they were engaged by a far superior force, in which
case they must expect " warm work ", he also ordered that food
and wine be served.   The enemy, until noon, had the option of
bringing the *Agamemnon* to action, but contented themselves
with carrying off the *Melpomene*.   Eventually, in an almost
sinking state, she got into Calvi.   The *Agamemnon* was, according
to her Captain's report to Lord Hood, " after a very few hours
at anchor, in many respects fitter for service than before ", an
additional tribute to officers and a ship's company who had
" conducted themselves entirely to my satisfaction ", for her
top-mast, main-mast and mizzen-mast had been shot to pieces,
and her fore-yard badly wounded.   Satisfaction in the
Agamemnon after her " little brush " was indeed general, and
with Christmas a Norfolk rectory received an enthusiastic description of her first engagement of this war.   Mr. William Hoste,
aged just thirteen, ended his long letter to his father, " Captain
Nelson is acknowledged one of the first characters in the Service,
and is universally beloved by his men and officers."

7

On one of the last days of November 1793, a small party of
European gentlemen, attired in the blue-and-white gold-laced
uniforms, black stocks, large cocked hats and long queues affected
by British sea-officers at that date, proceeded as swiftly as possible
through the tortuous streets of a walled city of North Africa
which included, amongst its outstanding features, many camels,
laden with charcoal, snake-charmers, separate markets for per-
fumes, carpets, saddlery and jewels, and a notable building of
green-tiled domes and walls, enriched with rose-coloured marbles.
    Commodore Linzee and his companions, formal in costume and
visage, had emerged from another wholly unrewarding interview
with the Bey of Tunis.   The Commodore's last letter from his
brother-in-law, Lord Hood, had opened, " You are to expostulate
with His Excellency, the Bey, in the strongest and most impressive
manner, on the impolicy of his giving countenance and support
to so heterogeneous a government as the present one of France,
composed of murderers and assassins, who have recently beheaded
their Queen in a manner that would disgrace the most barbarous
savages. . . ."   The Captain of the *Agamemnon* had produced
this argument, but the reply of the Bey, descendant of a Cretan
renegade of ability, had been exasperating.   His Excellency, by

means of his interpreters, had smoothly agreed that nothing could be more heinous than the murders of the King and Queen of France by their subjects. Yet, if the historians of the great country represented by his naval visitors were to be believed, the subjects of a King of England had once arisen and beheaded their sovereign.

Nelson, after his first glance at the Oriental potentate, had silently fixed His Excellency's price at £50,000. The French convoy from the Levant, lying in Tunis Bay, was worth at least £300,000, so England could have afforded the bribe. That the French had expected Linzee to attack had been obvious : they had, on his arrival, hauled their ships almost aground. When they had found, to their relief, that he was not prepared to do so, that the Bey refused to give them up, and that the English Commodore had patiently sent to Toulon for further orders, their bearing had been unforgettable, even considering that they were revolutionaries of a nation expert in polished malice. Nelson believed that the Bey, presented with a *fait accompli*, would have swallowed a sufficiently richly gilded insult. To attempt to negotiate with such characters only gave them the idea that England was weak. " The English seldom get much by negotiation, except the being laughed at, which we have been ; and I don't like it." He knew that the enemy had bought His Excellency, and although Linzee might hesitate to attack enemy ships which had sought the shelter of a neutral port, the fact was that Tunis was little better than a piratical stronghold. In the Commodore's place, he would have seized the French man-of-war and convoy first, and seen the Bey later. However, Linzee had not believed that his instructions authorised him to use force, and from the moment that the Bey and the enemy had realised that, the position had been hopeless. The officers of *Le Duquesne* had not shown even polite interest in the suggestion that they should hoist the white flag, the Bourbon flag, and return to loyalty to their lawful sovereign, Louis XVII, a small boy, reputedly locked in a black cupboard in the Temple prison. The Bey, surprised at the mild behaviour of the English, considering English superiority in these seas, had taken up a strong line. And after three weeks, the *Nemesis*, despatched to Toulon to describe the situation to Lord Hood, had brought word " nothing was to be done ". The squadron would have to retire, having accomplished nothing. Even Nelson considered that the golden moment had now passed. To attempt to use force at this stage would drive the Bey openly into the arms of revolutionary France, a thing undesirable from the point of view of trade.

Lord Hood himself, at Toulon, was having trouble, with Allies as well as with enemies. Only his personality held together a motley garrison of royalist French, Spaniards, Piedmontese and Neapolitans, unable to understand one another's speech, all desirous of acting independently, and mutually suspicious. The Spaniards, in particular, were behaving with odious cruelty in the town, cutting the throats and plundering the bodies of natives who had surrendered to the small body of English regulars. There were dark, demoralising rumours that they were secretly in communication with the invading General, Carteaux. "The English never yet succeeded in a negotiation against the French," wrote Nelson resignedly, "and we have not set the example at Tunis. Thank God! Lord Hood, whom Linzee sent to, for orders how to act after having negotiated, has ordered me from under his command, and to command a Squadron of Frigates off Corsica and the Coast of Italy, to protect our trade, and that of our new Ally, the Grand Duke of Tuscany, and to prevent any Ship or Vessel, of whatever Nation, from going into the port of Genoa. I consider this command as a very high compliment—there being five older Captains in the Fleet. . . . Lord Hood is certainly the best officer I ever saw. Every order from him is so clear, it is impossible to misunderstand him."

He prepared to see the last of Tunis without regret, except for an opportunity missed. Lord Hood, who had by now heard of the "little brush" of October 22, had sent him a letter quite in his old style. To be given a detached command was "most handsome", and to be empowered to deal with the frigates that escaped him was exhilarating. "The Lord" had written that he looked upon them as "certain, trusting to my zeal and activity". Nelson had learnt their names and strength now, and they had been, as he had suspected, part of the convoy now in Tunis harbour, under the protection of His Excellency the Bey. Two of them were at San Fiorenzo, one at Bastia, and the damaged *Melpomene* at Calvi.

Also, amongst the ships which he was to take under his command was one very old friend—the *Lowestoffe*, bringing memories of Captain Locker, "sea-daddy" of a fever-ridden lieutenant, now "never better, and in active service, which I like ".

8

When the *Agamemnon* arrived in Leghorn roads in Christmas week, to water and provision, she found the port in confusion, and received bad news. Lord Hood had been obliged to evacuate Toulon. " For England ", wrote Nelson stoutly to Hilborough Rectory, " a most happy event." On the forenoon of December 17, in the dark reception-room of a Toulon merchant's house which had been his headquarters on shore, while the dull thud of distant gunfire sounded, attired in the three weeks' mourning ordered for his fleet on receipt of the news of " the murder of the late good Queen of France ", Lord Hood, " the same good collected officer he ever was ", had dryly informed a consternated audience of six nationalities that he was about to order his fleet to put to sea, taking with it as many French ships as were ready, and setting fire to the rest. He would himself hold the fort of La Malgue as long as possible. The troops at his disposal had long been insufficient to control the land defences of the port, and gradually enemy artillery had gained command of the roadstead, making his position untenable. A Lieutenant-Colonel, aged twenty-four, with his fortune to make, had been sent from Paris to stir up General Carteaux. Nelson heard the facts, but the name of " Buona Parte " was first written thus by him two and a half years later.

The place had admittedly been held at great cost. Lord Hood would from the first have preferred to remove the French fleet to a place of safety; but the feelings of Allies had demanded consideration. The retiring forces under his orders had now wrecked the arsenal, burnt nine French warships and carried off a dozen frigates and four battleships, including the *Commerce de Marseille* (so large that no dock at Portsmouth could take her). Half the town was said to have been left in ashes. The fact remained that the British fleet now lacked an advanced Mediterranean base, and eighteen French sail-of-the-line had been abandoned, either unharmed or only partially disabled. It had not been possible for Lord Hood to achieve miracles, and he had made chivalrous efforts to save royalist troops and refugees, likely to be shot, guillotined or murdered, by a mob which had arisen in revolutionary fury, as revolutionary troops drew near. Nearly fifteen thousand unhappy Toulonese had been safely embarked.

At Leghorn, Nelson found home letters. His mare had not

been sold. The Rector wrote that his having been thrown had been entirely his own fault. He did not believe the poor beast " vitious " : he feared, however, that she might be going blind. . . . Mrs. William Nelson had heard of a delicious Mediterranean fish that could be salted; spelt " Tonges ", if her brother-in-law deciphered William's handwriting correctly. She would be glad if Horace could bring some home in his ship, since he seemed to think that France, torn by the internal feuds of Jacobin and Girondist, could not much longer continue war against England. The homely request sounded strangely at a moment when the young Captain of a British man-of-war was confronted by a collapsed French female, explained to him as the mother of five, penniless and homeless, whose husband had committed suicide sooner than be left to the mercies of the revolutionaries of his town. " What calamities do Civil Wars produce, and how much does it behove every person to give their aid in keeping peace at Home."

13

Vessel upon vessel packed with hysterical refugees was labouring into Leghorn, where there was a rumour that, as the port was already short of food, they might be refused admittance : ships bringing wounded troops must be given preference. Nelson never forgot the tales and scenes of horror following the fall of Toulon, which took him by surprise, in Christmas week 1793. " Fathers are here without families, families without fathers." M. le Comte de Grasse, Captain of the frigate *Topaze*, under his command, was distracted for news of a wife and nursery, and some reports estimated the number of men, women and children left screaming on the quay-sides of the burning town as over 6,000. Many had been drowned by the oversetting of boats, many had taken their own lives in despair, and many been trampled underfoot, swept into the harbour, or torn in pieces by their own countrymen. Lord Hood, who had attempted to rally the flying troops, had been the admiration of everyone, but " the torrent was too strong ". The Neapolitans, so swiftly despatched by General Acton in September, had panicked shamelessly. The French and Spanish had been at best inefficient. " Many of our posts were carried without resistance; at others, which the English occupied, every one perished. I cannot write all. My mind is deeply impressed with grief. Each teller makes the scene more horrible." Napoleon Buonaparte also never forgot a scene of which he had been an eyewitness. He enthralled audiences in St. Helena with descriptions of his feelings as he had

watched ship upon ship bursting into flames which had matched
the blood running into her gutters as the Red Terror took possession of Toulon.

The *Agamemnon* left Leghorn on January 3, to be blown off
her Corsican station by some of the hardest gales, accompanied by
the heaviest rains, that her Captain had ever trysted with. An
enemy frigate took the opportunity to slip down from San Fiorenzo
to Calvi, but he believed that his blockade had been so close that
the provisions carried by her could only feed the place another
fortnight at the outside. He had received further orders from
Lord Hood, entrusting him with a negotiation opened by Linzee,
but now suddenly of importance. Corsica had been decided
upon as a base of operations, and he was " to settle plans for the
landing of troops, etc." with the Patriot General Pasquale de
Paoli, who had agreed that the island should be ceded to Great
Britain on the condition that the British should assist the natives
to expel the French. Nelson sent as his " Ambassador to the
Chief of the Corsicans " Lieutenant George Andrews, brother of
the beauty of St. Omer. The situation needed delicate handling,
as Lord Hood was by no means convinced of the good faith of the
Patriot General. He had also his own troubles. English troops
took San Fiorenzo without difficulty in mid-February. Even
the garrison of the renowned Tower of Martello, after two days'
bombardment at a distance of a hundred and fifty yards, called
for quarter. One of the imprisoned frigates which had escaped
the *Agamemnon* was burnt. But General Dundas, supported by
Lieutenant-Colonel John Moore, refused, before the arrival of
reinforcements from Gibraltar, to proceed to attack Bastia,
little more than twelve miles distant across the hills in the north-
east of the island. The enemy were adding daily to the strength of
their positions there. Lord Hood took the event upon himself, and
keeping up a close blockade by sea, ordered Lieutenant-Colonel
Vilettes, of the 69th Regiment, and Captain Nelson to land with
a force consisting of 1,000 regulars and marines and 300 seamen.

Nelson prepared " to anchor and act with the army " in good
health and spirits. " Armies go so slow that seamen think they
never mean to go forward; but I daresay they act on a surer
principle though we seldom fail. . . . We are few, but of the
right sort." He had, during the weeks before San Fiorenzo
fell, as well as continuing the blockade, conducted a dashing
series of coastal raids—on one occasion " seized a happy moment "
to land sixty soldiers and sixty seamen to demolish an essential

mill; on another, burnt twelve vessels loaded with wine, and captured four. "At a place called Rocliniar, or Porto Nuovo", he had, with his own hand, struck the national colours hoisted by the natives on the top of "an old castle". At L'Avisena he had taken another fort, Miomo, and driven her garrison up to a position within gun-shot of the walls of Bastia. Naturally, such operations could not be carried out without some losses, but after "a very smart contest" which had ended in a courier boat being carried "in high style", he had a casualty list of no more than six wounded. "My ship's company behaved most amazingly well; they begin to look upon themselves as invincible, almost invulnerable. . . . They really mind shot no more than peas."

The siege of Bastia opened on April 4. Her husband reckoned Mrs. Nelson by now at Bath, where she should find, amongst other friends, Admiral Robinson, "my old Captain with a wooden leg". He told her that Corsica was a wonderfully fine island, her people brave and free. "Paoli has nothing to give them; no honours to bestow." He held out the usual hopes of coming home before long, on the conclusion of the war—not by France's return to a monarchy, but by England's decision to leave her to stew in her own juice, "perhaps the wisest method we could follow". He begged his wife "not to want for anything" at a spa where prices were always high. "Don't be afraid of money." His own expenses at present were not likely to be great.

9

Always foreseeing that it must be the next place to be attacked, and much hoping to be concerned, he had made himself thoroughly familiar with the appearance of Bastia long before he landed, three miles north of the town, under cover of darkness, during the night of April 3. He had guessed that San Fiorenzo had fallen before he got the news, for the red light from the frigates burning in the harbour there had lit the evening skies beyond the mountains on February 19. Next morning he had taken his second careful look at Bastia, running so close inshore, attended by two of the six frigates under his command, that the enemy had opened fire, from a new half-moon battery below the town, Fort St. Croix, beyond the town, and the forts of the citadel. The bursting of one shell, very close, had shaken the *Agamemnon*, and on their third appearance, merely to reconnoitre, during the afternoon, all three ships had been struck in the hull. But their damage had been easily reparable and they had sustained no casualties, whereas they heard from a Dane, coming out of the mole, that their very accurate replies had destroyed six French guns and killed several gunners.

Nelson felt the siege of Bastia particularly his. " I presumed to propose it." (Uncle Suckling, at Kentish Town, possessed a picture of the town, which did not, however, show the citadel.) He knew that his reports had decided Lord Hood to make the attempt, and therefore his reputation depended upon the result. An Engineer and an Artillery officer had been sent, at his request, to approve his choice of sites for a battery on shore and landing-place. Fortunately, both had been young and enthusiastic. He had now sent Lieutenant Duncan, R.A., in a fast frigate to Naples, to ask Sir William Hamilton to press the King and Prime Minister for mortars, shells, field-pieces and stores. He had not been perfectly frank with Lord Hood in his account of the expected strength of the garrison, fearing that if he was, his Lordship might incline to the opinion of General Dundas, shared by that gentleman's successor, General D'Aubant, that the project in hand was " most visionary and rash ". But, to do him justice, it was not until everything was fixed for the attack that he received certain information on this point. Personally, he felt strongly that to let the opportunity slip, merely because it presented great difficulty, would be " a National disgrace ". " What would the immortal Wolfe have done ? " " A thousand men would, to a certainty, take Bastia ; with 500 and *Agamemnon*, I would attempt *it*." " We are really without firing, wine, beef, pork, flour, and almost without water : not a rope, canvas, twine or nail in the Ship. . . . Not a man has slept dry for many months. The Ship is so light, she cannot hold her side to the wind : yet, if your Lordship thinks or wishes me to remain off Bastia, I can, by going to Porto Ferrajo, get water and stores, and twenty-four hours at Leghorn will give us provisions ; and our refitting, which will take some time, can be put off a little. My wish is to be present at the attack. . . ." He was relieved that at the end of a fortnight's repetition of such telling phrases, Lord Hood had told him to do his best with a force of 1,300.

All the defences of Bastia could be clearly viewed from the sea, as he had told Lord Hood, and the place was, as he had told Mrs. Nelson, highly picturesque, " the environs delightful, with the most romantic views I ever beheld ". The Promised Town rose from the rocky shore like an amphitheatre, and contained, in its

upper parts, in addition to the citadel, tiers of lofty white houses
with flat faces and many shutters, several churches, somewhat
florid in architecture, a Law Courts, Hôtel de Ville and Theatre.
The walls of the citadel, which dominated the port, enclosed a
keep—the original *bastille* from which the place took its name.
The lower portion of the town possessed humbler houses : some
of those clustering round the quays were of one storey, and had
their hearth in the centre of the chief living-room. A densely
populated quarter of labyrinthine, steep and narrow streets
joined the upper and lower quarters.   The picture was completed
by *La Flèche*, last seen by Nelson in Tunis, lying in the harbour,
dismantled. Her guns had, he knew, been removed to the out-
works. Bastia had always been the principal stronghold of the
north of the island, and her defences were now, to his regret,
much stronger than they had been a fortnight past. He reckoned
her garrison to number about 4,000 all told, but he also reckoned
upon " consternation, almost insurrection within her walls ".
The surrounding country, where cultivated, displayed the usual
Corsican prospect of straggling vineyard, cypress, citron and
olive grove, pale lower slopes on which goats and sheep picked up
what sustenance they could, villages perched like sea-fowl on sun-
baked cliffs, and, in the background, heights clothed by forests
of sweet chestnut, pine, beech and oak.   Corsica, island of barren
rock, rushing streams, bitter honey and excellent timber for
shipbuilding, looked her best in early spring, when the blossom
of apricot and apple was succeeding almond and cherry.   Even
her uncultivated districts, lying about the lagoons at the mouths
of her many rivers, were covered with a vigorous undergrowth
of arbutus, myrtle and other aromatic shrubs, called by the natives
maquis, and so pungent that their presence could be detected even
after dark, and from the sea.
    By noon on April 4, eight 24-pounders from the lower deck
of the *Agamemnon* and eight 13-inch mortars had been landed
under cover of gunboats without molestation, and the troops
commanded by Colonel Vilettes and Captain Nelson had encamped under a rocky height within 2,500 yards of the citadel.
Nelson perceived without dismay that the Corsican patriots
holding the adjacent tower of Torga, which they had taken during
the night of April 2, knew nothing except how to fire a musket.
They watched open-mouthed while Norfolk seamen who had
volunteered for a 64 commanded by the son of the Rector of
Burnham Thorpe (advertised as a flier, with prospects of good

prize-money) made roads, hauled up guns and cut down fragrant Corsican undergrowth and copses to make platforms for guns and cover towards their fort, the weakest point, from which attack might be expected.   The future Viceroy of the island was an admiring spectator.   The green face of the rocks leading to the fort was, said Sir Gilbert Elliot, steeper than Minto craigs at home.   " They fastened great straps round the rocks, and then fastened to the straps the largest and most powerful purchases, or pullies, and tackle, that are used on board a man-of-war.   The cannon were placed on a sledge at one end of the tackle, the men walked down hill with the other end of the tackle.   The surprise of our friends the Corsicans, and our enemies the French, was equal to the occasion."

When he had mounted a captain's picquet at Torga, with a sentry a hundred yards in front of it, and sent word to the *Scout* sloop to anchor as close as possible to the tower, Nelson resignedly hoped that the mere presence of his Corsican allies might be useful later.   In the middle distance of the warmly coloured picture, his sweating seamen had a comforting vision of the *Agamemnon* at anchor, and on the skyline, south of the town, " Lord Hood in the offing ".

During the next fortnight he realised that only time could bring success.   His first batteries were ready for action by the eighth day after his landing; none too soon, for the camp had been for two days exposed to heavy fire.   Lord Hood's flag of truce, sent in before his batteries spoke, had received from the Commissioner in the citadel the reply, " I have hot shot for your ships, and bayonets for your troops "; whereupon Lord Hood had hoisted a red flag at the main-top-gallant mast-head of H.M.S. *Victory*.   When Nelson, in reply, hoisted English colours on the rock above his tattered tent, and the order was issued to open fire upon the town, citadel and redoubt of Camponella, every man present gave three cheers.   They fired throughout the night and next day, and during the afternoon, Colonel Vilettes, Nelson, Duncan of the Artillery—happily returned from Naples with the desired mortars—and two other military officers, attended by a Corsican guide, advanced to examine a ridge about a thousand yards nearer the town.   Enemy musketry and grape were pouring towards their camp.   The guide was killed, the Brigade-Major was fatally wounded and Nelson received " a sharp cut in the back ", first mentioned by him in a letter to his wife four months later, and never again.   Next morning he began to superintend the building of two more batteries for mortars and guns from the *Agamemnon*; one close to the Torga tower, the other a little to the rear. They took eight days to complete, but after they had been firing for twenty-four hours, deserters from the town affirmed that the guns of the citadel had been twice put out of action. Nelson's first letters home, dated " Camp, near Bastia ", were mainly occupied with descriptions of " my poor seamen dragging guns up such heights as are scarcely credible ". Five men from his ship's company had been killed. " They are not the men to keep out of the way."

The Corsican patriots were now directed to make false attacks upon the upper and southern enemy outposts. More British troops were urgently needed, but General D'Aubant, with seven regiments at San Fiorenzo, continued firm in his resolution not to " entangle himself in any co-operation ". (" It is enough to make any lover of his Country run distracted.") Nor was co-operation in the camp ideal. Nelson had to write to Lord Hood, asking for a ruling as to whether the seamen landed were under his command or that of Captain Hunt. The enemy, having got their town batteries into " a tolerable state ", reopened very heavy fire, and one of Nelson's best men from the *Agamemnon*, working on repairs during the night, was killed by a shot from the Camponella redoubt. A letter, in neat, slanting Italian hand, was despatched on its long journey to a small home in Swansea :

" From the nature of our profession, we ever hold life by a more precarious tenure than many others, but when we fall, we trust it is to benefit our Country. So fell your Son, by a cannon-ball, under my immediate command, at the Siege of Bastia. I had taken him on shore with me, from his abilities and attention to his duty."

The next battery to be built was on the ridge examined a fortnight earlier, and within 700 yards of the town. Andrews (referred to by General Paoli's staff as " Mr. George ") was appointed to fight it with forty-five seamen, but was wounded almost at once. The end, however, was now in sight. In a letter begun on May 1 and ended on the 4th, Nelson was able to tell his wife " as a secret " that Bastia should fall before the month was out. He reminded her that, in the words of Shakespeare, not quite correctly remembered, " a brave man dies but once, a coward all his life long ". It was to a correspondent at Leghorn, to whom he had sent for provisions (and who had added to the butter, Dutch cheese and porter ordered, a personal gift of peas and asparagus), that he admitted, " I have had my escapes."

L

General D'Aubant was now expecting his Gibraltar reinforcements, and Nelson foresaw with irritation that their appearance would coincide with the fall of the town; depriving those who had done the hard work of the credit.   On May 8 Lord Hood sent in another flag of truce, which was refused, but four nights later a large boat coming out of the mole was captured, and her despatches (thrown overboard, but rescued by Lieutenant Suckling) disclosed that the Governor, unless succour arrived within a fortnight, intended to surrender.   By Lord Hood's orders, the crew and wounded were provided with a week's food and returned, and within twenty-four hours news of his humane act had filtered to the Camponella redoubt, with an unexpected result.   An oil-painting, hastily performed by a native artist, was hung out by the enemy all day.   At first the British were inclined to regard this likeness of an officer in their uniform as a fresh form of Gallic insult.   They presently learnt that it was intended to represent Lord Hood, as a mark of respect.

On May 18 a message reached Lord Hood from a brother of the Mayor of Bastia, begging that he would condescend to forward yet another flag of truce.   The garrison, terrified of falling into the hands of victorious Corsicans, and short of food and ammunition, were ready to enter into negotiations for unconditional surrender.   The army from San Fiorenzo made the timely appearance expected by Nelson.   At 6 p.m. on May 23 the British Grenadiers took formal possession of the town gates, and next morning, with daylight, the combined forces marched into Bastia to the strains of the National Anthem.

Two days later, Nelson sent a brief triumphant note to Sir William Hamilton, enclosing a letter for Lady Hamilton.   He promised, " We shall now join heart and hand against Calvi." The embarkation of stores for this purpose was discontinued on news that the French fleet was out of Toulon.   Admiral Hotham's blockading squadron had lost touch with it, and lost, as afterwards appeared, an excellent chance of an action much to be desired.   He had borne up hastily to join Lord Hood.   The enemy retired before superior force, and the *Agamemnon* was sent to Gibraltar, to refit before entering upon a bout of combined operations, which Nelson considered his first in this war, for of the siege of Bastia he commented pointedly, " I may truly say that this has been a Naval Expedition."

10

The siege of Calvi, a place, small but very strongly fortified by art and nature, on the western side of the island, differed in many respects from that of Bastia, chief commercial city of Corsica. The chief point of resemblance was that Nelson's seamen were again employed " dragging cannon up steep mountains, and carrying shot and shell to batteries built, armed and manned under his personal supervision ". But the rocks of the Calvi district were far more inhospitable than those of Bastia, and this time there was no question of the Army refusing to co-operate. From the moment that General the Hon. Charles Stuart (a younger son of Lord Bute) came on board the *Agamemnon* to express himself anxious to get on with the attack, if Captain Nelson thought it right to proceed with the shipping (to which the answer was " I certainly do "), affairs moved swiftly.

The Corsican port nearest to France, only 109 miles from Antibes, was crowned by an ancient town, on a beetling height, above peacock-blue waters. Its steep streets, paved with rock, were commanded by the star fort, Muzello. Its ample barracks had begun life as the palace of a sixteenth-century Genoese Governor. The lagoons below it, to the practised eye, spoke of malaria.

At 10 p.m. on the night of June 17, H.M.S. *Agamemnon*, *Dolphin* and *Lutine*, with sixteen sail of transports, victuallers and store-ships, anchored after much difficulty about a mile from the shore and three and a half miles west of Calvi, opposite a romantic-looking cove known as Porto Agro, and at 3 a.m. next morning, Nelson, with General Stuart, went ashore, in the hopes of discovering a better place for landing guns and stores. The *Agamemnon* was lying in fifty-three fathoms; sunken rocks, with very deep water between them, extended to within twenty feet of the beach. It was to be feared that with a common sea-breeze such a swell would set in as to prevent boats landing. They examined the enemy's outposts, Fort Monteciusco, close to the south-west of the town, Fort Muzello to the west, and between it and Fort San Francesco, on a rocky peninsula washed at the base by the sea, the Fountain Battery, well tucked away behind a mountain shoulder. The town itself, although not ditched, appeared well fortified. They reluctantly decided that in spite of its distance from their object, and bad landing, Porto Agro must be their base. Nelson repeated that he placed

the firmest reliance on the protection of the fleet, under Lord
Hood, who would see to it that the French fleet at Golfe Jouan
should not molest them, and disembarkation of the troops began.
The business of getting field-pieces and military baggage on
shore was still in progress when the picture took on dark colours.
For the next two days a Corsican thunderstorm of truly melodramatic variety raged over the scene. Most of the ships were
obliged to put to sea in such weather as to raise doubts of their
reappearance. The anxiety of those landed, however, was
nothing to that of Lord Hood, as he powerlessly contemplated
from Martello Bay the possible fate of a force, which had believed
itself " under his wing ", deserted on a hostile shore. " I
tremble ", he wrote to Nelson, " for what may have happened
from last night's wind." But that night, amidst thunder,
lightning, gale and downpour, Nelson's seamen had begun to
make a road for their guns. On the 22nd the weather became
" rather more moderate ", and although a great deal of surf was
running, he got boats off to such ships as were still visible, and
much-needed rations and some powder, shot and gun-carriages
were landed. The guns began to pass up towards the site chosen
for a battery against Monteciusco. On the beach, working-
parties of drenched soldiers set to work to fill sand-bags. Next
day more reassuring quantities of ammunition and guns were
landed, and the *Agamemnon* and transports returned to their
anchorage. The " Royal Louis ", first battery to be completed,
opened fire with dawn on July 4. Two more were in action within
three days; still progress was much too slow to satisfy General
Stuart, who slept every night in the advanced battery and suffered
" more than I can describe " when he was obliged to ask for
another night's grace before his working-parties could come up
to an intended emplacement where punctual seamen had been
waiting with the guns since sunset.

Amongst the first casualties was Captain Serocold of the
Royal Navy, " by a grape-shot passing through his head as he
cheered the people who were dragging the gun ". Nelson made
time to scribble a line to his always nervous Fanny, who might
see the fact in a newspaper, unaccompanied by the name:

> " I am very busy, yet own I am in all my glory. Except with you, I
> would not be anywhere but where I am, for the world. I am well aware
> my poor services will not be noticed: I have no interest; but however
> services may be received, it is not right in an Officer to slacken his zeal
> for his Country."

He had been dashed that in Lord Hood's despatch announcing the taking of Bastia, he had merely been mentioned as " commanding and directing the seamen, landing guns, mortars and stores ". Captain Anthony Hunt's name had appeared as " commander of the batteries ". Lord Hood had indeed dropped a hint that he wished to " push forward " Hunt, who had, by misadventure, lost his ship in the Mediterranean, some months previously. Nelson, while appreciating his Commander-in-Chief's kind intent towards an " exceeding good young man, zealous for the Service ", had hardly expected such a result. When poor Serocold had heard that Hunt was to be the officer sent home with the Bastia despatch—" a young man who never was on a battery, or even rendered any service during the siege. . . . (If any person says he did, then I submit to the character of a story-teller) "—he, who had himself commanded a battery under Captain Nelson, had hotly announced his intention of " publishing an advertisement ". The services of Duncan, the young Artillery lieutenant whom Nelson had sent with a personal letter of commendation to Sir William Hamilton at Naples, had also been singled out for praise; and Duncan, with a slight flesh wound, promoted to a Company, and an *aide-de-camp* on General Stuart's staff, was showing an inclination to condescension. " There is nothing like kicking down the ladder a man rises by." However, " Lord Hood and myself were never better friends, nor, *although his Letter does*, did he wish to put me where I never was—in the rear." By the newly appointed Viceroy of Corsica, Sir Gilbert Elliot, Captain Nelson knew that his efforts and position had been recognised; he believed that General Stuart, " a stranger and a landsman ", would probably do him the credit " which a friend and brother officer has not given me ". Disappointment from that quarter was yet to come.

The enemy, having allowed the British to land and bring guns over mountains which they had, apparently, considered inaccessible, now opened heavy and concentrated fire upon their works, demolishing two valued 24-pounders from the *Agamemnon* and a 26-pounder. On the morning of July 12 at 7 a.m. Nelson was struck with great violence, in the face and breast, by splinters, stones and sand from the *merlon* of a battery hit by an enemy shell. When the profuse flow of blood from his head-wound had been checked, he found that he had received several superficial lacerations in the face and a deep cut in the right brow, which had penetrated the eyelid and eyeball. The pain was great, but the surgeons who performed the first dressing held out hopes that the eye might recover a measure of sight. " I got ", he told Lord Hood, in the last sentence of his daily report forwarded the same evening, " a little hurt this morning : not much, as you may judge from my writing." Lord Hood, in the first sentence of his reply, asked for details and said that he would be sending someone next morning, " to know how you are, and whether you would not have assistance ". Nelson's answer was that if a more advanced entrenchment was to be begun the next evening he would be capable of superintending the work. " My eye is better, and I hope not entirely to lose the sight." Three days later he was " much better ".

The siege was now proceeding as well, though not as expeditiously, as even he could wish. The guns of the *Commerce de Marseille* had been landed, and the carpenter of the *Agamemnon*, a better man at making a gun-platform than any military gentry, had turned his energies to siege ladders. The news of Lord Howe's glorious victory of the First of June came as a restorative at an hour when an officer who never forgot the Nicaraguan expedition was beginning to receive alarmingly long lists of men down with " the fever ". " We have far more to fear from the Climate than the Enemy." His only consolation was that the Army was falling sick in far greater numbers than the Navy, a fact which he attributed to the greater activity of seamen. [15]

Fort Muzello was carried on July 19, two days later than Nelson had expected. The two breaches in its defences had long been of insufficient extent to satisfy Colonel Moore (whom he wished a hundred leagues off). A week later, the pile of ammunition at the back of the captured position reminded him of Woolwich Arsenal. Fort St. Francesco and the Fountain Battery were silent. Still the land-officers proceeded at their customary solemn pace, and, " Why ", asked Colonel Moore, " don't Lord Hood land 500 men to work ? Our soldiers are tired." Nelson's seamen, who had worked barefoot dragging field-pieces up roads built by them on dizzying heights, and had afterwards, under fire, mounted and fought every gun but three, were also tired, but " Our Jacks don't mind it ". At night they slept on the batteries, with their pikes and cutlasses always ready.

Lord Hood wrote daily, urging tact and silence, and Nelson assured him, " We will fag ourselves to death before any blame shall lie at our doors ", and, " I never write, or open my mouth, to anyone but your Lordship."

Thirty-five pieces of heavy ordnance were playing on the town towards the end of the month, and Calvi, although rejecting an offer to negotiate for terms of peace, asked for a twenty-five days' truce. Her defenders had learnt of the sickness in the English camp, and were playing for time. Lord Hood was reported unwell; General Stuart was visibly very sick. Nelson himself began to experience, in addition to pain from his eye, a familiar cycle of sickening symptoms which threatened to send him down to a hospital ship packed with malaria cases (the *Boreas*), but he hoped that " an active scene " would cure his shivering fits, to which he was so accustomed that they worried him less than those in his company. The weather, also, was becoming intolerable. He discovered that the unremitting glare of what an Englishman termed " the Dog Days " was called by the Corsicans " the Lion Sun ". It was certainly something that no man could endure.

Just in time for him, and many others, the enemy hung out a white flag. The garrison marched out on August 10, and amongst the warlike material relinquished by them was the *Melpomene*, " the most beautiful frigate I ever saw ". But his spirits were lowered by the realisation that two juniors to whom he was attached by more than Service ties were likely to die. " Little Hoste " returned from the brink of the grave. James Moutray, aged twenty-one, Second Lieutenant of the *Victory*, the only son of his mother, and she a widow, was laid to rest in the church of San Fiorenzo, and Nelson, before he sailed from Calvi (a place he hoped never to see again), composed directions for the inscription on a memorial tablet to be cut by his carpenter.

Back in his cabin in the *Agamemnon*, bound for Leghorn to refit, staring into a familiar small mirror, clapping a hand over alternate eyes, one of which was still painful, he was able at last to come to a decision about the injury sustained by him on July 12. He no longer had a pair of eyes. The pupil of his right eye was now large, irregular in shape and immovable. It nearly covered the blue part—he forgot what the doctors called it. Within four days of being wounded he had been able to distinguish light from darkness, but no object. The efficient, hard-drinking young surgeon who had performed the first dressing on shore had not promised much more. He had since taken two further opinions from more exalted quarters. It was in the sick-bay of the *Victory* that he had learnt for certain that he had now only one efficient eye.

While he waited for the *Agamemnon's* guns to be brought on board, he had gone out to consult the medical staff of the Commander-in-Chief's flagship, taking with him Captain Hallowell, a Canadian-born officer, who had been " always on the batteries ", even when suffering from the fever. The couple presented a contrast in types, for Hallowell, " though at present much reduced, poor fellow ", was of mordant humour, gigantic stature and great physical strength. General Chambers, Surgeon-in-Chief to the Forces in the Mediterranean, had, in a discouraging certificate, dated August 9, stated his opinion that Captain Horatio Nelson's right eye had been so materially injured by stones and splinters struck by shot from the enemy that he would never recover the perfect use of it. The amiable Dr. Harness, Physician to the Fleet, a person devoted to sick seamen and to citric acid as the antidote to scurvy, merely confirmed the diagnosis of Mr. Michael Jefferson. He wrote of " a wound of the iris of the right eye, which has occasioned an unnatural dilation of the pupil, and a material defect of sight ". Nelson had been absent from duty only a few hours, and his name had never appeared in the Calvi casualty list. On October 2 he enclosed the two certificates to Lord Hood, stating the loss of an eye in His Majesty's service. Since August 9 he had indulged in no false hopes. " As to all purposes of use ", the eye was gone. " I feel the Want of it but such is the chance of War, it was within a hair's breadth of taking off my head." His intention now, after fears of total darkness of which nobody knew, and a lucky escape, was to keep out of the awful hands of the medical fraternity as far as possible. " Nature does all for me, and Providence protects me." For a sea-officer with twenty-five years' service, to be short of an eye was nothing out of the ordinary. He now confessed to his wife the extent of the " slight scratch " first mentioned to her three weeks after receiving it. He assured her that " the blemish is nothing; not to be perceived, unless told ". He also assured her that his hurts had not kept him from his duty. Nothing less than the loss of a limb could have done that.

17

CHAPTER VI

1794–1796
(*ætat* 35–37)

"OLD MEDITERRANEAN MAN"

I

THE hour of the appointment offered by the Doge of Genoa to the captain of the first British man-of-war to enter his port since England had opened hostilities against France seemed typical of leisured magnificence. Nelson, making his way towards the Piazza San Lorenzo at a few minutes before seven o'clock on Sunday evening, September 21, 1794, was not, however, for many reasons, wholly at ease in his mind.

He had arrived in Genoa the morning before, his orders being to deliver despatches from Lord Hood to Mr. Drake, Minister at Turin, and await further instructions. The thick coastal fog which often precedes an autumn day of hot sun in the Mediterranean had hidden the *Agamemnon* from the authorities of the Genoese signal-house until she was in the mole. As nobody on board had ever been to Genoa, she had the signal up for a pilot. After a wait of a quarter of an hour, she had been startled by a salute of fifteen guns. The Genoese, suddenly recognising the Union Jack at the fore-top-gallant mast-head of a strange warship, had concluded themselves honoured by the visit of a British Vice-Admiral. Nelson had returned the salute without hesitation. He knew that he had been sent here to be civil. The case was only one more example of the inconvenience of using a national flag for signals. But he reflected gloomily, " I shall probably hear more of this." The morning proceeded badly. The British Consul, Mr. Brame, with whom he got in touch promptly, produced letters proving that Mr. Drake, who was expected this evening, was on his way to England for five months' leave; and it was impossible to imagine how Mr. Drake was disliked by all classes in Genoa, said the flustered Brame, whom Nelson wrote down, " a poor creature, more of a Genoese than an Englishman ". He was aware that after a month in Leghorn—her first month of repose in a year and a half—his ship still showed a sick list of seventy-seven—" almost all objects for the Hospital ". Lord Hood was inclined to take him home, in which case he might spend this winter in some snug cottage, instead of eternally " on the wing ", until his ship actually fell to pieces. Nothing could have been handsomer than the conduct of Lord Hood, who had offered him every 74 that had fallen vacant, and, appreciating his reluctance to part with a ship's company with whom he had gone through such hard service, had mentioned the possibility of transferring them bodily to a 74. Lord Hood spoke confidently of his return to the Mediterranean with the reinforcements which he was going to demand in London, but Nelson, without proof, doubted this.

His professional eye had instantly remarked two enemy privateers in Genoa mole, and three English merchantmen. He had asked whether the privateers ever went to sea, and been told, yes, occasionally, and that they had recently taken two vessels, one Spanish property, both bound from Spain for this port. He had made a note to mention that to Mr. Drake, but by Sunday evening Mr. Drake had not yet arrived, and he had been obliged to set out unsupported to pay his respects to an authority surrounded on state occasions by elaborate ceremonial, and accorded in international relations the status of a sovereign prince of the first rank. (Doges, in Genoa, were not so great as in Venice, as they were elected biennially, but the situation was delicate, since Genoese neutrality was being observed as closely as possible by England, and far from closely by France.) He had already realised that only as far as picturesqueness went, and when viewed from the sea, could Naples enter into competition with Genoa. Marble met the eye everywhere in this city concerned with products of the suavest sound—cut-velvet, gloves, steel, scented soap and olive oil. . . . The many mediæval churches on his route all presented striped *façades* of black and white marble. He entered to his audience, doggedly determined to do everything in his power to put the governors of such a place in good humour with Great Britain at war. His brief view of it had confirmed his belief that unless they were driven mad, they could not consider allowing " the Sans Culottes " to enter a city offering opportunities of such glorious plunder.

The interview which followed also reassured him, although it was quite as awe-inspiring as he had expected. The Doge, who was obliged to open despatches from foreign rulers in the presence of his senators, had considered this occasion of sufficient importance to summon his officials, although no despatches were to be presented. The scene was staged in a modern hall of impressive dimensions, brilliantly lit, and new-furnished every two years, "for the sake of commerce". The guest had no difficulty in discovering to which of these signors of patrician aspect, all clad in unrelieved black, he should address himself. The stately gentleman who did him the honour of advancing into the centre of the room to greet him had a friendly expression, and his speech of welcome, as translated, sounded all that could be desired. The Captain of the *Agamemnon*, finding it "absolutely necessary", then summoned a gift of extremely lucid statement, and in the vigorous style which he had used at need before—in his first interview with Lord Hood; in his early morning meeting with the Secretary to the Treasury—assured His Serene Highness that both by inclination and duty he should do everything in his power to improve the happy relations already existing between their countries. His Serene Highness, looking "much pleased", expressed his belief that a national friendship resumed so pleasantly must endure. He declared himself always glad to see English men-of-war in Genoa, hoped that his visitor would mention if he found difficulty in obtaining anything which he needed during his stay, explained that he should be happy to remove any obstacles, and concluded by announcing his gates always at the disposal of Captain Nelson. This courtesy had a literal significance, as Nelson found when he came to make a relieved exit. The Doge's order had arrived before him at the palace doors, and the captain of the guard came forward to explain that he had received orders to open them at whatever hour Captain Nelson chose to appear.

It was not for some months that Nelson learnt what problem had been adding a shade to the brow of Signor Giacomo Maria Brignole, member of a family which had several times given Doges to the Serene Republic. Throughout the audience His Serene Highness had been very much wishing to know, but had been too polite to ask, what was the age of this English sea-officer.

Something of the austere elegance of his reception hung about Nelson's phraseology when he addressed himself to his wife, during his first visit to Genoa :

"This City is without exception the most magnificent I ever beheld, superior in many respects to Naples. All the houses are palaces, on the grandest scale. However, I trust we shall soon quit these magnificent scenes, and retire to England, where all that I admire is placed."

1

2

When Lord Hood sailed for Gibraltar, and Portsmouth, without him, on October 12, Nelson was disappointed, but the duty on which he was ordered offered chances of prizes, and unless a peace should send him home, he was not, at heart, inclined to leave the Mediterranean at present.   He knew that after a period of eclipse, his interest was rising again ; and he had not yet seen a fleet action.   " I trust the time will come when I shall be rewarded, though really I don't flatter myself it is near."

His chief regret was for Mrs. Nelson, from whom letters were arriving to say that the prospect of seeing her dear husband and child so soon made her happy beyond expression.   " It has given me health, for before you wrote that you were well, and that Calvi was taken, I had fallen into the same way I was last year." Her anxiety had transferred itself to the possibility that her husband might still, of course, die on his way home to her.   " Let me beg you to be particularly careful of sleeping at the inns.   It is dreadful to hear of the fevers that rage in the West Indies."

His Fanny's letters from Kentish Town were read by Nelson in Golfe Jouan, which the fleet had christened " Gourjean ", and while he faced a boringly familiar prospect of inclining conifers and rocky islets, in increasingly bad weather, he was mentally transported to a scene typical of Georgian England.   Under Mr. Suckling's roof, on September 29, a large party had sat down to dinner, and drunk the health of the absent friend.   They had a couple of geese amongst the good fare, as the host was a Norfolk man.   In the background stood Price, the black butler, looking blue, poor fellow, since his son had been found drowned in Hampstead ponds.   Hickman, another old retainer, had also, on Mrs. Horatio Nelson's arrival, been full of enquiries for the Captain.   The blooming and attentive Mrs. Suckling was supported by her father, contemporary of her husband, and other members of her family from Hampstead.   The daughter of the house—born out of wedlock, but frankly acknowledged, as the eighteenth century had still some years to run—had a wistful look.   She had formed an attachment for an Army officer.   Her father knew of it, but said the young man must sell out—a hard saying, as he was at present with his regiment on the Continent, where the war was going poorly.   If any little thing should come in her husband's way, Mrs. Nelson wished he

would bring it home with him as a keepsake for his cousin.
" I feel for her." The party had been very merry, and Mr.
Suckling had quizzed his nephew's wife, as was his way, saying
that he could always tell what was in her good man's letters by
her expression. At the close of the feast, his present to her on
her husband's thirty-sixth birthday had been truly handsome—
" nothing less than £100 ". The trifle bought by Nelson for his
cousin Elizabeth was also handsome—a diamond ring; and,
since he would not now be home for Christmas, he sent £200 to
his father, to be spent on comforts for the poor of Burnham
Thorpe. He said that he thought a large N. could be woven
into the blankets.

Christmas saw him at Leghorn again. His itinerary for the
present was Gourjean, Leghorn, Porto Ferrajo in Elba and San
Fiorenzo in Corsica. His duty was blockade, and his expectation
that nothing much was likely to happen till the spring, when, if
the French should turn their attention to the invasion of Italy,
they would probably succeed. " We don't seem to make much
of this War." " Pray let me hear from you often ", he had
written to his wife, in his first moment of dejection at not coming
home; " it is my greatest comfort." But Fanny's letters, dated
from Bath now, did not bring great comfort. " This winter will
be another anxious one. What did I not suffer in my mind, the
last ! . . . My mind and poor heart are always on the rack ! "
She told him that his brother Maurice, who seemed at last to be
prospering, had grown quite stout, and that Mrs. Matcham was
ailing for the usual reason, and that Mr. Matcham, as usual, was
dissatisfied with his latest purchase. The manners of her
husband's brother William (to whom he was unalterably attached)
were growing more and more rough. Uncle Suckling had, since
her departure, alarmed his young wife and his daughter by
another of his coughing fits, in which he nearly strangled himself.
She was deeply interested in the Prince of Wales's forthcoming
match with the Princess of Brunswick, and much misinformed on
the subject. " Mrs. Fitzherbert has been long dismissed. . . .
The Prince, it is said, is quite happy at the thought of being
domesticated." In her husband's family, only his saintly father
escaped a Parthian dart. She did not know that he was writing
to Mrs. Matcham :

" No letters by Lord Hood from your Bro. His poor wife is continually in a Hurry and fret about him, and I find many others are the
same, and worse. In such a state, the blessings of a Marriage union are

thus made a torment, and most likely the Health is destroyed, or the temper soured, so as never to be recovered." 3

Lord Hood had arrived home, and presently news of him reached Nelson from several sources. All seemed to be going well. As the Commander-in-Chief from the Mediterranean had stepped out of his coach in London, the First Lord had been ready with a hand of greeting. From an inn at Devizes, on his road to Bath, Lord Hood assured " my dear Nelson " that he had taken the earliest opportunity of explaining to the First Lord the very illiberal conduct of General Stuart in making no mention of the services rendered by the Captain of the *Agamemnon* in the taking of Calvi. He had put into Lord Chatham's hand, with the understanding that it should be delivered to His Majesty, Nelson's letter enclosing the two medical certificates attesting the loss of an eye. " So you may be perfectly easy upon that subject." Three days later, Fanny took up the story. The Hoods had arrived at 5, Queen Square, and called at 17, New King Street. His lordship had been as affectionate as if she was a daughter, and held out hopes that within three months her grass-widowhood would come to an end. Lady Hood had privately assured her that if justice was not done to Nelson it would not be his lordship's fault. A week later she had dined with them, and been " cheerful and well-dressed ". Nelson had not received well her pathetic disclosure that sheer worry during the siege of Calvi had undermined her health. (" Why you should be uneasy about me so as to make yourself ill, I know not. . . . The Service must ever supersede all private considerations.") She realised that she must begin to think of Josiah, now nearing his fifteenth birthday, as " my young man ", no longer " my child ", but found this almost impossible. " My child ! I figure him to myself—good and obedient to you, and I hope tells you all his secrets. If he does, you will keep him good." After fierce storms, snow clothed the streets of Bath, a most unusual thing, and a sea-officer's wife could not resist the confession, " I never hear the wind but my dear husband and child are full in my thoughts." 4

Nelson's reports of his stepson were always favourable. " His understanding is excellent, and his disposition really good. . . . He is a seaman, every inch of him." He had begun to detect signs of what he cautiously termed " a warm disposition "— however, nothing could cool that so thoroughly as being at sea, " where nobody has entirely their own way ". 5

At Leghorn, on Sunday evening, March 8, he was interrupted for the third time while attempting to compose a letter to his wife. He had begun it over a week before, on his return from a very bad cruise, but so far it contained but two paragraphs. For twelve days of January the fleet had been under storm stay-sails. All his letters since the New Year had told of little but gales and lumping seas. "But in *Agamemnon*, we mind them not; she is the finest Ship I ever sailed in, and were she a seventy-four, nothing should induce me to leave her while the War lasts." He repeated that he wished Lord Hood would make haste out, and that much as he regretted his separation from his wife, it was best to take the long view. When two or three months' further absence might make all the difference to his career, it was obviously folly to repine. "I hope we have many happy days to live together." He was determined, however, as soon as he had collected round about two thousand pounds, to buy a home, in which Fanny could settle—nothing grand, just a "neat cottage"—"which we shall never have occasion to change".

He was now fast becoming what he called "an old Mediterranean man", well accustomed to brown shirts and scanty dinners, and he knew the free and neutral port of Leghorn as well as his native Lynn. The Tuscan sea-bathing resort, used by the Mediterranean fleet for refitting and victualling, had not many wholesome attractions for the exile, and when a sterner Admiral succeeded Hotham, he took ruthless measures to check behaviour which had resulted in a lamentable percentage of officers and men being invalided to Ajaccio Hospital. The second-rate hotel and opera charged exorbitant prices. Nelson haunted the house of the Pollards, Levant merchants, and together with Mr. Udney, British Consul, often agents for prizes taken by the fleet. He ordered his portrait in miniature from a local artist, who produced for the admiration of Mrs. Horatio Nelson a curiously pursy-looking sea-captain, with fashionably curly hair. The uniform was conscientiously attempted, but even the men-of-war, dramatically heeling over in the background, did not suggest British reality.

The third interruption to Nelson's letter of March 8 was unexpected, and caused him to close it immediately, with the words, "I have only to pray God to bless you." The fleet, "taken rather suddenly", got off at dawn, "pretty tolerably, as to order", and early on the morning of the 10th, Nelson's hope that they had gone to sea for some good purpose seemed likely to be gratified. The fifteen enemy sail-of-the-line reported to Admiral Hotham, by an express from Genoa, to be out of Toulon and steering for Corsica, were sighted at 10 a.m. and Hotham, with fourteen British warships and one Neapolitan, gave the signal for a general chase. Nelson reckoned the English fleet "half-manned", to have but 7,650 men at quarters, while the enemy had 16,900. His chief anxiety was lest the *Agamemnon* might not be able to acquit herself worthily, owing to being short of complement. It was during this day of light and variable winds and mists, typical of the Mediterranean in early spring, that he scrawled, in momentary expectation of his first fleet action, a jerky addition to what might be a farewell letter : " My character and good name are in my own keeping. Life with disgrace is dreadful. A glorious death is to be envied." The action which followed was scrambling and unsatisfactory, but a chance did come for him to distinguish himself.

At midnight on the 10th Hotham hoisted the signal to form in order of battle, but next morning no enemy was visible. Another uncanny day of sighing fickle airs and haze, accompanied by a heavy swell from the S.W., followed. The night was calm. With dawn the enemy were in sight again. Since his ship belonged to Vice-Admiral Goodall's division, it was to this officer, in the *Princess Royal*, that Nelson sent, at 9 a.m., a note expressive of strong emotion :

> " My dear Admiral,
>   " I most heartily congratulate you on our being so near the Enemy's Fleet, and have only to assure you that the *Agamemnon* shall ever most faithfully support you. I wish we had a hundred, or at least should have, fifty good men. Should any of our Frigates get near you, I hope you will order some men for us, even should Admiral Hotham forget us. Believe me as ever, but never more than on the present occasion,
> " Your most faithful,
> " Horatio Nelson."

A few minutes before 3.15, when Hotham gave the signal " Prepare for Battle ", Nelson saw Genoa lighthouse, about five leagues to the N.N.E., and, with that quickening of the visual sense usual at such moments, Genoa, surnamed " the Superb ", displayed in all her glory. In the *Agamemnon*, as the *Britannia* broke the red flag, a continual drumming began to sound, and every man hurried to his assigned duty. Wooden bulkheads and canvas screens vanished : tables, chairs, lockers and chests went to the hold : hammocks, piped from below, neatly rolled and corded, were packed in troughs along the tops of the bulwarks. The galley fire was doused, and the fighting decks watered and dressed with sand : the ship's company tied their silks round their heads and cast their footwear, and indeed all wear save their trousers, both in expectation of warm work and because surgeons preferred to operate on wounds uninfected by greasy textiles. The *toilette* of the guns was also completed and the port lids yawned, while along the sanded decks buckets of water, tourniquets and swabs were ranged handy. With the first roll of the drum, nets had been spread from the main-mast aft to the mizzen, and in the hatchway "fearnought" felt fore-screens were hammered into place. Finally, to the orlop, safe under the water-line, repaired a solemn company, including the carpenter with his gang, ready to staunch a mortal wound to under-water timbers, and Mr. Roxburgh, surgeon, with mates rolling their shirt sleeves to their shoulders. Six minutes was the time allotted for this transformation scene in a ship-of-the-line, but an hour passed on March 13, 1795, before Hotham gave the signal to form order of battle on the larboard tack; and his next signal, half an hour later, was for every ship to carry a light during the night. Nelson's opportunity did not come until the next morning, with fresh breezes and again the order for a general chase.

The enemy, refusing battle, were running as fast as they could, pursued by the English fleet, on a parallel line, the *Agamemnon* and half a dozen other ships well ahead, when suddenly Nelson beheld a French 80-gun ship (afterwards identified as the *Ça Ira*) run foul of another and carry away her own fore and main top-masts. Captain Fremantle, in the leading frigate, coming up fast, with great resolution at once attacked the 80-gun ship, and the first shots of the action were heard; but the little *Inconstant* received heavy punishment and was forced to retire. The *Agamemnon* then stood towards the *Ça Ira*, the *Sans Culotte* of 120 guns and the *Jean Bart* (which Nelson, better versed in the names of prominent members of the French Directory than French naval history, wrote down as the *Jean Barras*). It was at this moment that a sacrifice avoided the previous day when clearing the decks for action was performed, and seven live bullocks, purchase of a captain with strong views on the prevention of scurvy, were hove overboard. "We could", considered Nelson regretfully, "have fetched the *Sans Culotte*, by passing the *Ça Ira* to windward, but, on looking round I saw no ship-of-the-line within several miles to support me." He determined to direct

M

his attentions to the *Ça Ira*, presently taken in tow by a frigate, with the *Sans Culotte* and *Jean Bart* standing by to protect her. Moving fairly rapidly through the water, she began firing stern-chasers, with such effect that Nelson, who had intended to touch her stern before he gave the order to fire, decided to reply. " Seeing plainly from the situation of the two Fleets, the impossibility of being supported ; and in case any accident happened to our masts, the certainty of being severely cut up, I resolved to fire as soon as I thought we had a certainty of hitting." He continued to manœuvre and hit, unsupported, for upwards of two hours, and during this time had the satisfaction of observing " my poor brave fellows " carrying out his orders with as much calm and precision as if they had been working the *Agamemnon* into Spithead. " Scarcely a shot seemed to miss : the instant all were fired, braced up our after-yards, put the helm a-port and stood after her again . . . never allowing the *Ça Ira* to get a single gun from either side to fire on us." By 1 p.m. the French 80-gun ship was " a perfect wreck ", and her commander ordered his towing frigate to pull her round, so that she could bring her broadside to bear. Nelson ran on boldly, and her shots flew over the *Agamemnon*. Such was the state of the engagement when Hotham, instead of hastening reinforcements, hoisted the signal of recall.

Next morning all sail was made to cut off the *Ça Ira*, now towed by a 74, and as the enemy made an attempt to save two ships-of-the-line, a partial action ensued in which the *Agamemnon* was again engaged, and two British ships were disabled. But as soon as the enemy cripples had struck, Hotham, contented with a measure of success, decided against further pursuit.

Having sent the faithful Andrews to board the enemy prizes and hoist English colours, Nelson himself went on board the Admiral's flagship, to urge leaving the prizes, with the two damaged English 74's and some frigates, and continuing the chase in hopes of forcing a general engagement. Hotham, " much cooler than myself ", replied, " We must be contented. We have done very well." Nelson, far from contented, when he got on board the *Princess Royal*, carrying with him, by Hotham's orders, the captains of the two enemy prizes, found Goodall of his own mind. This more adventurous officer went so far as to send a hasty line to his Commander-in-Chief, backing Captain Nelson's opinion that, if they could but get close enough, they might have the whole enemy fleet, and " such a day as I believe

the Annals of England never produced ". " Sure I am," wrote
Nelson privately, " had I commanded our Fleet on the 14th, that
either the whole French Fleet would have graced my triumph, or
I should have been in a confounded scrape." But Hotham,
perceiving the possibility of the scrape, refused to make a
dangerous attempt, and contemporary comment did not criticise
him too severely. He had not, after all, done badly. Corsica
was temporarily saved, and two French sail-of-the-line had been
captured. Only a few persons of discernment summed up his
future from that hour. " I can *entre nous*, perceive ", wrote Sir
William Hamilton, from his Neapolitan palace, " that my old
friend Hotham is not quite awake enough for such a command
as that of the King's Fleet in the Mediterranean; although he
appears the best creature imaginable." Nelson was obliged to
be content with the reflection that he had been lucky enough to
command the only line-of-battle ship to get into single action,
and with an opponent " absolutely large enough " to have taken
the *Agamemnon* in her hold. While the *Ça Ira* and the *Censeur*
showed a casualty list of seven hundred and fifty, the *Agamemnon*
had, by what seemed like a miracle, since " our sails were ribbons
9 and all our ropes were ends ", only thirteen wounded. " The
Enemy, notwithstanding their red-hot shot and shells, must now
be satisfied (or we are ready to give them further proof,) that
10 England yet reigns Mistress on the Seas." Also, although
Hotham's despatch made no mention of him on the second day
of the battle, he soon discovered that in both the British and
enemy fleets his services had not been under-estimated. As " we
are too far from home to be noticed ", he told his wife " as a
secret " that out here now he was not unknown. The French
poetasters had given Captain Nelson a mistress—" no less a
11 personage than the goddess Bellona ".

3

His dissatisfaction with the results of the late engagement
was renewed when he heard that the French fleet had, before
being encountered, fallen in with and captured the *Berwick*, and
afterwards had been joined by six ships from Brest, which should
never have been permitted to get into Toulon unopposed.

For above three weeks, while the cautious Hotham kept his
whole fleet under his eye at San Fiorenzo or Leghorn, Nelson was
" absolutely in the horrors " lest a convoy, momentarily expected
from Gibraltar, might share the fate of the *Berwick*. In case the

enemy, encouraged by their superior numbers, might make
another attempt to take Corsica before the arrival of Lord Hood,
he wrote to the Viceroy, offering his services for the command of
any seamen landed for the defence of the island.   Twelve months
had now passed since he had first set eyes upon Sir Gilbert Elliot,
a figure who would, by anyone familiar with the type, have been
recognised by the gait and set of jaw alone as a Border laird.
The Scots Viceroy was one of the most admirable characters yet
encountered by Nelson.   He was, like most of his race, slightly
below middle stature, with a gift of silence and a lightning wit;
a man of parts and means, personally disinterested, impossible to
fret or daunt.   On the first occasion that her husband was a
candidate for the Speakership of the House of Commons, the
news had caused Lady Elliot to laugh more than ever in her life
before.   Fortunately, since the two things which she did bar were
a constant bore and a flowing wig, this ambition had not been
realised.   The Vicereine, indulgently described by her partner   12
as " my John Bull wife, who understands a Frenchman no better
than Molly housemaid ", had arrived safely at Bastia from   13
Roxburghshire in the previous December, with their six children
and a young cousin, Miss Eleanor Congleton.   From her " fairy-
tale palace ", overlooking an island-studded bay, Lady Elliot
now issued invitations to assemblies and balls at which regimental
bands played, and the company were at liberty to wander, in
moonlight, through great glass doors on to the terrace of an
immense garden, on a cape washed by the sea.   She also
astonished the natives by being out early for hard walks in
mountain scenery which reminded her husband of *As You Like
It* and *A Midsummer Night's Dream*, while he astonished her
by bringing to her table guests who were precisely her picture
of Bluebeard.   The elder of the six hardy little Elliots (who had
been trained not to howl when they injured themselves, but to
remember the sufferings of classic heroes and the deeds of their
ancestors) were as happy as the day was long, learning to sail
the boat moored to their garden wall, paying visits to His Majesty's
ships, and scrambling about the hills in correct Corsican undress,
with fowling-piece, pistol and stiletto.   Only occasionally did the
Vicereine regret what she described as the " stink " of their
capital, and the number of lizards, and gentry armed to the
teeth, encountered on her romantic strolls; while her husband,
after an official appearance at a Corsican native dance, nostalgi-
cally compared it with a Lochgelly Ball.   Even before he had

explained his reason for sending his second son into the Navy, Sir Gilbert had won Nelson's heart by his insistence upon the attack on Bastia. ("I like the sea better. The character of the profession is more manly. They are full of life and action, while on shore it is all lounge and still life.") There were other attractions in conversation with the Viceroy of Corsica, who had the high polish of a country gentleman educated at the *Pension Militaire*, Fontainebleau, before proceeding to a Grand Tour, Christ Church, Oxford, and Lincoln's Inn. Sir Gilbert, who had entered the House of Commons at the age of twenty-five (and confessed to having once completely dried up, from sheer "gallows-feeling", for what seemed the length of a Scottish sermon, after the first period of an important speech), was a born Whig, but one who had left the Opposition two years past with the Duke of Portland. He could not share Mr. Fox's admiration for Revolutionaries. A Coalition, "without the sacrifice of former principles on either side", was his war-time ideal. "All the ability of the country, united to direct all the resources of the country to the one good end, is a prospect which I hope is not quite out of sight." When Mr. Pitt sat, after having delivered one of his fighting speeches, "being right", Sir Gilbert could hardly help almost *liking* him. Only when having what he called "a crack" with intimates did a good party man confess that the habit of his leader, the Duke, when attacked, of admitting everything you said, and replying with nothing but feeling sobs, was depressingly reminiscent of George Elliot, aged ten. The Viceroy was openly in agreement with Nelson's despair over neglect of the Mediterranean by those at home. The news of the appointment of Lord Spencer to succeed Lord Chatham had been a personal blow to an officer still waiting for recognition of his loss of an eye. ("Now he is out, all hopes will be done away.") His chagrin vented itself in a long letter to Locker:

"When I am to see England, God knows! I have, in the present situation of affairs, determined on staying here till the autumn, or another Action take place, when all active service will probably be over in these seas. . . . One hundred and ten days I have been actually engaged at Sea and on shore against the Enemy; three actions against Ships, two against Bastia, in my Ship; four Boat Actions and two Villages taken, and twelve Sail of Vessels burned. I don't know of anyone who has done more, and I have had the comfort to be ever *applauded* by my Commander-in-Chief, but never *rewarded*; and what is more mortifying, for services in which I have been slightly wounded, others have been praised, who at the time were actually in bed, far from the scene of action.

" But we shall, I hope, talk my opinion of men and measures, over the fire next winter, at Greenwich."

Locker, now much of an invalid, was comfortably employed, together with an ancient Admiral called Forbes (who had lost the use of his legs and arms), supplying a painstaking younger gentleman, Mr. John Charnock, with material for a collection of volumes entitled *Biographia Navalis*. Locker was a storehouse of naval tradition, Forbes possessed a remarkable memory, and Charnock, an author by profession, and at one period in his career an enthusiastic naval volunteer, possessed the advantages of having been to Winchester College and Trinity, Oxford. The first volume had been forwarded to Nelson, and he gave it guarded praise.

As the spring passed, and no word came of the promised reinforcements, he began to fear that the new Lords were not to be an improvement on their predecessors—a thing he had scarcely believed possible. The junction of a single Neapolitan 74, towards the end of April, was " absolutely matter for exultation " in the fleet, " not so much neglected as forgotten are we at Home ". He was glad when Hotham, " I believe heartily tired of his temporary command ", at last took his fleet to sea, a proceeding not only more honourable, but also much safer than " skulking in Port ". But contrary winds held them in Leghorn, while the French Minister at Genoa triumphantly announced the signature of a peace between his country and Spain, and Sir William Hamilton wrote ruefully that if this story was true, we should soon be losing " our Naples friends ", quoting—" As do Spain, so do Naples."

The long looked-for store-ships and victuallers from Gibraltar made an essential appearance (" Had we lost them, the game was up "), but everyone felt indignation that they had been obliged to run such a risk of capture and that their Admiral was receiving " not the scratch of a pen " from London, where " they should know that half the Ships in this Fleet require to go to England ". Presently, unofficial reports of the reinforcements with which Lord Hood was waiting to sail from St. Helens were truly astonishing—only five of the line. " What ", demanded Nelson of Uncle Suckling of the Navy Office, " can the new Board of Admiralty be after? We expect the French Fleet to be at sea every hour." On June 15 a disaster which he had long dreaded was announced. Admiral Man joined the fleet with a squadron of seven ships. Lord Hood, while lying at Spithead in the

Victory, ready to sail, had found it his duty to remonstrate for the last time with their Lordships on the inadequacy of the force on the Mediterranean station, and when Lord Hood felt strongly the result was remarkable, for, in the words of the admiring William Hotham, he had even upon normal occasions " A Something " about him which put inferior officers in much awe. " He was a stranger to any feeling of nervous diffidence." Their Lordships, on encountering this side of Lord Hood, had ordered him to strike his flag and come on shore, which he had accordingly done, never to be employed at sea again. Nelson's dismay was equalled by his indignation. His hopes, like those of Sir Gilbert Elliot, had been " accustomed to rest on the *Victory's* anchor ". " Oh, miserable Board of Admiralty. They have forced the first officer in the Service away from his command. His zeal, his activity for the honour and benefit of his King and Country are not abated. Upward of 70, he possesses the mind of 40. . . ." Nelson's belief that his lost leader was a man " equally great in all situations " was justified. Hood, even at this moment, had taken care to send by Admiral Man a letter from Lord Spencer acknowledging the pretensions of Captain Horatio Nelson " to favour and distinction when proper opportunities offer ". It was dated before news of the action of July 13–14 had been received at the Admiralty, but also before Hood's difference with their Lordships—a serious consideration, as he had since written to another officer :

> " To be candid with you, I can be of no use to anyone, for Lord Spencer is not content with marking me with indifference and inattention, but carries it to all who have any connection with me. You will therefore do well, in any application to his Lordship, not to make mention of my name. I have neither seen or spoken to his Lordship since my flag was struck, and look upon myself as thrown upon the shelf for ever."

Lord Hood's retirement was dignified. In 1795 he expressed his intention of spending " the short remnant of my life " in the happy situation of a private gentleman. Ill-health had been offered as his reason for coming back from the Mediterranean last winter, but on a chill March morning his silver head and hawk-features were observed in the House of Commons at 6 a.m. In the following March he was appointed Governor of Greenwich Hospital, a post which he held for twenty years.

4

While Nelson was " waiting off Minorque, doing nothing . . . out of spirits, though never better in health ", he dealt with a matter which he had deferred in hopes of Lord Hood's return. He addressed himself directly to the Secretary at War, asking for the allowance usually made to a land-officer of equal rank (" which I understand is that of Brigadier-General ") in respect of his services on shore during the sieges of Bastia and Calvi. A chilly but quick reply informed him : " No pay has ever been issued under the direction, or to the knowledge of this Office, to Officers of the Navy, serving with the Army on shore." He sailed for San Fiorenzo at the end of June, at a tense moment. The French fleet was said to be at sea again, with twenty-two of the line and " innumerable frigates ", but a valuable convoy from Gibraltar (this time bringing ammunition and troops) had escaped. " So far, good." On his arrival in Corsica he found that he was to be given a detached command. By what seemed an ironic chance, considering the ill-success of his late application, he was, on account of his experience during the sieges of Bastia and Calvi, being employed to act with forces on shore. His mission had a sound of high romance—" to co-operate with the Austrian General, Baron de Vins, in the Riviera of Genoa ". The principal armies engaged against the French Republic now were those of Austria and Sardinia, and France was bringing increasing pressure to bear on technically neutral Genoa.

At San Fiorenzo Nelson found Hotham, happy in the belief that only seventeen enemy sail were at sea, and for no other purpose than to exercise their men. A courtly letter from de Vins at Genoa had assured him that the main fleet was in Toulon, and that allied arms had taken Vado Bay, which should be a useful base for the English fleet. Nelson sailed from San Fiorenzo with five frigates at dusk on July 4, and midway between Nice and Genoa, on the afternoon of the 7th, fell in with the enemy fleet in full strength. They immediately gave chase to his small squadron, and he needed all his seamanship to get back to San Fiorenzo. For seven of the twenty-four hours during which he was pursued Hotham's fleet had the mortification of watching him in imminent danger of capture. The wind was blowing right into the bay, and most of the British ships were watering and refitting. After great exertions they got to sea—" Twenty-three of the Line, and as fine a Fleet as ever graced the seas ", searching for an enemy equal in strength. Five days later they came in sight of their opponents, and Hotham, after spending a long time in dressing his line, hoisted the signal for a general chase. He was being given the second chance, rare in the career of a Commander-in-Chief. Many lesser Powers in Europe, and particularly along these shores, were waiting to see whether the English could hold the Mediterranean, or whether the star of France was in the ascendant. The night of July 12 had been wild, and several British ships had split their topmasts. With daylight the wind continued high, and there was considerable swell. The weather favoured the pursuit for a while, but by noon, when the *Agamemnon*, with half a dozen other ships of Man's squadron, leading the van, was in touch with the enemy's rear, the French coast near Toulon was also visible, and soon after the *Victory* had opened fire, the breeze swung round to the north, giving the three sternmost enemy vessels the opportunity of bringing their broadsides to bear. The *Victory* and the *Culloden* lost limbs, but the *Alcide*, last ship in the French line, was so badly damaged that she struck and surrendered. Before she could be boarded, she took fire and blew up. While the sun struggled through the clouds, about two hundred of her crew were saved by English boats. Nearly all the prisoners subsequently declared themselves royalists, and Nelson decided that, upon the whole, he found French republicans better specimens.

Although smoke from the gunfire had now produced a perfect calm, the *Cumberland* and *Agamemnon* were again getting into close action when Hotham, eight miles astern, signalled, "The whole Fleet will now retire." In his own words, "Those of our ships which were engaged had approached so near to the shore, that I judged it proper to call them off." Captain Rowley did his best to avoid seeing the unwelcome signal, but the *Victory* repeated it, hoisting the *Cumberland's* distinguishing pendant, and Rowley was obliged to obey. Once more the French fleet had escaped, and even the immediate results of the Battle of Hyères were obviously inferior to those of the disappointing action of the previous March. The eventual results were to include the abandonment of the Mediterranean by the British Fleet, the loss of Corsica, and Spain ranged by the side of France. Nelson wrote:

> "Thus has ended our second meeting with these gentry. In the forenoon we had every prospect of taking every Ship in the Fleet, and at noon it was almost certain we should have had the six near Ships. . . . To say how we wanted Lord Hood at that time is to say, 'Will you have all the French Fleet, or no Action?' But the subject is unpleasant and I shall have done with it. I am now co-operating with the Austrian Army, under General de Vins, and hope we shall do better there."

5

General Baron de Vins returned the first visit of Captain
Nelson on July 21, 1795, and according to the log of the
Agamemnon, was received with all the honours due to his rank.

His ship, ship's company and himself had long, in Nelson's
opinion, been in need of repairs.   There was not a mast, yard,
sail or any part of the rigging, outlined against Mediterranean
glare that late summer afternoon, which did not show the result
of enemy shot.   The hull of the old and battered 64 was secured
by cables, frapped round.   All had, however, been sufficiently
smartened to fill the eye of a foreign land-officer.

The morning had been a disturbed one, but there was no sign
of this as the marines fell in on the poop and quarter-deck, and at
the entry port; Joe King and his mates assembled with their
calls, and the formal shapes of Mr. Roxburgh, Principal Medical
Officer, and Mr. Fellowes, Captain's Secretary, appeared, ready
to be presented to the distinguished guest.   Nelson was closely
supported by Hinton, his First Lieutenant, and " an amiable
lad ", Charles Pierson, of the 69th Regiment (acting as marines),
who spoke the Latin languages better than English.   At length
the boatswain piped the side, the marines presented arms, and
fifteen guns spoke as the Commander-in-Chief of the Austrian
Army came on board.   To the owner of every pair of steady eyes
that perceived him, the same thought leapt unbidden.   General
Baron de Vins, handsomely figged out in a white uniform with
scarlet facings and much gold braid, and with the ribbon of some
illustrious decoration across his *jabot*, was pitifully old.

Four days had passed since Nelson had arrived in Genoa, and
picked up letters and newspapers from home which told him that
he had been gazetted Colonel of the Chatham Division of Marines.
For some months past the promotions rewarding the Glorious
First of June had been expected.   He had dreaded that they
might give him his flag and send him home.   He found that the
promotions to Admiral had stopped short seven above him.   As
he made his way through the streets of Genoa towards Mr. Drake's
house, which stood five miles outside the city, he saw in his mind's
eye the grey pile of Holkham presiding over the Norfolk fields
close by Burnham Thorpe, and pictured the " very small cottage "
now within his means, where he should be as happy as if in Mr.
Coke's famous Hall.   He decided to send his dear father a gift
of £200, " since at present I believe that I am the richer man ".

The recognition of his services, achieved without any interest, raised his spirits. After his evening with Mr. Drake his brow was not so light. He slept on their conversation, and next day sent the Minister a long letter ending, "When your Excellency considers the responsibility of a Captain in the Navy in these matters, I trust you will think it right for me to state my opinion fully." His Excellency had asked him to take a step justly described by him as "vigorous", his favourite adjective at this date. Mr. Drake wished him to stop, not only all enemy vessels, but all neutrals trading with the districts of the Genoa littoral under enemy occupation. Hotham's recent instructions gave him considerable freedom, but a circular order based on advice from London, issued by the Commander-in-Chief to his fleet only a month past, adjured all officers to take extreme care, in their dealings with neutral shipping, not to give just cause of offence to Foreign Powers in amity with His Majesty. He doubted whether Hotham would stand by him if he did give cause for complaint, and as a Captain in the Navy, he was well aware that should neutral owners sue him successfully for detention and damage he would be liable for the payment of sums amounting to so many hundreds of thousands of pounds that the exact probability was not worth his consideration. He therefore asked Mr. Drake to assure him that unless an entire stop was put to all trade, the army with which he was told to co-operate was unlikely to hold its present position. He also asked to be assured that the step proposed was for the benefit of His Majesty's Service. Mr. Drake did so, and with the words, "Political courage in an Officer abroad is as highly necessary as military courage", Nelson agreed without further hesitation to take the responsibility of acting, "not only without the orders of my Commander-in-Chief, but in some measure contrary to them". He issued "proper orders" to "the Squadron under my command", and taking Mr. Drake on board the *Agamemnon*, sailed for Vado Bay. There they found the Honourable John Trevor, now Minister at Turin, awaiting them, and the Baron de Vins, "extremely glad" to see them. Nelson was disappointed with the newly captured base. Had it not been called a bay, he would never have recognised it as one. It appeared to him to be a mere "bend in the land", and his first experience of going ashore from a warship at anchor was not encouraging. He grudgingly allowed that the water was certainly deep, with a good clay bottom, and that a fleet might ride there for a short

time during the summer months. With the Allied Army he was
better impressed—" 3,200 of the finest troops I ever saw "—and
the practised charm of an aristocrat of the Imperial Court was
not lost upon him. He thought the Baron de Vins an officer who
perfectly knew his business, and seemed disposed to act with
vigour. "A good man, and I verily believe a good General."
Listening to the flowery periods of the old Austrian cavalry
General, who informed him that the name and reputation of
M. le Commandant Nelson were perfectly known in his army,
indeed throughout Europe, he could almost fancy himself charging
at the head of a troop of horse. When his army entered Nice, as
they might do in six weeks, said de Vins, he expected to receive
the bâton of a Field Marshal, and the English fleet would have
Villefranche harbour. Once he was across the Var, Provence
would rise. "All War or all Peace" was his motto. It took
Nelson nearly two months to discover that talking dramatically
was General de Vins's strong point. The General, having
appreciated very quickly that the English Commander-in-Chief
had sent him a highly exhausting young companion in charge of
a few frigates, had privately decided not to move unadvisedly.
He meant to continue his careful tactics of spreading small forces
everywhere possible, thus never, as his critics claimed, having a
main body with which to attack.

The day on which he returned Nelson's first call opened
propitiously. The diplomats from Turin and Genoa had been
insistent on the necessity of impressing the Allies with Great
Britain's good faith. The officers of Nelson's small squadron
had already begun to act. In the morning, Cockburn, in the
Meleager, had brought in the *Nostra Signora di Belvedere*, bound
from Marseille for Genoa. The gold, silver and jewels found in
her deserted cabin were hastily transferred to the Captain's cabin
in the *Agamemnon*. The only persons found on board the prize
were a couple of indignant passengers, who had been forgotten
by the master and crew when making their escape. There was
no time, before the General's arrival, to move, or even inspect, a
cargo in the hold, said to be of great value.

The General's visit passed off very pleasantly, and Mr. Drake
and Mr. Trevor expressed their opinion that his Commander-in-
Chief ought to give Captain Nelson an order to wear a distinguishing pendant. Having said all that was necessary for the moment,
Nelson sailed again for Genoa, with their Excellencies, promising
to return to Vado Bay with all possible expedition. He did not

intend even to anchor, but a gale blew him into Leghorn roads, and a week passed before he returned to a business which he soon learnt to describe as " pushing the Austrian General forward ". De Vins gradually disclosed his difficulties. He had tried both flattery and abuse on the Piedmontese and Neapolitans under his command. The former were too poor in spirit even to defend their own territory. He had long been patiently awaiting their promised attack, under General Calli, in the Ventimiglia district. He believed that no Neapolitan vessel would stay at sea in winter to save an empire. Still, if Neapolitan gunboats could be obtained, they might serve to check enemy supply vessels streaming out of Genoa after dark, and creeping along the coast in shallow water. He apologised that " the politics of his court so constantly tied his hands ". A plan that Nelson should take five or six thousand troops round behind the enemy front and land them between San Remo and Ventimiglia received his polite consideration. The young Englishman himself admitted that it might be a risky undertaking.

Nelson began to suffer from nervous strain. On the bright side of the picture he still ranged the General, " inclined to go forward, if England will but play her part, which I hope she will ". Admiral Hotham was " said to be coming to look at us ", which sounded promising. With " the Squadron under my command " he was fully satisfied. The squadron, at the moment, consisted of eight little frigates, their names ranging from classic romance to English ports and descriptive attributes—H.M.S. *Speedy, Tartar, Inconstant, Southampton, Lowestoffe, Meleager, Romulus, Ariadne. . . .* In three of their captains, Hallowell, Fremantle and Cockburn, he had old friends. The Genoese authorities had begun to be very angry, " but that does not matter. . . . It seems almost a trial between us who shall be first tired—they of complaining, or me of answering them." He disregarded a warning that it would not, perhaps, be wise for him to land there at present. The capture of a Leghorn vessel or two would stop the Leghorn trade. The chief anxiety in London seemed to be lest the Dey of Algiers should be alienated. " But, Sir," he invoked Sir Gilbert Elliot, " is England to give up the almost certainty of finishing this war with honour, to the fear of offence to such beings ? "

The dark side of the picture kept him awake at nights, in a ship nearly as crank and in need of a refit as her Captain. After long days of ceaseless vigilance in heavy weather he had formed the disagreeable habit of waking suddenly with a most disquieting sensation, " as if a girth were buckled taut over my breast ", and staying awake—remembering that owners of neutral vessels might sue a Captain in the Navy successfully, remembering that Hotham, the best heart in the world, needed a new head, and hated " this co-operation ". His " good " eye began to trouble him. For ten days, in August, he was almost blind and in great pain. The strain of entertaining foreign officers who considered only his rank, not his pay, was having its effect upon his purse as well as his constitution. From Norfolk, Brother William, who believed that " the Brigadier " must be very rich by now, suggested the purchase of a desirable property at Tofts, now in the market. Nelson, who shared in all prizes with his squadron, replied that he had as yet seen more French shot than gold. He had another personal worry, which was an ever-present source of irritation. His servant, Frank Lepée, who had followed him up the dreadful green reaches of the San Juan river on his first expedition, would have to go. Ten months of reprimand and promises of amendment had dragged their weary course. The family circle, with whom the faithful sailor servant was a popular and picturesque figure, would expect an explanation. He achieved this in the least possible words—" Parted with Frank for drunkenness, and when so, mad; never will keep a drunkard another hour." Tom Allen, one of the Burnham Thorpe lads who had volunteered for the *Agamemnon*, was promoted to be what he proudly called " wally-de-sham ". He was black-haired, stunted, uncouth, entirely illiterate, and never wrong, but he knew his capacity : Nelson endured him for seven years. (" That beast Allen has left behind, or lost, all my papers. . . . I asked him, in the boat, for my red case, as I did not see it. His answer was, ' Sir, I put it in the stern locker.' I then desired him to take particular care in handling the case up the side, when he knew perfectly well he had not put it in the boat. . . . Huzza ! Huzza ! P.S., Allen is returned with my case.") Since it did not occur to Nelson to attribute his symptoms to accumulated fatigue and irregular meals snatched amidst the writing of " difficult " letters, he resorted unwillingly to the doctors, who said that he ought to be on shore for a month or two, " without the thoughts of service ". They prescribed a course of the waters of Pisa, which closely resembled those of Bath. But the harassed figure of Horatio Nelson, in a faded uniform, was not destined to wander, in Italian autumn weather, on a daisied plot covering

19

holy earth, below a Leaning Tower, beside slow waters reflecting a small perfect chapel dedicated to the Madonna who protects sailors. The French fleet was said to be coming out of Toulon, bound for the Archipelago, in which case there was another good chance for Hotham, or should they, as Nelson hoped, be bound for Genoa, to save their convoy, " rest assured they shall never do it as long as *Agamemnon* is above water ".

A small successful action on August 26 by " part of my Squadron "—actually six out of his eight frigates—made him feel " better every way ". De Vins had sent him word that provisions and ammunition had arrived at Alassio, a place occupied by the enemy. Within an hour of Nelson's appearance he had captured a National corvette, two galleys, one large gunboat and six or seven lesser vessels, one fully laden. Some enemy cavalry fired on his boats from the shore, but without killing or wounding anyone in his boarding parties. His sole casualty was little Hoste, who, in charge of a small boat, cut out a vessel loaded with ammunition, but broke his leg falling down her scuttle. Hoste, however, did not spend long picturing " the seat on the starboard side of Papa " at the family dinner-table in Norfolk, perhaps occupied by his next brother. He rather enjoyed his spell in the sick-bay, as Captain Nelson came down so often to see him. He was soon on crutches, loudly singing his favourite " Dearest Peg ", and a ship's company, dying with laughter at his efforts, decided that this boy had been born lucky, and began to entertain a partly superstitious affection for him. The capture of the corvette had pleased the men of the *Agamemnon*, for they all recognised *La Résolve* as " the long black polacca ship which came alongside the *Sans Culotte* on the 13th of July, and outsails us all ".

The next expedition of " part of my Squadron " was not so successful. On their passage to cut off a ship from Oneglia, Lieutenants Andrews and Spicer, in two small galleys, fell in with three tall Turkish merchantmen, who opened fire. One Turk was carried, but the other two got into Genoa, with six million pounds in hard cash. Nelson had to record—" My gallant Officers and men, after a long contest, were obliged to retreat ; and it is with the greatest pain that I have to render so long a list of killed and wounded." As September wore on and he began to despair of getting the Admiral to move, or the General into action, suddenly de Vins appeared to announce that his troops had carried an enemy outpost in the mountains, that they were now within half musket shot of some other point, which, if possible, he meant to attack, and that he was now going to the advanced post. The moment he knew that he had the transports necessary, he would lead his troops to larger encounters, with no doubt of success. He withdrew, and nothing further happened. His latest difficulty was whispered to be " the non-co-operation of the British Fleet ". He complained " heavily " of never seeing the Admiral. Nelson, in whose letters the words " frivolous " and " excuses " had begun to appear, at once went down the coast, as far as Nice, and sounded and examined every port. On his return he offered to land five thousand men, bag and baggage, with their field-pieces, and to ensure their safe convoys. The General, in reply, produced another scheme, which he considered preferable. The only drawback to it was that it entailed " a small degree of assistance from Admiral Hotham ". In his elaborate report, contrasting the bays of San Remo and Vado, to the detriment of the former, he quoted the lamented English Admiral Matthews, active here during the winter of 1745–46. So as not to leave him what he called " a 21 loop-hole ", Nelson wrote to Hotham, asking for transports, more frigates and at least one 74. He had hopes of the effects of Mr. Drake's appointment to reside at the headquarters of the Austrian Army, but, as he told Uncle Suckling, " My situation with this Army has convinced me, by ocular demonstration, of the futility of Continental Alliances." De Vins too wrote to Hotham, but only to say how much he and his staff appreciated the judgment, abilities and activity of Captain Nelson, and also the discernment of the British Commander-in-Chief in having made choice of so zealous an officer to co-operate with them. Mr. Drake duly forwarded this testimony to Lord Grenville, Secretary of State for Foreign Affairs, and for a space nothing more was heard of a complaint which had made the commander of the co-operating British squadron very angry indeed. In mid-October he went to see his Admiral, who was lying quiet in Leghorn roads, in the belief that the armies were unlikely to move until the spring, and that wholesale desertions in the Toulon fleet were keeping the enemy in port. Six of the line and eight frigates had got out of Toulon, and were said to be gone to the West Indies, but Hotham, content so long as month after month slipped past without any losses, let a fortnight elapse before he parted with equal numbers to pursue them.

The military action which Nelson had so long desired did

take place that year, although the season was so far advanced, but it was not engendered by the Allies. The first week of November 1795 was bitterly cold. In the Alpes Maritîmes, after north wind, the first snows of the winter had fallen, followed by frost. Austrian soldiers were said to be dying at their posts in the mountains. In the French camp, General Kellerman was reported to be going round every post daily, saying all that he could to encourage his troops. As both armies were strongly entrenched, the competition seemed to be which could endure hardships longest. De Vins, in a very bad state of health, had temporarily relinquished his command to General Count Wallis. For some time the Austrians had complained of enemy gunboats harassing their camp near Loano, fourteen miles west of Vado Bay. Nelson had done all he could. He had written to the Commander of the newly joined Neapolitan flotilla, who preferred to lie in Savona Mole. He had kept a frigate at anchor near Pietra, and persevered in doing so, until, as he indignantly pointed out, two of His Majesty's ships were very nearly lost. On November 7, being compelled by the weather to remove this defence, he had ordered a couple of brigs to cruise off Cape Noli. In accordance with his expectations, both were blown off their stations. The *Flora* eventually reappeared in Leghorn, but with the close of the year he still had no news of the *Speedy*. He had promised the ailing General that the moment he heard of an attack he would come round to the bay and give every assistance in his power. He had forwarded suggestions for a series of alarm signals.

On the night of November 10, while the *Agamemnon* lay at single anchor in Vado Bay, ready to proceed at the first sound of an enemy gun, the boats of *La Brune*, a French frigate of 26 guns, crept out of Genoa, attended by several privateers. An Austrian commissary, travelling to Vado Bay with £10,000 sterling, pay for de Vins's troops, was known to be spending the night at an inn in the small town of Voltri, nine miles east of Genoa. On that wild and bitter winter's night a landing-party of about three hundred from *La Brune* took the neutral post, unopposed and slenderly guarded, robbed the commissary, and seized the corn and flour magazines. Next day, flushed with triumph and rich in booty, their captain was publicly enlisting men for his army in the streets of Genoa. On the 13th about seven hundred were embarked, to sail under his convoy, to attack a strong post between Voltri and Savona. There a detachment of the French

N

army was to join them and the Genoese peasantry were to be incited to insurrection.

Nelson found himself "in a cleft stick". Mr. Drake, having put his wife and nursery on the road to Milan, was calling with all his might and main for the return of the *Agamemnon* to Genoa. De Vins agreed that the sailing of this expedition must at all costs be prevented. Nelson weighed, and made sail along the shore to the eastward, anchored the same night within Genoa mole, and there did the only thing possible in the circumstances—laid the *Agamemnon* across the harbour's mouth so that no French ship could leave the port. He was aware that while he was in this position he covered the Bochetta Pass (the only possible retreat for de Vins and a force of between eight and ten thousand, should they be worsted in an attack), but he also knew that by leaving Vado he was giving the enemy gunboats their chance to plague the Austrian left flank. He regretted that the *Agamemnon* could not be cut in two.

For several dark late November days he received no certain news. The weather was "so very bad that neither sails, nor ships nor people could remain at sea very long". For ten days, "very anxious and uneasy", he hoped against hope that accounts of a defeat, after a grand enemy attack near Loana, on the 23rd were exaggerated. Hotham had retired to Naples, and Goodall— a greater loss—much hurt at not having been chosen to succeed him, was on the first stages of a journey which was to end in permanent survey of the placidities of Teignmouth. Sir John Jervis, "who I understand is a man of business", had not yet arrived, and Sir Hyde Parker, in temporary command, had by now deprived Nelson of all but one of his frigates. By December 4 he knew the bitter truth.

> "The Austrians, by all accounts, did not stand firm. The French, half naked, were determined to conquer or die. General de Vins, from ill-health, as he says, gave up the command in the middle of the Battle, and from that moment not a soldier stayed at his post. . . . It was 'Devil take the hindmost.' . . . The Austrians ran eighteen miles without stopping, the Men without any arms whatsoever, Officers without soldiers, Women without assistance. Thus has ended my campaign."

On the same day he added a postscript to a letter to Brother William, begun a fortnight earlier. "I am on my way to Leghorn to refit. The campaign is finished by the defeat of the Austrians, and the French are in possession of Vado Bay." If he should fall in with the French squadron, which was now ready for sea again at Toulon, and with troops embarked, he thought the situation of the *Agamemnon* would be very precarious. " My Ship and Ship's Company are worn out, but the folks at Home do not feel for us." Actually, folks at home were beginning to hear vaguely of his exertions. An article in the *Gentleman's Magazine* for the following February, dealing with the nomenclature of H.M. ships, mentioned that the men of a certain 64 on the Mediterranean station, disliking classical titles, had renamed the *Bellerophon* the " Bully Ruffian ", the *Polyphemus*, " Polly Infamous ", and their own *Agamemnon*, " Eggs and Bacon ".

No untoward incident such as Nelson feared disturbed his passage to Leghorn, and at that port he learnt news of great interest to him. Sir John Jervis had arrived at San Fiorenzo from Spithead, in the *Lively* frigate, on November 27, " to the great joy of some, and sorrow of others ".

6

He had met Sir John Jervis once, years ago, but the chance *rencontre* was not one which the new Commander-in-Chief would be likely to remember. It had taken place in the dimness of the Treasury Passage of the House of Commons. The Member for Yarmouth had recognised an old messmate, from Captain Locker's singular habit of scanning a scene through an eye-glass fitted to the head of his cane. Sir John had stopped, and Captain Locker had begged leave to present his young *élève*, Captain Nelson.

Sir John Jervis, in his sixty-third year, had a reputation not altogether enviable. He was credited with a heart of stone, a most discerning nose for inefficiency, a grim turn of humour, an ungovernable temper and a tongue which did not spare even those of elevated station and birth. Professionally, his prestige stood high: he had a record of distinguished service in the Seven Years' War, the War of American Independence, and as Commander-in-Chief in the West Indies. Romance had touched his career with her wing. At the age of twenty-four, he had carried the dying message of General Wolfe (an officer who esteemed him) from the Heights of Abraham to a lady in a drawing-room in a London square. From visits to St. Petersburg, Stockholm, Copenhagen, Lübeck, and particularly Brest and L'Orient, he had brought home a valuable note-book, and proficiency in the French tongue. But the fleet which the *Agamemnon*, " as fit as a rotten ship can be ", joined on January 15, 1796, was not a happy one. On his arrival, the new Chief had

begun without loss of time the inculcation of a system of rigid
discipline and curtailment of customary privileges, far from
agreeable to the majority of his captains, and so much resented
that, four years later, the toast, " May the discipline of the
Mediterranean never be introduced into the Channel Fleet ", was
endorsed by a naval wife, " in full coterie ", with the rider,
" May his next glass of wine choke the Wretch ! "

He was an ugly but not insignificant-looking man, of middle
height, very broad shouldered. His strongly marked features
were of the gnarled variety, and his members seemed designed
for a taller person. He came of hard, sound Midland stock, of
old family, bitterly impoverished, and had learnt his first lessons
in a grammar school by the cold waters of Trent. A move to
Greenwich, in his twelfth year, on his father's appointment as
Solicitor to the Admiralty and Treasurer of Greenwich Hospital,
had proved fatal to schemes for his following his father's profession. Within a few months he had run away to sea. He was
brought back, but early next year obtained a grudging consent
to his entering the Royal Service, and went afloat in a ship
ordered to the Antilles. His stern parent, having given him £20
in farewell, three years later dishonoured a bill drawn by him for
the same sum. To the end of a long life, the Earl of St. Vincent
never forgot or forgave the humiliating penury of his early years
at sea. He had then disposed of his pay tickets (at a heavy
discount), sold his bed and slept on the deck, left the mess to
which he belonged, mended his top clothes and washed out his
underclothing.

Nelson, after his reception by this character on January 19,
1796, was greeted by a disgruntled brother officer with the
wondering words : " You did just as you pleased in Lord Hood's
time, the same in Admiral Hotham's, and now again with Sir
John Jervis ! It makes no difference to you who is Commander-
in-Chief." To this outburst, Nelson, fresh from a surprising first
interview with his new Chief, returned " a pretty strong answer ",
before sailing for his old station off Genoa. He was satisfied that
in Sir John Jervis he had, at any rate, met a man who meant to
act with vigour. For the Mediterranean fleet there was to be no
more peaceful lying at anchor in Fiorenzo Bay, or skulking
amongst the Balearic Islands.

He had taken care, as soon as possible, to mention Captain
Locker's kind remembrances. But whether or not Sir John
Jervis recollected their previous meeting did not matter, for he

had at once shown himself friendly, and made the offer of the
St. George, of 80 guns, or the *Zealous*, a 74. Nelson had respectfully declined either, whereupon Sir John, deserting that subject
abruptly, had demanded his knowledge, and even advice, on
several matters upon which, in Nelson's opinion, others in the
fleet should already have been able to inform the new Admiral.
At the end of a very long and interesting sitting, Jervis had
regretted that he had at present no means of giving Captain
Nelson a squadron equal to his merits, and then asked if he would
object to serving under him when promoted. Nelson's reply had
been that if the *Agamemnon* was ordered home before his flag
arrived, he had many reasons for wishing to go to England.
Should his flag arrive (which he could hardly expect) and the
war continue, he would be proud to hoist it under the command
of Sir John Jervis. He took his leave under the impression that
Sir John was writing to the Admiralty that day, to ask that, if
the fleet was kept there, his flag might be sent to the Mediterranean.
But, cautious after many disappointments, all he would admit in
letters home was that, as yet, he appeared to stand well with his
new Chief. He did not have to wait long for the appearance of
Sir John and the fleet off Toulon, and after his second interview
with the Admiral, in a February blizzard, sounded a more
confident note:

> " Sir John Jervis, from his manner, as I plainly perceive, does not
> wish me to leave this station. He seems at present to regard me more
> as an associate than a subordinate Officer; for I am acting without any
> orders. . . . He asked me if I had heard any more of my promotion.
> I told him ' No '. His answer was, ' You must have a larger Ship, for
> we cannot spare you, either as Captain or Admiral.' "

The French were making great preparations for opening their
spring campaign in Italy. Sardinia was in open rebellion. On
March 9, Nelson, who did not know when he had been so ill at
sea, stood for Leghorn, to get his damages repaired. The worst
north-easterly gale which he had ever experienced in the Mediterranean had stove in the stern of the *Agamemnon*, carried away
her starboard quarter-gallery and sprung her main topmast.
The coastline of the Riviera di Levante, under deep snow, was
intensely cold. Through Paris streets deep in slush, General
Buonaparte, aged twenty-six, was arriving late to hurry through
a civil marriage ceremony with a graceful widow. His choice,
like that of Nelson nine years past, was an elegant, neurotic
West India lady, some undiscovered months his senior, who had

borne to his predecessor, but by whom he was to have no children. No other points of resemblance existed between the romances.

Two leaders who were to know each other's names well, both at work, in hard weather, to achieve a remarkable personal touch with sorely tried men under their command, were drawing together. On March 27, Buonaparte, at Nice, issued his first inspiring order to troops whom he found sullen and half-starved :

" Soldiers ! you are naked, ill-nourished. The Government owes you much, but can do nothing for you. Your patience, the courage which has carried you amongst these rocks, do you honour, but give you no advantage, no *éclat*. I will lead you into the most fertile plains in the world, where you shall find great towns, rich provinces—within your grasp, Glory, Honour, Riches ! Soldiers of Italy ! shall you be found wanting in constancy, in courage ? "

In the *Agamemnon*, Mr. Midshipman Hoste was meanwhile writing home :

" Our Squadron at present consists of two Sail-of-the-Line and four Frigates, but is to be increased in the summer, when we shall not want for amusement, I make no doubt, as our Commodore does not like to be idle.

" I suppose your curiosity is excited by the word *Commodore* Nelson. It gives me infinite pleasure to be able to relieve it by informing you that our good Captain has had this additional mark of distinction conferred upon him, which, I daresay you will agree with me, his merit richly deserves. His Broad Pendant is now flying; therefore I must beg my dear father to draw an additional cork."

24

This appointment had been made on the day of Buonaparte's Nice order.

CHAPTER VII

1796–1797
(*ætat* 37–38)

"NELSON'S PATENT BRIDGE
FOR BOARDING FIRST-RATES"

I

THE end of a chapter came on June 11, 1796, when Commodore Nelson shifted his broad pendant from the *Agamemnon* to the *Captain*—a 74. Orders had come from England for a second-rate and the worst ship-of-the-line to go home with a convoy. There could be no doubt that the *Agamemnon* must go, and for a week Nelson seemed likely to go with her. However, Captain J. S. Smith of the *Captain* confessed to a very weak state of health and great anxiety to get home, whereas Commodore Nelson assured Sir John Jervis, on June 3, that in spite of insomnia and chest trouble, to tell the truth, when he was actively employed, he was " not so bad ", and on June 5, " Having slept since my last letter, indeed, I cannot bear the thoughts of leaving your command." In the end, he had four hours in which to " change all my matters ".

His last days in the *Agamemnon* were, with a single exception, entirely depressing. Throughout May, in strange changeable weather, amongst fogs, brilliant sun, heavy seas and sudden stark calms, his business was to forward to his Admiral news of uninterrupted French successes in Italy. He reported Buonaparte's defeat of the Allies at the battle of Montenotte on April 12, in the gorges of Millesimo, at the village of Dego and at the bridge of Lodi. Sardinia had made peace; Naples was preparing to desert; Spain was getting ready; Genoa had begun to be openly insolent ("Commodore Nelson is very much surprised that, whenever he approaches any Town belonging to the Genoese Government, they fire shot at him"). Milan presented her keys to the conqueror, and on May 15 Buonaparte rode into the capital of Lombardy through the Porta Romana on a little white horse. Nelson mentioned without comment that the first pictures of Italy were being sent to Paris " to decorate the Palace of the Louvre ", and that a demand had been made upon Rome for " the famous statue of the Apollo Belvidere ". Since his last hopes of assisting the Austrians to retake Vado Bay, or of landing English troops at St. Remo, were now washed out, and he knew that the French were in possession of every supply they needed, he enclosed a note to Jervis, asking that, if he could be in any way more active or useful, his squadron might be recalled, even if this meant that he must strike his distinguishing pendant. Before his Admiral could receive this letter, however, he had the satisfaction of a last small successful action in the *Agamemnon*. Under the guns of Oneglia, on May 30, his squadron captured the siege-train *en route* to Buonaparte at Mantua. His prize list included two gunboats and five transports, his casualty list one killed, three wounded, masts, sails and rigging a little cut, but of no material consequence, while " I have got ", he added happily, " the charts of Italy sent by the Directory to Buonaparte, also Maillebois' *Wars in Italy*, Vauban's *Attack and Defence of Places*, and Prince Eugene's *History*. If Buonaparte is ignorant, the Directory, it would appear, wish to instruct him; pray God, he may remain ignorant." He kept the Vauban when forwarding the remainder of Buonaparte's library to Sir John, since he believed that the Admiral would not, at present, be wishing to study that volume. He added, as postscript to his " List of prizes taken between the 1st of June 1794 and 1st of June 1796 ", a note that three years and three weeks had now elapsed since his sailing from Spithead in his first ship-of-the-line.

Inevitably he saw the last of the *Agamemnon* with mixed feelings. Her ground tier was giving way. Her appearance, which confirmed his assertion that not an ounce of paint had been sent to him for many months, was, he bitterly said, that of a tub floating on the water. (The last rope sent to him for repairs had been a mere insult, " without exception the worst I ever saw. The twice-laid we make on board is far preferable; indeed I never saw any so bad in my life.") She could have stayed out here, without a thorough refit, for another three months, but not for another winter. Still, as he watched her fade from view on June 18, from Fiorenzo Bay, with his new First Lieutenant, Mr. Edward Berry, by his side, the sum of his reflections was that although the *Diadem* (another 64) was certainly in better plight, yet in point of sailing the *Agamemnon* was much superior. All her officers had been changed, with the exception of the Master and Maurice Suckling (now heir to Woodton Hall, bent on marriage, and carrying home to Norfolk many small parcels from her late Captain). Hinton and Andrews had been promoted for their services in her. He was sorry to lose them, but had already every reason to be satisfied with the strict attention paid to his orders by his new First Lieutenant, who had the countenance of a poet, but the air and manners of an efficient officer and a gentleman. Neither could tell, as they watched the last of the "old and worn-out *Agamemnon*" from the quarter-deck of the *Captain*, on a midsummer's day of 1796, that she still had ten years' life in her and that Sir Edward Berry, newly appointed to her command, would join Lord Nelson's fleet off Cadiz in October 1805, just in time for the *Agamemnon* to be present at Trafalgar.

2

"If I hoist my Flag here," wrote his old pupil to Captain Locker, a few days later, "the *Goliath*, I fancy, will be my Ship!" She was new-coppered, but according to rumour, wretchedly manned and worse disciplined. "However," said he, "the latter I don't mind, if I have but good stuff to work upon." (Brother William received almost a duplicate of this sentence: "I don't mind, if I have but the stuff to work upon.") He had his eye upon a Captain Ralph Willett Miller as his Flag-Captain, a very solid-looking person, born in New York thirty-five years past, of a Loyalist family, educated in England, went to sea aged sixteen, three times wounded in action, served under Admirals Barrington, Rodney and Hood; a married man, a father. . . .

The Captain's log of the *Captain*, from the day that Nelson took possession of her in 1796, tells a tale of continual effort, of perpetual motion, under circumstances generally disadvantageous and sometimes heart-breaking. But the latest postscript of a Commander-in-Chief with marked leadership qualities had been "Go on, and prosper". He went on. A blockade of Genoa had to be proclaimed, and very soon of Leghorn, for late in June French troops seized that neutral port so suddenly that only remarkable exertions on the part of Captain Fremantle got away the English shipping and residents. The Pollards were just in time to get on board a French prize, with the best of their furniture and little Hoste, whom Mrs. Pollard had been nursing through malaria. Lady Elliot and her children, returning from a holiday at the Baths of Lucca, embarked with nothing except the clothes in which they had happened to be standing up when Fremantle appeared to hurry them down by-streets to the *Dolphin*.

Another British family, who had fled at top speed from Florence (and arrived at the Consulate to jettison two expensive coaches with scarcely a pang, in their relief to discover that a squadron of the fleet was there), claimed permanent attention from the young officer in charge of the evacuation. The Wynnes were perhaps hardly recognisable as an English family, since Mr. Richard Wynne (of Welsh extraction, son of a passionate Venetian mother and husband of a neurasthenic French lady) had despairingly sold the last of his property in Lincolnshire soon after the birth of his fifth successive daughter, and had since been expending the result in the best society on the Continent. He was an attractive, futile man of two-and-fifty, of the type sent to the guillotine in France, and his *suite* usually included, besides his Catholic wife, grown-up daughter (unhappily married to an Italian) and four schoolgirl daughters, some nineteen dependents, exclusive of dogs and horses. Miss Betsy Wynne, a small and fairy-like creature, chattering French and Italian, but able to remember England, met in Captain Fremantle of His Britannic Majesty's Navy probably the first straightforward and efficient man of her life. This was fatal to her peace of mind, and before he had left his charges in safety at Bastia, Fremantle too had lost his heart. The situation of the young lovers seemed desperate, for Sir John Jervis had often announced that " an officer who marries is damned for the Service ", and had been capable of asking the First Lord to order instantly " to the East or West Indies, to cool " a Captain who had rashly plighted troth with a naval store-keeper's daughter at Gibraltar (" a very bad party for him "). The Commander-in-Chief, however, took an unexpected view of romance when personified by a young lady of good physique, blood and fortune. He dubbed the decorative Wynnes " the Amiables ", invited them all on board his flagship, and sheltered them under a benevolent wing for many months. The result was invaluable to biographers of Nelson, for both Miss Betsy and Miss Jenny Wynne kept journals, preserved by their descendants. 3

From no other source is it possible to appreciate, so exactly, the impression made by Jervis's fleet on an audience to whom Britain's Navy had been previously nothing but a name. Its strong, fine frigates appeared to the bright eyes of these young ladies so remarkably clean. Its ships-of-the-line were " castles " (though the *Victory*, the same size as the *Britannia*, and in the highest order, was possessed of disappointingly smaller and less comfortable " apartments "). On the decks of the *Lively* and the *Inconstant*, " most elegantly dres't up, all the guns being removed ", they enjoyed famous suppers after dancing to the strains of crack bands, and the officers attendant always kind, gay and civil, " doing the honors so well ", under such difficult circumstances, seemed qualified to win everybody's heart. All were, at first sight, " equally complaissant and good-natured ". " They live like brothers together, and give all they have." A tiny, childish candle is held up to the rugged countenances of many of Nelson's daily companions. Foley kept a good table; his ship was " a little town—you get all your desires in it ". The penurious Cockburn was sprightly and fashionable, Saumarez the glass of fashion, Bowen could be satirical about a spoilt beauty, Drinkwater was the most agreeable society imaginable; General de Burgh, always writing angry letters, was, by general consent, always wrong. And since the scene was set in real life, on a closer view less happy characters flitted across it—Lieutenants, little, starved-looking and anxious, chattering and forward, married and miserable; Captains, stingy, dark and brutal; military gentlemen drinking remarkably hard. . . . There are brilliant *vignettes* of a convoy at sea—the *Inconstant* coming close enough to the *Achilles* for her Captain to roar out that he was in a great rage at having to run away from the French; " Captain F. going to the Fleet ", waving farewell (while the motion of the ship was terrible); " Old Admiral Jervis " bowing and smiling from his stern gallery to young ladies, " a curiosity in his Fleet ". Naturally, junior Captains and Lieutenants absorbed most of the attention of diarists in their teens. To such, the difference in age between Commodore Nelson, who was thirty-eight, and Admiral Jervis, who was sixty-two, was not discernible. And except that " the noise and crashing of the guns was most tiring ", and that when a frigate was cleared for action the ladies dining in the gun-room found the atmosphere induced somnolence, there are few references to the fact that they were guests of a squadron engaged in a death grapple for the possession of the Mediterranean.

3

After the departure of Captain Fremantle's squadron from Leghorn with the refugees, Buonaparte made a dramatic appearance, on a flying visit, took possession of the house of Mr. Udney, Consul, and at dinner with the Grand Duke asked to be shown the road to Rome. Nelson wrote to Sir Gilbert Elliot, in hopes that an attack on Leghorn by troops from Corsica might be engineered, but the Viceroy's reply was that the landing of small parties of Corsicans in the French service in the island was

becoming a menace and must be stopped, by the seizure of Elba.
Nelson successfully conveyed troops, under the command of his
old acquaintance, Major Duncan, from Bastia to Porto Ferrajo
and returned to blockade Leghorn and Genoa. It became his
duty to seek a second and less pleasant interview with the Doge,
and send to the Serene Republic letter upon letter complaining
of the detention of bullocks, purchased for His Britannic Majesty's
Fleet by Mr. Heatly, Agent Victualler. Last November, when
the date had arrived for the election of a new Doge, he had nourished hopes of the election of a firmer character, more kindly
disposed towards English interests. But a thing unprecedented
had occurred. Signor Giacomo Maria Brignole had been requested, in a period of extreme stress, to continue in office. The
French were to make the same request after their abolition of the
Genoese constitution in the following May, and keep him for six
months in nominal power. Nelson's efforts to persuade an
opportunist to remain at least neutral were vain, and on September 18 a letter of the Vicereine of Corsica described the hurried
appearance of the Commodore to consult with her husband on the
necessity of " the seizure of the island of Capraja, thirty miles
distant, which belongs to the Genoese and has been a nuisance to
us ever since we had Corsica ". This resolution was the result of
what she described as " a little fracas between Commodore
Nelson and the Genoese ".

" He had lost a boat in the night, and sent one out in the morning to
look into the little harbour to see whether it could be found; and he
told the crew, if the French battery, by which they must pass, fired upon
them, they might take a small vessel that lay close to the battery, which
was unloading stores for the French, but not to touch it unless they
fired. Nelson's boat was no sooner under the guns of the battery than
they fired, and the crew took the vessel and brought it off. The Genoese
then began to fire on our ships, and continued to do so, from seven in
the morning till one o'clock, without one shot hitting. Commodore
Nelson returned three shot only, to the battery, and none to the Genoese,
whereas he could have half destroyed the town."

On sending in a flag of truce to know what had occasioned
such conduct towards His Majesty's ships, and receiving the
answer that the port of Genoa was shut to the English and a
fuller reply should be forwarded in a few days, Nelson had not
lingered longer. The expedition against Capraja sailed on the
night following his arrival at Bastia, and Lady Elliot, from
her terrace, without the aid of a spy-glass, was able to follow the

progress of a combined operation considered by Nelson the best conducted in his experience.

The Vicereine's letters home were stoic. She described Corsica as " still as the sea ; we ride every evening till nine o'clock by moonlight, and have no more palpitation, when we meet a man with a gun, than in England a peasant with a stick ". But a fortnight later, when, after eight months' silence, despatches from London arrived for the Viceroy, her husband's brow grew very grave, and when Nelson made his second sudden appearance at the palace with great glass folding doors, on the night of September 29, the atmosphere was high tragedy. He came in haste from Leghorn, to protect Corsica from a French landing. Sir John Jervis had appointed him a Commodore, First Class, on August 11, and the sterling Miller was now his Captain. He had, on hearing of the rumoured French expedition, transferred his broad pendant to the *Diadem*, and sent the *Captain* down to Ajaccio, under the command of Berry. On his arrival at Bastia he had received orders from his Admiral, labelled " most secret ", which were indeed a thunderbolt. News of the decision of the Cabinet to " withdraw the blessings of the British Constitution from the people of Corsica " and the British fleet from the Mediterranean had reached Sir Gilbert Elliot and Sir John Jervis simultaneously. Only Sir John received part of these summary instructions without strong emotion. He had for some time considered that for England to retain Corsica, when at war with Spain, would not be possible. He now looked forward to an early meeting with the large but rotten Spanish fleet. To Nelson, all the instructions were " sackcloth and ashes ". There was a supreme irony in the fact that he, who had been chiefly respon- sible for the capture of Bastia, should be the officer ordered to conduct its evacuation. In London, the authorities had not yet decided whether his loss of an eye at the siege of Calvi constituted, financially, the loss of a limb. He had not forgotten, and never would forget, the unparalleled exertions of his seamen landed, the loss of Serocold and young Moutray, the Lion Sun and the fever. He had long since outgrown his love at first sight for the rust-red rocks and deep blue waters of a promised isle. Once his orders were digested, he was coolly prepared, if necessary, to " knock down Bastia ". But that the fleet should leave the Mediterranean seemed to him a sheer disgrace. " They at home do not know what the Fleet is capable of performing—anything and everything. Of all Fleets I ever saw, I never beheld one, in

point of officers and men, equal to Sir John Jervis's, who is a
Commander-in-Chief to lead them to glory." He had also, in
three years, conceived a strong possessive affection for the Mediterranean—that extraordinary compound of fickle seas, blazing
flowers, palm-crowned crags, ancient towers, turning a ruined
shoulder to warm sun in midwinter, and bleached towns, famous
for two thousand years for their gaiety and the cure of chest
complaints. "Indeed, this Country agrees much better with
my constitution than England." He foresaw that, shuddering
amongst what he called "the cold damps" of home, his fancy
would return to villages predominantly of the shade known as
"Naples yellow", couched amongst silvery olive-groves, under
lavender skies; to happy returns to quaysides, canopied by stars,
where music sounded from every open window; to autumn mists
parting at 10 a.m. to display Genoa the Superb; to the glow of
Vesuvius, above a ship-of-the-line, becalmed in full moonlight in
the Bay of Naples. . . .

He found Sir Gilbert "low and distressed". The Viceroy
repeated that he believed Corsica to be at the moment in a state
of most perfect loyalty to the King and affection for the British
Nation. His astonishment and disappointment at his orders
were profound. For two years now he had made unrelaxed and
even enthusiastic efforts to induce the natives of an island which
possessed features in common with the land of his birth "to take
an interest in roads, bridges, fountains and other public improvements". The embittered and theatrical quarrels between the
Corsicans friendly to England, whose thirst for place, and universal vanity, were incredible, had from the first made his life a
burden. In the patriot General Paoli, who had now retired to
London, disgusted with the favour shown to his compatriot,
M. Pozzo di Borgo, his interest had for some time been at a low
ebb. But his feeling of responsibility for those of the natives
who had committed their families, property and lives to his care
was poignant, and he resented acutely that no terms could be
made to protect them from their pro-French neighbours when
the landing, now inevitable, took place. He announced his
determination of removing all troops and stores no further than
Elba. Throughout the night Nelson and he conferred, keeping
in view the possibility of "an attack from a very superior Fleet ".
The evacuation was not to be announced until arrangements
were complete, but obviously the appearance of transports,
in large numbers, at Bastia, Calvi and Ajaccio was certain

to arouse the suspicions of a people hereditarily prone to intrigue.

Sir Gilbert believed that the number of French royalists and Corsicans whom he was bound to remove from the vengeance to come would not exceed six hundred. His own intention was to go directly to Naples, since Nelson agreed with him that no chance must be lost to keep the King, who had already made an armistice, from proceeding to a peace with France. Lady Elliot, Miss Congleton and the children (with the exception of George, now a midshipman) must return to Scotland at once. The prospect for the father of a family was not reassuring. Nelson offered the *Gorgon*, one of his fastest frigates, adding that if His Excellency wanted another ship, he must, and would, spare one. Sir Gilbert said heavily that the *Gorgon* would suffice, and that he would provision her. The childless Commodore could only repeat his confidence in Captain Dixon (who should be told, under all circumstances, to run and not fight), and suggest that Lady Elliot should be begged on no account to quit the " coach "—the apartment near the stern of the frigate usually occupied by the Captain. It was arranged that the *Gorgon* should sail from Gibraltar within the week. The morning of the 21st was settled as the earliest possible date for the embarkation of the Bastia garrison. With the assurance that, as far as his powers and abilities went, he could be relied upon, the Commodore then parted from the stricken but still stately Viceroy, to become very busy.

Their next private consultation took place a fortnight later, and after dark, but in a house from which the mistress and children were already gone, and echoing to the sounds of the removal of luggage. No sooner had the Viceroy given official notice to the Municipality of Bastia that the island was to be evacuated, than they had taken the law into their own hands. They had appointed a Committee of Thirty to carry on the government until the French should arrive, sequestered all British property, forbidden any vessel to quit the mole and sent a delegation to the Corsican Generals in the French service at Leghorn. Nelson arrived, this time, by the garden path. He had not waited for the *Diadem* to anchor. He found the situation fully as serious as he had been led to expect, but the Viceroy in typically resolute mood. Sir Gilbert's first request was that some confidential papers might be taken on board the *Diadem* without delay. Although he proceeded to explain that he believed a plot was on foot to seize his person that night (a thing which might easily be effected, since all the British troops except a small guard were in the citadel), he refused to consider a precipitate retreat. He said that he could scarcely blame the Municipality for making what terms they could. He still held that, until they had learnt that they were to be deserted, the bulk of the islanders had been loyal. The influence of a philanthropic master had been appreciated, and Nelson noticed tearful and trembling Corsican members of the household at work to render the eternal farewell of His Britannic Majesty's representative as painless as possible. During the next twenty-four hours he was fortunately too much engaged to reflect upon " miserable anxiety " for the safety of a gentleman of worth and wisdom. From the Viceroy's house he went, through black darkness and wild weather, to General de Burgh, who told him that there were as many hostile armed Corsican as British troops in the citadel, and that he had not a hope of saving any stores, guns or provisions. The gale, still raging, had driven H.M.S. *Southampton* and every transport from their anchors; a privateer was moored across the mole-head, by orders of the Committee, and Corsican musketeers mounted guard at every post. " Commodore Nelson," reported Sir John Jervis to Lord Spencer, " by the firm tone he held, soon reduced these gentlemen to order." His subordinates also were firm. Captain Sutton, of the *Egmont*, having despatched the Commodore's message that he would batter down the town if he noticed the smallest molestation to English property being embarked, took out his watch, held it in his palm and announced that he would give the authorities fifteen minutes in which to make up their minds. " This ", commented Nelson, " was effective." The Corsicans on guard at the mole-head downed muskets and ran; the privateer, having pointed her guns, took no further action, and sixty heavily laden vessels came out of the mole in good order.

By midnight on the 15th the streets of Bastia were silent as the grave. Nelson's suggestion to General de Burgh that the gates of the citadel should be closed, to prevent more French partisans entering, had produced peace, not a riot, as had seemed equally likely. The Viceroy was safe on board *La Minerve*, a French prize frigate, philosophically pondering fresh despatches from Whitehall which told him, if it was too late to counter-order the evacuation of Corsica, to retain Elba. " Wonderful ", commented Nelson. " Do His Majesty's Ministers know their own minds? " Since it was certainly too late, he set heartily to work to save what time, and a very heavy surf, would permit ; an effort which was continued until sunset on the 19th. " Our boats never ceased, night or day." The garrison marched out at midnight, and by 1 a.m. French troops were passing in to the back of the town. " From its blowing a gale," stated Nelson in conclusion, " it was dawn of day before the General and myself went into the barge, not one man being left ashore ; and we took with us the two field pieces brought down to cover our retreat." He stood for Elba, with a fine wind, at 6 a.m. (unaware that the Spanish fleet, consisting of thirty-eight sail-of-the-line and ten frigates, was already abreast of Cape Corse), and before dark was able to announce, " Every man and vessel safely moored in Porto Ferrajo, for its size, the most complete port in the world." The garrisons from Calvi and Ajaccio came in without an accident, within the week, and his arrangements for the Elliot family were as successful.

The Viceroy had vowed, on saying farewell to his wife, " This shall be our last parting. . . . God bless you, my dearest love. If I could hear of your safe arrival at Gibraltar, though I can see no further into your destiny, I should at least be without any immediate burthen on my mind." Actually, the *Gorgon's* worst trials came after leaving Gibraltar, when almost at once she was three times hailed, after dark, within pistol shot, by Spanish frigates. Captain Dixon, " going at a great rate ", gave no answer. A week later, he appeared to explain to Lady Elliot and Miss Congleton that, had not the wind changed just when it did, he must have returned to Lisbon, a prospect considered " shocking " by his audience, as at Gibraltar the news had been that Portugal was making terms with France. Lady Elliot's passage from Bastia to Weymouth occupied eight weeks, and included

" every danger that war and tempests can present—white squalls and black squalls and contrary winds. I never quitted the coach, and lay on two boards, just a month. Two days we spent under the storm-sails ; every sail was torn in pieces at different times, and our masts in continual danger. Even Dixon's face grew pale ; nevertheless, pray tell Nelson that I never was out of my coach, night or day, and got into a state of resignation."

Ten days after her arrival at a Wessex inn, Lady Elliot took roads made dangerous by frost to Bath, where she dined with Lord Hood at 5, Queen Square, and since her host had had the happy idea of asking that " good little woman ", Mrs. Horatio

Nelson, to meet the ex-Vicereine of Corsica, a very stalwart lady
was able to assure a very easily startled one that she was a devout
worshipper of Commodore Nelson. The future Lady Catherine   8
Boileau was safely born, at Minto, on July 2, and her father's
nickname for his "lucky" seventh child, begotten during the
last days of his troubled viceroyalty, was "Princess".

4

"I remember", wrote Nelson to Locker, from the *Captain*,
at sea, on November 5, 1796, "when we quitted Toulon we
endeavoured to reconcile ourselves to Corsica ; now we are content
with Elba—such things are." Worse were to come. When the
fleet arrived at Gibraltar, three weeks later, fears that Admiral
Man had, in defiance of orders, taken his squadron home, became
a certainty. All ideas of a meeting with the combined French
and Spanish fleets in the Mediterranean had to be laid aside by
the infuriated Jervis, and Nelson's next orders were to bring
away the troops from Elba. To a four-line note addressed to
Collingwood, in which he hoped that his friend had heard from
home, and prophesied dire consequences to Man, he scribbled the
postscript, "If we are at anchor, will you dine here at 3 o'clock?"

Collingwood, who had, five years past, concluded a somewhat
slow-paced wooing of a granddaughter of his old Captain (now
Admiral) Roddam, had been on the Mediterranean station, in
command of a 74, for above a year, but the old messmates met
so seldom that Nelson had to enquire by letter such facts as
"How many children have you?" They kept their friendship
in repair by gifts of fresh vegetables and old newspapers, jottings
of the latest dates on which they had heard from home, and on
their rare occasions of leisured encounter (prefaced by Nelson's
"Then we can Talk") they explored every aspect of private
and public affairs. Collingwood's confidence in "my friend
Nelson, whose spirit is equal to all undertakings, and whose
resources are fitted to all occasions", was a steady flame, but
the father of Miss Sarah and Miss May Patience Collingwood had
been shocked by the breakdown, within the year, of the Prince
of Wales's marriage, and could not understand the comment of
his less happily situated contemporary, "What have we to do
with the Prince's private *amours*? The World says there are
faults on both sides : like enough. Thank God, I was not born
in high life." Since he had not been born in high life, had heard   9
nothing more of his promotion, and knew that Sir Gilbert Elliot's

diplomat brother-in-law had been ordered to Paris to open peace
negotiations, one of the questions which two officers high on the
post list had to discuss after dinner on a December day of easterly
gale off Gibraltar was whether Nelson would do well to seek the
interest of newly made but influential friends, all of whom, he
believed, would give him a good character to those in high life at
home—" a public letter of my conduct, as has come under their
knowledge ". The fleet was to leave the Mediterranean, therefore he would probably see no more of their Excellencies the
British Ministers at Genoa, Naples and Leghorn, and the ex-
Viceroy of Corsica. Making such applications was not a very
pleasant business, but " God knows," said Nelson ruefully,
" ambition has no end." He knew that he stood well with Sir
John Jervis, who had done all that he could, and now could but
repeat that Lord Spencer had expressed his sincere desire to give
Commodore Nelson his flag. Sir John had his own troubles.
His frequent recommendations of the very uncommon officers
under his command were beginning, he feared, to give their Lordships the notion that he was " a puffer, like many of my brethren ".
" I never ", he stated coldly, when recommending Captain
Troubridge, " saw him before my arrival at San Fiorenzo, and it
is with great repugnance I say anything to your Lordship about
promotions, knowing how much you must be pressed upon at
home."

All Nelson's letters were written, and all had produced most
kindly response, before the first month had passed of a New Year
which was to bring him such an opportunity of distinguishing
himself as to render them unnecessary. He wrote also, before
he left Gibraltar, to his wife, telling her, " I am going on a most
important Mission, which, with God's blessing, I have little doubt
of accomplishing. It is not a fighting Mission, therefore be not
uneasy." Having hoisted his broad pendant in the *Minerve*, and
taken the *Blanche* in company, he then set out, on December 15,
on his extremely perilous passage up the Mediterranean to save
the Elba garrison.

Five nights later, off Cartagena, amongst fresh gales and
cloudy weather, the *Minerve* and *Blanche* encountered two
Spanish frigates (one of which carried a poop-light), hailed them,
and receiving a defiant answer, commenced action. The *Santa
Sabina*, engaged by the *Minerve*, after losing her mizzen mast,
her main and fore masts, and having a hundred and sixty-four
men killed or wounded, struck her colours. Her Captain, the sole

surviving officer, came on board the *Minerve* to surrender himself and give up his sword. His mien was haughty, even for a Spanish grandee. His swarthy visage of high features, which seemed marked by heredity for misfortune, struck some chord of memory. He introduced himself to Commodore Nelson as Don Jacobo Stuart, great-grandson of James II, one-time Lord High Admiral, and King of England, Scotland and Ireland. Nelson recounted:

"When I hailed the Don and told him, 'This is an English Frigate', and demanded his surrender, or I would fire into him, his answer was noble, and such as became the illustrious family from which he is descended—'This is a Spanish Frigate, and you may begin as soon as you please.' I have no idea of a closer and sharper battle. . . . I asked him several times to surrender, during the Action, but his answer was, 'No, sir; not whilst I have the means of fighting left!'"

The *Santa Sabina* was taken in tow, but three hours later another frigate, after hailing her in Spanish, fired a broadside into her. The *Minerve* cast off her prize and engaged the stranger, who, after three-quarters of an hour's warm action, wore and stood away. Daylight displayed her having joined two Spanish line-of-battle ships and a frigate. By 9.30 a.m. the *Minerve*, with all her masts shot through, and furniture much cut, was being chased, and saw, bearing to the east, a fleet which her commander could only suppose to be that of Spain. The *Santa Sabina* and the *Ceres*, both with prize crews on board, were re-taken, but after dark the enemy quitted the pursuit. "We very nearly", considered Nelson, on Christmas Eve, "escaped visiting a Spanish prison. Two lieutenants and a number of our men are taken, and we have lost near fifty killed and wounded; but 'tis well it's no more." He finished the day by capturing, off the south end of Sardinia, a French privateer, three days out from Marseille, and dictating letters to His Excellency Don Miguel Gaston, Captain General of the Department of Cartagena, and Admiral Don Juan Marino, couched in old chivalrous style.

"Sir,
"The fortune of war put *La Sabina* into my possession after she had been most gallantly defended; the fickle Dame returned her to you with some of my officers and men in her.
"I have endeavoured to make the captivity of Don Jacobo Stuart, her brave Commander, as light as possible; and I trust to the generosity of your Nation for its being reciprocal for the British officers and men.
"I consent, Sir, that Don Jacobo may be exchanged, and at full liberty to serve his King, when Lieutenants Culverhouse and Hardy are delivered into the garrison of Gibraltar."

On the wet afternoon of Christmas Day he arrived at Porto Ferrajo, to fresh troubles. These, however, were not at once evident. At Porto Ferrajo a Military Ball was toward, and Captains Cockburn and Fremantle had promised to send a barge for the Misses Wynne, who had been mentioning the Ball in their prayers, and had made all arrangements to change into their gala at the town house of their friends, the Cantinis. "Commodore Nelson, who was going to take the command of this place", was mentioned in Miss Betsy's carefully kept journal as the leader of the party that "had to trot about in the dirt" of a wet night towards the Theatre of the town, where the Ball was staged amongst very pretty decorations. It was essentially a provincial affair. Captain Woodhouse got "perfectly drunk". The principal Shylock of the place had managed to secure an invitation, several Italian and Corsican ladies, and some French girls, who, imagining that the Misses Wynne understood no language but their own, commented favourably on the unexpected elegance of the English misses. But as Commodore Nelson and the sea-officers of the station, escorting their countrywomen, entered to be formally received by General de Burgh, Commander of the Garrison, the band struck up "See the Conquering Hero comes!" and this was followed by "Rule Britannia". Before 3 a.m. the Commodore had been brought to realise that an arduous action which he had, in the chagrin of losing his prizes, written down as "an unpleasant tale" would be mentioned in the *Gazette*, "and I may venture to say, it was what I know the English like".

Later on the same winter's morning, he found time to visit Mr. Wynne's country house, and intimate to that vacillating displaced person that "as a friend" he would advise him to take the chance of sailing for Naples with Captain Fremantle, who was going there on an undisclosed mission. His troubles began with his call on General de Burgh, who was agreeable as ever, but "under a great embarrassment for want of precise orders". "My instructions," explained Nelson, "both written and verbal, are so clear that it is impossible for me to mistake a tittle of them." Sir John Jervis had sent him to take under his command the seventeen ships stationed at Porto Ferrajo, and to remove all troops and stores lately brought from Corsica. The Artillery and First Regiment of Foot were to be landed at Gibraltar; all other troops, British and foreign, were to be carried to Lisbon. The General replied that he had always been of the opinion that the signature of a peace between Naples and France ought

to be the signal for his quitting Porto Ferrajo.   Now that he was
advised that the British fleet would never again come there, he
believed that the troops under his command could fulfil no useful
object by staying in Elba.   But without written authority from
London, annulling the orders under which he had been sent to
Elba, he could not feel himself justified in taking the responsibility of quitting his post.   Restrained letters began to pass
daily between the embarrassed General and the impatient
Commodore, who declared that whether the troops came or not,
he was going to withdraw all naval stores, and as many ships as
possible.   " The object of our Fleet in future is the defence of
Portugal, and keeping in the Mediterranean the Combined Fleets."
He was on tenterhooks lest he should miss a fleet action under
the flag of Jervis, who had announced that his first meeting with
the enemy should be no " half-begotten " battle.   Presently,
the General was brought to agree that if the ex-Viceroy of Corsica
would assure him in writing that the Government wished him to
depart, his mind would be easy.   Nelson, who had already sent
Fremantle to Naples, with orders to stay, if possible, no more than
forty-eight hours, while awaiting Sir Gilbert Elliot, or the orders
from home which the aggrieved General said that he ought to
expect, began to collect his squadron.

Sir Gilbert and staff did not appear until 3 a.m. on January 22.
The ex-Viceroy had been upon a valuable tour of the Italian
states.   But the appearance of this wary Scots politician at Porto
Ferrajo by no means simplified the situation.   Sir Gilbert, whose
own experience of waiting for orders from His Majesty's Ministers
was bitter, refused to put his name to any document purporting
to interpret their possible pleasure.   He disagreed with the
Commodore and the General as to the advisability of quitting Elba,
and had a slight passage-at-arms with de Burgh, who let slip, with
a sneer, the word " politics ".   The ex-Viceroy of Corsica, fresh
from a most cordial reception at Rome and Naples, considered a
superior British fleet in the Mediterranean an essential measure for
securing Italy, and indeed Europe, from the domination of the
French Republic, " politics " which he believed represented the
sentiments of all His Majesty's Ministers.   After composing a
letter which he knew would cause his poor friend the Duke of
Portland to raise his spectacles to his forehead, sigh deeply and
do nothing for a fortnight, Sir Gilbert gladly went on board the
Minerve, and prepared for a protracted passage to Gibraltar, since
the indefatigable Nelson said that he must, in order to bring his

Commander-in-Chief the latest news of the enemy, look in *en route* at Toulon, Mahon and Cartagena.

The Captain's cabin in the *Inconstant* was filled with what Commodore Nelson, invited to view the glowing spoil, could only describe as "pretty things". The efficient Fremantle had managed, during his brief stay at Naples, to secure Miss Betsy Wynne, with £8,000. Two very weak characters had been swiftly overruled by two of great vigour. Mr. and Mrs. Wynne had proved no match for Lady Hamilton, instructed by a British sea-officer. The hasty wedding had been staged at the Embassy, and Lady Hamilton had taken complete charge. The impression made by "the well-known and admired" Ambassadress on a moist bride and bridesmaid had been remarkable. Miss Eugenia Wynne, attending her sister, had noted Lady Hamilton as "four or five and twenty, in the bloom of youth and beauty, full of graces and accomplishments", yet principally admirable for her delicate, warm and sincere attentions "to a husband of past 70".

The Pollards, also refugees from Leghorn, were now struggling to establish themselves at Naples, and Mrs. Pollard had sent Commodore Nelson her kind remembrances, a large box of the Neapolitan native ware which he liked, and an aggrieved message. The Commodore replied at once to say that the box was very handsome, just the thing he wished, that he was far from having forgotten Pollard, and if he had any interest in appointing agents for prizes, would certainly name him amongst them. He hoped that the Pollards might, before long, be happily restored to Leghorn. Since seeing the very handsome things Fremantle had got, he must request Mrs. Pollard to be good enough to lay out ten or twelve pounds on Naples gifts for Mrs. Nelson, anything "such as may please a most elegant woman". What he had particularly admired amongst Mrs. Fremantle's *trousseau* was the Italian silks—"shawls, particularly large handkerchiefs".

Although he viewed with apprehension Fremantle's addition to his cabin of a curly-headed young lady of seventeen in a white gown, who played upon the harpsichord and sang very sweetly, he shouldered some responsibility for the match, and accepted the invitation of the happy couple to dine in the *Inconstant*. Mrs. Fremantle recorded her little party of five sea-officers as "very noisy. Old Nelson very civil, and good-natured, but does not say much". Two mornings later, her bridegroom, with a brow of thunder, began to see Nelson's well-known point of view with regard to officers' wives going to sea. For Captain

Fremantle, with a very bad head after a " bachelor " party in the *Minerve,* had been obliged to order all hands to witness punishment, and the results had been unavoidably audible in his Betsy's bower.   One of the wretches had contrived to break a leg, and Betsy, who had replied with spirit to her lover's question, " What if the Ship comes to action? " naturally had not visualised floggings.   In vain a young officer went so far as to confide that they still made him ill.   They simply broke his Betsy's heart. Glad to get out of his ship, the bride of an Ogre went for a little walk out of town.   It rained, and in company with the Commissioner, tiresome Captain Hope, she had to shelter in a sentry-box for a whole hour.   Ten days later, the bride's journal ceased to mention listening to floggings, though these did not cease. Her younger sister, Jenny, had long since formed the convenient opinion that all sailors, like fishes, could not exist without unlimited drink.

Nelson during these days had been what he called " active ". Having left de Burgh sufficient transports to remove his troops in three days, and a small escort, he prepared to go down to Gibraltar, " sure of a pleasant party, let what will happen ". Sir Gilbert Elliot was the best company in the world; his advice was " a treasure ", and the ex-Viceroy had brought amongst his staff a successful author, Colonel John Drinkwater, whose *Siege of Gibraltar,* dedicated to His Gracious Majesty, had run into three editions in as many years.   The handsome Colonel had a singularly uninformed enthusiasm for life at sea (although his father had at one time been a naval surgeon), painted delightfully in water-colours, and, as *aide-de-camp* to Sir Gilbert, had very properly fallen in love with Sir Gilbert's eligible cousin, Miss Eleanor Congleton.   It was something of a blow to Nelson to discover that until after Gibraltar he could not offer Colonel Drinkwater accommodation in the *Minerve.*   For Sir Gilbert had also brought with him his late Secretary of State, M. Pozzo di Borgo.   Indeed, he had no choice at present but to carry this unfortunate and very sea-sick gentleman everywhere with him, for the name of M. Pozzo di Borgo had not been amongst those mentioned in the general amnesty when French troops landed in Corsica, and on his recent travels in Italy a demand had been made by the French Government for his arrest.   His politics at present seemed concentrated in loathing of the Buonaparte family (also of Ajaccio).   However, he was a nobleman by birth, and spoke fluent English in a penetrating voice.

Sir Gilbert's Italian tour had been rewarding. At Naples he had been received with more than civility. He had suffered a pang when he bowed over the hand of the Queen of Naples. A family likeness to her sister, the murdered Marie Antoinette, had carried his fancy instantly to the last public dinner attended by him at Versailles, " where the Queen of France, then Dauphiness, was in all the glory and lustre of Burke's morning star ". His report on Maria Carolina was favourable. He thought that she had a strong, powerful mind. Amongst her children she was charming and at her best. He had spent many pleasant quiet evenings with the royal family, and the Queen, having ordered the Theatre of San Carlo to be lighted up, had herself conducted him around it, taking his arm, " as gracious as any queen could be ". The King, toasting the English nation publicly at his dinner-table, and carrying his English guest to view the factory of Belvedere, " where he seemed like a father in the midst of his family ", had shown in a better light than after a morning's sport at Carditelli, when he had been sulky at securing nothing more than fifteen wild boars, four foxes, two fawns and a hare. The effusive welcome of the English Ambassadress, delighted to entertain any friend of England and her " Sir Willum ", had not been much to the taste of a Border laird. Sir Gilbert admitted that Lady Hamilton's face was beautiful. The pains she had taken to acquire education and accomplishments were remarkable and laudable. After a performance of her " Attitudes " his allegiance had almost been won. But a Scottish gentleman, slightly below middle height and by nature reserved, had recoiled instinctively from a voiceful, glowing, sea-side hostess whose person seemed to him " nothing short of monstrous for its enormity " ; and he could not but resent the spectacle of Sir William Hamilton, son of a Scottish duke, married in his senescence to a blooming mistress of doubtful antecedents. To his own lady he confided, " With men, her language and conversation are exaggerations of anything I ever heard anywhere ; and I was wonderfully struck with these inveterate remains of her origin : though the impression was very much weakened by seeing the other ladies of Naples."

The pleasant party bound for Gibraltar sailed on January 29, the *Minerve* for Toulon, the *Romulus* and *Southampton* in charge of a convoy of transports, in two divisions, and with orders to take different courses, so that one, at any rate, might escape the enemy. The wind was foul for Mahon, so Nelson cut Minorca out of his programme. Finding at Cartagena that the Spanish

fleet had left that port, he hurried.   At Gibraltar he learnt that
the enemy had passed the Rock to the westward, and that Sir
John Jervis, determined to intercept them on their passage to
Brest, had taken up his station off Cadiz.   He paused only to
collect his two Lieutenants, Culverhouse and Hardy, with the
prize crews taken in the *Santa Sabina*, and weighed in the forenoon of February 11.   Two Spanish sail-of-the-line and a frigate,
at anchor at the head of the bay, also weighed, and began to
chase him.   The *Minerve* cleared for action.   When Colonel
Drinkwater asked the Commodore whether he thought an action
possible, the Commodore replied, " Very possible.   But ",
looking up at his broad pendant, " before the Dons get hold of
that bit of bunting, I will have a struggle with them, and sooner
than give up the frigate, I'll run her ashore."

The Commodore and his party, which now included an author
taking notes, presently sat down to dine with true British phlegm,
the Spaniards meanwhile overhauling them.   Colonel Drinkwater was in the act of congratulating his neighbour, the large
and somewhat blockish-looking Lieutenant called Hardy, on his
escape from being a prisoner of war, when the warm hum of
conversation was arrested by the cold cry of " Man overboard ! "
The officers of the frigate sped to the quarter-deck.   Sir Gilbert
and *suite* hurried to the stern windows, and beheld, in February
dusk, a white wake whirling into design more intricate than those
of any Oriental magic carpet.   At first they could see nothing
but most intimidating-looking waters, through which they
seemed to be moving very fast, but in an incredibly short time
they got an excellent view of the lowering of a jolly boat, in which
Colonel Drinkwater recognised, as the officer in charge, his late
large dinner-partner.   The landsmen watched breathlessly while
the current of the Straits, running strongly to the eastward,
carried the little boat far astern of the *Minerve* and towards the
foremost pursuing Spanish sail-of-the-line.   After a breathless
interval Lieutenant Hardy made a signal, interpreted to them as,
" No sign of the missing man ".   The boat's crew pulled " might
and main " to regain the frigate, but seemed to make hardly any
progress.   When *Le Terrible*, the foremost Spanish sail-of-the-
line, was almost within gunshot of the *Minerve*, " By God ! "
exclaimed Commodore Nelson, " I'll not lose Hardy !   Back that
mizzen-topsail."   To   the   landsmen   in   the   *Minerve*,   their
destruction now seemed only a matter of minutes, but, to their
stupefaction, *Le Terrible* proceeded to shorten sail, in order to

16

allow her consort to join her, and in the time given, the *Minerve* dropped down to the jolly boat and took out Hardy and his crew. In the winding of the Straits she soon regained her lost distance and by sunset, steering further to the southward, lost sight of the enemy. The only explanation could be that the Commodore's daring action had been misinterpreted by the Spaniards. They had evidently supposed that the *Minerve* had sighted the British fleet approaching from the west, and was offering action.

Darkness succeeded sunset, and with darkness in the Straits on that February night came fog. The little *Minerve* found herself alone in clammy blue gloom, surrounded by strange sounds, strange sails. Colonel Drinkwater, an author, and in love, sharing the Commodore's cabin with Sir Gilbert Elliot, noticed with mingled admiration and surprise that his employer slept soundly through the Commodore's first wordless incursion. After Nelson's second *affairé* visit he felt himself obliged to arouse Sir Gilbert, and explain that they were apparently either amongst the Spanish fleet or a convoy bound for the West Indies. The Commodore had briefly said that if his second guess was correct, it would be his duty to give the earliest intimation to the British Commander on the West Indies station. Sir Gilbert, faced in the small hours, after an exhausting day, with the prospect of a trip to the Antilles, displayed his usual well-bred imperturbability. With the words, "We are only passengers, and must submit to circumstances", he fell asleep again. When morning broke the passengers learnt that they had passed unscathed through the Spanish fleet.

On the morning of February 13 the *Minerve* joined Sir John Jervis's fleet and Nelson moved back into his own ship, the *Captain*. After all, it seemed, he had arrived in time. During the Eve of St. Valentine's Day the wind shifted to the westward, Spanish signal guns sounded repeatedly, and Sir Gilbert Elliot, a Scottish country gentleman, a politician, forty-seven years of age and the father of six, discovered to Sir John Jervis his great desire to assist at "a general action of the British Fleet". The ex-Viceroy's application to be allowed to come on board H.M.S. *Victory*, as a volunteer, was rejected, but at his earnest request the *Lively* frigate, under orders to carry him home directly, was detained, to carry also the news of the approaching naval engagement.

5

At dawn on the sunless morning of February 14, 1797, the position of the British and Spanish fleets was twenty-five miles west of the Portuguese headland of St. Vincent, a hundred and fifty miles north-west of Cadiz, for which port the enemy were running, with a fair wind but in poor order. As far as numbers and size went, the fleets, moving one from the westward, the other from the northward, to a common crossing, were most unevenly matched, a fact which was not confirmed to Sir John Jervis until the dense morning mists clinging to the waters began to part. Amongst the many scraps of conversation recorded of that eventful day, none is more characteristic than that which opened between him and the First Captain of the *Victory* at 10.49 a.m.

" There are eight sail-of-the-line, Sir John."

" Very well, sir."

" There are twenty sail-of-the-line, Sir John. . . . Twenty-five. . . . There are twenty-seven sail-of-the-line, Sir John ; near double our own ! "

" Enough of that, sir ! If there are fifty sail, I will go through them. England badly needs a victory at present."

Captain Ben Hallowell, whose ship had been wrecked a couple of months previously, was serving on board the *Victory* as a volunteer, and happened to be walking back and forth beside the Admiral on the poop. The huge Canadian-born officer, who had been Nelson's constant companion on the batteries at Calvi, so much forgot himself at this exhilarating moment as to deal his Commander-in-Chief a thump on the back, exclaiming, " That's right, Sir John, that's right ! And, by God ! we shall give them a damned good licking."

The fleet under Jervis's command numbered fifteen sail-of-the-line, of which the *Victory* and *Britannia*, of 100 guns, the *Barfleur* and *Prince George*, of 98, and the *Blenheim* and *Namur*, of 90, were three-deckers. He had eight 74's—H.M.S. *Culloden, Colossus, Captain, Excellent, Egmont, Goliath, Irresistible* and *Orion*. The *Diadem*, a 64, four frigates, a sloop and a cutter completed the array with which he proposed to engage the Spanish Grand Fleet of twenty-seven of the line, ten frigates and a brig. Half a dozen of the Spanish three-deckers carried 112 guns, and the four-decker *Santissima Trinidad*, flagship of Don José de Córdoba, mounted 136. With the exception of one 80, the *San Nicolas*, the other Spaniards were all 74's. But these fine ships, graphically described by the Signal Lieutenant of the *Barfleur* as

" Thumpers, looming like Beachy Head in a fog ", had been forced to sea in haste, and were all undermanned. A large proportion of their ships' companies were pressed landsmen, and their officers were inexperienced. When they discovered the proximity of the British, they were taken by surprise. They were proceeding leisurely, in a long, straggling line, some side by side, in pairs, others in groups of odd numbers, and a gap of some seven miles stretched between their leading division of six and the remaining one-and-twenty. Jervis, before they had time to recover, took the risk he had announced of going through their line. Ten of his ships had been under his command for a couple of years, the other five had recently joined him from the Channel Fleet. " Confident in the skill, valour and discipline of the Officers and Men I had the happiness to command, and judging that the honour of His Majesty's arms, and the circumstances of the War in these seas required a considerable degree of enterprise ", at 11.42 a.m. he ordered six of his ships to put on a press of sail and get through the enemy gap. " We flew to them ", wrote Collingwood to his wife, " as a hawk to his prey." Troubridge led the van, in the *Culloden*, Collingwood brought up the rear in the *Excellent*.

As they drew near the enemy, nine Spanish ships had passed to the eastward. The gap in their loose formation was wide, but it seemed that as the two lines were steering, a collision between the tenth Spaniard and the *Culloden* was inevitable. Her First Lieutenant drew the attention of his Captain to this, and received the reply, " Can't help it, Griffiths. Let the weakest fend off." A distant cannonade broke out between the leading ships on either side, but the *Culloden* reserved her fire for the ship which threatened her with collision.

The Spanish backbone was broken, and Jervis's next signal was to tack in succession, his intention being to engage the bulk of the enemy fleet to windward, before the discomfited nine ships to leeward could assist them. By the nine now cut off but a feeble attempt at molestation was made, and only one, running down the British line, and passing to the stern of the *Excellent*, regained the eighteen.

The battle was half won, as the British ships proceeded, one by one, to turn towards the north, but the possibility remained that the larger Spanish detachment, by bearing up to pass astern of them, might rejoin the small division, and perhaps escape to Cadiz. It was at this point that a 74, third from the rear of the

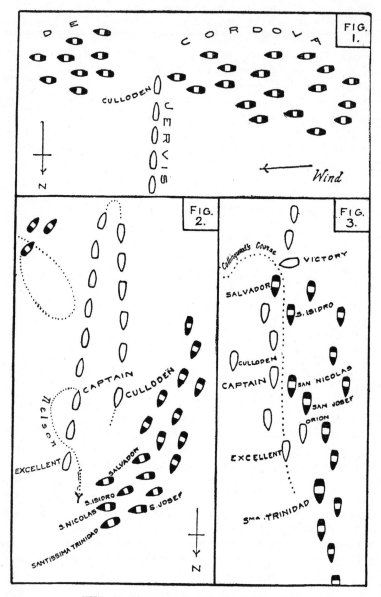

THE BATTLE OF CAPE ST. VINCENT
February 14, 1797

Reproduced from *Sea Kings of Britain*, by Sir Geoffrey Callender
By kind permission of Messrs. Longmans Green and Co., Ltd.

British line, altered course to the west and threw herself in defiance across the bows of the Spaniards. An independent squadron was needed in this position, to prevent the battle degenerating into the "half-begotten" engagement despised by Jervis; and Nelson, with the *Captain*, had resolved to represent it, offering himself to the attack of at least seven enemy sail-of-the-line. He wore out of his station, and came into close action with the *Santissima Trinidad*, largest fighting ship in the world. In quitting the line he was aware that he was not only acting without orders, he was deliberately disobeying them. A friend came to his assistance.

> "I was immediately joined, and most nobly supported, by the *Culloden*, Captain Troubridge. . . . For near an hour, I believe (but do not pretend to be correct as to time), did the *Culloden* and *Captain* support this apparently, but not really, unequal contest; when the *Blenheim*, passing between us and the enemy, gave us a respite, and sickened the Dons."

Two Spanish ships dropped astern, and "being fired into, in a masterly style" by Collingwood, the *San Isidro*, of 74 guns, struck. Nelson believed that the larger *Salvador del Mundo* had also struck, after being attacked by Collingwood, at a distance which that north-country officer reckoned as not longer than a certain well-remembered garden on the banks of the Wansbeck.

> "But Captain Collingwood, disdaining the parade of taking possession of beaten enemies, most gallantly pushed up, with every sail set, to save his old friend and messmate, who was to appearance in a critical state."

Jervis, having seen and recognised the brilliance of Nelson's action, had ordered the *Excellent*, last ship in the line, to support him instantly, and the *Blenheim* was soon followed by the *Prince George* and *Orion*. The larger enemy division resumed its former course, but by now the engagement had become close and general. "The *Blenheim*, being ahead, and the *Culloden* crippled and astern, the *Excellent* ranged up within ten feet of the *San Nicolas*, giving a most tremendous fire." At this moment the Spanish 80 luffed incontinently, and the great three-decker *San Josef*, which almost simultaneously received the fire of the *Prince George*, fell foul of her. Nelson's second opportunity of the day had come. His ship had by this time been so much mauled as to be incapable of further service, in the line or in chase. She had lost her fore topmast; her wheel had been shot away. "Not a sail, shroud or rope was left!" He ordered her helm to be put down, and called for a boarding-party. "Captain Miller so judiciously ordered her course" that the *Captain* was laid aboard the starboard quarter of the *San Nicolas*; her sprit-sail yard passed over the Spaniard's poop, and hooked in her mizzen shrouds. The first man to board the enemy 80 was Berry, "late my First Lieutenant", a passenger in the *Captain*, as he had recently been promoted Commander. Miller, anxious to lead, had been directed to remain in charge of the crippled *Captain*, while Nelson undertook this duty. Many "old Agamemnons" were equally eager. "The Soldiers of the 69th Regiment, with an alacrity which will ever do them credit", headed by "my poor soldier officer", the accomplished Pierson, were amongst the foremost. Nelson, with his boarding-party, which included three midshipmen, passed from the fore-chains of his own ship into the enemy's quarter gallery, where the butt of a marine's musket smashed an upper window for their entry. The doors of the cabin in which they found themselves were locked, and some startled Spanish officers discharged their pistols through the sky-lights, but the doors were quickly forced by the marines, who then opened fire, and amongst the enemy officers to fall, mortally wounded, retreating to the larboard side of the quarter-deck, was the Commodore, Don Tomaso Geraldino.

On the quarter-deck Nelson found Berry in possession of the poop, engaged in hauling down the Spanish ensign. The lower-deck guns of the ship were still replying to the *Prince George*, which was firing into her starboard bow, but as Nelson passed towards the forecastle, several officers delivered their swords. This ceremony was interrupted by a spatter of pistol and musket fire from the Admiral's stern gallery of the *San Josef*, and seven men of the boarding-party were instantaneously killed. This much larger ship, inextricably entangled aloft with the *San Nicolas* (now on fire), seemed determined to expel the handful of invaders from her. Nelson, without hesitation, decided to carry a Spanish first-rate from the decks of a Spanish 80. He ordered his marines to return the fusillade, stationed sentinels at the hatchways to keep the enemy below decks, called to Miller to push more men into the *San Nicolas*, and to the cry of "Westminster Abbey, or Glorious Victory!" charged on. Berry was at hand to help him into the main-chains, and another headlong scramble from ship to ship was painfully achieved. But the appearance of resistance from the *San Josef* was deceptive. As the depleted boarding-party came in view, a Spanish officer, looking over the quarter-deck rail, hailed to say that she surrendered. This news, "most welcome" to Nelson, was treated with caution until he found

himself on the quarter-deck of the first-rate, where her Flag-
Captain, on bended knee, presented his sword and explained
that his Admiral, Don Francisco Xavier Winthuysen, was dying
of his wounds below.   On being assured that the *San Josef* had
struck, Nelson gave her Captain his hand, and then asked him
to summon his officers and ship's company to hear an announcement of the surrender.   This was done, and

> " on the quarter-deck of a Spanish first-rate, extravagant as the story
> may seem, did I receive the swords of the vanquished Spaniards, which,
> as I received, I gave to William Fearney, one of my bargemen, who put
> them, with the greatest *sang-froid*, under his arm.   I was surrounded
> by Captain Berry, Lieutenant Pierson (69th Regiment), John Sykes,
> John Thomson, Francis Cook, all old Agamemnons, and several other
> brave men, seamen and soldiers.   Thus fell these ships."

17

6

As the announcement, in the Spanish tongue, of the surrender
of the *San Josef* died upon the foggy air, Nelson found his hand
seized by one of his boarding-party.   The man was muttering
that " he might not soon have such another place to do it in, and
was heartily glad to see me ".   Spirits were running high amongst
a ship's company who realised their achievement as something
new in the annals of naval warfare.   Nelson's own view of the
exploit was temperate.   He had had " good fortune " such as
did not fall to every man.   He afterwards told Locker that he
did not pretend that the ships might not have been taken had he
not boarded them, but it was far from impossible that they might
have forged into the enemy fleet, been taken in tow and reached
Cadiz.   This disappointing result did occur in the case of two
other disabled ships, the *Santissima Trinidad* and the *Soberano*.

He experienced the sensation of being " in a dream " a few
moments later, when the *Victory* passed the interlocked group of
the *Captain*, *San Nicolas* and *San Josef*, and her men, lining her
bulwarks, saluted him with three cheers, an example afterwards
followed by every ship in the fleet that day, when they distinguished Commodore Nelson's broad pendant.

The *Captain* was, for the present, useless, but Nelson believed
that there might be further work for him to do.   The *Minerve*
was sending a boat for him.   He returned to the *Captain*, and in
her cabin addressed himself to his second-in-command—" Miller,
I am under the greatest obligations to you."   The phrase was
modern, but accompanied by a mediæval gesture.   Captain

Miller found himself the possessor of a sword and a ring—the sword, very fine, lately the property of Don Tomaso Geraldino, the ring of no commercial value, a pale semi-precious stone set round with brilliants, drawn from the finger of a British sea-officer of better blood than fortune.   18

Nelson ordered Captain Cockburn to put him on board the nearest uninjured ship-of-the-line, which proved to be the *Irresistible*; but, as he regretfully discovered, " the day was too far advanced " for him to venture upon the project of taking possession of the Spanish Admiral's flagship. In February, in poor weather, light fails soon. Jervis was gathering his fleet to protect his prizes and cripples. He had decided to rest content with the possession of four enemy sail-of-the-line (two of them first-rates), more especially as he had only twelve ships left capable of fighting, while the enemy seemed likely to be reinforced by nine which had scarcely been into action. His casualty list was light, and the Spanish fleet had been demonstrably beaten. Córdoba, with his surviving Rear-Admiral and six of his Captains, was to be court-martialled and dismissed the service. By five o'clock all firing had ceased. Gradually the fleets separated, the British standing for Lagos, the Spaniards for Cadiz. Nelson's description of his reception by his Commander-in-Chief was marked by the same temperateness which distinguished all his accounts of personal adventure that day. " At dusk, I went on board the *Victory*, when the Admiral received me on the quarter-deck, and having embraced me, said he could not sufficiently thank me, and used every expression to make me happy." Many months later, in private conversation with his brother-in-law Bolton, he drew a more highly coloured picture of this darkling and dramatic scene. Jervis received him with open arms. Nelson's appearance was remarkable. Most of his hat had been shot away, his shirt and coat were in tatters, and his countenance was freaked with the smoke of gunpowder. (But, for that matter, the Admiral himself had been standing too near a marine killed by a shell.) " On my return on board the *Irresistible*," ends Nelson's narrative, " my bruises were looked at, and found but trifling, and a few days made me as well as ever." This was another understatement. His name appeared in the casualty list as " bruised but not obliged to quit the deck ". He had, in fact, received a superficial wound from a shell-splinter; he had not slept on the nights of the 11th and 13th, and he had been engaging in some violent activity. The surgeons, perceiving symptoms which might signify internal injury, were uncommunicative, and some rumour of their anxieties spread through the fleet that night. For a week Nelson's "contusion of no consequence" caused him acute pain, and though he reported himself "not near as much hurt as the Doctors fancied", he felt so unwell that he achieved only the briefest of lines to assure his wife—"I am well, Josiah is well." Something a little less perfunctory, to Collingwood, was a duty which must be achieved without delay.

"My dearest Friend," he wrote, discarding for the only time in a long correspondence his customary, "Dear Coll.",

> "'A friend in need is a friend indeed,' was never more truly verified than by your most noble and gallant conduct yesterday in sparing the *Captain* from further loss; and I beg, both as a public Officer and a friend, you will accept my most sincere thanks. I have not failed, by letter to the Admiral, to represent the eminent services of the *Excellent*. Tell me how you are; what are your disasters? I cannot tell you much of the *Captain's*, except by Note of Captain Miller's at two this morning, about sixty killed and wounded, masts bad, etc. etc. We shall meet at Lagos; but I could not come near you without assuring you how sensible I am of your assistance in nearly a critical situation. Believe me, as ever, your most affectionate
>
> "Horatio Nelson."

Collingwood, an officer renowned for his icy reserve and unbending demeanour, answered within the hour, offering "My dear good Friend" his congratulations on distinguished services. "You formed the plan of attack—we were only accessories to the Don's ruin. . . . It added very much to the satisfaction which I felt in thumping the Spaniards that I released you a little."

7

On the morning after the greatest naval battle since the Saints, Colonel Drinkwater was delighted to hear the voice of Commodore Nelson enquiring for Sir Gilbert Elliot. He was further delighted when the hero of the hour, finding that Sir Gilbert had gone with the Captain of the *Lively* to the *Victory*, said, "I hoped to have caught him before he saw the Admiral; but come below with me."

"Seated alone with the Commodore", the eager author began by offering, "in the most expressive terms", congratulations on his safety, and on the very distinguished part taken by his ship in yesterday's action, of which many particulars had by this time reached the *Lively*. He added (redundantly, since every officer in the fleet who could spare a moment on a morning which was busy was engaged scribbling a letter home) that, of course, the *Lively* would be bearing the glorious news to England. Nelson, who had received his congratulations with great modesty but evident pleasure, then, " in the most good-natured manner ", acceded to a pressing request to give as many details as possible of the proceedings of the *Captain* yesterday, and as he continued, after a brief professional statement, to let drop priceless musings, the author drew towards himself a sheet of paper and a pencil. Presently, the saga, begun with the words, " I'll tell you how it happened ", ceased, and the Colonel bound for London began to calculate comfortably the Honours List which must follow such an affair. " The Admiral will, of course, be made a peer, and his seconds in command noticed accordingly. As for you, Commodore, they will make you a baronet." He was arrested by a hand on his arm. " No ! "

21

Nelson returned to the *Irresistible*, to send a line to Sir Gilbert, but it stated little more than the condition of his ship, and his satisfaction that his Admiral thought his reputation " had not been diminished by the events of yesterday ". Sir Gilbert's answer, prompt, was in his best style :

" To have been foremost on such a day, could fall to your share alone. Nothing in the world was ever more noble than the transaction of the *Captain*, from beginning to end, and the glorious group of your Ship and her two Prizes, fast in your gripe, was never surpassed, and I daresay never will. I am grieved to hear you are wounded, however slightly you talk of it. . . . I was in hopes you were unhurt, by seeing you on board the *Minerve*, and hearing the cheers you were saluted with. . . . May you speedily recover, and enjoy your honours, and the gratitude and admiration of your Country for many years."

Encouraged by this " affectionate and flattering " letter from the man possessed of " interest ", who was accompanying the Admiral's despatches to London, Nelson wrote next day, " If you can be instrumental in keeping back what I expect will happen, it will be an additional obligation." After the victories of Lords Rodney and Howe, in 1782 and '94, baronetage had been bestowed on their junior flag-officers. Nelson mentioned that he was far from disposed to hold such a distinction light, but strongly felt that to accept; without having the means to support, an hereditary title, was a situation that should, if possible, be avoided. As things were, he was having difficulty to " make ends meet ", and on taking flag rank must forfeit his pay as a Colonel of Marines.

He tentatively added, " There are other Honours, which die with the possessor, and I should be proud to accept, if my efforts are thought worthy of the favour of my King."

22

The news brought by the *Lively* frigate reached London on March 3, and a *Gazette Extraordinary* was published the same night. Although his fleet had included two Vice-Admirals, a Rear-Admiral and a Commodore, Sir John Jervis's despatch mentioned by name only Calder, his First Captain. His accompanying private letter to Lord Spencer, explaining that " the correct conduct of every Officer and man made it impossible to distinguish one more than the other ", went on to name Vice-Admiral Waldegrave, Captains Troubridge, Collingwood, Berry and Hallowell, and Commodore Nelson, " who was in the rear, on the starboard tack, took the lead on the larboard, and contributed very much to the fortune of the day ". Nelson had certainly expected that the despatch would tell his family details of his actions which he had not had time to describe in his letter carried by the *Lively*, and when the despatch was seen it aroused criticism in the fleet. It was murmured that an original draft, giving due prominence to Nelson's outstanding services, had been suppressed on a reminder by Calder that the Commodore had, by his unauthorised departure from the prescribed order of attack, created a dangerous precedent. Nelson himself credited an anecdote that when Calder had reported—" Sir, the *Captain* and *Culloden* are separated from the fleet and unsupported, shall we recall them? " Sir John's reply had been, " I will not have them recalled. I put my faith in those ships." He also believed that Sir John was, like himself, not quite satisfied with the engagement, although he could not say so publicly. " We ought ", he was still fretting, two months later, " to have had the *Santissima Trinidad* and the *Soberano*, seventy-four. They belonged to us by conquest, and only wanted some good fellow to get alongside them and they were ours. But it is well, and for that reason only, we do not like to say much."

23

England, which had been badly needing a victory, had no doubt that " it was well ". Every gift in the hands of Government was showered on the victors. The thanks of both Houses of Parliament were voted by acclamation; His Majesty sent a personal message to the fleet, and gold medals to the Admirals, Commodore and every Captain of a ship-of-the-line. Sir John Jervis was, as Drinkwater had prophesied, made an Earl (it was said that the King himself had chosen the title—" of St. Vincent ").

Admirals Thompson and Parker became baronets, and Waldegrave, already possessed of a courtesy title, was presently
rewarded with an Irish peerage; Captain Calder was knighted,
and the Order of the Bath was conferred upon Commodore
Nelson.   Sir Gilbert had not failed him.

Congratulatory letters began to reach Nelson on April 1, but
they had all been written a week before the news of the Battle
of Cape St. Vincent had reached home.   On a promotion of
flags, dated February 2, he had become, in the ordinary course
of seniority, a Rear-Admiral of the Blue.

At Bath, on February 22, Captain Fane, of the Royal Navy,
literally ran from the coffee-house where he had been scanning
the newspapers, to carry the good tidings to a modest couple
established in Bennet St., and " I never ", wrote Mrs. Horatio
Nelson, " saw anything elevate our father equal to this."
Little more than a fortnight after the ageing Rector had accomplished a patriarchal screed, opening " My dear Rear-Admiral ",
came the news of St. Vincent, and he found himself obliged to
seek the shelter of his lodging in haste, to shed a private tear,
and, in his easy chair, in front of the fire, spend " a useless hour "
reflecting gratefully on " the various Events of a long life ".
On his daily potter to the Market perfect strangers were stopping
him to say " Hansom " things of Admiral Nelson's courage and
judgment.   The post was bringing more letters than Mrs. Horatio
could answer in a month.   Lord Walpole had written that
London was ringing with the name of his relative: at Bath it
was being mentioned at the theatre and in the grey streets by
the common ballad-singer.   The cities of London, Bath, Bristol
and Norwich had voted the Admiral their Freedom, and to the
capital city of the county of his birth he was sending the sword
of the Spanish Admiral Winthuysen.   The couple in Bennet St.
had a little celebration, but Mrs. Horatio was shy of attending
large gatherings, at which some kind friends were over-direct in
their enquiries as to prize money.   The Rector slyly told his
daughter-in-law that he believed he had the more spirit.   They
understood from the Admiral that they were not to be very rich
yet.   He still wrote of no more than a cottage, though his present
for the poor of Burnham this year was to be fifty blankets so
good that they should last seven winters.   A little before it
must be mentioned abroad, he warned them of his " mark of
the Royal Favour, which I was once given to understand I had
no likelihood of enjoying ", and Maurice was, at his request,

communicating with York Herald as to coat-of-arms, crest, motto, etc., for Sir Horatio Nelson, K.B.—

> " the supporters, on one side a Sailor, properly habited, holding in his hand the Broad Pendant, on a staff, and trampling on a Spanish flag; on the other side, the British Lion . . . *Crest*—on a wreath of the colours, the stern of a Spanish Man-of-War, proper, inscribed, ' San Josef '. *Motto*—what my brother William suggested, turned into English, ' Faith and Works '."

25

He added to a holograph copy of his " Few Remarks relative to myself in the *Captain*, in which my pendant was flying on the most glorious Valentine's Day, 1797 " a note, " There is a saying in the Fleet too flattering for me to omit telling—viz., ' Nelson's Patent Bridge for boarding First-Rates ', alluding to my passing over an Enemy's 80-gun Ship ", and he sent home " Commodore Nelson's Receipt for an Olla Podrida ", which showed that Mediterranean men could be merry.

> " Take a Spanish First-Rate and an 80 Gun Ship, and after well battering and basting for an hour, keep throwing in your force balls, and be sure to let them be well season'd.
>
> " Your fire must never slacken for a single Moment, but must be kept up as brisk as possible during the whole time.
>
> " As soon as you perceive your Spaniards to be well stew'd and blended together, you must then throw in your own ship on board of the two decker, lash your Spritsail yard to her mizzen mast, then Jump into her quarter gallery, sword in hand, and let the rest of your boarders follow as they can.
>
> " The Moment you appear on the 80 gun ship's quarter-deck, the Spaniards will all fly. You will then have only to take a hop, step and jump from your stepping stone and you will find yourself in the middle of a First-rate's quarter-deck, with all the Spaniards at your feet.
>
> " Your Olla Podrida may now be consider'd as completely dish'd, fit to set before His Majesty."

26
> " *Nelson's New Art of Cookery.*"

More letters than could be answered in a month penetrated to Nelson too, but much more slowly. The first set, congratulating him on his promotion, reached him off Cape St. Mary's; the second, on his performances in the Glorious Action of Valentine's Day, came in the same ship as orders from Jervis to sail for Corsica; the third, on his decoration, found him blockading Cadiz. The effort of Lady Parker, which fell into the second group, was typical. His old Admiral's lady, who addressed him simply by his surname, sent messages to the seventeen junior officers known to her in the victorious fleet, and had even a condescending word for " your truly able and gallant Commander-

in-Chief ".   Sir John Jervis should be henceforth "her
Valentine ".   " Your conduct on the memorable February 14th,
a proud day for Old England, is above all praise. . . . All that
I shall say is that your mother could not have heard of your deeds
with more affection. . . . Long may you live, my dear Nelson,
an ornament to your Country and your Profession, is the sincere
wish of your old Commander Sir Peter, myself, and every branch
of our family."   *27*

After the trumpet note of Volumnia came the still small voice
of Virgilia :

" My dearest Husband,
    " Yesterday I received your letter of February 16th.   Thank God
you are well, and Josiah.   My anxiety was far beyond my powers of
expression.   M. Nelson and Captain Locker behaved humanely, and
attentive to me.   They wrote immediately, Captain Locker assuring
me that you were perfectly well, Maurice begging me not to believe idle
reports, the ' Gazette ' saying you were slightly wounded.   Altogether,
my dearest husband, my sufferings were great. . . . I shall not be
myself till I hear from you again.   What can I attempt to say to you
about Boarding ?   You have been most wonderfully Protected ; you
have done desperate actions enough.   Now may I—indeed I do—beg
that you never Board again !   *LEAVE* IT for *CAPTAINS*."

Her next letter repeated her last injunction :

" I sincerely hope, my dear husband, that all these wonderful and
desperate actions—such as boarding Ships—you will leave to others.
With the Protection of a Supreme Being, you have acquired a character
or name which, all hands agree, cannot be greater ; therefore, rest
satisfied."   *28*

CHAPTER VIII

1797
(*ætat* 38)

IN-SHORE SQUADRON, CADIZ BAY:
SANTA CRUZ, TENERIFFE

I

On the fresh spring night of April 11, 1797, two old friends of East India days, seated in a patched-up cabin of His Britannic Majesty's Ship *Captain*, at anchor off Cadiz, held deep and private counsel. Their prey, as might be guessed from the maps and charts spread before them, and lit by swaying lanterns, lay in the Atlantic Ocean, in a Spanish-owned archipelago, some sixty miles west of the north-west African coast. Nelson's scheme for a daring combined operation, to which he brought characteristic enthusiasm, might, he claimed, not only immortalise the undertakers and ruin Spain, but actually put an end to the war.

On rejoining the fleet this morning, after a five weeks' cruise, he had not been much impressed by the appearance, after her partial refit at Lagos, of the ship which had taken so prominent a part in the events of St. Valentine's Day. He was assured that a new ship-of-the-line was to be assigned to him, as soon as a reinforcement arrived from the Channel Fleet—a thing which he would believe when seen. Alternatively, he hoped that his lot might not be H.M.S. *Gibraltar*, a three-decker ("not active enough for my purposes"), at present undergoing extensive repairs at Portsmouth, after parricidally striking on the Pearl Rock, Gibraltar.

He had gone to sea in the *Irresistible* on March 5, at the first possible moment after the last gasp of a formidable gale, taking with him *La Minerve*, the *Zealous* and the *Culloden*; his instructions being to look out for the Viceroy of Mexico. This dignitary, also with three of the line, two of them first-rates, was believed to be on his passage to Cadiz, from Havana and Vera Cruz, laden with the gold of the Americas, so a meeting with him might have brought gaudy reward, and was regarded as a most covetable chance. Spain depended so much on the safe arrival of these specie ships (reported to be carrying between six and seven million sterling) that some people were sure her fleet would be obliged to come out, to meet and protect them. Nelson, who had, as he expected, cruised in vain between Cape St. Vincent and the African coast covering the approaches to Cadiz, had no belief in the readiness of the enemy to see further action at present. On his arrival this morning he had found himself, though junior flag-officer, appointed to the command of the in-shore squadron, an honourable post, and in emergency practically independent; but not what he had wanted. Lord St. Vincent had decided on a strict commercial blockade of Cadiz, entailing the stoppage of every supply which might assist Spain, for her trade, for her navy and for her operations against Portugal. Nelson had accordingly circularised the captains of his squadron, the Danish and American Consuls and all neutrals in the port; but in a letter to his Commander-in-Chief he had recurred to his anxiety for the late Corsican garrison, now at last on their way to Gibraltar from Elba, with only a frigate escort, and very likely to encounter at least a couple of French warships from Toulon. He hoped that Lord St. Vincent, whom he knew to be very short of ships, and who had spoilt him by allowing him to speak his mind freely, would consider his name should a detachment be spared to protect General de Burgh's troops. Next morning he sent yet another letter, offering himself for even more vigorous employment. Troubridge, who had been on their recent cruise, and had come to dine in the *Captain* after picking up the gossip of the fleet, had mentioned that two frigates were being sent to look for the missing treasure-ships at Santa Cruz of Teneriffe, and that the Chief had said he would be interested to hear Nelson's opinion on the possibility of an attack on that place. Nelson forthwith disclosed " my plan ", which had long occupied his thoughts and during his late weeks at sea had been carefully considered.

His letter to Lord St. Vincent urging the attack on Santa Cruz had many points in common with past letters to Lord Hood pleading to be allowed to take Bastia. Given the means he asked, he was equally confident of success. He opened by dealing with the operation by sea. Santa Cruz of Teneriffe, or de Santiago, a sea-port, the capital of Teneriffe and of the Canary Islands, occupied a small plain, bounded by rugged rocks and seamed by water-courses, generally dry. Water was brought to the town in wooden troughs, so the stoppage of this supply should induce a quick surrender. The anchorage was good, and a mole facilitated landing.   The shore, although not easy of access, rose steeply from deep water, enabling transports to run in and land an army in twenty-four hours.   " I will undertake, with a very small squadron, to do the Naval part."   The bay was open to all winds between E. by N. and S.W., and a swell was generally setting in. From April to October the N. or N.E. wind blew upon the island, roughly from 10 a.m. to 6 p.m.   In summer this wind produced a dense stratum of sea-cloud, and as a rule, when making Teneriffe from the northward during these months, land was seldom recognisable till within twenty miles of it.   The approach by sea to the anchoring place was under very high land, and three valleys—Teneriffe and the adjacent Gomera being twin peaks of a volcanic mass.   Spanish ships generally moored with two cables to the sea and four from the stern to the shore.   " Therefore, although we might get to be masters of them, should the wind not come off the shore, it does not appear certain we should succeed so completely as we might wish."   A surprise attack by night was indicated, and " as to any opposition, except by natural impediments, I should not think it would avail ".   Details of the dazzling action of Admiral Blake at Santa Cruz, in April 1657, were clear in his mind, although he had not had the opportunity to refresh his memory.   Blake, if he remembered correctly, had succeeded in capturing six Spanish galleons laden with silver, and had engaged ten other ships, all of which he had burnt or sunk.   But Blake had been " much obliged ", for his safe withdrawal, to the wind veering to the S.W., a thing rare in these islands.   Fortune, however, had " favoured the gallant attempt and may do so again ".

Having given a fair picture of every possible difficulty besetting the attempt by sea, he proceeded to unfold " my plan ", which entailed military support.   By a happy chance, 3,700 trained men, with every necessary munition and store, were already embarked, and since Teneriffe, in its history of three hundred years of Spanish occupation, had never been besieged, the hills that commanded the town had no fortifications.   The troops, once landed, could not fail.   Three days, very likely less, should see the capitulation of the island.   The only drawback was that the detachments at sea were the old Corsican garrison, and he was doubtful whether General de Burgh (who had flatly refused to leave Porto Ferrajo for Gibraltar without London orders) would consent, however rich the prize and propitious the moment, to a suggestion of Lord St. Vincent that

men ordered for service in Portugal should be deflected to take
part in a combined action on an island of the Canary group.
Should General de Burgh refuse to act, he could only suggest
that General O'Hara, Governor at Gibraltar, should be approached.
This valiant gentleman, a native of County Sligo, known in the
fleet as " Old Cock of the Rock ", was constitutionally far from
averse from a sporting chance and sudden violent action.   *1*

2

Lord St. Vincent thanked Admiral Nelson for his friendly
hint about the danger of the Elba garrison and offer to go in
quest of it, of which he would avail himself. He mentioned that
he was sending H.M.S. *Dido* and *Terpsichore* to look into Santa
Cruz, and that meanwhile, far from having any news of his
promised reinforcements from the Channel Fleet, his last letter
from home, in His Majesty's own hand, had told him of nothing
but old Lord Howe's journey from Bath, in order to be invested
with the Garter, an honour never hitherto bestowed upon a sea-
officer.   (There was sufficient reason for silence from the
Admiralty, but it was not yet known off Cadiz.)   He had written
to the First Lord, suggesting that taking possession of the island
of Teneriffe, could troops be furnished, was a practicable
enterprise.

Nelson proceeded up the Mediterranean, with the *Colossus*
and *Leander*, on his last cruise in the *Captain*.   It was not without
minor incident.   On the day after he left the fleet three frigates
joined him, off Cabrita Point.   He took the opportunity of
sending with the mail for Gibraltar a letter to General O'Hara
saying that if the Governor could dispense with the Emperor of
Morocco's present for a little, he should like to have H.M.S.
Meleager.   O'Hara jovially replied that he did not care if the
Emperor did not get his English clock at Tangier this month, and
sent him the *Meleager* : Nelson then wasted no time in getting to
the eastward.   Every vessel he spoke declared that a French
squadron was off the south end of Minorca.   He passed within
gunshot of Port Mahon on the 19th, with a strong wind at N.W.,
which, he imagined, must have blown the French into a Sardinian
port, since there was no sign of them at sea.   The weather in
the Mediterranean was, he found, even worse than last Christmas.
At length, on the morning of the 21st, sixty miles to the westward of Corsica, " to my inexpressible pleasure ", he sighted
forty sail.   He also observed a French gun brig evidently

looking at the convoy, but his charge was too important to separate a ship in chase of her, especially as he had just sent his two frigates round to the north side of the islands, to get hold of some Spaniards reported there.   Finding Captain Fremantle's charge and arrangement of the convoy perfect, he ordered no alteration.   " It could not be in better hands, therefore I only overshadow them with my wings."

Except that a transport containing some of Dillon's regiment (isolated with contagious fever) parted company in a gale during hours of darkness, that the gunner of the *Seahorse* frigate committed suicide, and that her Captain seemed likely to die from natural causes, no further anxieties disturbed him before he saw the Rock.   The report of a Dane, four days from Malaga, that the Spanish fleet had positive orders to come out, probably on that British anniversary, the Glorious First of June, made him hurry on alone from Gibraltar with as much speed as he had made on Valentine's Eve.   He rejoined St. Vincent off Cadiz on May 24, and resumed command of the in-shore squadron, which had, during his absence, been given to Sir James Saumarez, an accomplished Guernsey gentleman, one year his senior, knighted after a skilful and very timely single-ship action off Cherbourg, at the opening of the war.

He found St. Vincent in a fine new flagship.   The *Ville de Paris* felt like a rock after the trembling, leaky *Victory*, so shaken by her efforts on Valentine's Day, and a subsequent accidental intrusion on board another ship, that the step of a man from the poop-ladder made her whole stern-frame tremble.   On March 7 the First Lord had written, " Admiral Nelson will, I find, prefer a two-decked ship to a larger one, and Admiral Parker may therefore have the choice of the *Victory* or the *Barfleur*."   It was from the *Ville de Paris* on May 27 that Nelson sent a note to Miller, telling him to anchor the *Captain* near the *Theseus*, and transfer his personal effects.   Such officers as wished to go with him into the *Theseus*, and such men as came from the *Agamemnon*, and volunteered, might make their preparations.   Miller and he could discuss details later.   In fact, they had much to settle. His new ship had also arrived from Portsmouth during his absence.   She was not the dreaded *Gibraltar*, but she came with the curse of a bad reputation.   St. Vincent called her " an abomination ".   However, the Commander-in-Chief was flatter-ingly confident that her condition, the result of a weak Captain and a bullying First Lieutenant, would soon be put to rights by

Admiral Nelson and Captain Miller. Amongst the three con-   3
gratulatory letters from his princely naval friend awaiting Nelson,
the one of latest date contained typically violent opinions of the
recent trouble at Spithead. " Pardon my gloom ", concluded
the bachelor Prince (after drawing a lurid picture of " the Fleet
at Spithead, during a War, for a whole week, in a complete state
of Mutiny ", and Ireland, in open rebellion, awaiting French
invasion). " I have a very large stake in this Country, and a
family of young children to protect." (The first detachment of
young Fitz-Clarences to be brought to him by Mrs. Jordan, the
famous comedy actress, was openly established at Bushey Park.)
Nelson's view of the respectfully expressed demands of the
Spithead malcontents was that shared by most well-informed
persons. " I am entirely with the Seamen in their first complaint.   4
We are a neglected set." At home, patriotic persons had learnt
with horror that the Navy's rations were maggoty and under-
weight, that their medicines were embezzled by their ships'
surgeons, and that their leave, wages and pensions were lamentably
in arrears and insufficient. Parliament had been quick to vote
the necessary sums for increased pay, the Admiralty had made
concessions, the sovereign had been prevailed upon to extend a
general pardon. For the far more dangerous and largely
politically inspired mutineers of the Nore, news of whose mis-
deeds was yet to reach St. Vincent's fleet, Nelson had presently
no sympathy whatsoever. They were scoundrels, and he would
be glad to command a ship against them. His immediate object
was to discover whether he had got scoundrels or " the stuff to
work upon " with the *Theseus*. She had certainly been sent to
St. Vincent from the Channel Fleet because she had been prominent
amongst the disaffected ships. In a letter to Alexander Davison,
headed " *Theseus*, changed from the *Captain* this day ", he made
no other mention of his new ship, though he expressed at length
his indignation that their Lordships, instead of adequately re-
inforcing St. Vincent, who was now faced with the possibility of
encountering forty-five enemy sail-of-the-line with a force of
twenty-two, had seen fit to spare a squadron to cruise, actually
on his station. The squadron had, apparently, been sent to
catch " the dollars " from Havana, which every veteran under
St. Vincent's command considered his perquisite. Davison (now
of Harpur St., Bloomsbury) had employed his talents for affairs
so successfully since their last meeting that he was now recognised
by his naval admirer as one of those happy few to whom money

was no object. Still, since his old friend " H.N." might happen to capture the Mexican six to seven millions sterling, believed in the City of London to be overdue at Cadiz, Mr. Davison had not neglected, in his last letter, to ask who were agents for St. Vincent's fleet.

On the same night, the report of Captain Miller, after that reliable officer's first inspection of the *Theseus*, was illuminating. The ship, carrying papers which showed that she had been provisioned in March for foreign service, was on May 27 absolutely destitute of stores of all kinds. The boatswain had nothing in his charge; the carpenter could not produce a single nail. As things were at present, should even a rattlin be shot away in action, she had no means of replacement. As she had, as yet, seen no service, nothing could have been used except for routine cleaning. His Flag-Captain withdrew, and Nelson presented his compliments to his Commander-in-Chief, thanked him for his confidential letter delivered by hand (" You may depend on me "), and warned him that the Captain of the Fleet would shortly be receiving a very heavy demand for stores for the *Theseus*. When some of these arrived, it was obvious to every " old Agamemnon " that Admiral Nelson was preparing for action of an interesting nature. They were being set to teach their new companions to make ladders, such as they had constructed before the sieges in Corsica. During the next few weeks, specimen escalade ladders, some over thirty feet long, kept on passing between the Commander-in-Chief's flagship and the *Blenheim* (whose carpenter was late of the *Captain*) and the *Theseus*. Admiral Nelson came to look at them often, and said that they would not take more than ten men at a time—" the actors in our *Comedy* must not be too anxious to *mount* ".

Admiral Nelson, it appeared, knew even when the fresh greens, which were always bought largely for his people, failed to arrive in sufficient quantities, and himself interviewed the Spanish market boatmen engaged to deliver them. He had, moreover, gone to the *Swiftsure*, where two poor fellows, suspected of shamming mad in order to get their discharge, were lying in irons, after an attempt to destroy themselves. The result had been that he had written to the Commander-in-Chief asking that Dr. Weir, Physician to the Fleet, should pay a visit to these cases. He had offered to pay fifty pounds out of his own pocket to send the younger and less afflicted fellow to a proper place for his recovery, and had recommended both men for discharge. . . .

Within a fortnight of his move into the *Theseus*, a soiled paper, of difficult script, found " dropped on the quarter-deck " during the middle watch, was brought to his hands :

> " Success attend Admiral Nelson !   God bless Captain Miller !   We thank them for the Officers they have placed over us.   We are happy and comfortable, and will shed every drop of blood in our veins, and the name of the *Theseus* shall be immortalized as high as the *Captain's*."

It was signed in large block capitals, " SHIP'S COMPANY ".   8

3

The Spanish fleet did not come out on the First of June.   On May 30, Rear-Admiral Nelson sent word to His Excellency Admiral Don Josef de Mazaredo that, as June 4 was the birthday of his royal master, Lord St. Vincent intended firing a *feu de joie* at 8 p.m., and desired him to mention this, " that the Ladies of Cadiz may not be alarmed ".   The answer of His Excellency was that " the Ladies of Cadiz, accustomed to the noisy salutes of the vessels of war ", would sit to hear what the British Admiral meant to regale them with, and that the Spanish nation, as a whole, could not but interest itself in so august an occasion.   Calling upon his Maker to preserve Rear-Admiral Nelson for many years, and kissing his hands, Don Josef (very courteous for a Biscayner) signed himself, " attentive servant ".   Nelson also was attentive. St. Vincent, out of a strength of twenty sail-of-the-line, eventually spared him ten.   The ships-of-the-line had to keep their distance, to avoid the shoals, but the small craft of the in-shore squadron kept a ceaseless guard on the harbour mouth, and with darkness every night they reported alongside the *Theseus*, their crews armed with pikes, cutlasses, broad-axes and chopping-knives. Every boat was provided with handspikes, sledge-hammers and ropes to tow off captured vessels, and when they had received their orders, Nelson visited them at their stations.   Even on his quarter-deck he was " barely out of shot of a Spanish Rear-Admiral ", and close enough to admire the languorous ladies of Cadiz, pacing the walls and Mall of their town, and the merchants peering out anxiously every morning to see whether the Havana convoy had fallen into the hands of the blockading British over-night.   Three ships from Lima were also now expected, and it was said that the merchants would sooner sacrifice ten warships than lose these galleons, that the ladies were mocking their sea-officers, and the " mobility " had gone so far as to pelt Spanish seamen in their streets.   An American reported that the townspeople, who had heard that a bomb-vessel was fitting at Gibraltar, were in perfect terror of a bombardment, and had petitioned their Government to order their fleet to sea.

On June 15 the combination of unusual signals, the unmooring of thirteen Spanish ships-of-the-line, and information that their men had been in the market buying much food, raised Nelson's hope of a meeting sufficiently for him to order all ships of his squadron to clear for action.   After nearly three weeks of existing in the miserable discomfort unavoidable when bulkheads were down, he was feeling " very indifferent ", and " almost tired of looking at these fellows ".   A Spanish report said that Mr. Pitt was out of office.   From England, first descriptions of the out-break at the Nore were worrying.   Austria had succumbed to Buonaparte and signed the Peace of Leoben, and a French army of invasion was waiting to sail from the mouth of the Texel under cover of a Dutch squadron.   By July 3, the *Thunderer* bomb-ketch and *Urchin* gunboat having arrived from Gibraltar, St. Vincent (who had been receiving almost daily letters from Nelson, on the subject of ladders, ammunition, artillery and a devil-cart necessary for the Santa Cruz Expedition) agreed to a bombardment of Cadiz, in the hopes of either bringing out the Spanish fleet or raising a revolution in the town.   Nelson wrote what should make a beautiful last letter to his lady—who had begged him to leave dangerous actions to subordinates—opening :   " Rest assured of my most perfect love, affection and esteem for your person and character, which the more I see of the world, the more I must admire ", and to St. Vincent two very cheerful notes, the first of which ended, " I intend, if alive, and not too tired, to see you to-morrow."   His second note asked that all the launches of the fleet, with their cannonades and ammunition, and all the barges and pinnaces, well provided with pikes, might be with him by 8.30 at latest.   He hoped to begin " to make it a warm night at Cadiz " at 10 p.m.   The town batteries and the fleet were, he knew, expecting him—" Gun boats advanced etc. So much the better.   If they venture from the walls, I shall give Johnny his full scope of fighting.   It will serve to talk of, better than mischief."   The enemy were expecting him on their " soft side ".   He stationed the *Thunderer*, with a detachment of artillery on board, within 2,500 yards of " the strong face of Cadiz ", near the Tower of San Sebastian, covered by the *Urchin*, launches and barges of the fleet.   The ketch began to do her duty, and several shells fell into the town, to be followed by smoke and

Q

flames, streaming towards the midsummer night sky. The town
was soon well alight in three places. The *Thunderer* was not, of
course, left long undisturbed. Seventy pieces of cannon on the
line-wall came into action; she was disabled, and a vigorous
attempt was made by enemy mortar-gun boats and armed
launches to carry her. " Rear-Admiral Nelson ", in the words
of St. Vincent, " always present in the most arduous enterprises ",
after signalling her to retire to the protection of three frigates
kept under sail for such an emergency, himself sped to her rescue.
In the *mêlée* which followed, the craft attending him boarded and
carried two Spanish gunboats, but the launch of St. Vincent's
flagship, the *Ville de Paris*, was sunk by a raking shot, and his
own barge was singled out for attention by the Commander of
the Spanish flotilla, Don Miguel Tyrason.

The attack on Cadiz on the night of July 3 was a small
affair, but it claimed a full paragraph in the succinct *Sketch of
my Life* later supplied by the Victor of the Nile to a biographer.
As yet he had never in his life been more nearly despatched in
hand-to-hand fighting. " This was a service, hand to hand, with
swords." His barge, with its common crew of ten men, a
coxswain, Fremantle and himself, was attacked by that of the
Spanish Commander, rowed by twenty-six men, and carrying
four officers. Fremantle was slightly wounded, and John Sykes,
coxswain, who had stood by his Captain's side on the quarter-deck
of the *San Josef* on Valentine's Day, twice saved his life by
interposing his person. On the second occasion, Sykes fell, with
severe head injuries. But the enemy, in overwhelming force,　⁹
were not only beaten off. By the time that the Spanish armed
launch of a much superior size had been captured, every survivor
had been wounded, and her Commander had been taken prisoner.

In the small hours, Nelson, with a hundred and seventeen
prisoners on board the *Theseus*, thirty of whom were not to survive,
was able to dictate a decidedly satisfactory report to St. Vincent,
who next day had the pleasure of learning that " the active
intelligent mind of Captain Fremantle " had got his launch up,
and was supervising repairs on board H.M.S. *Culloden*. Another
bombardment was planned for the 5th, this time on " the soft
side ", on the outside of the lighthouse, where Mr. Jackson,
Master of the *Ville de Paris*, knew of a good berth for the
Thunderer, now reinforced by the appropriately named mortar-
boats, *Terror* and *Stromboli*. St. Vincent's announcement that
" the Lieutenant who had the greatest merit, taking an enemy

brig, should immediately be given command of his prize " had Nelson's warm approval. He thought that the prospect could not fail to encourage zeal hitherto damped, though not quenched, by the consideration that after such an action promotion would come, not to " the poor gallant fellow responsible, but to some Great Man's son ". He was " merely a spectator " of the attempt of the night of July 5. From the first the shore batteries had got the exact range of his bomb-ketch and mortars, and as their gunboats kept close under the sea wall, no opportunity offered for Bowen of the *Terpsichore* to " make a dash at them ". When some forty-odd shells had been successfully landed in the town and harbour, and the *Thunderer* had been shot in the hull and both masts, Nelson signalled Bowen to tow her off.

St. Vincent had his own good reasons for ordering these nightly distractions. On the 7th and 8th four mutineers of the *St. George* were being tried by court-martial on board his flagship. Their trial did not terminate until after sunset on the Saturday, so he decreed that the sentence should be carried out at dawn on the following morning. Nelson, who was ordered to be present, with the boats of the in-shore squadron, approved the speedy carrying out of the sentence, though on a Sunday, but " Vice-Admiral Thompson having presumed to censure the execution on the Sabbath in a public letter, I have ", reported St. Vincent, " insisted on his being removed from the Fleet immediately." One of the mutineers, when interviewed by the chaplain, had disclosed that his scheme had been in contemplation for six months, and that he had confederates in the *Britannia, Diadem, Captain* and *Egmont*. The condemned men had asked to be allowed five days in which to prepare for death, " in which they would have hatched 500 Treasons. Had it been Christmas Day, instead of Sunday," said Nelson, " I would have executed them." He believed that if the same spirit of determination had been shown by the authorities at home, the disturbances in the Channel and North Sea fleets need never have got out of hand. But he still thought that old Lord Howe's sending back the Spithead men's first petition had been quite wrong.

On the hot and uneasy night of the 8th, after the court-martial had risen, his plan of a third operation on Cadiz having been frustrated by a gale which made it impossible to get the *Thunderer* up to the chosen point of attack, he summoned and addressed his ship's company, under, perhaps, the most difficult circumstances of his career. " We, in the advance, are night and

10

day, prepared for battle.   Our friends in England need not fear
the event." An unusual silence pervaded the men of the *Theseus*,
lately " an abomination ".   They dismissed very quietly.   They
were ordered to assist at to-morrow's scene, so Nelson hoped that
he had spoken with good effect.   Next morning the sentence was
duly carried out, and the action of twenty-seven enemy mortar
and gunboats, which advanced to cannonade his ten sail-of-the-
line, on observing the barges and pinnaces of his squadron
proceeding to the execution, was decidedly helpful to *morale*.

In the postponed third attack on the town, made on the night
of the 10th, since the *Theseus* " had the honour of every gun from
the southern part of Cadiz, and of every gun and mortar boat ",
she suffered a few casualties, but Nelson, who had much rather
see fifty men shot by the enemy than one mutineer dangling from
his yard-arm, welcomed the shot flying about her as likely to do
her good.   He had now forced the enemy from their outer into
their inner harbour, so his squadron should, in future, have
notice of the emergence of the Spanish fleet, and next morning,
to his great interest, he saw a red flag hoisted on board seven
enemy ships, including that of an Admiral.   He seized the chance
of sending a flag of truce into the town, with some ninety of the
prisoners taken on the 3rd, and the officer in charge reported, on
return, that when he had asked if the Spanish fleet was " *à la
Nore* ", he had received an unbelievably languid reply, " Yes,
that the men were demanding their wages ".   The merchants of
Cadiz, however, were offering a small fortune to any volunteer
who would board the dreaded *Thunderer*.

Quite suddenly, only a few hours after he had written to St.
Vincent asking for more mortars from the Rock, came the orders
for which Nelson had long been hoping.   After receiving them he
wrote to his wife, telling her that as he now had a prospect of
being absent from the fleet for a short time, she must not be
anxious if she heard nothing awhile.   On the morning of July 14,
at 8 a.m., he weighed, and stood towards the main body of the
fleet.   Noon was the hour appointed by the Commander-in-Chief
for a tense, though not long, interview, and next morning at   11
6 a.m., having received orders to take under his command H.M.S.
Theseus, Culloden, Zealous, Leander, Terpsichore, Seahorse and
Emerald, the *Fox* cutter and *Çacafuego* mortar-boat, Nelson made
sail to the westward.

4

The circumstances under which the expedition sailed for
Teneriffe on July 15 were by no means those visualised by Nelson
and Troubridge on the hopeful night of April 11.

St. Vincent had not been successful in persuading either de
Burgh or O'Hara to part with troops " to attempt the surprise
of Santa Cruz in the Grand Canary ". O'Hara, indeed, describing
himself as out of spirits, had counter-attacked, asking for an
addition to the naval force at Gibraltar. These refusals were
serious considerations, as Nelson, when presenting his original
plan, had stipulated for either the Corsica garrison of three
thousand seven hundred, or one thousand six hundred men from
the Rock. Nor, as St. Vincent admitted, was the capture of
Teneriffe quite the grand object that it had been when Nelson
suggested the enterprise. Captains Cockburn and Hallowell (sent
thither to cruise, with a roving commission, so long as their
provisions lasted) had ascertained that the Viceroy was not
sheltering in Teneriffe. " I long ", wrote Nelson, " for *poor*
Cockburn and Hallowell to enrich themselves." In answer to a
question from St. Vincent, who knew that he had married a West
India lady, of connections reported affluent and influential, his
reply had been bleak : " I believe my acquaintances in the
West Indies are but few : indeed, I can recollect none I am in the
habit of correspondence with."

The news from Lisbon was that, hearing of the result of the
engagement of Valentine's Day, and hoping for a peace, the
Mexican treasure fleet had decided not to run the enormous
hazard of attempting a homeward passage until the war was
over. It had not sailed. On the other hand, by the first week
in May, St. Vincent knew for certain that two register ships
belonging to the Philippine Company, bound from Manila for
Cadiz (one of them the famous *El Principe d'Asturias*), were at
Santa Cruz, and had not as yet unloaded their rich cargoes. And
O'Hara, although he would not part with troops and expressed
wrath at the request to do so, was willing to supply the train of
artillery, ammunition and devil-cart demanded by Nelson. As
this news gradually dropped in, St. Vincent kept Nelson advised,
by letter and by the impenetrably discreet Jackson, and finally
asked him to pronounce on the possibilities of a wholly naval
operation—" Turn this in your mind." Personally, St. Vincent
had always hoped to live to see the day when there was not a

foot-soldier left in Great Britain, or the colonies, except the King's Guards and the Artillery. " A very considerable corps of Marines " in their place was one of his dreams for a peace establishment. Nelson, without the least hesitation, answered [12] that given two hundred extra marines for his landing-party, " with ' General Troubridge ' ashore and myself afloat, I am confident of success ". Thereupon, St. Vincent agreed that the moment his fleet was reinforced by the four sail-of-the-line for which he had asked repeatedly and strongly, he would be ready " to dash you off ". His offer of material for the ladders to be prepared by every ship in the fleet, now that the time was drawing near " to make people guess ", was nicely calculated to touch the imagination of Nelson. Since Nelson had complained that the first specimens were heavy, the *Ville de Paris* should supply bamboo cut in the Martinique swamps, " by which we make nice ones ", resembling those " by which my late gallant friend Faulknor readily found his way into Fort Royal ". Nelson, on his side, said that the Duke of Clarence never wrote without expressing the hope that " the illustrious Jervis should now fall in with the Dollars ", and that the sentiments of Collingwood represented those of the whole fleet—" a great desire to see our Commander-in-Chief a Marquis this summer ".

On June 7 St. Vincent wrote, " We must have something from England soon, together with your ribbon, and the patents for the Admirals ", but a month later he had not been reinforced and he was trying mutineers. He was now convinced that the Spanish fleet was not coming out, at least during the season while he could keep his present station, and while Spain had between thirty and forty sail-of-the-line in port at Cadiz and a division at Cartagena he could not hope to return to the Mediterranean. In these black weeks he persuaded himself that hopes of a success at Teneriffe under a lucky commander were " well-grounded ". His temper at this period was at its most formidable, and not only mutineers felt it. " I dread not the seamen. It is the indiscreet, licentious conversation of the officers which produce all our ills, and the presumptuous discussion of the orders they receive." The *Captain*, under her new Captain, was not what she had been. Acting on a belief that her wardroom was enjoying the dainties of the fresh fare obtainable, the Chief issued a General Fleet Order that ships' companies were to be first served. " When at sea, we do not make snug for the night, as in the Westward Squadron." Colonel Flight, commanding officer of marines, being summoned to the quarter-deck of the *Ville de Paris* at 2.30 a.m., arrived armed at all points, imagining that the enemy were out. " I have sent for you, Colonel, that you might smell, for the first time in your life, the delicious odours brought off by the landwind from the shores of Andalusia. Take a good sniff, and then you may go and turn in again." On another morning, a too well-liking Lieutenant came on board to answer a signal. " Calder," observed the Commander-in-Chief, " all the Lieutenants are running to belly. They have been too long at anchor. Block up the entering port except for Admirals and Captains, and make them climb over the hammocks."

But to Nelson he could not have shown more spacious favour. He allowed him to choose the ships and officers to accompany him, although the old friends chosen by Nelson were the cream of the late Mediterranean Fleet—Troubridge, Fremantle, Miller, Waller, Bowen, the young Sam Hood. . . . The senior captain of marines was also Nelson's choice. The worthy Oldfield had been wounded in his company on the night of July 5. The Lieutenant of Artillery, Baynes, also direct from Gibraltar, belonged to the Rock, dynastically and professionally. Lord St. Vincent, who had long known both his parents, had commended this officer, of a good Service family, to Nelson before the young man had distinguished himself shelling Cadiz from the *Thunderer*. Thompson, the only Captain not present, had special knowledge of the Canaries, was cruising down there now, and would join the squadron at sea, as would Bowen, who had taken the *Terpsichore* to Lisbon for supplies.

An hour before the expedition sailed on the early morning of the 15th the Captains of the squadron came on board the *Theseus*. They were given their orders, and, in case of separation, the *rendezvous*. The scene was not peaceful, for the boats of the fleet were delivering scaling-ladders, ammunition and the marines to be transferred to the *Leander*; but Lord St. Vincent's instructions were as usual unmistakable. Admiral Nelson was to proceed with the utmost expedition to the Island of Teneriffe, to take possession, by a sudden vigorous assault, of the port of Santa Cruz. If successful, he was authorised to seize *El Principe d'Asturias* with her whole cargo, and all treasure in the port belonging to the Crown of Spain. Should the inhabitants object, he might levy a heavy contribution upon them and endeavour to take, burn, sink or otherwise destroy all enemy vessels of every description on the coast of Africa, even those engaged in the fishery. Lord St. Vincent's order closed : " And having performed your mission, you are to make the best of your way back to join me." Nelson had assured him : " Ten hours shall either make me a conqueror or defeat me ", and, " We shall get hold of something, if there is anything moving on the face of the waters." Still, in his note of farewell, the Commander-in-Chief displayed more good wishes than high expectations : " God bless you and prosper you. I am sure you will deserve success. To mortals is not given the power of commanding it."

At 9 a.m. on July 15, H.M.S. *Alcmene*, nearing the end of her passage from Portsmouth to Cadiz, in charge of a convoy, beheld a cheering and business-like sight. The British squadron which she spoke in the mouth of the Straits consisted of three 74's, a couple of frigates (one of 60 guns) and a cutter with a gunboat in tow. The early morning had been very cloudy, but the wind was now moderate from the S.S.W., and before the squadron passed from view the smaller frigate had parted. Waller, in the *Emerald*, had been sent ahead to look out for Bowen. The *Terpsichore* joined next evening, and Captain D'Arcy Preston of the *Blanche* carried to his relative, Lord St. Vincent, the news that at 6 p.m. on Sunday he had seen Admiral Nelson's squadron standing on for Teneriffe with light airs and clear weather.

Nothing further was heard of the Santa Cruz Expedition for exactly a month, when the swift *Emerald* arrived alone, with a despatch and two letters written in an almost indecipherable strange hand, the contents of which caused the Commander-in-Chief extreme anguish.

<h1 style="text-align:center">5</h1>

The expedition had sailed on a Saturday morning. On the Monday the Captains of the squadron came on board the *Theseus* again to bend their brows over a large-scale plan of Santa Cruz Bay, drawn by a Lieutenant of Engineers, in which the valley to the north-east of the town, known to the inhabitants as " Lion's Mouth ", was labelled " E ", and the heights and battery behind it, and commanding the port, were " F " and " G ". It was agreed that the boats carrying the landing-parties should proceed in six divisions, kept together by towing, that they should disembark their men simultaneously, and that the moment the attempt was discovered, the *Çacafuego* should open fire on the town and keep on doing her duty until she saw a flag of truce hoisted—" from either the Enemy or from us ". Frigates were to anchor as soon as possible after either the alarm had been given or the forces were on shore, and as near as they could to " F " and " G ", which would be immediately stormed. The Admiral recommended that every possible seaman disembarked should be provided with a marine's greatcoat or jacket; certainly canvas cross-belts. He had not the slightest doubt of the boldness and efficiency of his " Jacks ", but they were few. " Red-coats have their use in dazzling the eyes of the Enemy ", and of genuine marines he had but two hundred and fifty. The knowledgeable Thompson, whom he had summoned from Cadiz and intended to employ as second-in-command to Troubridge, had not yet joined. He empowered all Captains who wished to do so to land at Santa Cruz and command their men, together with as many men above the number detailed from each ship as wished to volunteer, only providing that sufficient were left to manage the ship and man her boats. The 74's would be kept below the horizon until the surprise night attack had been launched, and then make their appearance, ready to bring their broadsides to bear against the line-wall battery and mole-head. All Captains were instructed to set their men to work to make iron ramrods, since wooden ones were apt to break when used in haste, and Troubridge, Fremantle and Hood were, in addition, provided with a sketch, showing sections of gun platforms. Next morning the *Theseus*, too, echoed to sounds of carpentry. She was making a sledge to drag eighteen-pounders. Other ominous sounds startled the summer seas as the squadron drew nearer to the " fortunate isles' " of Plutarch and Ptolemy. After a general signal for midshipmen, small-arms men exercised themselves firing at a target. At 8 a.m. on Friday the 21st, the Captains came on board for their final conference. A blue cone, of barbaric contours, uncannily girdled by drifting cloud, and seemingly based on air, was looming momentarily larger. Indeed, since with sunset yesterday the visibility had suddenly become un-commonly good, the Peak of Teneriffe had been clearly discernible, against fading skies, at thirty miles distance.

The last conference was held. Captains Hood, Fremantle, Miller, Waller and Bowen " very handsomely " offered their services on shore. The ninety men detailed had been augmented by about a hundred volunteers. " General " Troubridge, " Commander of the Forces ordered to land ", was entrusted with his Admiral's formal summons to the Governor or Command-ing Officer of the port, which he was recommended to present, as he thought best, either before or after proceeding against the town and mole-head battery. His orders, which gave him great scope to use initiative, advised that his first step should be the capture of the mountain fort " G ", and ended, " Having the firmest confidence in the ability, bravery and zeal of yourself, and all placed under your command, I have only to heartily wish you success." The squadron wore to the eastward and hoisted out the boats which were to transfer the landing-parties to the frigates *Terpsichore, Emerald* and *Seahorse.* All oars for the boats designed for the night operation had been muffled with pieces of kersey or canvas. Scaling-ladders, each provided with a lanyard four fathoms long, many sledge-hammers, wedges, broad-axes, ramrods and " every implement I thought necessary for the success of the enterprise " were also transferred. Nelson, with his line-of-battle ships, then retired to the eastward, to wear and tack throughout the hours of darkness in increasing anxiety, as no unusual and hoped-for sounds disturbed the night. At 3.30 next morning, he bore up for the island, and through the clouds of daybreak could see three British frigates and a mortar-boat off Santa Cruz, and the ships' boats pulling off-shore. Evidently the dash in the dark had not taken place. At 6 a.m. a trio of solemn figures presented themselves to report a setback. Troubridge, Bowen and Oldfield wished " to consult what was best to be done ". Their lamentable tale was that, although the frigates had been within three miles of " Lion's Mouth " by midnight, by the unlucky conjunction of a strong gale of wind in the offing and a strong current against them in-shore, they had not been able to get within a mile of beach " E " before light came. The surprise attack had been frustrated by the elements, and the enemy were now well aware of their presence, and in high commotion. Still, Troubridge believed that if he could capture the mountain overshadowing " Lion's Mouth ", he might storm the fort, halfway up it, from the rear, and turn its guns upon the town. It was true that his forces were likely to be greatly out-numbered, but the veterans of St. Valentine's Day had not forgotten the pitiful lack of discipline and eagerness to surrender displayed by Spanish seamen in that very unequal action. (Officers taken prisoner had assured them that after the first broadside, neither threats nor punishment had availed to persuade a single Spaniard to go aloft to repair a rigging.) And although a complete surprise of Santa Cruz was now out of the question, it was likely that the enemy were, as yet, confused and unready.

Nelson assented, and by nine o'clock the frigates had anchored and begun, in broad daylight, to put the landing-party on shore. But Fortune again refused to "favour the gallant attempt", and his effort to "create a diversion" with his line-of-battle ships, by battering fort "G", was rendered impracticable by a flat calm and contrary currents. The 74's could not get within range of the fort, and were unable even to reach anchoring ground. They plied to and fro off the port, wearing occasionally, throughout a long day, during which it became increasingly obvious that the enemy had full possession of the heights and intended to keep them. With darkness came gales and cloudy weather. The 74's struck their top-gallant masts and wore. The sole success of the expedition took place with dawn, when the *Zealous* captured a merchant vessel from another of the Canaries, bound for Teneriffe with stock. At 7 a.m. Troubridge appeared, dead-beat, to announce that he had failed to get possession of "F" or "G", but had gathered his landing-party and re-embarked it on board the frigates. Nelson signalled the frigates to weigh and join him. The landing-party was carried back to its various ships, and all boats were hoisted in. As the wind still permitted of no closer approach to the shore, the squadron continued under sail for two days.

By Monday morning, July 24, "foiled in my original plan", Nelson was ready with another, so hazardous that all serious-minded persons, on hearing of it, made their preparations. After two failures, entirely owing to the "natural impediments", which he had always predicted as a possibility, he would have been justified in giving over the attempt to take Santa Cruz and returning to St. Vincent off Cadiz. But the moment was most inopportune for a return to St. Vincent's fleet with a tale of nothing achieved, and he felt, though he did not utter the belief, that had not Troubridge wasted three hours in coming to ask his advice, the attack on fort "G" might have succeeded. "Convinced there is nothing which Englishmen are not equal to, and confident in the bravery of those who would be employed", he had decided, during those two days of blowing weather, upon a direct attack on the town, in the centre of the bay, at the earliest possible moment; and this time he would lead it himself. The weather that day remained persistently unfriendly, with strong gales but good visibility, but by 5.30 p.m. he had anchored the squadron about two miles north of the town, and anyone who had not taken a closer look was able to satisfy his curiosity as to the attractions of Santa Cruz of Teneriffe on a wet summer's evening. It was a small old town, in the Spanish style, with an exiled air. It possessed one prominent square church tower. Its white houses, flat-roofed and faced, crouched, half in eternal shadow, below weirdly shaped and seamed volcanic heights. Most of the greenery in the picture was provided by cacti.

Nelson's display of every indication that he was about to bombard the heights had the desired effect. As dusk closed in, he was able to observe detachments of troops hurrying from the town to the mountain fort, which he meant to leave undisturbed. The only unexpected incident of the afternoon was a welcome one. The *Terpsichore's* signal for a strange sail heralded H.M.S. *Leander.* Her two hundred marines were added to the landing-force, and Captain Thompson, chosen for his knowledge of the island, was immediately ready to volunteer his services on shore. At 6 p.m. the boats of the squadron received the same directions as on the preceding Friday. Complete darkness could not be relied upon, even on a poor day, until shortly before midnight. As light faded in the *Terpsichore* Mr. Thomas Thorp, First Lieutenant, aged nineteen, carefully reckoned his fortune. He believed he left about £1,500 up to date, and wisely decided not to count upon what he might get after to-night's affair. He wrote to his parents that Mr. Cook, prize-agent, should produce £1,200. The £300 in his chest would be sent home by his messmates. " As I think there is a chance of my not returning, I leave this directed to you. . . . As I never intentionally did wrong, I do not feel affraid [*sic*]. I think you will have the satisfaction of saying your boy has done his duty, and believe me, the greatest concern I have, is the coming grief my loss will occasion you. My best Adieux to you, all I care for in the world." In the *Theseus*, too, young men were active. Lieutenant Nisbet, Officer of the Watch, summoned to his stepfather's cabin, found the Admiral busy, this July night, sorting and burning Lady Nelson's letters. The dress of Josiah announced that he was prepared to embark with the landing-party, and a dramatic dialogue followed his war-like entry.

" Should we both fall, Josiah, what would become of your poor mother ? The care of the *Theseus* falls to you. Stay, therefore, and take charge of her."

" Sir, the Ship must take care of herself. I will go with you to-night if never again."

That Josiah's memory did not exaggerate the tone abroad

that night may be judged from the letter written by his step-father, after his exit, to the Commander-in-Chief:

"*Theseus, off Santa Cruz,*
"*July 24th. 8 p.m.*

" My dear Sir,

" I shall not enter on the subject while we are not in possession of Santa Cruz; your partiality will give me credit that all has hitherto been done which was possible, but without effect. This night, I, humble as I am, command the whole, destined to land under the batteries of the Town, and to-morrow my head will probably be crowned with either laurel or cypress. I have only to recommend Josiah Nisbet to you and my Country. With every affectionate wish for your health, and every blessing in the world, believe me your most faithful

" Horatio Nelson."

" The Duke of Clarence, should I fall, in the service of my King and Country, will, I am confident, take a lively interest for my Son-in-Law, on his name being mentioned."

16

Before setting out for what he himself afterwards described as " a forlorn hope . . . I never expected to return ", Nelson proceeded to sup with Mrs. Fremantle, in the *Seahorse*.

Besides the logs of the various ships concerned, four first-hand accounts of the events of that dark and fatal night are available. Nelson's " Journal ", despatch and detailed report to St. Vincent, with which he enclosed a letter to himself from Troubridge, record in official language the events of a disastrous

17 night operation against hopeless odds in foul weather. Josiah Nisbet and an anonymous " officer who was present " add some valuable details, but their story was not collected for at least

18 seven years. Two young persons left behind to await the return of the party wrote their impressions on the spot. Betsy Fremantle

19, 20 kept her diary. William Hoste sent a letter home.

6

When Captain Fremantle, at Gibraltar, received orders to change into the *Seahorse* and join the fleet off Cadiz, he was not much pleased. His expectation had been to carry his foreign-bred bride home in the *Inconstant*, and settle her amongst his affectionate family while he pursued a brilliant career. But Captain Oakes of the *Seahorse* was in a deplorable state of health, the *Inconstant* was due for a thorough refit, and his Betsy was enchanted at the prospect of more of his company. When he got to Cadiz, and heard of the project in hand, his wife noticed " much better spirits ". He told her that there were good hopes

of peace, which, after two experiences of sitting up for him while
he was "out all night with Admiral Nelson to bombard the
town", she was glad to hear.   His outings with Nelson sounded
very noisy, and from one of them he returned, having received
"a blow".   On the day before the expedition sailed for Santa
Cruz, the bride felt "not well, but I don't know what makes me
feel so ".   Her husband had by now given her an explanation of
the duty on which they were bound.   "We are going ", she
calmly instructed her diary, "to take the island of Teneriffe."
The island, to be sure, did not seem quite so easy to take as she
had been led to expect, and after two days in a small bay at a
short distance from the town, but out of gunshot, she was delighted
at the order to weigh and join the Admiral and 74's.   "Had they
been with us, the place would have long been taken."   A German
merchant captain had brought news that Santa Cruz possessed
only three hundred regular troops, and that the inhabitants were
all crying and trembling at the appearance of the British squadron.

By the night of July 24, when the Admiral, attended by
Captains Bowen, Miller and Hood, came to sup with her in the
Seahorse, Mrs. Fremantle was "pretty well ".   The only drawback to her happiness as a hostess, that dark, rough night, was
the noise made by the men of the *Theseus* as they went on board
the boats bound for the mole of Santa Cruz.   During the last
three days she had found these three hundred and fifty guests
"the most tiresome, noisy, mutinous people in the world ", and
noted that they seemed to annoy Fremantle.   But it appeared
that their temporary presence was a necessary evil.   "They
are all ", she explained to her diary, "to land in the Town."
Satisfied by the brief explanations of her supper-party that
"the taking of the place seemed an easy, and almost a sure thing ",
she received their polite farewells with *aplomb*, and went to bed,
"apprehending no danger to Fremantle ".

He had fitted up a lower cabin for her, and for the past four
nights had seen to it that she had a woman within call—the sail-
maker's wife.   When she heard "much firing " during the night,
the ailing bride had no doubt that the English were by now
masters of Teneriffe.   "Great was our mistake.   This proved to
be a shocking unfortunate night."

7

Of what followed after the last of Mrs. Fremantle's guests
had gone over the side of the *Seahorse* into darkness, Troubridge's

experiences may be given first.   At 10.30 the marines and seamen from the various ships, numbering between six and seven hundred, began to go on board the heaving boats alongside the three frigates.   A further hundred and eighty men were embarked in the *Fox* cutter and eighty in the Spanish merchant vessel taken at dawn.   Fremantle and Bowen went with the Admiral, to lead the central division in the attack.   The Captains of the remaining five divisions had all received orders to land on the mole and make for the principal square of the town as fast as possible.   There, they were to form, in preparation for whatever services might be necessary.   By 11 the last boat had put off.   The night was pitch black, and there was a heavy sea running—circumstances which prevented the enemy from discovering the approach of the invaders, but also prevented them from finding their way. Troubridge's division was almost the unluckiest.   After more than an hour and a half's steady pulling against stinging rain and raving wind, he heard the roar of the surf breaking on rocks. He realised then that he must, as he had feared, have missed the mole.   Almost immediately he knew that someone must have been more successful, for a crackle of musketry sounded from end to end of the town, the sky lit, cannon opened fire close overhead and all the bells of Santa Cruz began to peal.   The expectation of the veterans of St. Valentine's Day that Spanish soldiers would show no more fight than Spanish seamen was quite mistaken.   Decadent Spain, like Rome, kept her best legions in her outposts.   There were tough men (though mostly irregulars), under a competent commander, awaiting the arrival of the English ; and although large detachments had been sent to the fort on the mountain-side, forty guns had been trained on the mole-head all day, and every house overlooking it had musketeers posted in the windows.   Troubridge found himself under the battery to the south of the citadel.   He pushed on shore, and landed safely on a narrow beach, at the same time as another boatload, whose commander he presently recognised as Waller.   But only two or three boats out of their two divisions followed them.   The surf was so high, many put back in despair ; many more, cast violently against the inhospitable rocks of Santa Cruz Bay, filled and sank instantly.   He collected what men he could, and, together with Waller, fought his way over the line-wall and battery, taking some prisoners, and managed to reach the central square.   At this *rendezvous* he waited, while the scene gradually but unmistakably took on every aspect of the night operation which has gone very wrong.

Most of the larger houses of Santa Cruz were built, Spanish-fashion, around a courtyard planted with shrubs. The sombre building which he had seized as his headquarters proved to be a convent. The alarm, firing and lateness of the hour had not driven all inhabitants from the flashing streets. He arrested two gentlemen and detailed them as escort to a sergeant of marines, whom he boldly instructed to demand the surrender of the citadel. (It may be said at once that he never saw or heard of the man again.) At the end of about an hour he decided that some fatal accident must have detained Nelson, and he must take some further and wholly independent action. His position was remarkably hopeless. He had no provisions; his men were all wet through, and, what was more serious, nearly all the ammunition in their pouches had received a thorough soaking. Every scaling-ladder had, apparently, been lost in the surf; for no enquiries could bring even news of a single one. It was therefore at present quite impossible to attempt to assault the citadel. He employed his men preparing fire-balls and collecting torches to set light to the town, which they did with such zest that the inhabitants of the convent fled to the Governor to demand the removal of the English, whatever the price. From some of the drenched lost seamen who appeared at the *rendezvous* during the next few hours, full of uneasy rumour and incorrect surmise, he heard that Captains Hood and Miller had made good their landing to the south-west of the place where he had managed to get ashore. They were said to have a body of men with them, but no one knew how many. Of the Admiral and his attendant Captains no one knew anything.

Dawn broke over the Spanish convent as Troubridge and Waller, with their party, marched out in search of their reported allies. After their encounter, their joint forces still only amounted to about 80 marines, 80 pikemen and 180 small-arms men. They took what ammunition they could get from their prisoners, and marched to survey the citadel in the light of day. But the streets, never quiet throughout that ill night, were now commanded by field-pieces, and down every avenue they could perceive advancing troops: 8,000 Spaniards and 100 French heavy gunners were said, by their prisoners, to be in arms against their force of less than 350. Being assured that all of their boats which were not stove in had delivered their landing-parties, and that no more men could come from the ships, Troubridge decided on another bold stroke. At 7 a.m. he sent Hood with a flag of

truce to the Governor to say that if the enemy advanced an inch
further, he would be reluctantly obliged to fire the town. As he
had no desire to injure the inhabitants of Santa Cruz, he was
ready to treat. He asked that all troops belonging to His
Britannic Majesty, with their arms, should be allowed to embark
from the mole in sufficient transport. In return he promised that
neither they, nor the ships of the squadron now before the town,
should take any further hostile action. Don Juan Antonio
Gutierrez, Commandant-General of the Isles of Canary, began in
leisurely fashion to tell Captain Hood (who spoke Spanish) that
he thought the English ought first to surrender their prisoners,
but the British sea-officer fiercely responded that his instructions
were that if the terms which he offered were not accepted, he
was to set light to the town within five minutes and order a
bayonet charge, whereupon the Governor hastily expressed great
willingness to treat. It was agreed that all prisoners on both
sides should be given up, and Troubridge, with his small band,
marched, with British colours flying, to the mole-head. Although
they were so few, many had swum ashore, and their own boats
were, as he had anticipated, quite insufficient to take them back
to their ships. The Governor supplied them with native craft,
sent them food and wine, and offered accommodation in the
hospitals of the town for the dangerously wounded. He could
afford to be generous.

8

William Hoste, midshipman of the *Theseus*, endured a most
wretched vigil after he had seen the ship's boat depart for
H.M.S. *Seahorse* and the mole of Santa Cruz without him.
Lieutenant Weatherhead, his best friend, and Lieutenant Nisbet,
to whom he was not so devoted, had both gone. Hoste, although
he had entered the Service at the same date as both these officers,
and was only three months junior to Nisbet, was still a midshipman. A serious attack of typhoid after the siege of Calvi, a
broken leg, from which he still sometimes felt twinges, and a long
experience of malaria at Leghorn last year, had deprived him of
many months of service afloat. He was, at the moment, recovering from a deep cut in the right palm, which he had got in
one of the hand-to-hand boat attacks in Cadiz harbour. Four
years and four months had passed since Captain Nelson had
commissioned the *Agamemnon*, and a noticeably small boy of
twelve, with the blunt, short features, direct, blue gaze and

R

flaxen hair of his Flemish ancestors, had said a wondering farewell to Godwick House, Norfolk.   He thought that if he was to
be set down at Tittleshall, he could still find his way to his father's
house ; but from no further village.   (He could not, in his home
thoughts from sea, remember the roads.)   And although he could
recollect the cast of the countenances of his father and elder
brother, the rest, he knew, would appear perfect strangers to him.

The *Theseus*, cleared for action, was not a " floating heaven ".
At 1 a.m. on the morning of July 25, Hoste's pricked ears were
rewarded by " one of the heaviest cannonades I ever was witness
to ".   It came from the town, and was doubtless directed upon
the boats which had pulled away into stormy darkness after
supper.   The attempt had been discovered, and the landing must
now be in progress ; the next few hours would be critical.

But less than an hour had passed when he suddenly heard,
above the confused clamour of a dirty night, the unexpected
sound of Admiral Nelson hailing the *Theseus*.   There was a very
brief pause after the suggestion had been repulsed of a chair
from the main yard-arm to hoist in the Admiral, wounded.   The
boat, it seemed, must immediately go back to the mole, where
men of the *Fox* were struggling in the surf.   Then William Hoste,
peering into the noisy blackness, straining his eyes and ears,
experiencing feelings so strong that he knew not how to describe
them, perceived " him, whom I may say has been a second father
to me, his right arm dangling by his side, while with the other he
helped himself to jump up the ship's side ".   He next heard a
familiar voice snapping at a consternated audience, " with a
spirit which astonished all ", " Tell the surgeon to get his
instruments ready, for I know that I must lose my arm, and the
sooner it is off the better."

9

As the central division of boats, led by Nelson, got within half
gunshot of the mole of Santa Cruz, rockets climbed the skies,
and blue lights threw a sudden ugly glare on the scene.   Above
the jangle of alarm bells he shouted to the boats to cast off from
one another, give a huzza, give way for their lives and remember
their orders.   Grape and canister began to tear the water just
outside of them.   Only the parties led by Thompson, Fremantle
and Bowen succeeded in landing at various points on the mole,
which they quickly carried, although it was defended by between
four and five hundred men.   They spiked its six twenty-four

pounders, but proceeded no further. By the time that this had been achieved " we were nearly all killed or wounded ". Nelson received his wound, a grapeshot shattering the right elbow, as he was in the act of drawing the dress-sword, regarded by him as a talisman. The gift of Captain Maurice Suckling, originally the property of Captain Galfridus Walpole, dropped from his right hand, but he snatched it up with his left. One account declares that he was, at the moment, stepping out of the boat, and that the same fire wounded seven other men in their right arms. Another describes him as having landed, being hit while pressing forward on the mole and falling, to lie for several moments in the dark confusion, until Josiah Nisbet, missing him, returned in search, and finding him senseless carried him on his back to their boat. (Nelson himself, according to his lady, " often said to me that, ' it was not so much Josiah's tying-up my arm, (the grasp he gave it stopped ye Blood immediately) but his judgment in getting me to the *Ship* ' ".)

He was laid in the bottom of a boat, and his stepson, noting that the sight of his blood seemed to increase the patient's faintness, took off his own hat and laid it on the Admiral's breast. A bargeman named Lovel had pulled off his shirt to form a sling, and helped to adjust a tourniquet. Nisbet, in this, his great hour, collected five other men, and after an alarming delay, got the boat, which had grounded from the falling of the tide, afloat again. He took an oar and shouted to the steersman to go as close as possible under the guns of the mole battery, which were firing. (" By All Accounts," wrote his mother, " he rowed very hard that night, and steered *well, too*, under ye Batteries—for which I am so thankful to Providence that I feel myself the Humblest of God's Creatures—for my son went to sea to oblige Me.") The young, raised voice attracted Nelson's attention, and the Admiral asked to be lifted, " that he might look a little about him ". The night was so dark that there was little to be seen except a stormy sea lit by gunfire, but his change of position was made at the moment that the *Fox* cutter went down, taking with her her commander and ninety-seven men. She had been hit in her under-water timbers, and sank rapidly. The water became alive with struggling figures, and Nelson insisted that his boat should go out of its way to pick up as many survivors as possible. After half an hour, the boat, pulling for the *Theseus*, got within hail of a frigate, but on hearing that she was the *Seahorse*, Nelson refused to approach her. He was strongly advised that further exposure in an open boat, over full of drenched men, might mean the loss of his life—" Then I will die ; for I would rather suffer death than alarm Mrs. Fremantle by her seeing me in this state, when I can give her no tidings whatever of her husband." The boat, accordingly, made on towards the ships-of-the-line, and although boarding on such a night was difficult even for a sound man, the Admiral, twisting a rope round his left arm, went up the side of his flagship unaided. " Let me alone !   I have got my legs left, and one arm."

The amputation to which he had resigned himself from the moment he was hit was performed as soon as possible, and it appears that the tale, often doubted, that Nelson's arm was taken off by a Frenchman is founded on fact.   M. Ronicet, Assistant-Surgeon of the *Theseus*, was a French royalist refugee, collected by Lord Hood at Toulon, in August 1793.   Like the Principal Medical Officer of the *Theseus*, he had followed Nelson, who had the highest opinion of him, from the *Agamemnon* into the *Captain*. [24] From the surgeon's point of view there was much for which to be thankful.   There were not many other wounded urgently needing attention, the ship was at anchor and her guns were not in action.   Nevertheless, the circumstances were far from favourable.   The lantern light was dim and shifting ; the ship was rolling ; and the patient was exhausted and chilled.   However, his unselfish resolution not to alarm Mrs. Fremantle seemed to have brought its reward, for after his ordeal he congratulated himself on " a good surgeon ", whereas Fleming, of the *Seahorse*, who attended Fremantle, got praise from no quarter.   Within half an hour [25] his Flag-Captain was by Sir Horatio's side, receiving necessary orders, " as if nothing had happened ", and a large outer audience presently heard that the Admiral had undergone his operation " with the same firmness and courage which have always marked his character ".   When asked whether he wished his limb to be embalmed and sent home for burial, he had said, " Throw it into the hammock with the brave fellow that was killed beside me." [26] " He was in a fair way of recovery."   He certainly did not get a fair chance.

Throughout the night the town batteries continued to fire, and at 4 a.m. a number of boats which had been tossing in the bay for five hours, unable to reach the mole, came alongside and began to discharge their landing-parties.   With first daylight came sudden and shattering noise.   In the market-square of Santa Cruz, Troubridge and Waller were marching out of their convent in quest of Hood. The enemy were responding by a bombardment of the English shipping in the bay. A shot went through a sail of the *Seahorse*, but Mrs. Fremantle, assisting at the dressing of her husband's wound, refused to obey repeated requests that she should descend to the cockpit. Since her marriage to a frigate Captain, she much fancied herself in the character of " an English girl ". In the *Theseus*, watched by Tom Allen, who had been present at the amputation, the patient stirred. Captain Miller was again summoned, and the Admiral, who had ordered the squadron to weigh, heard the measured clank of the capstan as the cable came in, the rumble of the guns being run out, and familiar patterings and bellowings as the port-lids opened. The *Theseus*, standing off and on the town, returned enemy fire regularly for the next two hours, during which time a boat which had managed to escape from the town arrived, bringing the dark tidings that every man of the landing-parties who had contrived to reach the *rendezvous* had been obliged to surrender. Persons who had begun to pride themselves on having silenced the enemy batteries fell silent.

Comparative peace continued until 9 a.m., when a flag of truce came off the mole, with Waller and a Spanish officer carrying the Governor's very handsome terms. Before noon Lieutenant Weatherhead was conveyed on board the *Theseus* in a cradle. William Hoste, again experiencing feelings so strong that he could not describe them, told himself that " this was not a time to give way ", and bustled round, getting everything in his power ready for the reception of his friend. With his first glance at John's changed face, some instinct told him that this was Death, and the surgeons, after examining the mute boy, held out no hopes of his long survival, a diagnosis confirmed by his collapse and quiet passing four days later. " I had almost forgotten ", added Hoste to his long letter home, " to say that on the death of Weatherhead, Admiral Nelson gave me a commission to act as Lieutenant in his vacancy; happy would it have made me, had it been in any other."

Nelson's arm had been taken off " very high, near the shoulder ", at an early hour on the 25th, and once the deed was done he eagerly reclaimed command of what he called " my carcase ". His medical officers, very ready with frequent wet dressings, found their examinations resented, and as far as possible avoided. Tom Allen, full of importance and invention, guarded his sick master, who would not be sick, with the devotion

of a dog, the jealousy of a woman.   In preparation for blowing
nights on their return passage to the fleet, Tom had rigged up a
cord, attached to his shirt collar, by which means Sir Horatio,
needing anything, need only give a twitch to summon his *valet-
de-chambre*.   By the 26th the patient was dictating a letter to   27
the humane and courteous Commandant of the Canaries, begging
his Excellency's acceptance of his sincere thanks and (in a
postscript) a cask of English beer and a cheese.   His Excellency
replied, sending his best wishes for the Admiral's recovery, and a
couple of flasks of finest Canary wine, whereupon the Admiral
gallantly offered to carry to Cadiz His Excellency's despatches
for the Court of Spain—" thus making himself the herald of his
own defeat ".   Next day he dictated a despatch to St. Vincent,
and to the enclosed list of two hundred and fifty-odd officers,
seamen and marines, killed, wounded, drowned and missing,
appended his second effort at a left-handed signature.   (Little Mrs.
Fremantle had already received a line of enquiry for her husband,
and assurances that he himself was " coming on very well ".)

   At last the weary preparations for leaving the Fortunate
Isles were complete.   The men of the landing-parties had all
been returned to their proper ships ; the squadron, provisioned
from the town, by courtesy of the Governor, was at liberty to
depart in peace, and Nelson might settle to the business of
recovery.   Only the wind stayed unfriendly and refused to carry
the vanquished out of sight of a shore now detested by more than
Mrs. Fremantle.   The body of Captain Bowen was brought on
board his ship, and committed to the deep.   As his squadron lay
becalmed, Nelson attempted his first letter.   The days of his
conventional, fine sloping hand, long since degenerated into an
over-driven scribble, were gone for ever.   His new writing, unmistakable, foursquare, at present spider-thin and tending to
wilt backwards, slowly and painfully came into sight.   With the
humiliating effort and the sudden heat and peace, came the
inevitable reaction.   He realised that of late he had received
" flattery enough to make me vain, and success enough to make
me confident ".   His memory recurred with futile insistence to
the loss of Bowen, and " a great many gallant officers and men ".   28
He believed the grey-headed Lieutenant of the *Fox* to have left,
in indigence at Hastings, " an only daughter, the darling of his
heart ".   The Admiral's attendants were obviously nervous, and
perhaps with reason.   His first letter rambled, in style as well as
script.

" My dear Sir,

" I am become a burthen to my friends, and useless to my Country; but by my letter wrote the 24th, you will perceive my anxiety for the promotion of my son-in-law, Josiah Nisbet. When I leave your command, I become dead to the World; I go hence, and am no more seen. If from poor Bowen's loss, you think it proper to oblige me, I rest confident you will do it; the Boy is under obligations to me, but he repaid me by bringing me from the Mole of Santa Cruz. I hope you will be able to give me a frigate, to convey the remains of my carcase to England. God bless you, my dear sir, and believe me, your most obliged and faithful,

" Horatio Nelson."

" You will excuse my scrawl, considering it is my first attempt."

During the long night, after achieving this, he remembered that he had failed, in his despatch, to make any acknowledgment of the services of the Artillery Lieutenant, young Baynes, son of the Rock, summoned from Gibraltar by the Commander-in-Chief, who was interested in his family; and Lord St. Vincent, as usual, had picked well. The *Emerald*, sent on to the fleet, was just
parting as he finished a hasty note, ending, " I am in great pain ".

29

10

On the afternoon of Wednesday, August 16, he came in sight once more of Lord St. Vincent's flag, and his spirits rose. The Commander-in-Chief's note of greeting combined in the happiest manner the grandiose and jocose: " Mortals cannot command success." He was sure that Nelson and his companions had deserved both success and fame. The *Seahorse* should waft him and Fremantle to England the moment she was provisioned, and they need not fear missing anything interesting here, as his Lordship had just betted £100 on the preliminaries of a peace being already signed, and a definitive treaty before mid-September. He sent his love to Mrs. Fremantle, and hoped to salute her, and bow to Nelson's stump, to-morrow morning.

But " a left-handed Admiral " who had asked nothing more than that he might get to some " very humble Cottage " as soon as possible, in order to make room for a better man, was now desirous to display himself as most suitable for further employment afloat. When the *Theseus* anchored at 3 p.m., Tom Allen had already got his master into his coat, and to the surprise of Captain George and Sir Charles Grey, a figure drawn in countenance but eager in speech appeared at Lord St. Vincent's dinner-table. He stayed an hour, and that night his host reported to the First Lord that Rear-Admiral Nelson had joined with his squadron, and in such health that nothing could prevent his coming on board the *Ville de Paris*. " He dined with me, and I have very good ground of hope he will be restored to the service of his King and Country." Privately, he had promised Nelson to ask for him again as soon as possible. 30

One letter very irritating to the invalid was awaiting him. Rear-Admiral Parker had heard from friends at home that " then Commodore Nelson ", in a statement of the action of Valentine's Day, had not given him that credit which properly belonged to him. To this letter, which was of great length, he received the curtest of replies, and not until after Nelson had sailed for England. For four days Dr. Weir, Physician to the Fleet, was allowed full access to his stump; then, in record time, the *Seahorse* was ready, and Admiral Nelson came on board in great spirits. Mrs. Fremantle, who now saw him for the first time since his loss, found " it looks shocking to be without one arm ". Sir Horatio had brought with him four years' luggage, a surgeon, an extraordinary body-servant and a number of sick and wounded from the *Theseus*, and Mrs. Fremantle liked the look of Mr. Eshelby sufficiently to confide her own symptoms before the day was out, whereupon the Principal Medical Officer of a ship-of-the-line valiantly supplied suitable pills and confirmed hopes which made her know that she was very happy, though feeling very ill.

What the Admiral described as " a fine fair wind ", and his hostess as " a nice breeze ", carried the frigate to the westward of Cape St. Vincent, and presently it seemed that the Admiral, although very hearty, was not free from pain. Next morning the *Seahorse* was rising at her fences, and Fremantle, whose flesh wound seemed to be getting larger and wetter instead of drier and smaller, was easily persuaded, after a bad night, not to attempt to get up. His ministering angel was utterly miserable; even the Admiral confessed that the motion of the ship hurt his arm. As for the sick and wounded of the *Theseus*, they suffered most noisily and with incredible persistence. " This ship ", Mrs. Fremantle entered in her diary, " is worse than a hospital ", and when a young lady wrote of a hospital in 1797, she wrote of something " amazing horrid ".

But being driven far to the westward, at great speed, was preferable to their next experience, a foul wind, which made the Admiral fume and become worthy to be acidly classed,

Theseus Augt 16th 1797,

My Dear Sir,

Soyuse at being once more
in Sight of your flag, and with your per=
=mission will come on board the Ville de Paris & pay
you my respects. If the Emerald has joined, you
know my wishes, a left handed Admiral will
never again be considered as useful therefore
the sooner I get to a very humble cottage the better
and make room for a better man to serve the State
but whatever be my lot Believe me with the most
sincere affection Ever Your most faithful
          Turn over   Horatio Nelson

Add. MS. 34,902, f. 150. (" Nelson Papers.") Reproduced by courtesy of the Trustees, the British Museum.

" To Admiral Sir John Jervis, K.B   *Theseus*, Aug. 16th, 1797.

" My dear Sir,
    " I rejoice at being once more in sight of your flag, and with your permission will come on board the *Ville de Paris* and pay you my respects. If the *Emerald* has joined, you know my wishes. A left handed Admiral will never again be considered as useful therefore the sooner I get to a very humble cottage the better, and make room for a better man to serve the State but whatever be my lot,
    " Believe me with the most sincere affection ever your most faithful

                      " Horatio Nelson."

" Turn over
" The papers I sent by Waller were, I find, neither *correct* or all which I wished to send   I send you the total by Captain Miller."

together with Mrs. Fremantle's adored husband, as "a very bad patient ". The succeeding complete calm was not reflected in the *Seahorse*. Fremantle, big-eyed, hot and restless, announced his resistance almost exhausted, and voiced in the same breath apprehensions of a lingering illness. His little wife drooped to see him so low. The Admiral wryly reported himself " very indifferent ". His unspoken belief was that Fremantle would have to face amputation before the month was out. " A great way from Portsmouth, as I can write but slowly ", he addressed himself to Uncle Suckling, to whom he feared he had always been a trouble. He must now ask his ever-kind relative to be good enough to arrange that the Controller of Customs should take charge of considerable lumber, including wines, " until I can find a hut to put my mutilated carcase in ".

In the fullness of time a fair wind was the only comfort of a party of wrecks. It brought them, by the penultimate day of August, in sight of Home, and Mrs. Fremantle, aged eighteen, who had not seen Home for nine years, thought " the light of Scilly, plain in the evening " had a lovely look. Next afternoon, when they should have been seeing land, came a foul wind again, and the Admiral mutteringly wished himself back with the old Mediterranean Fleet, off Cadiz. In the mist of a gloomy first of September, the pretty Isle of Wight did not display herself nearly clear enough for patriotic Mrs. Fremantle's taste. The *Seahorse* came to anchor at Spithead before dinner, and immediately after that meal, although the sea was much too rough for a lady to consider leaving the ship, a one-armed Admiral descended to his barge, and was pulled, in whirling rain, amongst swooping gulls, towards fishy smells, and wet house-faces, and the " George ", Portsmouth. The Admiral Superintendent of the Dockyard was his old friend Sir Peter Parker (more of a caricature than ever), and the result of Nelson's descriptions of his suffering fellow-passengers to the Commissioner's lady was evident within the week, when the bride, paying her duty call, found Lady Parker (a Personage who claimed that she had been a Mother to Fremantle in the West Indies) " the most civil kind woman I ever saw ".

Early on the drowsy Sunday morning of September 3 the lighter luggage of Sir Horatio Nelson, K.B., was cast on a fretting vehicle, and his odd and possessive sailor servant prepared to accompany him on an exhausting and not painless journey, half across England at war, unseen by master or man for four seasons, with autumn colours flying. The shabby, expensive vehicle threaded its way through the sprawl of Southampton towards a valley where the spire of Salisbury Cathedral pointed a finger at cloud and rainbow.   Rustic Warminster was half asleep for dinner hour.   Since he had commissioned the *Agamemnon* he had been engaged against the enemy upwards of a hundred and twenty times. . . . He had good reason to hurry on his homeward journey, for his wound still needed dressing, and he had left his surgeon in attendance on Fremantle.

Mr. Eshelby, bereaved of his more important patient, found consolations.   His old messmate Leeds, of the *Brunswick*, enticed the Chief Surgeon of Haslar down to look at an ugly arm, and throughout a meal at the Fremantles' Portsmouth lodgings, regardless of their wilting hostess, three healthsome gentlemen of the faculty kept the conversation strictly to medicine, wounds and fever.   32

CHAPTER IX

1797

(*ætat* 38–39)

DOCTOR'S ORDERS

I

WHEN a letter addressed in an unfamiliar handwriting, its incompetence suggesting rather senility than infancy, was delivered at a Bath lodging on Saturday, September 2, 1797, the grass-widow of a long-absent sea-officer suffered incapacitating anguish.

Since August 25 naval experts of the spa had been discussing an expedition on which Admiral Nelson was said to have been detached with a squadron of three sail-of-the-line and seven frigates. Lord St. Vincent's curt despatch, although sent by a lugger, had been over three weeks on its journey, and announced July 15 as the date on which the expedition had sailed. Absolutely nothing further had been admitted by official sources, and editors had been reduced to publishing surmises that the Admiral had called at Gibraltar for additional troops; and descriptions of Teneriffe as an island measuring forty-five by twenty miles, rich in wine, fruits and cattle. A long silence after such an announcement is not often a good sign, and painful rumours had prevailed. Actually, even the Admiralty had known nothing.

Fortunately, Mrs. Bolton, a lady possessed of balance and good eyesight, happened to be on a visit to her invalid parent and sister-in-law. Susanna, at the Rector's request, deciphered, and presently divulged to a shattered family circle, the contents of the difficult and troubled sheet, achieved by Nelson in snatches, during the dog days at sea, on his passage from Santa Cruz to Cadiz Bay. His opening paragraph said that he was sure his dearest Fanny would be as glad to receive a letter written by his left hand as his right. " It was the chance of war, and I have good reason to be thankful." He said that he was lucky in having a good surgeon on board his ship, but Josiah also had been instrumental in saving his life, a thing which would please the boy's mother. He begged that neither his wife nor father should think much of a matter to which his mind had long been made up.

His postscript told them that he had just joined the fleet,
" perfectly well ".　He should be with them, perhaps, as soon as
his letter.　Probably the next they would hear of him would be
" at the door ".　He was clearly taking the most cheerful view
possible of a sad business, and at first the family was too much
overcome with grief at the thought of his mutilation to rejoice at
the prospect of his return—a promise so often made, so often
cancelled.

Sunday, September 3, was a lovely day, sunny and pleasant,
and light lingered long, but shutters were closed against night
air, candles were lit and a very quiet family in the dead season
for Bath were thinking of bed, when suddenly a wife's ear
detected the sound of a familiar voice, accustomed to shouting
commands.　The house of the late Mrs. Searle, which the Rector
had rented furnished for three years, stood just round the corner
of the street, and Admiral Nelson was directing his coachman
where to stop.　A moment later he was in the room, " come
laughing back ", as he had always prophesied.

He had now attained the appearance made familiar by the
most famous series of his portraits, for which the original sketches
were made during the next few months.　Time and the enemy
were yet to strike a blow at him.　One more visible scar was to
be added to his brow.　He grew in the eight seasons remaining to
him more meagre and haggard.　At the last, shrunk inside a
weighty uniform and orders, almost as fragile as an autumn leaf,
he appeared to the uninitiated, on formal occasions, a truly
alarming compound of direct manners and elaborate dress.　But
essentially the unexpected figure which electrified the Bath parlour
that night was already that which would be recognised by members
of every succeeding generation as Nelson.　His hair, originally
light auburn, had been since the fatal Nicaraguan Expedition so
white as to require in his opinion no powder.　Fashionable women
wrote indulgently of his shock head, and, never a man of fashion,
it seems that after he was largely dependent upon a *valet* to
get him into a complicated costume, his dress and person
suggested additionally the mild dissociation early remarked by
Prince William Henry.　The fixed dim right eye, the empty
right sleeve, were painful novelties to his family, but that his
old infective high spirits were untouched was at once equally
obvious ; and these spirits were so distracting a characteristic that
witnesses called upon for a description of a great man often
confirmed on a note of surprise that he was not above middle

height, very slight, far from handsome, unaffectedly simple in address, and of no great dignity, " indeed, in appearance nothing remarkable either way ". In vain they catalogued a face of irregular worn features, a complexion whipped and spoilt by sea-winds, a grave nose, a vulnerable mouth, an eye still boyish. The outstanding impression of those who encountered Nelson while the radiant orb shone upon the burning glass was of a man so active in person, so animated in countenance and so apposite and vehement in conversation that little else was recollected.

Only one member of the party surprised that night seemed to the home-comer quite unchanged. He had been much fore-warned to expect alteration in his parent. To his delight, his good father looked to him exactly as he had done on a snowy morning of January 1793. Over four years of perpetual ailment and fret had inevitably taken their toll of the looks of a lady nearing forty, but his wife had always dressed well, and possessed fine features. He gladly pronounced on his return " my domestic happiness perfect ". His elder sister, as befitted a matron of daughters nearly marriageable, was now chiefly remarkable for a formidable cap, nose and chin, and the young lady by her side was, of course, quite unrecognisable as " the little Kate " remembered as a round-eyed child, sitting about disconsolate at Burnham Thorpe, wondering how her mama could have sent her to so dull a place. To this future Captain's lady the arrival of her distinguished naval uncle spelt romance. Her cousin and confidante, Mary Anne Bolton, had already received an offer from an " old Agamemnon ". Lieutenant Pierson, the bearer of letters to East Anglia after the battle of February 14, had not been idle when invited to spend some weeks of convalescence at Hollesley Rectory. News of Mary Anne's brother, also an " old Agamemnon ", was eagerly awaited. But it soon transpired that the traveller's arm, which still required attention, had not been dressed since dawn. Late though the hour, Mr. Nicholls, medical advisor to Lady Nelson, had to be fetched, and presently a lady so nervous that she dared not open a letter which might contain bad news found herself called upon to attend the dressing of an amputation case. Moreover, her husband expected her to acquire the skill to perform this business, when necessary, unaided. Since he was cheerfully firm, and she was devoted, resolution was summoned, and the first great effort made. After an interval, a paler Admiral and lady reappeared, and the Bath physician, accustomed to plucking the golden goose and prescribing for nothing more shocking than the results of English fare and weather after East or West Indian service, had no objection to offer to his patient's desire for a London opinion. Next morning Lady Nelson wrote to Mr. Maurice Nelson, asking him to engage London lodgings. Next morning also, and for several days, newspapers published full accounts of the total failure of the expedition against Teneriffe. Editors had stopped the press on Saturday night to announce the arrival of Captain Waller, who had landed from the cutter *Flora* at Falmouth on Friday, and set off express for Whitehall with despatches from Lord St. Vincent.

The journals scanned by the returned Admiral at Bath were typical of their date. In the advertisement columns, since Britain's Fleet was still fast expanding, sea-officers were tempted by offers of succulent ship's stores—Beef-rounds, Portable soups, Morello cherries, Anchovies, Truffles, white Walnuts, and particularly Mr. Skill's delicious genuine six-pounder Stilton cheeses. In the gossip columns, Margate was reported very vulgar, Ramsgate very gay, Tunbridge very full, Brighton extremely modish and Southampton deserted. Lord Spencer was on holiday at Althorp, and the Prime Minister, at his country house, was combining exercise and amusement by swinging a hatchet. All papers gave pride of place to the failure at Teneriffe, and no journalist had been able to resist dwelling gloomily upon the loss of the *Fox*. Otherwise, comments differed according to the political complexion of the organ. The *Courier* noted, with erudite and ghastly gaiety, that " the Fortunate Isle of the Ancients is evidently not one of Billy Pitt's ". Another Opposition leader-writer pointed the finger of accusation at Mr. Dundas, Secretary for War—doubtless jealous of the brilliant successes of his friends in their slaughter of our noble countrymen on their Dunkirk and Quiberon enterprises. A stirring reverse in the Canaries was caustically acclaimed as just the thing to distract the public eye from the failure of Lord Malmesbury's peace mission, described as " the late puppet-show and burlesque at Lille ". Several much mistaken persons represented ageing Lord St. Vincent as meekly submitting to bloodthirsty orders from Home ; others resented the brevity of the Commander-in-Chief's despatches, and there was bickering about contradictory numbers in the casualty lists. On one point only the Press were agreed. No blame attached to Rear-Admiral Nelson, " just landed after his gallant though unsuccessful attempt, in good spirits and health except the loss of his arm ". It was recalled that the Puerto Rico Expedition had been a failure, although it, too, had been entrusted to a commander of approved merit. Bad information as to the degree of enemy force to be encountered and as to recently strengthened defences was averred in his defence. A Bath journal was possessive : " Arrived at Bath— Lady Ann Mahon, Sir John Snow, Sir William Addington, Admiral Sir Horatio Nelson. . . . The Rear-Admiral, who was received at Portsmouth on the 1st with a universal greeting, reached Bath on Sunday evening in good health and spirits, to the great joy of his Lady and Venerable Father, and gratification of every admirer of British Valour." " The brave Admiral certainly owes his country no service ; he has signalized himself in as exemplary a manner as any hero that graces the Naval Annals of this country, and with the loss of a right arm—

> ' Having purchased in his youth renown,
> To make him lov'd and valued when he's old,'

it might have been supposed that he would set quietly down ' with all his budding honours thick about him '. But it is said that he eagerly longs to repair to that station on which his name has been the pride of the British Fleet and the terror of the enemy." One writer paid him the supreme compliment of alluding to him without title or Christian name : " Protected by such as NELSON we may defy the malignant threats of our Enemies, and look with contempt upon the wild project of an Invasion, confiding in the superintendence of Providence to afford us safeguard, and in our Wooden Walls."

On the Wednesday following his entry, pens were active in Mr. Searle's house. Lady Nelson wrote to Mr. Suckling explaining that they could not as yet come to Kentish Town, since the Admiral's wound required a daily dressing by a surgeon. " My husband's spirits are good although he suffers a good deal of pain— the arm is taken off very high, near the shoulder. Opium procures him rest, and last night he was pretty quiet." Her husband was simultaneously writing to William, " As to my personal health, it never was better, and my arm is in the fairest way of healing", but " the truly affectionate William " was already on his road to Bath, and on the following Saturday the weekly local sheet recorded his arrival amongst that of many important personages. Letters from distinguished quarters continued to surprise the quiet household. The Corporation of Bath presented congratulations on Admiral Nelson's safe return.

Lord Hood sent what Lady Nelson called " such a letter ! "   The First Lord wrote most handsomely, hoping to see Rear-Admiral Nelson in town as soon as possible. The Duke of Clarence longed to be one of the first to shake his old friend by the left hand, and considerately begged that Lady Nelson might report. In slow and laboured characters the old friend himself replied :

" Sir,
    " I trust your Royal Highness will attribute my not having sent a letter since my arrival to its true cause—viz, the not being now a ready writer.   I feel confident of your sorrow for my accident ; but I assure your Royal Highness, that not a scrap of that ardour with which I have hitherto served our King has been shot away."

There were other letters which he might not depute to the most willing amanuensis.   The family of Captain Miller must be reassured.   Coke of Norfolk would expect news of the two boys recommended by him, both of whom had done him so much credit.   One, young Weatherhead, alas ! was gone.   To little Hoste's father he added, " Your son is as gallant, and I hope he will long live to honour Norfolk and England."   The Corporation of Bath also got a specimen of left-handed calligraphy.

At last all the letters were written, the London surgeon and lodgings were engaged, and Sir Horatio Nelson and lady, the Reverend William Nelson, the Admiral's sailor servant and her ladyship's woman took the road for the capital.   The months of July and August had been remarkably tempestuous, and September was proving very wet, but warm, and with pleasant sunshine between the thunder-showers.   There were gossamer floats in the hedgerows of the clean-washed landscape through which the travellers passed, and although Provence roses were still to be seen in cottage gardens, the large golden leaves of the horse-chestnut were sailing to the ground through still airs, evenings were vaporous, the swallows were congregating and the song of the robin had been heard.   They broke their journey at Newbury, and it is possible that this was the occasion remembered by " John " of " The Pelican ".   After the knife-and-boot boy of the popular inn on the Bath road had brought up his slippers, the one-eyed and one-armed naval gentleman bade him sit, and demanded to be told " the news of the place ".   After more than four years on active service, sea-officers have been known to look upon Home and its inhabitants with a quizzical eye, almost as if they believed themselves spectators at the play-house ; and this one was the son of a country clergyman.   He well knew that

Sir Horatio Nelson, K.B., Rear-Admiral of the
Blue Squadron (*aetat 39*).

By Lemuel Abbott (1760–1803).   (30" × 25".)

Nelson gave sittings for this portrait (a " study " upon which a full-
length could be based) in the house of the Lieutenant-Governor of
the Royal Hospital, Greenwich (Captain William Locker) in
October, 1797, after the loss of his arm, but before the stump
had healed.   Abbott subsequently produced many other half-
lengths, with additional decorations and with and without a
hat, and several full-lengths, in the backgrounds of which Santa
Cruz was altered, at appropriate dates, to Aboukir Bay and the
quarter-deck of the *Victory* at Trafalgar.

This version, which has never before been reproduced in a
biography, was engraved by Richard Earlom, Dec. 7, 1798.

Reproduced by kind permission of the Trustees, the National
Maritime Museum, Greenwich.

though London correspondents might deplore that nothing worth staining paper with had befallen in their world, in such places as Newbury dramatic events would be crowding upon one another like geese upon a common. The first question of the Admiral, seated in the country inn bedroom, stretching cramped limbs after a fifty miles' coach journey, was, " Can I get to London from here by water? " to which John, recognising a great man, and playing for safety, smartly replied, " Yes, my lord. You can go by the Canal to Reading, and on by the River Thames to London."

The party next morning took the conventional route—by Maidenhead and Hounslow Heath—and on the evening of Wednesday, September 13, in sunshine after heavy rain, drew up safely at the doors of 141, Bond Street. The lodging-house kept by Mr. Jones stood on the west side of the fashionable street, a little south of Grosvenor Street, and near enough to St. George's, Hanover Square, for a wakeful man to hear the hours tolled from that modern classic building throughout the long night, after the last coach had rolled home, the last laugh had died away outside, the last pair of heels had ceased to trouble the pavements, and there was no other sound in the world remarkable, except the too-fast heartbeats bred by rising fever.

2

Nelson, who persisted in regarding his condition as the result of an accident, not an illness, and who realised that he had been arrested at a critical moment in his career, was disappointed after he had displayed his arm to his first London surgeon. Mr. William Cruikshank, late partner of Dr. William Hunter, brought his young son-in-law, Mr. Thomas, a person who had been chief dresser to the great but brusque Hunter at St. George's Hospital. After five days of their treatment, a most impatient patient found himself not the least better than when he had left the hands of good Dr. Weir at Cadiz. The London experts confirmed his gloomy opinion that only time would bring him about again. Meanwhile, since he would not be an invalid, and must perform the duty known as " keeping in touch ", he repaired nearly every morning to the Admiralty, and since in the autumn of 1797 the public took interest in all active Admirals, his pilgrimages did not pass unnoticed. A very junior clerk, staring from an upper window of the vast building, noticed a thin, spare officer, with only one arm, entering the vestibule at a smart step for many mornings in succession. What attracted his attention was

s

that this person, instead of taking, like everyone else, the smooth pavement round the sides of the quadrangle, invariably made for his goal by the direct but stony path across the round, rough cobbles. As an octagenarian, but still a clerk on the establishment, the spectator eagerly explained to the author of a forthcoming handbook to London that he had ceased to wonder when he learned that this frail officer was Admiral Nelson, "who always took the nearest way to the place he wanted to go". 7 "Admiral Nelson", recorded a newspaper of this autumn, "is now daily at the Admiralty." And lest the name might not be familiar to all readers, an instructive paragraph added the anecdote of the Admiral pausing, after the loss of the *Fox*, although severely wounded, to take into a small boat, under shell-fire, struggling survivors from the vanished cutter.

At the Admiralty Nelson learnt, amongst other things, the very welcome news that he was to get a pension of £1,000 a year. Custom decreed that he must first make a formal statement of his services to his sovereign. The document, when accomplished, was impressive. He could claim to have assisted at four fleet actions, three with frigates, six engagements against batteries, ten cutting-out expeditions and the capture of three towns; in which service, humbly submitted for His Majesty's consideration, he had lost his right eye and arm. But the business was by no means finished when he had drawn up his memorial and forwarded it with a covering letter to Lord Spencer. A fortnight passed before the Surgeons Company notified him that the hour of 6 p.m. on the first or third Thursday of every month had been appointed for such examinations as that of the injury to his eye. To an officer who possessed no carriage, and was enduring daily dressings after an amputation, an invitation to present himself in the City, after dark, in the height of the London fog season, for the examination of an injury sustained three years past, did not seem reasonable. He took a firm line; addressed himself to the 8 Commissioners of the Navy, offering to appear at Surgeons Hall any day between the hours of ten and four, carried his point, and presented himself in jocund mood, accompanied by his brother-in-law Bolton. (" Oh! this is only for an eye : in a few days I shall come for an arm : and in a little time longer, God knows, most probably for a leg.") 9

There were other advantages in daily attendances at Headquarters. The word that Nelson was in town, lodging in Bond Street, in the surgeons' hands, passed like lightning from the

outer chambers of Whitehall to the clubs, and particularly to
the coffee-room of an hotel at the Strand end of Oxford Street.
Callers began to knock at the doors of Mr. Jones's house : callers
who did not look like actors out of a comedy or tragedy—brother
officers. Mr. Richard Bulkeley, one of the survivors of the San
Juan Expedition, appeared one evening after candles were lit,
bringing two boys, to whom Sir Horatio showed his sword.
Three years later Mr. Bulkeley had to intercept a letter written
by his Dick, upon whom, at the age of nine, the personality of
Lord Nelson had made so strong an impression that he had now
addressed himself to a national hero, offering his services. " As
you have *bit* him," commented the parent, " you must be his
physician."

The Lieutenant-Governor of the Royal Hospital, looking
older and less rubicund, but benevolent as ever, came up from
Greenwich. He had been quite unable to wait to see a favourite
pupil until the *levée* at the end of next week. He had also a
confession to make, and a plot to weave. After Valentine's Day,
a small print-seller of George Street, Woolwich, had come to the
Hospital, begging leave to engrave any likeness of Admiral
Nelson which might be in the possession of his old Captain.
Locker had unhung from his gallery of future heroes the portrait
of a Lieutenant by J. F. Rigaud, R.A., and on August 14 (an
unhappy date in Nelson's story, when he was toiling back to the
fleet from Teneriffe) Mr. Shipster had given to the world a small
oval portrait in stipple, entitled " Horatio Nelson, Esq., now Sir
Horatio Nelson, K.B., Rear-Admiral of the Blue Squadron ".
The engraver had been obliged to guess as to the changes wrought
by twenty years' service, and had not guessed very happily. Lady
Nelson, also approached by a print-seller (who intended to
dedicate the result to H.R.H. the Duke of Clarence), had been as
guilty, but either more discerning or fortunate. The miniature
by an anonymous artist of Leghorn, sent to her two years past,
had been entrusted by her to Mr. Robert Laurie, of Messrs.
Laurie and Whittle, trading at the Golden Buck, Fleet Street,
and Mr. Laurie, a mezzotinto engraver of considerable merit,
working upon a portrait much inferior to that given to Shipster,
was still engaged altering a Captain's uniform to that of an
Admiral, adding the Star of the Bath, and removing Sir Horatio's
right arm. Locker now considered that it was the duty of his
friend to sit again as soon as possible for something authoritative,
and he had an artist in mind. Lemuel Abbott, who abode in

Caroline Street, Bloomsbury, in domestic disquiet and such penury that he could employ no assistants, was of a persevering disposition, and could present the speaking likeness of a sea-officer. He was willing to come to Greenwich when the Admiral was visiting the Lieutenant-Governor. Lady Nelson approved the idea. Her husband, waiting to get well, had unaccustomed hours of idleness to fill, and had already, at the request of Bulkeley's brother-in-law, Sir Henry Englefield, sat to a Mr. Edridge for a water-colour sketch. The thought that the moment was not favourable for a flattering likeness apparently troubled nobody.

About noon on the fine but sunless morning of September 25 Admiral Nelson, bearing with him the two gentlemen he was to present—his large, robustious elder brother and slight, diffident Captain Berry—performed the short journey downhill from Bond Street to the St. James's Palace, where the first *levée* of the autumn season was to be held. When an officer had newly lost an arm—no unusual occurrence—the procedure as regards uniform was conventional. The upper sleeve of the close-fitting coat was slit or gashed to allow a servant to insert his hand and ease the painful stump into the tight garment: three neat bows of black or navy blue ribbon fastened the opening. All portraits of Nelson showing three ribbon bows on his right upper coat sleeve belong to the four months before the stump healed.   11

The *levée* was typical of its date. The Turkish, Sardinian, Portuguese and Neapolitan Ambassadors were present. The diplomats, headed by a deaf peer with a high nose and waving white locks, were ranged to receive the first share of royal notice. Six blue and eight scarlet coats were marshalled into line below them. Old Lord Howe had many enquiries to make after Lord St. Vincent. The officers of the navy included one other survivor of the Teneriffe expedition—Waller. The King, who had come up from Kew for the day, with two daughters to look after him on the journey, walked into the long gallery of the old blackened red-brick palace at 12.30, attended by the Duke of York. Lord Malmesbury, fresh from his unsuccessful attempt at peace-making with France, presented two soft, handsome youngsters of his staff, drawn from the Grand Whiggery of Devonshire House—Lord Morpeth and Lord Granville Leveson-Gower. Admiral Nelson's turn came next, but did not find him unready. The obstinate, pink-faced old gentleman with a bright light blue eye, for whom he nourished the warmest and most reverential feelings, was suddenly exclaiming before him. "You have lost your right arm!" observed the King. "But not my right hand, as I have the honour of presenting Captain Berry." Few outside their immediate circle heard the *riposte*, but Berry repeated it to the girl he hoped to marry.

Afterwards came the ceremony of investing Admiral Nelson with the Order of the Bath, and a solemn procession of gentlemen in red cloaks came forth, attending a ribbon and order on a cushion, and the Admiral spoke his vow and appended a left-handed signature to a document, and received from the hands of George III the Star, which, like many other gentlemen of his day, he afterwards caused to be embroidered on his uniform coats. There was more talk with royalty, and a very sick-looking officer making light of his loss of a limb in the Royal Service received a kindly reminder, "But your Country has a claim for a bit more of you." His Majesty then duly asked after the general health of the Commander-in-Chief at Cadiz, and as suddenly as it had begun, the *levée* was over. The King departed to a council with Lord Malmesbury, to ponder the latest news from France. (Newspapers were describing Buonaparte's lady as holding *levées* in Venice.) It was just a happy chance that someone who so much appreciated the romantic fact should have been invested by the sovereign personally. Orders had been sent to Cadiz six months past for Lord St. Vincent to perform the ceremony, but by the time they had arrived Nelson had already sailed for Teneriffe. Strictly speaking, he had not been Sir Horatio until to-day, and St. Vincent and others of the fleet had been exact, but even the Secretary to the Admiralty and the Duke of Clarence had so addressed him. Times had much changed since the *levée* after which an ardent Post-Captain had repaired to Alexander Davison's Lincoln's Inn chambers to discuss every subject under the sun. Davison, like the officer whom he called "H.N.", had prospered during the past five years. At the opening of the war with France he had been concerned with the commissariat of the Duke of York's ill-fated Flanders expedition, and now that large bodies of troops were being retained at home in expectation of invasion, he was acting as a Government contractor on a large scale. His factories, furnishing barrack supplies, from tents and boots to coal and candles, covered an area of Milbank. He had bought a Northumbrian property called Swarland Hall, where he was making improvements. At a house in aristocratic St. James's Square he was forming a collection of historical oil paintings by British artists. The man who had deterred the young Nelson from an improvident love-match had practised what he preached. He had waited until the age of thirty-six to form an alliance with the daughter of a solid banker of Fleet Street, and, successful in everything, had promptly become a parent of fine male twins. Nelson, vaguely disturbed by the large talk of a man now deep in Cabinet, princely and City secrets, offered in vain a word of caution.

On October 5 a congenial party set out for the Royal Hospital, Greenwich. Sir Gilbert Elliot, invited to dine with the Governor, had gladly accepted the offer of a seat in the carriage bespoken by the Nelsons, bent upon a stay with the Lieutenant-Governor. The ex-Viceroy, who had just heard that he was to be raised to the peerage, as Baron Minto, and had decided upon a Moor's head as his crest, was chiefly exercised by the thought of having to face the criticism of his Eton son. However, he had written to tell his tutor to apologise to young Gilbert, and Mr. Reed reported that the heir had resignedly pronounced, " Well, if it is to be so, it must be so." Sir Gilbert, who had not seen Nelson since his loss of an arm, thought that he looked, nevertheless, " better and fresher than I ever remember him ". Nelson confessed that his arm was by no means well, and that he was still suffering a good deal of violent pain—taking opium every night. His surgeons were talking of a further operation, which, they warned him, would not be easy, as the stump was already very short, but to which he would gladly consent if there was any hope of success, as he was very impatient to get to sea again. Sir Gilbert himself was feeling far from well, and resented the gout which had first begun to afflict him during the nerve-racking last days of his Vice-royalty. He, too, was anxious to be employed abroad again for his country's good as soon as possible, and his lady, " less of a coward than myself ", wrote rousingly from Scotland, urging high deeds upon him. He had dined with the Great at the First Lord's house yesterday, and was due for a visit to Mr. Pitt, at Holwood. The Duke of Portland, Windham, Canning, etc., all reported that His Majesty had said over and over again that Lord Minto would be of the greatest use in the Lords ; a prospect which did not sound promising. His family were coming south for the winter, and he had taken a villa at Roehampton, where they would be close to their kinsfolk, the Malmesburys and Palmerstons, already settled amongst the chestnut groves of East Sheen and flowery shrubberies of Fulham. He was to kiss

13 hands on Wednesday or Thursday next, and poor Pozzo di Borgo still haunted him.

The carriage-full of cheerfully talking invalids jolted into the echoing grey precincts of the Royal Hospital, seen at its best on an autumn day of cloudless skies, when every massive building which had succeeded the ancient palace of Placentia rose clear-cut against a background of wooded heights and flashing, tumbled waters, well covered by slow and swift-moving merchandise, although England had now been at war again for nearly five years. The houses of Lord Hood and Captain Locker stood opposite one another, the Governor's facing the noble Grand Court on the west, and the Lieutenant-Governor's on the east—therefore, as far as outlook and prospects of summer sun went, infinitely preferable. The Nelsons passed through a commodious entrance-hall to a drawing-room in which Mrs. Locker and family awaited them, and afterwards through a panelled room to the dining-room. The panelled room, which was of notable charm and comfort—exactly the room pictured by an officer thinking of home on blowing nights—was generally used by the Lieutenant-Governor as his sanctum, and old Miss Elizabeth Locker loved in long-after years to describe to an author nephew how she had, as a child, helped Nelson on and off with his undress uniform coat, before and after every sitting given by him to Lemuel Abbott in her father's apartment *14* at Greenwich Hospital.

3

A few days later, when winter was beginning to settle down upon eighteenth-century London, deep sunk in brown fog and mire, an elegant caller presented himself at 141, Bond Street, where, although prices were high, guests could only be offered what Lady Nelson deprecatingly styled "a family dinner". Colonel Drinkwater soon mentioned a rumour current in Whitehall this morning that an engagement between our North Sea Fleet and that of the Dutch was hourly expected. The result surprised him. "Drinkwater!" exclaimed Nelson, starting from his seat, in his peculiar energetic manner, "I would give this other arm to be with Duncan at this moment." In the shadows, her constant *rôle*, Lady Nelson endeavoured in vain to restrain her *15* husband.

At dawn on October 13, a gloomy morning of black clouds, later discharging heavy rain, Lieutenant Brodie of the *Rose*

cutter arrived at the Admiralty with a despatch, and before dusk
the guns of the Tower and Park had fired salutes in honour of
what to-morrow's newspapers would describe as "Admiral
Duncan's total destruction of the Dutch Fleet at Camperdown".
Illuminations were ordered in official quarters, and late though
the hour and poor the visibility, most private houses in the
fashionable streets put out some evidence of enthusiasm. A
crowd of cup-shotten patriots thundered at the doors of 141,
Bond Street, where every window was dark. Their repeated
knockings and shoutings dragged back from the borders of drug-
induced sleep an invalid who had retired to bed early after a bad
day. They startled a gentle lady seated at her embroidery,
dreaming of sugar-canes, palm trees and sunshine; wishing that
"my Captain" would send her a line. Oddly enough, nobody
in this house most interested in a naval action had heard either
the guns or the news. Everyone leapt to the conclusion that the
visitors brought an alarm of fire. Presently the rough voices
faded apologetically and heavy boots retreated. On being
informed at Mr. Jones's house that Admiral Nelson, badly
wounded at Teneriffe, lodged there, their leader had withdrawn
the intruders with the words, "You will hear no more from us
to-night."

¹⁶

The mere thought of a decisive action at which he could not
assist had been maddening to Nelson, now beset by four surgeons,
a physician and an apothecary. The late Principal Medical
Officer of the *Agamemnon* had come to his old Captain's aid, and
at the request of Mr. Bulkeley, Dr. Benjamin Moseley, late of
Jamaica (now Physician to the Royal Hospital, Chelsea), had
been called in. Still the ligature applied on board H.M.S. *Theseus*
on a July night held fast to the artery and nerve. The stump
was now hot and swollen, requiring poultices. The patient had
decided that if he paid his promised visit to his family at Bath
next month, he would have to take a surgeon with him. The
advisability of cutting down upon the nerve-bulb had been
discussed *ad nauseam*. Mr. Cruikshank was nervous of a further
operation. Finally, the opinion of Mr. Thomas Keate, Surgeon-
General to the Army and Surgeon to the Prince of Wales, had
been sought. Mr. Keate, although little likely to agree with any
crony of Dr. Hunter (especially one given to intemperance),
pronounced himself averse from violent methods. He advised
that the cure should be left to time and nature. A patient who
knew that he was playing a game in which time mattered had to

resign himself to keeping up his spirits and proceeding with what activities were possible. He achieved an astonishing amount.

Norwich was preparing great festivities against Lord Mayor's Day, and from the capital city of the county of his birth, to which he had sent the sword of Admiral Winthuysen, he had accepted an invitation to appear in person to be enrolled a Freeman. On November 3, when his preparations for leaving London for Norfolk were well in train, two young visitors were ushered in to him. A lady, little more than a child herself, but within a few weeks of opening her nursery, possessively shepherded a tall naval Captain with an arm in a sling and the heavy, pallid look of one deprived of accustomed hard exercise. Mrs. Fremantle had asked for Lady Nelson (a person she had never met), but on hearing that her ladyship was not at home, the callers had leapt at an offer of " the good Admiral ". The Fremantles (who had no notion that they were pathetic) had been in London five days, and had been shopping, and to the Shakespeare Gallery, and to see the King go to open Parliament, " very grand, and amusing enough ". They had spent most of October as lodgers in a pretty farm-house at Purhook, where a Miss Fortnum (a very well-behaved delicate little girl, whose father kept a grocer's shop) had been their fellow-guest; and Fremantle had felt the benefit of being out of Portsmouth, but was still far from well. His arm, although his wound had healed, was intermittently so agonizing that he had to fly company, and had even, on one occasion, when out for a walk, been driven to enter a cottage and ask permission to lie flat. He had borne the jolting of a journey to the capital pretty well, but the inquisitors of the Surgeons Hall, at their favourite 6 p.m., had so pulled him about that he had subsequently been obliged to desert a family party at the play at Drury Lane. However, he had seen Lord Spencer, who had been very civil, and the surgeons had pronounced his wound equal to the loss of a limb, and he had been instructed to memorialise His Majesty with regard to a pension. The Nelson family, whose sense of humour was well-developed, had drawn up a remarkable memorial on the subject of missing limbs. It purported to be written by a bereaved twin, and although begun by William, and continued by Kate, was actually signed, " Admiral Nelson's left hand ". " The poor neglected survivor " was made to point out—" How often has your petitioner itched to take a lady by the hand, but yet never was permitted, tho' the right hand was engaged in all the offices of Gallantry. And in battle, when my noble Master, God

bless him, was hewing down the Dons with his right hand, your
petitioner remained unemployed."   *18*

At last Susanna's brother-in-law, Sam Bolton of Akenham
Hall, near Ipswich, seemed to have heard of a house of the right
size in the right position. The Nelsons' journey into a beloved
county was attended, on the first evening, by an atmospheric
effect sufficiently remarkable to find its way into the newspapers—" a singular horizon, at sunset of broad crimson stripes ".
On an early November day their carriage drew up at Roundwood
Farm, in the parish of Rushmere, two miles north-east of Ipswich.
The type of advertisement was familiar to an officer who had long
wished to settle his wife under his own roof—" An estate of about
sixty acres, with neat lawn and shrubbery, spacious lofts, well-
stocked, well-timbered, in the neighbourhood of Fox Hounds,
and bordered at several points by Trout streams ". The timber
at Roundwood, which was mostly elm and sweet chestnut, had
given its name to the estate. The present tenant, Captain Edge,
unlike the tenants of most houses advertised for sale, was ready
to quit, taking his furniture. The prospective purchasers, ghost-
like, as people in such a situation must always seem, began to go
over the house which might become their first home. There were
two parlours on the ground floor, one large enough to take
Abbott's full-length of the Admiral. The farm need not be a
care to Lady Nelson and the Rector, as it was let " to a very civil
tenant ". Roundwood, as they could call it, was not flimsy or
glaringly new. It had been built to last, in 1700. " All looks like   *19*
a gentleman's house." It was not the romantic cottage of
Nelson's early dreams, but neither was it one of the unmanageable,
decaying mansions thrust upon his notice, as so cheap, by the
large-minded William. Before Nelson had seen the house, the
Rector had guessed that he meant to buy it if at all possible, and
this expectation was fulfilled. The moment was suitable for the
setting up of a new home, for the Rector was thinking of retirement. He had already intimated to his family and Bishop his
relinquishment of the living of Burnham Sutton. He had always
hoped that his youngest and least satisfactory son might be
provided for there. The Admiral, " such a Son falls to the Lott
of few Fathers ", obediently discovered the correct procedure,
wrote direct to the Lord Chancellor (although some people said
he ought to have obtained an introduction), and received a most
civil reply (" Sir, you judged perfectly right "). Lord Lough-
borough expressed his great pleasure in marking his appreciation

of the public services performed by Admiral Nelson, but a further application for a Stall at Norwich, or, failing that, any residentiary stall, the nearer Norfolk the more agreeable to the Rev. William Nelson, did not bring equally happy result.

On the night of November 28, at 11 p.m., back in Bond Street, Nelson wrote to Berry, who had announced his engagement to a cousin, Miss Louisa Forster, elder daughter of Dr. Forster of Norwich. The Admiral's first paragraph expressed congratulations on the prospect of becoming " one of *us* ", and hopes of meeting Mrs. Berry. The second was important. Although his arm was still obstinate, his daily visits to the Admiralty had not been fruitless. He had heard to-day that he was to have the *Foudroyant*, of 80 guns, due to be launched in January and commissioned in February. Lord Spencer had also told him that he must be in town on December 19, which had now been fixed for the King's going to St. Paul's in procession to offer thanks for the naval victories of the war. To this pageant, likely to be very fine, Captains Berry and Noble should attend him. He wrote cheerfully, for he had just emerged from one of those functions his soul dreaded. In spite of his early political aspirations, and ample practice in addressing a ship's company, the thought of having to make a ceremonial speech of thanks to a complimentary civilian audience, to " be stared at ", still poisoned his life for hours beforehand. He had to study his few sentences carefully, and depart for the ordeal at last on the dogged note— " Anything better than ingratitude ". At the Guildhall this afternoon, Mr. Chamberlain John Wilkes, presenting the Freedom of the City of London, in a gold box of the value of one hundred guineas, had addressed him with penetration :

> " Many of our Naval Commanders have merited highly of their country by their exertions, but in your case there is a rare heroic modesty which cannot be sufficiently admired. You have given the warmest applause to your Brother Officers and the Seamen under your command but your own merit you have no tmentioned, even in the slightest manner. . . ."

Five nights after he penned his late line to Berry, Nelson went to bed as usual. Outside the streets were quiet, for on the 29th snow had fallen from 9 a.m. without intermission, and throughout the next three days there had been snow-showers, and although to-day no snow had fallen, the skies were heavy again, and it was Sunday night. He went to bed as usual, but did not stir till daylight—an extraordinary thing, something

which had not happened since last July.   He had slept the night
through, like a child, and woke almost free from pain.   He had
returned to a sane world, nothing resembling the distorted scene
through which he had been forcing his way, almost a soul dragging
about a corpse, from the moment that he had felt himself hit in
the right elbow, on the mole at Santa Cruz.

The reason might easily be guessed, and when the surgeon
(hastily summoned) undid the bandages, the ligature came away
at the slightest touch.   The knotted thread attended by evil
odours fell into the dressing like a spent snake, to trouble no
more.   Within a few days his stump was fast healing.   20

He attended another *levée*, and heard that the *Foudroyant*
would not be ready for him in time, now that he was well.   On
the night of December 8 he wrote two short notes.   The first was
to his future Flag-Captain:

" To Captain Berry, R.N., Dr. Forster's, Norwich.
" SECRET, except to Dr. Forster and Miss.
" My dear Sir,
   " If you mean to marry, I would recommend your doing it speedily,
or the to be Mrs. Berry will have very little of your company; for I am
well, and you may expect to be called for every hour.   We shall probably
be at sea before the *Foudroyant* is launched.   Our Ship is at Chatham,
a Seventy-four, and she will be choicely manned.   This may not happen,
but it stands so to-day,
                                   " Ever yours most faithfully,
                                        " Horatio Nelson."

But since he was also the son of the Rector of Burnham
Thorpe, he did not, in his moment of relief, forget another duty.
He sent across a note to the clergyman of the nearest parish
church, St. George's, Hanover Square: " An Officer desires to
return thanks to Almighty God for his perfect recovery from a
severe Wound, and also for many mercies bestowed upon him.
December 8th, 1797 (for next Sunday)."   21

4

The National Thanksgiving for the three great naval victories,
achieved under the flags of Lords Howe, St. Vincent and Duncan,
was, as the First Lord had prophesied, a grand affair.   The day,
which came between one of high wind and one of dense fog, was
the finest for many weeks, and long before dawn windows and
streets on the route were crowded.   The military, including three

Brigades of the Guards and mounted volunteers, mustered in Hyde Park at 7 a.m., and within the hour moved off down Constitution Hill to Pall Mall and the City. After Temple Bar, the streets were lined by the City Militia. The seamen and marines chosen to escort the captured enemy colours fell in outside the Admiralty—" fine-looking men ". Indeed, throughout the day it was noted that when the naval part of the procession came into sight, public enthusiasm waxed warmest. " The seamen and marines were universally cheered." The colours taken from France, Spain and Holland, labelled " June 1794 ", " February 1797 " and " October 1797 ", were carried on artillery wagons, each set escorted by Lieutenants and Petty Officers who had taken part in the actions, marching with drawn swords. A very large detachment of marines, with bands playing, followed the wagons, and the whole corps was ranged inside the Cathedral from the west door to the choir. Nelson was one of the seventeen Admirals, jolting in carriages, preceding those of the Lords and Commons, and it was noticed that " This was by far the most interesting part of the spectacle. The deportment of these gallant sons of the Ocean was extremely dignified." He had been pronounced fit for service six days past, and yesterday had seen his new ship out of dock at Chatham, and ready to receive men. At nine, the firing of the Park guns announced that their Majesties had left St. James's. Eight cream Hanoverian horses drew their coach. The Duke of York appeared with six greys, the Duke of Gloucester with six bays, the Duke of Clarence with roans, and the remaining twenty carriages, bringing the Household, were provided with well-matched, high-mettled, coal-black steeds. " The effect was, perhaps, the finest equestrian spectacle ever seen in any country."

The austere figure of Mr. Pitt was greeted with plaudits which drowned the hisses and cat-calls of a few malcontents. When the royal family had dismounted, to the sound of martial strains, it was observed, with a roar of appreciation, that every member had marked the occasion in a manner very flattering to the naval service. The King's uniform was dark blue, with gold lace. The small Queen, whose usual choice was several regal colours, had restricted herself to a diamond necklace and wreath, and brocades of the deep rich shade familiar to all collectors of Worcester porcelain as " Mazarine blue ", the " Bleu du Roi " of Sèvres. The Princesses, in powder, white and gold plumes, and gold " chainnet " head-dresses, all displayed " Mazarine " satin vests and petticoats, under white and gold silk hoops and bodices. There was an unrehearsed incident when the King, greeted at the West Door by the Bishop of London, the Bishop of Lincoln (Dean of St. Paul's) and the Lord Mayor, recognised Lord Duncan and Sir Alan Gardner and stopped for a word. During the momentary pause, when all eyes were turned towards the sudden rush of noise and sea-colour at the open great doors, the Queen paid the gallant sea-officers present the compliment of a superb curtsey, a gesture imitated *en passant* by the four fair, smiling princesses.

Afterwards, the organ rolled, and the choir burst forth with the Anthem, " I will give thanks to Thee, O Lord, with my whole heart ", and the flag-officers present, marching in two divisions, escorted the trophies of naval success to the altar. The sermon was noble, but the service was long, and the short winter's day was closing in by the time that the first part of the return procession reached St. James's. Except that some mischief-makers contrived to get into the crowd an overdrove ox, which ran up and down Ludgate Hill, causing a universal terror, no accident spoilt the splendour of a day of triumph. From Nelson's point of view, the only mistake was that Duncan's victory, " the last action and the nearest home being always the best ", had most engaged the attention of John Bull.

On December 21 his appointment to H.M.S. *Vanguard* was gazetted, and a gentleman of the Press, doubtless patriotic, announced that the gallant Admiral was said to be sailing shortly on a secret expedition.

CHAPTER X

1798

(*ætat* 39)

THE NILE

I

ON April 24, 1798, two handsome peers, seated in Whitehall, where the lilacs were budding in the First Lord's garden, held under the cloak of a casual morning call an interesting conversation. *The Times* that morning had published a circumstantial account of the French armament collecting in Mediterranean ports. Lord Minto, whose sources of information were reliable, had heard that the Government was at last thinking seriously of the Mediterranean. He supposed that Sir Horatio Nelson would be the fittest man in the world for such a command, and, glancing round the apartment in which he found himself, added, " He is as well acquainted with the Mediterranean as your lordship is with this room we are sitting in." He proceeded to eulogise Admiral Nelson as quick and sharp with the enemy when caused offence, conciliatory with all friendly neutrals and thoroughly experienced in dealing with the Courts and Powers of the Mediterranean. Our Consuls, with whom he always acted in the greatest harmony, as with all on shore, put confidence in him, and, what was most to the point at this hour, his name was dreaded by the enemy. His professional record was well known, but the ex-Viceroy of Corsica had perhaps possessed unique opportunities of observing the Man. He fancied that he knew more of Nelson's qualifications than Lord Spencer or any other person.

Lord Spencer listened patiently to an agreeable man who might himself get another important post abroad. He did not much relish being told that anyone appreciated better than himself the possibilities of junior Admirals, but any flag-officer who could serve under Lord St. Vincent for a considerable period without the noise of an explosion penetrating to Whitehall merited attention, and he had taken the trouble to study Nelson during his months of sick-leave, a thing rendered easy by the Admiral's zealous attendance in his waiting-rooms and drawing-room. Lady Spencer, the simplicity of whose grandeur sometimes startled her gentle sister-in-law, the Duchess of Devonshire, had thought Nelson an extraordinary-looking creature before he spoke, and after he had opened his mouth, more extraordinary still. The Lady of the Admiralty, who was determined that her husband's tenure of office should be marked by brilliancy and high moral tone, was undecided whether Nelson was an idiot or a genius. On his first arrival in her drawing-room he had appeared so shockingly ill she would rather not look at him. He had certainly performed a feat in getting a hostess of pronounced hauteur to break through her well-known rule of never noticing a sea-officer's wife. All officers of the rank of Captain and above received an invitation to dine at the First Lord's before they sailed to take up a new command. Nelson had said that he had not asked permission to introduce his lady, but that if Lady Spencer could notice her, after his departure, it would make him the happiest man alive. He was convinced that Lady Spencer must like Lady Nelson, who was beautiful, accomplished and, above all, an angel whose care had saved his life. He had been invited to bring the angel to dine that very day, and he had upset Lady Spencer's table arrangements by handing his own wife in to dinner and asking to be allowed to sit next to her. He had said that he saw so little of her that he would not voluntarily lose an instant of her company.   *1*

Lord Minto's panegyric ended, and Lord Spencer thought that he might venture to assure his companion that if the Government should take such a decision with regard to the Mediterranean, the name of Nelson would certainly be the first to suggest itself to him. Actually, Lord St. Vincent must nominate the officer. But he knew well how high was the opinion held of Nelson in that quarter. He would express to Lord St. Vincent his own and the Government's view. Making a great gesture of throwing off the official mask, he mentioned a squadron of eight of the line as the first reinforcement likely to be sent to Cadiz. Lord St. Vincent might be able to spare Admiral Nelson another four, and competent frigates. There was no chance of any other officer being chosen. He thanked his caller for confirming an opinion he had already held, and said that he would always be glad to hear the valuable suggestions of the ex-Viceroy of Corsica.

Lord Minto returned to his Roehampton villa to send a long letter to Nelson, confessing " the step I have taken on my own responsibility ", and Lord Spencer wrote five days later to Lord   *2* St. Vincent, pointing out that, if he determined to send a detachment into the Mediterranean, the activity, disposition and experience of Sir H. Nelson seemed to qualify him in a peculiar manner for this service. His letter marked " Private and Confidential " waited at the Admiralty until May 2 to accompany a long official document headed " Secret Instructions ", and arrived in Cadiz Bay on May 24, a date which found Nelson already on his way to Toulon, and overtaken by disaster. In the following winter, when people had long ceased to complain of so junior an Admiral being chosen, His Majesty's sailor son asked Berry to tell Nelson that, as a matter of fact, the person who had chosen him and " formed the whole plan ", resulting in the victory of the Nile, was his august parent.

[3]

Nelson's progress since he had seen the *Vanguard* out of dock on December 18 had been entirely successful, though not so speedy as he had hoped. In France, during the early months of the year, while General Buonaparte (abruptly summoned from Italy) was inspecting the invasion ports of the north coast, Nelson, at Bath, was receiving the usual flood of letters from persons who had relatives or friends to place. Poor Weatherhead's father, nothing deterred by his own loss, wrote on behalf of a boy called Meek, languishing in a guardship at the Nore. Unfortunately, Meek had been pressed, and, as Nelson pointed out, volunteers must come first. Nevertheless, Berry got the boy. The widow of Vice-Admiral Collier was assured that her second son, Francis Augustus, a very fine lad, should spend as little as possible. (" He will be a very lucky fellow if he gets on shore twice in a year.") At Bath, in the height of the winter season, Sir Horatio availed himself of the very attentive offer of Lord Lansdowne to occupy his box at the play. " But his Lordship did not tell me all its charms—that generally some of the handsomest ladies in Bath are partakers in the box, and was I a bachelor I would not answer for being tempted; but as I am possessed of everything which is valuable in a wife, I have no occasion to think beyond a pretty face." By early February the *Vanguard* had gone down the river to the Nore. Berry was bringing her round to Spithead, and if the present wind held, Nelson reckoned that the next thing he would hear would be orders to hoist his flag. He hoped to stay at Portsmouth not above forty-eight hours. The Admiral, " as usuall in Great Good Spirits, panting to be in Actuall Service ", said farewell to his father and moved up to Bond Street again, this time to No. 96. A fortnight later he had heard nothing from Lord Spencer. A large convoy, which he was to escort, was slowly assembling. On March 14 he made his final appearance

T

at a *levée*, and after that had nothing further for which to wait, except a line from the Admiralty. Lady Nelson would set off for Bath, taking with her little Kate Bolton (to whom she meant to be very kind), at the same moment that he took the Portsmouth road. William, come up from Norfolk to see the last of a hero, was given an affectionate letter for very old Miss Mary Nelson, the Rector's sister, and two pounds of tea, a gift easily come by at the moment, for stores of every description were beginning to shower upon the Admiral's lodgings. Already he knew of three passengers whom he would have to entertain at his table, and an Admiral must at least present the appearance of having everything handsome about him. To be remarkably shabby or frugal was bad for discipline. A crate labelled " China " was sent off by coach. The tailor, haberdasher and linen-draper delivered new gear, marked and numbered in cross-stitch. Lady Nelson, her maid and niece packed; still the collection of parcels seemed to increase, and Mrs. Cuthbert Collingwood might yet be sending treasures to be carried to her husband at Lisbon. The last days in London were trying, not the least of the difficulties being that the Admiral's sailor servant had taken the measure of the Admiral's lady. Lady Nelson's spirits were low as the hour of parting approached. Her orders were to settle as soon as possible at Roundwood. " I am clear it is right you should be in your own cottage."

At 8 p.m. on the night of March 29, Sir Horatio broke his flag, blue at the mizzen, on board the *Vanguard* at Spithead, and entered into his new kingdom. The scene for the next forty-eight hours was just as busy as that he had quitted in London, but much less distressing. " Berry is married, but still goes with me." He found very little wrong in his flagship. He greeted Captain Peyton, made the acquaintance of the two land-officers whom he was to carry to Lisbon, and began to employ a new character, his Secretary. The First Lieutenant, Galwey, another stranger, displayed every mark of the good officer risen without the help of friends. Michael Jefferson was Principal Medical Officer. Cork reports mentioned that the chops of the two channels were crowded with home-bound ships waiting the first spurt of a southerly wind to enter their destined ports. The *Vanguard* was off with the lark on April 1, but, the wind coming to the westward at noon, was forced to return to St. Helen's. All passengers went ashore, but Sir Horatio remained " fixed ". In the Admiral's state-room, amongst mahogany which would soon be reflecting Mediterranean sun, Tom Allen unpacked doggedly. Lady Nelson had kindly slipped in her own little blue pillow, but in the bustle of departure had gone off with the Admiral's old watch, and, apparently, the keys of his dressing-stand. Tom had obeyed her ladyship's orders to lock the bedroom door before he opened any of his master's luggage at the inn on the road down; all the same, many things were missing. Letters began to fly between the Admiral, detained for ten days by the wind blowing as foul as it could ("So much for Admiralty delays"), and her ladyship, watching the vane on Queen Square Chapel, Bath, to see whether the *Vanguard* had sailed. He could not find the old pieces of Portuguese gold given him by his father, or his black stock and buckle. (It was true that the buckle had only cost him 1s. 6d., but it was a friend of eighteen years standing.) In an evil hour, while it blew so strong as to prevent all intercourse with the shore, he went through his linen, and found it very different from his dearest Fanny's list. The brightest spot was sixteen cambric handkerchiefs instead of thirteen. The magnitude of the most serious deficiencies (eleven pairs of new silk stockings and ten huckaback towels) led him to hope that they had never been sent. Lady Nelson replied that Bath was over-full of country families who had run there supposing it a safe place in case of the Invasion. She was trying to exert her spirits. "Mr. Matcham last week fell from his horse, at 3 o'clock in ye morn: in Liquor. I wish very much it had been in my power to send your things more comfortably." She believed that his buckle and keys must come to hand. His papers, both private and professional, she had seen tied up; and Kitty had put three Genoese velvet stocks into the box of sundries, and Ryson was positive that a small parcel, written upon, probably contained the small silver. She would go out herself to buy anything further that he needed. "I will leave this mortifying subject." But the Admiral's lady, much more afraid of his servant than himself, could not leave it without the suggestion, "Don't say much to Allen, and I will give the search I promised." She sent her love to her "child", and invoked God to protect and bless her husband. "I rejoice to see you so exact. Times will make us all very careful." His last words were, "Nothing in the world can exceed the pleasure I shall have in returning to you", and, "I hope, when you travel, you will not trust yourself in a stage."

2

"I am very happy", wrote the First Lord to Lord St. Vincent, on March 30, 1798, "to send you Sir Horatio Nelson again, not only because I believe I cannot send you a more zealous, active and approved officer, but because I have reason to believe that his being under your command will be agreeable to your wishes." "I do assure your lordship", replied Lord St. Vincent, on May 1, "that the arrival of Admiral Nelson has given me new life. You could not have gratified me more than in sending him. His presence in the Mediterranean is so very essential that I mean to put the *Orion* and *Alexander* under his command, with the addition of three or four frigates, and to send him away (the moment the *Vanguard* has delivered her water to the in-shore squadron) to endeavour to ascertain the real object of the preparations making by the French."

Lord St. Vincent had continued to suffer since he had last seen Nelson. "What", he demanded, "do they mean by invariably sending me the mutinous ships? Do they think I will be hangman to the Fleet?" Captains were forbidden to entertain one another at dinner, and all officers to go ashore at Lisbon or Gibraltar, "on what is called pleasure", except in correct uniform. (The coloured clothes and round hats which the Commander-in-Chief had observed might, he feared, cause these supercilious and licentious-spoken young gentlemen to be mistaken for shopkeepers.) Lights out by 8 p.m. was the rule for ships' companies, and since the utmost frugality in fuel consumption was necessary, no fires were to be lit except between 11 a.m. and 3 p.m. Breakfast could be cooked on stoves. While the Captain of a ship newly arrived from home reported to the Admiral, one of his bargemen, perceiving the bronzed countenance of a veteran peeping out of a lower-deck port of the *Ville de Paris*, ventured to ask, "What have you fellows been doing while we have been fighting for your beef and pork?" "Take my advice", was the awful reply, "and say nothing at all about all that out here. For, by G—d if old Jarvie hears ye, ye'll be dingle-dangle at the yard-arm by eight o'clock to-morrow morning."

Raging neuralgia, mutineers and "the vain conceit and flippancy of manner of inexperienced officers" were not the worst things mourned by St. Vincent during the months of Nelson's absence. "The nerves of Mr. de Pinto are totally unstrung ! " Portugal, England's only remaining ally, gave her at present nothing but the use of the Tagus, and Portugal, like nearly every timorous neutral, appeared blind to the expediency of uniting openly and effectively with Great Britain, while time remained. All watched fascinated to see whom the revolutionary crocodile would devour next. Austria (never ceasing to lament that her Italian campaign had been ruined by the withdrawal of the British fleet from the Mediterranean) had signed the definitive Treaty of Campo Formio in October, relinquishing Belgium, and receiving in exchange the city and part of the former territories of despoiled Venetia. Holland, Switzerland and the Italian Republics were all occupied by French troops, and exercising government under French control. The death of the Anglophil Catherine of Russia had been immediately followed by the breakdown of Lord Malmesbury's peace mission, for France had little fear of obstruction from her successor. It was under these circumstances that Pitt " began to think of the Mediterranean ", where it was obvious that France was planning some new operation on a grand scale, but with commendable secrecy. Ireland, the West Indies, Naples, Sicily, Portugal were all considered as the possible destination of the fleet fitting out at Toulon, and the troops and transports collecting in large numbers at every southern French port, in Genoa, Civita Vecchia and Corsica. At all costs the junction of this force with the Brest squadron, or the Spanish fleet still held in Cadiz, must be prevented. A new coalition was now Pitt's dream—an auxiliary Russian squadron in the North Sea, France vexed by a renewal of war on the Continent by restive Austria and perhaps her satellite Naples; but before it could be realised, these Powers must be reassured that Britannia ruled the waves. While Nelson dined with Lord St. Vincent on April 30, Lord Spencer's letter urging " the appearance of a British squadron in the Mediterranean is a condition on which the fate of Europe may at this moment be stated to depend " was not yet despatched from Whitehall.

Nelson found his host very friendly, very violent, obviously unwell and, although he was close about this, hinting at retirement. (" The person to succeed me should possess both temper and good nerves, or he will be in continual hot water, and terrified at this anchorage.") Not only professional matters were discussed. The Commander-in-Chief had done his best for the large lowering lad of eighteen, who sent Nelson stilted notes beginning, " My dear Father ". The Captain of the *Dolphin*, according to Lord St. Vincent, had acquitted himself marvellously well as an officer on three recent occasions, and was improving in manner and conversation. (" Pretty quick promotion ", resignedly commented William Hoste.)

On Sunday evening, May 20, as the rays of a spectacular spring sunset gilded the green paint of his cabin, Nelson, pacing up and down it, knew himself " exhilarated beyond description ". Yesterday it had blown strong from the N.W. This evening the wind had dropped away, and the *Vanguard*, with top-gallants set, was not moving as fast as his wishes. Still, the picture framed by slanting stern-gallery windows was handsome, for she was attended by H.M.S. *Alexander* and *Orion*, seventy-fours, four frigates and a sloop. The Gibraltar garrison had been very civil and very merry. English beef and buttons, chained to the Rock, announcing themselves forgotten in London, generally were in spirits. But the scarlet coats had shown an inclination to *fête* sea-officers who had better be watering their ships, and having no taste at present for social gaieties, the Admiral had been glad to slip out of Rosia Bay with dusk, his eastward course marked by no unfriendly eye. Despite his loss of a right arm, he was up the Mediterranean again, with secret orders " to look after the French ", and the men of the corvette *La Pierre*, captured by one of his frigates four days past, and separately examined, all agreed that General Buonaparte had arrived at Toulon on the 6th, where fifteen of the line and numerous transports were ready to go to sea, and twelve of forty thousand men were already embarked. Cavalry had been pouring into the city as the polacca left the harbour. Nelson reckoned that he should now be in the exact position for intercepting enemy supply ships bound for Marseille and Toulon. He had sent the usual line to his wife, telling her that she must not be surprised if she did not hear from him again for a little. He would not be going on any fighting expedition. Nor need she now fear the invasion of England by Buonaparte this summer. (Although the Conqueror had now abandoned the Italianate version of his name, to Nelson he was ever " Buonaparte " and never, except in derision, " Napoleon ".) He had addressed the letter to " our Cottage ", where he hoped that she would soon be fixed in comfort. The evil months of his protracted convalescence, permeated by the sickly fragrance of dressings and opium, were safe wiped from his record, and almost from his memory, as the *Vanguard*, with her squadron about her, stood in towards Cape Sicie, with a moderate breeze. He knew that his squadron, " small but very choice ", expected much of him, and he returned the compliment. The sun sank, and the weather began to appear not so promising, but as the ship had been prepared for a gale, his mind was easy. By midnight the *Vanguard*, under a main storm-stay-sail, was at close grips with trouble. At 2 a.m. her main-topmast went over the side, with the top-sail full of men, followed within half an hour by the mizzen-topmast. The fore-mast soon gave an alarming crack, and at a quarter past three went by the board, with a resounding crash, falling in two pieces across the fore-castle. The shrieking of the wind began to be punctuated by an ominous thumping sound. The wreck of the fore-topmast and fore-mast, together with the best bower anchor, were beating against the ship's bottom. The smooth face of young Captain Berry, who could not help fearing that such a series of disasters might not have overtaken a more experienced officer, grew long. The *Vanguard*, without masts and rolling unspeakably, was shipping so much water that it became necessary for him to order the scuttling of the lower deck. Amongst those lost on that black night, during which no night-signals could be seen, was Mr. Midshipman Meek, " showing himself so particularly active at the time that everybody admired him ". Throughout Monday the tempest raged, and unrelaxed effort had to be made to prevent the ship drifting towards the hostile shore of Corsica. The wind did not drop until Tuesday afternoon, when the *Alexander* took the *Vanguard* in tow and made a daring attempt to bring her into Oristano Bay, Sardinia. Captain Ball, although signalled by the Admiral to shift for himself and leave the flag-ship to her fate, continued wonderful exertions. The worst moment for Berry was shortly before dawn on Wednesday, when a heavy western swell was driving them towards invisible rocks on which he could clearly hear the surf breaking. Daylight found the *Alexander*, with the flagship still in tow, about five miles off an island south of Sardinia. The imperturbable Saumarez appeared with the *Orion* to announce and guide them into the bay of St. Pietro. At about 6 a.m. a breeze at last filled the sails of the *Alexander*, and before noon the *Vanguard*, a perfect wreck, having weathered the rocks to the southward of the little isle, anchored in six fathoms and fine smooth water. The Admiral, as soon as possible, went on board the *Alexander* to express unreserved gratitude, and enter upon a new and lifelong friendship. There was irony in the chance that had made him so much obliged to Ball, for although they were almost contemporaries, their paths had never crossed, except at St. Omer, fourteen years past, when Nelson had decided that if he should ever come to know this well-favoured son of a considerable Gloucestershire landowner, he should very much dislike him. The impression had lingered, and when Ball had appeared at Gibraltar to pay his respects and place himself under Nelson's orders, he had been greeted with the dry query, " What, are you come to have your bones broken ? "

On the last day of May, Nelson addressed a four-line letter to St. Vincent :

" My dear Lord,
    " My pride was too great for man, but I trust my friends will think I bore my chastisement like a man. It has pleased God to assist me with His favour, and here I am again, off Toulon."

His pride was not entirely dead, for he had written to his wife that if the ship had been in England, months would have passed before she came out of dock. " Here my operations will not be delayed. The *Vanguard* will in two days get to sea again, as an English man-of-war." Captain Ball had again come to the rescue of young Captain Berry (who was nervous that the Admiral might shift his flag to a more effective ship), and a character of dour visage, with near thirty years experience in the Royal Service, had been lent to advise a newly commissioned ship's company as to the repair of very extensive damage. For three days and four nights the disappointingly unfriendly shores of St. Pietro echoed to sounds of sawing and hammering, while persons on their mettle, under the direction of Mr. James Morrison, shipwright of the *Alexander*, rigged jury masts; then Berry was able to announce that the *Vanguard* was not only equipped, but actually at sea, and " not bound (I would have you observe) to Gibraltar or any English port, to be refitted, but again cruising after the enemy on their own coast ! "

On the day after she left St. Pietro the *Vanguard* spoke a merchantman from Marseille, and learned that Buonaparte was at large. He had sailed from Toulon, on the day before the storm in which the *Vanguard* had been dismasted, and he had taken with him thirteen ships-of-the-line and four hundred transports. Nelson made all possible speed to his appointed secret *rendezvous*, where he hoped to find the frigates never seen

British Fleet at Anchor in Naples Bay, June 17, 1798, Waiting for news of the French Fleet, prior to the Battle of the Nile.

By G. Guardi (1764–1835). Gouache. ($11\frac{1}{2}'' \times 20\frac{7}{8}''$.)

since the gale. He reached it on June 9, but it was deserted. It was with dawn next morning that a despatch brig joined the seventy-fours, and the solid figure of Captain Hardy came on board the *Vanguard*. His news was startling, and almost wholly welcome. The frigates were safe, but at Gibraltar, whence they had betaken themselves, never doubting that a ship so severely damaged as the *Vanguard* must return to a dockyard. Urgent instructions from the Admiralty, dated May 2, had reached Cadiz Bay, and the Commander-in-Chief, promised reinforcements, and given the choice of either taking his whole fleet or sending a considerable squadron up the Mediterranean, had appointed Admiral Nelson to this detached command. Next day, at ten minutes past one, a strange fleet was sighted near Cape Corse, which proved to be ten of the line under Captain Troubridge, sent off by St. Vincent as soon as the reinforcement from Portsmouth, under Sir Roger Curtis, had been visible from the masthead of the *Ville de Paris*. Indeed, since every ship designed for Nelson had been ready to put to sea at a moment's notice, Troubridge had actually been out of sight, on his course to Gibraltar, before Sir Roger cast anchor at the British station off Cadiz. "Choice" and "active" were favourite epithets in Service diction at this date, and St. Vincent's private letter, accompanying Nelson's commission, promised him "some choice fellows of the in-shore squadron". He had, in fact, deprived himself of his best officers and ships, and at a moment when the Spanish fleet, in obedience to French pressure, was making a feint of coming out. Troubridge also brought additional secret instructions. Nelson was advised to exact every supply he might need from the Grand Duke of Tuscany, the King of the Two Sicilies, the Porte, Malta, and the *ci-devant* Venetian state. The Dey of Algiers was well-disposed, the Bey of Tunis perfectly good-humoured and neutral, and the Bashaw of Tripoli probably friendly. He was empowered, in his efforts "to take, sink, burn or destroy the Armament preparing by the Enemy at Toulon", to pursue the French to any part of the Mediterranean, the Adriatic, the Greek archipelago or even the Black Sea. "It is hardly necessary", ended the Commander-in-Chief, "to instruct you to open a correspondence with His Majesty's Ministers at every Court in Italy, at Vienna and Constantinople, and the different Consuls on the Coasts of the seas you are to operate in."

Three major difficulties confronted Nelson when he received these flattering but large orders. He was becalmed, he knew that Buonaparte had already sailed, " with a long start " (but he knew not in what direction), and he lacked the essential equipment for discovery—" Frigates, the Eyes of the Fleet ". Captain Thomas Thompson, " an active young man ", who had regretted orders to remain at Gibraltar a month ago, made a welcome appearance within twenty-four hours, with the 50-gun *Leander*, but he had to be left behind to redirect Ball and Saumarez, who had been detached to look out for Troubridge. Nelson's only recent information was that the troops gathered at Genoa had not yet sailed, so he hoped that Buonaparte might have given them a *rendezvous* in Telamon Bay. He told Hardy to look in there, set off himself round the north of Corsica for the Italian coast, and (since he must have frigates, and the King of the Two Sicilies, hourly expecting invasion, certainly possessed them) he wrote to the British Ambassador at Naples in very clear terms. Fortunately this official was Sir William Hamilton, with whom he had been in friendly correspondence at intervals ever since his visit to the Palazzo Sessa five years past. His letter of June 12, however, was entirely formal, and suitable to be shown to Sir John Acton, Chief Minister at the Court of Naples. His Excellency was asked exactly what co-operation was intended by the Court, whether all the ports of Naples and Sicily were open to His Britannic Majesty's fleet, and whether their authorities had received orders to give him supplies. If it was *convenient*, Nelson much wished for the loan of some fast-sailing vessels. " I want information of the French Fleet; for I hope they have passed Naples. I want good pilots, say six or eight, for the Coast of Sicily, the Adriatic, or for whatever place the Enemy's Fleet may be at, for I mean to follow them if they go to the Black Sea." 5

On the night of Friday, June 9, at Wimbledon, the Right Honourable Henry Dundas, Secretary for War, slept ill, and during the next two days twice addressed himself to the First Lord. " My dear Lord, Did the instructions to Lord St. Vincent mention that *Egypt* might be in the contemplation of Buonaparte's expedition? It may be whimsical, but I cannot help having a fancy of my own on that subject." " My dear Lord, *India* has occupied my thoughts all night. . . ." Such fancies 6 were no novelty to the First Lord, or, for that matter, to Mr. Dundas, who had received a mysterious warning in April that French officers were being sent to Egypt *en route* for Hindustan. A British sea-officer with a romantic record, prisoner-of-war in

France, had managed to send Lord Grenville, as long ago as last January, a message that the Directory had designs on Egypt and British trade in the Levant. On Captain Sidney Smith's escape, last month, the First Lord had given him breakfast and taken him to a *levée*. Lord St. Vincent seemed the person to deal with an officer of initiative, inclined to be rather talkative. Captain Sidney Smith's latest tall tale had been that Buonaparte's *troupe* included mathematicians, historians and geologists, ordered to report upon the antiquities, and develop the resources, of captured Egypt and India.

Five days after Lord Spencer had received Mr. Dundas's second note, Nelson wrote to him, from off the Ponza Islands :

> " The last account I had of the French Fleet was from a Tunisian cruiser, who saw them on the 4th, off Trapani, in Sicily, steering to the eastward. If they pass Sicily I shall believe they are going on their scheme of possessing Alexandria,—a plan concerted with Tippoo Saib, by no means so difficult as might at first be imagined."

Hardy had rejoined, reporting "nothing in Telamon Bay", and since the Admiral had not, as he had hoped, been welcomed by a cruiser from Naples, he had decided to send Troubridge in the *Mutine* to talk to Sir William Hamilton had General Acton, get the news and repeat his distress for frigates. (" Troubridge will say everything I could put in a ream of paper.")

On June 17, while he lay with his squadron, outside neutral waters, in Naples Bay, awaiting the return of his envoy, he received four letters from the Palazzo Sessa. The Ambassadress, as well as her husband, had written. Lady Hamilton's first note, well though hastily performed in a thin, slanting hand, expressed on behalf of herself and the Queen of Naples best wishes for his success and happy return.

> " God bless you, my dear Sir, I will not say how glad I shall be to see you. Indeed, I cannot describe to you my feelings on your being so near us. Ever, Ever dear Sir, your affte and gratefull Emma Hamilton."

Her second effort, an almost indecipherable scrawl on a scrap of the same paper, contained an enclosure.

> " Dear Sir, I send you a letter I have this moment received from the Queen. *Kiss it*, and send it back by Bowen, as I am bound not to give any of her letters, Ever yours, Emma."

The words " kiss it " were underlined, and Nelson replied, in equal haste, before sailing forthwith for the Straits of Messina.

"My dear Lady Hamilton, I have kissed the Queen's letter. Pray say I hope for the honor of kissing her hand when no fears will intervene, assure her Majesty that no person has her felicity more at heart than myself and that the sufferings of her family will be a Tower of Strength on the day of Battle; fear not the event, God is with us. God bless you and Sir William, pray say I cannot stay to answer his letter, Ever yours faithfully, Horatio Nelson."

The news with which Troubridge had returned within two hours was not entirely satisfactory. Sir William Hamilton had carried him and Hardy directly to General Acton, who had been the person to beg the Admiralty to send a fleet into the Mediterranean for the protection of the Kingdom of the Two Sicilies. It had been correct etiquette that the shifty, effeminate and anti-British Marquis de Gallo, Secretary of State, should be present at their interview, and the scene must have been a remarkable one, for both the sea-officers were, in appearance and manner, British oaks, and Troubridge, according to Sir William, "spoke straight to the point"; but the much-desired frigates were not forthcoming. An extremely delicate negotiation with Austria was in progress, and if the Emperor should learn that his brother-in-law had lent vessels of war to an English squadron, bent on the destruction of Buonaparte's fleet, he certainly could not be expected to continue to consider proposals to support Naples, should she suffer an unprovoked attack by France. The lethargic King, whose fears of invasion had been temporarily allayed by the French fleet passing Naples on the 8th to attack Malta, was "perfectly at peace with France", and by the terms of the late treaty with the Directory not more than four belligerent ships at a time might enter his ports. However, General Acton, "a true man of business", had furnished Troubridge with an informal order, "in the King's name" (what the anxious Sir William Hamilton described as "a sort of credential"), empowering all Port Governors of the Two Sicilies to give Admiral Nelson every necessary assistance and supply, "under the rose".

Nelson (who, on Troubridge's return, had not even waited to read Gallo's prevaricating replies to his previous letter to Sir William) achieved during his swift passage to the Straits a cheerful note headed "private", in which he begged Sir William, if he thought proper, to tell their Sicilian Majesties and General Acton that they might rest assured he would not withdraw his fleet from the Mediterranean, except upon positive orders from his Commander-in-Chief or (underlined) the *impossibility of procuring supplies*. He repeated that his distress for frigates was extreme.

" I cannot help myself and nobody will help me.   But thank God,
I am not apt to feel difficulties.   Pray, present my best respects to
Lady Hamilton.   Tell her I hope to be presented to her crowned with
laurel or cypress."

In a long official communication, dated two days later, " off
the Pharos of Messina ", he reminded the Ambassador that
although, on his arrival in the Bay of Naples, he had found
plenty of goodwill towards England and hatred of France, he
had also found no assistance, and no hostility to France.
The French Minister had been permitted to send off vessels
to Buonaparte's fleet, reporting the arrival, strength and
destination of the English squadron, but no corresponding
information had been available for Captain Troubridge.   When
His Britannic Majesty's Ministers heard that *no co-operation* had
been offered at Naples, who could say whether they would decide
to keep the squadron, so pressingly demanded, in these seas?
He drew to a close with a telling warning.   " I have said, and
repeat it, *Malta is the direct road to Sicily.*"

On the 22nd of June, off Cape Passaro, the *Mutine* fell in
with a Ragusan brig from Malta, and Hardy learnt the unpleasant
news that the French, having taken the island on the 15th, and
left a garrison there, had sailed again next day, it was supposed
for Sicily.   But as the wind had blown strong from the westward
since that date, and the Sicilian Government was not calling for
aid, Nelson was convinced that Alexandria was their goal.   He
immediately signalled four of his Captains to come on board the
Vanguard.   The handsome Saumarez, Troubridge, Ball and Darby
(a lively Irish officer whose nationality was proclaimed by both
his countenance and voice) made up the first of many councils
held in the Admiral's flagship during those hot, weary weeks of
vain search.   His own guess was that the enemy might at the
moment be safe in Corfu, and his officers agreed; but without
frigates they could only guess.   He sent Hardy ahead with a
despatch for the British Consul at Alexandria (" Pray do not
detain the *Mutine*, for I am in a fever at not finding the French ")
and prepared to follow with all possible speed—six days' passage.
Saumarez, as the squadron crowded all sail for the chief port of
Egypt, thanked Providence that the sole responsibility for the
decision did not rest with him.   It would have been too much for
his irritable nerves.

In Alexandria, on June 28, the roads were empty.   That is
to say, the old port displayed one Turkish ship-of-the-line and

four frigates; and what was called "the Franks' port" held about fifty sail of merchant vessels of various nationalities. The ship-of-the-line (alarmed by the tidings brought by an English brig, and a Leghorn report) was landing her guns, and the town was filling with troops. Alexandria, in midsummer 1798, as an officer of Buonaparte's army was to discover within the week, was far from the innocent's dream of the glamorous East. Under a brazen sky, scarcely enlivened by perpetually hovering birds, arose, it is true, palms, a picturesque Pharos and numerous white domes and minarets. The closer picture was entirely squalid—" mud houses, windowless, except for a few holes in the walls, covered with a rude latticing, and entrances so low that you stun yourself entering. In a word, picture to yourself a collection of dirty, ill-built pigeon-houses, and you have a fair idea of Alexandria."

An officer of the British Navy, of large stature, with a sweet Devon accent, had a sorry but clear tale to tell. Hardy had been obliged to bring back the Admiral's urgent letter to Mr. George Baldwin, British Consul, and the accompanying reviews and magazines, " pleasant though old ". Mr. Baldwin, according to the Vice-Consul (who was neither English nor intelligent), had left this place twelve weeks past. The disappointment was bitter, but the squadron did not waste time in vain regret. Ball, on being shown the long explanatory despatch composed by the Admiral next day, at sea, said that he thought it quite a master-piece of clarity and accuracy, but strongly advised that it should not be sent. " I should recommend a friend never to make a defence before he is accused of error." Nelson, who had good reason to fear that he was already being criticised, forwarded it on its long journey. He knew that he had been appointed in preference to senior Admirals. From Cadiz, on June 16, Sir John Orde had sent to the First Lord a letter, opening, " Sir Horatio Nelson, a junior officer, and just arrived from England, is detached from the Fleet in which we serve. . . . I cannot conceal from your lordship how much I feel hurt." He had not, either, concealed it from Lord St. Vincent, who, after a stormy interview, had ordered him home and presently announced " the removal of a certain baronet from this squadron has produced a wonderful effect ".

On July 12, off Candia, Nelson wrote again to his Commander-in-Chief, but he had now been without news of the enemy for a month, and the strain was beginning to tell. " After receiving

Captain Hardy's report, I stretched the Fleet over to the Coast of Asia." In the interval since his last despatch he had been up the Aleppo coast, and into the Turkish gulf of Antalya. Many years later he bade Troubridge, "Don't fret . . . I wish I never had." The return to Syracuse, he said, had broken his heart. July 18 was the date mentioned by him as finding him at his lowest ebb.

By July 20 he was back in Syracuse again, with ships some of which had not been watered since May 6, and all of which, although provisioned for another nine or ten weeks, lacked the anti-scorbutics which were part of his creed. His intention, if he heard nothing further within six days, was to try the Morea, Constantinople and, failing them, Cyprus. " The devil's children ", he wrote to Sir William Hamilton, " have the devil's luck." Addressing himself to His Excellency two days later, he found himself unfortunately obliged to send hot complaint of having been refused entry by the port authorities of Syracuse. " I understood that private orders at least would have been given." His postscript explained that it was only " as a public man " that he had to complain. Every personal courtesy

12 had been shown to him. Both these letters were endorsed, " Sent on shore, to the charge of the Governor of Syracuse."

To Lord St. Vincent, he reported on the 20th that he was watering, and " getting such refreshments as the place affords ",

13 and hoped to get to sea in a few days, and on the 22nd, " Our treatment in the Sicilian Ports is shameful. If they had the force, this Governor says, they are bound by their orders to prevent our entry. Acton promised to send orders. *None has been sent.*

14 What (do you) think of this? " Lady Hamilton, who had

15 written to him warmly, got an equally indignant note on the 22nd. Next day he suddenly announced to her husband, " The Fleet is unmoored, and the moment the wind comes off the land, shall go out of this delightful harbour, where our present wants have been most amply supplied, and where every attention has been paid to us." Then, before concluding with professions of respect to the Ambassadress (never omitted from his private letters), he added something irreconcilable with his first paragraph, and inexplicable, unless it was intended to exculpate those who had aided him " under the rose "—" But I have been tormented by no private orders being given to the Governor for

16 our admission."

The squadron, having got to sea two days earlier than Nelson had expected when he first wrote to Cadiz, made the Gulf of Coron, in the Morea, within the week, and Troubridge, sent to ask for news from the Turkish governor, returned in a few hours with an enemy wine-brig in tow, and news that Buonaparte's fleet had been seen steering to the S.E. from Candia about four weeks earlier. Another vessel confirmed this to the *Alexander* within the day. It now began to be clear to Nelson that after all he had been correct in going to look for the enemy in Alexandria, but that, far from having missed them by delay, he had arrived too soon. This was what had happened.

As he had no frigates to bring him information, he had twice missed the French by a matter of hours. The first occasion had been during the night of June 22, soon after leaving Sicily, in thick weather, when, having believed that Buonaparte had left Malta six days before, he had unwittingly crossed his route, and passed so close to his slow-moving Armada that British signal guns had been heard and caused Admiral de Brueys to steer in alarm for the security of Crete. On June 29 watchers from the Pharos of Alexandria had scarcely seen the sails of Nelson's squadron disappear rapidly over the north-eastern horizon than the immense French flotilla had begun to come in view from the N.W. Within three weeks of landing, Buonaparte had taken Alexandria, won the Battle of the Pyramids and entered " Grand Cairo " in triumph. Lower Egypt, with all its possibilities, was his.

Nelson's second passage to Alexandria occupied only four days. It had always been his hope to fall in with the enemy at sea, and the squadron had sailed in order of battle, in three compact divisions, two of which were to engage the French warships, while the third paid deadly attentions to the reported four hundred transports. Of the efficiency of that famous young Corsican, " the Conqueror of Italy ", as a General, he could not pretend to judge, but as a sea-officer of more than twenty-five years' experience he grimly longed " to try Buonaparte on a wind; for he commands the Fleet as well as the Army ". Throughout the cruise, gun and musketry practice had been kept up, and whenever possible he had summoned his Captains on board his flagship for conference. Consequently, the disposal and conduct of each ship, when attacking the enemy under every likely combination of circumstances, had been so often discussed and calculated as to render signals almost unnecessary. Nevertheless, some fresh ones, which might be needed, had been inserted

in his signal-book. When he approached Alexandria for the second time his theories and intentions were well known to his officers, and they appreciated that he had the highest opinion of, and reliance in, every Captain under his command. There was not a weak link in that chain. The squadron's health was good, and its *morale* as it reached the end of its long quest was high. In the *Vanguard* the Officers of the Watch who breakfasted with the Captain at 8.30 when they came off duty remarked that the Admiral had asked the time of night rather often. Not even Troubridge knew until afterwards that, as day after day had slipped past without bringing the hoped-for encounter for which he was momentarily ready, Nelson had reached such a state of nervous tension that the slightest unfamiliar sound sent his heart pounding as it had done during his experiences of high fever. This bad habit, he said, persisted whenever he was startled, either by pleasure or pain, in after years. He believed that those weeks had, in the colloquial phrase, " taken years off his life ". " More people perhaps die of broken hearts than we are aware of."

With dusk on the last day of July, he made the signal for his fleet to close, and early next morning the *Alexander* and *Swiftsure* were detached to look into Alexandria. The fleet came in sight of the Pharos and Pompey's Tower with a top-gallant wind, in clear weather, soon after noon on August 1. As before, neither harbour displayed French sails. The signal to turn eastwards down the coast was given, and in every ship-of-the-line the main meal of the day, usually served at 1.30, began. Looking back, Captain Saumarez did not recollect ever feeling more hopeless than when he sat to eat that day.

> " Judge what a change took place when, as the cloth was being removed, the Officer of the Watch came running in saying, ' Sir, a signal is just now made that the Enemy is in Aboukir Bay and moored in a line of battle.' "

As he reached his quarter-deck cheers were sounding. The masthead look-out of the *Goliath* had been the first man to sight sixteen enemy warships at anchor in a strange bay on the larboard bow, about fifteen miles east of Alexandria. Lord Minto's second son, Mr. Midshipman Elliot, had run direct to Captain Foley, without having hailed the quarter-deck; but before the *Goliath* could signal " Enemy in sight ", her jealous but devoted consort, the *Zealous*, had anticipated her.

In the *Vanguard*, Captain Berry noticed " the utmost joy which seemed to animate every breast " reflected in the countenance of

U

the Admiral, " perhaps more heightened ".   Having signalled his
squadron " Prepare for Battle ", Nelson then ordered his dinner to
be served, and on rising from that meal, remarked to his officers,
" Before this time to-morrow, I shall have gained a Peerage or
Westminster Abbey."   19

3

Admiral de Brueys had been ordered, after Buonaparte's
victorious disappearance inland, either to take the French fleet
into Alexandria, to sail for French-occupied Corfu or to assume
a strong position on the coast and prepare to repel attack.   The
old harbour of Alexandria was difficult of entry for large ships, he
still had army stores on board and he was insufficiently provisioned for the passage to Corfu.   After the event, when he found
the army which he eventually deserted cut off in Egypt, Buonaparte declared that he had repeatedly ordered de Brueys into
Alexandria.

When first accounts of a Fleet action penetrated to the
Admiralty, *via* a Paris newspaper, on September 21, the name
" Béguieres " puzzled experts until it was recollected that Béquier
was the old French form of the Arab " Al-Bekir ", distinguishing
a district including a bay of shoals, stretching for many miles
between a promontory, village and island, and the Rosetta mouth
of the Nile.   The shores of the southwards-curving bay were sandy,
with waters deepening so slowly that anchorage for ships-of-the-
line could not be found within three miles of the coast, and the
promontory at its western extremity was linked by rocks to the
small island, which it sheltered from north-westerly winds.
Aboukir Island, protected on its seaward side by further rocks
and shoals, had, when Nelson came in sight of it, been newly
fortified, and the French fleet, anchored in a single line, with a
slight bend in the middle, stretching from N.W. to S.E., was
actually composed of thirteen ships-of-the-line and four frigates.
But the ships-of-the-line included one of 120 guns—the inspiringly
named *L'Orient*, de Brueys's flagship—three 80's, *Le Franklin*,
Le Tonnant and *Le Guillaume Tell*, and nine 74's.   Nelson's
fleet, lacking at the moment the *Alexander* and *Swiftsure*, detached
on scouting duty, and the *Culloden*, nine miles astern with her
wine-brig in tow, consisted of his flagship, the *Vanguard*,
H.M.S. *Goliath* (Foley), *Zealous* (Sam Hood), *Orion* (Saumarez),
Audacious (Davidge Gould), *Theseus* (Miller), *Minotaur* (Louis),
Defence (Peyton), *Bellerophon* (Darby) and *Majestic* (Westcott),

all 74's, the *Leander*, of 50 guns (Thompson), and the *Mutine* brig (Hardy).

De Brueys, anchored on the edge of shoal water, with the fortified island to the windward end of his line, had reckoned correctly on the English being unprovided with charts of the reefs protecting his position. Ben Hallowell had given Nelson, a few days previously, a rough sketch of the bay, taken out of a French prize. Sam Hood possessed an English map which he soon discarded as useless; Foley, always well-found, had a good chart in a modern French atlas—" Bellin's Collection ". De Brueys, expecting attack from seaward, had taken the precaution of placing his strongest vessels, including his own flagship, in tee centre of his line. His next heaviest ships occupied the only other position which he considered vulnerable, his rear. His van, of which the leading ship should have been so close to the island as to make it impossible for the enemy to pass between it and the shore, contained his oldest and least effective craft. There was also room for ships to pass through his line.

When a French 74 signalled, in rapid succession, around two o'clock, " Strange sail in sight ", " Enemy in sight ", and " Enemy moving on the bay ", the French Commander-in-Chief proceeded to call a council of war. He was so short of provisions that his frigates had not been on the look-out, and the boats of many of his ships-of-the-line, with many men, were on shore, filling water-casks and digging wells, a business at which they had to be protected by guards against Bedouins. Only one of his flag-officers, Blanquet-Duchayla, advised that he should order his fleet to weigh and stand out to meet Nelson, and for three precious hours hopes were entertained that as the brief tropical twilight must be fading by the time that the sails approaching out of the west could enter the bay, the English would not attempt a night action in uncharted waters. During the hours of darkness, de Brueys considered, he might form his line in closer order, nearer the shore, or even contrive an escape. But the English ships continued to bear up for the bay, now with a whole sail breeze, and were presently observed to be coming to the wind in succession, so at 5.30, *faute de mieux*, he signalled that he intended to engage them, at anchor, and his ships were hurriedly cleared for action on the seaward side. The hot and weary working-parties had been recalled, but many men failed to return in time, and although " good seamen " were taken from the frigates to strengthen the crews of the 74's, eventually revolutionary France fought two-thirds short of complement.

De Brueys's preparations showed a complete misconception of his opponent. Nelson had repeatedly promised, " I will bring the French Fleet to Action the moment I can lay hand upon them ", and as all the possibilities of a night attack upon a stationary enemy had been discussed by him with his Captains, he had nothing for which to wait. Indeed, as he realised at once, dangerous though the attack must be under existing circumstances, delay could only advantage his adversary. In the words of Berry, he viewed de Brueys's dispositions, from the first moment, " with the eye of a seaman prepared for attack ". He gave the signals to prepare for battle, to get ready to anchor by the stern, and communicating his intention to attack the enemy's van and centre, as they lay at anchor, " according to the plan before developed ". At about 5.30 his fleet began to form line of battle " as most convenient ". " No further signal was necessary." Every Captain appreciated what Nelson had eagerly and instantly noted—" that where there was room for a French 74 at single anchor to swing, there was room for a British 74 to anchor ", and he was alive to the probability that the French would have lumbered up their guns on the in-shore side. It had always been his intention, if he found the enemy at anchor, to throw his whole weight on a part of their line and crush it, before assistance could come—" first to secure the victory, and then to make the most of it, according to future circumstances ". As de Brueys had disposed his line, this blow would fall on the oldest and weakest enemy vessels. The risks taken by Nelson were great, for he was entering a strange bay with nightfall, without charts or pilots ; and the possibility of his own ships firing into one another when attacking enemy ships lying between them could not be disregarded. That the batteries on the island were as ineffective as they proved, he could not guess ; all that he could do was to keep as far out of their range as reefs would allow.

The ten British 74's hauled sharp to the wind to weather the foul ground to seaward of the island, sounding as they came into the shallows—fifteen fathoms, thirteen, eleven, ten. . . . As they came abreast of the end of the shoal at the entrance, Nelson hailed Hood to ask him if he thought they were far enough to the eastward to clear it. Hood replied composedly that he was in eleven fathoms, and that he had no chart, but that, " If you will allow me the Honour of leading you into Battle, I will keep the lead going."

Nelson said, " You have my leave, and I wish you success ", and took off his hat. The lofty-statured Hood, attempting to return the courtesy in a fresh breeze, lost his hat, and his First Lieutenant caught the words, " Never mind, Webley! There it goes for luck. Put the helm up and make sail." The *Goliath* was on their larboard bow, striving for place. The efforts of the French brig *Alerte* to lure them on to the outer shoals and within range of the island batteries were coldly disregarded, though she man-œuvred almost within gunshot. (Afterwards, Contre-Admiral Blanquet-Duchayla, prisoner of war, remarked to his host, Ball, that the English Admiral had *sans doute* pilots of experience. " He did not pay any attention to the brig's track, but allowed her to go away; he hauled well round all the dangers ! ") At 6.28, the enemy having hoisted their colours and opened fire, the *Goliath* fulfilled her Captain's hopes of leading the fleet inside the French van. Foley crossed the bows of *Le Guerrier*, raking her with a broadside, but his sheet anchor hung, whereupon Hood took up the station he had intended. Foley brought up on the inner quarter of *Le Conquérant*, next in the line, and the *Orion*, *Theseus* and *Audacious* followed them round. As the fiery sun of August 1, 1798, sank below the horizon, the five leading English ships, all inside and at closest possible quarters, were bringing an overwhelming fire to bear upon the enemy van, the more distressing to its recipients because their larboard guns were not only loose, but piled up with baggage and mess furniture, a certain source of deadly splinters. The *Vanguard*, the sixth ship to come into action, was the first to anchor outside the French line, abreast and within pistol-shot of *Le Spartiate*, already engaged at longer range by the *Theseus*. But until the *Minotaur* had drawn the fire of *L'Aquilon*, fourth in the French line, the *Vanguard* was hard pressed.

By 7 o'clock, total darkness having fallen, and the scene being lit by nothing but gun-fire (as five French 74's, under-manned and able to fight only one broadside at a time, were being swiftly beaten into helplessness by eight British), Nelson signalled all ships to hoist distinguishing lights. Only one enemy Captain at the very rear of the French line, waiting horrified for inevitable destruction, spread his topsails in an appeal which brought no response.

The eighth and ninth of Nelson's ships, arriving to a smoke-hung and darkling scene, sustained the heaviest casualties. The *Bellerophon*, missing *Le Franklin*, first of the French 80's (at the moment most gallantly attacked by the *Leander* frigate), brought up abreast of *L'Orient*, and received the undivided attention of a vessel of double her own force. The *Bellerophon's* masts were entirely shot away, and she wore out of the line to the lee side of the bay. The *Majestic* ran her jib-boom into the main-rigging of *L'Heureux*, and while she hung in this position, suffered heavy loss. Her Captain, Westcott, was fatally struck in the throat by a musket ball; but her First Lieutenant, getting her free, and anchoring on the bows of the next enemy astern, instantly began an unsupported action with *Le Mercure* (and having fought his ship resolutely throughout the Battle of the Nile, Mr. Cuthbert was next morning promoted to the vacant command).

The battle had reached this stage, round about 8 o'clock, when Nelson, standing on his quarter-deck with Berry by his side (according to tradition looking at Hallowell's sketch of the bay), was struck on the head by a piece of flying langridge—the scrap shot much used by the French for the destruction of British sails. The fragment cut his brow to the bone, above his old wound, and a flap of flesh, falling down over his " bright " eye, accompanied by profuse hæmorrhage, blinded him. He fell, and Berry, catching him in his arms, heard the words, " I am killed. Remember me to my wife."

4

This was the end he had long foreseen, and it was indeed as good as he could ever have hoped, for he had fallen when a victory, to be greeted as " the most signal that has graced the British Navy since the days of the Spanish Armada ", was already assured. He proceeded to carry everything in the high style dear to him and Shakespeare. Towards the cockpit, inefficiently lit by lanterns curtseying to the roll and thud of gun-carriages, and amid unintelligible sounds, prefaced by shouts and followed by explosions, seventy-odd wounded were trooping with bent heads, or being carried. He would not allow the Principal Surgeon to be told that the Admiral was amongst them. To the relief and surprise of those about him, Jefferson, after probing the wound, pronounced the visible damage superficial. Since all wounds, and especially head wounds, were dangerous, he cautiously diagnosed " no immediate danger ". But the son of the Rector of Burnham Thorpe, struck on the head, and in total darkness at last, could not believe that this was not the end. He sent for Mr. Comyn, Chaplain, and messages were delivered for Lady

Nelson and for Louis of the *Minotaur*, who had so boldly and efficiently relieved the Admiral's flagship from the dual fire of *L'Aquilon* and *Le Spartiate*—" Your support prevented me from being obliged to haul out of the line." While he lay awaiting his dressing, cheering sounded above, and Berry entered, to acquaint him with what that young man described, with considerable meiosis, as "pleasing intelligence". *Le Spartiate*, long dismasted, had ceased to fire at 8.30. Berry had sent Galwey to board her with a party of marines. The First Lieutenant had returned with the French Commander's sword, which his Flag-Captain delivered to the Admiral, together with the assurance that *L'Aquilon* and *Le Souverain Peuple* had struck, and although *L'Orient*, *Le Tonnant* and *L'Heureux* were not yet taken possession of, " they were considered as completely in our power. . . . It appeared that Victory had already declared itself in our favour."

The surgeon had stitched and bandaged his brow, and urgently entreated him to remain quiet. Nelson withdrew, in order to clear the cockpit. A quiet place, at such a moment, and in a ship so shaken as the *Vanguard*, could with difficulty be found. He was settled in the bread-room, in the hold, a place of great capacity, far removed from the din of battle, where a man might walk upright, and it was to these surroundings that the Admiral's Secretary was summoned, to take down a despatch to the First Lord. But the sight of the Admiral, blinded by bandages, identifiable only by his stump and his St. Vincent medal, ghastly pale, cold as ice and highly impatient, was altogether too much for the newcomer, who had himself been hit. He afterwards explained his incapacity as the result of emotion on seeing his employer blinded and suffering much pain. He was dismissed from the bread-room, and, within a fortnight, from Nelson's life. (" My Secretary I have recommended to be Purser of the *Franklin*. He has not activity for me.") Mr. Comyn made another appearance, offering his services, but Nelson himself had taken up the pen and, pushing up his bandage, begun to trace the words, " My Lord, Almighty God has blessed His Majesty's Arms in the late Battle." This was the correct style for a victorious Admiral. He well knew that after the Battle of the Saints, Rodney had begun—" It has pleased God, out of His divine providence, to give His Majesty's arms a most complete victory."

He was interrupted by another entrance of Berry, this time to report that *L'Orient* appeared to be on fire, in her cabin.

Disobedient as usual to doctor's orders, Nelson demanded to be assisted on deck, and emerged into the soft but smoke-hung Egyptian night at about the moment that *Le Conquérant, Le Guerrier* and an unrecognisable 74 struck to H.M.S. *Audacious, Zealous* and *Minotaur*. Firing was still brisk. Gradually a ruddy light began to swell upon the battle scene, until it was so bright that the Admiral, focusing his imperfect and painful gaze on every quarter in turn, could distinguish the colours flown by the respective ships, and judge of the situation with some certainty.

L'Orient had been repainting, and the flames had spread to oil-jars and paint buckets lying on her poop. He at once told Berry to do what he could to save as many as possible of the crew of the enemy flagship, which he judged " completely beat ", and the indefatigable Galwey, with the only boat of the *Vanguard* in condition, set off towards a warm spot.

In the dramatic shadows, to the north-west of Aboukir Island, a British 74 lay at a dejected angle. This pitiful spectacle represented Troubridge, who, having received permission by signal to cast off his prize, and hastening to the engagement through the perilous defile with a failing wind, had struck the tail of the shoal. All his own endeavours, combined with those of the smaller craft commanded by Thompson and Hardy, had failed to get the *Culloden* off, and the only assistance that could be afforded during the Battle of the Nile by the Captain described by Lord St. Vincent as " the ablest adviser and best executive officer in His Majesty's Service " was serving as a beacon to the vessels coming up astern. Ball and Hallowell, arriving late on the scene, gave the *Culloden* and the island batteries as wide a berth as possible, and sweeping down to anchor on either side of the ships of the enemy centre, already heavily engaged, had presented the terrifying aspect of an untouched British reserve. Hallowell, with judgment, withheld his fire while a disabled and unlighted 74 drifted past him—the *Bellerophon*, with Darby and one-third of her crew casualties.

As the poop of *L'Orient* was alight, the new arrivals concentrated their fire on that spot, rendering all attempts to check the conflagration quite impossible. Men continued to serve her lower-deck guns until they were driven from them, but flames began to race up tarred rigging, along her newly painted sides and down towards her magazine. As her destruction became imminent, many gesticulating figures, silhouetted against

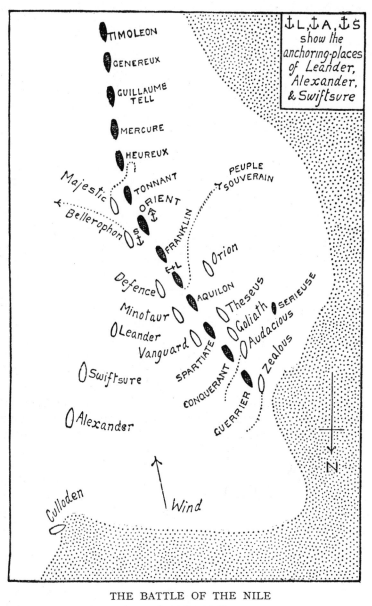

THE BATTLE OF THE NILE
August 1, 1798

the glow, leapt into the sea, and ships to the windward of her
veered, or slipped their cables.   Only Ball, having drenched the
Alexander, held his station until he was sure of the doom of
L'Orient.   She blew up at 10.5, with a detonation which startled
French troops at Rosetta, ten miles distant, and was believed
by workers below decks in the *Goliath* to signify an explosion
in the after-part of their own vessel.   Adjutant-General Moutard,
although wounded, swam to the nearest ship—the *Audacious*—
and several stunned men were tugged in to safety through the
lower ports of British 74's, but Commodore Casabianca and his
intelligent ten-year-old son, who had been clinging to the wreck
of the main-mast in the water, never reappeared, and it was   21
reckoned that Galwey's boat, and those from other ships which
had followed his example, rescued not more than seventy of the
four hundred odd men noticed in the water before the explosion.

L'Orient* took with her to the depths of Aboukir Bay the body
of Admiral de Brueys, dead of his wounds on his quarter-deck,
£600,000 in ingots of gold and diamonds wrested from the Swiss
Republic and Roman State to finance Buonaparte's Eastern
expedition, and, what was irreplaceable, the storied treasures of
the Most Venerable Order of the Hospital of St. John of Jerusalem.
Malta of the Knights, under her first and last German Grand
Prior, and well prepared by propaganda, had made the feeblest
show of resistance when the French fleet had appeared in Valetta
harbour, and for the past three months their treasure, with the
exception of three relics, had been in the hold of the French
Admiral's flagship.

For a few minutes after the explosion (calculated by various
eyewitnesses as between three and ten) complete darkness reigned :
then firing broke out again.   Meanwhile masts, yards, red-hot
ammunition, charred fragments of rope, timber, metal and corpses
rained from the eastern skies into the troubled waters and on
board the surrounding ships.   At the Battle of the Nile, republican France, crippled by every inevitable result of National
Revolution, fought with ardour, though largely uninstructed.
(" Fire, fire, steadily ", urged Admiral Blanquet-Duchayla in the
dismasted *Franklin*.   " The last shot may give us victory.")   As
the moon rose on the scene of triumph and wreckage, struggling
through a pall of black smoke, Nelson was persuaded to go below.
He did not rest, and continued to issue orders, but although until
3 a.m. firing continued spasmodically, and broke out again at
dawn with renewed vigour, the " follow through " of the Battle

of the Nile was not sufficiently effective to satisfy him. The
fact was that the experience of Miller was characteristic throughout the fleet :

> " My people were also so extremely jaded, that as soon as they had
> hove our sheet anchor up, they dropped under the capstan-bars and
> were asleep, in a moment, in every sort of posture, having been working
> then at their fullest exertion, or fighting, for near 12 hours."

With the light of day came the garnering of the fruits of
victory. Out of thirteen enemy sail-of-the-line, nine had been
taken and two burnt. Of the four frigates, one was burnt and
one sunk. Rear-Admiral Villeneuve, in his flagship *Le Guillaume
Tell*, accompanied by *Le Généreux* and the frigates *Diane* and
Justice, weighed before noon and stood out to sea, to fight
another day. Hood made an attempt to chase, despite the state of
the *Zealous*, but no other vessel was in a condition to accompany
her: he was recalled. The British casualties were estimated by
Nelson at about 200 killed and 700 wounded; the French loss as
5,225 taken, drowned, burnt and missing, 3,105 sent on shore by
cartel, and 200 kept to serve the fleet. During the first day
succeeding his victory (which he rightly styled a Conquest),
though jarred and sick, he knew little rest. His desk was littered
by letters written over-night by his Captains, of which Davidge
Gouid's was a fair example :

> " Sir,
> " I have the satisfaction to tell you the French ship *Le Conquérant*,
> has struck to the *Audacious*, and I have her in possession. The slaughter
> on board her is *dreadful*; her Captain is dying. Our fore and main-
> mast are wounded, but I hope not very bad. They tell me the fore-
> mast is the worst. I give you joy. This is a glorious victory."

Nelson signed Hardy's commission for the *Vanguard* (as Berry
was to go home in the *Leander* with despatches), and lest Berry
might meet with an accident, he decided to send his Signal-
Lieutenant, Capel, together with Hoste, to Naples in the *Mutine*,
with duplicates. He wrote to the French Commandants of
Aboukir and Alexandria to arrange for the reception, under
cartel, of their wounded into hospital, and he issued a memorandum of congratulation and thanks to all captains, officers,
seamen and marines of the squadron. In the evening he entertained French officers. A large proportion of the company, of
both nations, were suffering from head-wounds. The prisoners,
although some obviously came of monarchist stock, were frankly

atheist, and expressed their surprise and admiration at the discipline which had enforced attendance at the religious services of thanksgiving held throughout the victorious fleet in the heat of the day, this afternoon. The scenes on board the battered men-of-war had been picturesque—the ships' companies ranged around their black-gowned chaplains, on the quarter-deck, under an awning formed of the ships' ensigns, through which the sunlight of 2 p.m. had cast a rich glow. As darkness fell, Arabs and Mamelukes lining the shores of the bay kindled bonfires. The guests took these to mean that some military success had been achieved over Buonaparte, and took their departure heavily. Afterwards, Miller, visiting Nelson in his cot, found him " weak but in good spirits ".

5

The days following the Battle of the Nile, when the stricken victor lay in Béquier Roads, totally unable to communicate with the outer world, were amongst the strangest in his story. His Captains, headed by the mortified Troubridge, urged their men to superhuman efforts, under Egyptian sun, amidst unparalleled débris. The burial at sea of poor Westcott took place, and many enemy corpses were interred below the sands of Aboukir Island, now to be renamed Nelson's Island. Throughout the hours of daylight the sounds of carpentry never ceased, and ships' boats plied incessantly amongst the hulks aground on the shoals.

After their toil and labour, the gentlemen were not idle. On the night of August 2, in Saumarez's ship, Nelson's Captains inaugurated " The Egyptian Club ", and a solemn document, signed by all present, invited Sir Horatio to accept the gift of a sword and have his portrait taken for the Society. Berry, 22 scribbling replies on behalf of his Admiral, assured Miller, " He is now more easy than he was this morning, the *rage* being over." But for many days yet Nelson could not be easy. Until the *Leander* was ready, on the 6th, his despatches had to wait for transport. The casualty list as usual omitted his own name. (" Were I to die this moment ", he added in a note to Lord Spencer, " ' Want of frigates ' would be found stamped on my heart.") He enclosed a packet of intercepted enemy letters, including one from Buonaparte himself. " He writes such a scrawl, no one not used to it can read ; but luckily we have got a man who has wrote in his Office to decipher it." These letters, and a later packet (travelling to Buonaparte from France, and recovered from the waves by dauntless tars, when the crew of a French gunboat tried to sink them), were published in London before the year was out, and the second volume was provided with a frontispiece displaying Admiral Nelson's left-handed signature.

After studying the captured enemy correspondence, large issues troubled Nelson's brain. Buonaparte, blockaded in Egypt and Syria, could only attack Constantinople overland, and the Victor of the Nile was sending an express to advise the British Minister at the Porte that if the Grand Signior would but trot an army into Syria, the career of the Conqueror of Italy and Egypt was finished. But unless Indian waters were watched, Tippoo Sahib might still get French reinforcements by the Red Sea. It appeared that Foley's Fourth Lieutenant (a cousin of Drake of Genoa) was ready to travel by Alexandria, Aleppo and Basra to warn the Governor of Bombay. " A very clever young man " came on board the *Vanguard* and was provided with letters commending him to the British Consuls, Vice-Consuls and merchants on his route, and authorising him to draw upon the East India Company for his expenses. If the Company objected, Sir Horatio took their repayment upon himself. " As an Englishman I shall be proud that it has been in my power to be the means of putting our Settlements on their guard."

At last, by August 15, Capel and Hoste had left with the duplicate despatches for Naples, and Admiral Blanquet-Duchayla's sword for the Lord Mayor of London—" Relying on your zeal and judgement, I have only to wish you a good voyage by sea and by land." The fleet had unanimously appointed Mr. Alexander Davison sole agent for the prizes captured at the Battle of the Nile, and Saumarez had sailed for Gibraltar with six of the prizes and seven of the line. Sam Hood had received orders to blockade the coast while his Admiral departed down the Mediterranean with his three worst-damaged 74's. Reports from the friendly natives of the interior suggested that such of Buonaparte's garrisons as had not been murdered by them were being decimated by water-borne fever. At last, too, despatches and frigates from Cadiz had traced Nelson to the mouth of the Nile. The Commander-in-Chief, who had heard nothing since the squadron had quitted Syracuse for the second time, but who had never ceased to send messages of good cheer, and deprive himself of frigates which had been missing the squadron consistently, now forwarded urgent secret orders for it to return to the westward and co-operate in an expedition against Minorca.

Lord St. Vincent also sent Admiral Nelson's stepson to receive a scolding for bad behaviour, and letters which showed that the Victor of the Nile was in disgrace at home for missing the enemy— " such is the chance to which officers' characters are subject ".

Suddenly in touch with Europe again, kept from sleep by a perpetual cough, Nelson replied at once in his own hand, " My head is so upset that really I know not what to do; but by to-morrow will arrange matters in my mind, and do my best." Next day he ordered three enemy ships which could not be refitted within a month to be burnt. He could only hope that the prize money for them would be granted.

Then, thick-coming fancies crowding upon him, he succumbed. Now that there was, for the moment, no more to be done, " That fever of anxiety which I have endured from the middle of June " fastened down upon him. Jefferson, in charge of an illustrious but impossible patient with a long case-history, running a high temperature, began to answer enquiries sourly.   24

6

Nelson's despatches, sent by Naples, announcing the Victory of the Nile, took two months and a day to reach England, and were beaten by five days by a circumstantial message from Hamburg. A French brig which had made a dash for the open sea just before *L'Orient* blew up had reached Rhodes with a tale of disaster, and the Governor had informed His Britannic Majesty's Minister at the Porte, who had expeditiously notified his opposite number in Vienna. Fortunately for those whose   25 reputation was deeply engaged by the choice of so junior an officer as opponent to Buonaparte, the headlines of English papers were much occupied for many months of 1798 by rebellion in Ireland. Still, they had much to endure. On July 12 editors mentioned that a private letter seen at Lloyd's Coffee House reported that Admiral Nelson had taken five enemy sail-of-the-line and Buonaparte on board a transport. This colourful story was the first of many entirely without foundation. The press was stopped a fortnight later to announce the arrival of Sir Robert Calder with despatches from Lord St. Vincent, but Sir Robert, it presently appeared, had come home for health reasons, and the only news from Cadiz station was of " serious misunder-standings ", resulting in the execution of five men apiece on board H.M.S. *Marlborough* and *Princess Royal*. By August 1 the public, agitated by persistent dark hints of an action in which seven British warships had been lost, was getting restive, and one editor voiced their feelings in a querulous article headed, " Where is Buonaparte ? Where is Admiral Nelson ? " Pitt, supplied with French prints, some of which claimed a success of Buonaparte over Nelson, concluded that " something has happened ", and while waiting patiently for authentic accounts, resolutely supposed that even French authorities would not long be able to disguise entirely what that " something " had been. Admiral Goodall, when asked, " What is your favourite Hero about ? The French Fleet has passed under his nose ! " stoutly promised, " something capital ". " I am always in hopes ", wrote Mr. Dundas to Lord Spencer from a northern holiday, " we shall hear of Nelson doing something brilliant."

But by mid-September, tired of what the First Lord called " the extravagant accounts propagated nearly all over Europe of Sir Horatio Nelson having won a decisive victory ", Mr. Dundas was " in charity " presuming that when Sir Horatio reappeared to tell his own story he would be able to give a good reason for having missed Buonaparte. It was known at the Admiralty by now that Nelson had left Syracuse for the second time, and Lord Grenville was insistent that he must be ordered to protect the Kingdom of the Two Sicilies, and not attach himself to Buonaparte's fleet. The First Lord replied coolly that he hoped Sir Horatio Nelson would have " a pretty good story to tell, at least. His missing the French fleet both going and returning is certainly very unfortunate but we must not be too ready to censure him for leaving Alexandria when he was there, till we know the exact state of the intelligence which he received there." Only his staff realised, when the good news— far surpassing the most extravagant rumour—did arrive, what had been Lord Spencer's anxiety. On being told that the victory had been achieved without the loss of a single British ship he turned, and without speaking a word, fell flat in the passage outside his office. At Naples, both the Queen and the British Ambassadress had fainted, but Lady Hamilton had been well enough, before the day was out, to drive about the streets, with young Capel and Hoste, wearing round her forehead a bandeau inscribed " Nelson and Victory ". In London, the First Lord (equally resilient), after a spell " stretched upon his couch, pale as death ", rose to offer dinner to Mr. Pitt, come up from the country in haste.

Berry and Thompson did not arrive in London until the last

week of November, having passed through very trying experiences.   After a six-hour action off Candia, with *Le Généreux* (the French 74 to escape with Villeneuve from Aboukir Bay), the 50-gun *Leander* had been captured.   The Republicans treated Nelson's Captains with discourtesy.   They not only relieved Captain Berry of his full-dress uniform, they actually removed some of the instruments with which the ship's surgeon was at the moment operating upon Thompson.   Both officers were severely wounded, and Thompson was observed on the night of his arrival " walking halt up Whitehall ".   However, Berry had the satisfaction of being able to assure Lord Spencer at dinner that the Battle of the Nile had been won before *L'Orient* blew up, an important point on which he found the First Lord, together with the whole nation, at fault.   He was knighted on December 12 and Thompson in the following February.

The rewards conferred upon Nelson were many, but of most of them he did not hear for many weeks, and congratulatory letters from home did not reach him till mid-January. The first gifts to be announced came from the Sultan of Turkey, and were of Oriental profusion and magnificence.   The Grand Signior sent a sable pelisse, a purse of 2,000 sequins to be distributed among the wounded, a canteen, a dress sword, a gold-hilted scimitar, an ivory- and silver-mounted musket, and a diamond ornament called a " Chelengk ", taken from one of the Imperial turbans. (Hearing that Nelson was wearing this Eastern jewel in his hat, Lemuel Abbott, called upon to supply more and more portraits, attempted the Chelengk unseen, and got it very wrong.)   Many royalties sent diamond-studded boxes.   That from the criminal lunatic Czar of Russia contained his own likeness in miniature.   One of particular beauty, in the shape of a rose, came, it was whispered, from the Dowager Sultana, mother of the Grand Signior.   From the East India Company came a grant of £10,000.   The City of London, recipient of the sword of Admiral Blanquet-Duchayla, replied with swords for Nelson and his Captains, who all received gold medals from His Majesty; and before the year was out, Messrs. Potter, haberdashers of Charing Cross, were ready with the medal ribbon.   Mr. Alexander Davison, sole prize agent, also provided medals, at a personal cost estimated at £2,000.   Davison's medals, in gold for captains, silver and copper-bronzed for seamen and marines, were handsome.   The obverse presented Hope, with an olive branch in her right hand, supporting on a rugged

rock a medallion with the profile of Nelson. The reverse showed
the opposing fleets lit by the sinking rays of the radiant orb,
encircled by the opening words of the Admiral's despatch—
" Almighty God has blessed His Majesty's Arms ". Only the
peerage, bestowed in November, together with a pension of
£2,000 for three lives, was not considered by Nelson's friends
adequate. Lord Hood had told Lady Nelson, on the best
authority—that of Mr. Pitt—that she was likely to find herself
Viscountess Alexandria. Jervis had received an earldom after
St. Vincent, and Duncan a viscounty after Camperdown. Neither
of these victories had been so complete or in any degree comparable in importance with that of the Nile. The reason offered
for the award of nothing more than a barony was that as Nelson
had not been a Commander-in-Chief, but merely detached in
charge of a squadron, the Admiralty could find no precedent for
offering a higher rank. For some months people believed that
the barony was merely a preliminary to higher honours, but
presently Pitt said indeed the last word on the subject, when he
pointed out that Nelson's glory did not depend upon the rank to
which he might be raised in the peerage.

The news of the Battle of the Nile roused an enthusiasm at
home the echoes of which have never died. The good tidings,
so long and anxiously awaited, spread very quickly. In a west-
country cathedral city, within forty-eight hours, the landlord
of a leading tavern, having attired himself as a British Tar,
stood on his threshold welcoming guests, beneath a balcony on
which the local volunteers played " Heart of Oak " and " A
Royal Standard flew above the disgraced Tricolour ". In the
adjacent seminary, young gentlemen, given a holiday, were cutting
out silhouettes to be carried in a torchlight procession. Their
labours represented " the Hero of Italy in the mouth of a Crocodile, and the French Admiral delivering up his sword to our
single-handed Conqueror ". By a happy chance, the essential
features of this naval success of the first order were easily to be
understood and to the last detail dramatic. The public eye
fastened with eager comprehension on the picture of the Republican fleet anchored in a crescent formation, under Eastern skies of
turquoise and rose, while British 74's, eagerly watched by
turbaned and dusky natives from the roof-tops and shores of a
palm-crowned bay of shoals, advanced unhesitatingly out of the
west, after a long chase, to match a couple of ships to every
vessel of an ill-disposed van. The young Admiral's despatch,

X

in which he gave all credit to his subordinates ("My band of friends was irresistible "), his failure to enter his own name in the casualty list, his gift of the French Commander's sword " as a remembrance that Britannia still rules the waves ", were recognised by a seafaring nation as breathing the heroic spirit of an antique day. They touched a note which had not been struck with like vigour since the Renaissance. By the close of the year, a shower of souvenirs, ranging from the purely ornamental to the functional, and within reach of every purse, had been produced to meet a huge popular demand, and the likeness of the Victor of the Nile, on canvas, paper, porcelain, pottery, glass, muslin and metal, was as familiar in cottage and castle as that of His Majesty. " Nelson with his one lame arm and gallant fighting spirit " had won a place in British hearts from which he was never to be deposed.

CHAPTER XI

1798
(*ætat* 39-40)

NAPLES

I

" My head ", wrote Nelson to St. Vincent, off Candia, on the first day of September, " is splitting—splitting—splitting. . . ." He made three efforts at the word.

He had seen the last of Aboukir Bay at 8 p.m. on Sunday, August 19, and decided then that if " my half-head " was not particularly needed in the Mediterranean now, he would apply for leave to go home, for the complete rest so much urged by the doctors. At Naples he would say nothing, except that he was going to Cadiz in a fortnight's time. The mere thought of having to tussle, in his present state of health, with the Marquis de Gallo sickened him. He hoped that his command might devolve upon poor Troubridge. (" The copy is a d—d deal better than the Original.") His plan had been to put Troubridge into the *Vanguard*, " with the *Culloden's* masts, yards, etc.", but the *Culloden*, it soon became evident, must be hove down before she could be trusted out of port. With oakum and canvas fothering her damaged bottom, she sailed dreadfully. Nevertheless, she was to reach the dockyard of Castellammare, in the Bay of Naples, before the Admiral's flagship. His progress towards the Court of the Two Sicilies, with light and contrary winds (" I detest this voyage "), was necessarily slow, but correspondingly curative. By September 7 he felt so much better that he decided not to " give up " for a little while, and advised Sir William Hamilton that he intended to spend not more than four or five days in the most populous city of Italy. Syracuse should in future be his port, and his sphere of operations from Malta to Syria. " These times are not for idleness." He felt also, with returning health, more cheerful about his stepson, in whom he hoped that Lord St. Vincent had been a little mistaken. Josiah was young for his age, but " very active ". The stuff to work upon was there, the anxious proxy parent assured himself. " He may have lain too long at Lisbon." The lad, " certainly ungracious in the extreme ", brightened at the news that a request for " a good frigate " for him had already been forwarded to the First Lord. *1*

Within the week, off Stromboli, more frigates joined the small division, and, as always, the home mails for His Majesty's ships brought months-old news, important, trivial, glad and tragic. Troubridge, already wrestling with a dark hour, learnt that he was no longer a husband. Lady Nelson, at Roundwood House, was now sitting opposite her Admiral's portrait. " The likeness is great; I am well satisfied with Abbott." *2*

Next evening the *Mutine* joined, back from Naples, bringing the first letters of congratulation. Sir John Acton presented at length to the Saviour of Europe the felicitations of his royal employers. Sir William Hamilton, who had but once sheltered the victor under his roof, for four nights, five years past, but who had (especially recently) been in continual helpful correspondence with him, hailed, on behalf of " myself and Emma ", " our bosom friend ". " History ", announced a much-moved Fellow of the Royal Society, " does not record an Action that does more honour to the Heroes that gained the Victory, than the late one of the first of August. You have now completely made yourself, my dear Nelson, *immortal.*" Lady Hamilton also had written, enclosing two letters from " my adorable queen ", but her description of the Queen's emotion on hearing the news of the Nile was such as to make a convalescent hope that he might not be called upon to witness the renewal of such a scene. His apartment, wrote the Ambassadress, was preparing, and his hostess was dressed from head to foot, " *alla* Nelson. Ask Hoste. Even my shawl is Blue with gold anchors all over." She sent some " Sonets ", but a separate ship would have been required to carry all being produced by the Neapolitans, mad with joy. Lady Hamilton, who would sooner have been an English powder-monkey in Nelson's victory than an Emperor out of it, was walking on air with pride, " feiling I was born in the same land. . . . Write, or come soon." He had already written, *3* trusting that the fact that she would find him much mutilated would not cause him to be less welcome.

As before, his moment of elation was closely followed by minor tragedy. At 7 a.m. on the morning of the 15th, in a sudden squall, the *Vanguard* lost her foremast, the head of her main-topmast and her jib-boom. Four seamen were carried away with the main-mast, and several survivors of the Nile were severely wounded. The Admiral's flagship performed most of the remainder of her slow progress towards Castellammare dockyard in tow of a frigate. Nelson's cough and fever returned. He doubted whether he should see St. Vincent's face again.

The triumphal entry into the Bay of Naples of what he sadly called " the wreck of the *Vanguard* " was the subject of description by many pens. All eyewitnesses agree that from dawn, when the British men-of-war were observed, in picturesque silhouette against the rugged rock of Tiberius, off Capri, the day promised to be remarkably fine and warm even for southern Italy in the month when the fig and grape are dropping. The *Vanguard*, towed by the *Thalia*, and followed by H.M.S. *Minotaur* and *Audacious*, was visible many hours before she anchored; in any case, the festival-loving Neapolitans had been provided with something in the nature of a dress-rehearsal of welcome to the battered victors of the Nile, when Ball and Troubridge had brought the *Alexander* and *Culloden* into port four evenings previously. By 10 a.m. on Saturday, September 22, the waters of the famous bay, smooth as a mirror, reflected the many-coloured sails of more than five hundred pleasure-boats, overfilled with musically inclined parties. Professional bands, including one from the principal Opera House, well knew the British National Anthem, and had learnt for the occasion " Rule Britannia " and " See the Conquering Hero ". The quays were crowded by enthusiastic *lazzaroni*, a speciality of Naples—beggars, named after Lazarus, but masterful, highly organised and regarded by their monarch with paternal indulgence. In the city, where tier upon tier of houses, parchment-coloured, terracotta, yellow and coral, were backed by hazy heights clothed with cypress, many native as well as English residents had hung flags and bunting from balconies already loaded with dependent carnations and roses. The British Ambassador's barge, accompanied by a boat-load of musicians in his employ, was the first to come alongside the *Vanguard*, and was greeted by a salute of thirteen guns. Nelson himself, a few days later, from the grateful shades of the Palazzo Sessa, sent his wife an account of what followed:

" Alongside came my honoured friends : the scene in the boat was terribly affecting; up flew her ladyship, and exclaiming, ' Oh God, is it possible ? ' she fell into my arm more dead than alive. Tears, however, soon set matters to rights. . . . I hope some day to have the pleasure of introducing you to Lady Hamilton, she is one of the *very best* women in this world. How few could have made the turn she has. She is an honour to her sex, and a proof that a reputation may be regained. I own, it requires a great soul. . . . Her kindness, with Sir William's, to

me, is more than I can express : I am in their house, and I may now tell
you, it required all the kindness of my friends to set me up.   Lady
Hamilton intends writing to you.   May God Almighty bless you, and
give us, in due time, a happy meeting."

A further salute, this time of twenty-one guns, sounded from
the *Vanguard* an hour later.   The King of the Two Sicilies, in a
much-gilded state galley with spangled awnings, was paying the
British Admiral the extraordinary compliment of coming out
nearly three leagues to meet him.   Ferdinand I, perspiring in
powder, black velvet and gold lace, was five years grosser than
when Nelson had last obtained an interview with him.   The large
and loosely-hung Spanish-Bourbon king was still remarkable for
the nose which led his boon-companions of the fish-market to
call him " Il Rè Nasone ", but his swarthy features appeared at
their best illuminated by relief, and the royal oration of welcome
certainly came from the heart.   He warmly clasped Nelson by
the hand, hailing him as " Deliverer and Preserver ", and
expressed, with the boyish vigour which he never outgrew, his
wish that he could have assisted at the battle of Aboukir Bay
under Nelson's orders.   The Austrian-born Queen was unavoidably absent, detained by a bout of ague, aggravated by the
sudden death of her youngest child, the Princess Elizabetta, but
she was represented by the Hereditary Princess, born the Archduchess Clementina, seventeen years of age, doubly first-cousin of
her mate, and eight months pregnant.   The King, who prided
himself upon being a seaman, stayed three hours on board the
Vanguard, gently moving towards his capital, quite unconcerned
that his dismal daughter-in-law had swooned at an early stage
in their inspection of the ship.   He demanded to see the hat which
Nelson had been wearing when he got his head wound, and was
particularly gratified by the scene in the spotless sick-bay, where
a wounded seaman, attended by two lob-lolly boys, was being
read aloud to by a brother hero.   As the illustrious company sat
to an elegant breakfast, a further important guest made a brief
professional appearance.   Commodore Caracciolo, Bailli of the
Order of Malta, a man of aristocratic family, forty-six years of
age, who had learnt his seamanship under Rodney, was in charge
of the nautical education of the King's nine-year-old son, Leopold.
Caracciolo was known by at least one of the feasters present to
have expressed, within the last few days, long-smouldering
resentment of Nelson's conduct in the engagement on March 14,
1795.   The spectator to record with interest his " seemingly

genuine " congratulations to the conquering hero was an authoress. Miss Ellis Cornelia Knight, who had accompanied the Hamiltons in their barge, was a figure venerated by the English colony at Naples. She was the only child of the second marriage of the late Sir Joseph Knight, Rear-Admiral of the White, and for the past twenty seasons, in company with her accomplished but impecunious and invalid mother, had moved incessantly in the best Continental society. Their last move had been from threatened Rome. Miss Knight, highly intelligent offspring of elderly parents, noticed that Admiral Nelson, a person one year her junior, and of homely features, received royalty quite without embarrassment, and her sense of the romantic was touched by the attendance at their table of a small pure-white bird, which, she was informed, had come on board the *Vanguard* on the evening before the action of the Nile, and in spite of being fed and petted by all, made the Admiral's quarters its chief residence.

The flutter of the wings of many liberated birds, towards skies of intensified colour, had been arranged to coincide with the moment of Nelson's setting foot in Naples. A multitude of vociferous fishermen, holding aloft curiously-shaped wicker baskets, let loose their captives as he stepped on shore, amongst sun, dust and scattered petals. The Admiral, the British Ambassador and Ambassadress, and the authoress gained an open waiting carriage with difficulty, and clattered away over lava pavements, uphill, towards the Palazzo Sessa, easily recognisable by the particularly vivid hangings of not quite British scarlet, white and blue festooning its façade, on which, when darkness fell, the words " Nelson of the Nile " and " Victory " were to spring to life from three thousand lamps.

During the drive Nelson mentioned that except for a few hours on board his Commander-in-Chief in Cadiz Bay on April 30, this was the first occasion for six months that he had been out of his ship.

2

On the evening of Nelson's arrival, while his name blazed from its balconies, the doors of the British Embassy were closed except to a few favoured compatriots. Ball and Troubridge were amongst the blue coats seated by candlelight beneath the likenesses by modern artists of one of the most beautiful women of any age. Sir William, before possessing himself for life of the glowing original, now happily presiding at his table, had never

lost an opportunity of securing a copy.   The three three-quarter-
length portraits of Emma, now Lady Hamilton, by Romney,
decorating the walls of the Palazzo Sessa, showed her as herself
(a model, in her teens), in a pink silk gown and a black hat; as a
Bacchante, in classic weeds, with auburn tresses flying, casting a
bewitching glance over her shoulder; and in white draperies, with
palms closed and eyes raised to Heaven—Saint Cecilia.   The son   6
of the Rector of Burnham Thorpe most admired his hostess as a
Santa, and when Lady Knight, an acquaintance of Lady Nelson,
supposed that the day of his victory was accounted by him as
the happiest in his life, he replied repressively: " No; the
happiest was that on which I married Lady Nelson."

Everyone present was in need of rest, after an exhausting day
of triumph in strong sun, following weeks of anxiety.   Sir William
confessed himself much run down; Lady Hamilton was still
suffering from bruises sustained in her swoon on hearing the
news of the Nile.   The atmosphere on that first night, deceptively, promised opportunities for relaxation.

The room prepared for the Admiral was on the upper floor,
where a boudoir, unique in her experience, had long been a
source of admiration to the much-travelled Miss Knight.   The
semicircular window commanded a prospect of the bay, which
was reflected in mirrors covering the entire opposite wall.   When
the full moon seemed to arise out of the ruddy crater of Vesuvius,
illuminating a little flotilla of native craft engaged in the tunny
fishery by torchlight, the effect was romantic.   Nor did dawn,
broad daylight or dusk bring disenchantment.   From the
upper floor of the Palazzo Sessa the eye could discern, beyond
masts and sails, clouds resting upon the mountains behind
Sorrento, Vesuvius dominating the fertile Campania, gardens,
mainly filled in the unsatisfying Italian style with topiary and
statues (curving along the shore towards the grottos of Posilipo),
and a medley of flat-faced and flat-roofed dwellings of all sizes,
five and six storeys high, separated by thoroughfares, noisy,
steep and tortuous.   Nelson soon found that for him to venture
into these streets, either on foot or in a carriage, produced a mob,
and that his expectations of a rest at Naples were utterly illusory.
" Between business and what is called pleasure, I am not my own
master for five minutes."

Within, the large and echoing Italian house still presented to
the stranger a bewildering assortment of staircases, grand and
subsidiary, narrow, tall folding doors, minor galleries, spacious

and sombre, with unmeant-looking views of closely surrounding masonry, and an army of servitors, mostly native. The ground floor was given up to reception rooms, but since the Ambassador was a man of taste, these were not furnished in the perfunctory manner usual in official residences. At the moment, several redoubtable galleries, with walls and floors of carefully selected alabaster and marble, stood empty, as, in preparation for flight, he had recently transferred the gems of his Etruscan collection to packing-cases. But this circumstance was providential, for his wife had invited eighteen hundred guests to celebrate Admiral Nelson's fortieth birthday, on the 29th. Sounds of hammering penetrated to the upper floor, where His Britannic Majesty's representative and his lady untiringly entertained the hero of the Nile *en famille*. A rostral column, engraved with the words " Veni, Vidi, Vici ", and the names of the Captains of the Battle of the Nile, was to be unveiled by Lady Hamilton at a dramatic moment during next Saturday's revelries. It was, of necessity, solidly incorporated in an apartment destined to be shaken by the feet of so many rejoicing Neapolitans, and she declared that it should never come down while she and Sir William occupied this house.

Sir William, whose ideas of hospitality had been learnt in the great country-houses of the mid-eighteenth century, had been truly fortunate at an age when many single gentlemen, fond of comfort, are reduced to marrying their housekeeper. Travelling English, calling at the Embassy, were sometimes startled by being asked their business by an elderly person in apron and keys, and more surprised when they heard that *La Signora Madre* was their Ambassador's mother-in-law. But, as that astute gentleman had foreseen, most Neapolitans accepted without further question what they deemed a stock figure of light opera. Nelson, on coming to know her, joined heartily in a devoted daughter's admiration of Mrs. Cadogan, a strong spirit.

His new Secretary, Mr. John Tyson, late purser of the *Alexander* (who believed that his hostess was, like himself, Lancashire born), adapted himself to improved circumstances with speed, but Nelson, despite the kindness of an accomplished host and hostess, fretted throughout his first week at the Palazzo Sessa, and closer acquaintance with the outstanding characters of the Court of the Two Sicilies by no means bred regard. Even an old Mediterranean man was taken aback by much that the British Embassy, long inured to Neapolitan morals, took for

granted, and Admiral Nelson, attired, night after night, in full-dress uniform by a perfectly complacent sailor servant, read, unhappily, word from Captains Hardy and Troubridge that the squadron was in distress for slops and bedding. (Lady Hamilton, distressed by his small appetite, was at this moment offering him the services of the Embassy *chef* for his flagship.) The only idea of the leaders of the circle in which he found himself at present seemed to be competition as to who could offer him the most spectacular entertainment. Prince Esterhazy gave a magnificent ball, and Sir John Acton a banquet attended by representatives of the Church, State and Services, at the close of which Prince Leopold appeared, to present a letter from his mother, regretting that ill-health had so far prevented her from giving audience to *Nostro Liberatore*. The Queen had ordered a portrait of the Admiral, and the sailor prince said that he meant to stand beneath it every day, and say, " Dear Nelson, teach me to become like you." Sir John explained confidentially that the country   7
was determined to fight as soon as possible, and had no idea of waiting for support from Vienna. He said that he was well advised of the French plan of attack. In fact, he seemed to be alone amongst his kind in holding such views, and nobody took the slightest interest in the possible arrival of Russian, Turkish or most probably Portuguese allies. A visit to the King was followed by the good news that His Majesty had been graciously pleased to order that the Court mourning for his infant daughter should be suspended for one night, the anniversary of Admiral Nelson's birth. After an hour with the Marquis de Gallo, the English Admiral's ire was roused. The polished and not brainless   8
Marquis, elaborately studying his snuff-box, decorations and ring, managed very successfully to convey the impression that " he has been bred in a Court, and I in a rough element ". " But I believe ", added Nelson, " my heart is as susceptible of the finer feelings as his, and as compassionate for the distress of those who look up to me." Commodore Caracciolo, equally courtier-like, brought an invitation in the name of his royal master to dine on board a Neapolitan 74 at anchor in the bay. For the King to offer entertainment on shore to the British Admiral, until war was declared, would be inadvisable. General Mack, sent from Vienna to take command of the Neapolitan army, was hourly expected, but so was a new French Minister. Nelson hoped that M. La Combe St. Michel might make so tactless a speech on presenting his credentials that he would be given his *congé* forthwith, but

this wish was not fulfilled, and General Mack, who required five carriages for his personal effects, still lingered on the mountain roads. "What precious moments the two Courts are losing; three months would liberate Italy; this Court is so enervated that the happy moment will be lost."

The problem of Malta was pressing. A deputation had offered the island to His Sicilian Majesty, and his colours had been hoisted on every fort with the exception of those of Valetta. But at Naples the authorities could not be brought to declare more than that they had no official communication from Malta since September 5. They hoped that Nelson would be able to take the place for them. He sent off a frigate to the island, and meanwhile made an expedition to Castellammare to see the *Vanguard's* foremast stepped. As he had feared, not all the exertions of Hardy or scoldings of the bereaved and maddened Troubridge had availed to get the refitting of his damaged ships as far forward as he had intended. He reminded himself that he had always known Naples was a bad place for such a business. "Beside the rest, we are killed by kindness." The phrase had originated with Lady Hamilton. A tendency to quote her, verbatim, had become noticeable in his hurried letters, though he himself was not without his *bon mots* during these days of Court life. As the party from the British Embassy passed in the Admiral's barge, between the enemy ships taken in the late action, Sir William, referring to absurd French claims, said, "Look at those, and ask how they can call it a drawn battle!" Nelson's reply, treasured by the ubiquitous Miss Knight, was, "They are quite right, only they drew the *blanks* and we the *prizes*."

It was impossible, he wrote to his wife, not to be touched by the childlike eagerness with which Lady Hamilton gradually revealed all her surprises for his birthday. Sir William had not stinted, and Neapolitan fingers were clever at fashioning glittering trifles of tinsel and satin for carnival favours. Every button and ribbon to be distributed amongst Saturday's guests bore Nelson's name, and the new dinner-service, ordered from the royal porcelain factory at Portici, had "H.N." and "Glorious First of August" on every piece. An additional verse to the National Anthem had been composed for the occasion by Miss Knight, and more songs and sonnets than he would ever open were being delivered. Lady Hamilton was making translations, and her collection of newspapers for despatch to Lady Nelson was growing formidable. It was almost a relief when the auspicious day dawned with broken weather, though this inevitably meant a heavy swell in the bay, further retarding the process of refitting, and a packed assembly within the walls of the Palazzo Sessa.

Next morning the Admiral penned a memorable note to Lord St. Vincent :

> " I trust, my Lord, in a week we shall all be at sea.   I am very unwell, and the miserable conduct of this Court is not likely to cool my irritable temper.   It is a country of fiddlers and poets, whores and scoundrels. I am Etc.
>
> " Horatio Nelson." 10

One of his reasons for irritation was understandable. Captain Nisbet had chosen Lady Hamilton's *fête* as the scene for a display of juvenile inebriety.   Captain Troubridge and other officers had removed the young man swiftly, but not before a considerable section of the enervated Neapolitan aristocracy had gathered with amusement that the stepson of the Victor of the Nile was complaining that the British Ambassadress was receiving attentions due to his mother. 11

It was during this week of gaiety—his words are, " on my arrival at Naples " and " in September, 1798 "—that the hero of the hour laid his single hand in the palm of a soothsayer.   Naples abounded in such characters, some of whom, though of ferocious aspect, and summoned from the lowest quarters, enjoyed great reputation in fashionable *salons*, and it appears from a letter of Ball to Lady Hamilton that the Ambassadress herself sometimes pretended to read a hand.   (After thirteen years in a capital where everyone went about garlanded with charms of classic origin, particularly against the Evil Eye and death by drowning, the companion of an antiquary was inevitably fluent in the lore of the silver sprig of rue, the serpent, the sea-horse and the siren.) The task of the gipsy employed by a sea-officer was straightforward, since nearly all such gentlemen were satisfied by talk on three topics—promotion, loved ones at home and date of death. The sibyl who performed for Nelson evidently kept to the popular pattern.   That she refused to see further than seven years ahead was recalled by him in 1805, to his sister Kitty in London, a few days before sailing for Trafalgar. 12

Their guest made two expeditions with the Hamiltons during the early days of October.   At the royal factory of Portici, a service ordered by the Queen to be decorated with his portrait and scenes from the various engagements in which he had taken part was in hand.   Fine porcelain always attracted him, but he prudently and tactfully confined his purchases to a set of busts of the royal family. When he came to pay, he was told that anything chosen by Admiral Nelson was to be delivered free. " It was handsome of the King." The Queen was at last ready to receive him, privately. Miss Knight has left a picture of an audience with the Queen of the Two Sicilies in the Palazzo Reale, Naples. At the end of long progress through the state apartments and galleries of a building with windows overlooking 580 feet of sea-view (but passages so dark that a footman with a lantern must precede the guests and Her Majesty's Cameriere Maggiore, even on a spring evening), " We found Her Majesty standing beside a marble table, between two windows. She asked us a few indifferent questions." The setting for Nelson's audience may have been identical, but there is no doubt that the interview which followed his presentation by the British Ambassador was more interesting than that experienced by the travelling English ladies. His first comment after he had recorded, " I have been with the Queen, she is truly a daughter of Maria Theresa ", was, " This Country, by its system of procrastination, will ruin itself : the Queen sees it, and thinks as we do." The mentally un-developed, pleasure-loving King was, as the Admiral afterwards fully realised, " A philosopher, God bless him." Sir William Hamilton had aged, and lacked firmness in dealing with vacil-lating Neapolitans—a fact tactfully indicated to his wife by the words, " His Excellency is too good to them." But Lady Hamilton (as Lord St. Vincent was informed) " is an Angel. She has honoured me by being my Ambassadress to the Queen : therefore she has my implicit confidence and is worthy of it."

The royal stateswoman whose dignity and distress had so much impressed Nelson had never been accounted a beauty, and a grand air, a fine hand, a long throat and the unmistakable Habsburg lip completed the catalogue of the attractions of Maria Carolina in 1798. She was forty-five, and had borne eighteen children, of whom eight survived. Her complexion was waxen, her eyelids were puffy and her figure was at once gaunt and massive. Like her sister Marie Antoinette, she had been over-early married, to a boor whom she despised. The story of the sisters had much in common, as the glassy eye and frozen look of Maria Carolina proclaimed to all beholders. The rattle of a *berline* on the road to Varennes, the flaxen curls of the Princesse de Lamballe waving from a pike-head, the decreasing sobs of her little nephew, the Dauphin, in his prison-cupboard, were never absent from her waking eye and ear.   Her dread and hate of republicans were hysterical, and she honestly believed that her own day of reckoning was drawing near.   She had always been the subject of much scurrilous gossip, which might not have approached a princess in whose character levity was unsuspected, but the *façade* displayed to Nelson on that October night was convincing and bound to enlist his wholehearted support.   It was as the enemy of the French Anti-Christ, the daughter of Maria Theresa and the mother of many children that Maria Carolina appealed to a British officer whose unusual appearance proclaimed that he was not likely to be absent in the day of battle.   Of course, also, like all injured foreign royalties, she hoped for money from Great Britain.

Next morning, although resident under the same roof, Nelson addressed to Lady Hamilton a long letter on the political situation with reference to Naples, urging attack on France without delay. He ended with the words, underlined—" *The boldest measures are the safest* ", and a postscript explained :

> " Your Ladyship will, I beg, receive this letter as a preparative for Sir William Hamilton, to whom I am writing, with all respect, the firm and unalterable opinion of a British Admiral, anxious to approve himself a faithful subject to his Sovereign by doing everything in his power for the happiness and security of their Sicilian Majesties and their Kingdom."

General Mack reached the palace of Caserta, sixteen miles north of the capital, on October 9, and Nelson and the Hamiltons were bidden to meet him there two days later.   Nelson, who had bitter experience of Austrian Generals, and had already formed his opinion of this one (but prayed he might be mistaken), prepared to impress his personality with care.   He felt that it was important that he should gain the entire confidence of the military leader to whom their Sicilian Majesties were about to entrust their army. The setting also was impressive.   The Versailles of Naples, one of the largest and most sumptuous palaces in Europe, built of Travertine from the Capuan quarries, was famous for its four courtyards—of barrack-like exterior and unfinished—its marble chapel and arcades, its theatre, and the ornamental waterworks of its park, now receiving " improvements ", including an English garden, from a Mr. Graeffer, *protégé* of Sir Joseph Banks and Sir William Hamilton.   The party from the British Embassy arrived beneath a main portico one hundred and thirty-four feet high and divided into three vestibules by sixty-four columns, and ascended a state staircase to a first floor of gilded reception-rooms, decorated with frescoes and tapestries in which most figures were of much more than life size. The royal residence seemed primarily designed to make all inhabitants appear insignificant, but the atmosphere of the small party that presently sat to dine was from the first moment hopeful, in spite of the fact that the General sent to command Neapolitan troops understood no Italian, and the Admiral spoke no language but his own. French was employed, and the Hamiltons translated for Nelson. Their hosts introduced the British Admiral and the Austrian General to each other with every expression of esteem and regard, the Queen adding impulsively to Mack—" General, be to us by land, what my hero, Nelson, has been by sea ! " The Emperor had desired the King of Naples " to begin ", and promised support. Nelson returned from the entertainment to record, " I have endeavoured to impress the General with a favourable impression of me, and I think I have succeeded. He is active, and has an intelligent eye, and will do well, I have no doubt." Field-Marshal Baron Karl Mack von Leiberich was a much more promising person than he had expected. He was, unlike the Austrian Generals previously encountered, neither fine-drawn nor of noble birth. A visible scar testified to his services against the Turk. He was a blunt, dry-spoken Bavarian. The fact that the imported military leader was prepared to march in ten days had surprised and relieved Nelson, and Mack had privately agreed that the moment the war began, their confidence should be placed in the Queen and Sir John Acton. " Acton was going down, but we have set him up again. . . . This evening I shall have in writing the result of last night's ' Session ', the Queen calls it—not a Council, as in that case *Gallo* must have been at it; but he is tottering, and the Queen has promised he shall not be the War Minister."

Having set affairs at Naples in what he believed to be good train, and entertained the King and Prince Leopold to breakfast on board his flagship, Nelson sailed for Malta. Knowing that the French were well supplied, he was not so sanguine as the Neapolitans as to the fall of Valetta, and he was right. Malta, although closely blockaded under his supervision, held out for two years. He was thankful to get his squadron, with the exception of the *Culloden* (still waiting for the pintles of her rudder), out of Naples Bay, though he himself was now bound by promise to their Majesties to return there. He had given up, with reluctance, his plan of going to Egypt to complete the destruction of Buonaparte's shipping. Turkish and Russian squadrons should soon be on that coast to relieve Hood, but his unwillingness to return to Naples was not only because he was uneasy at entrusting any blockade to Allies. In a letter dated October 4, now speeding towards Cadiz Bay, he had confided to Lord St. Vincent:

> " I am writing opposite Lady Hamilton, therefore you will not be surprised at the glorious jumble of this letter. Were your Lordship in my place, I much doubt if you could write so well; our hearts and our hands must be all in a flutter. Naples is a dangerous place, and we must keep clear of it." 13

When this letter arrived at Admiral's House, Rosia Bay, the Commander-in-Chief wrote at once to the British Embassy, Naples. To Nelson he struck the professional note, mentioning his relief that the ladies of Naples had not detained him from duties that only he could perform. " You're great in the Cabinet as on the Ocean, and your whole conduct fills me with admiration and confidence." To Lady Hamilton he suggested: 14

> " Ten thousand thanks are due to your Ladyship for restoring the health of our invaluable friend, on whose life the fate of the remaining governments in Europe whose system has not been deranged by those devils, depends. Pray, do not let your fascinating Neapolitan dames approach too near him; for he is made of flesh and blood and cannot resist their temptations." 15

3

A Portuguese squadron had joined Ball off Malta, and on Nelson's arrival, after a very slow passage, the Marquis de Niza expressed every flowery courtesy. But it instantly appeared that these allies were going to be rather a burden than a help. The Marquis was written down by Nelson, after one interview, as " completely ignorant of *Sea* affairs ". He claimed to be considered as an Admiral commanding an English squadron, and since the officers commanding his ships were all Commodores, they expected to be given precedence over the English Captains, fresh from the Nile. " It is ridiculous to hear them talk of their rank, and of the impossibility of serving under any of my brave and good Captains." Nelson thanked the Marquis for his zeal in proceeding to the blockade of Malta, ordered him to take his ships instantly to Naples (where they were needed), and repeated that none but Portuguese ships were under His Excellency's

orders. He saw them weigh with the expectation that they
would all meet with disasters, and applied himself to become fully
master of the problem of Malta. This, too, was difficult. The
Marquis, before taking his departure, had gloomily assured him
that the islanders who had declared for the King of Naples had
no footing in Valetta, no arms or victuals, and that he had been
unable to get in touch with any Neapolitan officers organising or
supporting them. Maltese deputies came on board the *Vanguard*
on the day after Nelson's arrival, and he learnt, to his disgust,
that in spite of all Acton's and Gallo's assurances of secret orders
to the Governors of Syracuse and Messina, nothing had been
heard of any arms, ammunition or provisions from either source.
He sent a formal summons to the French General and Admiral in
command at Valetta, landed British stores and ordered Ball
down to the little island of Gozo, which was also flying French
colours. The French in possession of Gozo, threatened with
bombardment if they failed to surrender, did so with alacrity,
and leaving Ball with five sail-of-the-line to continue the blockade,
Nelson sailed again for Naples, after dark on the 30th of October.
Letters from Lady Hamilton had told him that he was urgently
needed. Since his departure, in spite of all her efforts, the
Government were dropping back into their former condition of
fascinated helplessness. General Mack had not even performed
his avowed intention of visiting the troops on the frontiers. He
said that he was working night and day, and that when he left
Naples it would be for good. " I tell her Majesty, *for God's sake,
for the Country's sake, and for your own sake, send him off.*" The
Queen, relieved by the arrival of Troubridge with one English
ship, in which she could embark her beloved children, vainly
abused Gallo and wished that the General would move. When
two couriers arrived, one from London, the other from Vienna,
Maria Carolina cried for joy at the lovely news that a British fleet
was to remain in the Mediterranean, and with rage after reading
the letters from her son-in-law and daughter, " cold, unfriendly,
mistrustful, frenchified, saying plainly, ' Help yourselves ' ". At
this juncture Lady Hamilton had felt called upon to give one of
her best performances—" I got up, put out my left arm, like you,
spoke the language of truth to her." The picture painted by
Lady Hamilton to the Queen had included " her friends sacrificed,
her husband, children and herself led to the Block; and eternal
dishonour to her memory, after for once having been active ".
The result had been satisfactory. A council had been summoned,
Y

and the King had agreed to join his army in a few days and not to
return.   " The Regency is to be in the name of the Prince Royal,
but the Queen will direct all."   The happiest passage in Lady
Hamilton's very long letter described the Grand Signior's gifts
to the Victor of the Nile, now on their way in a frigate from
Constantinople.   " I must see the present.   How I shall look at
it, smel it, taste it, to(u)ch it, put the pelice over my own
shoulders, look in the glas, and say, ' Viva il Turk ! ' "

She drew to a close with talk of children.   Little Prince Leopold had been detected yesterday attempting to run away to sea to
join Nelson, and had cried himself sick on being recaptured.   The
Court was at Caserta, awaiting the *accouchement* of the very pusil-
lanimous Hereditary Princess, and after being summoned to sit in
gala attire during a false alarm which had lasted twenty-four
hours, the English Ambassadress had retired with a headache,
humming the old English catch, " Oh dear, what can the matter
be ? "   She sent her love to her " dear little fatherless Faddy ",
the fourteen-year-old son of a Captain of marines killed on board
Nelson's flagship in Aboukir Bay.   " I will be his mother as
much as I can."   She ended, " Love Sir William and myself, for
we love you dearly.   He is the best husband, friend, I wish I
could say father allso ; but I should have been too happy if I had
the blessing of having children, so must be content." [16]

4

Nelson's next glimpse of Lady Hamilton was as hostess of an
Italian country house, but business as well as caution decreed
that it should be only a glimpse.   Sir William's " Villina " at the
gates of the palace of Caserta was amongst the many sources of
expenditure which had for some time caused that ageing gentleman
concern.   It was not small, although any building in the neighbourhood of a royal residence with a frontage of two hundred and
seventy-seven yards appeared necessarily modest.   Behind, its
views were of November parkland and woods, embellished with
groups of dramatically posed statuary and rushing cascades.   The
adjacent town of Nuova Caserta had been merely a village, called
" La Torre ", until Carlo III had ordered the erection of what he
chose to describe as a " hunting-box ".   At Caserta there was
almost as much affectation of rustic ways as there had been at the
Petit Trianon.

Nelson's journey of sixteen miles towards the Hamiltons'
country house at dusk on November 5 came at the close of a

wearisome day. Miss Cornelia Knight, through her telescope, had watched from her hotel window from the moment that Admiral Nelson in the *Vanguard*, together with the *Minotaur* (" Captain Louis from Malta "), had appeared over the horizon; " and they were all day coming in ".   When the Admiral reached the vicinity of the palace, the scene was one of unpromising confusion, and the air was rent by the pealing of bells and discharge of guns.   The Hereditary Princess had at last been brought to bed, though not of an heir.   Court officials who had been tied to the spot for weeks were departing in glad haste, and the King had announced his determination to join his army at the camp of San Germano.   Lady Hamilton, who had found it impossible to be happy away from Naples while " our ships " were there, was in good spirits, but after a visit to the palace, Nelson recounted in the heavy manner which had previously succeeded an interview with Maria Carolina, " I am, I fear, drawn into a promise that Naples Bay shall never be left without an English Man-of-War.   I never intended leaving the Coast of Naples without one; but if I had, who could withstand the request of such a Queen? "   He had presented to His Majesty the French colours captured at Gozo, and told Ferdinand that he had sixteen thousand new subjects.   Leghorn, where the attitude of their Majesty's son-in-law, the Grand Duke, was causing anxiety, was his next objective.   He returned to the *Vanguard*, not the Palazzo Sessa, but when summoned, within the week, to consult with Mack and Acton at the camp spelt by him, " St. Germaines ", he travelled with the Hamiltons.   The weather was fine, and the military spectacle stirring.   Thirty thousand of what Mack called " La plus belle Armée d'Europe " were drawn out for Nelson to see. He politely pronounced that as far as an officer of the navy could judge, the rank and file appeared healthy and good-looking. Privately, he noted that the force was, " with some few exceptions, wretchedly officered ", and he was much struck when the monosyllabic Mack, attempting " the courtier-like " to their Majesties, regretted that so fine an army should not have the prospect of encountering an enemy more worthy of its prowess.   French republicans could, as Nelson well knew, fight to the death, even when the inflammatory Buonaparte was not present.   (At the Battle of the Nile, Citizen-Captain Du Petit-Thours, after losing both arms and a leg, had ordered his trunk to be placed in a tub on his quarter-deck, and from that position refused to strike his colours, although *Le Tonnant* had not a mast left or a gun serviceable.)

After dark, after the long day of the review, a council in the field was staged. Torchlight fell upon many new uniforms, glittering with gold lace, the magnificent white and gold of an Austrian Field-Marshal and a solitary British blue coat. The tented air was heavy with patchouli and frangipanni, although no ladies were present. Indeed, had the Queen and her English *confidante* been invited, discussion might have been less prolonged. " Sir William ", reported his lady, " laughs at us, but owns that women have great Souls, at least, his has." (The phrase was that which Nelson had used to describe his hostess to his wife on his arrival in Naples.) It was ultimately agreed that a force of four thousand infantry and six hundred cavalry should be landed in the enemy's rear, at Leghorn. With the Emperor's advance, the French should be caught between three fires. Nelson volunteered to be responsible for transporting the infantry. He knew that three British sail-of-the-line and a store-ship were ready, and believed that two Portuguese warships could be prodded to sea. (" Not that I see they have any wants.") A Neapolitan ship was to bring the cavalry in a convoy after them. The King's order for the destination was entrusted to him, with instructions not to deliver it to the Neapolitan General Naselli until they were at sea. This unfortunate character was to be secretly told, before embarking, that Malta was their goal. Mack was to march on Rome on Saturday, the 17th. Information from that city told that two new French Generals had arrived.

At 6 a.m. next morning the Admiral went to take leave of their Majesties, and found a sad change. Despatches received overnight from Vienna had not brought any solid assurance of support from what Lady Hamilton called " their poor fool, of a son-in-law ". M. Thugut, the highly neurotic Austrian Minister to Naples, was evasive, and much wished that the French could be presented as the aggressors. Nelson, feeling far from well, ventured to tell their Majesties, without aid of an interpreter, that one of two things was bound to happen, and His Majesty had his choice—" Either to advance (trusting to God for His blessing on a just Cause), to die with ' *l'épée à la main* ', or remain quiet and be kicked out of your Kingdoms ". Ferdinand, startled, replied that he would go on, and trust his Maker, but Nelson was asked to delay his departure and hold further conference with Baron Mack on what their Majesties described (but he refused to recognise) as " a new face on affairs ". Two days later the question of financial support from Great Britain was again mooted,

17

and on the 18th Lady Hamilton received a letter from the Queen, "full of the idea" that English money was essential to their effort. The British Ambassadress was desired to show this letter to Admiral Nelson and ask him to say what he saw. Nelson's reply was blunt. He had long ago told the Queen that he did not think Mr. Pitt would go to Parliament to ask John Bull to throw good money after bad. When his country once saw that Naples was taking up arms on her own behalf, he had no doubt that an ally in distress would be supported. As to what he saw, he could say that briefly. He saw the finest territory in the world, full of resources, unable to supply her public wants, and all persons of influence who could get at public money or stores helping themselves. As a sea-officer, he could state that one Neapolitan ship-of-the-line would cost more than ten English ships fitting out. Five would ruin the country. "Everything else is, I have no doubt, going on in the same system of thieving." Reporting to St. Vincent before he sailed for Leghorn, he said that he believed Lady Hamilton had written so fully and so ably of the political situation here that he need add little. In a hurried line to Brother William, he stated that he thought it very unlikely that he would ever take his seat in the House of Peers. He signed his official account of the San Germano negotiations simply "Nelson", but Lord Spencer was not the first person to receive a letter so signed. On October 16, after receiving a private note from the First Lord, he had sent the following lines to the Palazzo Sessa:

"My dear Madam,
"I honour and respect you and my dear friend Sir William Hamilton
"And believe me ever,
"Your faithful and affectionate,
"Nelson."

Lady Hamilton added, underneath, on the same sheet—"The first letter written by our gallant and immortal Nelson, after his dignity to the peerage. May God bless him, and long may he live to enjoy the honour he so deservedly won, prays his true friend, Emma Hamilton." Like most of his friends, she was indignant at the sparing acknowledgment so far bestowed. "If I was King of England I wou'd make you the most noble present, Duke Nelson, Marquis Nile, Earl Aboukir, Vicount Pyramid, Baron Crocodile, and Prince Victory, that posterity might have you in all forms. . . . Your statue ought to be made of pure gold and placed in the middle of London."

At last, on November 22, he sailed for Leghorn, and two days later Mack's army crossed the frontiers into the Papal states. Nelson's part in the enterprise proceeded, if not without difficulty, to complete success. " It blowing a strong gale on that night and the next day, none but British ships kept me company." He anchored in Leghorn Roads on the afternoon of the 28th, and, in concert with Naselli, sent in a summons. By 8 p.m. the Governor of the city had come on board the *Vanguard* to surrender unconditionally. The Neapolitan troops were then landed, despite a heavy swell, together with their cannon and baggage, and having won a bloodless victory, proceeded to take possession of the town and fortress with loud rejoicing. Amongst the items of news to be brought to the Admiral's flagship by Mr. Wyndham, British representative at Leghorn, was the capture of Minorca on the 15th, by Nelson's old companion of Corsican days, Colonel (now Lieutenant-General) the Honourable Charles Stuart. Commodore Duckworth, an officer ten years Nelson's senior, had (in the parlance of military observers) " convoyed the troops and covered the operation". Nelson, who had, four months past, expected to be ordered to attend Stuart, said that he was sure his place had been much better filled. Not everything that the amiable Mr. Wyndham had to recount was equally pleasant. General Naselli and the Duke de Sangro, Neapolitan Minister at Leghorn (flying to him to interpret for them), wished him to explain at once that they did not think the British Admiral (engaged solely to transport Neapolitan troops) ought to seize the many French and Genoese privateers now in the port. Their reason was that their monarch had not declared war on France. This problem kept Nelson awake all night on the 29th. Next morning, having persuaded Naselli to agree to an embargo being laid upon the vessels, until orders arrived from Naples, and leaving Troubridge with wide powers, he sailed again for Naples. Troubridge, worthily representing him after his departure (upon which Naselli instantly wanted to release all the enemy vessels), settled the dispute by pointing out that unless they " got on with the business ", the mole, and probably the town, would be fired by Tuscan republicans, and the French, " in the bustle ", would seize the port. Acting on his own authority, Troubridge gave passports to two small Genoese craft, which put out, in terrifying weather, taking with them two hundred and fifty Leghorn undesirables, selected by the British commander, and despatched with the grim reflection, " Stowing them close, keeps them warm."

Two letters from Lady Hamilton met Nelson on his return journey to Naples. The first, beginning, " My dearest Lord,— How unhappy we are at the bad weather. How are you tossed about? Why did you not come back? " told him that the army had marched. Lady Hamilton, who had not slept for two nights, thinking of his sufferings, had not yet seen the Queen, who had arrived in the capital, nor could her ladyship hope to do so for another two or three days, as she was kept indoors by a feverish chill. She adjured the Admiral not to go ashore at Leghorn, where the stiletto of many a republican would be ready for him. Her second letter told a story that sounded too good to be true. On the approach of the Neapolitan army, General Championnet had retreated. The King had written to the Queen from Frascati, and was about to enter Rome in triumph. The Hamiltons, whose chief care was for the squadron of their own nation, at Leghorn, would not eat, sleep or drink in comfort till they saw their friend safe back again. Many enquirers at the Embassy had tried to discover where he was gone, but nobody had learnt the truth.

> " I wou'd have my flesh torn off by red-hot pinchers sooner than betray my trust. We send you one of your midshipmen left here by accident, Mr. Abrams; pray don't punish him. Oh, I had forgot I wou'd never ask favours; but you are so good, I cannot help it."

19

The *Vanguard* anchored in Naples Bay on December 5 after a very rough passage, and Nelson drove at once to the Palazzo Sessa under dark skies. Nothing could have been more unlike his sunlit arrival of September 22. Indeed, the atmosphere in the city, as well as the weather, was altogether reminiscent of an earlier scene in his career—his midnight entry by the garden path, on a blowing night, to the threatened palace of the Viceroy of Corsica, at Bastia.

5

The King had taken up his residence at the Farnese Palace, and held a reception to which all the old Roman nobility, having illuminated their palaces with wax lights, had hastened to kiss his hand. But two nights later a great concourse had waited in vain for his appearance at the Théâtre Alibert, and nervous characters whispered that although everything was being conducted as if the war was over, the French tricolour still streamed against grey winter skies from the Castle of St. Angelo (in which Championnet had left a force of five hundred), and His Majesty's carriages, carts and mules were being kept in instant

readiness for him to take the road again.   On December 7 he did
so, going, as a shrewd *Abate* of the house of Colonna noted, in the
wrong direction.

The Naples to which Nelson came back on December 5 was an
uneasy place, full of rumours.   On the last day of November the
British Embassy had heard that after a battle resulting in heavy
casualties, Mack had been taken prisoner.   There had been no
such bloody encounter, but many men who had marched with
the Baron were secretly home again, having shed their uniforms.
" La plus belle Armée d'Europe " had already suffered, though
not from the foe.   Its officers, as Nelson had foreseen, " did not
like fighting ".   Some were suspected, by those under their
command, of " liking the French ".   Its ranks had been stiffened,
at the last moment, by old soldiers, condemned by military
tribunals, and robust convicts from civilian gaols.   At the first
opportunity such leaders had shown recruits how to plunder a
countryside and their own convoys, and they had cause for
complaint, for already, on their road to Rome, they had been
left three days without rations.   Even the King and his staff
had been thirty-six hours without food or a change of clothing.
On the day following his return Nelson informed St. Vincent
that the French had thirteen thousand troops at a strong post
called Castellana, and that although the force with which Mack
had gone against them numbered twenty thousand, " the event
in my opinion is doubtful ".   If Mack was defeated, he had no
doubt that Naples would be lost within a fortnight.   " For if
the Emperor will not march, this Country has not the power of
resisting."   To Stuart, later, he prophesied that unless Mack
succeeded quickly in dislodging the French from Castellana, he
must fall back to the frontier, for " the French have driven back,
to say no worse, the right wing of the King's Army, and taken
all their baggage and artillery ".   He had gathered this unfortunate state of affairs during a painful audience with " the
great Queen ", who admitted that her husband's troops were
behaving in a manner which broke her heart, that Mack was in
despair, and that she put no faith in the remainder of her subjects,
whom she termed " rabbits ".   Nelson assured her that he had
no intention of quitting her or her family " until brighter prospects
appear than do at present ", and the interview had ended on a calmer
note, her Majesty hoping that " this horrid weather and detestable
dirty roads " might be responsible for much that had happened.
She heard with satisfaction that all arrangements had been made

by Nelson for the despatch by sea, in the Genoese pink, *La Madonna di Porto Salvo*, of the dismissed French Minister, his train and baggage.   For three days after this, nobody from the British Embassy was summoned to the royal palace, but from letters from the Queen to Lady Hamilton, "painting the anguish of her soul", and from other sources, Nelson was able to form a picture of the "bad behaviour" of her husband's troops deplored by Her Majesty.   This he pronounced with unusual sarcasm, upon the whole, not so bad as he had expected.   "The Neapolitan officers have not lost much honour, for God knows they had but little to lose, but they lost all they had."   Mack had applied to the King to sabre every man of the force led by Generals San Filippo and Micheroux, who had run away, almost at the sight of three thousand French at Fermi ; but this would be difficult, as many had run thirty miles without stopping ; they had numbered nineteen thousand and suffered only forty casualties.   San Filippo had been shot in the arm by one of his own sergeants as he had galloped off to join the enemy, and the King had stripped the Prince of Taranto of his *épaulettes* with his own hands.   Only one Neapolitan General—Prince Cette—was said to have collected some runaways and obliged them to advance.   Mack, with the main body *en route* for Castellana, had been equally ill-served. He had been wounded, when on foot, in a vain attempt to rally men who had begun to retreat at the first shots from a French trench.

Early on the 14th Naples enjoyed its most startling rumour yet.   Amongst the soldiers in civilian disguise who had slipped back home was His Majesty.   A large mob gathered in the square below the palace, and his *lazzaroni* roared until the figure of Ferdinand appeared on the balcony.

6

As early as October 3 Nelson had warned Lady Hamilton that it might become his duty to evacuate the English colony and the Neapolitan royal family at very short notice.   At the Palazzo Sessa, in early December, the Ambassador (whom his guest had come to look upon as a father) slippered unhappily amongst galleries shorn of all splendour, and directed the unostentatious packing of beloved possessions with pardonable acerbity.   The only comfort of a connoisseur called upon to leave a city where he had been happy for thirty-five years was that, owing to the kindness of the British Admiral, his best pictures, and the crates containing what he believed to be his most valuable vases, had already been despatched to England in H.M.S. *Colossus*. Against his judgment, he had been enticed by Gallo, newly returned from Vienna, to agree to the insertion of a secret clause in the Treaty of Alliance between England and the Two Sicilies. It promised an English subsidy, but he had made it conditional on the abandonment of their Majesties by the Emperor.

Nelson, meanwhile, took stock of his resources, and dealt with the paper work which had accumulated during his Leghorn absence. "Lady Hamilton's goodness forces me out at noon for an hour. . . . We are all united in our Squadron : not a growler amongst us." Unluckily, the victors of the Nile were at this critical moment united in spirit only. Troubridge was blockading the Roman coast with the *Minotaur* and two frigates, Ball with the *Alexander*, *Audacious* and *Goliath* was blockading Malta, and Hood with three of the line and two frigates was still awaiting allies to relieve him in Egypt. "I am", decided Nelson, "here *solus*, for I reckon the Portuguese as nothing."

A letter from the First Lord informed him that First Lieutenants of all ships engaged at Aboukir Bay would get promotion, a statement which caused him to address St. Vincent in haste. "I sincerely hope this is not intended to exclude the First of the *Culloden*, for Heaven's sake, if it is so, get it altered. Our dear friend Troubridge has suffered enough." To Troubridge himself he wrote instructions to keep some vessel in Leghorn Roads, "for I think it is very probable that I may be forced to send for you in a hurry. Everything you may send here, let them anchor cautiously, if my Flag is not here."

He learnt that Turkish and Russian lieutenants, as well as the Marquis de Niza, had missed him at Leghorn, whence the fatuous Duke of Tuscany sent him a sword and an invitation to stay at a palace in Pisa. He replied courteously, regretting that his stay at Leghorn had been brief, but his real answer to the Duke was contained in a letter to the Right Honourable Sir Morton Eden, in which he begged the British Minister at Vienna to assure the Empress that he was ready to save the sacred persons of her parents and her Imperial Majesty's brothers and sisters, including the sister who was consort of the Duke of Tuscany. "For all must be a Republic if the Emperor does not act with expedition and vigour. '*Down, down* with the French ! ' ought to be placed in the Council-room of every Country in the world." A postscript explained, "Whenever the Emperor acts with vigour, your Excellency may say that a proper Naval force shall attend to the safety of the Adriatic."

The 14th, the day of the King's ignominious reappearance, was a busy one in the Bay of Naples. " Arrived also ", noted the journal of the *Vanguard*, " the Marquis de Niza, in the *Principe Real*, and the *Alcmene* from Egypt, bringing despatches from Captain Hood of H.M.S. *Zealous*, and the Turkish Ambassador and his suite, bringing presents from the Grand Signior." Of all the allies so long heralded, only Theodore Ouschakoff, Vice-Admiral of the Russian squadron ("a blackguard " in Nelson's opinion, and with an eye for Malta), was now missing.

Lord Nelson notified Sir William Hamilton that in view of the invasion of the Two Sicilies by a formidable French army, he felt it his duty to acquaint His Excellency that three British transports were ready to receive the effects of any of His Britannic Majesty's subjects resident in Naples, and the whole squadron was ready to receive their persons, with as much secrecy and little bustle as possible. Lieutenant Lamb, Agent for Transports, was ordered to heave all condemned provisions overboard and expect refugees. The Marquis de Niza was told to send officers and seamen to assist Neapolitan men-of-war to get ready to go to sea. Two days later, in his reply to the greeting of the Grand Vizier, Nelson displayed that he well knew how to address an Oriental potentate :

" I beg that your Excellency will lay me at the feet of the Grand Signior, and express what I feel for the great and singular Honour conferred upon me, which I am sensible I owe to his Imperial goodness of heart, and not to my deserts. When first I saw the French fleet which, for near three months, I had in vain sought, I prayed that, if our cause was just, I might be the happy instrument of His punishment against unbelievers of the Supreme only True God—that if it was unjust I might be killed. The Almighty took the Battle into His own hand, and with His power marked the Victory as the most astonishing that ever was gained at sea : All glory be to God ! Amen ! Amen !

" I cannot allow Kelim Effendi to depart without expressing my thanks to him for the very able, dignified, and polite manner in which he has executed his mission, and I beg leave to recommend him to your Excellency's protection, as my dear friend. That your Excellency may long live in health to carry, by your wise councils, the glory of the Ottoman Empire to the highest pitch of grandeur, is the sincere prayer of your Excellency's most faithful servant,

" Nelson."

" I send my dear son-in-law, Captain Nisbet, to carry Kelim Effendi to Constantinople."

The smiling and unsuspicious old Kelim Effendi, attended by his long procession of staff, in charge of a Mr. Pisani, employé of Mr. Spencer Smith, Minister at the Porte, had been duly decanted at the Palazzo Sessa, where a group of armed *lazzaroni* stood on guard night and day, under orders from their chief, Egidio Pallio, to attend the British Ambassador wherever he went. Arms were now carried by many such persons, who met deserters at the gates of the city and relieved them of their equipment, and the King, who on his arrival home had declared that he would await the French surrounded by his loyal subjects, was beginning to share his wife's opinion that " *les scènes de Varennes avec toutes leurs suites* " were about to be repeated in his own capital. On December 18, a despatch from Mack, in full retreat, besought His Majesty to move before the French took possession of Naples. Eventually Ferdinand was unfavourably impressed by a spectacle witnessed on one of the many occasions when shouts from an excited mob had demanded his appearance with his whole family upon the balcony of his palace. The elderly man whom he watched dragged to the square by the legs, and clubbed before being despatched by a stiletto, had been a royal courier. Contradictory accounts in a disturbed city declared that the man had been an innocent old French-speaking Corsican *émigré* (who had been mistaken for a Jacobin by loyalists), one of the Austrian Queen's spies (who knew too much of her secret intrigues with her own country), and, finally, the victim of Maria Carolina's latest effort to persuade her husband to desert his loving people.

On the previous day Nelson had written to Spencer Smith, " I do not know that the whole Royal Family, with 3,000 Neapolitan *émigrés*, will not be under the protection of the King's flag this night." He had shifted the *Vanguard* to a new berth, out of range of the Neapolitan forts, an act that had brought residents—not all British—panting to the Palazzo Sessa, as much taken aback as if the Rock at Gibraltar had moved. The King's consent was not obtained until the 19th, when he suddenly became pressing to be gone, but from the 15th onwards the Queen had been delivering, under cover of darkness, to the British Embassy, the belongings of ten members of her family, " it may be for life ". Lady Hamilton sat up nightly, to receive an astonishing jumble, ranging from " the diamonds of the family, both male and female ", and three dozen casks of doubtful security containing gold ducats, to small coffers of linen which would be needed by the children on the voyage, tapestries, pictures, furniture, sculpture and plate.

Nelson reckoned the value of the royal property personally collected by Lady Hamilton, received by her at the Embassy, and delivered to his seamen and marines, labelled " Stores for Nelson ", at £2,500,000.   Sir William and he avoided the palace during these days of tension, but although Lady Hamilton visited the Queen as usual, Maria Carolina also wrote to her daily.   The Queen's letters testified that a flattered and ambitious woman, who in her springtime would have liked to do some good, did she know how, had failed in the hour of need to achieve self-restraint.

> " I abuse your goodness as well as that of our brave Admiral.   Let the great cases be thrown into the hold, the smaller ones are easier to dispose of.   Unfortunately I have such a large family.   Such distress drives me to despair, and my tears flow unceasingly, the suddenness of the blow has distracted me, and I do not think I shall ever recover from it, but it will sink me amazed into the grave.   Pray send me, my dear friend, information of everything, and be certain of my discretion.   My son has returned from Capua with dreadful accounts of the flying troops and unheard of misfortunes.   *Adieu, ma chère*, the effect of this horrible break-up is destructive of two-thirds of our existence, our accustomed habits. . . ."

The small ornamental mourning card attached by Maria Carolina, with characteristic love of unnecessary mystification, to her " special " list of " the unfortunate who have a note from me " is typical in its elegance and futility of her age and state.   It has come to rest amongst the Egerton MS. in the British Museum, and its design, in blue transfer, is of a wreathed *amorino* piping beside a tombstone, behind which two of his fellows are capering. On the tombstone, left blank for inscription, the Queen has written the words " *Embarqué, je vous prie*, M.C."

If one person in Naples knew of the proposed flight, a thousand must have done so, as the first paragraph of the list of passengers, drawn up by the Royal Chamberlain, Prince Belmonte, demonstrates :

First Embarcation

The King.
The Queen.
Prince Leopold.
Prince Albert, with his *Zafatta*, D. Vincenza Rizzi.
Three Princesses, daughters to their Majesties.
General Acton.
Prince Castelcicala.
Prince Belmonte.

Count Thurn.

The Hereditary Prince.

His Princess.

Their daughter, a child, with their *Zafatta*, Dalguero.

Duke of Gravina.

Nelson had originally fixed the flight for the night of the 20th, but until the 19th the problem of how to get the royal family from the palace to the landing-stage called Vittoria, on the little quay known as the Mola Figlio, had not been solved. The solution in an Italian palace was, of course, a subterranean passage.

The morning of the 21st dawned exceedingly foul, and Acton, who sent to Nelson and Hamilton during the day at least eight contradictory notes, suggested a further postponement on various pretexts, one of which was that the Admiral might find it impossible, owing to the swell, to transfer the sacred persons of their Majesties and household from the landing-stage to his expectant men-of-war. Nelson's reply was to postpone the first embarkation by an hour and a half. A note of the 20th, with underlined corrections in his own hand, preserved by Hope of the *Alcmene*, shows how detailed had been his preparations:

" *Most secret.*

" Three barges, and the small cutter of the *Alcmene*, armed with cutlasses only, to be at the Victoria at half-past seven o'clock precisely. Only one barge to be at the wharf, the others to lay on their oars at the outside of the rocks—the small barge of the *Vanguard* to be at the wharf. The above boats to be on board the *Alcmene* before seven o'clock, under the direction of Captain Hope. *Grapnells to be in the boats.*

" All other boats of the *Vanguard* and *Alcmene* to be armed with cutlasses, and the launches with carronades to assemble on board the *Vanguard*, under the direction of Captain Hardy, and to put off from her at half-past eight o'clock *precisely, to row half way towards the Mola Figlio. These boats to have 4 or 6 soldiers in them. In case assistance is wanted by me, false fires will be burnt.*

" Nelson."

" *The Alcmene to be ready to slip in the night, if necessary.*"

A note entirely in his own hand, delivered at Lady Knight's hotel, just as the invalid and her daughter were preparing to go to bed on the night of the 21st, secured immediate obedience:

" My dear Madam,

" Commodore Stone will **take** care of you. Do not be alarmed, there is in truth no cause for it.

" Ever your faithful servant,

" Nelson."

The widow of a Rear-Admiral of the White, recognising the voice of authority, called for her bill, took the arm of an unknown officer and ventured out into December darkness, followed by armed seamen, shouldering all her worldly possessions. Sir William Hamilton had kindly dropped a hint some days past, and the trunks were packed. The driving wind and rain which had made the morning horrible had abated, but the appearance of Naples Bay was shocking.

Amongst Nelson's larger instructions had been a summons to Troubridge from Leghorn ("For God's sake, make haste!"), and to Foley from Malta, and a warning to Ball not to send any Neapolitan ships with the *Goliath*. The Queen's fear that there were traitors in her husband's Marine had been confirmed. The ships' companies and several officers of the *Parthenope* and *Sannita* had abandoned their ships and come ashore. Caracciolo's application to be allowed to carry his royal master and mistress in a ship of their own navy had been refused, and Miss Knight, meeting the gentleman at a dinner-party a few evenings before the flight, had remarked that, "I never saw any man look so utterly miserable. He scarcely uttered a word, ate nothing, and did not even unfold his napkin." Amongst the ill presages which afflicted the Queen on the fatal morning was the news that Count Vanni, an officer once employed by her, had shot himself. "The White Terror of Naples", who had been responsible for the arrest and imprisonment of hundreds, could not face the prospect of republicans occupying Naples.

Nelson, in better health than recently, "my mind never better and my heart in the right trim", drove with the Hamiltons and Mrs. Cadogan after dinner at the Embassy to attend a farewell reception offered by Kelim Effendi. At the Palazzo Sessa servants proceeded to lay a supper-table. Their Excellencies' carriage, ordered to fetch them home in two hours time, was already outside the scene of the entertainment when all members of the Hamilton party withdrew on foot. Lady Hamilton noted that she had fifteen minutes in which to reach what she called "my post". Faithful to her dramatic promise to follow her royal companion to the scaffold if necessary, she hurried to the palace to support a royal lady who had repeatedly and unpromisingly announced, "My head is quite gone."

Nelson landed at the corner of the Arsenal at 8.30 and entered the palace by the long subterranean tunnel communicating with the Vittoria landing-stage, on which Count Thurn, an Austrian

Commodore in the Neapolitan service, was posted with instructions which included two pass-words—" All goes right and well ", and " All is wrong, you may go back ". The descent of the royal family, escorted by Nelson, began punctually, and soon the first party of hooded and muffled passengers urged towards a heaving barge had entered upon half an hour's experience of Naples Bay with a heavy ground swell. The Knights, who went with the main party of British refugees, were less fortunate.

23

24

> " The night was cold, for we were in the month of December, and it was between twelve and one before we were in the boat. There were several persons already in it, and an English child fell in the water, but was taken out unhurt. We had a long way to go, for the ships had cast anchor at a great distance from the city, to be beyond the range of the forts in the event of treachery or surprise. When we came alongside the Admiral's ship, the Captain, Sir Thomas Hardy stepped into the boat, and told my mother that the ship was so full there was no room for us. In vain we entreated to be taken on board. The thing was impossible."

The Knights passed on perforce to the *Rainha de Portugal*, commanded, they were assured,

> " by an Englishman, who had formerly been a Master in our Navy, but was now a Commodore. . . . The young midshipman who conducted us was constantly jumping about in the boat to keep himself from falling asleep, for during the last 48 hours he had been unceasingly engaged in getting the baggage and numerous attendants of the Royal Family on board."

In the chief cabin of the Portuguese man-of-war the Knights found many ladies of various nationalities, of whom only one, a Russian of high rank and great wealth, had secured a bed. They now heard, for the first time, that their destination was Palermo.

In the *Vanguard* conditions were not much better. Captain Hardy had set sailmakers to make cots for the royal family three days past, and the wardroom and offices under the poop had been hastily repainted, but his notice to get his ship ready for sea had been short, and throughout the week he had been obliged to send men on shore to fetch the royal valuables. " The first embarcation " of about thirty persons came on board between 9.30 and 10. The gentlemen passengers were directed to the wardroom; the Admiral's quarters had been prepared for the ladies and children. When the " second embarcation ", consisting of more than an equal number of royal attendants, several Neapolitan nobles and their *suites*, and many British merchants, arrived, about two hours later, the *Vanguard* (rolling at single anchor) began to appear uncomfortably crowded. It became known that their Majesties' linen and bedding was not to be found. That of the Hamiltons was successfully traced to the transport *Samuel and Jane*. Throughout the hours of darkness, boats bringing refugees swarmed around the flagship. The British were referred to the three transports of their nation and the ships of the Portuguese squadron. For the frantic royalist-French and Corsican *émigrés*, the British Ambassador had chartered two Greek polaccas, and arranged that they should be provisioned by English victuallers.

After a broken night, the dishevelled passengers arose to witness a storm so violent that for several hours no communication could take place between the ships. The King's Confessor fell out of his crib, and fractured a forearm. Nelson, hoping for the arrival of Troubridge to relieve his overcrowding difficulties, had worse problems with which to contend. A letter from Captain Sir Sidney Smith, containing enclosures from their Lordships, must be left to burn a hole in his pocket until he had leisure to attend to it. Not even the promise of double pay had availed to persuade Neapolitan ships' companies to return to their 74's. Such officers as remained explained that their men were naturally too anxious about the fates of their homes, which they would be leaving unprotected. It was Nelson's duty not to leave any men-of-war to fall into enemy hands, but their Majesties, who remembered what their 74's had cost, could not be reconciled to the prospect of their destruction. The Admiral did what he could—directed the Marquis de Niza to get all out of the mole, and equip as many as possible with jury masts for a passage to Messina. The remainder, if the French captured Naples, or the Neapolitan Jacobins revolted, must, he insisted, be burnt. He decided to leave the *Alcmene* behind under de Niza's command, and their Majesties left Count Thurn.

Next day, the weather being more moderate, several deputations from the town approached the *Vanguard*, desiring audience of the King. Ferdinand, however, had made up his mind for Palermo. Towards dusk came a visitor whom Nelson scarcely recognised. Baron Mack—" worn to a shadow "—had to announce that all that was left of his army was already at Capua, with the enemy on its heels, and that Tuscany had been invaded. He could only, before making a tragic exit, beg the King to sail as soon as possible. " My heart ", said Nelson, " bled for him." A month later Nelson had to admit that Mack

z

seemed lost. The Baron had taken refuge from the remnant of the Neapolitan army in the French camp.

    At 7 p.m. on December 23 the *Vanguard* weighed and made sail, in company with the Neapolitan corvette *Sannita* and the *Archimedes*, 74, the three British transports and about twenty merchant vessels. "Next day", in Nelson's opinion, "it blew harder than I have ever experienced since I have been at sea." The wind with which he had sailed had been easterly, but he had hardly cleared Capri when it chopped round to the westward, in heavy squalls, with rain. The *Vanguard*, with a disagreeable coast under her lee, began to labour prodigiously. Although all rest was out of the question, comparative quiet began to reign amongst the passengers. The horse-laugh of the King was no longer heard. Mrs. Cadogan, who attended sufferers in the ward-room, was acclaimed by him as an angel. All the Neapolitan servitors, who should have been performing the duties undertaken by the *Signora Madre*, were invisible, or on their knees engaged in last prayers. At about 1.30, at a moment when Nelson had just left the quarter-deck to look at the ship's position on the chart, a furious blast from the W.S.W. gave the *Vanguard* a heave, and blew her topsails to pieces, together with the driver and fore-topmast staysail. Count Esterhazy flung to the waves, in appeasement, an expensive snuff-box embellished with the likeness of his Italian mistress. In the ladies' quarters, the Duchess of Castelcicala cut her head on Admiral Nelson's side-board, and little Prince Alberto fell into convulsions. Tom Allen, assuming knowledgeable airs, had told the groaning ladies that they would be all right "while the sticks stand". Hearing bare-footed seamen hurrying with axes to cut away the wreck, they judged that the worst had happened and that they had escaped being torn to pieces on shore only to be lost at sea. Lady Hamilton and one of the Queen's stewards, Saverio Rodino, "a faithful and sure man", were the only passengers to keep their heads. The Ambassadress, in the words of the admiring Admiral, from the moment that she had come on board a British man-of-war, had put him and the whole royal family under an eternal obligation. When her own bedding and linen had been brought to light, she had instantly given up all to the party of women and children in his cabin (which included a swaddled princess, aged seven weeks), "and become *their slave*, for except for one man, no person belonging to Royalty assisted the Royal Family, nor did her Ladyship enter a bed the whole time they were on board".

" Good Sir William ", he added, " also made every sacrifice for the comfort of the august Family." Another officer told a tale which showed the aged antiquary in a more characteristic attitude :

> " During the height of the gale, when Lady Hamilton could think of nothing more wherewith to console the desponding Queen, she looked around for Sir William, who was not to be found. At length it was discovered that he had withdrawn to his sleeping-cabin, and was sitting there with a loaded pistol in each hand. In answer to her Ladyship's exclamation of surprise, he calmly told her that he was resolved not to die with the ' guggle-guggle-guggle ' of the salt-water in his throat; and therefore he was prepared, as soon as he felt the ship sinking, to shoot himself ! "

Next morning, although the wind moderated and drew round to the S.E., " there was still much for such passengers to endure ". The British officers made a brief appearance to express good wishes for the season and regrets that they could not offer more worthy fare for Christmas Day. Prince Alberto, apparently entirely recovered, ate a hearty breakfast. Soon afterwards the child began to display symptoms of agony, and by 7 p.m. was dead in the arms of Lady Hamilton. He had reached the attractive age of six, and was, she said, her favourite amongst the royal children.

The *Vanguard* anchored within Palermo Mole at 2 a.m. next morning, and Nelson escorted the stricken Queen and Princesses on shore, *incognita*, before day dawned, returning at 9 a.m. to assist at the entry of the King into his second capital. " Manned ship, and cheered him until on shore; could not salute him by reason of being in the Mole."

His Sicilian Majesty's royal standard flying at the main top-gallant masthead of a British warship had been visible for many hours, and the authorities of the town, including Mr. Tough, British Consul, had arrived to pay their respects. Ferdinand was received by his subjects with the loudest acclamations and apparent joy.

26

CHAPTER XII

1798–1800

(*ætat* 40–41)

" INACTIVE AT A FOREIGN COURT "

I

THE refugees' first impression of Palermo, in December rain, was wholly chilling, but on the day after he had taken the royal family on board the *Vanguard*, Nelson had received some instructions which had made him warm whenever he had time to think of them. Their Lordships had at last discovered a suitable way in which they might employ Sir Sidney Smith, whose address and pretensions were considerable. Good relations with Turkey were now of additional importance, he knew Constantinople well, and his own younger brother—who must be accustomed to him—was Minister there. He had been appointed to a vaguely defined combined naval and diplomatic post, and sent to St. Vincent with orders to forward him to the Levant. Sir Sidney's own view of his position was quite clear—in a splendidly engrossed and sealed passport, which presently found its way to Nelson's desk, he styled himself " *Chevalier Grand Croix de l'Ordre Royal et Militaire de l'Épée de Suède, Ministre Plénipotentiaire da sa Majésté Britannique près la Porte Ottomane, et Chef de son Escadre dans les Mers du Levant* ". (" We are not ", was Nelson's comment, " forced to understand French.") Sir Sidney had written to inform Sir William Hamilton that he was going to conduct operations in Egypt, and had been allowed by their Lordships to choose Captain Miller as his second-in-command. Sir William, at present, was in no fettle for strife. He was confined to bed by a familiar variety of bilious fever, brought on by anxiety, cold and fatigue, and he objected strongly to the house in which their grateful Majesties had established him after two nights as their guest in the gloomy Colli Palace. The Villa Bastioni was not gloomy : it stood upon the Marino promenade, where the view was of a wide carriage road and footpath along the shore, embellished by statues of the Kings of Sicily. It adjoined the beautiful gardens known as the Flora Reale, and being designed as a summer residence, was rich in marble decoration and contrivances to avoid heat and glare, but possessed no

fireplaces. Sir William had been far too unwell to attend the
effective, though hastily planned, Reception given by their
Majesties, this dark Sunday afternoon, to the nobility and gentry
of their second capital (a function which had entailed an apologetic
note from the Queen to Lady Hamilton, begging that the big
cases, which she had rashly said might be thrown into the hold
of our brave liberator's flagship, might be sent up to the Colli at
once, as they contained all the Court dress of the family).

The Ambassadress, who had been up to the palace several
times to weep with the Queen, was, after a succession of sleepless
nights—twelve, she claimed—and the loss of three elegantly
furnished houses and six or seven carriages, naturally, in her
husband's opinion, able to weep easily. She said that to do so
was now the only comfort of two women of sensibility, and
disliked being told that she was not yet a philosopher. Their
guest also was not yet a philosopher. A left-handed scribe, who
covered a sheet slowly and had waited a week, sat down in the
long-untenanted Villa Bastioni that night to tell Lord St. Vincent that, since much abler officers had arrived in a district
which he had believed to be under his control, he hoped that
unless his health (at present much affected by uneasiness of mind)
should shortly improve, he might be allowed to resign his command
to one of the brave officers who had so gloriously fought at the
Battle of the Nile. Next morning he addressed his Commander-
in-Chief privately:

> " *I do feel, for I am a man,* that it is impossible for me to serve in
> these Seas, with the Squadron under a junior officer :—could I have
> thought it !—and from Earl Spencer ! Never, never was I so astonished
> as your letter made me. As soon as I can get hold of Troubridge, I shall
> send him to Egypt, to destroy the Ships in Alexandria. If it can be
> done, Troubridge will do it. The Swedish Knight writes Sir William
> Hamilton, that he shall go to Egypt, and take Captain Hood and his
> Squadron under his command. The Knight forgets the respect due to
> his superior Officer : he has no orders from you to take my ships away
> from my command, but it is all of a piece. Is it to be borne ? Pray
> grant me permission to retire, and I hope the *Vanguard* will be allowed
> to convey me and my friends, Sir William and Lady Hamilton, to
> England."

Having ordered Sir Sidney to Alexandria, and assured him
that all instructions coming from their Lordships and the Commander-in-Chief should be most strictly complied with, he could
do no more than await results, which meant months of waiting.
But during them he became not too unapproachable upon a sore

subject to appreciate the very remarkable imitations of " S.S.S." given by Lady Hamilton, who had been privileged at Naples to undertake the unaccustomed rôle of mute and admiring hostess of an officer of the British Navy, one of whose boasts was that he could, when he chose, pass anywhere for a Frenchman.

The results of Nelson's letters began to be apparent in mid-February, when Lord St. Vincent wrote, " Employ Sir Sidney Smith in any manner you think proper." A long despatch from Lord Spencer, received at the end of April, mentioned " very great misunderstanding ", and Sir Sidney was obliged to relinquish his self-appointed rank of Commodore flying a broad pendant. His very gallant and successful services in Egypt fully confirmed their Lordships' hopes of him, but as far as his relations with Nelson went, his desire to re-establish the control of the Porte in Egypt (even though it meant giving passports to French troops deserted by Buonaparte and fast dying of malnutrition) was fatal to good understanding. " The Great Plenip: " continued, while Nelson remained in the Mediterranean, to be a thorn in the flesh.

Not only the inhabitants of the Villa Bastioni were miserable as the early weeks of 1799 dragged slowly past, bringing execrable weather and unrelievedly bad news from Naples. The plan of Palermo, a walled city of vast antiquity, displaying strong Byzantine and Saracenic influence, hinged upon two main thoroughfares running at right angles to one another—Il Cassaro (leading downhill from the Palazzo Reale to the Porta Felice and Marina) and La Nova (running east and west). The Queen, shuddering with cold and ague, amongst the flaking gilt and dusty plumes of the only habitable part of the Colli Palace, quickly perceived her new home to be the appointed background for royal assassination. She pointed out that if she had to make another escape from republicans, the only road to the quay was over two miles in length, and one of the main thoroughfares of the town. To add to her anguish, she found her influence with her husband and his counsellors much diminished. " I am neither consulted nor even listened to, and am exceedingly unhappy. I regret that I did not go elsewhere with my children."

The densely populated side-streets of Palermo presented many eating-houses, but only lodgings for bag-men. There was but one hotel in the town—in Sicily, said cynics—at which a French proprietress was accustomed to receive (and charge accordingly) an occasional English milor' who had read in a library overlooking green parkland of the mosaics of Monreale. The Knights were amongst the favoured few to obtain rooms under this roof. They faced the principal gaol of the town, and since the street was very narrow, the English ladies could hear the lamentations of the captives throughout the night. But one of the prisoners used to drape himself at his grating with a guitar, on which he played exceedingly well, and Miss Knight, an inveterate sightseer, was enchanted by the soft beauty of the Sicilian coast, the fair complexions and blue eyes of some of the islanders and the romantic Oriental aspect of the palaces. The hotel swallowed up about a score of the 2,000 unexpected exiles whose pallid but supercilious *valets* and *femmes de chambre* had not yet learnt that mention of Naples was loathed by Sicilians. The remainder gradually established themselves, in colonies, in vacant *palazzi*, with reception-rooms of great size, where ceilings were beautifully painted with cupids and clouds, but marble-topped tables and mirrors were cracked, and furniture was scanty and untrustworthy. To the more nervous of the refugees, the very independence of the Sicilian character suggested republican leanings, and their feeling of insecurity increased as they heard of Jacobinism spreading to the very toe of Italy, and Trees of Liberty planted in Calabrian towns. When the newly-appointed British Consul-General to Naples arrived from England, after a three months' passage, he found, " We should have been on ' le pavé ', but for the Ambassador's exertions, for a lodging is not to be had." The appointment of young Mr. Charles Lock (obtained through the influence of Lord Robert Fitzgerald and Lord Craven) was not a happy one. Mrs. Lock was first cousin to Charles James Fox, and stepsister of " the notorious Irish rebel ", Lord Edward Fitzgerald, husband of " La Belle Pamela ", illegitimate child of Philippe Egalité, Duc d'Orléans, who had voted for the execution of Louis XVI. Nothing in the subsequent conduct of the Locks persuaded their Majesties of the Two Sicilies from the opinion that the couple were Jacobins. The Locks conceived violent animosity against ' " Lady Hamilton, who governs the Queen and Lord Nelson ", and attributed all their troubles to her " female vanity which could not bear that any English woman should be admired by her countrymen except herself ".

After a short pause, consequent on the royal flight having outstripped news, dire tales of what had followed in Naples arrived, at irregular intervals, at the Colli Palace, where, as Nelson deplored, although sometimes three councils were held in a day, nothing resulted, except that the Sicilians, naturally concerned for the defence of their country, were estranged by the King's preference for Neapolitan advisers. General Pignatelli, who had been left as Regent in Naples, soon proved quite unequal to a task which he did not relish. He proceeded to treat with the French for a two months' armistice, in the terms of which his sovereign's name nowhere appeared, whereupon the *lazzaroni* revolted and elected Prince Moliterno and the Duke of Rocca-romana in his place. Of these, both presently joined the republicans, but the Duke eventually returned to royalism. Pignatelli fled to Palermo, where Ferdinand disgraced him and ordered him to the fortress of Girgenti. Amongst the complaints brought by the General was that Commodore Mitchell, one of the British-born officers of the Portuguese squadron, had taken upon himself to burn two Neapolitan ships-of-the-line in the gulf and sink one refitting at Castellammare. Nelson, believing that neither of the situations in which Mitchell had been empowered to take this action had as yet arisen, wrote to him in sharp reproof, but the Queen interposed to save the officer from court-martial. Actually, ghastly atrocities had already been committed in a city divided against itself, and terrorised by mobs led by the section of the community devoted to the dynasty. The *lazzaroni* had freed all prisoners in the gaols of the town, and massacred in cold blood all available characters suspected of Jacobinism. On the arrival of the French they put up a fierce though disorganised resistance, but by February 4 Nelson knew that what he called " the tricoloured flag " was flying from every fort in Naples, and that a provisional government, under French protection, known as the Parthenopæan Republic, had been established. A great number of persons lately holding Court appointments, some of whom were convinced republicans, or considered themselves deserted by the King, had accepted office in hopes of salvation from anarchy.

Nelson, who dubbed the new *régime* " the Vesuvian ", wrote to Brother William, " My situation here is not to be envied, and I hope very soon to be released from it " ; but in their hour of darkness he considered himself " tied so fast by their Sicilian Majesties that I cannot move ". A welcome convoy from Gibraltar which had arrived on the last day of January had brought him a flood of letters written in the week when the news of the Nile had reached home. The Rector of Hilborough, who, in his brother's words, now felt the Mitre tumbling on his head, demanded to know what the Ministry proposed to do for the Nelson family. The expenses of fitting out young Horace for Eton, and a Bath season, "for the improvement of Charlotte", had been heavy. The Admiral answered that he had written to Mr. Pitt, Mr. Windham and Lord Spencer. The two first-mentioned had not replied. Lord Spencer said that he did not know what he could do for Mr. Maurice Nelson.

Nelson shifted his flag to the *Bellerophon*, while she underwent repairs after her passage, and ordered Cockburn to take the *Vanguard* and *Minerve* to Malta to see if they could be of any use to Ball, who was calling desperately for corn. He told Ball that he hoped soon to be able to return her Purser to the *Alexander* for a few days, but at the moment was quite unable to spare Tyson. "My public correspondence," he explained to William, "besides the business of sixteen Sail-of-the-Line, and all our commerce, is with Petersburg, Constantinople, the Consuls at Smyrna, Egypt, the Turkish and Russian Admirals, Trieste, Vienna, Minorca, Earl St. Vincent and Lord Spencer. This over, what time can I have for private correspondence?" Nevertheless, all old friends who had sent congratulations received answers in his own hand, all on a note of deep dejection. Admiral Goodall was told, "Palermo is detestable, and we are all unwell and full of sorrow"; Lady Parker, "You who remember me always laughing and gay, would hardly believe the change"; Davison, "I am ready to quit this world of trouble, and envy none but those of the estate of 6 feet by two." To Louis, waiting off Leghorn to rescue the royal families of Tuscany and Sardinia, he wrote, "Darby will tell you what is *not* passing here, for none can tell what we *are* doing." His note to Lady Nelson was the saddest of all: "I wish I could say more to give you any satisfaction about Josiah, but I am sorry to say, with real grief, that he has nothing good about him. He must, sooner or later, be broke, but I am sure neither you nor I can help it." But on February 2, the wheels at the Admiralty having duly revolved, he was able to tell Josiah's mother that Captain Nisbet had been appointed to the *Thalia*.

The defence of Messina, the key of Sicily, was absorbing him on the early February date when persons scanning the *Gazette* in London coffee-houses read that, on a promotion of Admirals, Lord Nelson had risen from Rear-Admiral of the Blue to Rear-Admiral of the Red.

2

The climate of Sicily, although both the Hamiltons and Nelson abused it, was famous for its equability, and towards Easter-tide of 1799, when the *tramontana* ceased to blow, Palermo began to show herself in her true colours. Under dazzling skies, suddenly warm and wide, country girls, accompanying gaily painted carts loaded with spring flowers, pressed upon passers-by stiff bouquets of violets and freesias. Pastry-cooks' windows were filled with sugar lambs; every morning small new shops opened. They displayed embroideries, executed in cottages of the landscape, models of ships and Sicilian vehicles (eagerly demanded by Neapolitan children), tastefully arranged furnishing fabrics, native pottery and sailors' hymns (which last afterwards enjoyed great popularity in London). It appeared to Miss Knight that the Sicilians, an active and intelligent people, had only needed encouragement for their industries. " It was wonderful to see the improvement and resources which started up in Palermo after the arrival of so many strangers." The Sicilians, moreover, seemed to be an unusually healthy people. Their panacea, even for abrasions and bruises, was cold water. " It is no less worthy of remark ", noted the daughter of an Admiral, " that I cannot recall to mind a single scandalous story relating to any of our officers serving in that gay and fascinating latitude. There were no duels, no rioting. Our people were beloved and respected by the inhabitants." All that met the eye of the English authoress was admirable, but by the following winter, when Palermo had assimilated over 3,000 Neapolitan and Tuscan exiles accustomed to luxury, the jackals of the entertain-ment trade, having smelt money, had provided much that had hitherto been uncalled for in *La Città Felice*. In the crowded rooms of a *palazzo* on La Nova, leased by a committee of titled exiles for concerts and balls, in imitation of the *Accademia de' Nobili* of Naples, company was less closely scrutinised than it would have been at Almacks in St. James's, play was high, hours were late and liquor flowed. Nor did the newly arrived aristocracy confine themselves to such quarters. The hosts of taverns in cobbled side-streets, some offering delicate fare, hastened nightly in bad weather to greet patrons of too resplendent title driven to them by boredom or curiosity.

In the spring, however, *al fresco* entertainments were the most fashionable, and since with the spring came hope, they were, in addition, continual. The background of Nelson's life underwent a change. The Hamiltons had moved to what Miss Knight mildly described as "a larger villa near the Mole", where Lady Hamilton was again able to entertain on a resplendent scale. "I find", wrote Captain Ball, in February, "that you fascinate all the Navy as much at Palermo as you did at Naples." "Patroness of the Navy" was his name for her. Three travelling Scotsmen, Captain Pryse Lockhart Gordon (who was bear-leading delicate Lord Montgomery) and young Lord William Gordon (who wrote verse), were also frequently invited to view the spectacle described by their hostess as "Tria Juncta in Uno" (in witty reference to the motto of the Order worn by both Sir William and Lord Nelson). Tom Allen, bearing a note, a bouquet or a bottle of Tokay, now rolled up many marble steps towards a Palace of pretensions. The property had been, in fact, so much beyond the Ambassador's means that until Nelson had arranged to take up residence there and bear a share of expenses, Sir William had been doubtful of the wisdom of the move. Even when two other English families—the Gibbses and the Nobles—had arrived as paying guests, there was room to spare in a house which struck the happy mean between town house and country ; for the Palazzo Palagonia had the advantage over the Neapolitan palace of standing apart from all other buildings, in its own spacious gardens. Both the English families possessed attractive children. In the evenings, a man "tired to death", "almost blind and worn out", attended by "good Sir William's wit and inexhaustible pleasantry and Lady Hamilton's affectionate care", revived gratefully, though not to peace of mind.

Letters from Brother William and Alexander Davison, and a packet from Lady Nelson, dated December and February, reached him early in April. A paragraph in a newspaper had been his first intimation that during the dark week of the flight from Naples a character very important in his early life had passed away quietly at Kentish Town. William's letter told him that Uncle Suckling had left him co-executor with an unknown Mr. Hume, and a legacy of £100. "I love his memory," replied Nelson, "and am not sorry that he has forgot me, except as his executor, in which I will be faithful. I loved my dear uncle for his own worth." Three months later, when he heard of the death of his younger brother, his expressions of regret were less warm. To the tender-hearted Maurice and uninhibited William he was sincerely attached, but Suckling had never been anything but a source of anxiety. Davison wrote, somewhat enigmatically:

> " I cannot help again repeating my sincere regret at your continuation in the Mediterranean; at the same time, I would be grieved that you should quit a station, if it in the smallest degree affected your own feelings. You certainly are, and must be, the best and only judge. Yet you must allow your best friends to express their sensations. . . . Your valuable better-half writes to you. She is in good health, but very uneasy and anxious, which is not to be wondered at. She sets off with the good old man to-morrow—for Bath. . . . Lady Nelson this moment calls, and is with my wife. She bids me say, that unless you return home in a few months, she will join the Standard at Naples. Excuse a woman's tender feelings—they are too acute to be expressed." ³

Nelson already knew that his wife was no longer living under what he liked to think of as " my own roof ". His father had explained as long ago as September that " Lady Nelson is apprehensive this place may be too cold for the winter, and moreover the House wants paint etc." Mrs. Matcham had been desired to find a small furnished house in a good situation in which her parent and sister-in-law might pass another Bath season. A most dutiful son had hastened to assure the Rector that if Roundwood and the Ipswich neighbourhood were not as pleasant as could be wished, he trusted that the generosity of his country would soon allow him to choose a more comfortable resting-place for his family. The note of his reply to his lady, dated April 10, could not be called encouraging:

> " You must not think it possible for me to write even to you as much as I used to do. In truth, I have such quantities of writing public letters, that my private correspondence has been, and must continue to be, greatly neglected. You would, by February, have seen how unpleasant it would have been had you followed any advice which carried you from England to a wandering sailor. I could, if you had come, *only* have struck my flag, and carried you back again, for it would have been impossible to set up an establishment at either Naples or Palermo. Nothing but the situation of affairs in this country has kept me from England; and if I have the pleasure of seeing their Sicilian Majesties safe on their throne again, it is probable that I shall yet be home in the summer. Good Sir William, Lady Hamilton, and myself, are the mainsprings of the machine which manages what is going on in this country. We are all bound to England when we can quit our posts with propriety." ⁴

The outlook, like the weather, had begun to improve, suddenly and progressively, exactly a month before this letter was written. The arrival of General Sir Charles Stuart to occupy the garrison of Messina with two English regiments from Minorca had been hailed by Nelson as " an electric shock, both to good and bad subjects of his Sicilian Majesty ". A fortnight later came news of the capture of Corfu by the Russian and Turkish squadrons under Vice-Admiral Ouschakoff and Abdul Cadir Bey. That the Emperor should move had always been regarded by Nelson as essential to the re-establishment of the Neapolitan monarchy, and Austria, having waited to be attacked, had by mid-April inflicted some startling reverses on the enemy. Tales from Naples were all of strained relations between the authorities of the Parthenopæan Republic and their masters, and since the Roman State and Southern Italy were in revolt, the French were beginning to realise that the troops holding down their Neapolitan conquest were in a precarious position. The most unexpected item of the good news (which continued to pour in as inexorably as that of disaster had arrived last autumn) concerned a counter-revolution engineered from Palermo. Cardinal Fabrizio Ruffo, a politician of princely though impoverished family, had left the Court on a January night when *morale* at the Colli Palace had been low. He had landed in his native Calabria with only eight companions. Within a few weeks his " Christian Army of the Holy Faith " consisting mainly of peasants and brigands, but numbering 17,000, were carrying the Sicilian royal standard, and considerable terror, towards Naples, through a country in which he had great influence. Ruffo, described by Nelson as " a swelled-up priest ", had never taken orders. His Cardinal's hat had been bestowed upon him on his retirement from the posts of Papal Treasurer-General and Minister of War. His followers, termed by himself " all ferocious men ", were reinforced by some Turks and Russians who had crossed the Adriatic. His most spectacular lieutenant was a bandit called Michele Pezza, generally known as " Fra Diavolo ", and by Nelson as " The Great Devil ". Nelson's interest, during the spring months of good hope in 1799, centred in the progress of the one force in which he could repose entire confidence—the squadron under Troubridge, sent by him to the Bay of Naples, with orders to blockade it and get into communication with the royalists of that capital. Since their Sicilian Majesties considered the presence of Admiral Nelson (even without his flagship) as necessary to their feelings of security, and the Bashaw of Tripoli was intriguing with Buonaparte, he transferred his flag to the *Culloden* while the *Vanguard* went to show herself at Tunis, and for two days after Troubridge's departure and before the return of the *Vanguard*, to the transport *Samuel and Jane*.

Troubridge, who sailed on the last day of March, was able by April 3 to announce that all the islands in the immediate neighbourhood of Naples had re-hoisted the royal standard. A week later Salerno had fallen to Hood and the royal colours were flying at Castellammare. " Your Lordship ", wrote Troubridge, " never beheld such loyalty ", but he was embarrassed that amongst their expressions of loyalty the faithful had hastened to deliver on board his men-of-war all natives of their islands who had held prominent office under French control, seven or eight of whom, he was told, merited death. He wrote to ask that their Majesties would send Neapolitan troops and an honest Judge to conduct trials. Nelson, after a hurried visit to the Queen and Acton, replied that a Neapolitan ship-of-the-line should instantly bring what was desired. " Send me word some proper heads are taken off; this alone will comfort me." The Admiral's reason for present discomfort was that although he preached incessantly to the now rejoicing and relaxed Court that speedy rewards and quick punishments were the only foundation of good government, " unfortunately, neither the one nor the other have been practised here ". Cardinal Ruffo's theories that a general amnesty should be proclaimed to all who had conceived the error of their ways were far more agreeable to many influential officials of the exiled King's circle ; and the Cardinal could speak well :

> " In winning back Naples, I foresee that our greatest obstacle will lie in the fear of deserved punishment. Now, if we shew that we mean to try, and punish; if we do not make them believe that we are completely persuaded that it was necessity, error, the force of the enemy, and not treason, that occasioned the rebellion, we play into the hands of the enemy and cut off our own way to reconciliation. . . . It even appears that no matter how great a rebel falls into our hands, no matter how he may have distinguished himself in rebellion, he ought to be pardoned. Read the history of France, and of the many capitulations agreed upon with rebels. . . ." [5]

Examples from French history were little likely to appeal to Nelson. The Queen's impression after reading the Cardinal's letters was that Ruffo was hoping for the results of gratitude from pardoned Jacobins.

Their Majesties were now agreed upon only one point—that they would not return to Naples until it was " entirely cleansed ", and that they must be supported by British men-of-war and troops. Ferdinand was in no hurry to quit Palermo, which he, alone amongst the refugees, had always liked. Maria Carolina still nourished fears of assassination. The arrival of Vincenzo Speciale, forwarded to Troubridge with assurances from the Queen and Acton that he had a reputation for severity, only increased the troubles of a British officer in charge of prisoners whose countrymen were howling for their blood, and a heated scene took place on board H.M.S. *Culloden* on May 7. " Mr. Judge ", pronounced by Troubridge, " the poorest creature I ever saw ", and " frightened out of his senses ", had come at intervals during the past fortnight to hint that he needed support. At least seventy families were involved in the cases under his consideration : also he could not execute disloyal priests without their having been degraded by a Bishop. He wished a British ship could be spared to take the priests to Palermo. Troubridge, by now, had delivered all the provisions in his power to the islanders, put his name down for a relief fund for seven ducats (more than he could afford) and pledged his name that supplies promised by the Queen were hourly expected. The conduct of the trials which had dragged on for the past fortnight appeared to him curious. " Frequently the culprit is not present." When " Mr. Judge ", unwillingly impressed by an inflexible audience, proceeded to ask for the services of a British hangman, the temper of an increasingly grim officer (avowedly " completely stupid " after the examination since 4 a.m. of " vagabonds, none of whom ever give a direct answer ") broke in a thunderstorm. " This treachery fairly does me up." The storm broke, not upon the head of " Mr. Judge ", but upon that of the equally feeble Neapolitan General who refused to land the troops sent from Palermo. Realising that the odium for anything that aroused criticism would be thrown upon Nelson's squadron, Troubridge spoke his mind. " I desired the General and all his cowardly gang to get out of a British man-of-war. We want people to fight ; he does not come under that description. I told him plainly that his King will never do well until he has hanged half his officers."

Among the officers who had turned his coat was now, beyond doubt, Caracciolo. The Commodore had left Palermo for his own estates on February 4, his reason being that the Parthenopæan Republic were preparing to seize the property of all absentee land-lords. Ferdinand's farewell to him had been pointed. " Beware of intermeddling with French politics. Avoid the snares of

Republicans. I know I shall recover the Kingdom of Naples."
For as long as possible both Nelson and Troubridge had discredited
reports that an officer who had learnt his seamanship under
Rodney had deserted his royal master. There was reason to
believe that such of the nobility as had been unlucky enough to
find themselves in Naples under French control had been obliged
by the occupying enemy to undertake humiliating duties in the
militia. But by mid-May the fact that Caracciolo had taken the
offensive against his King was indisputable. On the evacuation
by the French of every part of Naples except the castle on St.
Elmo, the authorities of the Parthenopæan Republic had begged
him to take charge of their crippled navy, and on May 17, in an
attack upon the Island of Procida, he had fired upon the vessel
which had once been his own flagship.

Nelson was in hopes of embarking their reluctant Majesties
for Naples within a fortnight, when suddenly all such plans had to
be laid aside. A brig arrived at Palermo with news that a French
fleet of nineteen sail-of-the-line had escaped from Brest under
cover of a fog, and had been seen off Oporto steering for the
Mediterranean. The Spanish fleet, with which it was expected to
make a junction, was reckoned at twenty-five sail-of-the-line.
Having summoned Troubridge and Duckworth, Nelson put to sea
on the night of May 19. The decision had been difficult. " If
I go, I risk, and more than risk, Sicily, and what is now safe on the
Continent." But to stay, when there was the prospect of action,
would have broken his heart. A note to Lady Hamilton was
achieved before he sailed:

> " To tell you how dreary and uncomfortable the *Vanguard* appears,
> is only telling you what it is to go from the pleasantest society to a
> solitary cell, or from the dearest friends to no friends. I am now per-
> fectly *the great man*—not a creature near me. From my heart I wish
> myself the little man again ! You, and good Sir William, have spoiled
> me for any place but with you." [7]

3

On the afternoon of June 25 Cardinal Ruffo came on board
Admiral Nelson's flagship in Naples Bay and was saluted with
thirteen guns. Dusk had fallen before the prelate took his [8]
departure, and Nelson opened a fiery letter to Duckworth with
the words, " As you will believe, the Cardinal and myself have
begun our career by a complete difference of opinion." His [9]
experiences during the past month had been varied, but all

ultimately unsatisfying. He had put to sea four times. June 4,
the anniversary of the birth of His Britannic Majesty, had
fallen between the two first occasions, and since the desired
financial support from England now seemed likely to be forthcoming, and the weather was magnificent, the day had been one
of unbroken festivity. "A Grand Dinner" at the Palazzo
Palagonia had been followed by a Court Ball offered by their
grateful Majesties. "Two or three very fine India shawls—
the price is no object", purchased at the request of Nelson by
the British Minister at Constantinople, had arrived in time for
presentation to Lady Hamilton, who employed such adjuncts in
her "Attitudes". But Nelson's letter of thanks to Spencer
Smith, written the morning after the *fêtes*, displayed that grand
dinners and balls were not at the moment congenial. In short,
nervous sentences, he described what was keeping him "on the
alert". The French fleet, which had sailed on April 26 and had
been joined by five Spanish warships, had passed through the
Gut by May 5. Lord St. Vincent had left Gibraltar on the 8th
with twenty sail-of-the-line, and letters from his lordship were
dated the 15th, off Minorca. "This is the whole I know." He
did not mention that a report that St. Vincent had applied to go
home on account of bad health had caused consternation in his
squadron and evoked a passionate appeal :

> "For the sake of our Country, do not quit us at this serious moment.
> I wish not to detract from the merit of whoever may be your successor,
> but it must take a length of time, which I hope the War will not give,
> to be in any manner a St. Vincent. We look up to you, as we have
> always found you, as to our Father, under whose fostering care we have
> been led to Fame. If, my dear Lord, I have any weight in your friend-
> ship, let me entreat you to rouse the sleeping lion."

A fine new second-rate arrived in Palermo on the day after
this letter was despatched, and on June 8 Nelson shifted his flag
from the *Vanguard*, and took with him into H.M.S. *Foudroyant*
"Captain Hardy, five lieutenants, Mr. Comyn, Chaplain, and many
mates and midshipmen." "Hardy was bred in the old school.
I never have been better satisfied with the real good discipline of
a ship than the *Vanguard's*. An odd trophy of the Nile which
also accompanied the Admiral lay for several days on the grating
of the quarter-deck of his new flagship, arousing much interest
amongst such of his officers as were new to his command. They
heard with surprise that Lord Nelson was accustomed to dine
with a coffin behind his Windsor chair. Captain Ben Hallowell

A A

had recently sent his lordship this unusual gift, made by the carpenter of the *Swiftsure* from part of the main-mast of *L'Orient*. Coming out of his cabin one June morning to discover his officers staring at this blunt reminder that all flesh is grass, Nelson remarked, " You may look at it, gentlemen, as long as you please ; but depend upon it, none of you shall have it."   10

His second return to Palermo, on June 15, had been occasioned by a despatch from Lord Keith, who had now succeeded Lord St. Vincent, telling him that the Combined Fleets were believed to be bound either for Naples or Sicily.   He had just quitted Palermo, taking with him " my little squadron ", 1,700 troops and the eldest son of the royal house, entrusted to him by the Queen in a typical letter.   Considering " that the best defence for their Sicilian Majesties' dominions is to place myself alongside the French ", he disembarked the Prince and troops, and cruised off Maritimo for four days, but without seeing anything of the Franco-Spanish armada.   On the 21st, having been joined by Ball with the *Alexander* and *Goliath* from Malta, he sailed again for Naples, calling at Palermo for two and a half hours *en route*. He did not anchor, but he made an expedition to the Colli Palace, and he took with him as passengers the British Ambassador (much shaken by the tragic intelligence that H.M.S. *Colossus*, carrying the treasures of his classical collection, had been lost off the Scillies) and " my dear Lady Hamilton, my faithful interpreter on all occasions ", to whom he had written almost daily during his absence.   On the passage he learnt that Ruffo, panic-stricken by the news of the Combined Fleets being at sea, and sickened by the behaviour of his own army in Naples, had concluded a three weeks' Armistice with the enemy.   When Nelson arrived in Naples Bay, on the afternoon of the 24th, he found flags of truce flying on the sea-forts of Uovo and Nuovo (held by the Neapolitan Jacobins), from the castle of St. Elmo (held by the French) and upon the frigate *Seahorse*, whose commander, Captain Foote, had been left, on Troubridge's recall, in charge of a small flotilla. Foote's orders had been to co-operate with the Cardinal, and with the Russian and Turkish detachments in the blockade, and (as he explained, when he came on board the *Foudroyant* at 4 p.m.) he had supposed the Cardinal " the confidential agent of his Sicilian Majesty ", and the French fleet more likely to appear than Nelson's. But the document, " already signed by the Cardinal and the Chief of the Russians ", to which he had put his name, with much misgiving, yesterday morning was, so far as the Neapolitan

11   Jacobins were concerned, no Armistice, but a definite capitulation. Foote had thought its terms " very favourable to the Republicans ", as indeed they were, for the Cardinal had offered to his countrymen, in arms against their sovereign, that on their evacuation of the sea-forts they should be permitted to march out with the honours of war and all their property.   Such as wished to retire by land might do so, while those who had no desire to remain in their native city should be evacuated by sea to Toulon. The French commander in St. Elmo, General Méjean, had ratified the capitulation before Nelson's squadron came in sight, but made no terms for his own force beyond the three weeks' Armistice.   He still hoped for the arrival of the Franco-Spanish fleet to solve his difficulties.   Finally, the Neapolitan nobleman who had taken charge of the negotiations with Méjean—the Cavalière Micheroux, accredited to the Turkish and Russian forces—was regarded by the Cardinal as a supernumerary character, and was upon the worst of terms with him.

Nelson did not waste much time upon an officer left in charge of a detached squadron who said that he had been unprovided with " instructions or any document to assist or guide me ". He told the harassed Foote that he had blundered—" had been imposed upon by that worthless fellow, Cardinal Ruffo, who was endeavouring to form a party hostile to the interests of his Sovereign "—gave him credit for having acted in an unpleasant and arduous situation with all possible zeal, and dismissed him with orders to draw up a detailed narrative of his dealings with
12   Ruffo.

The *Foudroyant* anchored in thirty-five fathoms at 8 p.m., and during the hours of darkness, while the squadron stood on and off Naples Bay with light winds, the Hamiltons gave audience to a melodramatic old acquaintance.   Egidio Pallio, chief of the *lazzaroni*, had come out to offer the services of 90,000 loyal subjects of His Majesty, who were, however, without the arms
13   necessary for a sanguinary attack upon the Jacobins.   Next morning Pallio was promised arms, but adjured, for the present, to restrict his efforts to keeping peace in Naples until the arrival of the King.   Nelson, who had annulled what he had believed to be an Armistice, by signal, before anchoring, now moored his fleet of eighteen sail in a close line of battle before the city, and summoned the twenty-two gun and mortar vessels lying at the islands to flank his ships-of-the-line.   " If the French Fleet should favour us with a visit, I can easily take my position in the

centre." He sent to Ruffo, by Ball and Troubridge, his " opinion of the infamous terms entered into with the rebels " and two documents to be forwarded to the castles flying the white flag. He demanded unconditional surrender from the French. To " the rebellious subjects of His Sicilian Majesty, in the castles of Nuovo and Uovo ", he simply announced that he would not permit them to be embarked or quit those places. " They must surrender themselves to His Majesty's Royal mercy." His " Observations on the Armistice " were endorsed in his own hand : " Read, and explained, and rejected by the Cardinal ". Ruffo refused to forward either document, and replied to Troubridge's direct question, that if the British Admiral chose to break the Armistice, and reopen hostilities, he must do so without assistance. The Cardinal was " tired of his situation ". During the afternoon he appeared in person to repeat his theories that his Jacobin country-men who had taken office under the French had done so *faute de mieux*, and that the best hope for the peaceful re-establishment of the monarchy was a policy of forgiveness for all, except perhaps a very few, who should not be judged quickly. Nelson's un-varying and furious reply was that both the Treaty and Armistice were at an end by the arrival of his fleet, and that neither the Cardinal nor he had the authority to agree to a capitulation so entirely contrary to the expressed instructions of their Sicilian Majesties. Sir William Hamilton acted as interpreter during the early stages of an interview which soon degenerated into an altercation, and when he retired, worn out, Lady Hamilton took his place. How difficult was their task may be judged from the fact that when the Admiral spoke of " the rebels " and the Cardinal of " the patriots ", they were referring to the same body of men.

The ship was loading beef, lemons and fuel, and her launches were watering, at the pace of forty butt per launch. A great number of officers, arrived to pay their respects, also came along-side, but not even the Cavalière Micheroux gained admission to " the Great Cabin ".

Presently, since they seemed unable to agree upon first principles, Nelson broke off the discussion, convinced that " an Admiral is no match in talking with a Cardinal ". He would write. His written opinion could be condensed into a single sentence. " Rear-Admiral Nelson, who arrived in the Bay of Naples, on the 24th of June, with the British Fleet, found a Treaty entered into with the Rebels which, he is of opinion, ought not to be carried into execution, without the approbation

16 of His Sicilian Majesty, Earl St. Vincent, Lord Keith." Ruffo withdrew, saving his dignity by the announcement that he must consult his Russian and Turkish allies, and would let them know at the castles of St. Elmo, Nuovo and Uovo that he could not answer for Lord Nelson's allowing of the Armistice to continue. The night of terror prophesied by him followed in Naples, although not exactly according to his expectations, since most of the disorder was caused by natives attempting to fly from the capital, convinced that, between them, the French from St. Elmo and the British from the sea were about to reduce their homes to a heap of stones. Such of them as were unlucky enough to be mistaken for, or recognised by the *Sanfedisti* or *lazzaroni* as, Jacobins, were either murdered on the spot or carried prisoners to ships in the bay which took them to Justice, as practised at Procida.

Next morning, very early, the two documents which Ruffo had said that Nelson might send in " if he pleased " were despatched to the sea-forts and St. Elmo, and Sir William Hamilton sent the Cardinal a hasty assurance that Lord Nelson would do nothing, pending instructions from Palermo, to break the Armistice—a statement which Nelson (who had not altered his opinion that only the King could agree to a capitulation not yet carried

17 into effect) later confirmed in his own hand. Ruffo, for his part, was now asking for the marines, refused by him yesterday, to be landed for the defence of the city against Jacobins, and French troops reported to be marching on Caserta. In the expectation that hostilities were about to recommence, he had ordered his own irregulars and the Russians, covering the forts, to retire, an action which aggravated the tumult in the town. After receiving Nelson's note he put them back again. He had also privately offered the Jacobins of the sea-forts the option of seeking sanc-

18 tuary in Naples. They, however, having mostly no desire to fall into the hands of the *Calabresi* or *lazzaroni*, and realising that they could not sail for Toulon in defiance of Nelson's fleet, proceeded to surrender before the day was out. They were not accorded the honours of war mentioned in the terms of the capitulation, and the vessels to which they hurried were not

19 allowed to sail. Thirteen hundred seamen and marines at once invested the forts, and next morning Troubridge, having been joined by five hundred Russians and some *soi-disant* " loyalists " (half of whom Nelson believed to be rebels, and knew to be cowards), advanced to the siege of St. Elmo. From Castello

dell Uovo ninety-five persons had chosen to embark in the transports, and thirty-four to retire, under cover of night, to their homes in the town. The Cardinal attended a service of thanksgiving in the Church of the Carmine, and wrote polite letters of gratitude and congratulation to Nelson, and to Sir William and Lady Hamilton, to which the Ambassador replied cordially.

On the morning of the 28th letters from the Colli Palace arrived. Acton wrote that no conditions except unconditional surrender were to be made with the Neapolitan Jacobins. The transports were forthwith brought in under the guns of the fleet, some of their most notorious passengers were brought on board the British men-of-war, and Nelson issued a proclamation to those who had returned to their homes, to the effect that they must surrender to the King's mercy within twenty-four hours, or be considered as still in active rebellion. These actions caused an immediate termination of his brief harmonious relations with the Cardinal, who stepped back to his old position of refusing to assist in the siege of St. Elmo, and in addition published an order that nobody in the city was to be arrested except by his command. For a few hours, as Nelson wrote to Acton, it was " a toss-up " whether or not he arrested Ruffo, but eventually he decided to send Foote with the *Seahorse* and a cutter to Palermo to beg the King, the Queen (thrice underlined) and Acton himself to embark for Naples, while he endeavoured to " keep things tolerable ", until their appearance. He had come to Naples prepared if necessary " to take off the Cardinal's head ", and he did not now inform that inveterate intriguer either of his invitation to the King or the fact that he had been given authority, if he thought fit, to arrest him and forward him to Palermo to explain himself.

4

The weather on the morning of June 29 was noted in the Journal of the *Foudroyant* as moderate and cloudy. Captain Hardy was on deck, watching the arrival of the Portuguese *Rainha* and the *Balloon* brig from Messina, when his attention was distracted by a sudden clamour amongst the Neapolitans on board his ship. Several minutes passed before he understood that the reason for their unwholesome excitement was that " the traitor Caracciolo was taken ". The appearance of the Commodore, " pale, with a long beard, half dead, and with downcast eyes ", being urged on board the flagship in handcuffs, by a party of Ruffo's irregulars (who had brought him out from Naples

20 in a small boat), shocked Sir William Hamilton. Hardy immediately ordered that the prisoner's arms should be unbound, and
that while the officers commanding the Neapolitan ships in the
bay were signalled, the Commodore should be confined from the
violence of his countrymen in a cabin guarded by a lieutenant
and two marines. He sent refreshments, of which the prisoner
21 refused to partake.

Caracciolo had not been amongst the Jacobins to surrender
two nights previously. He had fled from one of the sea-forts as
long ago as June 17, and made his way in a peasant disguise to a
country villa in the neighbourhood, upon the estate of his uncle,
the Duke of Calvirrano. A warning that he had been betrayed,
and that a price was set on his head, had caused him to leave the
villa for a hut. Some of Ruffo's men, under a leader called
Scipione La Marra, had dragged him forth into Neapolitan sunshine from the depths of a well. His capture had taken place on
the 25th, and Nelson, who had received the news within twenty-
four hours, had sent a message to Ruffo on the 27th that if his
Eminence thought proper to deliver the Commodore, together
with the other rebels, on board his flagship, he would " dispose of
them ". Determined to choose a glaring case for an example of
the " quick punishment " he had always urged upon their
Majesties of the two Sicilies as the only foundation of good government, his plans were made before the prisoner was delivered.
By 10 a.m. a court-martial, convened at his order, and composed
of the five senior officers of the squadron in the Neapolitan service
under the presidency of Count Thurn, was in progress in the
wardroom of the *Foudroyant*. The proceedings, which lasted
two hours, were conducted in Italian, and Nelson was not present.
Caracciolo's actions were a matter of common knowledge to all
his judges, and undeniable. He had accepted the command of
the republican fleet and acted with considerable vigour. By
his attack with gunboats upon the British and Royal Neapolitan
ships approaching Castellammare he had, in Nelson's words,
" spirited up " the republicans of the naval arsenal. Off
Procida, firing impartially upon British and Neapolitan ships, he
had damaged *La Minèrva*, once his flagship. The charges made
against him were rebellion against his lawful sovereign and firing
at his colours. His request to be tried by British officers was
refused, and Count Thurn, after calling upon the court to identify
him, informed him of the charges and asked if he had any defence
to offer. Caracciolo, although obviously suffering from deadly

fatigue, roused himself to reply at length. He pleaded " not guilty ", saying that he had been given the choice of being shot or accepting the command of the republican fleet. Cross-examined by Thurn, he repeated that he had, on every occasion when he was called upon to attack His Majesty's ships, done so under compulsion. He admitted to having been with the division of gunboats which went out to prevent the entry of His Majesty's troops at Castellammare, but said that he had mistaken Ruffo's hordes for "insurgents". He confessed to having issued "written orders tending to oppose His Majesty's forces." Asked why he had not attempted to fly to Procida, he answered that he had feared to be ill-received there. Shortly after noon the court was cleared, and Thurn called upon the five officers to declare their verdict. Four, including himself, voted for death, two against. He reported to Nelson, who ordered that the sentence should be carried out at five o'clock on the same evening. A suggestion by Thurn, supported by Sir William Hamilton, that the condemned man should be allowed twenty-four hours in which to prepare his soul, was disregarded by an officer who had observed the results of Lord St. Vincent's methods with mutineers.　　²²

Mr. George Parsons, Signal Midshipman of the *Foudroyant* (who forty-five years later published *Nelsonian Reminiscences, Leaves from Memory's Log*), remembered Caracciolo as a "short thick-set man of apparent strength, but haggard with misery and want, his clothes in wretched condition, but his countenance denoting stern resolution to endure that misery like a man ". Caracciolo spoke a sentence to Parsons in good English when summoned to the court, and according to the young officer, his defence included a dramatic period unrecorded by Thurn. When accused of treason, he retorted that his King had deserted him and all loyal subjects. Though the accused was, in fact, forty-seven years of age, Parsons remembered him as " a wretched old man and grey-haired, who, however, walked with a firm step when conducted to the British Admiral's barge for removal to the scene of his execution ".

At 5 p.m., accordingly, Commodore Caracciolo was drawn by his own men to the foreyard-arm of His Sicilian Majesty's frigate *La Minèrva*, which he had once commanded, drums rolled, a gun was fired, and English seamen, clustering like bees on the rigging of eighteen ships-of-the-line, on a heavy evening, watched him launched into eternity. At sunset, in obedience to Nelson's orders, the body was cut down and thrown into Naples Bay.　　²³

Next day Ruffo came on board the *Foudroyant* to dine, having withdrawn his hostility towards the attack on St. Elmo. " Certainly ", wrote Sir William Hamilton, " this quick justice had had a great effect." The King's letter to the Cardinal and order to Nelson for the Cardinal's arrest remained throughout the meal locked in the Admiral's writing-box, in a sunlit cabin decorated by the gaily-dyed French and Parthenopæan flags, collected on the evacuation of the forts. Nelson's first comment on hearing of Caracciolo's defection had been, " This man was fool enough to quit his master when he thought his cause was desperate." Maria Carolina, who had always believed Caracciolo's actions the premeditated result of professional chagrin, wrote, " All his rage was at not having us embark with him, to have us at his disposal and at the disposal of his felon and traitor friends." After his death she alluded to " the sad but merited end of the unhappy and crazy Caracciolo ".

Sir William Hamilton was in great uneasiness until July 10, when the Royal Standard fluttered from the mast-head of the *Foudroyant*, signifying that His Sicilian Majesty had arrived to take up his headquarters there ; but his anxieties were quite unnecessary.

Lord Spencer, on October 7, wrote to Nelson, " In answer to your letter of the 23rd of July . . . I can only repeat what I believe I have before said on the subject—namely, that the intentions and motives by which all your measures have been governed, have been as pure and good, as their success has been complete."

24

Not until the following May did Nelson hear any criticism from England of his proceedings in the Bay of Naples in mid-

25 summer 1799.

5

On February 3, 1800, a day upon which Nelson was writing a letter beginning, " My dear Lady Hamilton, Having a Com-mander-in-Chief I cannot come on shore till I have made *my manners* to him ", trouble for the Admiral was blowing up in the House of Commons. On the Motion for the Address, thanking His Majesty for refusing to negotiate with the French repub-licans, Mr. Fox had arisen to suggest :

" I wish the atrocities, of which we hear so much, and which I abhor as much as any man, were indeed unexampled. I fear they do not belong exclusively to the French. When the Right Honourable Gentleman speaks of the extraordinary successes of the last campaign he does not mention the horrors, by which some of these successes were accompanied. Naples, for instance . . ."

Mr. Fox believed that a party of Neapolitan republicans, sheltering in the fortress of Castello dell Uovo, had made terms with a British officer which, although absolutely guaranteed, had resulted in their being delivered, not, as they had expected, with all their property, into safety at Toulon, but to dungeons and strangulation. His source of information was probably his cousin-by-marriage Charles Lock, who had written home privately, from Naples, on the previous 13th of July :

> " You will hear with grief of the infraction of the articles convented with the Neapolitan Jacobins and of the stab our English honour has received in being employed to decoy these people, who relied on our faith, into the most deplorable situation. . . . But *the sentiment of abhorrence expressed by the whole fleet* will I hope exonerate the nation from an imputation so disgraceful, and charge it where it should lie, upon the shoulders of *one or two*." [26]

Nelson on hearing of Fox's speech on May 9, 1800, wrote at once to Davison, forwarding amongst other papers his " Observations on the infamous Armistice entered into by the Cardinal ". He begged his friend to show them to the Right Hon. George Rose, and if necessary, give them to the Press. But he was too late to efface the impression, founded upon fact, that Neapolitan royalist vengeance had been ferocious, and when Captain Foote arrived home on leave in the same year, that worthy but not brilliant officer was dismayed to discover that Nelson's part in the transactions in the Bay of Naples last summer had become the subject of violent controversy, and, amongst some level-headed persons, sincere regret. He was dissuaded by Service friends from asking for a public inquiry, but the wound festered, and seven years later, two years after Nelson's death, he published a " Vindication " of his own conduct (which had never been attacked by any authoritative person) and a notably confused criticism of that of Nelson, which he had not, until now, made any attempt to question. [27] Meanwhile, he had been provided with additional material. In 1801, Miss Helen Maria Williams, an English authoress in her fortieth year, who during residence in France had adopted the principles and ideas of the Revolutionaries with a whole heart, published a work in two volumes, called *Sketches of the State of Manners and Opinions in the French Republic, towards the end of the Eighteenth Century*. It included a lively but unconscientious report of the Neapolitan revolution and counter-revolution. She accused Nelson of having tricked and trapped the garrisons of Uovo and Nuovo, including Caracciolo, and she passed very severe comment on the assistance of Lady Hamilton at the scene. A copy of what Nelson wearily called "that Miss Williams' book", with marginal corrections in his own hand, is to be seen in the British Museum. His final comment is, " Miss Williams has, in my opinion, completely proved that the Persons she has named deserved death from the Monarchy. They failed, and got hung or beheaded."

The next writer to inflame the brooding Foote was Lady Hamilton's *protégé* Harrison, who published for the first time, in 1806, Nelson's letter of July 13, 1799, to Lord Spencer, in which the Admiral described the capitulation arranged by Ruffo as "Infamous". That Foote had not heard the word used upon the occasion is improbable, but he resented Harrison's strictures on his part in the transaction exceedingly, and took up an unaccustomed pen to defend himself and the document to which he had put his name in Naples Bay. Harrison, delighted at the consequent demand for a further large edition of his book, refused to delete the passages objectionable to Foote, who thereupon commenced pamphleteer. He censured Nelson for the execution of Caracciolo, and for having acted, with regard to the capitulation, without consulting Lord St. Vincent and Lord Keith. Following the lead of Miss Williams, he accused him of having been influenced by guilty passion for Lady Hamilton. The fact that Nelson soon detached him on immediate service " to some distance from Naples " now appeared to him suspicious. The Rev. James Clarke, engaged upon an unhappy chapter in his biography of the Admiral (due for publication in 1809), involved himself in an ultimately acrimonious correspondence with the pamphleteer. Dr. Clarke, after conversations with Admiral Foley and Sir Thomas Hardy, had been forced to revise his unfavourable opinions of Nelson's behaviour, but believed that Lady Hamilton had " indecently and unjustly accelerated " the trial and execution of Caracciolo, and that " this wicked siren " had attended the carrying out of the sentence. Three years later, Robert Southey, Poet Laureate, added to his chapter on the events of midsummer 1799 the inaccuracies of Miss Williams and Captain Foote, and some of his own invention.

It was left to Captain Edward Pelham Brenton, in 1823, to insert in his *Naval History* a fiction that Lady Hamilton had made an expedition with Nelson in his barge, expressly to gloat over the pendant corpse, a spectacle which had haunted her midnight hours to the day of her death, evoking " horrid screams ". " A lady who lived many years with Lady Hamilton and who scarcely ever quitted her room during the last few weeks of her life " bravely ventured into print to say that Lady Hamilton had not been in the habit of having nightmares and never mentioned the name of Caracciolo. Commodore Sir *32* Francis Augustus Collier, whose widowed mother had delivered him to Nelson's care at a tender age, loudly denounced " an arrant falsehood ", and what Brenton described as " a person signing his name John Mitford, R.N." sent a polished letter of denial to the *Morning Post.* " I called on this man, but could never find him ", said Brenton. " I discovered he lodged over a coal-shed in some obscure street near Leicester Square, and that he was not an officer in the Navy." Had Captain *33* Brenton persevered, he would have discovered further that Mr. Mitford, who since his discharge from the Royal Service as insane, in 1814, had been in and out of the mad-house, and whose sole possessions now were a candle, a pen, a strip of bedding, a bottle of ink and a bottle of gin, had indeed been a midshipman in a ship-of-the-line at Santa Cruz, and an eyewitness of the death of Caracciolo.

But Lord Holland, in his *Memoirs of the Whig Party*, had spoken of Lady Hamilton's " baneful ascendancy " over Nelson's mind as the chief cause of indefensible conduct at Naples, and Lord Brougham and Mr. Alison, the historian, had credited Miss Williams and the Laureate. In 1830, Major Pryse Lockhart Gordon, who had been present in the bay, in Hood's ship, published memoirs of remarkable inaccuracy. Until Commander Jeaffreson Miles took up the defence in 1843, lacking essential *34* documents and with unskilled impetuosity, no author attempted the task of catching up a contemporary rumour that Nelson, languishing under the spell of Lady Hamilton, *confidante* of a bloodthirsty and dissolute queen, had acted towards a guiltless Neapolitan with ill-faith, precipitance and cruelty.

6

Cardinal Ruffo's pronouncement that the English were hateful, even to the well-disposed amongst the Neapolitans, " because they burned our Fleet ", had not been forgotten by the royal exiles. Ferdinand I returned to Naples, with a convoy of troopships and escorted by H.M.S. *Seahorse,* but in a Neapolitan frigate. He had been loath to leave Palermo, where he was comfortably settled in a new country house, from which good sport was available. As his wife told her daughter, the Empress, " *Naples est pour lui comme les Hottentots* ". Throughout the four weeks of blazing midsummer Mediterranean weather spent by him in Naples Bay, while Nelson completed the reconquest of his kingdom, he never once went ashore. He conducted all his business of state on board the English Admiral's flagship, and held *levées* on her quarter-deck. Some months later, wishing to describe a scene of irritating confusion, Troubridge said that it reminded him of the " buzz " above the gangway ladder of the *Foudroyant* when at Naples. A number of the nobility and officials who hastened to welcome their increasingly hilarious King brought their ladies, and in the Great Cabin which had witnessed a heated interview between Ruffo and Nelson, Lady Hamilton, acting for the absent Queen, received messages protesting devotion from many congratulatory persons, some of whom she remembered as having been openly pro-French before the flight of the royal family. She also received a flood of heartrending letters, begging for her intercession on behalf of political prisoners languishing either in the polaccas or the gaols of the town ("compared to which", said Troubridge, " death is a trifle "). It was difficult, even for British officers present, to realise that the chief source of influence available to the Ambassadress was the Queen, whose advice was anathema to the King. Domenico Cirillo, a scholarly and benevolent man, Court Physician, and formerly medical attendant at the Palazzo Sessa, was a personal friend, and it appears that in his case, at least, Lady Hamilton did break through her rule never to ask favours from Admiral Nelson, who described the correspondence received by her as " excuses from rebels, Jacobins and fools ", and was determined not to interfere after the arrival of a King upon whom he had always urged speedy punishment of the guilty and reward of the loyal as the only foundation of good government. The result of efforts on behalf of the humanitarian Cirillo, who frankly confessed in his letter to very mild co-operation with the enemy, under compulsion, was mortifying. The Doctor, according to Nelson, " might have been saved, but that he chose to play the fool, and lie ; denying that he ever made any speeches against the government, and that he only took care of the poor in the hospitals ". Cirillo was hanged on October 29, a date

which supports the story of Clarke and M'Arthur that Maria
Carolina went on her knees to beg this life from her husband,
who had by then rejoined her at Palermo. The Queen's letters   *35*
to Lady Hamilton during the weeks while her unpopular Majesty
was what she called " banished " from her husband's triumphal
reappearance all repeated her resolution not to appear to question
Neapolitan sentences on her former ill-companions. An English
gentleman, writing from Posilipo to Lady Hamilton, apologised
for troubling " again " " your Ladyship, who is the general
patroness of the distressed in these perilous times "; yet, before   *36*
the year was out, Neapolitan Jacobin refugees, and even royalist
representatives in Pisa, Vienna, Paris and London, were spreading
the tale that the sanguinary vengeance still in progress in their
capital was inspired by the Queen and her English friends. The
task of throwing the odium on the British was, as Troubridge had
foreseen, thoroughly accomplished, and a century later English
visitors, touring Neapolitan public and private collections,
viewed with dismay the portraits of noblemen of liberal sentiments and baby-faced ladies of birth, all attended by gruesome
anecdotes of execution while eighteen British sail-of-the-line,
under Nelson's command, lay at anchor in Naples Bay. That
the Bourbon dynasty overthrown in the nineteenth century was
entirely corrupt and decadent was by this date obvious : but
that Nelson, when called upon to support it, believed himself to
be saving Naples from a Terror analogous to that which in Paris
had outraged humanity, was by no means understood.

Public executions in the Piazza del Mercate were a permanent
feature of entertainment in Naples from July 1799 until the
following May. Nightly during the King's stay, boats plied to
and fro amongst the polaccas, collecting victims required for
interrogation by the Junta sitting in the Castel di Carmini. As
at Procida, some of the accused were condemned without being
present at their trials; others, having given evidence against
fellow delinquents, were, as surprisingly to British spectators,
released. By mid-August, when the polaccas sailed for Toulon,
only one-third of their original passengers survived. The execution, on the 20th, of a particularly brilliant group, noted by
Troubridge as " princes, dukes, commoners and ladies ", led that
officer to hope that the judges would " soon finish, on a great
scale, and then pass an act of oblivion ", but the gallows were
not taken down for another nine months. Ferdinand I had been
badly frightened. For three days after his arrival the bombard-

ment of St. Elmo formed a noisy background to the scenes of festivity on board the *Foudroyant*, and in the following week he had a bad moment. A fisherman at dawn had brought a story that Caracciolo, " who had risen from the bottom of the sea ", was coming as fast as he could to Naples. The wind being favourable, Nelson obliged the curious King by standing out to sea. A body, moving upright in the water, was presently noticed to be directing its course towards the flagship. Sir William Hamilton saved the situation by saying in courtier-like vein to a mentally unstable royalty that Caracciolo had been unable to rest until he had implored his monarch's pardon, and the horrible corpse was towed by Nelson's orders to Santa Lucia, where it received Christian burial in the fishermen's church of Santa Maria La Catena.

The anniversary of the Nile brought the news that Capua and Gaeta, the last Jacobin strongholds in the kingdom, had fallen to Troubridge's seamen and marines, and the rejoicings in the Bay of Naples were sufficiently superb to evoke a description from Nelson to his lady :

> " The King dined with me ; and, when His Majesty drank my health, a Royal salute of 21 guns was fired from all his Sicilian Majesty's Ships of War, and from all the Castles. In the evening there was a general illumination. Amongst other representations, a large Vessel was fitted out like a Roman galley ; on its oars were fixed lamps, and in the centre was erected a rostral column with my name ; at the stern were elevated two angels supporting my picture. In short, my dear Fanny, the beauty of the whole is beyond my powers of description. More than 2,000 variegated lamps were suspended round the Vessel. An orchestra was fitted up, and filled with the very best musicians and singers. The piece of music was in a great measure to celebrate my praise, describing their previous distress. *But Nelson came, the invincible Nelson, and they were preserved and again made happy.* This must not make you think me vain ; no, far, very far from it. I relate it more from gratitude than vanity. I return to Palermo with the King. May God bless you all. Pray say, what is true, that I really steal time to write this letter, and my hand is ready to drop."

On the day that St. Elmo had hoisted Royal Neapolitan colours he had received a second despatch from Lord Keith, who had been out of touch with the French fleet for three weeks. The Commander-in-Chief, who believed Minorca to be threatened, ordered Nelson to send him, at once, as many ships as could be spared from Naples. Nelson, believing Minorca to be in no danger, had decided that " at this moment I will not part with a single ship ". " It is better to save the Kingdom of Naples, and risk Minorca, than to risk the Kingdom of Naples to save Minorca." " I am fully aware ", he wrote to Lord Spencer, " of the act I have committed, but, sensible of my loyal intentions, I am prepared for any fate which may await my disobedience. . . . Do not think, my dear Lord, that my opinion is formed from the arrangements of any one. *No*, be it good, or be it bad, it is all my own." When Keith wrote again, peremptorily demanding " the whole or the greater part of the force under your Lordship's orders ", Nelson sent Duckworth with three sail-of-the-line and a corvette. None of his letters of explanation reached his Commander-in-Chief until Keith had left the Mediterranean and the French fleet was again back in Brest, a fact which probably prevented strong action being taken by the Admiralty. In due time he received a measured rebuke from Whitehall, but also temporary succession to the command left vacant by Keith. That he had been right as to enemy intentions, and Keith wrong, was a fact, but that he had disobeyed orders was not forgotten, and bore fruit. It was true that in attaching himself so unreservedly to the Royal Neapolitan interest he was acting under previous instructions, but more than a suspicion that he was held in such close and prolonged attendance on the Court by private considerations was by now current.

7

Nelson sailed for Palermo on August 5, leaving Troubridge in command in Naples Bay with orders to hoist a broad pendant, so that his authority over the expected Turkish and Russian squadrons could not be questioned. His opinion of the allies was not high. " The Russian Admiral has a polished outside but the bear is close to the skin. . . . He is jealous of our influence. . . . As for the Turks, we can do anything with them. They are good people, but perfectly useless."

Ferdinand I did not scruple to make the return voyage in the *Foudroyant,* and on their arrival, in the heat of noon, his Queen and children came on board to dine, after which, to the sound of a salute of twenty-one guns, answered by every fort of the capital, the royal family went on shore. A richly-gilded stucco landing-stage, of classic pretensions, on which were grouped the Senators of Palermo, sweltering in togas, had been erected opposite the Porta Felice. Their Majesties, attended by Lord Nelson and Sir William and Lady Hamilton, mounted into state carriages and drove to the cool of the cathedral, to take part in a service of thanksgiving. Two days later, Lady Hamilton, at the Queen's request, broke to Nelson the news that the King intended to bestow upon him the Sicilian duchy of Brontë, accompanied by feudal domains reported to produce an annual income of about £3,000. From the Palazzo Palagonia, in weather of a moist warmth denounced by him as intolerable, Nelson wrote to offer his father an immediate gift of £500 a year. It was all he dared promise until he had seen a year's returns from the duchy, for he had refused payment for their Majesties' expenses while on board his flagships, and did not yet know whether the Admiralty would refund him. The grateful King, whose gifts included a diamond-hilted sword, had written to England for permission for him to bear the Sicilian title, and empowered him to settle the succession to it as he chose. It should pass, in Nelson's opinion, to his father, brothers and their children, and after them, sisters and their children. (Five lives at the moment stood between the dignity and the eventual heiress, the twelve-year-old Charlotte, daughter of his brother William.) Actually, the duchy, represented as belonging to the Crown, was Church property, sequestered a century past, and in a state of decay. It did not include the small mediæval mountain town from which it took its name. Its predominant architectural feature, the fortress of Maniace, was a picturesque ruin. A farmhouse called " La Fragila " was the only habitable dwelling of any size on the estate, and since they lacked roads to send their produce to market, the tenants made no active efforts to improve their condition. However, London journals presently published romantic accounts of a duchy with Etna for background, where, down lava lanes shadowed by giant cactuses, goatherds and shepherds piped their flocks towards fragrant gorges, and after a call from a travelled gentleman who had actually seen Brontë, Nelson's wife, born a West Indian, sighed for an invitation to a land of sunshine. A spinster sister of Berry, Miss Patty, had offered her services as *femme de chambre* to her grace, whose health was really very indifferent.

Nelson, who was determined that the Brontese should know a model landlord and English methods, appointed Graeffer, the landscape gardener, *protégé* of Sir William Hamilton, as his agent. His first letters after his adoption of the title were signed " Brontë Nelson "; later he chose the form " Brontë, Nelson of the Nile " and finally, " Nelson and Brontë ". According to Sicilian

legend, the original Brontë, one of the Cyclops, had forged the
trident of Neptune and thunderbolts of Jove, so the name was
judged particularly suitable to the Admiral of the *Foudroyant*,
who had reseated the Bourbon monarch on his throne; and in
the fullness of time Lady Hamilton and Nelson's sisters proudly
alluded to a person mild in the family circle as " Great Jove "
and " My Lord Thunder ".

Sir William Hamilton, now professionally complacent, accustomed to the Neapolitan midsummer habit of turning night into
day, and much restored by his cruise, was the most cheerful
inhabitant of his house during the month of unbridled festivity
which succeeded the King's return. The bereaved Miss Knight,
who had been entrusted to him with her mother's dying breath,
was now a permanent guest at his table. His wife and even his
mother-in-law were prostrated by the heat. The Admiral was
suffering from eyestrain. On the 16th of August, writing to
Duckworth to inform him that he was sending Hardy in the
Foudroyant to Malta, Nelson mentioned apprehensively, " We
are dying of heat, and the feast of St. Rosalia begins this day.
How shall we get through it? Our dear Lady has been very
unwell, and if this fête to-night does not kill her, I daresay she
will write you." Maria Carolina, while deserted, had been busy.
The *festa* of the patron saint of Palermo, for which she had urged
the return of the victors of Naples, was generally disposed of
in five days, but the Queen's characteristic efforts did not
culminate until September 3, when all officers of His Britannic
Majesty's fleet were invited to a midnight *fête champêtre* in honour
of her British friends. The occasion left an indelible impression
on the memory of Midshipman Parsons, whose account casts a
sudden beam of light into the cockpit of an eighteenth-century
ship-of-the-line while young gentlemen are getting into ballroom
order. The midshipmen of the *Foudroyant* dressed to shouts of
" Two dirty shirts nearly new for one clean one ", and " Who
will lend a pair of uniform breeches? " A clumsy, apple-cheeked
English boy who had ruined a shipmate's " number one " coat
at his last turn-out promised a new one made by Stultz " when
we both reach old England ", if his friend, who was on duty to-
night, would but part with a pair of breeches not yet worn out by
pipe-clay. As they were unaccustomed to hiring transport,
their joint resources when they assembled on the Prado amounted
to fivepence. They commandeered a nobleman's carriage for
their four-mile journey uphill, and fifteen of them packed into

or upon the box of the roomy vehicle. The "fairy scene" at which they alighted surpassed Vauxhall on a gala night, and after witnessing a display of fireworks, representing the blowing-up of *L'Orient,* they flocked with a crowd, which included grave Turkish officers and the fairest of Italy's nut-brown daughters, towards a Temple of Fame. This edifice was surmounted by a goddess blowing a trumpet, and occupied by waxworks of Admiral Nelson, the British Ambassador and "Lady Hamilton, Britannia's pride". After the playing of a patriotic air, the nine-year-old Prince Leopold, who was represented by his fond mother as the originator of the *fête,* placed a laurel wreath on the head of the very life-like effigy of the Victor of the Nile, and running to thank "the guardian angel of his papa for recovering his realm", was received into the kneeling Nelson's one arm. Tears coursed down the weather-beaten cheeks of the Admiral as the trumpets blew to a point of war, and bands struck up "See the conquering hero". Midshipman Parsons, searching for a handkerchief, remembered too late that he had been obliged to place the leg of an old white silk stocking in the pocket designed to display the missing article. The entertainment ended sadly as far as he was concerned, for towards its close some of his ebullient contemporaries charged the King's Foot-Guards with dress dirks, whereupon one insulted guardsman fired "and shot a fine boy through the thigh, who did well. For this notable and ill-timed feat Lord Nelson stopped our leave for six months."

A clash of temperaments more serious in its result summoned the ailing Commander-in-Chief from the Palazzo Palagonia on the following Sunday night. A quarrel had broken out in the over-hot and over-full town between some Palermitans and Turks. A considerable number of Cadir Bey's seamen had been killed, and their fellows, forbidden to take worthy vengeance, had proceeded to mutiny. Nelson went on board the Turkish Admiral's flagship, "and subdued the disturbance". His private opinion was that the Sicilians were to blame, and he wrote to Spencer Smith at Constantinople, obliquely suggesting this, and to the Grand Signior himself, representing the bloody encounter as "a little disturbance" for which Cadir Bey was in no manner responsible. But he made no efforts to dissuade these allies from sailing for the Bosphorus forthwith.

Plans for the forthcoming winter already occupied his busy mind, although Lady Elgin, bride of the peer appointed to succeed Spencer Smith, was "literally gasping" on board H.M.S. *Phæton,*

39

at anchor before Palermo, and only kept from swooning by bathing her brow with vinegar while " the thermometer in the shade " stood at ninety. In what was called the cool of the evening, a little hot air puffed seawards from cobbled streets crowded with seamen of many nationalities, but at 8 p.m. eighty-two degrees were still registered. The Portuguese squadron had been recalled to Lisbon. Admiral Ouschakoff had explained that no Russian ship could be expected to keep the sea during the cold and blowing months. For that matter, as far as Nelson could observe, they had shown no desire to do so in the summer. He began to consider which of his own ships must go home for a thorough refit, and which could be dealt with at Gibraltar or Minorca; for if he was to be continued in his present command, he was determined not to keep a single useless ship devouring stores in the Mediterranean next season. He was disconcerted by the undeniable fact that the King preferred to stay, and spend, in Palermo, a state of affairs which roused justifiable discontent amongst Neapolitans. " Indeed, sick and tired of this want of energy ", he mentioned emphatically that if he found it impossible to be of use to His Majesty he must retire from his present " inactive service ". In the end of September, Troubridge, still unaided by English troops, but supported by a Russian division forwarded by Marshal Suvárov, reported the capitulation of Rome and Città Vecchia. Nelson, amused by the fulfilment of a prophecy, made to him in Naples by an Irish priest, " that I should take Rome with my ships ", pointed out that the last objection to the return of the royal family to their Neapolitan capital had been removed. Still the King would not move. " I am almost mad with the manner of going on here."

" The unpleasant paragraphs in the newspapers " regarding their Commander-in-Chief, deplored by Commodore Troubridge in letters to Governor Ball, were not in very wide circulation in England as yet, but Gibraltar was so full of gossip on the subject that the Elgins had arrived determined to accept as little hospitality as possible at the Palazzo Palagonia. " They say ", wrote young Lady Elgin to her mother in Scotland, " that there never was a man turned so *vain glorious* (that's the phrase) in the world as Lord N. He is now completely managed by Lady Hamilton." Her husband found that " they " had not spoken strict truth as far as Lord Nelson was concerned. On business, particularly in private, the young diplomat was penetrated by the " infinite fire ", decision and refusal to be daunted by difficulties

displayed by a prematurely aged man, who appeared to have a
film growing over both eyes. But in private, too, the Admiral
told him solemnly that he had now lived a year in the same house
as Lady Hamilton, and that her beauty was nothing in comparison
to the goodness of her heart. Sir William, in Lord Elgin's
opinion, ought to go home, and he wrote to England to say so.
Lady Elgin found that Lady Hamilton was pleasant, sang remarkably well, and at dinner, quite in an undress, looked very
handsome. " My Father would say, ' There is a fine Woman for
you, good flesh and blood.' She is indeed a Whapper ! " The
famous Emma, however, appeared to her fellow Ambassadress
lacking in reserve, and Lady Elgin felt really humiliated as she
watched Nelson's obvious devotion. " Lord Nelson, whenever she
moved, was always by her side. . . ." " He seems quite dying, and
yet as if he had no other thought than her." The young critic had
also to acknowledge that " you never saw anything equal to the
fuss the Queen made with Lady H.", and that the Chinese *fête*
which she attended in Palermo on October 4 surpassed anything
she had ever seen in England. It was said to have cost £6,000,
and the company, served in a garden at innumerable round
tables by a vast quantity of servants all in Chinese costume,
supped in view of an avenue seemingly a mile long, lit by coloured
lanterns. " It really outdid the Arabian Nights." Fortunately
the bride, who had attired herself in " my finest white gown, a
Crazy Jane with a yellow handkerchief on it, and my fine white
lace cloak ", was able to attach herself to Mrs. Charles Lock. " I
took her up, and left Lady H." Next morning, when the
Foudroyant sailed for Minorca, and probably Gibraltar, Lord Elgin
had so much fallen a victim to the Admiral's personality as to give
the toast " Lord Nelson " at Sir William Hamilton's table, whereupon, to Lady Elgin's amusement, " my-Lady actually *greeted* ".

Nelson had warned Ball and Sidney Smith that he was going
to Minorca to get together ten sail-of-the-line in order to meet a
squadron of fourteen enemy warships, including one three-
decker, reported off Finisterre. He was satisfied that they were
not bound for the Mediterranean, and that the British outward-
bound convoy was their prey. This consisted of seven hundred
sail, escorted by a few frigates, English authorities having been
assured—quite correctly—that the French were blockaded in
Brest. On the evening of October 12, having called at Port
Mahon, the squadron of the temporary Commander-in-Chief on
the Mediterranean station, under sail for Gibraltar, fell in with the

Bulldog sloop of war, and Sir Edward Berry, recovered of his wounds of the Nile, and fresh from England, brought news from Admiral Duckworth that the supposed French were Spaniards who had already put into Ferrol. The squadron returned to Port Mahon, but in a four-hour interview with Sir James Erskine, Nelson did not succeed as he had done with Lord Elgin. The military commander could not at present consider sparing 2,000 men to assist in the reduction of Malta, where the conciliatory Ball, appointed Governor, was on the best of terms with the afflicted natives, but still without the troops necessary to drive " the accursed French " out of Valetta. General Fox (brother of the statesman whom Nelson had hoped to " unkennel " in the Westminster Election) was expected by Sir James and might decide otherwise. Amongst other business despatched by Nelson at Port Mahon, on the same day as a court-martial, was a literary effort, " which I am sensible wants the pruning knife ". Mr. John M'Arthur, who had been Secretary to Lord Hood, and Purser of the *Victory*, had explained that the first volume of his *Naval Chronicle*, for which a " Sketch of my Life " by Lord Nelson was essential, was already in print. Nelson's " Sketch of my Life ", which he realised would be read in English homes, closed on a trumpet note. " Perseverance in any profession will most probably meet its reward. Without having any inheritance, or having been fortunate in prize-money, I have received all the Honours of my Profession, been created a Peer of Great Britain, and I may say to the reader, ' *Go thou and do likewise.*' " The moment was a sad one for him to address himself to the rising generation. His sister Susanna, whose family opened with daughters, had at last been able to fulfil her dream of sending a son into the navy. The Admiral had just heard that George Bolton, aged twelve, had died on his passage from Gibraltar to Minorca.

When the *Foudroyant* returned to Palermo on October 22, Berry was again her Captain, " my friend Hardy " having gone into the *Princess Charlotte*, " to make a Man-of-War of her ".

8

The English Press, as the last months of the old century wore out, was principally concerned with the ignominious end of Tippoo Sahib at Seringapatam, something in the nature of a *coup d'état* in Paris, and what Nelson knew as " the Secret Expedition ". The Fourth Lieutenant of the *Goliath* had safely performed his

long journey to the Governor of Bombay, and Lord Mornington
and his military brother, Colonel Wellesley, had acted promptly
in India on hearing of the victory of Aboukir Bay. On the day
after Nelson, delighted by Sidney Smith's successes, had written
to Troubridge, " *Adieu, Mr. Buonaparte !* " that character had
deserted his army in Egypt. Buonaparte had landed six weeks
later at one of those small French Mediterranean ports so well
known to officers of Hood's and Jervis's fleets, and had been
received with enthusiasm by a handful of surprised and obscure
inhabitants. In his own phrase, " the pear was ripe ", but
" the Secret Expedition ", which had just been launched, appeared
to all English readers of newspapers much more important.
After a year of preparation, since invasion of their own shores
had been frustrated by the Battle of the Nile, English troops
had invaded the Continent. Holland had been their choice for a
landing-place, and, so far as Nelson knew, affairs were proceeding
according to plan ; but the Mediterranean fleet, while affairs
in Mediterranean waters were " pretty nearly at a standstill ",
seemed to him quite forgotten, and in his darker moments he
suspected that this neglect was intentional. He had attempted
to justify his failure to obey Lord Keith :

> " Much as I approve of strict obedience to orders—even to a Court-
> Martial to inquire whether the object justified the measure—yet to say
> that an Officer is never, for any object, to alter his orders, is what I
> cannot comprehend. The circumstances of this War so often vary, that
> an Officer has, almost every moment, to consider—What would my
> superiors direct did they know what is passing under my nose ? The
> great object of this War is—' Down, down with the French.' To accom-
> plish this, every nerve and by both services, ought to be strained."

Two days before Christmas, writing to his Flag-Captain, he
mentioned that he had heard nothing from home since October
22, " and then only a miserable letter from the Admiralty ",
indeed " a severe set-down ". His offence now, of which he
felt himself quite guiltless, was, ironically enough, failure to
keep their Lordships informed. He had replied that, as an
acting Commander-in-Chief, without the usual appointments or
salary, he had been " thrown into a more extensive correspondence
than ever, perhaps, fell to the lot of any Admiral, and into a
political situation, I own, out of my sphere ". His situation
for some months now had been, as he mourned to Lord Spencer,
" most uncomfortable. Plain commonsense points out that the
King should return to Naples, but nothing can move him. . . .

Unfortunately, the King and Her Majesty do not, at this moment, draw exactly the same way. Do not, my dear Lord, let the Admiralty write harshly to me—my generous soul cannot bear it, being conscious it is entirely unmerited." He was "almost ⁴¹ in desperation about Malta ", and in anxiety lest the long-suffering Maltese, when they learnt that England was deferring to the Czar's desire to restore the Order of St. John with his Imperial Majesty as Grand Master, should give up the long struggle. He was working night and day to get them troops from Messina and corn from Girgenti. He was ready to sell the Czar's diamonds, and had pledged Brontë. " Nothing in this Country is well done." Acton continued to promise, but not to act. The Bashaw of Tripoli, who was now far from averse from concluding a peace with His Sicilian Majesty (which should ease the passage of supplies for Malta), wished first to know what sum he would be paid for it; as if he made peace with King Ferdinand he must find some other monarch to fight, or lay up his cruisers. " Very good reasons for being at war ", wrote Nelson on the back of the English Consul's explanatory letter. " Well said, Bashaw ! " Lord Elgin was calling for a strong squadron in the Levant, and the Austrians for one to blockade Genoa. The murder of an English seaman in Palermo by two Genoese who could be identified had been reported. For the last twelve months British ships ·had been losing valuable men in tavern and quayside affrays with Genoese. A firm letter to the Marquis Spinola was sent on its way.

Mr. Charles Lock, " mortified beyond what I ever was in my life ", had been persuaded by Sir William Hamilton to send Lord Nelson a letter of abject apology for spreading " malicious and scandalous " rumours that the Victualling Board were grateful to him for exposing Captains' and Pursers' frauds, and saving the Government forty per cent on the provision of stores for Lord Nelson's fleet.

> " I declare that circumstances compelled me against my will and against my sense to appear in the light of a Public accuser. As it was far from my intention to assail your Lordship's integrity by any expression which may have fallen from me, and as every purpose of Justification is already answered which a further inquiry could produce, I trust your Lordship will deem it unnecessary to press the matter further."

But Mr. Lock still felt sore, for he had been thanked by the Victualling Board for his zeal—though unofficially. His interest at home was good, and his father had written to him that Mr.

Marsh, a Commissioner of the Board, felt very much obliged to him for "interference"; and Miss Lock reported that Sir William Bellingham, Chairman, at a family dinner-party, had repeated the sentiment. Suggestions by Mrs. Lock, however, that "Lord Craven and Lord Bathurst should be informed of it all", had been disregarded by her prudent father and father-in-law; and unfortunately, in one of many heated letters to the Admiral, Mr. Lock had accused Lord Nelson of forwarding false statements of his conduct to the Board. ("I wish I had said 'erroneous' instead of 'false', as the expression is offensive.") The Board, disingenuously, replied to a complaint from the Admiral that they had never had correspondence with Mr. Lock; but the Admiral's letters also had been heated, and one had contained a sentence bound to arouse criticism at home—"Nelson is so far from doing a scandalous or mean action as the Heavens are above the Earth."

Palermo, this Christmas-tide of hard gales, was very gay, gayer than ever, and Troubridge, whose letters of warning were becoming a familiar feature of Nelson's correspondence, had produced a maddening theory that the Queen, an inveterate employer of secret agents, was privately acting against the British she favoured so openly. The Commodore believed that his letters to his Commander-in-Chief were seen by Her Majesty before they reached their destination. Last September he had believed "some person about Sir William Hamilton's house sends accounts here, as I have frequently heard things which I knew your Lordship meant to keep secret". Now a story that Nelson was gambling was driving him frantic. The facts were that Nelson, who began his day at 5.30 a.m. and had told the Secretary to the Admiralty, "till after 8 o'clock at night, I never relax from business", had fallen into the habit, during the winter months, of attending the Hamiltons to the concert, ball and card rooms on La Nova. Supper-parties at the Palazzo Palagonia were also enlivened by high play at Faro. Nelson never played, but Lady Hamilton had begun to do so, and the mere appearance of the British Commander-in-Chief dropping asleep at the table, by the side of a gambling lady, had been delightful to the Jacobin Press, and Neapolitans who loathed the Queen and her English friends. At the Chinese *fête* Lady Elgin had heard fellow-guests laying bets that Lord Nelson would not be able to tear himself away from Lady Hamilton to put to sea next morning. A story that Sir William had challenged the

Admiral had not survived, as they were always seen together on
the best of terms, but one that the Admiral and Ambassadress, in
disguise, haunted quayside taverns *incognito* was popular.   " You
may not know ", wrote Troubridge heavily to Lady Hamilton,
" that you have many enemies.   I therefore risk your displeasure
by telling you."   To his relief, she took his admonition in good
part, saw his point and gave up playing.   The mischief, however, was done, and Sir William Hamilton's successor was told,
and reported to London, that Lord Nelson had ruined his health
and fortune playing Faro, and other games, at Palermo, in the
company of Lady Hamilton.   *43*

The new century opened with a week of pacific skies and
sunshine, at the end of which Nelson learnt that his acting command had come to an end.   Lord Keith, from Vigo, announced
that the Admiralty had directed him to proceed into the Mediterranean.   He was going to look into Genoa, and ordered Nelson
to join him.   The report of the retiring Commander-in-Chief
was a model of clarity, and within ten days Nelson had sailed
for Leghorn ; but despite the frigidity of his recent relations with
their Lordships, he was shocked and sore at having been, as he
considered, set aside in favour of a senior, steady, persevering,
and cautious, but something of whose mental capacity might be
judged from the fact that in 1800 he insisted upon the retention
of the pigtail in the Naval Service.   Lord Keith received, without
any assumed pleasure, a chagrined and personally unsympathetic
officer whom he intended to treat with great tact.   He fixed a
critical eye upon the *Foudroyant* and brilliant young Sir Edward
Berry, one of Nelson's " swans ".   Lord Keith had brought
his lady with him, and this personage, though like Lady Elgin
a Scottish heiress, and of far more formal manners, availed herself of an invitation to the Palazzo Palagonia while the *Queen
Charlotte* was in port.   The moment was not a happy one.   During
his absence a thunderbolt had fallen upon the house in which
Nelson abode with the Hamiltons.   Sir William had been abruptly
informed that the Honourable Arthur Paget, in a fast frigate,
was on his way to relieve him of his duties.   It was true that in
1798 Sir William had mentioned to Lord Grenville that he would
like to come to England to look after his Pembrokeshire estates,
and that if leave could not be granted the Foreign Minister
might dispose of his post; but he had heard nothing further on
the subject, either publicly or privately.   Now, their Sicilian
Majesties' representative at St. James's had blandly written to

Sir John Acton that Sir William's retirement was at his own wish. A philosopher, Sir William valiantly supposed that he was the victim of " a Cabinet job " (some provision for a young son of Lord Uxbridge being necessary at the moment), but his lady was horrified at the prospect of retirement, and the Queen, according to her own account, was " half dead with grief ". All rallied. Sir William announced that after thirty-six years' service he had been " either kicked up or down out of my post ". Time would show which. " I have now not a doubt but we shall have the extreme satisfaction of returning home with our dearest friend, Lord Nelson." Lady Hamilton spoke of a Season at home, before return to Naples. The Queen promised that the amiable Prince Castelcicala should proceed to St. James's and ask for Sir William's reappointment. But when Nelson sailed for Malta, with Lord Keith, on February 12, after what that dour character described as " the *long* eight days I was at Palermo ", all felt that the end of a chapter was drawing near. The capture of Valetta and the two enemy warships which had escaped from the Nile was all that remained to bring Nelson's professional career in the Mediterranean to a triumphant finish. The *Guillaume Tell* was known to be in Valetta harbour, and had received some attentions from Ball's squadron, but the whereabouts of *Le Généreux* was a mystery.

Amongst the unpleasant news received by Nelson, after a long, ominous silence, was that Marshal Suvárov had retired to Prague, ready to act either with or against the Austrians, as events proved; for a French envoy was treating for peace at Vienna. That the combined English and Russian invasion of Holland had not been a success was becoming apparent. The Czar was passing into disgust for both his allies. Consequently, Admiral Ouschakoff had accomplished his long-threatened withdrawal from his station off Malta. Ball, looking back upon the events of the following week, said that Nelson was indeed a lucky Admiral. For sixteen months the blockade had been carried on without any serious enemy interference. No sooner did Nelson arrive than a frigate brought word that a French ship-of-the-line, in charge of a convoy bringing 4,000 troops and grain from Toulon, for the relief of Valetta, had been seen west of Sicily. Keith, with his division, approached the island in unusually good weather for the season, but Nelson's journal on the anniversary of the Nile was achieved in low spirits:

" At 9 o'clock went on board the *Queen Charlotte*. Lord Keith just got up. Went into the breakfast-room. (N.B. Everything very dirty,

and the table-cloth not changed since we sailed.) Got no information
of Lord Keith's intentions about me. Came on board very unwell.
Had all the officers and midshipmen of the ship, who were in the battle
of this day, to dine with me. Blew fresh all night.'' [Next morning
they were close off St. Paul's.] '' Asked the Admiral, by signal, if I
should lead into port. Answer, ' No.' ''   44

He realised, what he had foreseen, that Keith had no
intention of admitting him to the confidence or giving him the
free hand to which the leadership of St. Vincent had accustomed
him. On learning from the *Lion* of the approach of the enemy,
Keith signalled to Nelson to chase to windward, with four of the
line, and for three days and nights, carrying all sail possible,
in very dirty weather, Nelson gloomily entered, '' Nothing in
sight ''. The Sicilian troops embarked on board the *Foudroyant*
suffered, and he grimly noted, '' Nothing is off Valetta to prevent
the entry of any vessel. The Commander-in-Chief knows best.''
To Lady Hamilton he misquoted Shakespeare, '' If it be a sin to
covet glory, I am the most offending soul alive '', adding dismally,
'' But *here I am*, in a heavy sea and thick fog ''. Next morning,   45
through the mist, he heard the note of cannon, and steered towards it. The scene is henceforward illuminated by the irrepress-
ible Midshipman Parsons, whose description, recollected for an
early-Victorian audience, opens at the moment that the mast-
head look-out is hailing the quarter-deck:

'' ' The stranger is evidently a man-of-war—she is a line-of-battle
ship, my lord, and going large on the starboard tack.'
'' ' Ah! an enemy, Mr. Staines. I pray God it may be *Le Généreux*.
The signal for a general chase, Sir Ed'ard ' (the Nelsonian pronunciation
of Edward). ' Make the *Foudroyant* fly! . . . This will not do, Sir
Ed'ard, it is certainly *Le Généreux*, and to my flagship she can alone
surrender. Sir Ed'ard, we must and shall beat the *Northumberland*.'
'' ' I will do the utmost, my lord. (Get the engine to work on the
sails—hand butts of water to the stays—pipe the hammocks down, and
each man place shot in them—slack the stays, knock up the wedges,
and give the masts play. Start off the water, Mr. James, and pump
the ship.) '
'' The *Foudroyant* is drawing ahead, and at last takes the lead in
the chase. ' The Admiral is working his fin ' (the stump of his right
arm). ' Do not cross his hawse I advise you.' ''

'' A strange sail ahead of the chase '' is the next report, and
Parsons, ordered to the masthead, after being damned by the
Admiral for starting to climb without his telescope, shouts:

'' ' A sloop of war, or frigate, my lord.'
'' ' Demand her number.'

" ' The *Success*, my lord.'

" ' Captain Peard; signal to cut off the flying enemy—great odds, though, thirty-two small guns to eighty large ones.'

" The *Success* has hove-to athwart hawse of the *Généreux*; and is firing her larboard broadside. The Frenchman has hoisted his tricolour, with a Rear-Admiral's flag.

" ' Bravo—*Success* ! *At her again ! '*

" ' She has wore round, my lord, and firing her starboard broadside. It has winged her, my lord—her flying kites are flying away altogether.'

" The enemy is close on the *Success*, who must receive her tremendous broadside. The *Généreux* opens her fire on her little enemy, and every person stands aghast, afraid of the consequences. The smoke clears away, and there is the *Success*, crippled, it is true, but bull-dog like, bearing up after the enemy. . . .

" ' Then signal for the *Success* to discontinue the action and come under my stern,' said Lord Nelson, ' she has done well for her size. Try a shot from the lower deck at her, Sir Ed'ard.'

" ' It goes over her.'

" ' Beat to quarters, and fire coolly and deliberately at her masts and yards.'

" *Le Généreux* at this moment opened her fire on us, and, as a shot passed through the mizzen stay-sail, Lord Nelson, patting one of the youngsters on the head, asked him jocularly how he relished the music; and observing something like alarm depicted on his countenance, consoled him with the information that Charles XII ran away from the first shot he heard, though afterwards he was called ' The Great ', and deservedly from his bravery. ' I therefore ', said Nelson, ' hope much from you in future.'

" Here the *Northumberland* opened her fire, and down came the tricoloured ensign, amidst the thunders of our united cannon."

Nelson gave the signal to cease fire, and Berry boarded the prize, soon to return with the sword of Rear-Admiral Pérée, who was dying of wounds. The convoy had scattered, never to return, and a large armed store-ship, loaded with meat, brandy, wine and clothing, had fallen to Nelson's sole attendant brig. But the victor's reception by his Commander-in-Chief next day was very unlike that usually given by St. Vincent to a favourite and successful officer. Not a muscle of Lord Keith's face moved as he listened to Nelson's report, and when Nelson added that he had made a vow that if he took *Le Généreux*, he would strike his flag, crushing silence followed. Nelson believed that he had again disobeyed Keith, in leaving him without a signal (" The way he went, the *Généreux* never could have been taken "), but Keith, writing to the Admiralty, gave him credit for skill and address in comprehending signals in very bad weather, and prepared to leave him in charge of the blockade of Malta, offering him the

choice of Syracuse, Augusta or Messina as a more convenient
rendezvous than Palermo. " I could no more stay fourteen days
longer here than fourteen years ", explained Nelson, in a private
letter, accompanying his request for a fortnight's sick leave,
" to go to my friends at Palermo ". To Lord Minto, he burst
out, " Greenwich Hospital seems a fit retreat for me, after being
evidently thought unfit to command in the Mediterranean."
For a few days hopes that the *Guillaume Tell* and other enemy
ships were likely to come out of the harbour detained him ; then,
in spite of anguished protests from Troubridge, he sailed. The
Speedy brig, from England, brought him a note of warning from
another good friend shortly before he weighed. Old Admiral
Goodall, seated in a mansion of Mayfair on a short November day,
had brought to a duty letter all his wonted address.

" My good Lord,
" I hope, as the sailor says, ' this will find you well, as I am at this
present.' I have wrote at different times three letters to you in favour
of my protégé, Captain Broughton of the *Stromboli* Bomb, and flattered
myself that I should have heard you had had an opportunity of giving
him Post. Keep him in your mind's eye, and let it be so.
" They say here you are Rinaldo in the arms of Armida, and that
it requires the firmness of an Ubaldo, and his brother Knight, to draw
you from the Enchantress. To be sure 'tis a very pleasant attraction,
to which I am very sensible myself. But my maxim has always been—
Cupidus voluptatum, cupidior gloriæ. Be it as it will, health and happiness
attend you."

47

Nelson replied at length to a man who had himself known
what it was to be passed over for the command in the Mediterranean, but did not mention the Hamiltons except as his present
hosts, and in that capacity " nonpareils ". The weather was
most unfavourable for an invalid suffering from symptoms which
he believed signified fatal heart trouble, and he was again without
a secretary. (" I wish ", said Ball, " he could be prevailed upon
to write less, because I am very apprehensive he impairs his
health by leaning so much.") Tyson, who had been left in *Le
Généreux* to act as prize agent, and who was sitting in his overcoat, with a high temperature and agonising throat, thought
the gales of early March 1800 worse than those he had experienced
in the royal flight to Naples. The infuriated French had broken
every pane of glass in the ship before Lord Nelson's officers took
possession of her.
On his arrival in Palermo, Nelson sent Berry back with the
Foudroyant, to take part in the blockade of Valetta, and again

hoisted his own flag on board a transport, in view of the windows of the Palazzo Palagonia. The latest festivity to take place in that hospitable house had been depressingly characteristic of Neapolitan Court circles, and confirmed his growing mistrust and dislike of their Majesties' chief Minister. Sir John Acton, aged sixty-four, had been married, by dispensation, to his niece, who still lacked three months to her fourteenth birthday.

The *Foudroyant* arrived back on her station just in time to capture the *Guillaume Tell*, and from the moment that he got the news Nelson's plans for going home began to take active shape.

> " My task is done, my health is lost, and the orders of the great Earl of St. Vincent are completely fulfilled. I hope the *Foudroyant* will be able to come here, to carry us first to Malta, and from thence, taking the Queen of Naples to Leghorn, proceed with us, at least to Gibraltar, if not to England."

9

The censorious young gentleman called by the Queen " the fatal Paget " had arrived some weeks past. On April 22 Sir William Hamilton presented his letters of recall, and next day a party from the Palazzo Palagonia sailed with Nelson in the *Foudroyant* for Malta. Miss Knight had at first declined the Admiral's invitation, but on being assured that it was his intention to visit Syracuse, could not resist the temptation. Since there were two authors on board, vivid glimpses of this cruise are available. Miss Knight noted in the Admiral's Great Cabin an immense tricoloured plume, carved in wood, a relic from the figure-head of the *Guillaume Tell*, four muskets taken from the *San Josef*, the flagstaff of *L'Orient*, and many new publications, sent from England by Lady Nelson. The officers of the ship were in turn invited to dine, and the Admiral kept a good table, although nothing about his appointments was ostentatious. Owing to contrary winds, their passage to Syracuse was slow, and Lady Hamilton's birthday, April 26, was celebrated on board with toasts and songs, one of which, composed by Miss Knight for the occasion, was set to the old tune " Heart of Oak ". It was coyly dedicated " To a lady who is leaving Sicily with great reluctance ", and opened:

> " Come, cheer up, fair Delia, forget all thy grief,
>   For thy ship-mates are brave, and a Hero's their chief."

After two days sightseeing in ancient Syracuse, the party again set sail, and late in the evening of May 3 joined the blockading squadron off Malta.   Parsons, who had been an admirer of " the fair and beauteous Emma " from the moment that he had first beheld her, " bending her graceful form over a superb harp, on the *Foudroyant's* quarter-deck, every day, after dinner in Naples Bay ", thought her presence not entirely conducive to a high state of discipline in a man-of-war.   He observed her, with her tablets in her hand, writing down the names of seamen who explained to her that they had been " freshish, but not drunk ", and concluded their requests for a word from her ladyship to the Admiral with the exclamation, " God bless that handsome face, for it is the Sailor's Friend ! "   However, he was himself presently grateful for her mediation, as, scampering up the companion-ladder in reply to a message that Sir Edward Berry wanted the Signal-midshipman, he violently overset Sir William Hamilton, " tottering down with all the caution of age ".

On the night of their arrival off Valetta a breeze unexpectedly came in from the sea, with the result that the *Foudroyant* dragged her anchor, and, being given cable, brought up within gunshot of the shore batteries.   Sir Edward Berry, roused from slumber by the Officer of the Watch, said, " Very well, Mr. Bolton, we will shift our berth at daylight ", but with dawn the enemy began target-practice upon the flagship.   " Lord Nelson was in a towering passion, and Lady Hamilton's refusal to quit the quarter-deck, did not tend to tranquilize him."   Their welcome by all the English authorities at Malta was hearty.   General Graham and Commodore Troubridge invited the whole party to dine on several occasions during their stay of seventeen days.   Governor Ball addressed Lady Hamilton as " my dear sister ".   An application of the Admiral to the Czar (as Grand Master of the Order of St. John) to notice the bravery of Captain Ball, and the exertions of the lady of the British Minister at the Court of the Two Sicilies to procure supplies for the Maltese, had resulted in the arrival of decorations for both.   Ball had been named *Commandeur Grande Croix*, and Lady Hamilton *Dame Petite Croix*.

Everyone concerned wished that Nelson would wait to witness the fall of Valetta, which they represented as imminent, but on May 20, having been at anchor in the little bay of Marsa Sorocco since the 11th, the *Foudroyant* got under weigh.   Ball's last letter to Lady Hamilton, who had failed to attend a farewell dinner, wished her prosperous gales and every blessing in this life.   He attributed Nelson's heart-attacks to fatigue and anxiety.   " I therefore rejoice at your being on board."   Their return passage was not attended by the desired favourable winds, and during it a report that Lady Hamilton was suffering from fever caused stillness to be observed in all parts of what Parsons called "this Noah's Ark". Only "the infernal regions", inhabited by midshipmen, still echoed to mirth, centring around the figure of the black steward (a prince, by his own account), charged by his young masters with stealing their pomatum. To give Lady Hamilton rest by night, the Admiral ordered the ship to be run off before the wind, with her yards braced. To his great joy, and indeed to the pleasure of all on board, this remedy appeared efficacious. She was pronounced convalescent when they made the port of Palermo, late on the last night of May.

Full strength was necessary to face the week of official leave-taking which lay before the party. On June 5 Sir William responded with a farewell banquet (also celebrating the birthday of his sovereign). At the last moment the Queen, in a flutter caused by the news that Buonaparte was crossing the Alps to recover Italy, postponed her departure for three days. Her alleged object in going to Vienna was to exert diplomatic pressure upon the Court of her daughter and son-in-law, but it was common knowledge that the King was thankful to be relieved of her company. She was taking with her her three unmarried daughters, her younger son and a *suite* calculated at about fifty. Nelson, who had sent for the *Alexander*, prophesied, "The ship will be overflowing." The Queen came on board the *Foudroyant* eventually, early on the morning of the 10th, thanked the Admiral again and again as he bent to kiss her hand, and turning to his officers, with inimitable grace, ordered their presentation to her daughters, the future Queens of Spain, France and Sardinia. The passage of the royal family to Leghorn was swift, and Parsons was in a seventh heaven, as the most ravishing of the princesses was a good sailor, and when her mother and sisters were presently prostrated, much enjoyed herself on the quarter-deck, being taught by the younger officers to use the speaking-trumpet. They came in sight of their destination on June 14, and as Tuscan guns fired a royal salute, the Queen murmured, in tones of rapture, "Leghorn! Leghorn!" "No doubt", decided Miss Knight, "as being on the way to her native land." A boat was sent ashore, with great difficulty, and the Queen began to present her parting gifts. To Lord Nelson she gave a miniature of her unheroic husband, in a setting of oak leaves and laurel,

C C

designed by herself. His Flag-Captain and Sir William Hamilton received diamond-set snuff-boxes, Lady Hamilton a diamond necklace (composed of the initials of the royal children) and all the principal officers of the *Foudroyant* liberal acknowledgment of their services. Her Majesty had also ordered her offspring to write letters of thanks to the Admiral in his own tongue, which they were all learning. Her own effort opened, " My dear and respectable Lord Nelson, To the numerous obligations, wich all Europa and we particularly have to you, is to be added our gratitude for the care you have taken to transport me." It was therefore something of an anticlimax that, owing to the weather, she was detained on board a further two days, but at the end of that time she landed, to be received by the Governor and conducted to a service in the cathedral. The doors of her ducal son-in-law's palace closed upon her, much to Nelson's relief; the Hamiltons drove on to the official residence of Mr. Wyndham, British Consul. But the Admiral's troubles, far from being at an end, were only beginning. Boarding on such a night was not easy, and when he regained his cabin, it was " truly a hog-stye ". Many of his belongings were afloat. The results of the *Foudroyant's* sharp action with the *Guillaume Tell* were apparent after rough weather, and a cold which had kept him in bed for four days of the past week was still heavy upon him. Although he knew that he would see her next day, he wrote to Lady Hamilton before he slept. He reflected that when the Commander-in-Chief saw the state of the ship, he could not object to her being sent to refit in England, or at least Gibraltar, although by the wreck of the *Culloden* and loss, by fire, of the *Queen Charlotte*, the Mediterranean fleet had recently been seriously depleted.

The Queen, on parting from him, had admitted that she was not perfectly satisfied with the news. Lord Keith's capture of Genoa on the 5th was well-confirmed, but Leghorn reports of a major encounter between the Austrian and French armies differed. At midnight on June 18 a despatch from Keith told Nelson that the Austrian Commander had signed a convention abandoning Northern Italy, as far as the Mincio, to the French, to whom were to be given up all fortresses, including Genoa. On the day that the Austrian-born Queen had come in sight of Leghorn, her countrymen had been totally defeated by Buonaparte at Marengo. Keith ordered Nelson to sail at once for Spezia, to take possession of the garrison of that place; next day a further despatch directed

that, in view of the changed situation, should the Queen wish to
return to Palermo, no British ship-of-the-line must be employed.
An earlier order, which had missed Nelson, had forbidden him
to take ships off the blockade of Malta to transport royalty.
Nelson sent off the *Alexander* and one frigate, but remained himself, with the *Foudroyant*, ready, if necessary, to evacuate " my
sacred charge ". Keith's next communication, labelled " most
confidential ", explained that he had just seen " a man who has
come from Buonaparte. Let the Queen go to Vienna as fast as
she can." Buonaparte had said publicly, " There is one Power
still in Italy to be reduced before I can give it peace ", and Keith
believed that if the French fleet got a day's start of his own,
Sicily would be captured. Nelson, who had no belief that the
Brest fleet would come into the Mediterranean, commented,
" But if they do, Lord have mercy upon them ! " With regard
to the Queen, he said, " Until I have got rid of my charge, nothing
shall separate me from her. I should feel myself a beast, could
I have a thought for anything but her comfort."

On the 24th Keith arrived in person, to land fugitives from
Genoa, and, as he informed the First Lord, " to be bored by
Lord Nelson for permission to take the Queen to Palermo, and
prince and princesses to all parts of the globe ". The Queen,
now highly hysterical, asked with tears for the *Foudroyant* to
carry her back to her husband. According to the British Consul,
whose relations with Sir William Hamilton had never been
harmonious, Keith had added to his refusal that " Lady Hamilton
had had command of the Fleet long enough ". He had already
ordered the *Foudroyant* to Minorca for repairs, and informed
Nelson, who had shifted his flag to the *Alexander*, that if he was
determined to accompany the Queen to Vienna from any Adriatic
port, he must send the *Alexander* to Mahon. The Commander-
in-Chief had further formally offered Lord Nelson and Sir William
Hamilton and party, should they wish to return to England by
sea, accommodation as passengers in the *Seahorse* frigate, or a
troopship from Malta.

On June 26 Nelson sent to his lady " a line, not to say that
I am contented or happy, for neither the one nor the other is
near true—but enough of that ! " He told her that he wore the
Order of the Crescent above that of the Bath, and that he was
going to give up two years' rent from his Sicilian estate for its
improvement. " It is my intention to fulfill a Prophecy that one
day it should be called Brontë, the Happy."

50

On the evening of July 9 the Queen and her children suddenly came on board the *Alexander*. News that the French were within twenty-four miles of the town had roused excitement, and the sister of the murdered Queen of France believed that the mob gathered below the palace windows meant to hold her and her family as hostages. Actually, the populace (who had illicitly armed themselves from the arsenal, and were strongly anti-French) were calling for Lord Nelson to be their leader against Buonaparte. Next day the idea of sailing round the peninsula to Trieste was abandoned, and the Queen returned to the palace. Lady Hamilton (translating for the Admiral) had successfully adjured the mob from the balconies to return their stolen weapons of war and depart in good order. Nelson struck his flag on the 13th, and it was announced that the whole party were about to travel overland, by way of Florence to Ancona, and there embark in small Austrian vessels for Trieste. Miss Knight heard of her future with dismay amounting to wrath, and in her farewell letter to Sir Edward Berry glanced severely at her hostess. She was astonished that the Queen, a sensible woman, should consent to such a journey. Poor Sir William Hamilton said he should die by the way, and looked likely to do so. Lord Nelson, although well, and keeping up his spirits amazingly, was clearly going upon an expedition of which he disapproved. Everyone, in short, was to be inconvenienced, because Lady Hamilton had suddenly discovered that " she cannot bear the thought of going by sea. . . . She hates the sea, and wishes to visit the different Courts of Germany." But, as Miss Knight broodingly realised, [51] " The die is cast, and go we must."

The Queen left on the 15th, and they followed two days later. A letter delivered to Nelson before the *Foudroyant* sailed was cheering :

" My Lord,
" It is with extreme grief that we find you are about to leave us. We have been along with you (though not in the same Ship) in every Engagement your Lordship has been in, both by Sea and Land ; and most humbly beg of your Lordship to permit us to go to England as your Boat's crew, in any Ship or Vessel, or in any way that may seem most pleasing to your Lordship.
" My Lord, pardon the rude style of Seamen who are but little acquainted with writing, and believe us to be, my Lord,
" Your most humble and obedient servants
" Barge's Crew of the *Foudroyant*." [52]

Two communications from Lord Spencer which had reached

him during his Leghorn stay were less calculated to bring him comfort. The First Lord expressed his regret that the state of Lord Nelson's health had obliged him to quit his station off Malta. Should the enemy come suddenly into the Mediterranean, Lord Spencer would be concerned to hear that Lord Nelson had learnt of this either on shore or in a transport at Palermo. It was by no means Lord Spencer's wish or intention to recall Lord Nelson, but he believed that all friends would join with him in deciding that Lord Nelson would be best advised to come home at once, rather than remain inactive at a foreign Court while active service was proceeding in other parts of the station.

53

CHAPTER XIII

1800–1801

(*ætat* 41–42)

STORMY HOMECOMING

I

THE four months of 1800 spent by Nelson travelling across
Europe with the Hamiltons are less satisfactorily documented
than any period of his career since he took command of his first
ship-of-the-line.   An Admiral who has struck his flag need keep
no journal.   No ships' logs disclose his whereabouts at every
hour of any day.   He was on his road home, so he scarcely wrote
a letter ; he met no brother-officers and hardly any old acquaintances.   An authoress was daily in his company, but Miss Knight
eschewed the hospitality of the Hamiltons within a week of
reaching England, and consequently lost his regard; her autobiography compresses their pilgrimage together into a few
paragraphs.   From the moment that he stepped into the first
of two large hastily purchased coaches outside the British
Consulate, Leghorn, early on the morning of July 17, amidst sun,
dust and noisy rumours of advancing French, the man almost
vanishes.   The dates of his arrival in capital cities, accounts of
pageantry in his honour, are to be found, and the figure of the
Hero of the Nile, playing his part with heraldic gesture, is just
recognisable.   The weeks spent by him in Vienna and Dresden
are annotated by letters of the Minto family and various other
English residents, less well-disposed, most of which owe their
survival to the fact that the writer once saw Nelson plain.
Scandal had outstripped him, and to many who beheld with
curiosity a caravan likely to be unacceptable in official London,
nothing but three familiar characters of the ballet was suggested.
They saw a particularly senile Pantaloon, anguished Harlequin
and superbly posturing, though massive Columbine.   Nearly a
century and a half later, English visitors traversing acres of gravel
and parquet in palaces of Austria, Bohemia and North Germany
were still sometimes startled into surmise by the statement that
the English Admiral Nelson had been entertained here by a
prince or archduke.   The many redolent, lively posting-houses
and hotels in which Tom Allen packed and unpacked his master's

much-decorated uniform had for the most part either forgotten
the fact or been replaced.

2

According to Miss Knight, the officers and ship's company of
the *Alexander* saw the last of the Admiral with additional regret
at the thought of the dangers to which he was going to expose
himself.   His first day's journey must take him within a couple
of miles of advanced enemy posts.   Another disadvantage of the
overland *route* was already obvious.   His sole experience of
Continental travel, as a private person, was a trip to Northern
France at the age of twenty-six.   His body-servant was illiterate.
Sir William Hamilton had penetrated to Muscovy, but with an
efficient staff, and when he was a much younger man.   His lady
and her mother, carefully shepherded, had twice reached Naples
from London.   Almost at once Miss Knight began to deplore
" the helplessness " of her travelling companions, and as days
passed the impression deepened.   In Vienna, to her relief, a
factotum called Oliver (long known to Sir William in Naples, and an
accomplished linguist) was engaged.   The authoress had promised
Sir Edward Berry that if she did not die on the way, or find herself
in a French prison, she would keep him informed of the Admiral's
progress, and from Ancona and Trieste she was better than her
word.   Owing more to good fortune than prudence, in her
opinion, the party, pressing on through the heat of the day and
darkness of the night, reached Florence in twenty-six hours.   On
the next stage of their journey, near Castel San Giovanni, the
leading coach overturned.   Nelson reported no injury, but both
the Hamiltons were bruised, and a wheel of the equipage was
broken.   It was repaired, but fell to pieces again at Arezzo.   The
Queen and her *suite* had now gained two days on the road, and
the French were said to be again on the move.   " It was therefore
decided ", explained Miss Knight with simple dignity, " that they
should proceed, and Mrs. Cadogan and I remain with the broken
carriage, as it was of less consequence we should be left behind, or
taken, than they."   It was true that nobody could have been
more attentive than the inhabitants of Arezzo, the most loyal
city of Tuscany, but Miss Knight was painfully struck by the fact
that only " poor Sir William " expressed distress at having to
desert her.   Lord Nelson was, apparently, lost to every consideration except the well-being of Lady Hamilton.   Two English-
women, left with a broken coach, spent three days awaiting its

reappearance, and when that glad moment came it was coupled with the tidings that the French were now about to cross their road, and Neapolitan deserters were streaming down it. A couple of soldiers were detailed by an Austrian officer to see them across the threatened stretch of country. The roads were in a wretched condition, and crowded with miserable refugees. The couple travelled day and night, and rejoined the important members of their party in a state of exhaustion. On their arrival at Ancona, they learnt that the Queen had given up the idea of going in an Austrian ship. The *Bellona*, having reduced her guns to twenty-four in order to accommodate eighty passengers, was in no condition to deal with the armed light vessels waiting off the enemy-held coast, and there had recently been a mutiny in the *Bellona*. It was decided that the Queen, Nelson and the Hamiltons should embark in the flagship of Count Voinovitsch, the officer in command of a Russian squadron, about to sail. Nelson would clearly have preferred to go with the unimportant members of the party, in a frigate commanded by an old English sea-dog, Captain Messer. (Whatever was done to turn off the conversation, the *Foudroyant* was the Admiral's constant topic, and Miss Knight heard him talking with Messer, who had once served with Lord Howe, of the manœuvres he intended if he accepted another command.) When the travellers met again, after an uneventful passage, those who had sailed with royalty had a sad tale to tell. Count Voinovitsch had never made an appearance, pleading illness, and his First Lieutenant, a Neapolitan, had displayed himself as the most ignorant and undisciplined of beings. (" Think what Lord Nelson must have felt ! ") Nelson's only comment was that a gale of wind would have sunk the ship. They had now reached safety, so far as enemy action was concerned, but un-accustomed hours and diet had taken their toll, and the physicians of Trieste had to be summoned to attend the Queen and thirty-four of her *suite*, Miss Knight and Sir William, all of them " very unwell ". " Lord Nelson, whose only comfort was in talking of ships and harbours with Captain Messer ", was recovering from his cold, but whenever he tried to take a stroll his figure collected a crowd, and his constant sigh, in a city where many houses had hung out illuminations spelling " Viva Nelson ", was, " Where is the *Foudroyant* ? " Providentially, the British Vice-Consul, a Mr. Anderson, was bound for Vienna and ready to escort the party when convalescent.

In Vienna the British Ambassador awaited their appearance

with feelings of almost unalloyed vexation. Lord Minto appreciated that the visit of the Queen of the Two Sicilies at a moment when national prestige was low was regarded by her daughter with trepidation, and by her son-in-law (who laboured under the disadvantage of being also her nephew) with as much truculence as could be summoned by an unwarlike character. The Queen was known to be inimical to crooked old Baron Thugut, the Foreign Minister (who had recently signed a treaty of subsidy with England), and to have left behind her an unappreciative mate and disturbed realm. She had not fixed any limit for her stay. Lord Minto's speech in the Lords upon the occasion of a vote of thanks to the Victor of the Nile had been a little masterpiece, and he had particularly stressed the lofty moral character of his gallant friend. A Mr. Rushout, a son of Lord Northwick, who had taken part in the royal flight from Naples, had brought incredible gossip from Palermo, confirmed by Mr. Wyndham, fresh from Florence, and judging by Nelson's letter to him, the British Ambassador feared the worst. That the Admiral should be coming in the train of Maria Carolina was bad enough, but the addition of the Hamiltons to the party was devastating. He had hoped that Nelson would not strike his flag, or at any rate not until he had taken Malta.

> " He does not seem at all conscious of the sort of discredit he has fallen into, or the cause of it, for he writes still, not wisely, about Lady Hamilton and all that. . . . He tells me of his having got the Cross of Malta for *her*, and Sir William sends home to Lord Grenville the Emperor of Russia's letter to Lady Hamilton on the occasion. All this is against them all, but they do not seem conscious."

From Palermo, Mr. Charles Lock had written home : " *She* is now gone, thank my stars ! "

In the narrow but very crowded streets of Vienna the tall houses of the great were all shuttered; only occasionally did a running footman, clad in tinsel and crowned with flowers, announce the passage of a fashionable coach. All persons of means had betaken themselves for the hot months to country houses in a landscape of wooded hills, rocky glens, smiling cornfields and fruitful vineyards. Nelson found the British Ambassador established in a palace on the slopes of St. Veit, " from Vienna, about Roehampton distance from London ". The house, which had been a monastery, possessed gardens " in the old style ", with temples, water-spouts and cascades, and needless to say the Mintos' household included many kindred spirits; several young

relatives sent to Vienna for advantages, and, as a member of the
staff, Pozzo di Borgo, in his element.

Nelson walked into one of the " extremely spacious " reception-
rooms of the Mintos' hired home, and straight back into their
hearts. One of his first utterances to his hostess was that he
owed everything to her husband. But for the interest taken in
him by Lord Minto he would never have been rewarded for his
services after his first successful action, or been placed in a
situation to obtain his second. With regard to Aboukir Bay,
he frankly admitted that the attack had been very hazardous,
" there was little room ", but knowing the men he had to trust
to, he had been sure that every Captain " would find a hole to
creep in at ". " He is just the same with us as ever ", exclaimed
Lady Minto in delight. " I don't think him altered in the least."
" I wish ", she said to him presently, " that you had the command
of the Emperor's army." " I'll tell you what ", replied Nelson,
with the schoolboy directness which later fascinated and horrified
political luminaries. " If I had, I would use only one word—
advance."

The British Ambassador prepared to present Lord Nelson and
Sir William Hamilton at the Imperial Court, while Lady Minto
presented Lady Hamilton, and Nelson appeared, " a gig, from
ribands, orders and stars ". The Crescent sent to him by the
Grand Signior was dazzling, but Lady Minto was disappointed in
the famous Chelengk, which she thought ugly in design, and
" only rose diamonds ". Having found that he had not altered
his " honest simple manners ", she was disappointed also as to
" Lady Hamilton and all that ". " He is devoted to *Emma*,
thinks her quite an *angel*, and talks of her as such to her face and
behind her back, and she leads him about like a keeper with a
bear. She must sit by him at dinner to cut his meat, and he
carries her pocket-handkerchief." But gradually, with amused
relief, the British Embassy realised that Nelson's visit to Vienna,
at a moment when England was not popular, was a great personal
triumph. The Viennese gathered all day outside the house in
which he was lodged, and when his carriage drew up at its doors,
the street became blocked. When he arrived at the playhouse,
the audience rose to applaud a hero—a thing unusual in the
Imperial city. It was told that on his road villagers had brought
their children to touch him, and when he had hoisted a little boy
in his single arm, the mother, bursting into tears, had cried out
that now her son should have a lucky life. In fashionable society

throughout Europe dress was undergoing a violent change. No
hoops were now worn in Vienna, even at Court. The classic
style, of which Lady Hamilton was a leading exponent, reigned
supreme. Dressmakers, reduced to decorating muslins with gold
and silver, hung out a portrait of the Victor of the Nile to attract
custom, and milliners produced " the Nelson cap ", in cocquelicot
velvet.

The English visitors, so kindly received, lingered in a
city notoriously romantic in the golden weeks of early autumn,
and invitations to country palaces flowed in upon them. The
Empress showed them her nursery at Schönbrunn, and Nelson,
enjoying " the noise of five fine healthy children for an hour ",
made his bow to an Archduchess aged eight, the future second
wife of Buonaparte. Prince Esterhazy, an old Naples acquaintance, was his host for four days. Nelson and the Hamiltons drove
out through the Vienna woods to Eisenstadt, after dinner on
Saturday, September 6, having spent the morning with the
Queen, who was satisfied that her son-in-law was departing that
evening to take command of his dispirited troops. On Sunday
the Prince offered a display of fireworks, on Monday a ball, and
on Tuesday a banquet, at which a hundred Hungarian grenadiers,
not one below six feet in height, waited behind the feasters'
chairs, and the toast " Admiral Lord Nelson " was followed by a
flourish of trumpets in the hall, and a salute from cannon fired in
the park. The Prince, scion of a house as musical as it was
magnificent, had arranged for four concerts during Lady
Hamilton's stay, and summoned from retirement in the Mariahilf
suburb a modest, sensible person, nearing his seventieth year,
who had been Oberkapellmeister to two successive heads of the
Esterhazy family. Mr. Franz Josef Haydn, who had met the
Hamiltons on one of his London tours, brought with him a copy
of his solo cantata for voice and pianoforte, " Ariadne in Naxos ",
and when Lady Hamilton sang, to his accompaniment, the
" Nelson Aria ", composed at her request, to words by Miss
Knight, the authoress found the effect grand. Young Lord
Fitzharris was shocked that during one of the concerts Lady
Hamilton retired to the Faro table, and, playing Lord Nelson's
cards for him, won between £300 and £400, but another member
of the house-party noticed that as soon as Haydn had ceased
conducting he hastened back to her side, and it is certain that a
maestro singularly slow to take offence left in his will engravings
of Lord Nelson and Aboukir Bay.

Miss Knight's " Ode on the Battle of the Nile " was on sale in Vienna, and Nelson presented copies to the Imperial and University libraries, decorating that given to the University with his signature—and (since he was presented with a virgin pen) with a large blot. Prince Stanislaus Poniatowski showed Lord Nelson his collection of jewels; Count Bathàny had good weather for an elaborate programme of aquatic events on the Danube, and the benevolent banker Arnstein was indefatigable in delicate attentions. On September 19, accepting a last invitation to St. Veit, Nelson repeated a suggestion that " the neglected Queen of Naples " would be gratified by even an informal call from the British Ambassador. Luckily, Lord Minto (reflecting that in some ways a great hero could be a great baby) was relieved from the necessity of excusing himself. Maria Carolina, after the departure of her best friends, was going to take a Baden cure. Her farewell letter to Lady Hamilton, prophesying that she foresaw clouds lowering upon her fortunes, sent " a thousand compliments to the Chevalier, and to the hero, and to you— everything ". She still hoped to see her " dear, dear Emma " again at Naples; in any case, her attachment and gratitude to " my friend and sister " would terminate but with her existence. " To you, I shall never change."

3

One of Nelson's last acts before leaving Vienna was to write to Davison, repeating orders to take a house or good lodgings in London—" not too large, yet one fit for my situation, to be hired by the month ". He also wrote to his lady saying that he expected to be in London about the middle of October, and desired her to be, by then, in the house which he had told Davison to engage " for the very short time I shall be in London. . . . Expect to find me a worn out old man."

The Rector of Burnham Thorpe had accepted his son's often-deferred homecoming with his usual humility. " He soars in spheres unknown to private Stations." Personally, the Rector would have preferred to stay the year round in East Anglia, alternating between Burnham Thorpe, where a curate was now installed in the Parsonage, and Roundwood, although nothing of the proposed improvements had been carried out there. His hopes had run high, last year, when his daughter-in-law had announced Yarmouth Baths instead of Brighton as her choice for the cure, but June 1799 had seen Lady Nelson in London

again, where the Walpole family, now very attentive, had lent
the lady of the Victor of the Nile their chairmen, etc., to carry
her to their Majesties' drawing-room, at which her husband had
told her to make an appearance. Eventually, only a few odd
weeks of July and October had been spent at the country house
to which Nelson continued to address letters, which reached his
lady redirected to 92, Sloane Street. A year past he had
sympathised with her complaints of the narrowness of Ipswich
society, and admiringly told her, " My dear Fanny, until you can
game (and talk scandal, that is)" her company would most
probably never be coveted by " Country Town Tabbies ".

For the winter of 1799, since the hero still tarried, what the
Rector described as " a house engaged until the Sun returns to us "
was taken at 54, St. James's Street, a modish address. Although
they were paying seven guineas a week, their accommodation did
not sound very inviting. The Rector slept in the back drawing-
room, and Lady Nelson promised " a light closet, on a floor, quite
large enough for you and my Josiah should you think it right for
him to come home ". Her letters never ceased to express hopes
for her husband's safety, but she explained that, living so quietly
and writing so often, she found little to say. She believed that
fashionable Mrs. Walpole would soon give her up, " for being too
humdrum ". She could not honestly say that she thought the
manners of Brother William at all improved. " When my lord
comes home ", prophesied William, " things will be in better
style." " My answer is, we are keeping two houses, and this is a
very expensive one." A proposal by William that she should
drop a gentle hint to Mr. Windham on the subject of recognition
for the Nelson family had thrown her into a flutter of righteous
indignation. " Some women can say and do anything ; I cannot,
and feel happy it is my disposition, by which I never get myself
into any scrapes." In September she mentioned that she had
taken her husband's niece, Susanna, to the concert, " for the
sake of driving your horses ". Miss Knight had noted at Leghorn
a remark which suggested that Lady Nelson was not an ardent
music-lover. The Admiral had said that after he and his lady
had dined with Sir William and Lady Hamilton—which he hoped
that they might do very often—" while the latter couple went to
their musical parties, he and Lady Nelson would go to bed ".

Stories of her attentions to his father were always, his lady
knew, welcome to Lord Nelson. Indeed, only in talking of the
Rector and her son did she ever display emotion. (" Rest

assured, my dear, no one thing that can be done for our good father shall be omitted.") In early March 1800 she had a fine tale to tell. Sir William Beechey was the fortunate man chosen by the Rector to paint his portrait. She had ventured to the artist's studio at her father-in-law's command, with instructions to look at the pictures, ask prices, and then, if the great man would come to an invalid. Sir William's answer had been, " No ". He really never went to any person outside the Royal Family. " But, may I ask, madam, who is the gentleman? " " Yes, sir, my Lord Nelson's father." " My God ! I would go to York to do it ! Yes, madam, directly." For a week, while sittings for what promised to be an excellent likeness proceeded, she did not know whether the result was to be a gift to the Rector's son or daughter-in-law, but presently it became clear that the surprise—a profound secret—was for the Victor's return. In the last letter from his wife received by Nelson before he left Leghorn, delighted at the news that Lord Keith had sailed (since she believed that this meant that her husband would come home), she stated, *apropos* of nothing, " I can with safety put my hand on my heart and say it has been my study to please and make you happy." The Rector also sent praises of her to a quarter where, if disturbing rumours were to be believed, they were very necessary. " I well remember, that on my receiving a wound, you promised to heal it, by giving to me another daughter. Indeed, you have, Lady Nelson's kindness as a friend, a nurse, a daughter, I want words to express." But he set off for Round-wood this spring, to assure himself that the shrubs were all trimmed up to receive my Lord, alone, but for servants.

News of relations, acquaintances and the fashions helped to fill Lady Nelson's dutiful sheets. " Truly, my chit-chat is hardly worth reading, but, such as it is, you must accept it." In London, powder had quite gone out. " You cannot think how much Lady Martin admires my black locks." Her chit-chat included constant fears of over-spending, and the hard facts that beef was 9s. 4d. the stone, and coals were very dear. It seems that the recent publications noted in Lord Nelson's cabin by Miss Knight must have been sent out at his order, for not a single mention of a book is to be found in the correspondence of a lady who declared Cale her favourite vegetable, and only noticed the weather in the streets. Her health was a constant topic, and in October 1799, when a young officer, who kept a chaise waiting at the door, called to say that he had left Lord Nelson quite well at

Palermo on September 9, the joyful surprise was altogether too much for her nerves. " It had such an effect on me that I could not hear or see, and was obliged to call in our good father, who made many enquiries."

Loving enquiries from his lady for a son who did not write much had caused the Admiral many pangs during a painful period in his career. His directions when sending Josiah down to Constantinople in charge of the Turkish Ambassador had gone into detail on the subject of discipline, and a few weeks later, on learning that his application to Lord St. Vincent on behalf of his stepson had been successful, and that Captain Nisbet was " on his own bottom now ", his anxiety had become acute. " I *wish* he may deserve it; the thought half kills me." His fears were soon realised. Apologies to an indignant St. Vincent were called for within four months. Josiah, finding the state of a Captain lonely, had fallen into the habit of messing in the gun-room. A reprimand in the handwriting of his stepfather's secretary recalled him to his senses, and in his abject and somewhat disarming letter promising to reform all his conduct, he declared that he well knew his dear father was the only person in this world that had his true interest at heart. After another four months, when sending H.M.S. *Thalia* to Admiral Duckworth with regrets that he could say " nothing in her praise, inside or out ", Nelson hoped, " Perhaps you may be able to make something of Captain Nisbet; he has, by his conduct, almost broke my heart." Silence fell for nine months. Then in June 1800, at a moment when Nelson could stand very little more criticism, came a shattering letter. Knowing the near connection of Captain Nisbet to his Lordship, Admiral Duckworth had to divulge with the gravest concern that H.M.S. *Thalia* had joined his squadron at Gibraltar in a low state of discipline. He proceeded to enumerate such facts as the Principal Medical Officer (above three months under arrest) asking for a court-martial on his Captain, and the First Lieutenant ready with a string of complaints, designed for Lord Nelson's eye, some of which, to say the least, would be sufficient to destroy the reputation of Captain Nisbet. Needless to add, while the Captain and his officers were visibly at daggers drawn, minor characters had taken liberties, rightly resented by a young gentleman of a warm disposition. Duckworth believed that possibly his Lordship's having given the First Lieutenant authorisation to advise an inexperienced Captain might in some degree be responsible for the present dilemma. He had taken action which he was confident would result in the whole affair being buried in oblivion, and after some labour—having represented to all parties that they were at fault—had arranged a compromise, by which the surgeon was released and requests for a public investigation had been dropped. There could not, however, be two opinions as to the necessity for the parties being divided, and, if he might suggest, the state of H.M.S. *Thalia* justifying her being paid off, his prescription for Captain Nisbet was "a few months with Lady Nelson ".

6

4

Lord Nelson and party arrived in Prague after dark on September 27, and the Hôtel Rothes Haus was splendidly illuminated in their honour, but, as Miss Knight afterwards noted, the host did not forget to charge for the lights on their bill. The Archduke Charles, who was sitting in the Hradčany, "as immovable as the Lady in ' Comus ' ", feasted his aunt's friends on Nelson's birthday. It had been hoped that he was to assume the chief military command, but Lord Minto's staff knew that epilepsy was one of the reasons for his unemployment.

A passage to Dresden by water had been advised by the Mintos, and for two days the English tourists proceeded at a gentle pace, in a canopied boat, down an alternately shining and sombre river, presented with a succession of views of forest-clad crags and mouldering mediæval castles, in the high romantic style dear to the artists called upon to decorate the panelling of contemporary palaces. After dark, the Admiral played cribbage with the ex-Ambassador.

The party arrived in the small but picturesque Saxon capital in holiday spirits, and took up residence in the Hôtel de Pologne, whence they joyfully apprised the British Minister of their arrival. They were aware that the many beautiful children whom they found running about the garden of his summer villa, like so many Cupids and Psyches, were the offspring of a second wife, of humble birth. Mr. Hugh Elliot had divorced a fascinating but faithless German heiress some years previously. It is possible that they had not been forewarned that Lord Minto's far more handsome and brilliant younger brother was already a disappointed man. Amongst his talents was that of finding himself generally superior to his company. In Dresden, languidly described by him as "a good sofa to repose upon ", they savoured a foretaste of the reception to be accorded to them in some circles in London. The Elector, whose gaze was bovine, the Electress, who had discontinued balls while Europe was in its present sad state, were so strictly bound by etiquette that when the Elector's uncle had lain dying they had been unable to visit him because he was not living within the walls of their palace. Sunday was their usual evening for receiving guests, but it soon appeared that no such assembly was to be held this Sunday, and an invitation from Madame de Loos, wife of the First Minister, did not include Lady Hamilton. " Sir," said Lord Nelson to Mr. Elliot, " if there is any difficulty of that sort, Lady Hamilton will knock the Elector down ", whereupon, after a flustered call from the humourless British Minister, Madame de Loos asked the whole party to dine.

A young Irish widow, herself an authoress, musician and beauty, had been playing chess with Mr. Elliot when he received the dire news of Lord Nelson's approach, and Mrs. Melesina St. George had been called to the rescue. She let Lady Hamilton borrow several of her gowns, but accepted gushing praise of them with reserve, as she thought the lady's own taste in dress frightful. (" Her waist is absolutely between her shoulders.") She listened without sympathy to indiscreet after-dinner doubts whether Queen Charlotte would condescend to receive the ex-Ambassadress, and after accompanying Lady Hamilton upon the piano, elegantly explained that she had never before " seen or heard of, the sailor's way " of ending all songs with " a bumper, and the last drop on the nail ". (To the Elliots she confided alarm at the quantity of champagne enjoyed by all the visitors.) She came, at Lady Hamilton's request, to see Lord Nelson attired for his audience with the Elector, " a perfect constellation of stars and orders ". But none of the party grew upon her: she found Sir William's affectation of youthful agility ridiculous, Miss Knight a person who never opened her mouth except to flatter her friends, Lady Hamilton more " stamped with the manners of her first situation than one would suppose, after having represented Majesty, and lived in good company, for fifteen years ", Lord Nelson " a willing captive ", and Mrs. Cadogan " what one might expect ".

The British Minister's guests occupied his box at the Opera, and were escorted to view the Elector's collection of porcelain, which included the Dragon China made for none but the electoral family, many accurate representations of bouquets, and many figures of fine ladies as shepherdesses, with their hats on one side,

D D

and attendant shepherds, dogs and sheep, all partaking in what witty Mrs. St. George called "the general smirk". The Court artist, Johann Heinrich Schmidt, was summoned to the Hôtel de Pologne, and obtained sketches for pastels of Lady Hamilton wearing her decoration and Lord Nelson in full-dress uniform. Two breakfasts, after which Lady Hamilton performed her "Attitudes", amidst applause, were endured by Mr. Elliot; then, having heard from a King's Messenger that a frigate awaited his guests at Hamburg, he "ventured to announce the fact". On his return from seeing what he called "Antony and Moll-Cleopatra" embark upon the Elbe, he plaintively begged his wife and Mrs. St. George, "Now don't let us laugh tonight. Let us all speak in whispers, and be very, very quiet." ⁷

He never again played host to Lady Hamilton, of whom he prophesied incorrectly, "She will captivate the Prince of Wales, whose mind is as vulgar as her own, and play a great part in England"; but, by an unkind turn of Fortune's wheel, in May 1803, on his appointment to the post once held by Sir William Hamilton, he was obliged to Lord Nelson for a passage in the *Victory*, and, as his young family now numbered twelve, was thankful to place two fine boys as midshipmen in the flagship of the Commander-in-Chief in the Mediterranean. The sequel to his Neapolitan appointment was sad, for he found Naples intolerable, but became so indiscreet a champion of Lord Nelson's and Lady Hamilton's, "Queen to the backbone", that he was summarily re-called. He could never again be employed diplomatically, but since the brother of Lord Minto (by that date Governor-General in India) could not be left without some honourable post, he was successively Governor of the Leeward Islands and Madras.

To Mrs. St. George, Fate was kinder. At the age of thirty-five she remarried, and became what Nature had intended, a happy wife and mother. She suffered four painful years of detention in France, as a prisoner of Buonaparte, together with a second husband, six years her junior, and after the births of nine children and the loss of four, became so stout as to abandon all interest in her appearance, but (inspired by the example of Elizabeth Fry) a benevolent figure. Her journal was published in 1862 by an eminent and devoted son, and the lamentable passages recording her meeting in 1800 with "a man deeply entangled" were quoted in every succeeding life of Nelson. But no biographer drew attention to the fact that in 1814, after reading the anonymously produced *Letters of Lord Nelson to*

Lady Hamilton, she pronounced Lord Nelson's sentiments, on subjects unconnected with his fatal attachment, to be elevated, liberal and candid. He appeared, indeed, "indifferent to the common objects of pursuit".

8

5

In North Germany the riverside inns were poor. The party found small rooms with sanded floors, no carpets or upholstered furniture, and but scanty fare. On their arrival in Hamburg, after a journey of eleven days, they were disappointed to discover that Mr. Elliot's information had been incorrect. Nelson wrote to England to ask for a frigate, and they settled down to waiting, and more feasting. Their only old acquaintance in the place was a link with Nelson's Jamaican service—Mrs. Parish, mother-in-law of Hercules Ross; but the British Consul at Altona was a brother of Captain Cockburn. Their welcome was warm. The English merchants of the town arranged a Grand Gala, consisting of dinner, concert, supper and ball. Baron de Breteuil gave a breakfast, at which all the other guests were titled *émigrés* with the manners of the *vieille cour*. Towards its close a short, shabby gentleman, with a military air, stumped in, as if by accident. General Dumouriez had, in fact, been very curious to meet Admiral Nelson. The Victor of Jemappes was living in retirement, having refused to enter the service of the First Consul, and was supporting himself by his pen. Nelson, who had not forgotten what he called " the pinch ", managed at a further meeting to secure the acceptance, by a brave officer, of a gift of £100. An elderly German poet called Klopstock, engaged in writing sublime odes, not to be understood of the people, also welcomed the English party, and while they were in his parlour, an unexplained reverend person, attired in canonicals, entered to them, with a book in his hand. Although upwards of seventy, this country pastor had journeyed forty miles to obtain the signature of a Christian hero on the fly-leaf of the Bible belonging to his village church.

The travellers had set out from Leghorn, in July, in intolerable heat. At Hamburg, in late October, candles flickered in hotel rooms at midday, the air was distractingly raw, and beneath banks of fog the sea was in motion, and noisy. Miss Knight, who had for some time been "uneasy on many accounts", went shopping with the Admiral, and assisted with pleasure in the choice of splendid lace to decorate a Court gown for Lady Nelson.

On the last day of October, their patience being at an end, the party sailed from Cuxhaven in the *King George* mail-packet, and after a very stormy passage landed at Yarmouth at noon on Thursday, November 6. The weather was thoroughly English, but so was their welcome. " The frugality of our Administration " in failing to send a frigate to fetch the Victor of the Nile had been resented in Norfolk. Bells began to peal, stout volunteers were ready to drag his carriage up from the quayside to " The Wrestler's Arms ", and the band of the Infantry quartered in the town struck up a national air as Lord Nelson appeared on a balcony of an inn overlooking a harbour in which every vessel had colours flying. While rain fell steadily, Lady Hamilton stood by his side, attired in a muslin gown designed for a Sicilian *fête*, with a border of oak-leaves and laurel enclosing the words " Nelson " and " Brontë ". The Mayor and Corporation, " with promptitude which did them credit ", shrugged into their regalia, and came to present the Freedom of the town and escort the Admiral to a religious service of thanksgiving. Before he had set out on his journey across a continent suddenly disturbed again by Buonaparte, an officer who had gone to sea at a tender age, and left part of his heart with the *Foudroyant*, had faced facts. When blue dusk filled the bottle-end windows of a cosy seaport hostelry, outside which muskets crackled and bonfires spluttered, two letters in his hand were already in the post. He had written to the Secretary to the Admiralty announcing his health perfectly restored and his desire to serve immediately. " I trust that my necessary journey, by land, from the Mediterranean, will not be considered as a wish to be a moment out of active service."

His second letter was addressed to " Lady Nelson, Round-wood, Ipswich, Suffolk " :

⁹

"Nov. 6th, 1800.

" My dear Fanny,
    "We are this moment arriv'd and the post only allows me to say that we shall set off tomorrow noon, and be with you on Saturday, to dinner. I have only had time to open one of your letters, my visits are so numerous. May God bless you and my Dear Father, and believe me ever, your affectionate

"Brontë Nelson of the Nile.

"Sir [*sic*] and Lady Hamilton beg their best regards, and will accept your offer of a bed. Mrs. Cadogan and Miss Knight with all the servants, will proceed to Colchester.

" I beg my Dear Father to be assured of my Duty and every tender feeling of a son."

6

Next morning, an unheralded corps of cavalry drew up outside the inn in which the Admiral had spent the night, and
escorted him, not only to the town's end, but to the boundary of
the county. Ipswich was equally ready with improvised
compliments, and in Colchester the streets had been lined ever
since the news of his arrival at Yarmouth had become known;
but when the carriage containing Lord Nelson and his friends made
a short détour in the neighbourhood of Ipswich, on a late autumn
afternoon of heavy clouds enlivened by occasional lightning, no
one in the party had any expectation of enjoying more than a
private welcome that night.   His attempt to show hospitality to
the Hamiltons at his small country house, however, was a failure.
At Roundwood silence reigned, and it presently became known
that Lord Nelson's father, who had been living there alone, had
left early on Friday morning to join her ladyship in town.   Letters
for Lady Nelson were being forwarded to 64, Upper Seymour
Street, Portman Square.   It was true that, in his letter from
Vienna, the Admiral had told his lady not to attempt to come to
Portsmouth, but to be ready to greet him in the house which
Davison was taking for them; but this address could not mean
that she had obeyed those instructions, as he had particularly
told Davison to avoid the Portman Square district.   The carriage
bringing Nelson home turned away down the short drive from a
house in which he had never spent a night and was never to see
again, and the journey to London was resumed by easy stages.

He met his wife and father, eventually, in the hall of Nerot's
Hotel, 17, King Street, St. James's, at 3 o'clock on the
afternoon of Sunday, November 9, to the accompaniment of a
thunderstorm.

The worst storm since 1703 had been threatening ever since
he had landed, and the tempest broke over London when he was
two hours short of the capital.   Several members of suburban
congregations, returning from Sunday morning service, were
killed by falling masonry, and outside Kensington Palace trees
were torn up by their roots.   After a few days came country tales
of drowned infants and cattle, and even a casualty list from Paris.

" The Arrival of Lord Nelson and Sir William Hamilton " was
a heading likely to sell many copies of a journal, and one had
printed in full, on Saturday morning, " Miss Knight's clever
song " the " Ode to Lady Hamilton on her Birthday ", boldly

substituting " Emma " for the discreet " Delia " of the original. A reporter from the *Courier* was on the spot when " Sir William Hamilton's German travelling carriage " ended its long journey at last, in a dark, narrow street, amongst huzzas from drenched admirers. He noted that Lord Nelson (looking extremely well) was wearing full uniform, two medals and two stars, and that although both the Admiral and the ex-Ambassador were thin in person, " Lady Hamilton looked charmingly, and is a very fine woman ". A black female, attendant upon Lady Hamilton, followed the party into the hotel, and ten minutes later the Duke of Queensberry, to enquire for Sir William Hamilton, was announced. The Honourable Charles Greville, nephew to Sir William, had called earlier, on the same errand. The Nelsons and Hamiltons dined together at 5 o'clock, and at 7.30 the vigil of a damp but dogged gentleman of the Press was over for the day. Lord Nelson had left the hotel for the Admiralty, to report to the First Lord, followed after a short interval, in a separate carriage, by Lady Nelson, bound, it was hazarded, for a friendly hour with Lady Spencer.

In Albemarle Street, meanwhile, unnoticed by any reporter, the burly and concerned figure of Sir Thomas Troubridge was approaching a " family " hotel, in which Miss Cornelia Knight had just dined with Mrs. Cadogan. The Commodore, who was on his way to take up his appointment as Captain of the Channel Fleet, under the command of Lord St. Vincent, had come to suggest to a spinster lady that she had better dissociate herself from the Hamilton party immediately. The welcome given by John Bull to Nelson was by no means echoed in well-informed high places. The daughter of a deceased Admiral thanked a true friend for his advice, and flew next morning to the protection of the wife of the Secretary to the Admiralty. " Mrs. Nepean made me take possession of a room in her house till her children come home for the holidays."

On the same evening Lord St. Vincent was writing to Nepean, from a west-country house :

> " It is evident from Lord Nelson's letter to you on his landing, that he is doubtful of the propriety of his conduct. I have no doubt he is pledged to getting Lady H. received at St. James's, and everywhere, and that he will get into much *brouillerie* about it. Troubridge says Lord Spencer talks of putting him in a two-decked ship. If he does, he cannot give him a separate command, for he cannot bear confinement to any object; he is a partisan; his ship always in the most dreadful disorder, and never can become an officer fit to be placed where I am. . . ."

10

All through the night of Nelson's arrival at a close fashionable hotel of St. James's distant thunder growled and winds sighed. It appears that the Admiral had an awful homecoming in every sense. Two brief notes from his saintly father, announcing to other members of the family the safe arrival of the hero, breathe joy tempered by bewilderment. Lady Nelson had, with her own eyes, begun to appreciate what she called " the wonderful change, past belief ". Her husband's own pen had informed her of his boundless admiration for another man's wife. Gradually, after his triumphal return to Naples from the Nile, he had become a perfunctory correspondent. A letter in which he had been mad enough to tell her of the marvellous " improvement " wrought in her rough and mannerless son by Lady Hamilton had been angrily annotated by a doting mother. He had arrived after long delay, involving professional reprimand, in the company of an enchantress of doubtful antecedents, and beyond doubt displaying every symptom of a man in the condition generally known as " madly in love ". A delicate lady, who would have been at home in the pages of a novel by Miss Austen, found herself called upon to play a part in a tragedy in the style of Shakespeare's " dark period ". For as long as possible Lord St. Vincent had tried to pass off lightly a sad state of affairs. Unhappily attempting the character of the man of the world, he had admitted that " the Almighty had been in a glorious mood when he had formed Emma ", and alluded to the couple as " a pair of sentimental fools ". Devoted officers of the Mediterranean squadron had been amazed, and naturally had not much relished, the spectacle of their Chief with his Famous Woman in tow, behaving with all the ingenuousness of a lad in his first affair, changing colour like a maiden when she sang of his victories, and confiding to all and sundry praises of her enormous kindness, angelic nature and brilliant understanding. Some of those who loved him best protested to the last that a devotion so openly expressed was innocent, and were persuaded that " the attraction between her and our hero was something of a kindred enthusiasm in the cause of their Country ", but by the time of his arrival in London the cynics had no doubt that the struggle between love and duty was over, and they were right, though they much under-estimated its violence and duration. It had lasted from September 1798 until February 1800. " Ah ! my dear friend," he wrote a year later, " I did well remember the 12th February, and also the two months afterwards. I never shall forget them and never be sorry for the consequences."

The time had now come when all persons important to him had to make up their minds that the situation was serious, and they were beholding, not a preternaturally drawn-out Mediterranean *amourette*, but a passion which would be remembered with the name of Nelson. Hugh Elliot, at Dresden, had not been wide of the mark when he slightingly referred to " Antony and Moll-Cleopatra ", but at the time hardly any spectator of events realised this. There is no satisfactory contemporary authority for the often repeated statement that " Lady Nelson's reception of her husband was extremely cold and mortifying ", but that ¹⁵ their remaining few weeks together were miserable is borne out by his outburst to Davison in the following March, " sooner than live the unhappy life I did when last I came to England, I would stay abroad for ever ". Lady Hamilton, for her part, was soon ¹⁶ confiding in Mrs. William Nelson (with whom she formed one of her " friendships at first sight " scorned by Mrs. St. George) that on meeting the terrified glare of Nelson's wife " their [*sic*] was an antipathy not to be described ". She also believed that the hero's ¹⁷ lady had not asked him a single question as to the Battle of the Nile, but had preserved for his delectation all the scurrilous passages reflecting on his conduct at the Court of the Two Sicilies which had been quoted from Jacobin journals by English newspapers. ¹⁸

The Hamiltons had been invited by the millionaire William Beckford (whose wife, Lady Margaret Gordon, had been a cousin of Sir William) to consider his house, 22, Grosvenor Square, their own. Having discovered that Beckford really meant this, Sir William, who was now more than £2,000 in debt to Nelson, gratefully moved from Nerot's. The house taken by Davison for Nelson was 17, Dover Street, and Davison had interpreted his friend's instructions liberally, for he had taken the house for a year, and though it was not small, he had staffed it so amply that the astonished Rector commented, " The Suite of nobility is long." He found his son " active and well, but always on the wing. I myself can only see him for a moment. He has asked for employment."

Although they were no longer under the same roof, the Nelsons and Hamiltons met daily, and since the situation, agonising to Lady Nelson, was *piquante*, reporters chronicled every appearance of the family party. In any case, the arrival of Nelson had been a godsend to the Press of a capital disturbed by bread riots, and his movements from the moment that he landed can be traced from many sources. November 9th was a Sunday, therefore the festivities of Lord Mayor's Day were transferred to the 10th. On the Monday morning following the Great Storm Sir William sought out Lord Grenville at the Foreign Office, and Nelson, after reporting at the Admiralty, repaired to the Navy Office in the Strand, in which neighbourhood he was recognised and mobbed. Davison's carriage rescued him for a private expedition. They went together to a large dog shop in Holborn, and it appears that a dog of strong personality captured the imagination of an officer who had never before been commanded to make such a purchase, for " poor Nile ", although provided with a silver collar announcing that he was " Nileus ", the property of the Right Hon. Lord Nelson, strayed, or was stolen, within six weeks. Advising Lady Hamilton as to a further companion, Nelson suggested that a less active dog might be more amenable to London life. He could not describe his unlucky choice as " a domestic animal ". He went on to watch the procession of peers to the House of Lords from the Duke of Clarence's apartments, and later that winter's day was guest of honour at the Lord Mayor's Banquet. His carriage was dragged by the populace from Ludgate Hill to the Guildhall doors, where seamen had been admitted to a prominent position by an affected mob. " The illustrious Tar, landing from his carriage ", shook several " old Agamemnons " warmly by the hand, and displayed unerring memory for names and services. A pompous scene followed, at which gold plate and show fruit were lit by the soft glow of many candles, while London fog settled outside. Nelson's reply to the oration of the City Chamberlain was brief, but having been conducted to his station under a triumphal arch, he " hoisted the sword of the value of two hundred guineas " voted to him by the City, and promised that he hoped soon to use it, to reduce to due limits Britain's implacable and inveterate enemy.

John Bull was vociferous, but the Press had provocatively announced that morning that Lady Hamilton, who was a Woman of the Bedchamber to the Queen of Naples and had been decorated by the Czar, was to be presented at the next drawing-room, while, in fact, the only member of the royal family to express any desire to behold her was the Prince of Wales. Their Majesties, who had been adamant on Sir William's marriage, had issued no such command, and Sir William, to Nelson's dismay, was resignedly prepared to make his bow alone, at a Court which would never countenance his wife—" and such a wife ! "

Accordingly, on the morning following the Lord Mayor's Banquet, Sir William Hamilton, on his return from the Court of Naples, and Baron Nelson of the Nile and Burnham Thorpe, upon striking his flag in the Mediterranean, attended a *levée*. At St. James's Palace the scene was unchanged, but the King, after a curtly expressed hope that his health was improved, turned from the Victor of the Nile without waiting for his answer, and engaged in nearly half an hour's earnest conversation with a military officer. " It could not be ", wrote Collingwood furiously from Cawsand Bay, " about *his* successes."   20

Nelson, after this experience, arrived to dine at Admiralty House looking like thunder.   Lady Spencer's duty dinner-parties had never been renowned for their conviviality, and in November 1800, guests at her board were being rousingly presented with the choice of a potato or rice in lieu of the staff of life.   On the last occasion that she had entertained the Nelsons, the Lady of the Admiralty had been ruffled by a homely request that a husband might sit next to his wife.   After this evening she announced, " Such a contrast I never beheld ! "   At table, according to her spirited description, Lady Nelson, " perhaps inadvisedly, but with good intention ", pushed across to her lord a wine-glass filled with walnuts, which she had attentively peeled for a one-armed man. He thrust it aside so awkwardly that it hit a dish.   Lady Spencer remained mistress of herself, though china fell, but Lady Nelson burst into tears, and afterwards, in a stately and frigid drawing-room, while the gentlemen in the adjoining dining-room settled to their wine and talk, " she told me how she was situated ".   Lady   21 Nelson's reserve broke seldom, but the wife of an officer applying for employment could not have chosen a more disastrous scene or *confidante*, for the tongue of Lady Spencer, a high-priestess of the conventions, was dreaded even by her *débutante* nieces.   It   22 may have been upon the Nelsons' homecoming together, after this dreadful entertainment, that an incident gloatingly described by Harrison took place, and the Admiral, " in a state of absolute despair and distraction ", set out on foot, alone, to spend the remainder of the night wandering the streets of London.   " He rambled as far as the city ; perambulated Fleet Market, Blackfriars Bridge etc., and, exhausted with fatigue, as well as overpowered by mental suffering, reached the house of Sir William Hamilton in Grosvenor Square about four in the morning."   Harrison claims that the ex-Ambassador suggested to his unexpected guest " to seek that happiness in his professional pursuits which it

23 seemed unlikely he would ever find at home." Meanwhile, as far as the world could see, the Admiral was enjoying the pleasures of leave.

Davison gave a banquet in honour of his celebrated friend at his mansion in St. James's Square, where every delicacy of the season was served up, and the other guests were the Prince of Wales, five Cabinet Ministers (headed by Mr. Pitt), the First Lord and a couple of Admirals. The East India Company feasted Lord Nelson at the London Tavern. It was known that he was sitting to Mrs. Damer, the aristocratic sculptress, for a bust to be placed in the Guildhall. On December 8 he sat to an artist called De Koster for a little sketch, of which engravings were soon on sale at Brydon's, the printseller most affected by him. The profile likeness was not flattering, but he said it was the best he had yet seen, adding doubtfully that not one picture of him seemed to resemble another. When he began to visit theatres, the discovery of his figure in the stage box caused the audience to rise and applaud until he came to the front of the box and acknowledged their greeting. At a performance of " The Mouth of the Nile " at Covent Garden his lady was observed on his left hand in an undescribed *toilette* and Lady Hamilton glowing in dark grey silk in the seat of honour. Behind them sat as dissimilar a trio as ever went to the play together—the Rector of Burnham Thorpe, Sir William Hamilton and Captain Thomas Masterman Hardy.

On the 20th Lord Nelson took his seat in the House of Peers, and after a dinner and concert given on the following night by the Hamiltons in Grosvenor Square, at which minor royalty were present, Lady Nelson was reported slightly indisposed; but she was at her post again four days later, to witness Kemble as Rolla in " Pizarro " at Drury Lane. An announcement that Lord Nelson had taken seats had filled the house to suffocation, and when his party entered the stage box at 6.10, it was eagerly scanned. It comprised his father and wife, the Hamiltons and the Neapolitan Princess Castelcicala. Lady Nelson was dressed in purple satin, with white sleeves and a turban with two up-standing ostrich plumes. Lady Hamilton's classic draperies were all white. Lord Nelson clapped Rolla heartily during the first act, and Mr. Kemble, playing up to a great house, over-reached himself. (" The pantaloons were cut through and the knee bled profusely.") During the second act, at the conclusion of the scene in which Rolla and Elvira plan the death of Alonzo, a scream from the stage box threw the house into confusion. Lady

Nelson had shrieked and fainted. Her father-in-law and Lady Hamilton took her home, but her husband saw the piece out. She made her last publicly recorded appearance in his company a few days later, when they drove down together with the Hamiltons (who were bound upon a week-end visit) to dine with Lord Abercorn at his Stanmore villa. Nelson set out with his friends for a mock-Gothic Yuletide at Beckford's Wiltshire country seat but without his lady. The invitation to a national hero from an admirer who pronounced himself " dead to the world in general ", but still " a genuine Briton ", had reached him *via* Lady Hamilton, and had not included his wife.

At Salisbury, on a very foggy day, he received the freedom of that city enclosed in a box of Heart of Oak, and amongst the crowd outside the Council House recognised old shipmates, one of whom had actually assisted at his amputation. The people of a cathedral city, even before learning that the Mayor had been presented with a very liberal benefaction for the poor of their town, decided that " Lord Nelson unites a feeling and generous heart, a quick discernment of occasion, and popularity of manners." Mounted volunteers, with a band of thirty playing " Rule Britannia ", led his carriage at a processional pace through the park of Fonthill to its grand entry, where Beckford stood posed under a tower 278 feet high, in a marble hall, surrounded by local gentry and Londoners of distinction, including Mr. Wyatt, the architect, and Mr. West, President of the Royal Academy. For three days of poor weather a large house-party enjoyed the splendours of a modern palace, built at a cost of a quarter of a million derived from West India property, and the brilliant conversation of a spoilt man. In the evenings the voice of Lady Hamilton mingled with that of the famous Banti, just returned from a successful French season. This character, born Brigitta Giorgi, whose powerful soprano had first startled a Paris boulevard *café* a quarter of a century earlier, became, together with her husband, a constant guest at the Hamiltons' London house, and Nelson provided for one of her sons by taking the boy to sea with him, a step which he had reason to regret, as the offspring of a *prima donna* and a professional dancer, reared in Continental hotels, proved " a knowing one ".

On Tuesday, December 23, the Fonthill festivities were transferred to the ancient Abbey in the grounds. The party drove through plantations of illuminated conifers, in eleven carriages, accompanied by mounted men carrying torches, to an edifice where they were served with a mediæval *menu* planned by a *cordon bleu* in a groined hall known as " the Cardinal's parlour ". Buffets loaded with remarkably heavy silver plate were lit by a fire of cedar logs and pine-cones, blazing in a tremendous hearth, and after the meal the company were directed up a winding staircase, upon which " at mysterious intervals " hooded figures, bearing fat wax tapers, stood sentinel. They found themselves in a saloon decorated in yellow damask, as foil for black, scarlet and grass-green Oriental lacquer furniture, and (having been refreshed by a further collation of spiced wine and confectionery served in gold baskets, in a library adjoining a gallery 250 feet long) they adjourned to a " great room " in which Lady Hamilton at once appeared upon a space prepared for a display of her " Attitudes ". Her representation of Agrippina bearing the ashes of Germanicus in a golden urn won general applause, but a later performance in which she played the part of a tender mother, to a little girl drawn from the audience, was so lifelike as to draw tears from many beholders.

24

On the 26th, amidst the first snow of the season, the party broke up, the Hamiltons to return to Grosvenor Square until their new purchase, No. 23, Piccadilly, was ready to receive them, and Nelson to 17, Dover Street. The London in which his wife and father had spent Christmas without him had been, by all accounts, unrelievedly gloomy. Miss Knight, who had been accustomed upon the Continent to hear the English capital acclaimed as the most flourishing and potent in Europe, had been horrified by the shortness and darkness of London days, and by fashionables who spoke of " the impossibility of going on ", and their desire for peace at almost any price. When she had asked a shivering Italian caller, " How do you like London ? " she had hardly been surprised by his reply, " I daresay, madam, I shall think it a very fine city when it comes to be daylight ". She had withdrawn from all connection with the Nelson and Hamilton circle, and for a month past had steadily refused invitations to Grosvenor Square. Princess Castelcicala, realising that her English acquaintances were *mal vus* at the Court of their native land, was following suit. In Naples and Palermo it had been indulgently accepted that both the British Ambassador and his lady were " bewitched by the gallant Admiral ", but in London not only the Press was busy with the names of Nelson and Hamilton. James Gillray, the caricaturist, whose sketches, exhibited in Mrs. Humphrey's print shop in St. James's Street, always gathered a

25

crowd, and who had produced a very complimentary cartoon of
the Hero of the Nile two years past, was again at work, and in his
most brutal vein. His first comment upon a *ménage* which was
attracting criticism, published on February 6, 1801, and labelled
" Dido in Despair ", depicted a lady of mountainous figure
lamenting with outstretched arms and large tears the departure
of a fleet, visible through the open window of a bedroom littered
with classic busts and unpaid bills, in which a night-capped
septuagenarian still slumbered. Below this sketch ran the
doggerel verse—

> " Ah ; where, and oh ! where is my gallant sailor gone ?
> He's gone to fight the French for George upon the throne.
> He's gone to fight the French, t'lose t'other arm and eye,
> And left me with old Antiquity, to lay me down and cry."

A companion picture, published six days later, and called
" Cognoscenti contemplating the Beauties of the Antique ",
represented Sir William, senile and slippered, peering through his
spectacles in a gallery where the exhibits included likenesses of
himself as Claudius and of his lady as the Serpent of the old
Nile, pledging her Antony in a bumper.

At 5 a.m. on the first Saturday of the New Year Nelson arose
in the lowest of spirits to struggle into uniform by artificial light
before embarking for the parish church of Addington, Kent.
" I will assuredly attend the remains in my own carriage." He
left his house wishing that the funeral could have been his own.
A note was sent to Grosvenor Square, saying that he hoped to call
that night, and the redundant staff of Dover Street were notified
that his lordship would not be home to supper. The death of 26
his old sea-daddy had not been unexpected. Judging by Lady
Nelson's accounts, Captain Locker had been failing for some time.
Indeed, it had been almost a relief to her when the old gentleman
had ceased to call, to desire her to say everything that was
affectionate and kind on his behalf to Admiral Nelson, always
coupled with the explanation that although he still had his legs,
he could not use his hand to write nowadays.   His habit of saying
the same thing twice over in a visit had tended, she thought, to
irritate the Rector, who, although he was not bodily active,
retained a perfectly clear brain, and disliked being called " old "
Mr. Nelson.   " Child," he would instruct his daughter Susanna's
offspring, " nothing is old but cows and horses." 27

7

Nelson, whose promotion to Vice-Admiral of the Blue had been gazetted on New Year's Day, 1801, had known since mid-November that he was to be employed again, and " mine will not, I hope," he wrote bitterly to Berry, " be an *inactive* service ". The word repeated in Lord Spencer's letters of reproof received by him at Leghorn had not been forgotten. Ball, notifying him of the fall of Valetta, told him that the Mediterranean Fleet much hoped for his appointment in succession to Lord Keith, who was said to have quarrelled with their Lordships and asked to be re-called ; but Nelson knew that second-in-command of the Channel Fleet was his probable fate. Hardy was to be his Captain, and St. Vincent, from Torbay, told him that the *San Josef* had long been in his eye as the most appropriate ship for the officer who had boarded her on Valentine's Day. There was at the moment an additional awkwardness in the prospect of serving under his old Chief, for their respective agents were still engaged in a long-drawn-out tussle on the subject of prize money. The solicitors employed by Davison on his friend's behalf were Messrs. Booth and Haslewood of Craven Street, and on a morning shortly before Nelson left London, one of the partners of that firm was invited to the breakfast-table of a man whose days were overcrowded with appointments. Mr. William Haslewood was the witness of a painful scene in which Lady Nelson, upon her husband mention-ing something said or done by Lady Hamilton, suddenly rose from her seat and burst forth, " I am sick of hearing of dear Lady Hamilton, and am resolved that you shall give up either her or me ! " Her manner was very vehement, but his attorney noted with approval :

> " Lord Nelson, with perfect calmness, said, ' Take care, Fanny, what you say. I love you sincerely, but I cannot forget my obligations to Lady Hamilton, or speak of her otherwise than with affection and admiration.' Without one soothing word or gesture, but muttering something about her mind being made up, Lady Nelson left the room, and shortly after drove from the house. They never lived together afterwards. I believe that Lord Nelson took a formal leave of her ladyship before joining the Fleet under Sir Hyde Parker ; but that, to the day of her husband's death, she never made any apology for her abrupt and ungentle conduct above related, or any overture towards a reconciliation."

28

The details of an anecdote recollected forty-five years later are inaccurate, but that a husband and wife who were not to meet again parted on January 13, after an unhappy scene, is certain. It is equally certain that neither as yet guessed that they had said their last farewell. Roundwood, in which Nelson had never spent a night, had been disposed of, to a Mr. Robert Fuller, before the old year was out. The Rector wrote to his daughter Kitty, on January 9, that " as things are now circumstanced ", he expected to leave for Bath soon after his son's departure, but made no mention of his daughter-in-law's intentions. Nelson's last words to his wife were, according to her testimony, " I call God to witness, there is nothing in you, or your conduct, I wish otherwise." His four lines, written the same night, ran :

> " Southampton,
> " January 13th, 1801.
>
> " My dear Fanny,
> " We are arrived and heartily tired; and with kindest regards to my father and all the family, believe me, your affectionate
> " Nelson."

He left her in the Dover Street house, which had been taken for a year, and before leaving London he had instructed his agents to pay £400 into her account. Whether a copy of the following undated and unsigned letter was ever despatched by Lady Nelson is not to be discovered :

> " My dearest Husband,
> " Your generosity and tenderness were never more strongly shewn than your writing to Mr. Marsh yesterday morning for the payment of your very handsome quarterly allowance, which far exceeded my expectations. Knowing your income, and had you left it to me, I cou'd not in conscience have said so much. Accept my warmest, my most affectionate and grateful thanks. I could say more, but my heart is too full. Be assured every wish, every desire of mine is to please the man whose affection constitutes my happiness. God bless my dear husband. . . ."

29

The Rev. William Nelson (who had been living in lodgings opposite to his brother, at 6, Stafford Street) was travelling with him to Plymouth, and after leaving Southampton they went out of their road to call at Rose's country house, near Lyndhurst. But Rose, who was, together with Pitt, to offer his resignation to his sovereign early next month, had unexpectedly left home for town, so Nelson's last effort to press the case of his brother Maurice, after so many years' loyal service, still, as he bitterly pointed out, no more than " a clerk in the Navy Office ", was frustrated. During this day's journey William had to call their carriage to a halt and fling open all windows while the Admiral panted for breath. " Anxiety for friends left, and the various workings of my imagination," explained Nelson to Lady Hamilton, " gave me one of those severe pains of the heart." But from Axminster he again made an 8 a.m. start before a long day.

At Honiton he sought out the mother of the late Captain Westcott, " poor thing, except for the bounty of Government and Lloyd's in very low circumstances. The brother is a tailor, but had they been chimney-sweeps, it was my duty to show them respect." Hearing from the old lady that she had never received her son's Nile medal, he detached the one he was wearing, and left it in her hands. He was neither in spirits nor health to enjoy a welcome at Exeter, wearily described by him as having been on the same lines as that Lady Hamilton had witnessed at Salisbury.

Lord St. Vincent, who had staggered his physician at Bath, last April, by the gleeful announcement, " Baird, I am going afloat ! " had received permission from the Admiralty to fix his headquarters for the winter months at the house of his cousins, Mr. and Mrs. George Cary. Torre had been selected as the site for an abbey by holy men of Norman date. Its many out-buildings included a Great Hall reminiscent of that at West-minster, in which Spaniards had been held prisoner after Don Pedro's galleys had been towed into Torbay by Elizabethan seamen ; its noble elm avenue stretched to a sandy beach. The hall of the modern mansion, overlooking the bay, possessed deep window-seats in which a schoolboy nourishing sea-dreams might stare away a winter's afternoon undetected, and the fruits of its sheltered walls and hothouses were renowned, even in the west country.

Nelson found his Commander-in-Chief so cheerful that he guessed him to be " riding post for something good ", and he had hardly entered when the arrival of a letter from Sir Hyde Parker gave their conversation a confidential and highly interesting turn. They parted next morning without a word having been said on the subject of prize-money, so Nelson was not compelled to bring into action " a broadside, as strong (and backed with justice), as any he can send ". His carriage rattled over the cobbles of Plymouth dockyard with dusk on January 17, and when his flag was hoisted, blue at the fore, in the *San Josef*, it was cheered by

E E

the whole fleet.   Hardy reported that as far as he was concerned, the ship was ready for sea, but the dockyard had not nearly done with her.   The Admiral's cabin was not finished, not even painted yet.   Hardy's, however, had been vacated, and contained two splendid easy-chairs of green morocco and mahogany, designed by Messrs. Foxhall and Fryer, who worked for Beckford at Fonthill.   The chairs had side pockets, into which a one-armed man might slip documents; a pad on the right arm had been provided, and the bill was £20.   Lady Hamilton was thanked for her thoughtful choice, but Lady Nelson's efforts had been more than usually ineffective, and " a letter of truths about my outfit " was despatched to that withdrawn figure.   Hardy, the ideal Flag-Captain, never in the way and never out of it, proceeded silently to take an unframed portrait of Lady Hamilton to the carpenter's shop, and the people of the dockyard, who had not believed that Admiral Nelson would want to go to sea until the winter was more worn away, suddenly became all bustle.   His statement that he wished to get the *San Josef* alongside the Commander-in-Chief's flagship in Torbay within seven days (coupled with a mention that she would be the finest ship in the world) had produced a wonderful effect.

From newspapers which published the fact on January 24 her husband learnt that Lady Nelson had left London for Brighton, and also that Mr. Davison was taking the lease of a fine London mansion for Lord and Lady Nelson.   His comment as he sat watching deep snow on Plymouth roofs was, " Let her go to Briton [*sic*] or where she pleases.   I care not ", and that if she was to take Shelburne House, " I am not, thank God, forced to live in it ".   30

He had heard, four days past, that Lady Hamilton was alleging " a very serious cold ", and since he had believed that he would be in Torbay before the 26th, he had told her to address all further letters to Brixham.   Almost frantic himself, he urged her, against his own belief, " Keep up your spirits, all will end well. . . ."   Letters redirected from Brixham began to arrive, but when he sailed for Torbay at last, in the teeth of a south-westerly gale, on January 31, he had received nothing dated later than the 27th.   31

8

The *San Josef* anchored in Torbay early on the morning of February 1, and Nelson went at once to report to St. Vincent at

Torre Abbey. From the first moment all the news that wild Sunday morning was good. An order was awaiting him to transfer his flag to the *St. George*, a three-decker, of lighter draught than the *San Josef*, and therefore considered more suitable for Baltic service. The First Lord had settled that he was " to go forth as the Champion of England in the North ". The expedition fore-shadowed by Sir Hyde Parker had been decided upon, with Nelson as second-in-command, but he was not to lose " my *San Josef* ". She was to be held for his return, which he believed would be within a few weeks, after which he hoped to be given the chance of another knock at his chosen foe, republican France. He had to acknowledge that their Lordships had behaved handsomely in this instance, and that his prospects " could not be better ". From Portsmouth he would ask for three days' leave " on my private affairs " and fly to London.

He got the letter from London for which he had been waiting on his return to the ship. It was blowing fresh, and he had been two hours pulling from Lord St. Vincent's house. When he had mastered the contents of a mysteriously worded message, he burnt it, with the exception of two lines which he cut out, and

32 meant to keep for ever. The child begotten in the *Foudroyant* last April was safely and secretly born, and Lady Hamilton was well. He was the father of a daughter. He found himself laughing and crying at once as he tried to offer a prayer of thanks for " this gleam of future comfort ". Since he must not show any of his feelings, he thought at first he would go mad. The post was just leaving, so he was obliged to sit down to write immediately, amidst disturbance. Captain Darby, entering the cabin, noticing a newly framed likeness of the famous Emma, and an engrossed figure, waggishly desired his compliments to her ladyship and sent wishes they could see her down here, instead

33 of merely her portrait.

As letters sent by the post were liable to fall into unintended hands, a fictitious couple had been invented. Thompson, or Thomson (for they carelessly spelt his name both ways), was supposed to be a young father in Nelson's ship, on whose behalf he wrote daily to Lady Hamilton (at present kindly looking after " Mrs. Thomson " and their new-born child). An uncle stood in the way of the lovers' marriage. In his letters of the next few days Nelson offered marriage " as soon as possible ", as often and contritely as any village lad, and indeed his fancy painted, in one such declaration, a country scene in humble life.

"If you was single, and I found you under a hedge, I would instantly marry you." Now that his child was in the world, his mortification that it must be unacknowledged was so enormous that he could not bring himself directly to mention the fact, and he hastened to do all in his power to repair the damage. "Aye, would to God our fates had been different!" Soon he had brought himself to believe that a union so unlike his marriage, and so promptly fruitful, must have been intended by Heaven and would be blessed by more children, born in wedlock. He harped upon the innocence and probable loveliness of the daughter of "the most beautiful woman of the age". Her baptism occupied his thoughts much, and St. George's, Hanover Square, was his first choice for the ceremony. As the son of a clerical family he was well aware that a private christening, if necessary, could precede a public one, but that the place of birth and names of parents would be demanded in either case. He could only suggest "born at Portsmouth, or at sea", and that he and Lady Hamilton should take the child to church, and stand sponsors, before he sailed, stating to the clergyman that both the Thomsons were at the moment "out of the kingdom". From the day that he learnt of her existence, he never failed to send his love and a blessing to "our little girl". As he had not dared to count upon the infant's survival, no names had been chosen. He now hoped for an "Emma", but Lady Hamilton had decided upon "Horatia". A lock of Horatia's hair was put by him into the case containing that of his shadowy mother, and as far as he could judge, the bright colour resembled what he remembered of his own in childhood. His "good eye" was giving him such trouble that he had been driven to consult the Physician to the Fleet, who prescribed an operation as soon as possible, meanwhile, no writing, and green shades. ("Will you, my dear friend, make me one or two?") He took far-sighted measures to provide for mother and child in case of his sudden death. Since a married woman could possess no property, he must ensure that in the event of both Sir William and Lady Hamilton predeceasing his child, her little fortune (which he hoped to make great) should not fall to Sir William's heirs, headed by Greville, described by him as "that other chap" who had used his love "ill enough". In his wilder moments of impatience, he proposed that when he returned from the Baltic, they should fly together to Brontë, and there settle, with Horatia, the world forgetting. But in time of war he was tied to his profession, and Sir William was visibly failing. For the present all he could offer was that they should marry on the death of " Mrs. Thomson's uncle ", or on a declaration of peace. Still another " impediment " which he said that God alone could remove remained, for such plans, never very hopefully suggested, presupposed his own freedom, and divorce never entered his calculations. The word never appears in his letters.

His admiration for the woman whom he had considered perfection even before she had become hallowed in his eyes as the mother of his child swelled into lyrical language. His thoughts turned to his favourite playwright, and a paraphrase of Romeo's speech in Capulet's garden—" Good-night, and good-night. I could say it till to-morrow ! " On one of the four occasions when he was able to deliver a letter by the hand of a private messenger he gave full vent to his passion. Davison, who had taken the trouble to travel upwards of two hundred miles from his Northumbrian estate in early February, came to Torbay to discuss his friend's impending lawsuit with St. Vincent. He had called on Lady Hamilton on his way through London, brought a letter from her, and carried one back with an enclosure. Troubridge and Captain Edward Parker also took charge of packets, of the contents of which they were entirely ignorant. Oliver, the factotum picked up in Vienna, went down to Spithead in March, and carried back a letter which settled for posterity the question of Nelson's relations with Lady Hamilton and the parentage of Horatia.

In one of the Davison letters, Nelson, regretting that duty forbade him to be the bearer, paid characteristic tribute to his " non-pareil ". The figure of Elizabeth Tudor, " our Elizabeth, a victorious and high-spirited woman ", had early captivated his fancy.

> " I know you are so true and loyal an Englishwoman, that you would hate those who would not stand forth in defence of our King, Laws, Religion, and all which is dear to us. It is your sex that makes us go forth, and seem to tell us, ' None but the brave deserve the fair,' and if we fall, we still live in the hearts of those females who are dear to us. It is your sex that rewards us, it is your sex who cherish our memories. And you, my dear honoured friend, are, believe me, the *first*, the best, of your sex. I have been the world around, and in every corner of it, and never yet saw your equal, or even one which could be put in comparison with you."

34

In the letter carried by Oliver, opening, " Now, my own dear wife, for such you are in my eyes, and in the face of heaven, I can give full scope to my feelings ", he proceeded, " I love, I never did love any one else. I never had a dear pledge of love till you gave me one. You, my beloved Emma, and my country, are the two dearest objects of my fond heart—*a heart susceptible and true.* My longing for you, both person and conversation, you may readily imagine. It setts me on fire. . . ." He ended incoherently— " My love, my darling angel, my heaven-given wife, the dearest only true wife of her [sic] own till death. . . ." His postscript adjured her—" Kiss and bless *our* dear Horatia—think of that ! "   35

9

He had no notion, when he thanked God that his non-pareil had never borne a child to anyone else, that a younger Emma, the result of a very early indiscretion, was already nineteen. Greville's cynical suggestion for the future of a snub-nosed, low-statured young woman who spoke with a bad accent and showed no signs of any but rural origin and upbringing had been—" a little money might be an inducement for a clergyman to marry her, and then I could help him on; but if she does not make an impression on a good sort of man, I am sure I cannot find one for her ". Nelson, when he heard, in the autumn of 1801, that Sir   36 William objected to his lady entertaining her connections, the Connors, at 23, Piccadilly, at once offered the hospitality of his own country house, and added, " I hope, Emma, you take care of your relative; when you can get her well-married and settled, we will try and give her something." Five Miss Connors, including the Sarah to whom his words probably refer, came, but there is no evidence that he was ever told that " Emma Connor " was half-sister to his own child. Sir William had not known of her existence until Greville, infuriated by the news of his uncle's marriage, had forwarded the pathetic bills for her keep.   37

The weather in which Nelson's Torbay letters were written suited their matter. " My dear amiable friend, could you have seen the boat leave the ship, I am sure your heart would have sunk within you." Sometimes for two and three days together it was impossible to send a boat ashore, either to send or receive the post. The sea came over the *San Josef's* forecastle, and in the Admiral's after-cabin the motion was so great that he could not sit. But " a miserable fellow, shut up in wood ", thanking Providence, " who keeps a look out for Poor Jack ", that his ship had new cables, still swore himself, " in fair or foul weather, at sea or on shore, for ever yours ".

Too often during the gales of this new year neither the writing nor receipt of his love-letters brought anything but misery. A usual accompaniment of illicit passion was driving him to the borders of insanity, both just before and for many weeks after the birth of his child. Jealousy, of the strength observed by Shakespeare before he drew the characters of Leontes and Othello, put him on the rack and brought him almost to a condition of trance. Since the woman whom he could not claim as wife professed herself equally untrusting, the situation was degrading, and both images suffered distortion. His fears, which were reasonable, though unreasonably expressed, centred around the figure of the Prince of Wales, who had idly told a circle, which had hastened to repeat it, "how Lady Hamilton had hit his fancy". After a few efforts to dine in Sir William Hamilton's house *en famille*, discouraged by Sir William's lady at her lover's command, a royal personage unaccustomed to rebuffs troubled no more. Lady Hamilton's fears included all women, and imposed refusal of all invitations at which any might be encountered, and, to satisfy her, her lover disparaged any whom he might chance to meet.

The diction of Nelson's love-letters of these weeks is unmistakably that of the early nineteenth century, but the cadence, especially of those which he believed would be instantly burnt after being delivered by hand, is that of the passionate lover of all time. He scribbled them late every night, after the day's interruptions had ceased, and he set down everything that came into his head.

10

At 7 a.m. on the morning of Tuesday, February 24, 1801, a carriage which had travelled through the night drew up at 23, Piccadilly, one of the smaller houses overlooking the Green Park. Nelson's three days' leave in London passed unnoticed by the Press. Twenty-four hours after his arrival journals predicted that he was likely to come to town before he sailed for the Baltic in order to attend councils and fix plans of campaign. Throughout his stay the Park was crowded by the equipages of loyal subjects, all bent in one direction. The King, who had caught cold in chapel on the 15th, was now unconscious. A Regency seemed inevitable, the accession of George IV, at any moment, a dreadful possibility. That the monarch had suffered a return of his "old disorder", brought on by the worry and excitement of a

change of Government, caused more grief than surprise, but the
rock upon which Pitt had foundered was unexpected.   The man
who had long been pressing the more vigorous prosecution of a
war of which his country was tired had been unable to satisfy
his sovereign on the subject of Catholic Emancipation.   Personal
encounter with the statesman who had been Nelson's idol in the
days when he had nourished political aspirations had not developed
into friendship, and two characters so diverse were never to
approach intimacy; nevertheless, he had been heartily sorry to
hear that Mr. Pitt was " out ", because " I think him the greatest
Minister this country ever had and the honestest man ".   The
change also interested him professionally, for under the leadership of the late Speaker, Mr. Addington, Lord St. Vincent had
succeeded Lord Spencer, and Troubridge had become a Lord of
the Admiralty.   The appointment of two such resolute officers
at a moment when Great Britain's command of the sea was her
only cause for congratulation had been popular, but a very
general opinion of the new Government had been neatly expressed
by the member for Calne, " They have got up the ' Beggar's
Opera ' without Macheath."   London, in February 1801, was
not a cheerful city.   An expedition under Sir Ralph Abercromby
should have arrived in Egypt by now, but nothing was known of
its progress.   The news from the Continent was all deplorable.
Paris was celebrating, with a Grand Fête organised by the brother
of the First Consul, the treaty between France and Austria
signed at Lunéville on the 9th.   From Vienna, Lord Minto, who
had looked upon Pitt as " the Atlas of our reeling Globe ", had
sadly written to Lord Grenville asking for his letters of recall.
The Neapolitan Government had bound itself to close its ports to
British ships and admit French garrisons.   Leghorn, Arezzo,
Ancona, every restless, sun-baked city in which Nelson had
received so noisy a welcome on the first stages of his journey home,
was back under Buonaparte's heel, and Portugal, threatened by
Spain, was wavering.   The First Consul, whom even Nelson still
failed to recognise as the sole inspiring figure of a perfectly new
alignment of French ambition and enmity, had most successfully
courted Paul of Russia.   Denmark, Prussia and Sweden had
agreed, at the suggestion of the Czar, to revive the " Armed
Neutrality of the North "; no new thing, but at the moment
particularly agreeable to France.   The result might break the
blockade of Brest, and must close the Baltic to British
trade.

Nelson arrived in London " almost beside himself with expectation ". He had little doubt that the result of this leave
38 would be a brother or sister for Horatia. But Lady Hamilton announced herself in health only " so-so ", though in spirits, to-day, excellent. A month ago he had written to her as strongly as he dared, advising her to keep her bed for a week at least after her " very severe cold ", and to make no attempt to go out of the
39 house for a fortnight. Her dangerous business having been despatched with complete success, a very resilient character, obsessed with the idea of keeping her secret, had over-taxed a remarkable constitution and was now paying the penalty. Three days had seen her not only out of child-bed, but in full dress. Her appearance on her husband's arm at a Grand Concert in the St. James's Square mansion of the Duke of Norfolk, on the night of February 1, had been noticed in the Press the following day, and amongst her fellow-guests had been Sir Harry Featherstonehaugh, Mr. Charles Greville and the Prince of Wales.

But face to face with " Mrs. Thomson " at last, " poor Thomson " forgot " all his anger, anxiety and sorrows ! " His arrival had been unexpected : their time together was short. As he had found his Dover Street house shut up, he had taken rooms at Lothian's Hotel, Albemarle Street. Essential matters were discussed at break-neck speed, between interruptions. He feared that, as a second-in-command, Lord Nelson might be given no scope. " Everybody except you, tears him to pieces." Lady
40 Hamilton stalwartly assured him that he would find " much to do ". Her opinion of the Czar was lower than his. . . . Eight weeks should, he hoped, conclude the Baltic campaign (therefore, " Cheer up ! fair Emma ! ") and then, " Peace in a cottage, with a plain joint of meat, doing good to the poor, and setting an example of virtue, even to king and princes ", was his breathlessly expressed theme, in a newly decorated Piccadilly drawing-room. Arrangements in case there should be any discovery of " poor dear Mrs. Thomson's business " during his absence had to be made, and an officer who was about to proceed on active service promised recklessly to be at hand, at need. If her " uncle " persisted in bringing bad characters to his house, she must quit it. A less dramatic plan for inviting Mrs. William Nelson up to London again, to bear her constant company, was originated. " What signifies a few hundred pounds to make your dear mind a little at ease ? " When intrusive

royalty found that Lady Hamilton was always from home, dining with the Nelsons, Sir William would soon discover that His Royal Highness did not come for the pleasure of his company. But " Reverend Sir ", who could be a bore, and his little woman, whose tongue never lay still, must have beef-steak in their own lodgings two or three times a week, for it must never be said that Sir William Hamilton supported the Nelson family.

At the Admiralty Lord Nelson did not neglect to press for a frigate for Captain Nisbet. At Davison's house all his business was confidential. Lady Hamilton had sold her diamonds in order to furnish 23, Piccadilly (which included a Nelson Room), and Sir William was selling some of his best vases and pictures. To her lover's dismay and wrath, he had learnt that amongst the pictures to be put up to public auction was Romney's " Lady Hamilton as St. Cecilia ". This cold-blooded and decidedly ignominious procedure revived all his terrors that a husband who could act so would be prepared to sell the original, when a Prince Regent was the bidder. (" Can this be the great Sir William Hamilton? ") He entrusted Davison to secure the picture privately and keep it for his return, packed up, without mentioning the transaction or showing it " to any soul breathing ". In a legal document beginning, " Whereas the Rt. Honble Sir William Hamilton, K.B., is in my debt the following sums ", he left the total, some £2,276, in trust to Alexander Davison, Esq., of St. James's Square, and Thomas Ryder, Esq., of Lincoln's Inn, for the use and benefit of Emma Hamilton. His executors were each asked to accept £100 to buy a mourning ring, and were directed to pay the income from a capital sum of £20,000 left to Lady Nelson.   *41*

Business done, he offered to tell his friend what he would do if he had been going to the Baltic in command. Davison sent a messenger running to Faden's at Charing Cross for a chart of the Cattegat, and when it arrived, after a very short pause for contemplation, Nelson said that as the Government would be only able to spare twelve ships-of-the-line this time, he would place them thus—marking the chart. Two months later Davison discovered that he had been granted a prophetic glimpse of the dispositions preceding a brilliant victory, but the confidant of a sea-officer kept the anecdote to himself until long after Nelson's death.   *42*

On the second day of Nelson's leave, after another visit to

the Admiralty and the Navy Office, he brought back with him as guests to dinner at 23, Piccadilly, Troubridge and his brother Maurice. A cultured clergyman from the neighbourhood of Sir William's Pembrokeshire estates had been invited to supper, and a party of three gentlemen and one lady talked politics until 2 a.m., the hostess being, in Nelson's opinion, "not only one of the most intelligent women of the age, but in Council the superior of most men." The Prince of Wales's postponed visit was now fixed for the following Sunday, and Nelson was ready to "let out" on the subject, but a much older man of great personal charm, who had been in the diplomatic service for thirty-six years, kept the conversation to other matters, and the Rev. Mr. Este was presented with nothing but the spectacle of " Tria Juncta in Uno ".

At some hour during the earlier half of this or the following day the last of the principal objects of Nelson's flying visit to London was accomplished. His first sight of a golden-haired, blue-eyed, month-old infant, arrayed in fine linen, whose physical perfection was emphasised by the presence of a crippled female child, brought him entire reassurance : his own word was " felicity ". Lady Hamilton, who had been enabled to pay well, had also chosen well. Mrs. Gibson, of 9, Little Titchfield Street, Marylebonne, was beyond doubt a good woman, and a good reason for a widow in reduced circumstances having accepted the sole care of a new-born child of gentle birth whose parents were unknown to her was present in the shape of an attendant figure—a little daughter of her own, " Mary ", slightly deformed. A widow who had been a mother herself had remarked that the infant brought to her on a winter's night by " Hond: Lady Hamilton ", unattended, in a hackney coach, was not more than eight days old, but whatever questions troubled the brain of a very quiet woman on that winter's morning, as she watched an open-handed, quick-spoken naval gentleman, with one ʻeye and one arm, take more than civil interest in a brother-officer's child, she asked no questions. His unspeakable thoughts were, " A finer child never was produced by any two persons. It was in truth a love-begotten child."

On the third morning of his leave he received orders to embark 600 troops under Lieut.-Colonel the Hon. William Stewart and proceed to join Sir Hyde Parker, who had already left London for Yarmouth. He cancelled his room at Lothian's, told Allen to pack and prepared to drive through the night to Spithead. The farewell of a lady renowned for her classical attitudes was interpreted by him as that of the Roman matron, " Return with your shield, or upon it ", and his own was, " No fear of death, except of parting from you."

44

CHAPTER XIV

1801

(*ætat* 42)

COPENHAGEN

I

By an extraordinary coincidence, the crowned heads of three of the four northern countries banded together in a Confederation directed against Great Britain were insane, and the fourth, Frederick William III of Prussia, was a character so amiably indecisive as to be personally negligible. Prussia had no fleet, but the remaining three allies represented a force double the strength of that which sailed from Yarmouth on March 12, 1801, under the command of an Admiral " a little nervous about dark nights, and fields of ice ". In Sweden the great house of Vasa was almost bred out, and a most desirable realm and industrious people were nearly ready for a new dynasty, founded by the only one of Buonaparte's Marshals to keep his crown on the fall of his master. The abnormal piety of Gustavus IV was occasioning his councillors uneasiness, but seven years were to pass before more startling manifestations were to cause a party of exasperated officers to compel his abdication. In Denmark the Crown Prince had long acted as Regent for an imbecile sire. Nelson had once seen Prince Frederick, and although the Prince had then scarcely attained his fourteenth birthday, remembered him as an un-promising type. (When trying to call up for Lady Hamilton the picture of a young man whose physique proclaimed his inheritance of more blue blood than red, he referred her to their memories of a son of Prince Esterhazy). In St. Petersburg the violent and embittered Paul I, physically remarkable for his cat's face and unco-ordinated gait, was by far the most fascinating figure, both from the medical and political points of view. His sudden seizure of the persons and property of all British merchants in his ports and cities had precipitated the present crisis, and his alliance with Buonaparte threatened Britain's possessions in the East. Nelson viewed Paul as the first enemy to be disposed of, and thought that his lesson should be severe. The trunk being cut down, he foresaw no difficulty in lopping off the branches. His hope, therefore, was to proceed directly to attack the Russian squadron ice-bound at Revel, and the fact that Lord St. Vincent had recommended to him a Captain Thesiger, late of the Russian service, who was sailing with the expedition as a volunteer, seemed to him to augur well. He was anxious to meet the Russian fleet, not only because the sooner the Baltic confederacy was dissolved the sooner he would see home. He had been privileged to hear Mr. Pitt's reflections on exactly the situation which had now arisen, and he realised that with every day that passed the Northern Powers would be strengthening their defences. A lightning blow at Russia would have been his advice. But he found himself, as days passed, ostentatiously excluded from conference.

Sir Hyde Parker was a respectable officer, aged sixty-two, who had gone afloat at twelve. His family, as his Christian name indicated, had been eminent at the Stuart Court, and his elder brother was a baronet. His knighthood was of his own winning, the reward for a distinguished minor action in the American War. He had grown rich during four years in command at Jamaica and had recently married a bride of eighteen, who reminded Lord St. Vincent of batter pudding. It may have been that he had observed expressions of pity mingled with the congratulations of friends when they learnt that he had been provided with a thunderbolt as second-in-command. The arrival of the squadron from Portsmouth had certainly surprised him. The *St. George* had gone to sea in such haste that she had carried her caulkers and painters to St. Helen's. ("If the wind proves fair, they shall be sent up the harbour; if unfair, no time will have been lost.") The appearance of Nelson at Portsmouth had produced more than the usual activity, for on dismounting from his carriage, his lordship had sent for the officer in charge of the military and announced that he meant to sail with the first tide. Colonel Stewart, an ardent young man, had received the intended impression, and the detachments of the 49th and 95th regiments waiting on Southsea Common to be embarked for special service in the North Sea had all been on board their long-attendant transports within two hours.

At Yarmouth, nine days later, Lord Nelson received many thanks from the First Lord for "using the spur", and Sir Hyde Parker an express ordering him to take his fleet to sea. Lady Parker's ball had to be cancelled. Sir Hyde, who on Nelson's courtesy call, accompanied by Hardy, had told him nothing, remained thereafter invisible. At first Nelson merely regretted that this would mean his having to go on board his Commander-in-Chief at sea. (His stepson, after observing the humiliating efforts of a one-armed man to go up the side of a ship in blowing weather, had hoped that some day he would slip and break his neck—and the observation had been mischievously repeated, cutting Nelson to the heart.) The newspapers and Yarmouth fisher-women had said that he was going to the Baltic. The rumour in the fleet was that they were to wait outside Cronenburg while Mr. Drummond, British Minister in Copenhagen, negotiated. (" I disapprove most exceedingly. . . . Weak in the extreme. . . . A fleet of British men-of-war are the best negotiators in Europe.") Dommet, the Captain of the Fleet, had apologetically revealed that Sir Hyde had struck his pen through every recommendation made by his second-in-command. Colonel Stewart, already a confirmed admirer, was disgustedly noting " studied neglect " of a hero. (His hundred sharp-shooters were " ready to fire out Paul's right eye ".) Presently, stratagem had to be employed to establish closer relations. Lieut. Layman (a great rattle) had observed that he had once caught a very fine turbot on the Dogger Bank over which the fleet must soon pass. Lord Nelson, to his surprise, ordered that an attempt must be made to repeat this feat. After a few tries, on a wild evening, a small turbot was secured. " Send it to Sir Hyde." Something was said in suggestion of the risk of employing a boat after dark in such high seas, but the second-in-command repeated that the Chief must have his turbot. The boat returned safely, bringing a civil message, and Lieut. Layman always held that the victory of Copenhagen had been made possible by a tactful turbot.

The season was the worst in the year for an expedition to the Baltic. The tedious passage of Nelson's squadron from Spithead to Yarmouth had been achieved, in his own words, " blindfold ". Fog, as thick as mud, had been all that was visible from gunport or stern-window, and he had always left the quarter-deck hoary or wet through. As the fleet of eighteen of the line, eleven frigates, and sloops, brigs, cutters, fire-ships and bombs, amounting in all to fifty-three sail, battled its way northwards, the temperature fell, and gentlemen from England, where daffodils had begun to peer, entered upon a second winter. Ice glistened on the rigging, and snowstorms alternated regularly with sleet. On March 15 the violence of the gale caused Lord Nelson in the *St. George* and Captain Fremantle in the *Ganges* to lay aside half-finished letters. The Admiral regretted that in the Great

Cabin of his hastily refitted flagship enough draught came through
to turn a mill; Fremantle complained that the hacking coughs of
his ship's company ceased not day nor night. It was a relief
when, early on the 18th, through flying snowflakes, a long, low
sandy arm of land became intermittently visible. This was the
Skaw, northernmost point of Jutland, last seen by Nelson twenty
years past. The fleet, which had been in some measure scattered,
collected, and next day turned southwards down the Cattegat.
Nelson observed a frigate sent away by the Commander-in-Chief,
and guessed that it carried a diplomat bound for Copenhagen.
(" I hate your pen and ink men.") On the following morning,
so that no attention should be wanting on his part, he paid a
further call upon Sir Hyde, and at the end of an hour's conversation had " ground out something ". The rumour that negotiation was to be tried first was evidently true, but he could not
achieve anything approaching the confidential note which he
considered essential as between a Commander-in-Chief and his
second. Next evening the fleet anchored eighteen miles from the
boasted defences of Cronenburg and Elsinore, and there waited
three days, although the wind was now fair for Copenhagen. At
last, on the 23rd, Sir Hyde called a council, and Nelson attended in
revived spirits. The *St. George* had been cleared for action a
week past. Hardy assured him that the ship's company " would
do ", and " I take the *Ghost's* word ". Amongst his efforts to
" brush up " strangers had been the importation of a band,
borrowed from the Channel Fleet. Before leaving his cabin he   3
scribbled a line to Lady Hamilton. During the passage he had
added a codicil to his will, in which he had left her the Sultan's
sable pelisse and the Chelengk. " Now we are sure of fighting ",
he wrote, " I am sent for. When it was a joke I was kept in the
background; tomorrow will, I hope, be a proud day for England."   4
    But on board the *London* the atmosphere nothing resembled
what he had pictured. Lieutenant Layman, who steered his
gig, noted with awe that " all the heads were very gloomy ".
The mission of Mr. Nicholas Vansittart, in conjunction with Mr.
Drummond, had been a failure. The Danes were not only far
too frightened of Russia to accede to Great Britain's request for
their withdrawal from the Confederation : they were actively
hostile. Moreover, the diplomats had returned with dreadful
accounts of newly strengthened defences at Elsinore and Copenhagen. When Nelson arrived, a long-faced council had come
to the conclusion that to stay in the Cattegat until the united

naval force of the Danes, Russians and Swedes came forth to offer battle was the only prudent course. To attempt to deal with Russia first, and separately, would mean leaving an undefeated enemy behind them, and was quite contrary to Government instructions. Even if they succeeded in reaching Copenhagen without having been severely damaged passing Cronenburg, to risk line-of-battle ships in shallow waters and such weather, against defences as described by Messrs. Drummond and Vansittart, would be hazardous in the extreme.

Colonel Stewart had noticed that when Lord Nelson was highly dissatisfied, he generally gave vent to less than he felt. Nelson now began by questioning the hushed gentlemen from Copenhagen in close detail, not only as to the strength, but as to the position of the enemy. Having gathered that the Danes had placed their strongest ships at the head of their line, he proceeded to consider the possibilities of coming up to take their rear by surprise. This would mean an entry into the Baltic by the Great Belt, which would entail loss of time, a most important factor. However, attack as soon as possible was his advice—" Let it be by the Sound, by the Belt, or any how, only lose not an hour ", and his enthusiasm was so infectious, his eloquence so potent, that by the time the council was dismissed an approach to Copenhagen by the Great Belt had been decided upon. He had warmly advised the necessity of disregarding Government instructions in view of an unexpected situation, and in giving farewell to the diplomats who were sailing for England he heartily wished them so slow a passage that the question might have been settled by a victory before they reached London. On his return to his own ship, he addressed himself to his Commander-in-Chief, and next day forwarded probably the ablest letter he ever dictated :

" My dear Sir Hyde,
" The conversation we had yesterday has naturally, from its importance, been the subject of my thoughts; and the more I have reflected, the more I am confirmed in opinion, that not a moment should be lost in attacking the Enemy. They will every day and hour be stronger; we shall never be so good a match for them as at this moment.
" The only consideration in my mind is how to get at them with the least risk to our Ships. By Mr. Vansittart's account, the Danes have taken every means in their power to prevent our getting to attack Copenhagen by the Passage of the Sound. Cronenburg has been strengthened, the Crown Islands fortified, on the outermost of which are twenty guns pointing mostly downwards, and only eight hundred yards from very formidable batteries placed under the Citadel, supported by five Sail-of-the-Line, seven Floating batteries of fifty guns each, besides Small-

F F

craft, Gun-boats &c. &c. And that the Revel Squadron of twelve or fourteen Sail-of-the-Line are soon expected as also five Sail of Swedes.

" It would appear by what you have told me of your instructions, that Government took for granted you would find no difficulty in getting off Copenhagen, and in the event of a failure of negotiation, you might instantly attack; and that there would be scarcely a doubt but the Danish fleet would be destroyed, and the Capital made so hot that Denmark would listen to reason and its true interest. By Mr. Vansittart's account, their state of preparation exceeds what he conceives our Government thought possible, and that the Danish Government is hostile to us in the greatest possible degree.

" Therefore here you are, with almost the safety, certainly with the honour of England more entrusted to you than ever yet fell to any British Officer. On your decision depends, whether our country shall be degraded in the eyes of Europe, or whether she shall rear her head higher than ever : again do I repeat, never did our Country depend so much on the success of any Fleet as on this. How best to honour our Country and abate the pride of her Enemies, by defeating their schemes, must be the subject of your deepest consideration as Commander-in-Chief; and if what I have to offer can be the least useful in forming your decision, you are most heartily welcome.

" I shall begin with supposing you are determined to enter by the Passage of the Sound, as there are those who think, if you leave that Passage open, that the Danish Fleet may sail from Copenhagen, and join the Dutch or French. I own I have no fears on that subject; for it is not likely that whilst their Capital is menaced with an attack, 9,000 of her best men should be sent out of the Kingdom. I suppose that some damage may arise amongst our masts and yards; yet, perhaps there will not be one of them but could be made serviceable again. You are now about Cronenburg : if the wind be fair, and you determine to attack the Ships and Crown Islands, you must expect the natural issue of such a battle—Ships crippled, and perhaps one or two lost; for the wind which carries you in, will most probably not bring out a crippled Ship. This mode I call taking the bull by the horns. It, however, will not prevent the Revel Ships, or Swedes, from joining the Danes; and to prevent this from taking effect, is in my humble opinion, a measure absolutely necessary—and still to attack Copenhagen.

" Two modes are in my view; one to pass Cronenburg, taking the risk of damage, and to pass up the deepest and straightest Channel above the Middle Grounds; and coming down the Garbar or King's Channel, to attack their Floating batteries &c. &c. as we find it convenient. It must have the effect of preventing a junction between the Russians, Swedes and Danes, and may give us an opportunity of bombarding Copenhagen. I am also pretty certain that a passage could be found to the northward of Southholm for all our Ships; perhaps it might be necessary to warp a short distance in the very narrow part.

" Should this mode of attack be ineligible, the passage of the Belt, I have no doubt, would be accomplished in four or five days, and then the attack by Draco could be carried into effect, and the junction of the Russians prevented, with every probability of success against the Danish Floating

Latteries. What effect a bombardment might have, I am not called upon to give an opinion; but think the way would be cleared for the trial.

"Supposing us through the Belt, with the wind first westerly, would it not be possible to either go with the Fleet, or detach ten Ships of three and two decks, with one Bomb and two Fire-ships, to Revel, to destroy the Russian Squadron at that place? I do not see the great risk of such a detachment, and with the remainder to attempt the business at Copenhagen. The measure may be thought bold, but I am of opinion the boldest measures are the safest; and our Country demands a most vigorous exertion of her force, directed with judgment. In supporting you, my dear Sir Hyde, through the arduous and important task you have undertaken, no exertion of head or heart shall be wanting from your most obedient and faithful servant,

"Nelson and Brontë."

Communications in 1801 were slow. As this letter was being carried from the *St. George* to the *London*, off Elsinore, on the night of March 24, a party of Russian officials, mostly in, or dismissed from, the Imperial service, were advancing through the streets of St. Petersburg upon the Mikhailovsky Palace. The night was calm but moonless. All the gentlemen had dined over well. By the time that a British fleet bent upon the Battle of Copenhagen, as a preliminary to the defeat of the Northern Confederation, had weighed and turned for the Great Belt, Paul I had been strangled, and his large and visionary son, whose tendencies were anti-French, was giving audience to his father's murderers, headed by Counts Pannin and Pahlen. But since communications were slow, Nelson did not learn of "the death of Paul" for three weeks.

2

On March 25 it blew too hard for men-of-war to lift their anchors. Next morning, after a few hours' progress in the direction of the Great Belt, the fleet was brought to, and orders were issued for a return towards the Sound. Sir Hyde's Flag-Captain, Otway, was sent to apprise his second-in-command of the reasons. Nelson's unofficial reply was, "I don't care a d——n which passage we go, so that we fight them." But Sir Hyde now found it necessary to send a message to Governor Stricker, of Elsinore, inquiring his intentions if a British fleet were to pass the Sound, and two officers from Copenhagen (the younger an aide-de-camp of the Regent) came on board the *London* in defiant mood. While writing a note in Sir Hyde's Great Cabin, the younger soldier called out, "Admiral, if your guns are no better than your pens, you may as well return to

England." He was very curious to hear who commanded the various ships, and the name of Lord Nelson startled him. (" What, is he here? I would give a hundred guineas to see him ! Then, I suppose it is no joke, if he is come ! ") Governor Stricker's reply, of course, was that he could not suffer a fleet whose intentions were not known to pass Cronenburg, and this was interpreted by Sir Hyde as a declaration of war. For a further three days, then, head winds and calms detained the fleet six miles from Cronenburg. Meanwhile, Nelson's general scheme for an attack on Copenhagen having been provisionally adopted, he made a complete change of personal plans. He must leave the *St. George* for a lighter ship. His choice was H.M.S. *Elephant*, a 74, commanded by the omniscient Foley, who had led the victors of the Nile inside the French line in Aboukir Bay. On the 30th, the wind coming fair, the fleet again weighed, and drew towards " the fancied tremendous fortress of Cronenburg ". This landmark was a four-square mediæval pile, crowned by turrets of unfamiliar design, likely to remind English observers that they were now approaching Scandinavia and Russia. The passage through the narrows was achieved in perfect order and with surprising ease, for, finding that the Swedes did not open fire from Helsingborg, the stately flotilla kept close to the Swedish coast, and clear of the Danish guns, which blazed away ineffectively. The *Elephant* did not even trouble to reply.

During that afternoon Nelson at last came in sight of Copenhagen. Eighteen days had passed since he had sailed from Yarmouth. If he had been in command, he would have been attacking the Danish capital in eight. The fleet anchored some five miles below the city, and Sir Hyde, Nelson and a party of senior officers at once embarked in the *Skylark* lugger, to reconnoitre the harbour and channels. It was soon apparent that their delay had been most obliging to the enemy, and that the accounts of Messrs. Drummond and Vansittart had erred, if anything, on the side of understatement. The Trekroner (Three Crowns) battery had been admirably strengthened, and all buoys of the North and King's Channels had been removed or misplaced.

In the *Elephant*, the Scottish Principal Medical Officer, up late, was disturbed at grim preparations by the sound of a gig coming alongside. He recognised, amongst the cloaked figures who had been out amongst floating ice-blocks during the hours of darkness, the officer whom he had already accepted as " the

first man in the world ". Presently " light showed me a path
which had been trackless ". Under the personal supervision of
Nelson, British masters and pilots had begun to place the buoys
necessary to guide his squadron to the attack.

Nelson's opinion of the Danish line of defence was : " It
looks formidable to those who are children at War, but to my
judgment, with ten sail-of-the-line I think I can annihilate them;
at all events, I hope to be allowed to try." On the afternoon of
the 31st another council was called, at the end of which he knew
that he was to be allowed to try; but he had to fight for permission,
for Sir Hyde was, not without reason, alarmed at the prospect.

Copenhagen was always protected by the Trekroner fort,
mounting seventy-odd guns, commanding the point at which the
entrance to the harbour branched off from the Inner or King's
Channel. Any ships approaching from the north would come under
its fire; shattered vessels would have no hope of retreat, and no
obstacle would prevent the promised Swedes and Russians
arriving to assist their allies. Also, in the present emergency,
the Danes, working day and night, had moored eighteen dismasted warships, mounting 634 guns, in a line a mile and a half
long, stretching from the Trekroner along the King's Channel.
Two more hulks, and a squadron of two ships-of-the-line and a
frigate, guarded the mouth of the harbour. A shoal known as
the Middle Ground lay between the Outer and Inner Channel.
Nelson's proposal was to pass with a northerly wind up the
Outer Channel and then wait for a southerly wind to take him
with ten of the line and all the small craft available down the
Inner Channel, to fall upon the rear, the weakest part of the long
line stretching south-east from the Trekroner. This plan offered
the undoubted advantage that damaged ships could retire after
action to join the fleet, which would be lying between the enemy
and reinforcements. When he had sketched his plan and offered
his services, in the most energetic manner, he had to listen to
discussion and criticism, for although most of his audience were
agreed upon " the necessity for striking a blow ", even some of
his greatest admirers thought him sanguine. (Admiral Graves
feared that they would be " playing a losing game, attacking
stone walls ". Captain Fremantle secretly held that they were
already a week too late.) Nelson, who had slept only in snatches
for the past six days, paced the cabin impatiently. He dismissed
fears of a Swedish squadron of superior force with the sharp
observation, " The more numerous the better ", and when the

Russians were reported as likely to be even more formidable, repeated, " So much the better—I wish they were twice as many. The easier the victory—depend upon it." (Afterwards, he explained to Stewart that he did not believe that either the Swedes or Danes could handle their ships, and that consequently the larger the force to approach a particularly difficult channel in haste, the better were the chances of their falling into confusion and running ashore.) " Close with a Frenchman, but out-manœuvre a Russian " was his dictum. He had been out with the leading Artillery officers that morning, in a frigate, to take the closest possible view of the Trekroner defences—and inci-dentally, in approaching the leading ship of that line, had come under its fire. These experts, called upon for their opinion, said that once the eighteen hulks were even partially out of action they thought they could bring their seven bomb ketches to play most effectively on the town and harbour.

Sir Hyde, once his decision was taken, acted handsomely. He offered two more ships-of-the-line than Nelson had asked (although his own position, should the Russians or Swedes appear upon the scene during the action, would then be very unpleasant) ; he thenceforward left all arrangements to Nelson's direction. That night the buoying of the Outer Deep was completed, and next morning (April 1) Nelson made a final examination, in the Amazon frigate. The activity and skill of her Captain, Edward Riou (a man whose scholarly countenance was shaded by what contemporaries described as " a pleasing gloom "), had impressed him, and when he gave the signal to weigh, at an hour after noon (which was received with cheers in every ship), the Amazon led the division down the Outer Channel to moor at the southern end of the Middle Ground. The wind was light but favourable. As the Elephant dropped her anchor, the Admiral called out loudly, " I will fight them the moment I have a fair wind ! " His thirty-four ships, crowded close together, were lying within range of the mortars of Amag Island, as a few shots discharged around 8 p.m. demonstrated, but the Danes, preoccupied with their defences, failed to avail themselves of the opportunity.

That evening, at a late hour for the date, Nelson sat down to dine in Foley's well-appointed ship, with a large but choice party of comrades in arms. The signal to prepare for battle had been given. Darkness had hidden the sullen line of enemy hulks and substantial fortress guarding a northern capital of fantastic towers and steeples. Candle and lantern light illuminated the

faces and figures of Nelson's second-in-command, Admiral
Graves, an old and valued acquaintance; Colonel Stewart, whom
he had met for the first time at Portsmouth; Riou, whom he had
met for the first time yesterday; Hardy, Fremantle and many
others whose names would be for ever remembered together
with his own. He was in the highest spirits, and drank to a
leading wind and to the success of the following day.

Soon after 9 o'clock the Captains departed to their respective
ships, with the exception of Riou, who retired to the after-cabin with
Foley and Nelson, to arrange the Order of Battle and detailed
instructions for every vessel. About 11 p.m. Hardy appeared.
He had been out taking soundings in the channel, and with a long
pole had personally explored the depths round the rearmost of
the enemy ships. At 1 a.m. a procession of secretaries was
settled in the Great Cabin, ready with quills poised to transcribe
orders. Nelson, since the embarrassingly attentive Tom Allen
insisted, had gone to his cot, or rather had caused it to be placed
on the deck in a position from which he could still dictate. His
urgency for the clerks to hurry increased during the small hours,
when reports of the wind coming fair were brought in to him.
He was up and dressed before six, when the scribes finished their
complicated labours, and an hour later he made the signal for
Captains. After the Captains had all been provided with their
instructions, the pilots came on board. These men, mostly
mates of vessels accustomed to trade from Scottish and northern
English ports to the Baltic, were unanimous in displaying " a
very unpleasant degree of hesitation ". All declared that to
take ships of deep draught up the channel indicated would be a
desperate business. " At eight o'clock in the morning of the
2nd of April ", noted Nelson, " not one pilot would take charge
of a ship. I experienced . . . the misery of having the honour
of our Country intrusted to pilots who had no other thought
than to keep the ships clear of danger, and their own silly heads
clear of shot." One was found, at length. Mr. Alexander Briarly,
Master of the *Bellona*, volunteered to lead the column. He was a
veteran of the Nile, where he had been Master in Davidge Gould's
ship, the *Audacious*. At 9.30, the signal to weigh in succession
having been thrown out, " the *Edgar* proceeded, in a noble manner,
for the channel ". The morning was cloudy, but fine. " Not a word
was spoken through the ship save by the pilot and helmsman, and
their commands, being chanted very much in the same manner as
the responses in a cathedral service, added to the solemnity."

3

The Battle of Copenhagen opened disastrously. The *Edgar*, passing along the front of the enemy line, took the shot of the rearmost Danes without reply, anchored abreast the third ship, in seven-fathom water, and opened fire, according to programme; but the *Agamemnon*, who should have followed her, failed to do so. She could not weather the shoals at the entrance to the channel and never came into action. Signal was then made for another 64, the *Polyphemus*, who should have been last of the line, to take up the station assigned to the *Agamemnon*. She promptly obeyed, and was very roughly handled. The *Isis* followed, and took the berth always intended for her, and the *Glatton* and *Ardent* were equally successful. The *Bellona* then grounded, on the east side of the Middle Ground, within range, but at too great a distance for fully effective fire upon the southernmost hulks which covered the front of the city from bombardment. (Later in the day the bursting of her lower-deck guns caused heavy casualties in this ship.) The *Russell*, last but one in the order of sailing, lost sight of her leader, the *Defiance*, owing to the smoke of battle, and mistakenly following the *Bellona*, shared her fate. From the outset, Nelson's division was reduced from twelve to nine of the line, and the gunnery of the Danes was superior to his expectations. His agitation on perceiving the *Agamemnon* signalling inability to proceed, and two 74's failing to obey his orders to engage more closely, was extreme, but the signal to advance was kept flying. He starboarded the *Elephant's* helm, passed to larboard between the grounded ships and the enemy line, gaining comparatively deep water, and made for the position left vacant by the failure of the *Bellona*. As the *Ganges* passed, he hailed Fremantle to place her as close as possible ahead of his flagship. (By one of the many unhappy chances of this forenoon, the only men in the *Ganges* to be hit before she anchored were the Master, who was killed outright, and the pilot, who lost an arm. Fremantle himself carried his ship in.) The *Monarch* imitated the example of the *Ganges*, and dropped into the berth originally intended for the *Elephant*. By seventeen minutes past eleven the battle had become general, each ship, as she arrived opposite to her number in the Danish line, anchoring by the stern and presenting her broadside to the enemy. Graves, in the *Defiance*, was the last to take up his position, ahead of the *Monarch*, who had already

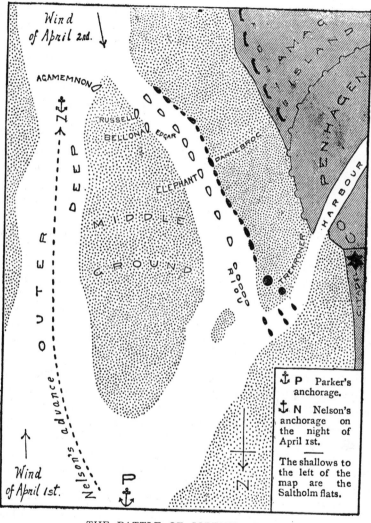

THE BATTLE OF COPENHAGEN

April 2, 1801

Reproduced from *Sea Kings of Britain*, by Sir Geoffrey Callender

By kind permission of Messrs. Longmans Green and Co., Ltd.

lost her Captain. From that moment, in Nelson's words, " Here was no manœuvring. It was downright fighting." Riou led his squadron of small craft to attack the Trekroner batteries. He knew that it had been intended, if opportunity served, during the smoke of battle, to land the military (from the flat-boats towed by every ship-of-the-line) to storm these two heavily fortified artificial islands. Nelson had left him a free hand, and owing to the accidents to the *Agamemnon, Russell* and *Bellona* the Trekroner was going unmarked. It had also been intended that Sir Hyde, with the remainder of the fleet, including the heavy ships, should make a menacing appearance from the north; but the Commander-in-Chief was still more than four miles distant, beating up against Nelson's fair wind. He had heard the enemy batteries open at 10.40. Two hours later the fate of the day still hung in the balance, and according to Danish accounts, their fire was undiminished. As their crews fell, fresh men were sent from the shore to the Trekroner batteries, and to the hulks, and in some cases rehoisted colours which had been shot away, with the result that ships which appeared to have struck reopened fire, much to the wrath of English boarding-parties.

About 1 o'clock, Sir Hyde, who could see little of what was happening, but realised that Nelson had met with mishaps, and that the Danish resistance was stronger than had been expected, began to feel himself called upon to discontinue the action. He was strongly dissuaded by his Flag-Captain, who obtained permission to go on board the *Elephant* to discover what had happened, but before Otway reached Nelson, Sir Hyde had acted.

Nelson, at 1.30, was, as he had been throughout the action, walking the starboard side of his quarter-deck. The *Elephant* was hotly engaging the Danish flagship *Dannebrog* and two floating batteries ahead of her. As a shot passed through the mainmast of the *Elephant*, sending a few splinters flying about them, he remarked with a smile to Colonel Stewart that this was " warm work ". He stopped at the gangway for an instant, and his look and next sentence were imprinted on Stewart's memory for ever. " But, mark you, I would not be elsewhere for thousands." When Sir Hyde's signal was reported to him he continued his walk. The Signal Lieutenant, meeting him at the next turn, asked whether he should repeat it to the squadron. Nelson ordered him to acknowledge its receipt but to keep " Number 16 ", the signal for close action, still flying.

" Mind you keep it so." Stewart noticed that his companion now walked with increased speed, working the stump of his right arm, and after a few more turns, Nelson asked, "in a quick manner ", " Do you know what's shown on board of the Commander-in-Chief? Number 39." Stewart had to admit that he did not understand what that number might signify. " Why, to leave off action ! " explained Nelson, adding, " Leave off action ! Now damn me if I do."

He gave a shrug, and addressing himself to Foley, said, " You know, Foley, I have only one eye. I have a right to be blind sometimes." He raised his spy-glass to his right eye, and announced, " I really do not see the signal."

4

About 2 p.m. the Danish ships astern of the *Elephant* had been silenced. When Fremantle came on board at 2.30 he found Nelson exercising what the Press called his quick discernment of occasion and popular manners. Floating gun-boats and batteries were drifting helplessly from the enemy line. The Great Cabin was filled with strange uniforms, and the English Admiral was heartily telling melancholy Danes how he wished they had been Russians, and how he longed to see the Russians down. He thrust a note into Fremantle's hands, saying that he had sent for him to get his opinion whether it would be practicable to advance, with such ships of the division as were least damaged, upon the uninjured northern end of the enemy line of defence. Fremantle read :

" To the Brothers of Englishmen, The Danes.
" Lord Nelson has directions to spare Denmark, when no longer resisting; but if the firing is continued on the part of Denmark, Lord Nelson will be obliged to set on fire all the Floating-batteries he has taken, without having the power of saving the brave Danes who have defended them.
" Dated on board His Britannic Majesty's ship *Elephant*, Copenhagen Roads, April 2nd, 1801.
" Nelson and Brontë, Vice-Admiral,
under the command of Admiral Sir Hyde Parker."

Fremantle was strongly averse from the further attack suggested. He pointed out that the Admiral had several ships aground, and most of those engaged were so crippled that it would be advisable to attempt to remove them from a very difficult channel while the wind was yet fair. Foley agreed, and Captain

Thesiger, fluent in Danish as well as Russian, was immediately
sent off in a flag of truce with the original of the note they had
just read. It was waiting, signed and sealed, and was in the
Admiral's own hand. He had scribbled it on the casing of the
rudder-head, with Foley's purser at his elbow, taking a copy as
he wrote, and he had surprised his audience by sending to the
cockpit for a candle and wax, as he wished to make a seal. The
first man sent did not return, and it was reported that a cannon-
ball had taken off his head. The Admiral's comment was, " Send
another messenger for the wax." It was pointed out to him that
there were wafers on his table, by which a folded sheet could be
well secured, but he repeated, " Send for the sealing wax." It was
brought, and he inspected with satisfaction a perfect impression
of his own coat-of-arms. Afterwards he explained to Stewart
that a wafer would still have been damp when the note was
delivered, telling a tale of stress and haste to end the action ; the
wax would be cold and hard. Forty-two years later, a painter
who specialised in the dramatic wrote to Foley's purser to ask for
details of an historic occasion, and Mr. Wallis, who was dying at
Hove, replied with pleasure that to the best of his recollection
Lord Nelson had been wearing a plain sort of a blue greatcoat and
plain cocked hat, but that gold lace and several orders on his
breast had made appearances as he leaned to write. His own dress
had been a blue coat and trousers with a white kerseymere waistcoat. They had both been standing at the extreme after-part of
the ship, and the decks of H.M.S. *Elephant*, fore and aft, had
been perfectly clear.   10

While his note was being carried to the enemy, Nelson
summoned several officers to receive thanks for their support.
Fremantle was much pleased at being thanked " before everybody on the quarter-deck ". Shot beat all round his boat as
Admiral Graves obeyed his summons to come on board the
Elephant. Lord Nelson's second-in-command, who was in a
condition not uncommon towards the end of a long and critical
action entailing close concentration for many hours, was entirely
taken by surprise on being told that he was likely to be made a
baronet. He had been principally impressed by the damage
done to British ships, far exceeding, he had gathered, that sustained at the Nile, and had hardly realised that he had taken
part in a victory second in importance to none ever gained by
Nelson.

Nelson's note was delivered by Captain Thesiger to the Prince

Regent himself, whom he found near the sally port, " animating his countrymen in a spirited manner ". The two leading ships of Sir Hyde Parker's division had now arrived on the scene, causing the remainder of the Danes ahead of the *Elephant* to strike. Commodore Fischer had shifted his broad pendant from the *Dannebrog* to the *Holstein*, the second ship from the north end of his line, and finally to the Trekroner. The *Dannebrog* was drifting in flames before the wind, spreading confusion in her path. Only the four ships within the harbour were still intact and, together with the Trekroner and the battery on Amag Island, still firing. Half of their shot was unavoidably striking a group of their own ships which had surrendered, and the British replies were causing more havoc in these unmanageable and unresisting hulks. Adjutant-General Lindholm was directed by the Prince to go to Admiral Nelson without delay, " to ask the particular object of sending his flag of truce ". On his way, he ordered the Trekroner to cease fire, whereupon the *Elephant* made the same signal to her division.

An action which had endured for five hours closed about 4 p.m. Nelson's reply to the Crown Prince was again in his own handwriting, but this time the document did show signs of having been composed in haste:

> " Lord Nelson's object in sending on shore a flag of truce is humanity, therefore, consents that hostilities shall cease till Lord Nelson can take his prisoners out of the Prizes; and he consents to land all the wounded Danes, and to burn or remove his prizes. Lord Nelson, with humble duty to His Royal Highness, begs leave to say that he will ever esteem it the greatest Victory he ever has gain'd if this flag of truce may be the happy forerunner of a lasting and happy Union between my most Gracious Sovereign and His Majesty the King of Denmark."

Wallis afterwards corrected the grammar in his copy, but the Admiral's own holograph was that delivered by Thesiger. The Adjutant-General was referred to Sir Hyde Parker, and no sooner was he gone than the signal was made for the *Glatton*, *Elephant*, *Ganges*, *Defiance* and *Monarch* to weigh in succession. The *Monarch* immediately hit on a shoal, but was pushed over it by the *Ganges* taking her amidships. Within a mile of the now silent Trekroner both the *Defiance* and *Elephant* ran aground, and in spite of all efforts made by their fatigued crews, remained fixed for the night. Nelson ordered his gig, and prepared to follow the Adjutant-General to the *London*, four miles distant. As he embarked to encounter his Commander-in-Chief, he exclaimed in Stewart's hearing, " Well, I have fought contrary to orders, and perhaps I shall be hanged. Never mind; let them ! " The *Dannebrog*, having also grounded, had just blown up, with heavy loss of life. Graves had not been able to make out the response of the *Elephant* to the Commander-in-Chief's signal of recall. He had therefore repeated the signal, and the gallant Riou, hauling off his battered light craft to safety, with the words, " What will Nelson think of us ? " had been cut in two by a raking shot from the Trekroner. The Captain of the *Bellona*, Thompson, one of the heroes of the Nile, had lost his left leg. The calculation of casualties, the scene of devastation through which he passed in the light of a northern sunset, seemed to his companions to have lowered Lord Nelson's spirits as he drew towards the *London*. " First to secure the victory, and then to make the most of it " had been his programme in Aboukir Bay. Physical exhaustion may have been taking its toll, but he was, in fact, considering how best to secure by negotiation what he had won to-day by force. The future of the whole Baltic campaign hung upon his taking the right decisions, and his opinion of his diplomatic talents was not high. (" A negotiator is certainly out of my line.") When the Adjutant-General took his leave at 8 o'clock that night a twenty-four hours' truce was all that had been agreed upon, but it had been suggested by Sir Hyde that his second-in-command should go on shore to converse with His Royal Highness.

Nelson slept in the *St. George*. Before he slept, he wrote to Lady Hamilton, to tell her that all the flower of the Danish marine was in his possession. " Of eighteen sail, large and small, some are taken, some sunk, some burnt, in the good old way." He enclosed a verse, entitled " Lord Nelson to his Guardian Angel ", endorsed, " *St. George*, April 2nd, 1801, at 9 o'clock at night very tired after a hard fought Battle ".

12

5

Next morning, while daylight was still growing, officers of the *Elephant* were pleasantly surprised to find a gig—the Admiral's favourite conveyance in these waters—alongside. He, too, was pleased and highly congratulatory to find his flagship no longer aground, but at anchor, in Copenhagen Roads, in 6½ fathoms. He took one of his characteristic snatched meals, and set off at once to interview a Danish Commodore. Two co-incidences marked this minor incident. The 70-gun block-ship in which the Commodore had his flag flying was the *Elephanten*, and the officer proved to be a very old acquaintance. Nelson's call concerned the irregular conduct of a Danish 74, the *Syaelland*. She had been driven by the waves under the protection of the Trekroner batteries and was refusing to acknowledge herself a captured ship. He had ordered a brig and four long-boats to approach her. The celebrated English Admiral's affable explanation to his old West India friend not only gained his point: he left the *Elephanten* as much admired by her officers as he was by those of the *Elephant*. (His personal arrival had indeed taken them by surprise, for when they had opened by saying that the 74 would surrender to no one but Lord Nelson, their early-morning caller, casting off an old green boat-cloak to disclose a coat decorated with three stars, and an empty sleeve, had briskly identified himself, " I am Lord Nelson. See, here's my fin." In the *Syaelland*, however, as active British tars lashed a cable to her bowsprit, preparatory to their gun-boat taking her in tow, feeling ran high, and Captain Stein Bille, in a burst of patriotic despair, hurried to ask the commander of the Trekroner why he had not opened fire and sunk their fine 74, sooner than allow her to be thus tamely carried off.

On his return to the *Elephant* Nelson made the necessary change in his costume before proceeding to the Amalienborg Palace to dine with a nephew of His Britannic Majesty. Hardy was the only officer ordered to accompany him on an expedition deemed by many who watched them set out to be dangerous. It was known that the carnage in the enemy vessels had been terrible, and Nelson's arrival would coincide with that of the Danish wounded. The morning of Good Friday, 1801, was overcast and hazy. In Copenhagen Roads English men-of-war were refitting with as much precision as if they were at Spithead. Their prizes had, with two exceptions, been secured over-night, but many boats were still plying to and fro, distributing prisoners at the rate of a hundred per ship-of-the-line. The word had gone forth from on high that these prisoners were patriotic fellows, mostly artisans and agricultural labourers, with a stiffening of Norwegian seamen. Young gentlemen from the University, serving as volunteers in the batteries, had, it was whispered, put in the charge before the shot. The Danes, a peace-loving, God-fearing people, were England's natural friends. They had never heard a shot fired in anger until their leaders had been seduced, for his own ends, by the Tyrant of Russia. British pursers, who had been insisting on the necessity of a return to Yarmouth or Leith, as they watched so many plump prisoners come on board, were relieved to learn that the prizes had been found excellently well provisioned.

Colonel Stewart afterwards heard that Nelson's passage through crowded streets to the palace had evidently been expected to be a touch-and-go business. The strong military guard on the *route* had been ordered as much from fears of an incident as from compliment. In the event, " the populace showed an admixture of admiration, curiosity and displeasure ". Nelson saw and heard only what he had intended, and next morning, over breakfast, told Fremantle that they had been welcomed with cheers, to the annoyance, he fancied, of H.R.H. and Count Bernstorff. " I hate the fellow." (This dislike was not based on personal contact, for Count Bernstorff had been delivered into his clutches for a moment only. In that moment the Foreign Minister heard that he had acted very ill in involving two countries that ought never to quarrel, in their present situation : a Court official immediately announced that His Royal Highness was ready to receive Lord Nelson, and on Nelson's reappearance, the Count was called to go in to the Prince.)

At the banquet which preceded his audience the chief guest worked hard, the cynosure of many eyes, for the townsfolk were permitted, not only to throng the hall and staircase of the palace, but to watch the lordly ones eat. " The people ", recorded Nelson, who trusted his touch with them, " received me as they have always done." As a one-armed English Admiral won his way through the many courses of a Danish state dinner, he told his host that he had been in 105 engagements, but that yesterday's had been the greatest. The French, in action, generally behaved well, but could not for one hour have stood what the Danes yesterday had endured for four. He tactfully recognised the name of Lieutenant Willemöes, who had fought a 24-gun raft right under the guns of the *Elephant*, offered the young officer his hand, and, turning to his royal employer, said that this lieutenant deserved to be an Admiral. The Prince, with dignified melancholy, said that if he was to promote every Dane who had fought heroically yesterday he would have no rank and file left.

At the interview which followed the Regent was supported by Lindholm ; Nelson stood alone. The Prince opened by graciously thanking Admiral Nelson for his humane attentions to the Danish wounded, but Nelson, going straight to the point, said that every

man in England, from His Majesty down to the lowest person,
would be painfully affected to hear that Denmark, leagued with
her furious enemy, had fired upon the British flag. His Majesty's
nephew interrupted to say that Admiral Parker had declared war
on Denmark, whereupon Nelson, with equal sharpness, requested
royalty to send for the papers to read the direct contrary, and in
the silence which resulted, asked if he was permitted to speak his
mind freely. When his freedom of speech had included the
suggestion that if Denmark was to pursue the policy outlined by
the Prince, the Baltic would soon be known as the Russian Sea,
his host, shying perceptibly, countered with imitative frankness,
" For what is the British Fleet come into the Baltic? " Nelson's
answer (intended to be unmistakable) was, " To crush a most
formidable and unprovoked coalition against Great Britain."
The Prince spoke much and unhappily of " misunderstandings ",
said that his uncle had been deceived, and presently was rash
enough to acknowledge that it was not to the interest of a peace-
loving commercial country to see England crushed, to which his
guest dryly acquiesced. He repeated, again and again, that he
had offered his services as mediator between his uncle and the
Czar, but Nelson held that a mediator must be at peace with both
countries. The Admiral's plain offer was, " Either join your fleet to
ours, or disarm." He asked, first, for a free entry of the British
fleet into Copenhagen (and the Prince interrupted eagerly to say,
" That you shall have with pleasure "). The demand that
Denmark should suspend her treaty with Russia, while Sir
Hyde Parker, for his part, suspended his plain and positive orders
for an attack upon the Danish capital, caused a royal personage
who had seemed " to quake on many points " obvious misery.
He finally said that he hoped Sir Hyde would not begin to-morrow,
as he must call a council on so important an occasion. Nelson
recognised his *congé*, and the interview ended pleasantly with the
English Admiral offering apologies if he should have said anything which His Royal Highness might consider too frank, and
His Royal Highness very handsomely begging that his guest
would show him the same lenience. Before Nelson departed
he was presented to a younger brother and nephew of the Regent,
and as he put off from a still crowded quayside cries which a
[14] Mediterranean man described as " Viva Nelson " broke out.

Nothing that occurred during the next five days was calculated to cheer him. He went with Fremantle to call upon Sir
Thomas Thompson. In the *Bellona*, four wounded midshipmen

had heard that their Captain was not dangerously ill, after the amputation of his leg. Thompson (whose private view was, " I am in great pain. . . . I am now totally disabled and my career is run through, only at the age of 35 ") pronounced himself as well as could be expected, and Fremantle found his spirits very good, but was staggered at the prospect of getting an officer " of very full habit " from the *Bellona* to the *Isis* for a passage home, on a day when it was blowing so hard that communication with the shore was difficult. Mosse, of the *Monarch*, had left a widow and six children; Riou, an invalid mother. Nelson's " heart ran out at his eyes ", as he began a letter to St. Vincent, recommending to the protecting hand of the First Lord the wives and families of those men who had lost their lives for their King and Country under his orders. The catalogue brought too freshly to his recollection his hand-grasp and good wishes to every Captain on the morning of April 2. The armistice was being renewed at twenty-four-hour intervals, and Count Bernstorff sent vague and unsatisfactory notes to Sir Hyde. When Nelson suggested that the Foreign Minister should meet him for discussion, Count Bernstorff took to his bed. If he had been in command, Nelson would by now have pushed on to Revel, to attack the twelve sail-of-the-line still icebound there, before they could join the main Russian fleet at Cronstadt; but Sir Hyde would not even consent to despatch him to cruise off Carlskrona. While the Commander-in-Chief stayed inactive, his second-in-command was so busy by day he had not time to turn round, and at night could not sleep. " All here hang on my shoulders." Fremantle, in letters home, was meanwhile describing him as " the life and soul of the squadron ". After Nelson had, with great labour, in bad weather, got out his prizes (some of them, in his opinion, in good condition and easily reparable), he was obliged to organise their immediate destruction. Sir Hyde, who was in no great need of prize-money, and was nervous of the approach of the Russian and Swedish fleets, had decreed that all except one 74 (which he had commissioned as a hospital ship, and was sending home) must be burnt.

At last, on the morning of April 9, the terms of a sixteen-weeks Armistice were ready for presentation, and Nelson prepared to land again. He was not entirely satisfied with the terms, and not sanguine as to their acceptance, for he was convinced that fear of Russia, not desire for further slaughter, was keeping the Danes from receding, even temporarily, from the

Armed Treaty of Neutrality. He wrote to St. Vincent that he only wished to finish Paul and then retire, and to Addington that if the Armistice was not approved, he hoped he might be superseded and allowed to seek the shade of a chestnut tree on his estate of Brontë. Captain Lindholm, Adjutant-General of the Fleet, and Major-General Count Ernst Walterstorff, Royal Chamberlain, had been appointed by the Regent to act on the part of Denmark. Lord Nelson and Colonel the Honourable William Stewart, Member of Parliament for Wigtownshire, were named by Sir Hyde Parker, who was lending his own Foreign Secretary, the Rev. Alexander John Scott, to act as interpreter. Nelson also took Foley, young Edward Parker and Fremantle with him, and they went in Fremantle's barge. Cold rain was lashing a capital which required sunshine to display its charms, and since the sea was very rough, uniforms suffered, in spite of " dreadnought " boat-cloaks. Briarly, on the morning of the battle, had mentioned as landmarks by which to steer, a small red house, a mill, a church and a wood, and as the negotiators approached Copenhagen, they were able to discern that its environs were principally rich in such features. In spite of the weather, the crowd upon the quayside was much larger than it had been on the preceding Friday, and this time it included many women and children, who had been evacuated when bombardment was expected. Lindholm had come to meet his fellow Commissioners, and the warmth of the dignified greeting between him and the famous Englishman produced a good effect upon a mourning people who had now buried their dead and were hoping for peace. Stewart gathered that their aspect was much less lowering than it had been upon the previous occasion. An impressive public funeral for the fallen had been staged two days past, in which a group of white-robed virgins, each attending a widow, orphan or walking case wounded in the action, had headed the long *cortège* to the naval churchyard. The hospitals were still busy, but had been obliged to ask that no more comforts for the wounded should be delivered.

The Commissioners met in a ground-floor chamber of the Amalienborg Palace, and after several hours' conference nearly parted upon Article VII, the clause fixing the duration of the Armistice. Nelson, who had represented his Commander-in-Chief and himself as " English Admirals come to treat with open heart and hand ", frankly admitted that he needed sixteen weeks in which to deal with Russia. When an angry Dane muttered in French that they had better renew hostilities, he picked up the phrase and repeated, " Renew hostilities ! Tell him " (turning to Dr. Scott) " that we are ready at a moment; ready to bombard this very night." The Commissioner, who had believed that because an English Admiral did not speak in any tongue save his own, he understood nothing else, apologised in confusion, and business recommenced with increased amicability : but by 2 o'clock, when the conference broke up to attend a *levée*, Articles VI and VII were still in dispute. The state apartments had been cleared of valuables, in apprehension of the city being shelled, and the quantity of timber employed by the architects of a northern palace was unusually visible. As he climbed a grand staircase, on the arm of one of his compatriots, stiff, hungry and tired of being what he described as " shut up in a room in a palace half-wet-through ", Nelson murmured, " Though I have only one eye, I see all this will burn very well." A banquet for which fifty covers had been laid awaited him upstairs. He buckled to his task again, and blonde ladies of the Court, looking in at the doorway during the feast, to see a celebrated figure seated on their Prince's right hand, observed with relief that much cordiality prevailed. Even Fremantle presently thought that if the weather had not been so cold and rainy, the party from the British squadron might have passed a very pleasant day in a Court, inferior of course to St. James's, and not even so splendid as Naples. Nelson, while his well-chosen *suite* made a strong impression on peace-loving, patriotic Danes, was closeted with the Prince for a long final tussle, and after much hesitation, the Prince agreed to an Armistice for fourteen weeks, instead of the sixteen mentioned in the treaty. He did not enter into further thorny dispute on the subject of neutral ships-of-the-line being stopped and their convoys searched for contraband of war by belligerents. His fatigued suggestion was that some means might be contrived by which such mortifications might be prevented. A smiling British Admiral replied, " I think there might very easily ", and later went into the problem in close detail with the efficient Lindholm, promising to forward the result of their discussion to Mr. Addington. He did not take his leave without a last cheerful shot : " Now, Sir, this is settled, suppose we write ' Peace ' instead of ' Armistice ' ? " But a Prince who had already gone too far could only muster a smile in return, and say that such a happy state of affairs must be brought about slowly, so as to cause no new wars. Darkness was falling by the time that the Commissioners proceeded, through cheering crowds, to the *London*, for the signature of the Armistice.

Nelson reached his flagship fagged out, to find letters from home awaiting him. While he devoured them, gentlemen at the Amalienborg Palace were also heaving sighs of relief. A message had arrived from St. Petersburg that the Czar had been found dead in his bed, on the morning of March 25. This was the form in which the news of the assassination of Paul I first reached the courts of Europe.

6

" I do not believe ", wrote Nelson to Lady Hamilton, on April 13, " we shall fire another shot in the Baltic."

Acting on this belief, he had written to St. Vincent, asking for leave to come home, and begged Lindholm to get him passports to travel overland, by Lübeck, to Hamburg, where, if no better chance offered, he intended to take the Yarmouth packet. Colonel Stewart had sailed, with the terms of the Armistice, and instructions to call at 23, Piccadilly, to introduce himself and collect " Lady Hamilton as St. Cecilia ". This portrait (which, having been privately secured, had never left Sir William Hamilton's house) had cost the purchaser £300. " If it had cost me 300 drops of blood, I would have given it with pleasure." Still, he marvelled at Sir William's *sang-froid*. Captain Bligh (" one of my seconds on the 2nd "), bearing a letter in which he was commended as a steady seaman and a good and brave man, was being entrusted with a gift of Copenhagen porcelain to be delivered at the same address. " It will bring to your recollection that here your attached friend Nelson fought and conquered."

In London, at Brooks's Club, Mr. Coke of Holkham was laying Sir T. Miller fifty guineas " that Nelson is neither taken prisoner or capitulated ". In Copenhagen the rumour ran that the new Czar was willing to give up all English vessels, goods and subjects detained in Russia. Sir Hyde hesitated no longer to enter the Baltic along the Grounds, between the islands of Amag and Saltholm. All his heavy ships had been ordered to remove their guns; nevertheless on their passage most touched, and several grounded, underlining how perilous had been their situation on the 2nd. Fremantle, who had brought his 74 to draw only twenty-two feet two inches, led the fleet the whole way, though very nervous to be running in four fathoms and a half, and frequently less, for more than four miles. The squadron

was safely at anchor in Kioge Bay by nightfall on April 12, with
the exception of the *St. George*, the *Agamemnon* and a few frigates.

While he was lying, detained by foul winds, some twenty-four
miles from his Commander-in-Chief, a message from Sir Hyde
told Nelson that a British look-out frigate had seen the Swedish
fleet at sea. The hour was 6 p.m., the temperature was, even in
the opinion of tough Mr. Alexander Briarly, " pretty sharp ".
This admiring Scottish expert, who had stayed in the *St. George*
to see her over the shallows, was the witness and chronicler of a
characteristic minor incident. The moment that Nelson received
the news he ordered a boat to be manned and jumped into her
(without even waiting for a boat-cloak), calling for Briarly to
attend him. His fear lest the fleet should have sailed before he
got on board a ship was his only topic during six hours of hard
pulling, mostly in darkness, against wind and current. Briarly,
offering a greatcoat, received the answer, " No, I am not cold ;
my anxiety for my Country will keep me warm." He heard
Nelson's voice repeating, " Do you not think the Fleet has sailed ? "
and ever replied, " I should suppose not, my Lord." But even
he was shaken by the Admiral's next decision. " If they are,
we shall follow them to Carlskrona, in the boat, by God ! "
Fortunately they were not called upon to cover a distance of
some fifty leagues in a six-oared boat, without a morsel to eat or
drink. They reached the fleet about midnight, and went alongside the *Elephant*, where her commander gave a warm response
to an inquiry, " in true Norfolk drawl ", whether Captain Foley
could be so good as to be plagued again by Admiral Nelson.   ¹⁶
The fleet proceeded in the leisurely manner typical of Sir Hyde
Parker's command towards " the Swedish Portsmouth ", and
Nelson vented his irritation in letters of complaint to Lindholm
of an official report of the action of the 2nd, composed by Commodore Fischer, who had commanded the Danish line on that
occasion. On the 19th, back in the *St. George* again, he came off
Carlskrona, to be presented with a beautiful picture of eight
Swedish sail-of-the-line and two frigates, " very snug ", shut up
in their fine harbour, where they were protected not only by their
batteries, but also by a profusion of the bronzed and glistening
rocks typical of the Scandinavian coastline. Nelson sadly
commented, " Thus all our hope of getting alongside them is at
an end ; they will not trust themselves out again this summer ",
and Sir Hyde, having received a letter from the Russian Minister
at Copenhagen saying that the Czar had ordered his fleet to

abstain from all hostilities, returned to an anchorage in Kioge Bay, near the Danish capital, there to await further instructions from England.

Warmer and longer days succeeded one another. Fremantle, who landed and spent a late April day on " a little bit of an island called Ertholmar ", thought himself almost at the end of the world. Innumerable tanned children, with linty locks, scrambled fearlessly by the side of the splendid Captain of an English man-of-war as he solemnly promenaded with an amiably slow-witted Governor around a kingdom consisting of seven rocky islets, covering not more than a square mile, and containing nothing but a lighthouse, barracks and fishermen's huts. Two days later he received one of those reminders for which Admiral Nelson's most devoted officers did not much care :

> " My dear Fremantle,
> " If you don't come here on Sunday to celebrate the Birthday of Santa Emma, Damn me if I ever forgive you. So much from your affectionate Friend, as you behave on this occasion,
> " Nelson and Brontë."
> " *St. George*, April 24th, 1801."

Two dozen guests, including Sir Hyde and " his parson secretary ", assembled on the 26th to drink Lady Hamilton's health in a bumper of champagne. She was possibly in Wales by now, on a tour of Sir William's Pembrokeshire estates. Her last letter showed that she had been vexed by persistent newspaper reports of the purchase of a house for Lord and Lady Nelson. Her lover had assured " Mrs. Thomson ", " he has never wrote his aunt since he sailed, and all the parade about a house is nonsense. He has written to his father, but not a word or message to her. He does not, nor cannot, care about her ; he believes she has a most unfeeling heart." Before he issued his invitations to Lady Hamilton's birthday feast he had sent a note of instructions to Davison :

> " *St. George*, April 23rd, 1801.
> " My dear Davison,
> " You will, at a proper time, and before my arrival in England, signify to Lady N. that I expect, and for which I have made such a very liberal allowance to her, to be left to myself, and without any inquiries from her ; for sooner than live the unhappy life I did when I last came to England, I would stay abroad for ever. My mind is as fixed as fate ; therefore you will send my determination in any way you judge proper."

Before he sailed, he had written again to old William Marsh, senior partner of Messrs. Marsh and Creed (now Marsh, Page and Creed), who had been his agents for seventeen years, asking him to pay £400 quarterly to Lady Nelson. He intended the sum as a permanent arrangement, a separation allowance, but had not stated this explicitly, and the " parade about a house " was not quite all nonsense. His brother Maurice's account of him on his last leave (obliged to lodge in a London hotel) had alarmed his family. His sister Susanna had bravely addressed herself, from Norfolk, on March 8, for the good of the family, to a person whom she had never liked:

20

" Will you excuse what I am going to say ? I wish you had continued in Town a little longer, as I *have heard* my Brother regretted he had not a house he could call his own, when he return'd. Do, whenever you hear he is likely to return, have a house to receive him. If you should absent yourself entirely from him, there never can be a reconciliation. Such attention must please him, and I am sure will do, in the end. Your conduct, as he *justly* says, is exemplary in regard to him, and he has not an unfeeling heart. I most sincerely love my Brother, and *did quite as much* before he *was Lord Nelson*, and I hope my conduct was ever the same towards you *as* Mrs. Nelson as ever it was as *Lady Nelson*, I hope in God I shall have the pleasure of seeing you together as happy as ever. He certainly, as far as I hear, is not a happy man."

21

The Rector had written, four days later, even more tactfully. He said he had heard nothing of his daughter-in-law for a long time. He asked if he could have done anything which might have offended her, and if there was any acceptable way in which he could exert himself on her behalf. But both these efforts arrived too late. The birth of Horatia, of which he had learnt since his last unhappy interview with his wife, had decided Nelson to seek no reconciliation. What he intended to be his last letter to her had been achieved as he lay in thick fog, in the Downs:

22

" Josiah is to have another ship, and to go abroad, if the *Thalia* cannot soon be got ready. I have done *all* for him, and he may again, as he has often done before, wish me to break my neck, and be abetted in it by his friends, who are likewise my enemies; but I have done my duty as an honourable, generous man, and I neither want or wish any body to care what becomes of me, whether I return or am left in the Baltic.
" Living, I have done all in my power for you, and if dead, you will find I have done the same; therefore my only wish is to be left to myself; and wishing you every happiness, believe that I am,
" your affectionate Nelson and Brontë."

His wife superscribed the sheet, " This is my Lord Nelson's letter of dismissal, which so astonished me that I immediately sent it to Mr. Maurice Nelson who was sincerely attached to me, for his advice. He desired me not to take the least notice of it, as his brother seemed to have forgot himself." She spoke of her brother-in-law in the past tense, for on the day that Nelson was sending his final instructions to Davison, Maurice was dying. (In the preceding year she had complained to her husband, " We see very little of Maurice.")

It has generally been asserted that when Lady Nelson swept out of a breakfast-room in Dover Street, she departed from her husband's life. It is true that they met but once more, for a formal leave-taking, a few days later, and that after March 4, 1801, he never again addressed her directly; but as this was a tale of true life, and a broken marriage of many years' duration, the end was neither so dramatic nor so tidy. He was yet to be reminded of her existence many times, and it was long before he had persuaded Lady Hamilton not to mar his picture of the ideal woman by hot allusions to " that Person ".

By the night of May 4 he was ready to leave the Baltic. His heavy luggage had gone on board the *Blanche*, a frigate which was only awaiting the arrival of the next despatch vessel from England to sail with return letters. He had been feeling so fagged that he had given up the idea of a journey to Hamburg by land; but his spirits improved as he gave his Flag-Captain orders for the forwarding of his private correspondence, and watched Hardy and young Parker sealing up his valuables. The first wounded from Copenhagen had arrived at Yarmouth, where he hoped soon to visit them in hospital, and his reply to a congratulatory address from the Mayor of that familiar port was jocose: " The French have always, in ridicule, called us a nation of shopkeepers—*so*, I hope we shall always remain, and like other shopkeepers, if our goods are better than those of any other Country, and we can afford to sell them cheaper, we must depend upon our shop being well resorted to." He had warned Lady Hamilton that the next packet she would receive would be himself, and that he looked for a line of welcome in her hand at the " Wrestler's Arms ".

The vessel, expected for a week past, joined the fleet late that night, and Colonel Stewart came on board the *London* at 1 a.m. Sir Hyde Parker, who had been well satisfied with his Command, found himself abruptly ordered home. Nelson, who was already in spirit in England, was appointed, with much compliment, to succeed him. The blow to both was painful, and Nelson (who had been resigned to the possibility of his Chief becoming " Lord Copenhagen "), in his first moments of bitterness, believed that Sir Hyde had " worked his leave " and deserted him, " to die a natural death " on a station where there would be no more fighting and (since he was forbidden to take prizes in the Baltic) no prospect for a penurious Admiral but " prison for debt ". An interview with Sir Hyde soon convinced him that he had wronged that unhappy man, and by 4.30 p.m., his baggage having been removed from the home-bound frigate, and that of Sir Hyde having taken its place, the *Blanche* sailed, carrying to eternal retirement an officer verging on old age, undisguisedly " low ".

Nelson's first signal as Commander-in-Chief was to hoist in all launches and prepare to weigh. He had sent St. Vincent an urgent note asking that another Admiral might be sent out, and begged the influential Davison to do all that he could to get him relieved of a most unwelcome Command. His letter to Lady Hamilton (which he was convinced would be seen by ten people before her) told her, " We must cheer up for the moment, at the present we are in the hands of others ", and that meanwhile, since activity must be his watchword as a Commander-in-Chief, " I am on my way to Russia ".

7

All the news in letters carried by Stewart had been ill, and the amiable Colonel had not even been able to bring with him the likeness of Lady Hamilton by George Romney. He feared that poor Saint Cecilia would think him a very uncivil sort of gentleman, but the fact was that his last day in London had been a nightmare of tedious immurements in the War Office, the Admiralty and Downing Street, culminating in orders which brooked of no delay, and offered no excuse for a farewell visit to Piccadilly. He had therefore left without her ladyship's promised letters to his friend, and the last received by Nelson had explained that Lady Hamilton was distressed for " Mrs. Thompson's child ". She had dismissed an unsatisfactory wet-nurse. The class, Nelson knew, was essentially untrustworthy, and too often disease, occasioning the loss of her own child, was the proxy's reason for availability. The hireling summoned by the lady of fashion always tended to be lazy and greedy. He

26

pictured Horatia, hastily weaned, losing weight and colour, ailing and wailing. Painful tears coursed down the cheeks of a remorseful father ("Dear innocent! she can have injured no one ") as the Baltic fleet, bound for Russia under his command, approached Bornholm Island, in blowing weather. He had at last been granted the Victory near Home which always filled the eye and ear of John Bull (and which he had, years past, from a sick-bed, envied Duncan), and handsome things had been said of him in both Houses, but the Prime Minister's letter told him that the Armistice achieved by him after so much labour had only been approved "considering all the circumstances ", and Davison, whose intelligence was good, reported in disgust that a Viscounty was likely to be his sole reward. " *That* you ought to have had long ago, and any additional distinctions short of an Earldom, in my humble opinion, would be degrading." Davison, who received "several epistles daily " from 23, Piccadilly, had naturally, but maddeningly as events had turned out, supposed that Colonel Stewart would be carrying all the latest from that quarter. He was, at the moment, confined to his house, after a carriage accident, and had therefore been unable to visit Mr. Maurice Nelson, who was dangerously ill, with what he described as an inflammation of the brain. He had sent his own physician to take charge of the case, and Sir John Hayes, who attended the Prince of Wales, was hopeful.

On the evening of May 12, in cold, clear light, which reminded him of a January day in England, Nelson came in sight of Pakerot Lighthouse in the Gulf of Finland. He had left the main body of his fleet, under George Murray, off Bornholm Island, to watch the Swedes and cover his communications, and had taken with him, on a visit to be represented as complimentary to Russians now supposed to be friendly, a chosen squadron of ten of his best-sailing 74's, two frigates, a brig and a schooner. But at Revel, next day, to his disappointment, he found that the twelve Russian sail-of-the-line had got out ten days past and gone up to Cronstadt. A polite note to the Governor of the Esthonian capital, requesting pilots, brought French-speaking Russian officers on board the *St. George*, and Lord Nelson was obliged to accept an invitation to land and visit the Governor of a picturesque city of great antiquity, which, in his present mood and health, charmed him not at all. Revel possessed an upper town of old, steep, cobbled streets, dominated by a church and fort, and a lower town, mainly modern, which owed its development to bathing facilities. A heavy cold on his chest was the Admiral's excuse for refusing a Russian dinner which, judging by the fine beef, fresh greens and soft, sweet-smelling bread surprisingly supplied for his squadron in a landscape devoid of vegetation, should have been worthy of acceptance. The crowd to which he had become accustomed followed him attentively during his three hours on shore, and all the Russians seemed to have taken it into their heads that he resembled a national hero. Everywhere he heard murmurs of " Suvárov ! ", " Le jeune Suvárov ! " The Military Governor 27 assured him that his letter to Count Pahlen, Foreign Minister, announcing his arrival, had been forwarded by express to St. Petersburg, but M. Balaschoff could not, without further authority, allow him to bring armed vessels within range of cannon-shot, so he had a seven-miles pull from his flagship to the town. He was amused at the surprise evidently felt by both his own squadron and the Russians at finding a British fleet in Revel, but he could not help reflecting with irritation that if, in February, he had been given the Command which he now held, and come straight here, he could not only have destroyed half the Russian fleet : many lives lost at Copenhagen might have been spared. On the following day he returned hospitality, and made his cough much worse escorting innumerable gentlemen of high-sounding title round his ship. Stewart noticed that the Cossack officers showed most intelligent interest in a British man-of-war, and that the disgraceful circumstances attending the death of the late Czar were by no means concealed. The Colonel, despite a wretched head-cold, had completed a plan of the Bay of Revel, which he was assured should be lodged in the hydrographer's office at the Admiralty, and Lord Nelson, after careful observation of the harbour, mole and anchorage, told him that he was decidedly of the opinion that had the Russian fleet been hostile, it might have been attacked with success by firing the wooden mole behind which it always moored during the winter months. A three-decker placed across the mouth of the harbour could rake the whole dock from end to end. The Admiral was also satisfied that, " We now know the navigation, should circumstances call us here again."

Count Pahlen's reply arrived about 3 p.m. on May 16, as the Commander-in-Chief was about to dine. He studied it with evident displeasure, but did not speak. During the meal he left the table, and in less than a quarter of an hour summoned his secretary. The signal to weigh was immediately thrown out, and although contracts had been made for provisions not yet delivered, the squadron stood out to sea, leaving the *Skylark*, a three-masted 14-gun lugger, to collect and settle. At this time of year, in this latitude, darkness lasted but a couple of hours, and with dawn the squadron proceeded down the Baltic. Count Pahlen's letter had not been civil. He had announced, on behalf of his Imperial master, astonishment that the whole fleet of a nation expressing friendly intentions should have come into the Gulf of Finland. The only guarantee of loyalty which he could accept was its instant withdrawal. Nelson's quickly composed answer had pointed out that, far from bringing his whole fleet, he had not brought one-seventh of the vessels at his disposal, and had deliberately left behind all his smaller craft of a distinctly hostile character, such as bomb-ketches and fire-ships. He had not entered even the outer bay of Revel without the consent of their Excellencies, Governor Balaschoff and Admiral Spiridoff. His intention had been to show very particular respect to his Imperial Majesty, either at Revel or Cronstadt, but since his pacific appearance had been so entirely misunderstood, he would immediately sail into the Baltic.

On the 20th, at night, the squadron fell in with the *Latona* frigate, having on board Lord St. Helens, newly appointed Ambassador to St. Petersburg. A very mild nobleman of attractive address discoursed for three hours in the Great Cabin of the *St. George*, but dashed an Admiral who liked quick results, by saying that he hoped, in a month, to be able to send him some decisive intelligence as to the attitude of Russia. Nelson (who had written to the British *chargé d'affaires* at the Russian capital asking him to call a meeting of British merchants to decide how he and his fleet could be useful to them) considered that two hours should have been sufficient. He was saddened, as he made on with a fair wind, by a letter of condolence from the Comptroller of the Navy, delivered to him by St. Helens. At last his brother Maurice had been promoted, but a rather unlucky man had not lived to enjoy the fruits of thirty-three years' conscientious toil. Maurice, who had obediently departed from a Norfolk parsonage at the age of fifteen to drive a quill in Seething Lane, had died a bachelor, but had left dependants. The Commander-in-Chief in the Baltic remembered with a pang that an elder brother's slender purse had always been open to a struggling Lieutenant, and forgot that he had more than once settled Maurice's debts. He wrote urgently, by three channels, to

Davison, asking him to do all that was kind for a lady whom he would always regard as his brother's honoured wife. (" Be liberal.") He begged Lady Hamilton to call upon and comfort " poor blind Mrs. Nelson " (who was legally Mrs. Ford). Maurice's irregular household had been no scene of guilty splendour, although of recent years it had included an elderly black butler. At an age when he had much ado to shift for himself, a young clerk of the Navy Office, who had inherited an over-tender heart, had made himself responsible for a little creature with a hard tale to tell. Of recent years his means had run to the lease of a pleasant small house in a green lane of the Thames valley, and an Eton boy's duty-letter had described to Admiral Nelson a magnificent day's expedition down the river with his Navy Office uncle, to Deptford, to christen an East-Indiaman after his famous godfather. A note which would have to be read aloud to her told Mrs. Maurice Nelson that Lord Nelson desired she should stay on at Laleham, keeping her horse and " whiskey " carriage for as long as she liked. James Price, " as good a man as ever lived ", should be taken care of and have a corner in his house for life. All his memories of hospitality at the Hampstead mansion of Uncle Suckling opened with the picture of big Black James beaming in the hall.

23

8

At dawn on May 23 the squadron from Revel joined the main fleet off Bornholm, and Rear-Admiral Totty, newly arrived from home with a reinforcement, was directed to relieve Captain Murray on that station. Detachments were ordered to Kioge Bay to water, and to Dantzig to buy bullocks, hay, biscuit and particularly wine (the Commander-in-Chief owning himself a strong advocate for serving wine to ships' companies instead of spirits). All his business having been completed by dusk, he proceeded, with eight of the line and a frigate, to provision at Rostock. On the first night after his arrival there he was amused and satisfied by the sequel to his Russian expedition. Count Pahlen was now singing to a very different tune. He most warmly invited Lord Nelson to visit his Imperial master at St. Petersburg, was horrified by their previous misunderstanding, and added that, as a first step towards solid peace, the Czar had instantly taken off the embargo from English shipping in all parts of his domain. As the Russian lugger left the fleet with a gracious reply to a gracious letter, she fired a salute, and Colonel

Stewart heard Nelson say to Wallis, " Did you hear that little fellow salute ? Well, now there is peace with Russia, depend upon it. Our jaunt to Revel was not so bad after all." It had, however, cost him dear.

Since April 27, when he had done what he called " the civil thing " at Revel, he had not been out of his cabin. The keen air of the North had cut him, he said, to the heart. He had written to Troubridge that he hoped his successor might be as strong as a horse. He seemed to have lost the art of sleep, and was coughing up what he believed to be the last of his lungs. He could not find out from his medical attendants whether they shared his fears, but they told him that the prevalent sickness in his flagship was undoubtedly " the influenza ". To his dismay, he found that his appearance upon the German coast of the Baltic with men-of-war that had fought at Copenhagen was regarded as an excuse for a seaside holiday by thousands of inhabitants of a small principality ruled by a brother of the Queen Consort of England. The Senate and University sent deputations to invite him on shore. Distant inland towns had forwarded their public books of record for an illustrious signature. The military Governor wished to pay him a visit, and in spite of a response that he could not expect an honour which he was unable, for health reasons, to return, an old General and three aides-de-camp arrived to walk all over such a ship as they had never before seen. He gave orders that no visitors were to be allowed on board the *St. George*, and that the *London* was to be the show ship. Boatloads of well-dressed sightseers bobbed around his flagship all day hoping for a glimpse of him.

Hearing that " the prince or duke of these parts " had left for the coast, he hurried on his preparations, and was ready to sail for Kioge Bay with a fair wind, when a letter from the Duke of Mecklenburg-Strelitz told him that His Serene Highness, who had come to Rostock to see him, desired he would appoint the time for his coming on board. A very homely country gentleman, sixty-one years of age, bringing with him " no less than a hundred men, women and children ", presented himself next afternoon. Queen Charlotte's brother, who offered ten thousand apologies for bringing such a large family, was obviously made happy by two salutes of twenty-one guns and the gift of a " Davison " Nile medal. In the Admiral's quarters he paused to admire three likenesses of a beautiful woman, and waited in vain for the proud explanation, " Lady Nelson ". Admiral Totty had brought

" St. Cecilia " from London.   The other two portraits of Lady
Hamilton had been " in the Battle " at Copenhagen, for their
owner had carried them with him to Foley's ship.   One was a
sketch by Miss Knight of her hostess laying a laurel wreath on the
rostral column at Palermo.   The other, the pastel performed in   *30*
Dresden, seemed to its anxious owner to have grown paler in
northern waters.   He hoped that this might not mean that the
original was ill, or changed in heart.   But he had been much
relieved by the safe appearance of the whole packet of letters
unavoidably left behind by Stewart.   " Little Parker ", who had
come out again with Totty, had brought them, and had also been
able to assure the Admiral that at 23, Piccadilly, Lady Hamilton
had shown him his lordship's godchild, " the beautiful Horatia ".

May slipped into June.   By June 11 Nelson reckoned that it
was thirty-seven days since he had received a post.   By every
vessel he had desired their Lordships to relieve him.   His case
against St. Vincent on the subject of prize-money should have
come on more than a month past.   His eye was almost worn out
searching " that point of land where ships came from England ".
Stewart, whom he had sent to Copenhagen to lodge a complaint
on non-observance of the Armistice terms, had tried in vain to
get him some English newspapers.   There were three in the
club-room of the Colonel's hotel, but no blandishments had
prevailed upon a grumpy old proprietress to part with one.   With   *31*
warmer weather, coughs and colds vanished, and a Commander-
in-Chief who possessed what the First Lord described as " the
magic art of infusing the same spirit into others ", was happy
to report " a finer fleet never graced the Ocean ".   For his own
part, he found that either the warm milk forced upon him at
4 a.m. every morning with Captain Foley's compliments, or
Captain Murray's lozenges, had produced a miraculous cure.   His   *32*
return to health had certainly been accelerated by the kindness of
everyone.   " I should be a wretch not to cheer up."   Even Totty,
an entire stranger, had written to say that he hoped to God it
was not true that Lord Nelson was going to England, or, if true,
that " your Lordship will take us all with you ".

On the night of June 12, Nelson could not sleep for joyful
expectation.   A cutter, reported in sight during the afternoon,
had joined at 11 p.m.   His old friend, Charles Pole, now a very
portly Adonis, was coming to relieve him.   His Viscounty had
been gazetted, and he was directed to invest Graves with the
Order of the Bath.   Two days later, Hardy having " trimmed

out the quarter-deck of the *St. George* in his usual elegant manner ", the ceremony was performed, with all possible dignity under the circumstances. The green morocco armchair from the Admiral's Great Cabin (chosen for him by Lady Hamilton) represented the Throne. It was draped in the Union Jack, and set under a canopy made of the Royal Standard. A guard of marines and men of the 49th Regiment was ranged on either side the quarter-deck, and all Captains of the squadron attended in full-dress uniform. The red ribbon, Star and Commission were carried on a blue satin cushion (also provided by Lady Hamilton), and Nelson, acting the King " as well as I could ", dubbed Sir Thomas knight with the gold crocodile-hilted sword presented to him by the Captains of the Nile. A salute was fired as he put the red ribbon over the shoulder of the new Companion. Above the scene of closely packed, rigid figures and primitive colours blazed a cloudless sky, and all around it a glassy sea. Silently, the Commander-in-Chief was wishing that he had a rope fast to Admiral Pole, who would never get on in such weather.

The *Æolus* frigate pathetically lacked a wind for a further five days. His release from a station where there was little hope of any further action came on June 19, when he quitted the Baltic for England, sailing in the *Kite* brig, so as not to deprive the fleet of a larger vessel.

CHAPTER XV

"SQUADRON ON A PARTICULAR SERVICE"
AND
"EXPERIMENTAL PEACE"

I

AT 5 p.m. dinner, at the Bush Inn, Shepperton, near Staines, on a mid-July day of 1801, Lord Nelson was heard to declare, amongst much laughter, that he did bar barbel. Sir William Hamilton was responsible for the appearance at the table (together with the succulent hams and chicken for which the hostelry was famed) of the uncouth fish caught by him in the Thames.

Since his arrival at Yarmouth, on July 1, the name of Nelson had been daily in the papers. Every reporter had drawn the picture of him passing slowly from bed to bed of the Naval Hospital and presenting every nurse with a guinea, before departing for London in a garlanded post-chaise and six with postillions attired as British tars. The toast in the Baltic Fleet on the day of his departure was said to have been, "May he, who is no longer our Commander, be our Example." At the Annual Meeting of the Durham Florists' Society, the first prize for pinks had been awarded to Mr. Donald, for his exhibit, "Donald's Lord Nelson". The royal family was at Mr. Rose's Wiltshire seat, bound for Weymouth. Cheltenham was filling, and amongst the persons of quality noted at Lymington were the Duchess of Somerset and Lady Nelson. The first choice for a few days' country quiet of a man who had no home in England had been a picturesque inn well known to sea-officers. "A very pretty place, and we are all very happy." Burford Bridge, set   1
in a green shade under the yew-covered shoulder of Box Hill, was also a haunt of artists and poets. But a Portsmouth road posting-house at all seasons was a scene of activity. At Shepperton, host Tom White could provide patrons with ideal recreation. Sir William was an expert angler; the Admiral had, in boyhood, and during his years of unemployment, often whipped a Norfolk stream. Their engrossed silhouettes were daily attended by   2
others, much junior. The party to assemble on the banks of the Thames had both the look and sound of a family party. The

466

Rev. William Nelson had brought his small, talkative lady and well-behaved daughter. (It had been possible to extract Charlotte from Mrs. Voller's seminary for a week-end, but only leave of absence for an afternoon could be obtained for her thirteen-year-old brother, who had been at Eton twelve months now, and liked it very much, but would be obliged if his Lordship could, when he had the time, send an occasional line, directed to Mr. Horatio Nelson at Mrs. Middleton's.) Merry little Captain Edward Parker, who needed a holiday but could ill afford one, had been invited to act as aide-de-camp. He made arrangements for the Admiral to visit the Staines Quarter Sessions dinner, at which, after the usual three cheers, three times three were voted for the British Navy. A day which the Admiral remembered as very happy had been spent at poor Maurice's house at Laleham. Parker ordered the transport, settled the bills, dealt with the tipping and presented the receipts to his Lordship. (There was a jest between the young Captain and Lady Hamilton that when he was rich and famous—say some sixteen years hence—he should present himself as a candidate for the hand of the Admiral's adopted daughter.) The caravan was completed by Sir William's Neapolitan body-servant, her Ladyship's black woman, Fatima, and Tom Allen. The Duke of Queensberry and Lord William Gordon, pressed by Lady Hamilton to join the anglers, had sent regrets in verse composed by Lord William, who wrote that nothing would have pleased him more than to see Antony and Cleopatra (" I mean you and Henry ") afloat in a wherry on the bosom of Father Thames.

An almost unclouded reunion was brought to a close on the 20th by a summons which caused a man invalided home from the Baltic to hurry up to Whitehall and Downing Street. On the day of his arrival at Yarmouth a statement that preparations on the coast of France were in great forwardness had been prominent in the Press. Buonaparte, relieved by the Peace of Lunéville of war on the Continent, had been for four months at leisure to reconsider his favourite scheme for invasion of England. Nelson realised when he accepted the command of a large squadron of light craft, for the defence of the coast between Orfordness and Beachy Head, that a reassuring name had been needed by those making an emergency appointment necessitated by popular apprehension. He believed that both St. Vincent and Troubridge were at work to keep him from the company of Lady Hamilton. But a bare three weeks' experience had convinced him that he could not happily make holiday in time of war. Besides, if the war continued, he wanted the Mediterranean Command. He had seen Horatia, and told Lady Hamilton to look out for a country house for him. At 4 a.m. on July 27 he left Lothian's Hotel for Sheerness, having met his father for a brief interview at the hotel on the preceding day. The Rector, who was on his way from Bath to Burnham Thorpe, was made happy by being told that his son had been appointed to the " most Important and most Honourable employment that any Navall officer has been entrusted with for many many years,—not since the Armada business ". His letter to Mrs. Matcham described the Admiral as " in Great Spirits and seems well ", but did not mention whether a delicate subject had been approached.

A letter received by Nelson during his Shepperton stay had run :

" My Dear Husband,
    " I cannot be silent in the general joy throughout the Kingdom. I must express My thankfulness and happiness it hath pleased God to spare your life. All greet you with every testimony of gratitude and praise. This Victory is said to surpass Aboukir. What my feelings are, your own good heart will tell you. Let me beg, nay intreat you to believe no Wife ever felt greater affection for a Husband than I do, and to the best of my knowledge I have invariably done everything you desire. If I have omitted anything, I am sorry for it.
    " On receiving a letter from Our Father, written in a melancholy and distressing manner, I offered to go to him, if I could in the least contribute to ease his mind. By return of post he desired to see me immediately, but I was to stop a few days in Town to see for a House. I will do everything in my power to alleviate the many infirmities which bow him down. What can I do more to convince you that I am truly,
                                 " Your Affectionate Wife,
                                        " Frances H. Nelson."

The direct question, the tacit suggestion of a meeting, had been alike disregarded by a husband who had closed his ears to the voice of duty, but a too candid lover had duly reported the call from the past, and since (finally very angry) protestations on his part had failed to convince the mother of Horatia that she was not being played false, a heavy cloud, culminating in a storm, had preceded his daybreak departure " on a particular service ".

2

As he dined at Sheerness, after a quick and easy journey, he privately considered that England's Defenders, as here exemplified, would make a good caricature. Vice-Admiral Graeme,

Commander-in-Chief at the Nore, who lived in one of the hulks, was, like himself, short of a right arm. The officer in charge of the military proved to have a wooden leg. An easterly gale rattled the windows as they feasted, and he thought, " If the Dutch mean to put to sea, this is their time." His flag was flying in the *Unité* frigate, and he had gone on board at once, " in order to show we must all be at our posts as speedily as possible ".

During his week at Lothian's Hotel he had carefully studied the mass of material available in the Admiralty and elsewhere on the subject of Buonaparte's avowed design of invasion. At Downing Street Mr. Addington, detained in town by the growing alarm, had been frank. In Hyde Park the Prince of Wales was reviewing volunteers. The capital was, as usual in late July, almost empty of fashionable folk, but John Bull was alarmed. The facts seemed to be that there were some 36 gun-sloops, over 200 gunboats and a large number of smaller vessels collected along the northern French coast, from Flushing to Cherbourg; in the Pas de Calais and Flushing districts a considerable number of troops, possibly 40,000. The picture which filled the eye of the gentry on holiday, and the dusty crowds cheering in Hyde Park, was of a calm night or hazy day, during which the French flotilla might slip across and land their invasion army on British soil while Britain slept. The reports of secret agents (mostly French *émigrés*, who had to live) were probably exaggerated, but the Grand Army mentioned by them exceeded in number any British regular army ready to offer opposition, and there had recently, beyond doubt, been much building of flat-boats in enemy ports. The Press had succeeded in killing the holiday season for most sea-bathing resorts of Kent, Sussex and Essex, and refugees from south-eastern towns were pouring inland, whilst heated volunteers on the coast erected beacons. After considering the evidence, Nelson had drawn up and submitted a Memorandum on the defence of the mouth of the Thames and the coasts of Kent, Sussex and Suffolk. His plan was based on the supposition that a descent on London might be made from Flanders and Flushing, in conjunction with an appearance of the Dutch Fleet. An officer of the naval service accustomed to using his own judgment was convinced that in order to gain the advantages created by a diversion, Buonaparte would divide his force, and land troops at two places simultaneously.

He was all day at his desk on the 28th, issuing orders to the little ships of his new command, some of which bore names very appropriate to their present duties—H.M.S. *Defender, Conflict, Attack, Cracker, Boxer, Bruiser, Firm, Haughty, Gallant, Ardent.* . . . Seven o'clock next morning saw him in his chair again. By noon, to the awed admiration of Parker, he pronounced himself ready to leave for Faversham and Deal, by post-chaise, having dealt with thirty of the ships at Sheerness, "made everyone pleased, filled them with emulation, and set them all on the *qui vive*". A line in the heroic vein from Lady Hamilton, received just as he set out, had chimed with his mood, and "naturally called forth all those finer feelings, of the sort none but those who regard each other as you and I do, can conceive". At Faversham, where his business was "to examine the organisation and readiness to serve of the Sea Fencibles", his arrival gathered staring and cheering crowds. The Reservists looked "with wild but most affectionate amazement at him who was once more going to step forward in defence of his country". A local gentleman, passing rich ("got it by the Fair Trade", was the Admiral's private comment), explained that the men, "always afraid of some trick", lacked, he was sure, nothing but a word from Lord Nelson, on behalf of the Admiralty, to reassure them that when the invasion was frustrated they would be allowed to return to their own homes. Until Lord Nelson's appointment had been published, nobody had rightly realised that "the thing" was serious. Lord Nelson, who had not himself realised that his new duties might include having to get up and harangue like a recruiting sergeant, supposed that if necessary, since he was "come forth", he could undertake something very disagreeable as well as any other. His immediate instructions to an eager audience on a windy day were easily to be understood. "Whatever plans may be adopted, the moment the Enemy touch our Coast, be it where it may, they are to be attacked by every man afloat and on shore; this must be perfectly understood. *Never fear the event.*" He reached Deal at 9 p.m., having had no food since breakfast, and supped an hour later with his homely old Captain of the Arctic expedition, now Admiral Lutwidge, Mrs. Lutwidge (who united an extraordinary appearance and a kind heart) and the military officer now in charge of the Deal Fencibles. Young Parker, invited to join the party, was quite overcome by his good fortune in being attached to "the cleverest and quickest man, and the most zealous in the world". He only feared that the favour shown him must arouse criticism. He longed for the opportunity to justify his patron's choice, and hoped it might come very soon, as the Admiral seemed to intend " to take a peep at them on the coast of France " as soon as the *Medusa* frigate was ready for him. Lord Nelson's flag had been hoisted in the *Leyden*, 64, and if the surf allowed, he said he meant to go on board early. " I shall have no bed, but that does not matter. I wish to show good people that they have not mistaken their man."

The anniversary of the Nile saw Nelson at sea, in the *Medusa*, trying to get off Boulogne. A report that the enemy were coming out had caused him to put to sea in a bustle at 10 p.m. on the preceding night, attended by some bomb-ketches. He saw already that the report had been incorrect.

Three days later, as first light revealed a mouse-coloured old *Haute-Ville*, clustering on the slopes of a wooded hill, and a *Basse-Ville*, where soldiers were already busy erecting new guns and mortar batteries, he prepared to make Boulogne an unpleasant spot, though without doing unnecessary damage to the civilian population. The enemy had moored two dozen gunboats in front of the pier, to guard the harbour-mouth and little port, from which no smacks had put out to fish since his approach. There were troops encamped along the coast to the south, but in no great number. The brilliant sun of a late summer's day broke through, and the people of Dover, hearing gun-fire, collected in crowds on the cliffs to hear " Nelson speaking to the French ", and since the visibility was very good, to see what they could. By noon his bombs had sunk three flat-bottomed boats and a brig, and disabled six more. As he visited the ketches, the enemy were " most attentive ", both to his barge and the various vessels visited by him. By 6 o'clock, when another French vessel went on shore, he was writing to the Secretary to the Admiralty that to-day's business was of no great moment, except to show the enemy that they could not with impunity come outside their ports. He assured St. Vincent, the Duke of Clarence, Davison and the Hamiltons that wherever invasion was coming from, he could now venture to predict that it was not Boulogne. In his second hasty note to Lady Hamilton, swearing himself " in fire, or out of fire, yours ", he urged, " Buy the house at Turnham Green. I can pay for it." It struck his sense of humour that he, who had been pushed forward to animate the nation to Home Defence, should not himself possess a house in England. To proceed, to reconnoitre Ostend and Flushing,

had been his intention as he withdrew after a noisy day, but the
wind coming easterly, he decided to go to Margate roads to look
at the Fencibles of that quarter, and do his utmost to get more
afloat.   The figures shown to him two evenings later were damp-
ing.   Of the 26,000 enrolled in the district under his command,
only 385 had volunteered to go on board a man-of-war.

A mountain of paper-work was awaiting him at Margate.   The
announcement of his appointment had brought the inevitable flood
of letters from friends, acquaintances and strangers.   A person in
Yorkshire hoped that Lord Nelson would lend £300 to open a
school.   The Rev. Mr. Comyn, picturing him in a first-rate, was
eager to serve him again as a chaplain.   That Lord Nelson's present
command entailed pitching about the narrow seas in nothing
larger than a frigate, and " running to every port " to drum up
pier-men (who professed themselves ready to fly on board as
soon as the enemy approached, but unable to leave home for
more than a couple of days at a time), had not penetrated to the
brain of any but the expert.   Even Lady Hamilton had forwarded requests from Reservist Captains.

Count Walterstorff, of Copenhagen, thought that he would
like to spend next winter in England, in a diplomatic capacity.
Mr. Julius Angerstein, on behalf of Lloyd's, wished to announce
that the Committee had voted £500 to be laid out in presentation
plate by the Victor of Copenhagen.   Prince Castelcicala wrote
sadly of the situation of their Majesties of Naples, and a merchant
of Ancona to complain that his house (in which Lord Nelson would
remember particularly fine oil paintings) had been pillaged by
Buonaparte's troops, with the words, " I leave the frames for
your English lords."   Sir William Hamilton was visiting his
Pembrokeshire estates, where Mr. Greville's developments seemed
likely to yield satisfactory financial results, and Lady Hamilton
was making expeditions from Piccadilly to look out for country
houses within easy reach of London.   The one at Turnham
Green had proved to have no furniture—a serious consideration
in days when all furniture had to be made to order.   She had
seen a villa at Chiswick which might do, and so nearly taken one
at Harrow that the Press had announced the fact.   The Rev.
William Nelson thought it would be an admirable thing if Mr.
Addington made him Dean of Exeter, when the vacancy occurred.
The Prime Minister's secretary acquainted Lord Nelson that His
Majesty had graciously acquiesced in his application that the
Barony of Nelson should be extended.   The patent of a new

peerage, to be called " Nelson of the Nile and of Hilborough in the County of Norfolk ", had been granted, and in default of male issue by his lady, Lord Nelson's father, brother, and heirs-male, and the heirs-male of his sisters, should inherit. Lord William Gordon enclosed his latest song, and an old Crocodile had gained a brilliant victory off Algeciras; " Sir James Saumarez's action ", wrote the First Lord, " has put us on velvet." More than a hundred of the letters required replies, and the Admiral, " half-sea-sick ", prophesied, " I believe my head will be turned with writing."

When Mr. Spence, maritime surveyor of this part of the coast, came on board the *Medusa* during the morning of August 10, he found a famous stranger of fascinating manners " in a fix ". Admiral Nelson, who had been out in a cutter since 6 a.m., explained, " We have got the *Medusa* into this hole, but cannot get her out again, through the proper channel, while this wind remains, and although I have two or three pilots on board, neither they nor the Harwich pilots will take charge of her. I must get to the Nore to-night in her." The *Medusa* had been lying at anchor in the rolling ground off Harwich for two days, imprisoned by an easterly wind. In her passage between the Ridge and Andrew's Shoal, she had touched once or twice, and pilots who were nervous of trying to bring her into Harwich or Hollesley Bay absolutely refused to consider taking her over the flats extending seawards from the Naze. Mr. Spence, adjured to devise some means to get her into the Swin (a distance of some eleven miles), immediately agreed to take the risk at high water, and to the satisfaction of an Admiral who thought he ought to know all that there was to be known of the navigation, and believed he had been a tolerable pilot for the Thames-mouth in his teens, his flagship achieved a hazardous passage which created a record for ships of her size, and was thereafter known as the *Medusa* Channel.

8

While he waited for the Admiralty to pronounce upon a large project for an expedition with 5,000 troops against Flushing, he went " over the water " again. His preparations for a boat attack on the vessels moored outside Boulogne were elaborate, and he believed that it should be possible to destroy or carry off the whole flotilla. Fifty-seven boats, manned by picked officers and men, and divided into four squadrons, each commanded by a captain, were detailed for the attempt. Every boat was allotted combustibles, a broad axe, picks, cutlasses and

tomahawks, and two in each division ropes and grapnels. Their
orders were, not to be content with taking a single enemy prize.
" There must not be the slightest cessation until their destruction
is completely finished." They were advised to be ready manned
at 10.30 p.m., and on observing a signal of six lanterns hung over
the guns of the *Medusa*, to put off in silence and row under her
stern, whence they would start as soon as all were assembled.
The watchword for the night was " Nelson ", and the reply
" Brontë ".

By 11.30 on August 15 the boats were rowing quietly
in, with muffled oars, each division in tow. Nelson, who could
on this occasion only order and arrange what others must
execute, abided the result miserably, his only solace being the
reflection that he had taken much more precaution than he would
had he himself been engaged. Toothache and headache were no
doubt partially responsible for a nervous disquietude quite
strange to him, but as the dark minutes passed, he resolved never
again to put himself into such a position. (" Would it were bed-
time, and all were well.") Shortly before one o'clock he heard
the division of mortar boats (directed to throw their shot
into the camp and batteries) come into action. His hope had
been that on finding themselves suddenly under fire, the French
would panic and scramble for the shore, in which case " our
folks have only to go on—never think of retiring ". In fact,
every vessel was defended by poles headed with iron spikes, and
strong nettings, and manned by military : moreover, they were
all chained, both together and to the shore, so that although
several were taken, after hard fighting, they could not be brought
off. The four British divisions, pulling hard against strong
uncertain currents in darkness, failed to attack " at the same
happy moment ". Parker's (the second) squadron, arriving
first and alone, was beaten off after a struggle in which some of
the *Medusa's* best men fell, and the young officer himself, with a
shattered thigh, only escaped being killed or taken prisoner
owing to the address of an acting lieutenant whom Nelson had
already written down as a rough diamond. The Hon. William
Cathcart, coming to the rescue in the *Medusa's* cutter, towed off a
boat entirely filled with dead or disabled men, and drifting towards the enemy line. Of the three other divisions, two, coming
up later, were separately disposed of by a fully alert enemy, and
the fourth lost its way until daybreak. Desperate attempts to
burn captured French craft were a costly failure, as the boarders

came under fire from musketeers on the shore, who took action
9 regardless of their own men.

Two mornings later, in London, where a heat-wave was in
progress, Cathcart's father, who had been out early to see some
young horses worked, was surprised by a note from Lady
Hamilton. He flung down the newspaper, jumped on a horse,
and according to his own account, devoured the distance from
Gloucester Place to Piccadilly in two minutes. Lady Hamilton
had sent for him in order that she might read aloud to him a
passage from a letter of Lord Nelson, mentioning that his " Bill "
was safe, " was in the hottest of it, and is distinguished ". Lord
Cathcart, forwarding " Lady H's note " to his wife, commanded,
" Do not show it, or talk of it. She was kind to me, and the
10 world are ill-natured and injurious about her correspondence."

3

On August 16 Nelson reported to St. Vincent, " I am sorry
to tell you that I have not succeeded in bringing out or destroying
the Enemy's Flotilla moored in the mouth of the harbour of
Boulogne. The most astonishing bravery was evinced by many
of our officers and men." His casualty list was 44 killed and
128 wounded. " No person ", he was careful to state, " can be
blamed for sending them to the attack, but myself. . . . All
behaved well, and it was their misfortune to be sent on a service
which the precautions of the enemy rendered impossible."

He anchored in the Downs the same night, and himself chose
lodgings in Deal for Parker and his Flag-Lieutenant. Frederick
Langford went ahead steadily, but from the first the case of
Edward Parker was serious. Seated between their beds,
Nelson wrote to St. Vincent offering to try a bombardment
of Calais, and to Lady Hamilton, " You ask me, my dear
friend, if I am going on more expeditions. And even if I
was to forfeit your friendship, which is dearer to me than all
the world, I can tell you nothing. For I go out if I see the
enemy, and can get at them; it is my duty, and you would
naturally hate me if I kept back one moment." He had warned
St. Vincent that he would like to be relieved before the equi-
noctial gales set in, and already he was ruefully ending a despatch,
" Heavy sea, sick to death—this sea-sickness I shall never get
over." He agreed that it was perfectly right to be prepared
against a mad Government, but he could not now see where an
invasion was to come from. " Nothing to be done on the great

Scale " was his description of his present duties, and he repeated his request that a junior officer of less damaged frame might be appointed. " The services on this coast are not necessary for the personal exertions of a Vice-Admiral." His belief that Buonaparte's invasion threat was a mere empty menace was perfectly correct, as were his suspicions that peace was in the air. As early as June 23 the First Consul had informed General Augereau, " You will receive instructions for the formation at Flushing of five divisions of gunboats, which, added to the sixteen divisions in Channel ports, will impose on England."

Another consideration which was causing Nelson anxiety was that he had only £3,000 in hand, and at any moment Lady Hamilton might find a house for him. " The Baltic expedition cost me full £2,000. Since I left London it has cost me (for Nelson cannot be like others) near £1,000 in six weeks. If I am continued here, ruin to my finances must be the consequence, for everybody knows that Lord Nelson *is amazingly rich.*" Before he left the *Medusa*, for instance, he must do something handsome in return for Captain Gore's hospitality, and Lady Hamilton, given welcome orders, had chosen at Messrs. Salter's a silver tea-urn, to be suitably inscribed, for which the estimate was £65 18s. 6d. A request for leave, in order to come to London for consultation with their Lordships and to settle his affairs, was discouraged. " The public mind is so very much tranquilised by your being at your post, it is extremely desirable that you should continue there." Only one difficulty, foreseen by St. Vincent, never developed. The district assigned to Nelson was taken out of the commands of senior Admirals, who still retained their authority. He was particularly warned that at the Scheldt he was impinging upon the province of Dickson, Commander-in-Chief in the North Sea. Not the slightest friction resulted, and his relations with Lutwidge, easy from the first, increased in cordiality after Mrs. Lutwidge had expressed the belief that Lady Hamilton was an Angel.

The arrival of Francis Oliver, on August 19, with Gore's tea-urn, letters from Lady Hamilton mentioning a house at Merton in Surrey, and the news that Sir William, on his return from Milford Haven, was likely to bring his lady and Mrs. Nelson to the coast for sea-bathing, threw Nelson into a fever of expectation. He hurried to engage bedrooms at an inn, and reception-rooms, with a gallery overlooking the beach, at the " Three

Kings ", Deal. A bathing-machine was secured for the ladies. On the day that his guests were due to arrive, duty called. Captain Owen of the *Nemesis* had reported from off Flushing that he believed a successful attempt might be made against an enemy flotilla there. A squadron from Margate joined the Admiral off North Foreland, and he stood for Flushing with a force numbering thirty sail, and including bomb ketches and fire-ships. He took with him several Artillery officers and half a dozen pilots, and, when he was at sea, summoned for conference one of the odd characters with whom he had become more closely acquainted in the pursuance of his present duties. The opinion on the ground of old Yawkins, an ex-smuggler, " a knowing one ", now Master of the *King George* cutter, weighed more with him than that of Captain Owen, whose zeal, he suspected, had caused him to overlook such trifles as tides and sandbanks ; and two days later, after an expedition up the Welling Channel in the *King George*, he was satisfied that he had come on a wild-goose chase. The reported enemy flotilla consisted of a single Dutch ship-of-the-line, one or two French frigates and three or four brigs; and Yawkins, whose local knowledge was considerable, pointed out that even supposing the Admiral was able to get alongside the enemy, they could, whenever they pleased, with the flood-tide, cut their cables and retreat, leaving him with nothing possible to do except silence the Flemish shore batteries.

On his return to the Downs, Nelson entered upon a fortnight of mingled toil and holiday. He escorted his guests over his flagship, to the Naval Hospital, and daily to the lodgings of Langford and Parker. Lady Hamilton promised to leave behind her chaise, to take out the convalescents, and sent to Piccadilly for a sofa for the Flag-Lieutenant. Sunlit excursions to Ramsgate, to Dover Castle and Walmer (where Mr. Pitt was not yet in residence) were successfully undertaken. One evening, when the carriage which should have met them failed, Nelson found himself deserted with Emma on an English country road. Something symbolic in the situation struck his imagination, and when he passed the stretch of road alone, on an autumn day later in the year, tears sprang to his eyes. The *Amazon* had come in, and he shifted his flag to her. Three dozen of the best champagne, ordered from London, had also arrived, and there was entertainment of the squadron in the galleried rooms at the " Three Kings " (overlooking a beach where there was the noise of a continual surf), and of the visitors at the house of Admiral Lutwidge.

Yawkins, commanded to find fishing for Sir William, did so, apparently with good effect, for on the paying off of the *King George* cutter, this worthy volunteer, who had never failed to send his respects to Sir William and lady, made a complacent reappearance in the Milford packet service. Not all officers of the squadron, however, were happy at the situation. " Lord Nelson ", wrote William Cathcart to his father, " is, I believe, still at Deal, and if he is wise, he will stay there during the equinoxes. . . . He talks of sailing directly Sir William goes to town. I hope and trust he will not, as his so acting will give rise to a good deal of newspaper chit-chat, which to me will be very unpleasant."

The condition of Parker was already lowering Nelson's spirits when the day drew near for the party to break up. An amputation had been decided upon, and unexpectedly elderly and ingenuous parents had been summoned from Gloucester. The poor father sent Dr. Baird on board the *Amazon* to explain that he had arrived penniless, his pocket-book, containing £20, having been stolen on his journey through London. The Hamiltons put off their departure for four days, and the operation was pronounced successful, but the little Captain, who had told Lady Hamilton, " To call me a *Nelsonite* is more to me than making me a Duke : I would lose a dozen limbs to serve him ", was now so altered that when the Admiral had to quit his bedside, " he got hold of my hand, said he could not bear me to leave him, and cried like a child. . . . I came on board, but no Emma. No, no, my heart will break. I am in silent distraction. . . . My dearest wife, how can I bear our separation ? Good God, what a change ! I am so low that I cannot hold up my head." He despairingly noticed that he could not even enjoy the sight of a hundred West Indiamen coming through the Downs. He determined to go to look at his Dungeness squadron, but bad news, and lack of a wind, brought him back from Folkestone. Several deceptive rallies led him to hope that Parker might yet " take possession of his room at the Farm ". Dr. Baird kept him advised of every change in the patient, and the Admiral fondly repeated, to many correspondents, details of the gradual dissolution of an obscure junior officer. " He was my child, for I found him in distress." On the morning of September 29 Parker died, and since he had youth and hope on his side, died hard. Nelson, who attended the funeral next day as chief mourner, was observed to shed tears as a body which represented to him hopes unfulfilled in his stepson was lowered into the cold earth. All the circumstances connected with the loss of Parker were painful, for the Admiralty refused to pay for his lodgings or interment. " He might have stunk above ground, or been thrown in a ditch." His accounts had to be inspected, in company with his helpless father, and it appeared that when already surprisingly involved, the young man had lent Langford a sum which that officer hoped might not be called for in a hurry. After Nelson had made himself responsible even for mourning for the bereaved and a coach to carry them away, it came to light that Captains Hardy, Sutton and Bedford had also all been " touched ". The last straw was a notification from Langford's agents that a Mr. Parker had called on his way through London for the money owing to his late son, adding nine pounds to a debt of which unfortunately the Lieutenant had kept no record. Nelson, who had written to ask their Lordships to commend a deserving case for a pension to the notice of His Majesty, and appealed to Lady Hamilton's kind heart for hospitality to un-accustomed travellers, had to warn all quarters in haste against a snivelling rogue. " I am so vexed that he should have belonged to our dear Parker."

He went under Dungeness in deep dejection, and planned another attempt on the Boulogne flotilla, this time with a fire-brig commanded by the indefatigable Owen, to be attended by H.M.S. *Eugénie* and *Jamaica* and the *King George* cutter. Yawkins had volunteered as pilot. While the Admiral was thus engaged, a Public Letter from Nepean instructed him that as the French Minister might have occasion to send despatches to his Government, their Lordships had directed that no vessels or boats of any description should at present proceed to France. This could mean only one thing, and on October 4 Nelson learnt that preliminaries of a peace treaty had been signed. He ordered his squadrons to abstain from putting into the Channel, but not for a moment to relax vigilance, as hostilities had not yet ceased. A farewell gift to Dr. Baird arrived in the nick of time. Desiring to express in solid form his gratitude to the Scottish Surgeon for his attentions to the Boulogne wounded, especially Langford and Parker, he had asked Lady Hamilton to choose another piece of plate—this time a silver-gilt cup. The actual scene of presenta-tion was not a social success, as Dr. Baird was so overcome that he fled from it, and immuring himself in his own cabin, sent a message that he was too unwell to dine. A note from the Admiral, however, presently evoked a personal explanation, and Lady Hamilton received a stately letter of thanks, which included

interesting details of the exfoliation of bone, as exemplified in
the leg of the Flag-Lieutenant. The days while the peace
awaited ratification were remarkable for their beauty. Nelson
noted, with growing calm, " a beach remarkably smooth,—not
a curl on the shore ". A neat note from his schoolgirl niece
called forth from a weary man the grateful comment, " Hers is a
nice innocent letter ". He had expected to be granted leave on
the morning of the 6th, and Allen had actually packed, when,
instead of the looked-for order of release, came a letter from the
Prime Minister expressing the opinion that it was of the utmost
importance that Admiral Nelson should keep his flag flying till
the definitive treaty had been signed. Troubridge, on behalf
of St. Vincent, mentioned a fortnight as the probable interval
between the ratification and cessation of hostilities, after which
everything that could be attempted to meet his lordship's
wishes (short of striking his flag) should be done. " I must
submit, for I do not wish to quarrel with the *very great folks* at
the Admiralty, at the last moment ", explained Nelson to Davison,
whose offer to lend any sum necessary for the purchase of a house
had aroused a reply in the style of a Walter Scott hero. (" Can
your offer be real ? Can Davison be uncorrupted by the depravity
of the world ? I almost doubt what I read ; I will answer, my
dear friend, you are the only person living who would make such
an offer.")

On the day that he had told St. Vincent, " Whenever I am
released I shall always be ready to come forth again ", descriptions of the welcome given by London to a French General bringing the ratification threw him quite out of temper. Like many
other officers in His Majesty's service, he was doubtful of the
durability of a peace which seemed very convenient to Buonaparte. After a spectacular gale, the autumn rains set in, followed
by fogs, and he contracted one of those devastating colds in the
head which he believed might last the season, if he was kept
" thumping in the Downs ". Mr. Pitt, calling on the afternoon
of October 13, found him in a frigate's cold cabin, half sea-sick
and racked with toothache, convinced, " I should have got well
long ago in a warm room, with a good fire and sincere friends."
The Statesman agreed that it did seem very hard that he should
be kept here still, " now all is over ", and an invitation to dine
at Walmer was issued, but Nelson, although he privately believed
that " Billy Pitt " might yet be of use to him, would not face
being dragged through a night surf to dine with the Angel Gabriel.

Merton Place, Surrey, the Seat of Admiral Lord Nelson (north façade).

From an engraving by W. Angus, published 1804, after a painting by Edward Hawke Locker (1777–1849), Commissioner of Greenwich Hospital, youngest son of Captain William Locker, R.N.

Troubridge, " one of my Lords and Masters ", had advised him not to think of leaving his station, to take health-inducing walks ashore, and wear flannel next the skin. " Does he care for me? *No*; but never mind." He made formal application to be allowed to strike his flag, pointing out that the service for which he had been called forth was now at an end, and the state of his health required repose. His request was crossed by a notification that he might have ten days' leave from the 22nd. " What a set of beasts ! "

He had assured Lady Hamilton that he meant to get away from Deal very early on the longed-for day, and reach Merton, at latest, in time for 4 o'clock dinner on Friday the 23rd. As the date approached, he remembered with anxiety that he had often found himself left for a week, and once for a fortnight, without communication with this shore. On the 20th the surf was so great that he could not have landed dry, if at all. Sutton offered to get the *Amazon* under sail and take him down to Dover, but he was busy parting with ships ordered to the Nore to be paid off; besides, he could not endure the prospect of having to wait unoccupied for two days at a seaside hotel. The 21st dawned so dirty, and with promise of such a gale, that both Sutton and Hardy recommended his going ashore while he could. He ordered a Deal boat for the following morning, and planned, if it was impossible to land there, to go to Ramsgate Pier. On his last day he had so much to do that he had scarcely time to notice the weather, except to realise that, despite a fire in his cabin, he was starving with cold and could not feel the pen in his fingers. On the 22nd, however, all went so well that he was able to advance his programme. He landed early, without difficulty, and took a carriage to Walmer to return Mr. Pitt's call. He paid his last visit to the wounded in Deal hospital before proceeding to dine with the Commander-in-Chief in the Downs. Each farewell showed him that he left his little squadron accompanied by the sincere regret and good wish of every creature in it. His flag was struck on board the *Amazon* with sunset of the late autumn day, and at 6.30 he left the " Three Kings " in a post-chaise and four. He would, if he travelled throughout the night, arrive at his unknown home in time for early breakfast instead of late dinner, but for Nelson to rattle through a sleeping England in the small hours, with a terrible cold and a fast-beating heart, would be nothing new, and this time, at last, he was going to a *11* country house of his own.

4

Merton Place, Surrey, which, even after he had set eyes upon it, he persisted in calling " the Farm ", had been his since September 18, when, after a brisk negotiation (in the later stages of which Lady Hamilton feared that Mr. Haslewood had not been very civil to Mr. Greaves), it had been secured, furnished, for £9,000. Possession had been promised for October 10, and Lady Hamilton had conducted all the business with the lawyers unaided. (Davison was in Scotland, and Sir William, who had not taken his famous lady with him when he visited his Milford property or his relatives at Warwick Castle, had, after their Deal jaunt, departed again alone, this time to Newmarket.) Nelson, who could not at the moment command more than £3,000, had borrowed from Davison and his late secretary, Tyson, and had so far paid £7,000 in two instalments. " As to asking Sir William, I could not do it. I would sooner beg." He was of opinion that everything in the house should be his, " even to a Cook and a Book ", and that Sir William and Lady Hamilton should contribute nothing. " You shall have the whole arrangement. . . . To you I may say that my soul is too big for my purse, but I do earnestly request that all may be mine in the house, even to a pair of sheets, towels etc. . . . You are to be, recollect, Lady Paramount of all the territories and waters of Merton, and we are all to be your guests, and to obey all lawful commands." He wrote to his solicitor, urging him to get Mr. Greaves out, and Lady Hamilton in, by the 6th, so that Sir William should be presented with a *fait accompli*. (" I wish I could have got up for four or five days. I would have roused the lawyers about.") Mr. Greaves held to his date, but an old diplomat, having once stated that he would be paying half the household expenses while he and his wife stayed in the country house of their best friend, reported on October 16, in his most imperturbable manner:

" We have now inhabited your Lordship's premises some days, and I can now speak with some certainty. I have lived with our dear Emma several years. I know her merit, have a great opinion of the head and heart that God Almighty has been pleased to give her; but a seaman alone could have given a fine woman full power to chuse and fit up a residence for him without seeing it himself. You are in luck. . . . The proximity to the capital and the perfect retirement of this place, are for your Lordship, two points beyond estimation; but the house is so comfortable, the furniture clean and good, and I never saw so many conveniences united in so small a compass. You have nothing but to come and enjoy immediately; you have a good mile of pleasant dry walk around your own farm. It would make you laugh to see Emma and her mother fitting up pig-sties and hen-coops, and already the Canal is enlivened with ducks, and the cock is strutting with his hens about the walks. Your Lordship's plan as to stocking the Canal with fish is exactly mine. I will answer for it, that in a few months, you may command a good dish of fish at a moment's warning."

Sir William congratulated him on a bargain, struck just before the prospect of peace sent up all prices, but his Jamaican friend, Hercules Ross, now patriarchally settled at "Rossie Castle, N.B. a new mansion in the ancient castle style; new church to correspond", regretted that a Norfolk peer had not invested in a Norfolk estate, particularly as "a London villa" must always be "a pick-pocket possession". His farm had filled Nelson's thoughts and letters as he pitched and rolled at anchor in the Downs. If Mr. Greaves's furniture was not good enough, they could get rid of it, little by little. "There are sales every day." In any case, "all will probably go to Brontë, one of these days". He must leave his cot behind him until his discharge, but it should come to the farm presently, for cots were the best things in the world for sea-friends, and he believed Sir William would agree with him that they should lay themselves out to entertain well-informed sea-officers rather than "country squires, lords, etc." He greatly hoped to see "my little charge" under his own roof, and tentatively suggested, "Probably she will be lodged at Merton; at least in the spring, when she can have the benefit of our walks. It will make the poor mother happy, I am sure." Lady Hamilton had beautifully described the little stream running through his grounds, "The Nile", on which she proposed to row him in a boat; otherwise he had been able to form but the vaguest of pictures of a place which he knew that he would admire, as it had been the choice of a person whose taste in laying out land was, he was sure, as fine as in music. His hope was for a thoroughly English country home. Gore, who had paid a visit of inspection, had mentioned that there were statues in the garden. If this was correct, they had better be banished, for they would accord very ill with the poultry, sheep and cattle with which his "farmer's wife" was going to make him a rich man. He pictured his flocks folded in peace in view of his windows. "Take care that they are kept on the premises all night, for that is the time they do good to the land." He had no fears that his stock would

decrease, " for I never expect that you will suffer any to be killed ".
Indeed, he foresaw Emma " getting all the old dogs in the place
about her ", and also two-legged and lame dogs—" for every
beggar will find out your kind heart ".   The egregious Allen was
bringing a remarkably fine goat, presented to him by Captain
Sam Sutton, who, together with Captain Bedford, was coming
to eat brown bread and butter at Merton.   Hardy sent a message
that he had not lost his appetite. . . .

It was with dawn of Friday, October 23, 1801, that his chaise-
and-four charged underneath a village-made triumphal arch,
past an unpretentious lodge and gates, and up a drive of no great
length (thickly planted towards the high-road) to the principal
entrance of a red-brick house of two storeys, about a century old,
facing east, and overlooking grounds intersected by a small
branch of the river Wandle, spanned by a light Italian bridge.
Lady Hamilton had regretted in her latest letters that the leaves
were falling in Surrey, and feared, as she looked at her hasty
purchase in the cold light of autumn, that her confiding friend
might not like Merton.   His first sight of it was at the hour when
vitality is at its lowest, and before fires were lit on a sharp morning,
but a weary traveller never doubted that he had found Paradise.

Verandahs shaded the bow-windows of the larger rooms on
the right and left hand of the owner entering up garden steps
from a winding gravel sweep.   Both the " withdrawing-room "
and " eating-room " were well-proportioned and well-lighted,
and a visitor to the house on an August day found the withdrawing-room, which had plate glass fitted to the doors, " magnificent ".   A fragment of the mainmast of *L'Orient* and a bust
of the Victor of the Nile had been given prominent positions in a
hall, beyond which came a smaller hall, designed to receive hats
and cloaks, and affording, through glass doors, a shining glimpse
of lawns and ornamental water.   The remainder of the wing
behind the dining-room was occupied by kitchen premises.   The
north wing, which boasted a garden front of classic aspirations,
with a pediment, niches and urns, contained a third hall, a breakfast-room (in which the owner presently sat to a meal off his own
Colebrook Dale service) and, opening out of it, a ground-floor
gentleman's dressing-room, and a spacious library, facing west,
with full-length windows giving access to greensward.   A staircase, liberally decorated with engravings of naval actions and
heroes and portraits of Emma and various crowned heads, led
to an upstairs drawing-room, five best bed-chambers, with

adjacent powdering-closets, and eight servants' rooms. Excellent cellars for wine and beer, a detached dairy and ice-house, a well-stocked kitchen-garden, orchard and greenhouse, an old barn, and a paddock of rich pasture land, skirted by extensive shrubbery walks, completed the advertised attractions of " the newly-acquired seat of the gallant Admiral ".

5

" To be sure," he had written from the Downs, " we shall employ the tradespeople of our village, in preference to any others, in what we want for common use, and give them every encouragement to be kind and attentive to us." On the night of his arrival, a rustic community, glad that so celebrated and reputedly generous a man should have taken up residence in their midst, marked the occasion by illuminations. Merton was, as he had hoped, a village, no more, and the names of the tradesmen supplying Merton Place were incredibly bucolic. Greenfield was the butcher, Woodman the chandler, Peartree the stable-keeper. Messrs. Wyld and Gadd were his cheesemonger and baker, Mrs. Cummins took in washing, and his next-door neighbour was Mr. Halfhide. The problem of neighbours had troubled him as he lay in the Downs. Lady Hamilton set the highest value on her " regained reputation ", which had been assailed by no tongues during the ten years that she had spent at the Neapolitan Court since Sir William had raised her to what she proudly called " honors, rank, and what is more, innocence and happiness ". There could be no doubt that her reputation had suffered since the appearance of the Victor of the Nile as her outspoken admirer. Her regard for the conventions was so strict that he had hesitated to suggest that he should come to Piccadilly, and run down to see Merton in her company, while Sir William was away. (" You would not, perhaps, think it right for me to come.") She had never lost a chance of assuring embarrassed acquaintances that Lord Nelson's regard for her was " the purest flame ". Nevertheless, in fashionable London there had been galling scenes when he had attempted to thrust her, in the character of " my particular friend ", upon eminent company, and he blamed himself for them. His decision for the future at Merton was, " No person can take amiss our not visiting. The answer from me will always be very civil thanks, but that I wish to live retired." Almost at once, however, it appeared that at Merton Lady Hamilton was not to be reduced,

as in Piccadilly, to the society of gentlemen who came without
their ladies, leading ladies of the stage and opera, and a very few
ladies of the *vrai monde* who remembered Neapolitan hospitality
with gratitude, realised that the situation was now quite different,
but had always been a law unto themselves. The largest landowners of the district were the Goldsmids, of a family devoted to
music and acts of charity. When Abraham Goldsmid gave a
fête at Morden Hall, descriptions occupied a full column in London
newspapers. An elder, but lesser, brother, Benjamin, resided
in competitive state at Roehampton. At Wandle Bank House,
Mr. Perry, editor and proprietor of the *Morning Chronicle*, was
always ready to extend to anglers an invitation to fish in waters
which nearly surrounded his mansion and were decorated by
many species of water-fowl, including swans. A demolished
monastic foundation was considered at the date indispensable to
a romantic country setting, and amongst the water-meadows
behind the orchard of Lord Nelson's new house lay ruins of
Merton Priory, at which Becket had been educated, and from
which in the days of the third Henry, Parliament had issued the
Statutes of Merton. A curious old brick bridge, with the head
of a river-god in the centre (believed to have been built by the
first Tudor owner of sequestered church property), now led across
the Wandle from the grounds of Gate House, originally the
guest house of the Priory. Rear-Admiral Smith resided here
with his elderly cousin, Mrs. Cook, widow of the Circumnavigator.
Amongst smaller householders, the Newtons and the Halfhides
(who had a field to sell to Lord Nelson) were profuse in friendly
attentions. Dr. Parrett, the medical practitioner, introduced
himself promptly, and the Vicar of the parish church, Mr.
Lancaster, whose appointment dated from the previous April.
Almost immediately Lady Hamilton was able to announce with
aplomb to Mrs. William Nelson, " We *could* have plenty of visiting
in the neighbourhood, but we none of us like it."

   The punctual appearance of the Merton Place party at matins
in the church of St. Mary the Virgin on the first Sunday after the
great man's arrival had aroused feelings of interest and reassurance. " Have we a nice church at Merton ? " the son of a country
clergyman, now a landed proprietor, had eagerly inquired. " We
will set an example of goodness to the under-parishioners."
Merton parish church, which stood in lush fields, irregularly
filled at harvest-time with lumpish haycocks, and shaded by tall
trees, had been built of soft Surrey stone some seven hundred

years past. The churchyard displayed the memorial of an embroiderer to King Charles II. The new parishioners passed beneath an open-traceried timber porch to an appointed pew on the north side of the chancel, near the pulpit, from which it was possible to behold the traditional features of the English country church. Under a king-post roof of chestnut, which was one of the glories of the county, were gathered a Norman arch with zig-zag mouldings, an oaken door with scrolled iron straps, a glowing but much-varnished contemporary copy of a devotional Van Dyck, and the monument of a Cofferer to Queen Elizabeth, kneeling, with his wives and children, beneath heraldry, painted vermilion, indigo and gold. The old parishioners beheld three figures, each of which in a different way was remarkable, attended by a fourth, all innocence. Charlotte, who had been fetched for the week-end from the expensive London seminary at which she was learning pretty manners, spontaneously helped "the old gentlemen" on and off with their overcoats. ("So now", explained Lady Hamilton, good-humouredly, "I have nothing to do.") Throughout the service a charming little schoolgirl, with a smooth black head, found the places for her celebrated uncle, and gravely handed his prayer-book to a man who had lost his right eye and arm in the service of his country. Only two descriptions of Nelson in civilian dress survive. There is unreliable mention of him strolling the Hamiltons' London house in a crumpled hat, with a
15   striped brown overcoat thrown round his shoulders. (This garment may have been a boat-cloak, since these were generally supplied in brown plaid camlet lined with green baize.) A nephew remembered him, very neat, in a simple suit of black,
16   doing the honours of his Merton table. In uniform, his "old checked *surtout*" and "cocked hat put on square, and much lower than the others" were famous.

On Monday mornings, since Merton was, as the owner of Merton Place explained, "exactly one hour's drive from Hyde Park or the Bridge", the landowners of the district, almost without exception, took the London road early. The chariots of the Goldsmid brothers hastened to Finsbury Square, in order that their occupants might direct the hidden channel of gold flowing towards London from their native Amsterdam and further capitals; Mr. Perry posted to Fleet Street; Sir Robert Burnett's carriage took the accustomed route to the Vauxhall Distilleries; Sir William Hamilton's emblazoned equipage carried the owner to the British Museum and Mr. Christie's auction rooms, Miss Charlotte Nelson to her desk, and his lady to 23, Piccadilly. The Admiral had appointments with the First Lord and Lord Hood, and had told Messrs. Webb to send a representative to collect his peer's robe, which must be altered to that of a viscount before Thursday. Lady Hamilton also had made an appointment for him. A letter directed on Saturday to a quiet house off Oxford Street had desired—

" Dear Mrs. Gibson,
" Will you come to Piccadilly with Miss Thomson on Monday at 10 o'clock, not later? I hope my dear god-child is well.
" Ever yrs, E. Hamilton." 17

Nelson returned out of the fog to the roaring fires and welcoming candle-light of his country house from his first London expedition, alarmingly exhausted, to describe himself, " Not yet well. The cold of the Downs gave me a severe shake ", and Lady Hamilton reported to his sister-in-law in some agitation, " I am sorry to tell you I do not think our Dear Lord well. He has frequent sickness, and (is) Low, and he throws himself on the sofa, *tired, and says ' I am worn out '*. But yet he is better, and I hope we shall get him up. He has been *very very* happy since he arrived, and Charlotte *has* been very attentive to him. Indeed, we *all* make it our constant business to make him *happy*."

Lord St. Vincent was no longer to be found in Mortimer Street. The First Lord had moved into Admiralty House, and Nelson, whose memories of that august mansion had not generally been happy, had found this morning's interview depressing. The Earl, gruffly pronouncing himself " very unwell, a most severe cough ", had received an indispensable officer, whose actions in private life were causing him deep displeasure, much as might have been feared. Nelson's letters to various Service applicants, dated from his country study during the following week, stated wearily, " Your letter shall be given to Lord St. Vincent, with a note from me on the back of it. I have very little interest." " I wish I could have congratulated you on your good son's being made Post, but I can assure you I have not the smallest interest." " I have not a scrap of interest, but believe me, I am ever your most obliged and affectionate friend." He had thought that the thriving ten-months-old child displayed to him at Piccadilly had a look of the mother about the brow. He had a heavy list 18 of public appearances before him, and after his introduction in the Lords must produce a maiden speech for the following day. His task was suitable—seconding a vote of thanks " to Rear-Admiral Sir James Saumarez, K.B., for his gallant and distinguished conduct in the Action with the Combined Fleet of the Enemy, off Algeciras ", but after all was over he thought he had acquitted himself only fairly well.   To sit for Ipswich, in the Commons, had been his desire when he was younger.   He had toiled for Rachel, and they had given him Leah.   John Bull, personified by a butcher of Cheapside, seized him by the hand in an uproarious City crowd scene, lit by rosy winter sunshine, this Lord Mayor's Day.   " How are ye, my hearty?   Glad to see ye back ! " shouted the butcher, as a carriage long since relieved of its horses rocked the Admiral towards the Guildhall. His weeks were assuming a regular pattern.   From Monday to Friday he drove down to Merton every night, after fagging London days.   He commonly took a turn in his grounds before setting out, and held confabulation with Thomas Cribb, his head gardener, who had known and loved his property long before him, and was to do so long after.   In the " detached dairy " across the ornamental bridge a *protégé* of the ex-Ambassador reigned supreme, and of all the wonders of Lord Nelson's farm, his young nephews and nieces voted " Mr. Sancho " the most impressive. A gift of plants for Lady Hamilton had arrived from the Marquis of Abercorn, together with a pony, on which Sir William might take the gentle exercise suited to his age.   On November 12, the owner of Merton Place told Captain Sutton :

" Yesterday was a busy day—between gardening, attending the House, and eating, drinking, and hurraing . . . 150 dined at the London Tavern, and I, being the Cock of the Company, was obliged to drink more than I liked; but we got home to supper; and a good breakfast at eight this morning has put all to rights again."

A few days later the best authority in his world found him " in better health, and happier in himself, than in good truth I have in any past time observed him to be ".   The first adult guest to stay under his roof was his father, and to have won the Rector to Merton was a triumph, for there had been times during the past twelve months when the happy relationship of a lifetime appeared threatened.   Lady Nelson had taken a London house, in Somerset Street, Portman Square, and it had been customary for her father-in-law to spend his winters with her.   Some tale that she was acting with harshness to Captain Nisbet (who still lacked

employment, and some months after the separation had still
been calling at 23, Piccadilly) had, apparently, been credited by
Nelson, for on September 26 he wrote, " I had yesterday a letter
from my father; he seems to think that he may do something
which I shall not like.   I suppose he means going to Somerset
Street.   Shall I, to an old man, enter upon the detestable subject;
it may shorten his days.   But I think I shall tell him that I
cannot go to Somerset Street to see him. . . . If I once begin,
you know, it will *all out*, about her, and her ill-treatment to her
son."   More than a week later, when he had not yet composed   20
a reply, he reported a second communication from Burnham,
" which has hurt me ".   The Rector, already disturbed, had been
incensed by an anonymous letter accusing him of unkindness to
his famous son.   " This is unexpected indeed."   He had written
with some frigidity to ask if he might be personally informed as
to his son's plans for future residence, now that peace was happily
returned to Britain.   A country clergyman, who had never
lacked moral courage, and had inevitably, in the course of forty-
five years of pastoral duty, observed the misery of the broken
home, stated firmly, " If Lady Nelson is in a hired house, and by
herself, gratitude requires I should sometimes be with her, if it is
likely to be of any comfort to her."   (To his daughter Kitty, he   21
was deploring, " No prospect of better times for her, nay I think
worse.")   For five days Nelson toiled at drafts of an explana-   22
tion—" that I shall live at Merton, with Sir William and Lady
Hamilton—that a warm room for him and a cheerful society
will always be there happy to receive him—that nothing in *my
conduct* could ever cause a separation of a moment between me
and him. . . ."   " Tell me, my dear Friend," he appealed to
Lady Hamilton, " do you approve?   If he remains at Burnham
he will die, and I am sure he will not stay at Somerset Street."
At length he achieved something (" I could not say less ") which
he endorsed, " When read, send it to London to be put in the
post ", but the result was only moderately encouraging, for the
Rector's acknowledgment of " many kind invitations " from his
son and Lady Hamilton, " which it is my intention to accept ",
went on to explain that for the present he had engaged to be elsewhere.   November 9 found him at Somerset Street, where, he
announced, he meant to stay a fortnight, but within ten days the
carriage and man-servant which a victorious son had provided
for an invalid after the Battle of the Nile made a quiet arrival at
Merton Place, and a character who always brought out the best

in all with whom he came in contact tremulously entered Circe's
cave. "My part is very distressing."

When Brother William had been expected, Nelson had
specially begged that a good dinner be provided, "for these
big-wigs love eating and drinking". For his austere parent
attentions more acceptable had been prepared, though, judging
by tradesmen's bills, at Merton the loaded board always accompanied the heaped fire and glowing wall. The Rector was greeted
by his own portrait, hanging in a place of honour, flanked by
those of Davison and Sir William Hamilton. Three grandchildren—his eldest daughter's twins, and William's Charlotte—
were his fellow-guests, and his letter of thanks, after a visit of
ten days, showed that an ex-Ambassadress had excelled herself
in well-considered arrangements for his comfort, and an ex-
Ambassador in delicate eulogy of a national hero. The Rector
retired to spend the winter with the Matchams at Bath, sadly
convinced that his son never meant to live with his wife again,
but relieved that "the Breach" in his family need extend no
farther. His children were instructed that the love and affection
of their famous brother for all of them and theirs "depend upon
it is very sincere and unshaken", whereupon the Matchams,
last of the family to take the decision, offered themselves for a
visit, and entered upon terms of warm and lasting friendship with
Lady Hamilton at the cost of relinquishing the acquaintance of
Lady Nelson. They could not, however, be quit of the injured
shade. Their sister-in-law haunted them like an unquiet spirit.
Society moved in a comparatively small circle, and there were
unavoidable *rencontres* in places of entertainment. At Bath, in
the winter before Trafalgar, Mrs. Matcham and her daughters
sailed past Lady Nelson in a ballroom with heightened colour, to
be told afterwards by busybodies that nothing could have exceeded the look of contempt bestowed upon them by the small
lady whose habit of using her hands in conversation had always
irritated them. The Rector's offer of hospitality to his daughter-
in-law was refused, with a bitter thrust. Lady Nelson replied
that she had better not come to Burnham Thorpe. "Lord
Nelson's friends, and he, would not like it." ("I have seen Tom
Tit once", wrote Kitty Bolton to Lady Hamilton, in March 1805.
"She called in her carriage at Lady Charlotte Drummond's, who
lives next door. The lady was not at home, but she got out of her
carriage, walked as stiff as a poker about half a dozen steps,
turned round, and got in again. What this Manœuvre was for,

I cannot tell, unless to show herself. She need not have taken
so much pains if nobody wanted to see her more than I do. She
is stiffer than ever.") That the William Nelsons and the Boltons   25
were influenced by anxiety to provide for their young is arguable,
but no such consideration can explain the conduct of the
Matchams, and George Matcham left amongst his papers a
character sketch of " Lord Victory ", which contains illuminating
passages. In the opinion of his brother-in-law, Nelson's marriage
had been a failure from the first, and long before Lady Hamilton
came upon the scene, " his heart sickened and revolted " by
perpetual complaint and reproach, Nelson had made up his mind
not to attempt further home-life in England. After long separation, two very unsuited persons might perhaps have managed to
spend the sunset of life together peaceably and comfortably (as
was desirable), but, on the other hand, if Lady Hamilton had not
filled the gap, some other artful female would certainly have
hastened to do so. " Generous in heart, feeling, and full of
sympathy, he would readily have been engaged in friendship,
and as readily have been attached in love. . . . He early felt the
want of that domestic comfort." Nelson's daughter, who never   26
knew that Lady Hamilton was her mother,

" always heard from the Matchams and Boltons that the fault was Mrs.
Nelson's originally. The Matchams said repeatedly, ' However beautiful
and fascinating Lady Hamilton was, it would have had no effect upon
Lord Nelson, had not his affections been chilled, and thrown back, as
it were, upon himself.' He was treated with coldness by his wife. His
home was not made happy, and though I know he was wrong, still with
his warm and enthusiastic feelings, he felt the want of someone to love,
and be loved by in return. Alas ! for his fame, his regards were not
wisely bestowed. Had Lady Hamilton's character in early youth been
irreproachable, I question much if Lord Nelson would have incurred
the suspicions under which he laboured."   27

With mid-December 1801 the Rector sent thanks to Merton
Place for a box of gifts—an elegant set of porcelain for
the Matchams and for himself a plaid, chosen by Lady Hamilton,
shyly acknowledged as " very handsome ". " From an old man
you will accept the old-fashioned language at the approaching
happy season, which is, ' I wish you a merry Christmas and a
happy New Year.' " The weather had turned bitterly cold, and
after the House rose Nelson did not visit London, except for a
couple of hours on business, for a full month. He watched a
heavy fall of snow from his Merton window on November 27,

and by Christmas week skating parties. Lady Hamilton took drastic measures to ensure that he was happy.

(Postmark, 12 o'clock, December 14th, 1801 Nt.)

" My dear Mrs. Gibson,

" If you will take a post-chaise to-morrow, Tuesday, and set off at half-past ten o'clock, and bring my god-daughter and your little girl with you, I shall be glad to see you. Tell them to drive you to Merton, and the best way you can come is over Clapham Common. Hire the chaise for the day. You can go back at three o'clock. *Do not fail.*

" Ever yours sincerely,

" E. Hamilton."

28

The owner's first Christmas at Merton, before a number of acquaintances with no real claim upon his hospitality had found their way to a comfortable house, was quiet enough. Only Brother William and family were guests under his roof. Count Walterstorff came down for a day, and promised a further call, frustrated by a fashionable cold known in Paris as " La Grippe ". Mr. Greville, similarly indisposed, sent his uncle a gift of moor game, and regrets. Lady Hamilton received a long letter from her beloved Queen, who magnanimously sent a thousand compliments to the Hero of the Nile, despite his recent speech in the Lords on the subject of Malta. The peace made by England with France, and the failure of her friends to condole with her on the untimely death of her sainted daughter-in-law, had also caused Her Majesty pained surprise. She thought, with the spring, of rejoining her husband (a situation described by her as " going to die at my post "), and was glad to hear a rumour that " the Chevalier " had bought an estate near London. Sir William, in fact, since Government was still insufficiently grateful, was at present primarily concerned with getting through one more winter tolerably, in an abominable climate. He thought that the air and early hours of Merton seemed to agree with him, and believed that if he could hire a post-chaise by the month to carry him to such London diversions as he still affected, he might subside into retirement, solvent. But to be paying half expenses in another man's country house while a Mayfair house of his own, fully staffed, yawned untenanted, vexed him, nor was he favourably impressed by his wife's latest " Attitude " as Lady Paramount. In Italy he had never failed to remind a very headstrong young woman, for her own good, of her shortcomings. He feared that entirely uncritical encouragement of a lavish *châtelaine* by the heroic owner of Merton Place would benefit nobody, and confided in his nephew and heir on January 24 :

" Nothing at present disturbs me but my debt, and the nonsense
I am obliged to submit to here to avoid coming to an explosion which
would be attended with many disagreeable effects, and would totally
disturb and destroy the comfort of the best man and best friend I have
in the world.   However, I am determined that my quiet shall not be
disturbed, let the nonsensicall world go on as it will."

He had also, in reserve, a plan, not quite his own, for regaining
prestige and, incidentally, comparative affluence.   Last Christmas, at Fonthill, his kinsman by marriage had sounded him on
a scheme which he thought might succeed.   A peerage for Sir
William, in recognition of his diplomatic services, with reversion
to Beckford, was the prize to be demanded.   In return, Beckford
offered to Sir William an annuity of £2,000, to Lady Hamilton
(upon widowhood) an annuity of £500, and to " H.M. Minister,
two sure seats in the Commons " (and two more which might,
under favourable circumstances, be secured).   He suggested that
the first approach to the fount of honours should be made by Sir
William, *via* the head of his family, the Duke of Hamilton.   He
had good reason to believe that the Duke's heir was likely to
make Miss Beckford Marchioness of Douglas.

But, upon reflection, an old diplomatist, hibernating, upon the
whole very comfortably, in the London villa of a hero, during the
first winter of what His Britannic Majesty himself called the
Experimental Peace, decided to let this matter wait awhile.

6

The correspondence with which the owner of Merton Place
laboriously dealt, in a country library, was not much less than
that which had oppressed him while in command in the Mediterranean and Baltic.   Indeed, with the prospect of peace, and
the sweeping economies in the Service proposed by Lord St.
Vincent, a certain feature of it rather increased.

" To Lieutenant Baker, R.N., Dover-Street.
" Sir,
    " Every officer who has lost a limb has certainly a right to a pension,
and by application to the Admiralty you would certainly have one
granted.   I have, I can assure you, no power whatever to meet your
wishes by getting you to the West Indies."

The Chairman of Lloyd's was approached on behalf of Captain
Johnson, promoted after the Battle of Copenhagen.   (" In nine
days from the loss of his arm, he did his duty again as First
Lieutenant of the Ship.   Such spirit in the Service is never to

be overcome.") The Rev. Mr. Scott wanted a recommendation to the Governors of the Charterhouse, and the Rev. Mr. Comyn a country living. The case of Mr. Fellowes, "a man of the strictest principles who served with me as a Purser during the whole time I commanded the *Agamemnon*", was pressing, for Mr. Fellowes, "involved with a wife and family", was under arrest for debt. His lordship's old secretary, Tyson, wrote from Malta in misery, afflicted like Job after two months' slow fever. Tyson's efforts to send agricultural implements and seeds to the duchy of Brontë had been attended by a variety of mischances, and the only payments from the estate as yet forwarded to him by Graeffer amounted to less than £800. The Admiral cast up his accounts, and wrote in haste to Messrs. Marsh, Page and Creed, telling them to have £2,000 ready to pay to Mr. Tyson on his arrival in London, even if this meant that they must sell Lord Nelson's India Stock. He also wrote to Davison, asking him to have some cherished Mediterranean trophies, the gifts of foreign royalty, privately shown to dealers. The contrast between the reputed value of these diamond-set *bibelots* and the offers presently submitted by Davison struck the owner as shameful, but both they and the India Stock had to go. Amongst the thirty-five younkers to sail for Copenhagen in his flagship, three had been *protégés* of Lady Hamilton. Young Banti and the engagingly nicknamed "little potatoe Harris" must take their chance, but for her ladyship's cousin he wrote thrice to Sutton, asking him to keep Charles afloat if possible, and if not in his own ship, with any good frigate captain who would give the lad his chance, preferably of foreign service. A stricken-looking guest, on a long visit, drowsed opposite the Admiral as he ended his letter to Sutton, "What a gale!" Poor Langford's leg was still throwing out fragments of bone, and the shadow of amputation now hung over him. Distinguished foreigners were still addressing themselves in compliment to the Victor of the Nile and Copenhagen. The Baron d'Eiker and Ekoffen wrote from Bamberg to announce that the West of Europe had not waited for the conclusion of peace between England and France to testify its veneration for Viscount Nelson. The Chapter of the Order of St. Joachim had universally, and by acclamation, decreed that the dignity of a Knight Grand Commander be offered to him. The East also had not been neglectful. His old acquaintance, Admiral Cadir Bey, wrote from Alexandria, and Lord Elgin from the Porte, to congratulate him on the Sultan's bestowal of a further honour

in recognition of the victory of April 2. When writing to the
Prime Minister to ask for the permission of his own sovereign
to wear these alien decorations, Nelson reverted sadly to an
omission which had been the subject of many of his letters this
winter. He had long been concerned that as yet nothing except
his own Viscounty and Graves's K.B. had been awarded after
Copenhagen. In July he had understood from St. Vincent that
medals would be issued, and had accordingly reassured his
Captains. When the City had voted its thanks to the two
services for operations brought to a successful close in Egypt,
his anxiety that protracted silence as to Copenhagen was intentional had become acute. He had written to Downing Street and
Whitehall, enclosing copies of a letter of complaint to the Lord
Mayor, and after waiting three days for any answer, posted the
original. St. Vincent dryly but promptly thanked him for
letting him see a document which he had seen fit to forward, and
in two longer letters, while regretting that worry was making
Lord Nelson ill, stated that no recommendation for any issue of
medals celebrating the Action at Copenhagen was going to be
made. Addington, after a week's delay, asked him to call.
What was said at the ensuing interview did not reach the public
ear. It was surmised that His Majesty's Ministers did not wish
to give offence to the part of Sir Hyde Parker's fleet not engaged
in the action : the feelings of Denmark must be considered.
The visible result was that Nelson dropped his inquiries about
medals or promotions, and asked the Lord Mayor to consider his
letter withdrawn. But in the following June he requested that
a motion of thanks to him for his subsequent efforts in command
of coast defence against invasion should not be tabled, and in
September 1802 he refused to dine with the Corporation at the
Guildhall, and in November with the Lord Mayor. " Never,
till the City of London thinks justly of the merits of my brave
companions of the 2nd of April, can I, their commander, receive
any attention from the City of London." On a change of
administration, in May 1804, he wrote from the Mediterranean,
asking a new First Lord for a reconsideration of the decision of
his predecessor. A quarter of a century after Nelson's death his
surviving Captains were still petitioning in vain that the most
difficult of his victories might be recognised as he would have
desired.

Inevitably, amongst the correspondents of a public character
were numbered the lunatic, the charlatan and the abusive letter-

Horatio, Viscount Nelson, Duke of Brontë (*aetat 43*).

By John Hoppner, R.A. (1758–1810). (92″ × 58″.)

Nelson gave sittings for this portrait, of which several versions
exist, before March 1802, when Joseph Farington, R.A. saw
it in Hoppner's studio, at 18, Charles St., St. James's Square.
An engraving by Meyer was published on November 4th, 1805,
and an enamel, by Bone, was exhibited at the Royal Academy
in that year. The naval engagement in the background of the
original oil-painting is Copenhagen, but in engravings published after Nelson's death it was altered to Trafalgar.

writer. When a person signing himself Thomas Tugbear begged His Honour to bring back with him the Emperor Paul of Russia (as Mr. Tugbear needed an outlandish wild beast to carry about with him as a show, in order to support a wife and six children), the Admiral, just setting off for the Baltic, replied in his own hand that he would do his best. After the unsuccessful attack on Boulogne, a Mr. Hill, who gave Lord Nelson the choice of forwarding a bank note for £100 by return of post or seeing an exposure of his conduct in the Press, received an answer at once so suave and terrifying that he never stirred again. There is only one recorded instance of an appeal addressed to the most generous and punctilious of correspondents being crudely returned to the author without any word of solace. A sheet in a familiar handwriting reached Merton in Christmas week, 1801.

> "16, Somerset St.
>
> " My dear Husband,
>
> " It is some time since I have written to you; the silence you have imposed is more than My affection will allow me and in this instance I hope you will forgive me in not obeying you. One thing I omitted in My letter of July, which I now have to offer for your accommodation, a comfortable warm House. Do, my Dear Husband, let us live together. I can never be happy till such an event takes place. I assure you again I have but one wish in the world, To please you. Let everything be buried in oblivion; it will pass away like a dream. I can only now intreat you to believe I am, most sincerely and affectionately,
>
> " Your wife,
> " Frances H. Nelson."

On this redirected letter appear the words " Opened by mistake by Lord Nelson, but not read ", signed " A. Davison ".

7

Lord Minto arrived to stay at Merton Place, in time for dinner on Saturday, March 20, 1802, determined to disapprove of all he found. He stayed until the Monday morning, and on his return to London, wrote to his lady in Scotland :

> " The whole establishment and way of life is such as to make me angry, as well as melancholy; but I cannot alter it, and I do not think myself obliged or at liberty to quarrel with him for his weakness, though nothing shall ever induce me to give the smallest countenance to Lady Hamilton. She looks ultimately to the chance of marriage, as Sir W. will not be long in her way, and she probably indulges a hope that she may survive Lady Nelson; in the meanwhile she and Sir William and the whole set of them are living with him at his expense. She is in high looks, but more immense than ever. She goes on cramming Nelson

K K

with trowelfuls of flattery, which he goes on taking as quietly as a child does pap. The love she makes to him is not only ridiculous, but disgusting : not only the rooms, but the whole house, staircase and all, are covered with nothing but pictures of her and him, of all sizes and sorts, and representations of his naval actions, coats of arms, pieces of plate in his honour, the flagstaff of *L'Orient*, etc.—an excess of vanity which counteracts its own purpose. If it was Lady H's house there might be a pretence for it; to make his own a mere looking-glass to view himself all day is bad taste. Braham, the celebrated Jew singer, performed with Lady H. She is horrid, but he entertained me in spite of her. Lord Nelson explained to me a little the sort of blame which had been imputed to Sir Hyde Parker for Copenhagen."   [31]

Three days later the Peace of Amiens was signed. England had surrendered all her colonial conquests of the late war, except Trinidad and Ceylon. Malta was to be restored to the Knights of St. John, Minorca to Spain, the Cape to the Dutch, and Martinique and Guadeloupe to France. France's part in a most advantageous bargain was to evacuate Egypt and Naples, recognise the integrity of the Turkish Empire and Portugal, and indemnify the House of Orange. Buonaparte, elected Consul for life by a grateful country, henceforward signed only his Christian name, or initial, on all documents.

Nelson was sitting for more portraits. In May Sir William Beechey was paid £36 13s. for a half-length, exhibited at last year's Academy. Joseph Farington, R.A., after a visit to the studio of Hoppner on March 29, noted that this year " Hoppner had intended not to exhibit, but has been persuaded by Lord Carlisle to send a Kit-cat portrait of a girl leaning, which he painted with a view to Rembrandt's works. He will also send a portrait of Lord Nelson, full-length." Two likenesses of Lady [32] Hamilton—one as a Bacchante—were also on view at Burlington House this year. Lord Nelson had lent them. In the following year's Exhibition an enamel by Henry Spicer was applauded as " critically just, and displaying all that decision in the features which so eminently characterises Lord Nelson, that Hero of our Nation ".

A few weeks after his first Merton call, Lord Minto found himself alongside his friend in an unexpected place—on the witnesses' bench at the Old Bailey. On the morning of April 6 Colonel Montgomery of the land forces and Captain Macnamara of the Royal Navy, both on horseback in Hyde Park, and both attended by favourite dogs, had in vain adjured one another to " Call off your dog, sir ! " After the duel of the Newfoundlands had

followed a duel between their masters, in which both officers had been wounded, the Colonel fatally, and the coroner's inquest had brought in a verdict of manslaughter. Lord Minto, giving evidence as to the disposition of Captain Macnamara, of whom he had seen much in Bastia, believed him not to be pugnacious. Lord Nelson, who had known him for nine years, was certain that, although he was not the man to take an insult, yet he was so good-tempered that he would not himself insult man, woman or child. Admirals Lord Hood and Hotham, Sir Hyde Parker and Sir Thomas Troubridge also deposed favourably as to the good character of the accused, and the naval Captain, who appeared leaning upon a stick, clad in an olive-green *surtout* with velvet facings, was reported of most prepossessing manners, and although stoutish in figure, with perfectly the air of the man of fashion.
33   The jury returned a verdict of " not guilty ".

8

A letter to the landlord of " The Star " Inn, Oxford, from George Matcham, Esq., of Bath, bespeaking rooms and dinner for himself and eight guests at 5 p.m. on Wednesday, July 21, 1802, had not aroused in that quarter any suspicions that the hostelry of a university city was to harbour a national hero. Indeed, it would appear that " The Star ", Cornmarket, favoured by a stranger with a large order in the peak of the tourist season, had declared itself full. His brother-in-law, explaining that he knew nothing of Oxford, had asked Mr. Matcham to make all
34   arrangements (" need not say for who "). Eventually, " The Angel " in the High Street, on the south side of the sacred bend, almost opposite Queen's College, was the appointed *rendezvous* of a party consisting of a large clergyman attended by a young Etonian, three gentlemen, all of unusual appearance, though very different stature, a smaller schoolboy and three ladies, two of whom were in deep mourning. The Matchams, with their first-born, aged twelve, had come from Bath. The William Nelsons, who were going to accompany Sir William and Lady Hamilton and Lord Nelson on a three weeks' tour, had come with them direct from Merton, crossing the Thames first at Maidenhead, again at Henley, and finally at Magdalen Bridge, on all occasions, unfortunately, in a steady downpour.

The Rector of Burnham Thorpe had died rather suddenly on April 26, and his famous son, although warned that the end was near, had not been present at either the death-bed or funeral of a parent who had never failed to hold up the highest ideals to him. The only person to perform the miracle of keeping upon terms with both Lord and Lady Nelson was now gone, for although his daughter-in-law refused to visit him, the Rector had never ceased to write to her, and a letter in his enormous childish handwriting, opening simply, " My dear " (his usual form of address to the ladies of his family), had been dated April 18. George Matcham, writing on the 24th, had merely asked for instructions from Lord Nelson, who had replied two days later, " Had my father expressed a wish to see me, unwell as I am, I should have flown to Bath, but I believe it would be too late; however, should it be otherwise, and he wishes to see me, no consideration shall detain me for a moment."   On April 26, Lady Hamilton's birthday, Merton Place was the scene of a christening, and Cribb, the gardener, always remembered the procession of three carriages to the village church, for the baptism, by the names of Fatima Emma Charlotte Nelson Hamilton, of her ladyship's black maid, a great favourite with her, " taken out of a slave-ship ", and entered in the parish register as " from Egypt, a negress, about 20 years of age, under the protection of the Right Hon. Lady Hamilton ".   The Admiral, on hearing the expected sad news next day, had cancelled an engagement to appear at the Academy Banquet, and decided not to attempt a pilgrimage to Norfolk.   Lady Hamilton wrote to his brother, describing his condition as probably necessitating a surgical operation.   William, who had been advised from Merton, not Bath, and too late, had taken huff, and in his character as sole executor of a very small estate had " not half liked " the sharpness of Mr. Davison, representing Lord Nelson.   However; he had excelled himself in arrangements for the interment, and everything (paid for by the Admiral) had been as the deceased would have chosen—the funeral order given to the local undertaker, and an old body-servant and Bath apothecary handsomely remembered.   " I don't think ", said William, whose bulletins arrived daily, " any proper people were left out.   We have sunk ye grave in the chancel, alongside our mother's—plenty of room." Dr. Nelson (who had reminded Lady Hamilton that this was his correct style, since the degree of D.D. had been conferred upon him in January by his own University) arrived in Oxford in what his relations described as " a diamond humour—that is in the very best ".   The Dean of Exeter had at last expired, but should his brother's application to Mr. Addington fail, he had just read in a newspaper that Stalls were vacant at Durham and York. A Peace Election was disturbing the country, and on his recent visit to his old college for the purpose of voting for Mr. Pitt, he had been gratified by " a bow from Billy " in the Senate House. " So I made up to him and said a word or two."

Other characters in the Admiral's immediate circle were thinking of preferment. Beckford, on hearing that the Duke of Hamilton had honoured Merton to partake of a family dinner and make the acquaintance of Lord Nelson, had jogged his kinsman's elbow, and Sir William, before leaving Merton, had
35 accomplished his difficult letter to the Marquis of Douglas. He urbanely presented " an old plan of Beckford's " as one " which Lord Nelson and Lady H. have taken up warmly ". In fact, Nelson's comment on Beckford's scheme, privately delivered to Lady Hamilton, was not flattering. He thought it " dirty "
36 and " a rub-off ".

Until April 10, when Admiral Nelson had received permission to strike his flag and come on shore, he had been nominally on leave, and still in command of his " squadron on a particular service ". Repeated applications for his discharge had been met by steady refusals until peace was signed, an event which had been cele- brated throughout the country with somewhat unbridled revelry. To inspect Buonaparte's Paris, unless detained at the hustings, was the popular programme for an English gentleman this season. For an Admiral who loathed everything French, and took no great interest in the Election, a tour of various towns of his native land which had offered him their Freedom, combined with a visit to Sir William's estates, in the company of his dearest friends and a contingent of his family, seemed a preferable way of obtaining a change of air and scene while Merton underwent some improvements. He had paid £23 for Halfhide's strip, and was now in treaty with an elderly Mr. Axe of Birchin Lane for a field which alone separated Merton Place from the abbey wall. Mr. Axe was agreeable, but a tenant to whom the field was let was not, so he could only suggest that his Lordship should buy the whole farm, consisting of 150 acres, for £8,000. The Matchams were going to share in the investment, so while Oxford bells tolled outside on a wet summer's day, business as well as pleasure was under discussion. Upstairs, two competent Italian *valets*, who had travelled in the second coach from Merton, were pre- paring the Stars and Orders for to-morrow's ceremonies. The red ribbon worn by both distinguished gentlemen was that of the

English Order of the Bath; that of the Neapolitan " St. Ferdinand and Merit " was blue with a narrow red border; a moss-green accompanied the laurelled cross *patée* of St. Joachim, and a fondant pink belonged to the golden Crescent, bearing the sign manual of Selim III. Tom Allen, discharged from His Majesty's Service, master of £95 and a bride to whom Lady Hamilton had been attentive during his absence in the Baltic, had retired to raise a family in his native Norfolk. To Francatello and Gaetano their task was reminiscent of Embassy days, and indeed for all the principal members of the party the next three weeks bade fair to resemble their homeward journey of two years past.

On Thursday, July 22, the City of Oxford bestowed the Freedom, in a golden box, upon Lord Nelson, and the Senior Burgess, a fair, stout, untidy gentleman, with a very polished manner, had a kindly paw for young George Matcham, introduced as a future lawyer. Sir William Scott, friend of Samuel Johnson, and a very good friend of the Bodleian, put into his pocket a copy of Lord Nelson's *Plan for Manning the Navy*, with professions of much interest. Friday, a day of boisterous weather, was dedicated to the University. In full Congregation the Honorary Degree of Doctor of Civil Law was conferred upon Lord Nelson and Sir William Hamilton, presented by Dr. Blackstone, Vinerian Professor of Civil Law. Dr. Collinson, Lady Margaret Professor of Divinity, presented the Rev. Dr. Nelson of Christ's College, Cambridge, Doctor of Divinity of the University of Cambridge, on his admission to the same degree in the University of Oxford. Having left behind him a present to be distributed amongst the prisoners in the city gaol, Nelson left Oxford after dinner. The party spent the night at a Woodstock inn, and next morning prepared to view the splendours bestowed by a grateful sovereign upon a military hero.

But at Blenheim a disconcerting incident occurred. Neither Lord Nelson nor Sir William Hamilton was acquainted with the owner, a nobleman whose habitual hauteur was translated by friends as partially the result of shyness. The ducal family, although in residence, made no welcoming appearance. After a lengthy pause (necessitated by the carrying out of an order issued to the kitchens of a palace), refreshments in the park for Lord Nelson and friends were announced. Last season newspapers had published daily, with uncharitable comment, the highly ingenuous love-letters of the heir of the house (the father of a young family) to the unhappily married lady of the Member for Bridport. Nothing could have been less desired at Blenheim than a party containing any more famous names linked by scandal. It does not appear that any of the rebuffed sightseers realised anything but personal affront. Sir William expressed pained surprise, Lady Hamilton wrath. The collation so coldly proffered was as coldly declined by Nelson, carriages were called for, and, as his careful accounts of the expenses of his Tour record, horses from Troymill to Burford, their next stage, cost £3 14s. The Victor of the Nile and Copenhagen crossed the Evenlode and Windrush, and saw, for the first time, deep country, very different from the " Petit Trianon " chosen for him in Surrey, obscure Oxfordshire villages, little changed since Elizabeth Tudor set eyes on them, complete with their pattern of mill, pond, church, manor house and home farm. Under skies full of racing clouds, which cast shadows over tree-belts, the fresher colour of after-grass springing in hayfields, and brilliant stretches of grain, three carriages bound for Gloucester by Witney and Cheltenham Spa covered the bedward miles rapidly.

At Gloucester the footfalls of what the Press called " Lord Nelson's tourists " sounded in cloister and aisle, and here, after an affectionate farewell, the Matchams turned off for Bath, taking with them the bad weather. High summer heat settled upon the increasingly sylvan landscape through which the diminished party headed for the very tip of South Wales, where belief in fairies, witches and ghosts was general, and fisherwomen wore scarlet cloaks and steeple hats. But the glades of the Forest of Dean spoke to a sea-officer primarily of wooden walls : he inquired much as to the cultivation and preservation of oak-timber from the landowners in whose company he sat during the following month in public hall and private house, and the results were noted, in his own hand, for a report to the Prime Minister. At Ross, having breakfasted at the " Swan ", the travellers embarked upon a winding, lion-coloured stream. Their boat was garlanded with laurel, many small craft attended it, and the river-banks and balconies of houses overlooking the Wye were lined with cheering spectators. The first deputation, whose pattering speech struck strangely on his ear, beset the Admiral when he landed, and he fixed a date on his return journey to receive the freedom of Monmouth. Brecon was ready for him, so, after passing through Abergavenny and the nobly-set little town written down by him as " Myrter Tidder " (where his unexpected appearance caused " a delirium of joy "), he went out of his way, up roads of alarming gradient, to be feasted by farmers very unlike the English picture—small, black-browed, vehement, sinewy men, whose spokesman shed tears as he noted the mutilations suffered in His Majesty's Service. At populous Carmarthen the tourists patronised the playhouse, and a ventriloquist was the recipient of a guinea from Lord Nelson. They made an early start next morning, and breakfasted at St. Clears, so as to reach Milford before nightfall. Greville was waiting for them there, and in a district in which Sir William's name also was potent his heir had drawn up a list of engagements which included laying the foundation stone of a new church, attendance at a Fair, Rowing Match and Cattle Show (which it was hoped might become an annual event on the anniversary of the Nile), and a Banquet. The Lord Lieutenant was coming, Lord Kensington, Captain Thomas Foley and Lord Cawdor (whose 750 rustic volunteers, together with a couple of naval lieutenants, had captured an invading force of 1,400 French on a freezing February night five years past). The company was well chosen, and the setting was cheerful—a perfectly modern marine hotel, with a dazzling view. It was remarked that Lord Nelson looked particularly happy on the night of August 1, and his praise of their splendid harbour pleased both the purely patriotic and those who had commercial interest in its development. He compared Milford favourably with Trincomalee, in the East Indies, and Sir William closed the festivity by presenting to the room in which they were gathered a remarkable oil-painting of his renowned friend performed by Guzzardi of Palermo, at a date when the hero was suffering from the wound on the brow sustained at the Nile.

Seaside days, beneficial to all, slipped away easily, though perhaps not quietly, since some expedition into a landscape of mild airs and sub-tropical vegetation was undertaken every day. Greville and his uncle prepared the scheme for a naval dockyard at Milford which the Admiral was to present to the First Lord. Nelson examined the yards of a French refugee shipbuilder whom he had first met at Toulon, bought oysters, and sailed for Picton, to dine with Lord Milford. His visit to Ridgeway was a success from the moment that his carriage turned into a lantern-hung avenue displaying the prospect of a family mansion illuminated by every candle to be got from the shops of Haverfordwest. After a Public Breakfast, attended by the Mayor, the Admiral, skilfully dropping grapes into the open mouth of the eldest Miss Foley, aged six (who had been doubtful when a one-armed gentleman hoisted her on to his knee), lingered long, blissfully unaware that his offer to call upon the brother of an old Crocodile had produced a black squall at Ridgeway. But Mrs. John Halbert Foley's objection to play hostess to Lady Hamilton had been overruled by a man who was master in his own house.

The travellers swept through Pembroke (destined to secure the dockyard and arsenal hoped for by Greville and Sir William for Milford), and at Swansea "a choice body of exultant tars" drew the Admiral to receive the Freedom of the town, where his speech of thanks containing a word on National Service addressed to the rising generation was printed for distribution by an enterprising Portreeve. The carriages were greased that night, in preparation for the long homeward journey through the Midlands, and the day of their second arrival at Monmouth was ideally spent, for the ruins of Chepstow Castle were admired before dinner at Piercefield Park, and those of Tintern Abbey by sunset. Next morning, early, the Admiral drove in a carriage and four up to the Kymin Pavilion to inspect the only Naval Temple in England and partake of another Public Breakfast, during which a band played and cannon were discharged; and since the day was very fine, he walked back to the town through the Beaulieu Grove to dine with the Mayor and Corporation. Venison had been sent by the Duke of Beaufort to the "Beaufort Arms". "Lady Hamilton charmed the company with several songs sung to the tunes of 'Rule Britannia' and 'God save the King'", and again the speech of thanks made by a happy man was felicitous:

> "It was my good fortune to have under my command, some of the most experienced Officers in the English Navy, whose professional skill was seconded by the undaunted courage of British Sailors; and whatever merit might attach itself to me, I must declare that I had only to show them the Enemy and Victory crowned the Standard. . . . In my own person I have received an overflowing measure of the Nation's gratitude— far more than I either merited or expected; because the same success would have crowned the efforts of any other British Admiral, who had under his command such distinguished Officers and such gallant Crews. And here let me impress it on the mind of every Officer in the Service, that to whatever quarter of the Globe he may be destined, whether to the East or West Indies, to Africa, or America—the eyes of his Country are upon him. . . ."

Ross had now created an arch of oak and laurel, spanning the Hereford road. That Friday night he attended a ball and supper, offered by Mr. and Mrs. Westfaling, friends of Naples days. Fireworks shot up into the midnight skies, and the sound of the flute and violin trembled through the groves of historic Rudhall until after 2 a.m. At Hereford the Freedom was presented to him by the Duke of Norfolk, in a box of apple-wood, and his footsteps followed those of a bishop's butler to an upstairs sickroom. At Downton, where Mr. Knight, the numismatist, had built an eccentric castellated home, the Admiral, traversing heavily wooded property at a moment traditionally fruitful of confidences—Sunday evening, after dinner—mentioned to a fellow-guest, Mr. R. W. Spencer, the vision of the Radiant Orb. [41] Worcester offered its Freedom appropriately, in a porcelain vase, and at Messrs. Chamberlain's factory the Admiral ordered a dessert service, "to be decorated in the most splendid style, with his coat of arms, insignia etc.". (Twelve years had passed since the Matchams had been shown, in the Worcester factory, "a dinner sett, for the Duke of Clarence; the figure of Hope in different attitudes in the middle, a very rich border of purple and gold".) [42]

Nelson's arrival at Birmingham was prudently timed for two hours before he was expected. The piece presented at the playhouse that night was *The Merry Wives*, and " Blissett, the Bath actor, supporting the character of the Fat Knight extremely well ", " set the house in a roar by turning to the stage box as he rolled forth the line, ' Before the best Lord in the land, I swear it ! ' " Citizens carrying torches escorted the guests back to Styles's Hotel, and the tour of the factories of " the first toy-shop in Europe " undertaken next morning was conscientious. From the japanners and sword-makers Lord Nelson and friends proceeded to watch the creation of buckles and rings, buttons, stained glass, and the Patent Sash. A medal commemorating his visit was struck in his presence. The bells of St. Mary's welcomed him to Warwick. Lord Spencer, at Althorp, was his last host. The tourists struck Watling Street at Towcester, and, moving fast thereafter, reached Merton on Sunday, September 5, having been absent six instead of the intended three weeks. " We have had ", wrote Lady Hamilton to Davison, " a most charming Tour, which will Burst *some* of *Them*." Mrs. Matcham was more elegantly informed: " Oh, how our Hero has been received ! I wish you could come to hear all our Story—most enteresting." [43]

Nelson's 1802 Tour is important in his story for several reasons. He had made holiday before, unnoticed, in the days of his obscurity. He had been enthusiastically received in English towns before, and was to be again, but always on his way to or from a campaign. Accustomed to long hours of nervous strain and far worse discomforts, he returned from his Tour in glowing health and confirmed in his belief that John Bull and he understood one another. Upon the many who caught sight of him, arriving in a dusty carriage, bowing from a balcony, escorted through institution, aisle and factory, or rising to reply to a toast, his image was fixed, the embodiment of the vigilance and resolution of the Service he represented. His speech was unvarying in essentials. By the grace of God it had been his good fortune to command in many engagements officers and seamen of unmatched courage, skill and discipline. Should this nation ever be called upon again to repel attack, he had no fear of the result.

> " You have but to say to your fleets and armies—' Go ye forth, and fight our battles, whilst we, true to ourselves, protect and support your wives and little ones at home. . . .' I have not the slightest doubt, from the result of my observations during this tour, that the native, the inbred spirit of Britons, whilst it continues as firmly united as at
44   present, is fully adequate."

He brought back from his Tour another conviction upon which he did not publicly enlarge. Within a few weeks of his return he had ascertained that if hostilities should recommence he was
45   to command the Mediterranean Fleet.

9

Sir William Hamilton, after a very exhausting experience, found himself soon called upon to take the road again, and to a place devoid of resource for the elderly antiquary—a fashionable seaside resort in the height of the season. A most unsatisfactory letter from the Marquis of Douglas had reached him. His kinsman politely but flatly refused to touch Beckford's peerage scheme. Shortly after their arrival at Ramsgate his wife addressed a remarkable note to him. (Her temper, too, had been frayed, and by an accident which she could not announce. She had lost the address of the Margate lodgings to which Mrs. Gibson had been
46   ordered by Nelson to take Horatia for a seaside holiday.)

> " As I see it is a pain to you to remain here, let me beg of you to fix your time of going. Weather I dye in Piccadilly or any other spot in

England, 'tis the same to me; but I remember the time when you wished for tranquility, but now all visiting and bustle is your liking. However, I will do what you please, being ever your affectionate and obedient E.H."

The ex-Ambassador's comment written on the back of the sheet was characteristic :

" I neither love bustle nor great company, but I like some employ-ment and diversion. I have but a very short time to live, and every moment is precious to me. I am in no hurry and am exceedingly glad to give every satisfaction to our best friend, our dear Lord Nelson. The question, then, is what we can best do that all may be perfectly satisfied. Sea-bathing is usefull to your health; I see it is, and wish you to continue it a little longer; but I must confess that I regret, whilst the season is favourable, that I cannot enjoy my favourite amusement of quiet fishing. I care not a pin for the great world, and am attached to no one so much as to you."

That storm blew over, but before the month was out he found himself obliged to address her again in dissatisfaction much more seriously :

" I have passed the last 40 years of my life in the hurry and bustle that must necessarily be attendant on a publick character. I am arrived at the age when some repose is really necessary, and I promised myself a quiet home, and altho' I was sensible, and said so when I married, that I shou'd be superannuated when my wife wou'd be in her full beauty and vigour of youth. That time is arrived, and we must make the best of it for the comfort of both parties. Unfortunately our tastes as to the manner of living are very different. I by no means wish to live in solitary retreat, but to have seldom less than 12 or 14 at table, and those varying continually, is coming back to what was so irksome to me in Italy during the latter years of my residence in that country. I have no connections out of my own family. I have no complaint to make, but I feel that the whole attention of my wife is given to Ld. N. and his interest at Merton. I well know the purity of Lord N.'s friend-ship for Emma and me, and I know how very uncomfortable it would make his Lp. Our best friend, if a separation shou'd take place, and am therefore determined to do all in my power to prevent such an extremity, which wou'd be *essentially detrimental* to all parties, but wou'd be more sensibly felt by our dear friend than by us. Provided that our expences in housekeeping do not encrease beyond measure (of which I must own I see some danger,) I am willing to go on upon our present footing; but as I cannot expect to live many years, every moment to me is precious, and I hope I may be allow'd sometimes to be my own master, and pass my time according to my own inclination, either by going my fishing parties on the Thames or by going to London to attend the Museum, R. Society, the Tuesday Club and Auctions of pictures. I mean to have a light post chariot or post chaise by the month, that I may make use of it in London, and run backward and forwards to Merton or to Shepperton, etc., This is my plan, and we might go on very well, but I am fully determined not to have any more of the very silly altercations that happen but too often between us and embitter the present moments exceedingly. If really one cannot live comfortably together, a *wise* and well *concerted separation* is preferable; but I think, considering the probability of my not troubling any party long in this world, the best for us all wou'd be to bear those ills we have rather than flie to those we know not of. I have fairly stated what I have on my mind. There is no time for nonsense or trifling. I know and admire your talents, and many excellent qualities, but I am not blind to your defects and confess having many myself; therefore let us bear and forbear for God's sake."

47

The result was that no separation took place, and during October he accomplished many excursions on the Thames, from one of which he brought back, in revived spirits, more than sixty pounds of fish. With the opening of the autumn season, Nelson accompanied him to meetings of the Literary Society. On Christmas Day a young party sat down to Merton turkey, and fifty wood bavins formed the Yule fire. Lady Hamilton told Mrs. Matcham, who was hopeful again, "here we are as happy as Kings, and much more. We have 3 Boltons, 2 Nelsons, and only need two or three Little Matchams to be quite *en famille*." She gave a Children's Ball for the country-house party early in the New Year, and, his nieces and nephews having been allowed by an indulgent hostess to dance till 3 a.m., Nelson found next noon that so far he was the only soul about in his house. He went up to 23, Piccadilly, with the Hamiltons in mid-January, and a tottering courtier, who had not lost hope, presented himself at Her Majesty's Birthday Drawing-Room. Lady Mansfield had promised Lady Hamilton to get poor Sir William near the King. Nelson's winter, so far as professional life went, was quietly spent. " I really am so little in the world ", he explained to Davison, " that I know little, if anything, beyond [what] newspaper reports say, respecting our affairs on the Continent." The First Lord was out of town for a long spell, ill, but he saw both St. Vincent and Troubridge occasionally. Neither ever offered to visit Merton. He submitted to the Admiralty careful memoranda on three subjects—Manning, Desertion, and Prize-Money—and having, in his own opinion, entirely failed to carry his points, was too disheartened to forward a fourth document dealing with the flotilla for Coast Defence. He had two ports of call during this winter at which his repeated appearances passed unsuspected by the world. He often sent in his name at an unfashionable hotel in which a Naval Chaplain was lying collapsed after a disastrous trip to the Jamaicas. He had long had his eye upon the Rev. A. J. Scott, an expert in languages, as a desirable member of an Admiral's staff. Before proceeding to his next inconspicuous destination, he sometimes paused at a toy-shop, and on one occasion gave sixpence for a watch which would tick audibly. ("She was always fond of my watch.") Mrs. Gibson, whose charge was unafraid of her illustrious god-father, would tactfully withdraw, having brought in Horatia, and the couple would play together for hours, upon the carpet. 48

A call from a nightmarish past reached the Admiral in the first week of February. He had, like the rest of the newspaper-reading world, been aware since November that one of the Despard brothers, well known to him on the San Juan expedition, had been under arrest on a dreadful charge. The career of Lieut. Edward Marcus Despard, of the 50th Regiment, since Captain Nelson of the *Hinchingbrooke* and he had served together, nearly a quarter of a century past, had been unhappy. Colonel Despard, recalled to England from Yucatan in 1790 to answer a number of charges for cruelty and illegal action brought against him as Governor by the settlers, had been kept hanging about the Secretary of State's office for a couple of seasons before being informed that, although his post had been abolished, he would not be forgotten. Six years later a violently spoken unemployed man had been arrested and imprisoned for a few weeks. In 1800, during a third period of detention, he had begun to plot against the Government. According to the evidence given at his trial by his spies, his scheme had been to seduce the Guards, seize the Tower and Bank of England, stop the English outgoing mails and assassinate the King on his way to open Parliament. Nelson, to his discomfiture, found himself subpœnaed to give evidence for the defence, at the New Sessions House, Horse-monger Lane, on February 7. He could not refuse, and duly testified that in the year 1780, "on the Spanish main, we were together in the enemies' trenches and slept in the same tent. Colonel Despard was then a loyal man and a brave officer." The Attorney-General, prosecuting, paid a tribute to a national hero, "a man on whom to pronounce an eulogy were to waste words", and Nelson's testimony produced a recommendation to mercy from the jury. But the evidence was too strong, and at 3 a.m. on the 9th Colonel Despard was condemned to death for High Treason, a sentence which included hideous details. Every circumstance of the remaining days was horrible, for between his sentence and execution the condemned man sent a high-flown letter to Nelson, saying that he would ask no further inscription on his tomb than the character provided by his old comrade-in-arms. He enclosed, almost without mention, a petition which Nelson forwarded in equal silence to Addington; and the Prime Minister and family, studying it together after supper, were moved to tears. Despard was dragged to the block on a hurdle, together with half a dozen of his poor associates, on February 21. He had refused the Sacrament, and he made a long speech on the scaffold, before being first hanged, then decapitated. The remainder of the sentence was remitted. Nelson, visiting Lord Minto in Spring Gardens on the following day, divulged that Mrs. Despard, who had insisted on being present at the final scene, was " violently in love with her husband ". He had solicited a pension for her from the Government, but believed that Despard's shocking conduct in denying the Chaplain admittance must render it ineffectual.

Throughout the Session, Admiral Nelson spoke in the Lords on professional subjects with growing ease and eloquence. On March 8 a message from the King to Parliament stated that, in view of the activity in French ports, His Majesty had judged it expedient to make suitable preparations for the security of his realm. That night, at 23, Piccadilly, while London traffic slurred through melting snow, the Admiral sat late at his desk. Some months had passed since, on the eve of a campaign, he had mentioned to Lady Hamilton that he was going to dine quietly with an elderly officer " forced to go to sea, owing to the extravagance of his children ". With child-like faith he had applauded his ideal woman when she had told him that she was settling a few small debts before the move to Merton. " You are right, Emma. Poor trades-people cannot afford to lay out their money." A gentleman who had felt the pinch in youth kept very exact record of the weekly expenses shared by himself and his friends in London and the country. At Merton, as he had desired, local tradesmen had been employed, but to entertain in Embassy style it had been necessary to call in the aid of London specialists. Mr. Birch had provided turtle soup, and Mr. Twining tea. Merton could not produce oranges, lemons, shell-fish, cases of " maccarone ". It was indeed alarming how many entries of London extras appeared every week. The bill for Merton Place stationery alone had been £18 17s. 6d., though that, like china and linen, would not recur speedily. The sheet achieved by him on the night of March 8 ran as follows :   50

LORD NELSON'S INCOME AND PROPERTY

My Exchequer Pension for the Nile	£2,000	o	o
Navy Pension for loss of one arm and one eye .	923	o	o
Half-pay as Vice-Admiral	465	o	o
Interest of £1000	30	o	o
	£3,418	o	o

OUTGOINGS OF LORD NELSON

To Lady Nelson	£1,800	o	o
Interest of money owing	500	o	o
Pension to my Brother's Widow	200	o	o
To assist in educating my Nephews . . .	150	o	o
Expenditure	£2,650	o	o
Income	£3,418	o	o

The result, as the most elementary mathematician could see, was " For Lord Nelson £768 os. od. per annum ", and in a single week of this year (to be sure an exceptionally heavy one, that following the return from his Tour) bills at Merton and Piccadilly had amounted to £117 8s. 2½d. The Tour itself had cost £480 odd. Next afternoon, while the Debate on the King's Speech was in progress in the Lords, he left his seat to scribble a reminder to the Prime Minister, " Whenever it is necessary, I am *your* Admiral."   51

More than a week later " nothing positive concerning Peace or War " was generally known. The reason for the King's message had been kept a close secret. The Militia had been called out, but it was guessed that as the strong measures taken in London had not produced an instant rupture with Paris, negotiation was still proceeding. Nelson returned to Merton, reasonably sure that in any case he would soon find himself afloat again. He was known to be in favour of a continuation of the peace, if possible, and therefore unlikely to act provocatively, and his mere appearance in the Mediterranean might cause Buonaparte to hesitate. His flagship was named, much to his satisfaction. " For I know the weight of the *Victory* in the Mediterranean." Towards the end of the month an event threatened which affected him personally, but did not alter his plans. Sir William Hamilton suffered a sudden collapse, entailing a period of unconsciousness. He recovered, to summon gentlemen of Lincoln's Inn to Merton

Place and add a codicil to his Will, but he had recognised unmistakable symptoms, and he desired to be moved up to London, to await the inevitable hour with all possible dignity, under his own roof. His physicians, headed by Moseley of Jamaica, pronounced his case hopeless. He felt no pain, and welcomed members of his family to his bedside, but he lay, after his safe arrival, " going off ", said Nelson, " as an inch of candle ".

As the lengthening spring days dragged by, in a hushed town house cut off from London activities, Nelson declared, " I shall almost hate April. Look at the last three years ! " The month which would bring the anniversaries of the deaths of his brother Maurice and his father opened, and he pictured the outside world hanging on news from 23, Piccadilly. " All London is interested in such a character." Actually, although obituaries were graceful, the departure of a retired Ambassador, a notable collector of classical antiquities, was quickly forgotten. Sir William, wandering in mind at last, ceased to breathe on the morning of April 6, without a sigh or a struggle, in the arms of his wife, and with Nelson holding his hand. Both attendants were exhausted from nights and days of watching and previous false alarms; both uttered the language of genuine grief. " The World ", wrote Nelson, " never lost a more upright and accomplished gentleman. . . . I lose a friend who has spoken well of me for thirty-seven years." Lady Hamilton tragically noted, " April 6th. Unhappy day for the forlorn Emma. Ten minutes past ten, dear, blessed Sir William left me." The proprieties were strictly observed. Mrs. William Nelson had already arrived from Norfolk, but despite his sister-in-law's presence, Nelson at once took lodgings at 19, Piccadilly, over a saddler's shop, and never again dated a letter from 23. Lady Hamilton directed Mrs. Gibson to keep Horatia indoors until after the funeral, " as we are very close and sincere mourners ", and applied to Greville to know what provision had been made for her, whether he would pay her debts, and how long she might remain in her late husband's house. A hatchment, displaying the sable ship of Arran and the bleeding heart of Douglas supported by silver antelopes, ducally gorged, was delivered and erected over the front door of 23, Piccadilly, and Sir William's coffin set off on its long journey to his Pembrokeshire estates and burial by the side of his first lady.

Early in May his Will was read, in the presence of his assembled noble kin, in a house of mourning noticeably gaunt. As all the furniture was hers, Lady Hamilton had already installed it in a smaller

L L

house in Clarges Street, close by. The actual Will contained ⁵⁴
no surprises. Greville was, as had always been understood, his
uncle's heir; the provision for Lady Hamilton was, as Nelson had
always anticipated, insufficient to keep her in the style to which
she had been accustomed as Sir William's lady. She received
an immediate gift of £300, and an annuity of £800, of which
£100 a year was to be paid, while Mrs. Cadogan survived, to her
mother. However, Lord Melville had responded promisingly
to applications from Greville, Nelson and the widow herself
for some continuation of the ex-Ambassador's pension, and
Merton should be hers (with £100 a month from the owner, for
housekeeping). The codicil, added after Sir William's seizure, ⁵⁵
displayed anxiety that his nephew should complete his engagement "to pay Emma's debts" (calculated as no more than
£450), but suggested as the source "the arrears due to me from
the Treasury as the King's Minister at Naples", an old grievance,
unlikely to yield profit. There was affectionate particularisation
of a violin, admired by the Marquis of Douglas, and long designed
for that valuable connection. Only the legacy to Nelson was
worded in a style which must arouse comment :

> "The copy of Madame le Brun's picture of Emma, in enamel, by
> Bone, I give to my dearest friend, Lord Nelson, Duke of Brontë; a very
> small token of the great regard I have for his Lordship, the most virtuous,
> loyal, and truly brave character I ever met with, God bless him, and ⁵⁶
> shame fall on those who do not say 'Amen'."

Nelson meanwhile had been warned to prepare for departure,
and had summoned to 19, Piccadilly the tradesmen to be favoured
with orders to supply the Commander-in-Chief of a Mediterranean
Fleet. He had been down to Merton to settle matters there.
He had seen his new Secretary, Mr. John Scott, lately Purser of
the *Royal Sovereign*. On May 13 Mrs. Gibson, provided with
written instructions to give the clergyman and clerk double fees
and bring back a record of the baptism, carried her charge to
Marylebonne Parish Church, to be christened by the names of
Horatia Nelson Thompson. ⁵⁷
A ceremony of Installation of Knights Elect of the Order of
the Bath had been fixed to take place in Westminster Abbey on
May 19, and Nelson had invited his old secretary, Tyson, and his
nephews Horace and Tom, to be his esquires. Dr. Nelson was
having a full-length oil-portrait painted of his handsome son, in
page's costume. The preparations had been great, and the
family disappointment at the prospect of a cancellation was

commensurate. But on Lord Nelson's requesting that a young connection in His Majesty's Service might act as his proxy, he was informed that not only might Captain William Bolton, R.N., represent him; his proxy would receive the honour of knighthood on the preceding day. The compliment gave pleasure, for the young man (one of the boys to go to sea with him in his first ship-of-the-line) was engaged to be married to a first cousin, the little Kitty Bolton who had been present in a Bath lodging on a Sunday evening when her famous uncle had returned to his family from Santa Cruz. Lady Hamilton had furthered the match (" The girl may thank you (if it is worth thanking) for her husband "), and the wedding, at which the Admiral would not now be present, was to take place at Clarges Street on the night of the 18th. He left London at about 4 a.m. that morning. The Duke of Queensberry had offered an equipage to carry him and his single trunk on the first stage of his journey, and he employed a ducal flunkey to take back a brief message from Kingston to Clarges Street : " Cheer up, my dearest Emma, and be assured that I ever have been, and am, and ever will be, your most affectionate and faithful Nelson and Brontë."

He breakfasted at Liphook, and arrived at Portsmouth, almost smothered with dust, at exactly 1 p.m., to be greeted by Captains Hardy and Sutton, the former in very high spirits. The harbour was dark with merchantmen awaiting convoy. The *Victory* was lying so far out that he could scarcely distinguish her, and the *Amphion*, the frigate in which Hardy was going to accompany him to the Mediterranean, was entirely beyond his powers of vision. During his past months of better health he had been haunted by fancies that the sight of his " good " eye was failing, and there had been discussion with Moseley of an operation. His own opinion had been that if it was necessary, the sooner it was done the better, but Moseley (given *carte blanche*, with a cheerful reminder that his patient could not very well spare another eye) had hesitated.

Portsmouth two days after a declaration of war was much as might have been expected. An Engineer officer, ordered to take up the duties of second-in-command on the Gosport side, had also just arrived, and this young man, who was never to attain eminence, but who kept a very painstaking record of first impressions, found the scene one of unparalleled bustle. In the town itself Motley's Library was filled with officers of both Services asking for the latest Army and Navy lists, the *Hampshire*

Telegraph and any London papers. The bow-windows of the
" Crown " and " Fountain " inns were also bright with uniforms.
There were regiments proceeding on foreign service, led by their
bands, marching down from Hilsea Barracks to embark, and, in
the contrary direction, trains of raw recruits, just landed from the
Isle of Wight, straggling uphill, all as merry as larks, with red,
white and blue ribbons streaming from their hats. On the heels
of both processions followed a noisy gang of fiddlers, mounte-
banks, fortune-tellers, pickpockets, screaming women and children,
barking dogs and Jewish pedlars (pressing the sale of such
treasures as gold wedding rings, price fourpence). An inadvisable number of ladies had made the expedition to see the last
of a loved officer, and when gunfire sounded, their embarrassed
escorts gladly hurried to the platform to inquire and report the
reason. The thunder of 13 guns about 3.30 p.m. signified that
Admiral Lord Nelson, who had hoisted his flag on board H.M.S.
Victory, was saluting the Commander-in-Chief. The High Street
and Parade were blocked by carriages and post-chaises, but the
heaviest wheeled traffic converged upon the landing-point, where
a continual service of tradesmen's carts, delivering live-stock,
groceries, liquors and crockery for newly commissioned ships-
of-the-line were in competition with halooing porters trundling
officers' luggage over the cobbles on barrows. With dusk the
pandemonium increased. Heated and vociferous midshipmen
scudded along the row of drinking- and dancing-houses for which
the back of the Point was infamous, and forcibly recovered from
the arms of their gaily dressed but tipsy Dulcineas the crews
which must be waiting to pull the Captain to his ship. Sailors,
clustering on the tops of hired coaches, waved their tarpaulin
hats and cheered as their vehicles collided, and shouted witticisms
to one another and their admirers.

Lord Nelson's heavy luggage began to make its appearance
after dinner, and his new secretary ran about in a promising
manner. His lordship's sofa and a treasured large chair were
not in any list. His wine was still in the Customs House ;
the parcels containing his table linen had not been so labelled,
and his cot had been sent to the *Amphion*, in the belief that the
Victory could not be ready. She seemed, indeed, to her new
master, " in a pretty state of confusion ", and he was inclined to
be vexed with the amiable Sutton, who, when the wind was fair,
reported that the ship would be ready in every respect for sea
by Friday morning. " A good man, but not so active as Hardy "

was told to try to make it Thursday night, and the Admiral retired genially, after a quiet meal, to write to their Lordships ("must keep them in good humour") and to assure Lady Hamilton that, as far as personal belongings went, he had never gone to sea so well provided. To his relief, the Commander-in-Chief had been engaged to dine out. ("They say there is much drinking.") Next morning, after an interview with Lord Gardner, he comforted himself with the old adage, "We shall get no rest, till we get to sea", but the fact that the *Victory* would have to sail half manned was, besides alarming, maddening to an expert whose suggestions for manning H.M. ships had been shelved at Whitehall. Dinner with Lord Gardner on Thursday could not be avoided, but his lordship had most civilly invited Mr. Davison (who was not going to leave the *Victory* until she was under sail) and Lord Minto, also just arrived from London, with his brother, Mr. Hugh Elliot, who had been ordered at twenty-four hours' notice to Naples, to take up the post once held by Sir William Hamilton.

On Friday, May 20, 1803, Portsmouth reporters ended a chapter in Nelson's story. "Such was the anxiety of Lord Nelson to embark, that yesterday, to one that spoke of his sailing, he said, 'I cannot, before to-morrow, and that's an age!' This morning, about 10 o'clock, his Lordship went off, in a heavy shower of rain, and sailed with a Northerly wind." Letters began to trickle back to Clarges Street. The first came from the "George", Portsmouth, "By Messenger": "The boat is on shore, and five minutes sets me afloat. I can only pray that the great God of heaven may bless and preserve you, and that we may meet again, in peace and true happiness. I have no fears." He wrote again before noon, from a Great Cabin which had been the background for the figures of Keppel, Kempenfelt, Howe, Hood and St. Vincent, and in which the smell of fresh paint was no worse than he had anticipated. "You will believe that, although I am glad to leave that horrid place, Portsmouth, yet the being afloat makes me now feel that we do not tread the same element."

Five days later, his voice sounded distant indeed: "Here we are, in the middle of the Bay of Biscay—nothing to be seen, but the sky and water. . . ."

CHAPTER XVI

1803–1805
(*ætat* 44–46)

MEDITERRANEAN COMMAND

I

THE Rock was surprised on the night of Friday, June 3, 1803, when Lord Nelson, appointed to the Mediterranean Command, appeared flying his flag in a 32-gun frigate. At Gibraltar nobody had even known that England was at war again.

His orders were to make the best of his way to Malta, and having conferred with Governor Ball and taken Sir Richard Bickerton's squadron under his command, proceed with all possible despatch off Toulon. His last instructions, brought on board the *Victory* at Spithead at 1 a.m. on the morning before he sailed, had been on no account to miss making the offer of that first-rate to the Commander-in-Chief of the Channel Fleet. He did not himself believe that Cornwallis could want the *Victory*, and after going to the Black Rocks off Brest, and hearing from a frigate that his old friend had a *rendezvous* at sea, he was assured that fears of the enemy putting out from that port were at present groundless. He searched for Cornwallis for twenty-four hours (losing a wind which would have carried him to Portugal) before deciding to act in strict obedience to his orders but against his judgment. The saddened Sutton was told that if he did not fall in with Admiral Cornwallis within a week he must return to Plymouth for further orders; a change made very difficult by a strong wind and heavy sea was effected shortly before dark on May 23, and at 10 p.m. that night Nelson lost sight of the *Victory*, " to my great mortification ". His letter to Cornwallis had begged that, if the Channel Fleet did not need the *Victory* " to add to the show off Brest ", she should be ordered to join him without a moment's loss of time, and he had left behind in her his steward and all his stock, with the exception of a few trunks of linen.

He had expected that in the *Amphion* he and his staff must be truly uncomfortable, and a foul wind, blowing fresh, and a nasty sea, were soon their lot. Not a vessel was to be seen on the face of the waters as they laboured off Cape Finisterre. The Admiral's Interpreter saw a whale, and noted it in his diary.

The Admiral caught a head cold, and began to imagine that the worst might happen, owing to his delay in getting to his station. In feverish moments he feared that Buonaparte might even seize Sicily. But he told himself, " Patience is a virtue at sea ", and gradually came to realise that his *suite*, in spite of sleeping seven and eight in a cabin, were not unhappy; that, in fact, a particularly invigorating atmosphere pervaded a small frigate in the highest possible order, doing her utmost. (" Hardy takes good care of us and the *Amphion* is very comfortable.") Hardy, like their Lordships, was triumphant at having recovered Britain's first fighting Admiral from Circe's cave, but nobody could have guessed this. Even the supercilious Mr. Elliot, who had been woebegone at Portsmouth, began to look up. There were no complaints, or clashes of personality, amongst the civilian passengers, or, if there were, the Admiral heard nothing of them.

A pastel of a fashionably dressed woman, wearing a foreign decoration (an excellent likeness, and one of the handsomest Mr. John Scott had ever seen), was toasted in the third and last bumper every evening. The secretary's engagement had come at a very welcome moment from the financial point of view, but from the domestic, tragic. Lady Hamilton had promised to send him news of Mrs. Scott's confinement. He had been provided with the remedy for the Admiral's spasms, and took care to report regularly. Below the picture of Lord Nelson's Guardian Angel hung a crayon sketch of his adopted child—a stout two-year-old, with cropped, fair hair and rosy cheeks, dressed in a mob cap, ankle-length muslin gown and morocco shoes, standing in a garden, with its finger in its mouth. Their owner felt revived every time he looked at his hostages to fortune, and prayed for a short war—" just long enough to make me independent in pecuniary matters ".

After passing Lisbon, the *Amphion* was blessed with a gentle fair wind, which so much freshened during hours of darkness, off Cape St. Vincent, that she entered the Straits at 2 p.m. on June 2, having made a run of more than a hundred leagues since eight o'clock on the previous morning. She captured a French brig shortly before coming to anchor in Rosia Bay, and learnt that Buonaparte's brother, Jerome, had passed a few days before, in the *Jemappes*, from Martinique. " If we had proceeded direct in the *Victory*, we should have had her to a certainty." A single night and forenoon were spent in Gibraltar. Mr. Elliot sent a messenger to Hookham Frere, his opposite number at

Madrid, to ask how England's declaration of war had been received in that capital. The British Consul at Cadiz thought that Spain must join Buonaparte, but his theories were not supported by any signs of activity in the Cadiz Naval Arsenal. Lord Nelson landed at 5 a.m., paid his respects to the Lieutenant-Governor, Sir Thomas Trigge; gave instructions to Mr. Pownall, Naval Store-keeper, and the officers of the dockyard; saw the surgeon of the Naval Hospital; detailed the frigates to guard the entry to the Straits and keep up communications with the Barbary coast; and made arrangements with the agent of a Quaker gentleman, Mr. Edward Gayner, merchant of Rosas, who was to prove useful. He took his leave of all before dinner, and the *Amphion* weighed at 4 p.m. In Tetuan Bay she cleared for action, and next day, Trinity Sunday, captured a French and a Dutch brig. A week later, in full view of the mountains of Mauretania, Mr. Elliot, supplied with letters both official and personal to every influential character at the court of the Two Sicilies, was transferred to H.M.S. *Maidstone* for a direct passage to Naples. He took with him also the bodyservant of his predecessor. Gaetano Spedilo, who had been *valet* for thirty years to Sir William Hamilton, promised to return to Lord Nelson when he had seen his wife and children, but his present master doubted whether he would ever see the efficient Neapolitan again.

The remainder of the *Amphion's* progress to Malta was distressingly tedious. The Admiral (as he watched coral-fishing fleets fade into summer haze, and a familiar, eternally brown, burnt-up coastline, presenting the silhouettes of mosques) dictated letters announcing his appointment and arrival to the various authorities of the Mediterranean coasts. The temperature had been rising ever since they left the Rock, and on July 1, as he ascended between cheering crowds towards the white courtyards of the Governor's Palace at Valetta, attended by the Governor, to visit General Vilette and the lady of General Bickersteth, and to drink tea with Lady Ball, he found himself cured of his cold but gasping for fresh air. His brief call was, upon the whole, unsatisfactory. Malta, like Gibraltar, had heard nothing of the war. Sir Richard Bickerton's squadron had sailed to cruise between Sicily and Naples on the same day that Lord Nelson had left Portsmouth. Governor Ball was very pleased to see him, but the man seemed to have become sadly desiccated. Drawing around him the solemn mantle of *le Corps Diplomatique*, Sir Alexander hinted that there were negotiations which could not be divulged to an Admiral. Nelson paid a Captain of the Nile the compliment of believing him to be secretly longing to be afloat again, but the truth was that an officer virtually retired from the Service had found an ideal niche, and was indeed during his lifetime being accorded some of the privileges of the beatified. When their tall, high-nosed English Governor stepped down their streets, affectionate Maltese uncovered and stood in silence. His appearance in their market-places stopped business, and evoked reverential applause. His devoted secretary, a Mr. Coleridge, of poetical aspirations, was eulogistic.

Nelson's thirty-six-hour call to the island convinced him that " this out of the way place " would never suit him as a base for operating against an enemy in Toulon. " The Fleet can never go there if I can find any other corner to put them in. It takes, upon an average, seven weeks to get an answer to a letter." His present experience was a three weeks' passage. In the Straits of Messina what he described as " the lower class of boat-people " swarmed on board, bringing fruit and flowers. Their expressions of loyalty to their King and delight at seeing the English were strong. When asked if there were any Jacobins in their city, they replied with appropriate gesture, " Yes—the gentry who wear their hats so—on one side of the head ! " " Bond Street loungers ", commented the Admiral, receiving their protestations of affection with extreme caution. On June 25 he came in sight of " *Dear* Naples, if it is what it was. God send me good news ! " The shape of Vesuvius, the circle of palaces and villas ranged around that radiant, sickle-shaped bay, aroused so many memories that he could scarcely restrain himself from flying on shore ; but he had resolved not to add to their Majesties' difficulties by presenting himself at their court as yet. French troops had begun to take possession of Pescaro, Brindisi, Otranto, Taranto. The constant presence of a British ship-of-the-line in their Bay, always ready to take on board the complete royal family, would be at the moment a more tactful attention. The frigate which had carried Mr. Elliot to his new appointment reappeared, and brought reports that the news of Lord Nelson's approach had inspired all Naples with confidence.

Nearly everyone to whom he had written had answered by the *Maidstone*. He was a little disturbed that the Queen's reply did not mention her particular friend, of whose impoverished widow-hood he had sent a clear account. He comforted himself with the reflection " hers is a political letter ", and vowed, " If she can forget Emma, I hope God will forget her ! " (Emma's belief was, he knew, " She never will, or can.") Mr. Elliot had not as yet been summoned to the King, who was said to be very dejected, living mostly at the Belvedere. Rumour declared that His Majesty would like nothing so much as to resign the throne of Naples, at least, to his son, and retire to Sicily—a situation often prophesied by Sir William Hamilton. To his master's surprise, Gaetano had returned, having apparently seen enough of conditions at home to realise himself lucky in his employment. The *valet* gave a vivid description of the greeting of the women of the Santa Lucia fish-market, who, when they had seen him, had thought that he came as herald of his mistress. Mr. Elliot had taken a house on the Chiaia, and the Palazzo Sessa had degenerated into an hotel, the Marquis, the owner, retaining some upper rooms. Most of the old Embassy servants seemed to have fallen on evil days, and the son of one, who now kept a small shop at a loss, had wanted to fly in the *Maidstone* to Lord Nelson— an example which must not be encouraged. Musical names, each recalling a glowing southern countenance, were catalogued by the *valet*, together with their fates. Only Sabatello Sabatini had entered Mr. Elliot's service. Nicolo and Mary Antonia had left Mr. Gibbs for some cause, perhaps *amore*. Francesca, with two children living, had a third coming. She was the luckiest one. Pasquale had gone to the Duke Montelione, and Joseph to an old Russian gentleman.

The owner of Brontë had heard, while upon his Welsh tour, that Graeffer, his residential agent, had died at his post. He had applied to his banker friends, Gibbs and Noble, for tidings of his estate, but Gaetano had found that both gentlemen were gone on business to Malta, so, as he did not wish to trouble Sir John Acton unnecessarily, an absentee landlord could only wait for their return, and hope that Sicily was not attacked meanwhile.

Other frigates had by now joined, bringing him official letters containing the first of the peck of minor troubles which must be the fate of a Commander-in-Chief. The Captains of H.M.S. *Cyclops* and *Experiment*, when at anchor in Naples Bay, had sent their boats to capture a couple of French merchantmen entering those neutral waters. A letter of censure, suitable for Acton to display to the French Minister, must be composed, and must contain salutary mention that English ships would not be allowed to act in a manner which could not with impunity be attempted by the French. The British Consul at Algiers had been summarily dismissed by the Dey. The reason alleged was—"the very worst. Women in his house—an offence which will never be forgiven by the Moor." This story needed confirmation. But the Admiral had caught a glimpse of the rejected Mr. Falcon languishing on the Rock, and feared his part of the story might not be quite correct. Sir Richard Bickerton was not a favourite with the First Lord, who thought him feeble, but on hearing of the war, from a French source, off Naples, he had at once steered for Toulon. . . . The British Consul at Leghorn, together with the leading merchants, had, most weakly and unaccountably, on the arrival of French troops, signed undertakings far beyond the necessary parole of a prisoner of war. The ex-Ambassador to the Porte was a prisoner. On the morning of May 2, a fortnight before England had declared war on France, Buonaparte had struck his first lightning blow. He had summoned the Governor of Paris to his study at 1 a.m. and delivered to him an order to seize the persons of all Englishmen, from the ages of sixteen to sixty, at present in France. Amongst the visitors to Paris that week had been Lord Elgin, on his way from Constantinople to London. Mr. Drummond, from Naples, had been sent to succeed him, but the Earl's prestige in the Levant had been high, and his present ignominious situation must arouse undesirable reflections in the Oriental mind.

As he toiled slowly past Monte Cristo, Bastia and Cape Corse, Nelson concluded a report to the Prime Minister, marshalled under place-headings in block capitals. At *Gibraltar* he had left Sir Thomas Trigge not unjustifiably worried that Dillon's Regiment, composed entirely of foreigners, was part of his garrison in war-time. With regard to *Algiers*, he forwarded the Consul's statement with a warning that if the Dey was given way to in the least degree, at a moment when he considered England embarrassed, his insolence would increase. At *Malta* Lord Nelson had found the populace vociferous in their desire never to be separated from England, but having admitted that he regarded the island as a most important outwork to India, and its possession valuable in connection with all Levantine and South Italian dealings, he repeated that nothing but dire necessity would force him to take the fleet there under present circumstances. The General in command of the military had been resigned but gloomy when asked to hold troops in readiness to embark for service in Sicily. Governor Ball, on the other hand, was confident that if half the troops of the island were removed, the gallant Maltese, supported by a British fleet, would defend it against any force Buonaparte could send. " Truth probably lies between." *Sicily* called for a long paragraph. He thought its condition as bad as possible. It possessed no troops worthy the name. The decadent nobility were rightly unpopular, the middle class were ready for almost any change of rule, and the peasantry were starving. However, should the King of the Two Sicilies be driven out of Naples, to establish himself in Palermo, one happy consequence might result, from the point of view of the British fleet. The very fine bay and port of Gaëta might be secured for its use. How long British troops would be able to hold the Neapolitan fortresses Lord Nelson did not think himself sufficiently a military man to judge. *Sardinia* had declared herself neutral, and was allowing no foreign troops to land. He could only hope that she might be able to defend herself against a French invasion. It was difficult to know whether to look upon unfortunate *Tuscany* as friend or enemy. The French had declared Leghorn in a state of siege. Perhaps H.M. Ministers would consider the possibility of blockading it while the French were in occupation. *Genoa* was undoubtedly as much French as Toulon, and its blockade ought to be declared instantly. " If not, it will be what it has always been, the granary of the South of France, and the north part of Italy." He came last to the *Morea*. He had no doubts that the French agents at work there were preparing it either for the arrival of an army of their own or a Greek revolt against the Porte. In either case it would be used as a base for another attempt on *Egypt*, the mention of which brought to his mind that Mohamed Bey Elphi desired a passage to England in order to solicit Britain's aid against Turkish oppression. " Government will know how to steer between the Turks and Mamelukes." His long letter ended with a calculation of the number of French troops now in Italy—13,000 in the Kingdom of Naples, 8,000 in Leghorn and more arriving every day. Buonaparte was drawing them even from Switzerland.

The *Amphion* was off Monaco on July 5, " looking out sharp for the *Victory* ". Three days later, at 2.43 a.m., she saw a strange fleet. At 4.30 she made a private signal, which on its repetition ten minutes later was answered. She bore up, to salute Sir Richard Bickerton, with 11 guns, and at 7 o'clock Nelson took under his command H.M.S. *Gibraltar* (of 80 guns), the *Triumph, Belleisle, Superb, Renown, Donegal* and *Kent* (all 74's), the *Agincourt* and *Monmouth* (64's), the *Medusa* frigate and the sloops *Termagant* and *Weazle*.

2

Before they had heard of the war, all the ships had been expecting to go home. This fever would have to be overcome. As far as outside show went, they looked well enough—quite well enough to frighten the French—but their Captains, with one voice, declared that they were in need of docking repairs. They had fuel for one month, and having been six months at sea, dependent upon Malta, no provisions. What men they had were good, but they had got much scurvy. Of the 74's, only the *Superb*, *Renown* and *Kent* could be termed new, and their rigging was a reflection upon Portsmouth dockyard. The *Triumph's* bowsprit was in such a state that she must be sent to the Rock at once, and the only 80-gun ship of the squadron had sprung her mizzen-mast and main-yard. The *Monmouth* and *Agincourt* sailed so ill that they would never be able to keep company with a fleet on a winter's cruise. It would not be wise to risk them either at Leghorn or Genoa. ("Compared to them, the *Britannia* was, in her last days, a flyer.") Lord Nelson had left a hole in a letter home to add the force of the French in Toulon, and Captain Gore of the *Medusa*, who had reconnoitred the harbour yesterday, said that there were seven of the line clearly to be seen, fully rigged or nearly so, five frigates, and six or seven corvettes, and possibly two or three more men-of-war in the Arsenal.

A Chief of renowned ability, who had come amongst " perfect strangers ", announced himself without a finger's ache since he had left England, and firmly of the opinion that the Mediterranean was about to become an active scene. His intention was to send his ships into port in turn, to prepare for a winter's cruise. " We are not very superior if anything, in point of numbers. . . . We must keep a good look-out, both here and off Brest, and if I have the means, I shall try and fight one party or the other before they form a junction." Officers were reminded that they must always have lead, or plenty of shot, attached to their despatches. . . .

The response, from the first, was promising. Sir Richard Bickerton hastened to ask Lord Nelson to mention to the First Lord that he was very desirous of remaining in the Mediterranean. Captain Keats, a character recommended by the Duke of Clarence, affirmed that he was recovering from an illness, but looked so shocking that he was at once ordered to Naples, with leave to remain there for a fortnight. He was back within nine days, knowing his lordship so short of ships at his *rendezvous* off Toulon.   Frigates had been despatched to San Fiorenzo, Genoa and Leghorn, to get the number of troops there, and to look out for an enemy squadron reported to be coming either from the West Indies or Brest to join the Toulon fleet.   Sloops were gone to the Bay of Rosas and Barcelona to inquire as to watering facilities, and the purchase (under the rose) of bullocks, fresh greens, oranges, lemons and onions.   The *Agincourt* had sprung a leak, and must accompany Sir Richard's flagship, the *Kent*, to Valetta.   The *Victory* was " in this country ".   She was at Malta, having taken a French frigate and two or three ships from San Domingo, worth £8,000, but within the limits of Admiral Cornwallis's station—" my usual prize luck ! "   At this time of year, thanks to calms and contrary winds, her progress would be stately. She could not be looked for before the end of the month, by which time even the *Amphion* would be almost down to salt beef.   A French newspaper sent by Mr. Elliot said that Lord Nelson's brother had kissed hands on his appointment to a prebendal stall at Canterbury;   an Italian journal announced hopes of peace negotiations, a change of administration in England and new heads at the Admiralty.

The first " scrap of a pen " to reach anyone in the squadron which had sailed from Portsmouth on May 20 also arrived from Naples in the *Phœbe*, on July 29.   Lady Hamilton, who had been writing without cease, had chanced a line, fit for any eye, to the care of Messrs. Gibbs, Falconet and Noble, of Naples and Palermo. She was going to visit Lord Nelson's family in Norfolk, before a trip to Southend for sea-bathing, and she sketched plans for winter retirement with Lord Nelson's adopted daughter, at Merton, where she intended improvements.   She enclosed a packet of business letters from Davison, and one item of news mentioned by his friend in his accompanying private note gave Nelson such a shock that for several days his thoughts recurred to it persistently.   He had already been caused " very serious uneasiness " by paragraphs in English papers headed " Ilchester Election ", reporting the first of the evidence being given before a select committee of the House of Commons.   According to a Mr.   *3* Oldfield, Mr. Davison had cut a great dash when he came down to the Ilchester district to offer himself as a candidate ; and at breakfast in company with Mr. Oldfield and Mr. Welsh, a solicitor of Somerton, at the house of Mr. White Parsons of West Camel, Mr. Davison had accepted without much demur the statement of his host that " the contest lay between that gentleman owning the property in the borough and the person who will give £30 a man to the voters. . . ." " When Mr. Lockyer was the owner of the property and gave £30 a man, Mr. Lockyer always carried the borough." Mr. Davison, who had spoken of himself as one to whom money was no object, and mentioned that " my Lord Nelson was to dine with him on such a day ", had said that he would be happy to pay £3,000 into the Yeovil Bank if such a sum would carry the Election. A Mr. Hopping, whom Mr. White Parsons had known from a lad (and who fortunately happened to be in the next room), was introduced to him as a perfectly confidential person who had a list of the men amongst whom £30 a head was to be distributed. Mr. Davison had, upon the spot, engaged Mr. Hopping to do so—not, of course, for love. Mr. White Parsons had mentioned £300 as Mr. Hopping's fee, but Mr. Hoppings himself had fancied £500. It had also been necessary to erect cottages to receive " the people who had voted against Colonel Wallis ", and some twenty had been built for Mr. Davison, by a relation of Mr. White Parsons, on ground belonging to that gentleman and a friend. They were now known in Ilchester as " Davison's Folly ". For, although Mr. Davison had departed from West Camel in a blaze of affability (offering to get one of Mr. White Parsons' sons out to India, and hoping that Miss Fanny White Parsons would be his partner when he opened his Grand Election Ball), back in St. James's Square he had become " a good deal alarmed about the bribery ". He had begun by jettisoning Hopping (who was accustomed at Election times to appear in some state, in a chaise decorated with favours, and by the name of " Sir Thomas Armstrong "). He had proceeded to withdraw his candidature.

Davison himself was confident that he could surmount a situation engineered by his personal enemies, but Nelson longed to hear that his friend was quit of a business in which he smelt danger. " Not a day has passed without that I have thought of you."

Every day, too, he noted his longing for the *Victory*. She came in sight, at last, on the morning of July 30, while he was at his desk, and that evening her log recorded : " 5.30. Joined this Ship, Captain T. M. Hardy, and superseded Captain Sutton. Hoisted Lord Viscount Nelson's Flag."

The scene was now set, and many of the principal characters were assembled for the final act, for although he had two years and two months of life to run, Nelson was to spend but twenty-six nights of this time out of the *Victory*. " We are all well ", he reported six weeks later. " Murray is measuring soap and coals, Hardy rigging the main-yard on the booms ; and we are caulking and refitting for a winter's cruise, unless the French will be so good as to prevent us."

But the schemes of Buonaparte did not at present include ordering a fleet into the Mediterranean. He was preparing for an Invasion of England. Only when he had laid that plan aside did he take the action which resulted in Trafalgar.

3

Lord Nelson had two officers in the *Victory* named Scott, obviously an inconvenient circumstance. He solved the problem by calling his Chaplain, the Rev. Alexander John Scott, " Doctor ", an anticipatory promotion, as the degree of D.D. was not conferred upon Mr. Scott by Cambridge University until after Trafalgar. This uncomplaining character, who had first attracted his attention as the Chaplain of a 74 in Lord Hood's fleet at Toulon, and afterwards as " Sir Hyde's parson-secretary ", was an Original. Languages were his prey, and to his noble employer, who never attained proficiency in a single one, there was fascination in presenting a person of cadaverous countenance and luminous orbs with a captured French despatch, letter, pamphlet or foreign newspaper, out of which they would together tear the heart in a few minutes. On his death at the age of seventy-two, volumes in forty tongues were discovered in the library of the Vicar of Catterick, though he had modestly claimed mastery of no more than eight, and admitted that elementary Danish had taken him three days, and Russian several weeks. Amongst the more improbable but well-attested anecdotes of his career was that when sleeping in the Captain's cabin of the frigate *Topaze*, on a passage to Kingston, Jamaica, he had been struck by a flash of lightning, which had rent the mizzen-mast, killing and wounding fourteen men, melted the hooks to which his hammock was slung, and, communicating with some spare ammunition on a shelf above his head, caused an explosion from which he was rescued, in flames, suffering from severe concussion and the loss of his front teeth. Sometimes Nelson agreed with the victim of this catastrophe in attributing his oddities to the fatal stroke of lightning, but, upon the whole, the Admiral blamed learning. " Absolutely too much learning has turned his head." As

Admiral's Interpreter, Dr. Scott received £100 per annum in addition to his pay as Chaplain of the *Victory*, but he was often useful in an unsuspected capacity. No Tuscan, Neapolitan, Algerine, Sardinian or Spaniard, beholding an invalid archæologist admiring their ancient monuments, guessed him to be collecting information and provisions; and in fashionable circles Lord Nelson's Chaplain on sick-leave was more than once able to arrange amicably a concession which could not be granted on paper. His *Recollections of Life in the " Victory "* did his employer as much posthumous service, for Dr. Scott's was the voice to assure early Victorian England that Lord Nelson had been " a thorough clergyman's son. I should think he never went to bed or got up without saying his prayers." Every Sunday it was the Admiral's custom either to congratulate his Chaplain on the sermon or suggest that it was not as well adapted as usual to the needs of the congregation; and Dr. Scott often preached from a text suggested by and discussed with the Admiral. Every morning, unless other duties interposed, the pair met, after breakfast, to sit in two leathern armchairs supplied with ample pockets, stuffed with matter awaiting translation, and the translator was repeatedly startled by his companion's skill in investigation, and ability to sift the few grains of intelligence lost in a bundle of apparent rubbish; though Lord Nelson's theory that no author ever put his pen to paper without having some new idea to communicate to the world was not altogether shared by the man of learning. Dr. Scott's considered opinion was " that man possessed the wisdom of the serpent with the innocence of the dove ".

Mr. John Scott, official Secretary, bore equally enthusiastic testimony within a few weeks of taking up his duties. " I have heard much of Lord Nelson's abilities as an officer and statesman, but the account of the latter is infinitely short. In my travels through the Service, I have met with no character in any degree equal to his Lordship; his penetration is quick, judgment clear, wisdom great, and his decisions correct and decided : nor does he in company appear to bear any weight on his mind, so cheerful and pleasant, that it is a happiness to be about his hand." Nelson in the same month was writing, " My Secretary, I esteem a Treasure. He is not only a clever man, but indefatigable in his business, and an extraordinarily well-behaved modest man. In short, I feel very well mounted at present."

In the *Victory* he had three commodious rooms at his disposal,

M M

under the poop, immediately under those of Hardy. They consisted of state room, " great cabin ", or reception room, dining cabin and sleeping cabin, and, taken with his gallery and steward's room, accounted for rather more than a quarter of the whole upper deck. The state room, in which his labours with his secretaries were conducted, was fifteen feet long, and had a row of nine sash windows in the stern, where its width tapered to twenty-five feet. It had two doors communicating with the thirty-five-foot-wide dining-room, in which he had a staircase constructed so that he could reach the quarter-deck without loss of time. Two further doors from the dining-room led to a lobby, subdivided for kitchen and pantry, and his sleeping cabin, measuring twelve feet by twenty. The decks of all were covered with canvas, painted with a pattern of black and white squares, and the furniture, although solid and handsome, was strictly functional. He had, like Buonaparte and other men of action, formed the invaluable habit of being able to sleep in short snatches, from which he would arise filled with new vigour. Sometimes, according to Dr. Scott, he used the two black leather armchairs in his state room, lashed together, as a couch, but the *suite* included an ottoman and a folding bedstead. A dining-table, circular pedestal tables, other chairs, a sideboard, tall-boy and washstand, all of mahogany and typical mid-Georgian design, used during these years, have been preserved, and a replica of his cot is still to be seen in his sleeping cabin. [6]

A Physician to the Fleet and a Surgeon of the *Victory*, neither of whom took up his appointment until the following season (a time when conditions were unchanged), also recorded impressions of daily life in the *Victory*. Dr. Gillespie was called at 6 a.m. by a servant who brought a light, and informed him of the hour, wind, weather and course of the ship. He presented himself for breakfast at the Admiral's table at about quarter to seven, together with Murray, Hardy, the two Scotts and one or two other officers, and their fare was tea, hot rolls, toast and cold tongue or other cold meat. Afterwards, in fine, or at least moderate, weather, they repaired upon deck to enjoy a majestic sunrise above a watery perspective, hardly ever obscured by cloud. The *Victory*, " a floating city ", mounting 110 guns, and designed to carry water and provisions for four months and a ship's company of nine hundred, went through the Mediterranean with the greatest steadiness, followed, in regular train, by other " lofty and tremendous bulwarks of Britain ". During the last three-quarters of an hour of his morning's professional duty the physician worked to the accompaniment of a band, and the Admiral's 3 o'clock dinner was announced by a drum beating to the tune of " The Roast Beef of Old England ". Three courses were usually served, followed by a choice dessert, and accompanied by three or four wines, including champagne and claret. " If a person does not find himself perfectly at his ease, it must be his own fault, such is the urbanity and hospitality which reign here, notwithstanding the four orders of Knighthood worn by Lord Nelson, and the well-earned laurels which he has acquired." After coffee and liqueurs the company walked the deck again, while a band played for nearly an hour. Tea was served before seven, and this was the hour after which the Admiral, if not otherwise occupied, sent for " my family, to sit and talk ", and generally " unbent himself ", although he was " at all times as free from stiffness and pomp as a regard to proper dignity will permit, and is very communicative ". At eight a rummer of punch, with cake or biscuit, was the prelude to wishing the Admiral a good night. Mr. Beatty noticed that Lord Nelson partook sparingly of the good things at his table, liked vegetables and eschewed salt. A liver or wing of a fowl, and a small plate of macaroni, sometimes taken with a glass of champagne, often formed his main meal, and after dinner he never exceeded four glasses of wine, and seldom drank three, all of which were diluted by Bristol water. He was generally on deck six or seven hours in the day, and generally, in the opinion of the medical man, insufficiently protected from the weather.

4

When Mr. à Court, Secretary of Legation at Naples, came on board the *Victory* just before dinner on August 9, he was asked to stay all night. He was on his way to England, *via* Madrid, carrying Mr. Elliot's despatches, and Sir Richard Bickerton, from Malta, was expected to join the fleet next morning. He had brought a most obliging letter from Mr. Gibbs, who would be willing to do anything possible with regard to Brontë from Palermo, and Mr. Elliot had written that, knowing the superstitious dread of sailors of having a corpse on board, he was having the remains of Frederick Augustus, Earl of Bristol, and Bishop of Derry (who had expired at Albano on July 8), crated for a passage in the next man-of-war going to England, invoiced and labelled " Antique statue ". Mr. à Court's Naples news was that their Majesties were now hoping that the mediation of Russia might save them from the clutches of Buonaparte. " Poor souls ", was the dictum of the Admiral, who did not share the diplomatist's faith in the young Czar, and only hoped that old Acton, trying to save Naples, would not lose Sicily too.   He had heard privately from Captain Capel, whose frigate had recently returned from duty in the Bay, that Sir John was so scared of France that he dared not ask an Englishman to dine, and that Mr. Elliot loathed his post.   Mr. à Court said that Prince Castelcicala was now in high favour at court, and it was believed that if Sir John " went ", the Queen would try to have him as Prime Minister.   " Then ", considered the Admiral, " the country would be well governed."   After dinner he showed Mr. à Court some newspaper advertisements of English vessels captured by the French, which the Spaniards were offering at public auction, and asked him to draw the attention of Mr. Frere to this behaviour.   8

Next morning, early, the *Kent* joined, and having gathered from his second-in-command that all was in order at Malta, the Commander-in-Chief did not detain his guest a moment longer than was necessary to add a postscript to his letter to Mr. Addington, in which he announced all in his fleet well, and only needing a sight of the French at sea to make them completely happy.   He had, during the night, composed another letter to be entrusted to the inviolability of the diplomatic bag.   It was his belief that anything in a square but toppling hand addressed to Lady Hamilton would be opened at every post-office between here and London, even when he had taken the precaution of writing as from an officer of his squadron sending messages to a Mrs. Thomson, and had signed them merely " yours ".

A week after Mr. à Court's departure, Lord Nelson's fears that the Admiralty had forgotten him were assuaged by the arrival of H.M.S. *Canopus* from Plymouth, under the command of Rear-Admiral George Campbell.   She was welcome, though small craft were his pressing need, and she brought the great batch of letters for the Mediterranean Fleet which had been collecting in London up to July 3.   His own large portion contained one piece of confidential intelligence not uncommonly received in a squadron three months after leaving home.   Either the recipient or the subsequent thief of his ecstatic reply, addressed to " Mrs. Thomson ", obliterated passages with the intention of making it incomprehensible.

" My dearest Beloved,

" To say that I think of you by day, night, and all day and all night, but too faintly express my feelings of love and affection towards you ********** unbounded affection. Our dear excellent good ******* is the only one who knows anything of the matter; and she has promised me, when you ****** again, to take every possible care of you as a proof of her never-failing regard for your own dear Nelson.

" Believe me that I am incapable of wronging you in thought, word or deed. No; not all the wealth of Peru could buy me for one moment; it is all yours, and reserved wholly for you and *** certainly ********* from the moment of our happy, dear, enchanting, blessed meeting. The thoughts of such happiness, my dearest, only beloved, makes the blood fly to my head. The call of our country is a duty which you would deservedly in the cool moments of reflection reprobate, was I to abandon; and I should feel so disgraced by seeing you ashamed of me; no longer saying—' This is the man who has saved his country ! This is he who is the first to go forth to fight our battles, and the last to return ! '

" And then all these honours reflect on you. ' Ah ! ' they will think, ' What a man ! what sacrifices has he not made to secure our homes and property : even the society and happy union with the finest and most accomplished woman in the world.'

" As you love, how must you feel. My heart is with you, cherish it. I shall, my best beloved, return—if it pleases God—a victor; and it shall be my study to transmit an unsullied name. There is no desire of wealth, no ambition that could keep me from all my soul holds dear. No ! it is to save my country, my wife in the eye of God, and ********** ********** will tell you that it is all right; and then, only think of our happy meeting.

" Ever, for ever, I am yours, only yours, even beyond this world.
" Nelson and Brontë."

9

" For ever, for ever, your own Nelson. August 26th."

But the arrival of Admiralty instructions after so long a hiatus had coincided with symptoms which led him to believe that the enemy were on the verge of putting to sea. Nine days passed before he gave vent to this passionate response, and since he had no safe means of despatching something so unguarded, he kept it, perforce, until an opportunity offered, which was not for three months. For two years, his only perfectly secure method of ensuring that a letter reached Lady Hamilton unopened was to see it go into the breast-pocket of somebody who would deliver it into her hand. This generally meant a Captain taking a ship of his squadron home for repairs. He was not often able to employ a despatch brig—the swiftest means of communication—and their Lordships, sending matter to which they needed an answer, together with everything else which had collected at headquarters, always expected him to return the vessel instantly. He began to write letters almost in journal form, adding a paragraph as a fancy or an anniversary suggested. Lady Hamilton often replied c/o Messrs. Gibbs, Falconet, and when Falconet, the French refugee partner, became so terrified of Buonaparte that he dared not oblige Lord Nelson by the purchase of a little macaroni, an unexpected character stepped into the breach. A Quaker merchant of Rosas Bay was already getting intelligence from inside Spain, which he transmitted to Nelson's officers when they called to water and provision. On a wild December night of 1803 a small Spanish merchantman joined the fleet off Toulon, and a solemn figure came on board the *Victory*. Friend Gayner, who had never before set foot in a man-of-war at sea, had taken a romantic fancy to see Lord Nelson. " I was, of course, very attentive to him and he is gone back quite delighted with our regularity." The guest was duly carried next morning by the Chief to attend Sunday morning service with a ship's company, " very healthy and very unanimous ". Henceforward he sent private letters for Lord Nelson, enclosed in his own correspondence, to a business connection at Bristol. *10*

5

An old Mediterranean man had noted that the strength of the north-west gales did not seem to have deteriorated since he was last in this country. " The happiness of keeping a station is always to have a foul wind, and never to hear the delightful sound, *Steady*." The *Victory* was so easy at sea that he hoped she might never sustain any material damage, but the *Canopus* had lost her fore-yard within a few days of joining. However, his mind was made up : " Never to go into Port till after the Battle, if they make me wait a year, provided the Admiralty change the ships who cannot keep the Sea in winter ", nor, as the season advanced, and he heard from St. Vincent, " We can send you neither ships nor men ", did he alter his resolution. " I bear up for every gale, I must not, in our present state quarrel with the north-westers. By always going away large, we generally lose much of their force, and the heavy sea. By the great care and attention of every captain, we have suffered much less than we could have expected. . . . We either run to the southward, or furl all sails and make the ships go as easy as possible." He believed that the three danger points in his command were the Straits of Gibraltar, the heel of Italy, and Toulon. This view entailed keeping a division on the watch over the mouth of the Adriatic and the Straits of Messina (through which narrowing trade-routes merchant vessels were continually requiring convoy); and whatever the Admiralty might say, he was determined always to keep at least a frigate in the Bay of Naples, ready to remove the royal family. His desire " to send many of our ships who want what I cannot give them, to England, towing a line-of-battle-ship " was appreciated in his fleet, and the anti-scorbutics in which he put great faith, and which he had acquired for his ships, at sea, with much difficulty, had also done their work. As early as August 24 he was able to state, " This day, only six men are confined to their beds in the whole Squadron ", and by early October his description had a familiar ring. " We are healthy beyond example, and in great good humour with our-selves, and so sharp set that I would not be a French Admiral in the way of some of our ships for something. I believe we are in the right fighting trim, let them come as soon as they please." He ended less happily, " Would to God the ships were half as good, but they are what we call crazy. I know well enough that if I was to go into Malta, I should save the ships during this bad season, but if I am to watch the French, I must be at sea, and if at sea, must have bad weather."

A position thirty to forty miles west of the harbour mouth had been his summer *rendezvous*. He admitted that it was unusual. He had chosen it to prevent the junction of the Spanish fleet, and to be able, if necessary, to take shelter within a few hours, either under the Hyeres Islands or Cape San Sebastian. He was indignant when congratulated from home on the success of his blockade of Toulon. His intention had always been to let the enemy fleet come out, and annihilate it. " Nothing ever kept the French Fleet in Toulon or Brest, whenever they had a mind to come to sea. I have no Frigates to watch them, and must take my chance." If he missed them, " which God forbid ", he was provisioned for a voyage to Madras, and ready to follow them to the Antipodes. " Our weather-beaten ships, I have no doubt, will make their sides like a plum pudding."

Nevertheless, autumn mornings, " as thick as buttermilk, and blowing a levanter ", found him " confoundedly out of humour ". Desertion from ships in Spanish ports was not yet stamped out, and he had found all his ships short of men. To St. Vincent he confided on October 5, " I am—don't laugh—dreadfully sea-sick this day." Another old friend was told, " Our gales are incessant and you know I am never well when it blows hard." Ten days later he was " absolutely in a fever of the mind ", for the latest rumours were that 10,000 troops embarked in Toulon and Marseille were bound for Ireland, for Sardinia, for Messina, the Morea or Egypt. " I have as many destinations sent me as there are Countries." The *Canopus*, ordered to water off the north-east end of Sardinia nearly three weeks past, had not yet returned (" I am uneasy about her "), and the attitude of Spain to his ships was so uncivil that he expected to hear at any moment of her having entered the war. He had written to Mr. Frere, asking to be personally advised from Madrid, as, if he was to wait for the official intimation from England, he would have to wait two or three months. To crown all, on a morning following a storm which had blown him off his station, " a lame story " had been brought to him, from a Spanish source, of a strange fleet of twelve sail seen off Minorca, steering to the westward. " If I should miss these fellows, my heart will break. I am actually, only now recovering from the shock of missing them in 1798, when they were going to Egypt."

It was on such occasions that a surgeon of the *Victory* noticed 11 with professional disapproval that " his lordship's wonderful activity of mind prevented him from taking ordinary repose ", and even kept him on deck throughout the night, attired in a thin overcoat, his favourite leather and flannel waistcoats, and light footwear. (He always preferred shoes, which he could kick off in his cabin, where, sooner than summon a servant to undertake a duty very difficult for a one-armed man, he would pace the carpet in his stocking-feet until they were dry.)

The worst of his anxieties of October 15 were banished during the hours of darkness by a signal from the *Seahorse*. She had been sent in to reconnoitre Toulon in company with the *Renown* five days earlier, but his expectation had been that his frigates would neither be able to see the enemy, nor find him if they did. " Relieved for the first time in my life by being informed the French were still in Port ", he retired to consider a scheme for running with his whole squadron to water at an open roadstead on a neutral coast recommended by one of his officers. Towards the end of the month, when the moon would be full, a couple of frigates could be left to watch an enemy very unlikely to move. His own private journal of his first voyage to the Maddalena Islands conjures up a fearsome picture. The distance was only 12 two hundred miles, but four days after leaving their Toulon *rendezvous*, daylight found a fleet with many split sails no more than five leagues directly to leeward of Rosso, an islet which it had left the night before, and with a very strong current against it. "The Fleet being absolutely in distress for water, I determined to persevere. . . . We worked the *Victory* every foot of the way, from Asinara to this anchorage, the wind blowing from Longo Sardo, under double-reefed topsails." On the evening of the eighth day the whole squadron tacked under Sardinia, and stood into "a beautiful little bay, or rather harbour", hitherto unnamed, and next morning the Governor of Maddalena, coming on board H.M.S. *Victory*, was saluted with nine guns, and Captain Ryves was sent a highly congratulatory note on a most correct chart of "Agincourt" Sound. This officer had been in command of the *Agincourt* in March of the preceding year, when he had been sent with a small detachment to prevent the French seizing these islands. The French had made no such attempt, but a man of resource had filled in his time in carrying out a survey of "one of the finest harbours I have ever seen", which possessed, moreover, the decisive advantage of two entrances.

During the next week processions of peasants in native costume of black kilt and scarlet jacket urged mules laden with onions, solid-wheeled ox-wains, ample flocks of skinny mountain sheep, and what bullocks could be mustered at short notice, towards a marshy shore, and boats collecting wood and water plied without pause between the fleet and a village boasting about fifty roofs and no chimneys. Nelson, having found the "hole to put the Fleet in" for which he had been searching ever since he had dismissed Malta from his considerations, repaired there six times before the following May, and since the Physician to the Fleet had represented that the country into which the wooding and watering parties must be sent bred fever, he ordered a dose of Peruvian bark to be administered twice a day to every man on this duty.

6

He told himself that in the Mediterranean the weather was not so raw as what they would have experienced in the Channel at this season, but it was undeniable that the monotony of their existence could not have been surpassed. "Our days pass so much alike that having described one, you have them all. We now (October 18) breakfast by candlelight; and all retire at 8 o'clock to bed. . . . We cruise, cruise, and one day so much like another that they are hardly distinguishable." In October he noted wanly that days could be remembered " by the difference of a gale of wind, or not ", but for a month from mid-January this distinction was absent. Despite the horrible link between the inscribed page and sea-sickness, he entered always twice, and sometimes as many as six times a day, in his own hand, in two small books, the state of the barometer, weather and wind. (His best barometer in variable weather, however, was always, he said, his stump.) How to combat monotony—what he described as " not allowing the sameness of the prospect to satiate the mind "—was his over-riding problem. He attacked it by changing the cruising ground continually, " sometimes by looking at Toulon, Ville Franche, Barcelona, and Rosas; then running round Minorca, Majorca, Sardinia and Corsica; and two or three times anchoring for a few days, and sending a Ship to the last place for *onions*, which I find the best thing that can be given to Seamen; having always good mutton for the sick, cattle when we can get them, and plenty of fresh water. In the winter it is the best plan to give half the allowance of grog, instead of all wine. These things are for the Commander-in-Chief to look to; but shut very nearly out of Spain, and only getting refreshments by stealth from other places, my Command has been an arduous one." " You will agree with me ", he added to his old medical friend Moseley, " that it is easier for an Officer to keep men healthy, than for a Physician to cure them." Acting on this belief, he sent to Malta for sweet oranges (which he knew could be packed in paper at the proper season), and deputed his second-in-command to discover on the spot why all the bread from this quarter should arrive infested with weevils. He wrote to Gibraltar to order more cheese, cocoa and sugar and less rice. To his chagrin, ships' companies in general did not much like rice, or, when in health, the macaroni so sonorously recommended by Dr. Snipe as " a light wholesome and nourishing food ". A Captain who had forwarded vouchers for five bullocks and six bags of hay was asked to explain so large a purchase of fodder for beasts immediately slain. The mystery of a transport which had arrived at Malta an eighth short of her normal stowage was solved by the discovery that the Master had not known that baskets of coal should be heaped. A complete specimen of a seaman's cot was sent to Naples, with enquiries as to the time and cost of supplying duplicates in bulk. Lord Nelson recommended that the Guernsey jackets, of a new pattern, should be made three inches wider and up to ten inches longer so that they should not work out of the trousers of seamen on the yards; and he sent back to England, with a message that "the Contractor who furnished such stuff ought to be hanged", frocks and trousers of "coarse wrapper stuff". "Best Russia duck" was his demand for the seamen of H.M. Navy. The Naval Hospital to be established in a palace at Valetta occupied his thoughts much. It must have a garden in which convalescent seamen and marines could take the air and enjoy gentle exercise.

Stores were as difficult to collect as food. The dockyards of Gibraltar and Malta had been left bare by the recent economy programme. Malta was finally desired to confine its principal rope-making to upwards of four inch. Provided hemp was forwarded to the fleet in butts, the line-of-battle ships could make their own, up to that specification, the best rope-maker in the fleet, mentioned the Admiral, being the Master-Ropemaker of the *Victory*—" a child of 13 years of age ".

As to the state of affairs at home, and elsewhere in Europe, during these weary months, he had to guess from newspapers obtained through Spain and never less than ten days old. In April 1804 he complained, " I have only had two dispatches sent me since leaving England."

When Sir William Bolton joined, in the *Childers*, on October 6, 1803, he brought an answer to the Commander-in-Chief's first long letter to the Prime Minister on Mediterranean politics, two bundles of respectively forty-eight and fifty-four printed Admiralty orders for distribution to officers of the squadron, instructions to proceed to the blockade of Genoa and Spezia, and a few private letters for the Admiral, of which only one packet was not dated " Admiralty ". The bearing of the Admiral's official Secretary became very uneasy. Fortunately it soon appeared that Lady Hamilton had mentioned Mrs. Scott's being brought to bed. The *Childers*, a 14-gun sloop, the result of Lord Nelson's repeated requests on behalf of his nephew, had been ordered to join him in such haste that no mail for the fleet had been carried. Her Captain had looked out until the last possible moment for some promised packages from Mr. Davison. The Rev. Mr. Este (who had particularly desired to provide a gallant son with a letter to the Commander-in-Chief) had almost wept, when led panting to Sir Thomas Troubridge's room, to be very kindly told that he was come too late.

Not all the matter brought out with such speed was agreeable to its recipient. The Prime Minister, not having time to read

Lord Nelson's political letter, had passed it on to Lord Hobart, Secretary of State at War and for the Colonies. Their Lordships desired Lord Nelson to summon and interview Mr. Falcon, the dismissed Consul from Algiers, and send a discreet officer to demand satisfaction from the Dey, who had now extended his insolence to detaining Maltese vessels, appropriating their cargoes and putting their crews to the galleys. Lady Hamilton was shocked at her expenses, especially as Davison seemed to think that she was going to pay for the improvements at Merton out of the £100 a month allotted to her for housekeeping. She wished to come out to the Mediterranean. The Commander-in-Chief had heard something of this plan already, from Davison, and reasoned with her gently. " How would you feel to be at that nasty place Malta, with nothing but soldiers and diplomatic nonsense, and to hear that the Fleet is gone out of the Straits? " It was true that Lady Bickerton had been unwise enough to maroon herself at Valetta. Knowing what attachment was, Lord Nelson took every opportunity of ordering Admiral Bickerton to Malta. But for a Commander-in-Chief watching Toulon, Malta was about as useful a base as Spithead. " I assure you that Merton has a greater chance of seeing me." The same applied to Sicily and Naples, with the additional disadvantage that if he did ever see them it would be during an action, and only for a few days; besides, sad to say, " nobody cares for us there ". A wilder suggestion was quickly quashed. " Imagine what a cruize off Toulon is! Even in summer time we have a hard gale every week, and two days heavy swell. It would kill you, and myself to see you. Much less possible to have Charlotte, Horatia, etc. on board ship! And I who have given orders to carry no women to sea in the *Victory* to be the first to break them ! "

With regard to her financial anxieties he was equally gentle, but much less firm. " I am not surprised, my dearest Emma, at the enormous expense of the watering place, but, if it has done my own Emma service, it is well laid out." Indeed, he did not find it easy to admonish a lady who, upon receiving from his own eldest sister a family saga of school-fees, doctor's bills and wish for more remunerative employment for the master of the house, had instantly forwarded £100. " Your purse, my dear Emma, will always be empty " was all that he could say, except that he wished Mr. Addington would give her £500 a year pension, and if the Queen of Naples had so far done nothing he should begin to write her down as a time-serving woman. On second thoughts, he did not wish his Emma to be beholden even to Addington. " Whilst I have sixpence, you shall have fivepence of it. . . . We can live on bread and cheese. . . ." He instructed Davison a little curtly that there must be no question of Lady Hamilton being called upon to pay for alterations at Merton, and that everything ordered by her must be undertaken.

Two more features of the " dear delightful letters " for which he waited with so much joyful expectation were not calculated to set his mind at ease. As before, during his absence on foreign duty, his idol could not resist telling him of the attentions paid to her by other gentlemen, and glancing at his wife. But he no longer responded on either count, and as far as her " titled offers " went, was jocular. " I hope one of these days you will be my own Duchess of Brontë, and then a fig for them all ! " While she had been the wife of a man who might compel her to receive dissolute royalty he had been anxious, but now she could choose her own company, and his belief in her constancy was absolute. A lady of experience took the hint, and neither of these topics recurred: But she did not settle at Merton, or have Horatia there, except for short visits, and she kept on her London house.

Horatia's name had begun to appear increasingly often in her father's letters. He had studied nursery growth sufficiently to know that she must now be running and talking all day. " How I long to hear her prattle ! " He was not happy until she had been " inoculated with the cow-pox ", and was most unhappy when the result was a very bad arm. " I dreamt last night, I heard her call ' Papa ', and point to her arm, just as you describe." On October 21, 1803, he set himself down to write to her.

" My dear Child,
" Receive this first letter from your most affectionate Father. If I live it will be my pride to see you virtuously brought up, but if it pleases God to call me, I trust to Himself. In that case I have left Dear Lady Hamilton your Guardian. I therefore charge you, my Child, on the value of a Father's Blessing, to be obedient and attentive to all her kind admonitions and instructions. At this moment I have left you in a Codicil, dated the sixth of September, the sum of 4,000 Pounds Sterling. . . ."

The thought that the child might be left unprovided for, dependent " upon smiles and frowns ", haunted him. He had already sent a note to his solicitor, headed, " Private for yourself—and most secret " and opening, " I send you home a Codicil to my Will, which you will not communicate to any person breathing." Amongst its clauses was a high-handed scheme to ensure that his daughter got an amiable husband, and bore his name. If his dear nephew should prove worthy, in Lady Hamilton's estimation, of such a treasure, it was his wish that the boy Horatio should marry " my adopted daughter ". He heard with pleasure that Horatia showed spirit. " Aye ! she is like her mother ; will have her own way, or kick up the devil of a dust." " You ", he was confident, " will cure her. I am afraid ", he added, " I should spoil her." He believed that he might have promised her a watch, and wrote to Falconet to produce one that would tick for a month at least, with a train *full* of trinkets. (" I have it in my possession now ", wrote Horatia forty years later, " a small French watch, set round with pearls, a chain and seals attached.") He was sure that he could not have promised a dog, " as we have no dogs on board ship ". Dreadful fears for his darling assailed him. He, who had seen the dogs of the Mediterranean coast, and hydrophobia, would never give a child " a pet of that sort ". He explained for the infant ear that he was not sending a dog, lest Horatia should come to love it more than Lord Nelson. A gold chain with a medallion of a greyhound in the centre was sent instead. He wrote twice to ask that a strong netting should be placed round the " Nile " at Merton, " that the little thing may not tumble in ". On pitch black nights, when the wind was blowing half a gale and the rain was coming down in torrents, he " whose whole soul is at Merton " could see the red-brick English country house almost as clearly as if the nine windows of the aft-most wall of his state room had looked forth on ornamental waters of Surrey, instead of " the stormy gulph of Lyons ".

" The entrance by the corner I would certainly have done ; a common white gate will do for the present, and one of the cottages, which is in the barn, can be put up as a temporary lodge. The road can be made to a temporary bridge, for that part of the ' Nile ' one day shall be filled up. Downing's canvas awning will do for a passage. For the winter, the carriage can be put in the barn. The new building the chamber over the dining-room, you must consider. The stair window, we settled, was not to be stopped up. The underground passage will, I hope, be made, but I shall, please God soon see it all."

It had always been his intention with the first prize money he got (" I *long* to be out of debt ") to pay Mr. Greaves, whose last instalment was due on October 1. Next on his list came

Davison, whose latest letters mentioned that he was opening a banking-house in company with Messrs. Noel, Templar, Middleton, Johnson and Wedgwood, at 43, Pall Mall.

He was well pleased with the steward provided by Davison, and indeed often told the astute Chevalier that he wondered he had not set up an hotel years past. But even " living as frugal as my situation will permit ", he was saving practically nothing, and he now knew why he had received no rent from Brontë for three years. The obliging Gibbs had made a pilgrimage to the estate on the wrong side of Etna. The last thirty miles had to be accomplished on horse-back. The spreading building under the volcanic mountain which had startled the eyes of the equestrian Englishman had explained all. The deceased Graeffer, letting his æsthetic sense overrule his reason, had been fitting up a perfect palace there, far more worthy to receive the Duke of Brontë than the best existing farmhouse on the estate, which was what he had been told to put in order for occasional residence. Graeffer's widow was demanding a pension of at least £200 per annum for herself and her orphan child. By 1805, with care (said Gibbs), a rental of £2,000 should be forthcoming. The hour was not propitious, but as he had already orders to *let*, might he inquire, would his Lordship (supposing his Sicilian Majesty himself suggested the idea) find the *sale* of his property anything against his inclination ? " Quite the contrary " wrote his lordship in the margin. As affairs were marching, he thought the French were likely to see Brontë before its Duke. He had, in any case, quite given up ideas of settling there. His instructions to Gibbs included a melancholy paragraph :

" I paid more attention to another Sovereign than my own ; therefore the King of Naples' gift of Brontë to me, if it is not now settled to my advantage, and to be permanent, has cost me a fortune, and a great deal of favour which I might have enjoyed, and jealousy which I might have avoided. I repine not on these accounts. I did my duty, to the Sicilifying of my conscience, and I am easy. . . . All I beg is that the just thing may be done immediately, and that I may have it permanent. I shall never again write an order about the estate."

[15]

He introduced his new agent to the new British Ambassador at Naples (" I believe I am to call Mr. Gibbs a Banker "), and hoped for the best. He was glad to be able to express his gratitude to the Gibbs family in practical form. Her widower father had now decided to part with his Mary, one of the children who had sat on the Admiral's knee in the Palazzo Palagonia. Miss

[16]

Gibbs, aged nine, got her passage home in a man-of-war, and may
have found companions of her own size, for when the Admiral
entertained five guests at his table in Christmas week, 1803, he
noted that one of them was " not three feet high ".   " All the
Grandees dined with Campbell, and I had a midshipman's party."

7

Early in the month of January 1804 he prepared to stand over
to Algiers, " to settle a little account with the Dey ".   Mr.
Falcon had been duly fetched from Gibraltar for his inquisition,
and had proved better in person than on paper.   " Spirited "
was the Admiral's approving word for a little man who had
apparently done his best to maintain British prestige when
attacked by a noisy and ignorant Oriental who would not stop at
personal violence.   Mr. Falcon was a little man.   He had been
secretary to the former Consul, a fact which perhaps explained
some of the liberties taken by the Dey.   But his evidence was
clear and consistent, his conduct seemed to have been " most
correct ", nor did he display any hesitation at the prospect of
being re-installed in a dangerous post.   His own explanation
was that the reason for casting him forth was a mere pretext.   He
had never seen a Moorish woman in his house; if any had been
entertained there it must have been in the servants' quarters and
without his knowledge.   The Commander-in-Chief, having heard
his story, and summed him up more favourably than at first
sight, sent for " my right trusty friend Richard Goodwin Keats
Esq., Captain of His Britannic Majesty's Ship *Superb* ", and this
officer received his orders with much satisfaction.

A melancholy minor incident of Mediterranean diplomacy
opened on January 9, when Mr. Falcon and *suite* were transferred
to the *Superb* for a passage to Algiers.   The fleet which was to
make an impressive supporting appearance was off Cape San
Sebastian, the Rendezvous No. 97 so often mentioned in the
Commander-in-Chief's letters of this winter.   The instructions
given to Captain Keats were complicated and interdependent.
They included two Admiralty orders, an extract from a letter of
Lord Hobart, a Memorandum from Lord Nelson and several
other letters and papers.   If the Dey refused to receive Captain
Keats unless his ship returned a salute, he was not to give any,
but to send in a letter announcing that he would sail in twenty-
four hours.   Supposing this difficulty did not arise and he got an
interview, he was to open by enlarging upon the indignity offered

to his sovereign in the person of Mr. Falcon, and unless the Dey consented to sign a note of apology couched in humiliating terms, break off the negotiation. If he carried his first two points, he must proceed to demand the restitution of all the Maltese vessels, crews and cargoes captured by Algerines, and try what he could do to get possession of the Sicilians with British passports carrying British cargoes for distressed Maltese. He was on no account to allow the Dey to digress to fresh complaints, and to promise nothing with regard to peace or war, "so that it may hang over his head". In conclusion, should the Dey (as would be in character) fly into a passion and stalk from the council chamber, he was to send in the letter provided for the previous contingency.

While the *Victory*, with the fleet in company, followed the *Superb* towards the coast of Barbary, the Commander-in-Chief accomplished much correspondence. An armed cutter, the *British Fair*, had joined just as he weighed from the Maddalena Islands. She had been chased in the Gut, and seemed to him lucky to have got away, for she sailed so ill that she had to be taken in tow the whole way to Cape San Sebastian. The orders for her return had been peremptory to the verge of incivility, so he had sent her to the Rock for repairs, and meanwhile parted with the *Childers* to carry his replies to the despatches. The *British Fair* had brought him many private letters. Davison, in fighting form, except for the gout, had become Colonel of a Westminster Volunteer Corps raised to repel Buonaparte's invasion, and buoyantly believed himself likely to be made a knight, if not more, having baffled the " dirty dogs " who had tried to pull him down. Moreover, he sent news that his noble friend's lawsuit with Lord St. Vincent on the subject of prize money was at last settled, and in favour of Lord Nelson. " I have no fears ", wrote Nelson, " for Old England whilst we are true to ourselves, and in this belief I send your Banking-house a Bill for £1,000." The relief of receiving this almost despaired-of windfall was great, for he had for some months been troubled by reports that, in hard times, another dependant needed his assistance.

" I could not bear that poor blind Mrs. Nelson should be in want in her old days, and sell her plate. . . . I would rather pinch myself than she, poor soul, should want. Your good angelic heart, my dearest Emma, will fully agree with me. Everything is very expensive, and even we find it, and will be obliged to economise if we assist our friends."

But he was sure that they could feel more comfort in such deeds
N N

than " in loaded tables and entertaining a set of people who care not for us ".   Brother William, looking ahead as usual, thought that, after Eton, the diplomatic service might provide a suitable opening for his Lordship's nephew.   But his lordship's reply to this was depressing.   " The road to ruin ! "   A letter to his sister Susanna, explaining that he had no influence to get her husband a good appointment, was friendly and colloquial.   He engaged himself to do all that he could, and promised to bear at least a part of young Tom's college expenses.   When some of his present pensioners were removed by Time, when, for instance, " poor Blindy goes the way of all flesh ", he hoped to do more. Davison was generally the friend to whom he confided intimate details of his health.   (" I have often heard that Blind people are cheerful, but I think I shall take it to heart.")   At present he did not wish to trouble a man who, in spite of keeping up a jaunty front, might, he shrewdly suspected, be in distress by the time his letter arrived.   Lord Minto was the person to be told (after a long description of the state of the various parties in the Mediterranean, and disquisition on the importance of England's investing Sardinia), " You will scarcely credit, after all I have wrote, that the Medical gentlemen are wanting to survey me and to send me to *Bristol* for the re-establishment of my health." But the Commander-in-Chief in the Mediterranean was careful to add, " Do not mention my health, (it is my concern), I beg of you."

Ten days had been the time allotted by him for absence from his station off San Sebastian, and with daylight on January 17 he came in sight of H.M.S. *Superb*, backed by the lighthouse and mole-head of Algiers.   She was too far away for signals, so a frigate was detached with a message, " You need only say, ' We go on well, or ill ', ' Stay off here ', or ' You may go '."   For some fifty hours the fleet lay to off and on Algiers, whilst many letters passed between the *Superb* and the *Victory*; then on the afternoon of the 19th it made sail, and the Governor of Malta was heavily advised, " The Dey is violent, and will yield no one point."   When Keats came on board the *Victory* at sea it was to say that he had got as far as a conference with his Highness— if indeed an interview could be so described in which one party had simply stood firm, while the other gave way to rage and violence.   After the British Captain had assured his gnashing Highness that he could prove that the British Consul had not known of Moorish women in his house, the answer had been,

" Well, they were in his house, and he is answerable. Besides, two years ago, his servant rode over a Moor, and killed him."

Nelson's hopes, on hearing the full story, were that he might now receive orders to open hostilities, in which case Mustapha might gallop off into the Desert and presently have his head cut off. The eventual sequel irritated him, and provided, he thought, a classic example of ministerial weakness in dealing with such pests. Lord Hobart wrote in the following May that His Majesty's Ministers wished to make another application to the Dey to see whether, if provided with a Consul to whom he could take no exception, he might release his prisoners. The long-expected change of administration took place while the whole subject was still under discussion, and in the following autumn Lord Camden, who had succeeded Lord Hobart, regretted that in spite of Lord Nelson's mention of Mr. Falcon as a person worthy of preferment, he could not promote him. The gentleman already selected by his lordship's predecessor in office seemed in every way qualified. (The post upon which the undaunted Falcon had been waiting to swoop was in Upper Egypt, a vacancy having occurred by the death from plague of Consul Lock.) " I have sent Keats ", explained Nelson, dispiritedly, " to do everything possible not absolutely to degrade us. We should never have given up the case of Mr. Falcon." But even he had to admit that it would now be useless to send anything less than ten to twelve of the line against Algiers, " and I feel a Fleet is not at this moment to be crippled on such a service ".

The Dey held on until January 1805 to a *bona fide* English merchant vessel called the *Ape*, which made many pathetic appearances in Nelson's official correspondence. Mustapha's pretext was that more than two-thirds of her crew had been Sicilians.

As January and February 1804 wore out, in spectacular snow-storms, Nelson's anxiety to hear that Lady Hamilton had recovered from an unexplained illness became frantic. On February 10, in an unsigned letter, he told, " My dearest friend ", " I only hope our dearest friends are well, and happily past all danger." On the 25th he was " anxious in the extreme to hear that you are perfectly recovered from your late indisposition ". On March 14, all he longed to hear was news of her health, and again " *perfectly* recovered " was the phrase employed. The *Royal Sovereign*, of 100 guns, joined the same evening, and he got letters dated January 15 and 28, which gave him " a raging fever all night ". His postscript bade her " kiss dear Horatia for me, and the other, I approved of the name you intended ". Four days later (again 19 in a postscript) he described himself as " very restless for these several days and nights past, and not likely to be relieved until I hear you are quite recovered ". At the close of a couple of un-dated paragraphs on the same sheet he repeated his injunction, " Kiss dear Horatia for me, and the other ", and added, " call him what you please, if a girl, Emma." 20

At home, in the first week of February, Mrs. Matcham had written to Lady Hamilton complaining of long silence, and hoping that illness was not the reason. On February 3, Dr. Este sat in 21 Lady Hamilton's house in Clarges Street, watching while " the most noble creature living " wrote letters of introduction to be carried by another of his sons suddenly ordered to the Mediterranean. 22 Nelson's anxiety was not relieved until the *Phœbe* joined the fleet on March 31, with a mail brought by the *Thisbe* to Gibraltar.

> " I opened—opened—found none but December and early in January. I was in such an agitation ! At last, I found one without a date, which, thank God ! told my poor heart that you was recovering, but that dear little Emma was no more ! and that Horatia had been so very ill—it all together upset me. But, it was just at bedtime, and I had time to reflect, and be thankful to God for sparing you and our dear Horatia. I am sure the loss of one—much more both—would have drove me mad. I was so agitated, as it was, that I was glad it was night, and that I could be by myself." 23

No suspicion of his private anxieties at this or any other time ever reached his officers. Indeed, the happily married young Captain of one of his ships-of-the-line gravely explained to his lady :

> " Dear domestic happiness—my only boon—never abstracted his attention. He had not, or however did not, acknowledge any incum-brances, such as I have. The rule he inculcated was that every man became a bachelor after he passed the Rock of Gibraltar, and he was not very tardy in showing that he practised what he preached." 24

8

Minor vexations, close under his eye, were not lacking as " a most terrible long winter " gave place to Mediterranean spring, and the tact and experience of a Chief singularly happy in his personal relations with subordinates were exercised, particularly in suggesting to young blood the most expedient way through, or around, or out of the " scrape ". A wretched but still heated Lieutenant who had sent him a sad tale of wrongs was serenely advised:

"I have just received your letter, and I am truly sorry that any difference should arise between you and your Captain, who has the reputation of being one of the bright Officers of the Service, and yourself, a very young man and a very young Officer, who must naturally have much to learn. Therefore the chance is that you are perfectly wrong in the disagreement.

"However, as your present situation must be very disagreeable, I will certainly take an early opportunity of removing you, provided your conduct to your present Captain be such that another may not refuse to receive you."

Charles Connor, the young cousin of Lady Hamilton, was reminded, on receiving his commission:

"As you from this day start in the world as a man, I trust that your future conduct in life will prove you both an Officer and a Gentleman. Recollect that you must be a Seaman to be an Officer, and also that you cannot be a good Officer without being a Gentleman."

Charles, however, was to prove a source of nothing but distress. Captain Capel, with whom he was first placed, soon had to report that he found this midshipman, though clever, odd in manner, complaining of pains in the back of his head and having seen a ghost in H.M.S. *Phœbe*—a most unpopular accomplishment at sea. Nelson took the lad into his flagship (" Nothing, my own Emma, shall be wanting on my part "), and came to the hopeful conclusion that except for " a kind of silly laugh when spoken to ", he was not much less sensible than many of his fellows, and that if he did not drink, he might yet do well. (Perhaps Capel was too kind to his younkers. The debts and wardrobe disclosed by Charles had amazed the Admiral.) In the *Victory*, daily coached by Dr. Scott, Charles made his fresh start. He lost the sight of an eye " through a midshipman heaving an olive-stone at me ", and suffered a relapse. After Dr. Snipe, Physician to the Fleet, had examined him, it became necessary to apply to Lady Hamilton for information as to family history. Was there any record of insanity? While this trouble was dragging its course, Chevalier, the ideal steward supplied by Davison, sent to ask if he might speak privately with the Admiral. This interview was brief. " I beg pardon, my Lord, but I find myself so disagreeably situated in the Ship that I beg of your Lordship to send me to England by the first opportunity." " Certainly, Mr. Chevalier." Chevalier thought again, and was present in attendance upon his master in the cockpit of the *Victory* at Trafalgar, but Connor had another and more serious outbreak a few weeks later, and in March 1805 Captain Hillyer of the *Niger* had to write to Lady

Hamilton, regretting that he had been obliged to leave her *protégé* in hospital at Plymouth, " with his hands bound, violently insane ".

But in spite of " the same faces and almost the same conversation " day in and day out, variances in the Mediterranean Fleet remained minor and rare, and the health record became unprecedented. The Chief, in despair of satisfying a tithe of his distinguished correspondents who wished to recommend a friend or relative, humorously explained that they had out here so far, " thank God ! no Court-Martials ", nobody asked to be sent home. " The Admiralty fill all vacancies except *death*, and nobody will die." He could not even get a ship for his dear Berry, whose face brought battles.

On St. George's Day, 1804, on a general promotion, Viscount Nelson was gazetted Vice-Admiral of the White (the highest rank he ever attained), but as communications were in the state so often deplored by him, he did not receive his commission until the last day of July. In the same week he, who had recently complained to Lady Hamilton, " Well, this is an odd War—not a battle ! " read something in a French newspaper which surprised him greatly. As the weather grew warmer, La Touche Tréville, in command of the Toulon squadron, had begun to exercise his ships outside the harbour, as best he could, singly, and in small groups. (" My friend Monsieur La Touche sometimes plays bo-peep in and out of Toulon, like a mouse at the edge of a hole.") " We are as usual ", Nelson had told Hugh Elliot on June 8. " The French Fleet safe in Toulon ; but upon the 14th Monsr. La Touche came out with eight Sail-of-the-Line and six Frigates, cut a caper off Sepet, and went in again. I was off with five Ships-of-the-Line, and brought to for his attack, although I did not believe that anything was meant serious, but merely a gasconade." His irritation was strong on August 3, when he discovered that La Touche had misrepresented the incident in a special despatch to Buonaparte as a refusal of the British Fleet to be brought to action, and that the letter had been given to the *Moniteur*, to be copied by the Press of Europe. " You will have seen ", he wrote to Brother William, " Monsieur La Touche's letter of how he chased me, and how I *ran*. I keep it ; and, by God, if I take him, he shall *Eat* it." La Touche was personally obnoxious to him, as an aristo who had turned republican, and professionally, as the officer who had attempted to bully the Neapolitan Court in 1793, and who had been in command of the

Boulogne flotilla which had repelled his boat attack of August 1801. But he was not destined to settle accounts with this French Admiral, for on August 18 La Touche died, of sheer exhaustion, solemnly stated the French editors, from walking so often up to the signal post upon Sepet to watch for the English fleet. " I always pronounced that that would be his death ", commented Nelson, mollified. The successor appointed by Buonaparte, after some delay, had also crossed Nelson's path before. Admiral Villeneuve had something of the same background as La Touche Tréville, but his promotion had been much more rapid. He had commanded the enemy rear at the Nile, and made his escape with two of the line and two frigates, to fight another day.

From two-months-old English newspapers which he got in July, the Commander-in-Chief in the Mediterranean learnt that Mr. Alexander Davison had been sentenced by the Court of King's Bench to twelve months' imprisonment in the Marshalsea prison. To Lady Hamilton he confessed that he was not surprised. " He never would take a friend's caution, and he has been severely bit. . . . After what passed in Parliament I did not expect so little. . . . He would only consult Lord Moira, and such clever folks, but an ignoramus like me could only warn him not to touch boroughs. He has, poor fellow, been completely duped, and who cares ? Not one of those great folks."

To Davison himself he wrote in much more sympathetic vein, urging a man of mercurial temperament, " Keep up your spirits. Do not take it to heart. It will soon pass away." At first he promised to come to see his friend in the Marshalsea, but as months passed without hope of his getting home, he was reduced to counting the days until Davison would be at liberty again. " It is some comfort that I shall be in England to shake you by the hand in St. James's Square, where I hope you will live many years, and that I will often breakfast with you. . . . Before you receive this letter you will again, thank God, be a free man." He never ceased to write, and never ceased to suggest that no consideration should ever again tempt Davison to dabble in politics—advice which was followed.

29

For the Mediterranean Fleet the summer of 1804 was boring. All Europe was waiting breathlessly for Buonaparte's Invasion. In England able-bodied males between the ages of fifteen and sixty had been called upon to enrol in their parishes for Home Defence ; seventy-five Martello towers had been hastily erected, and the beacons were ready for conflagration. "An awful and trying period for us all", wrote Nelson's younger sister, whose family party now sat down to dinner fifteen. "My neighbour Edwards", reported his even more resolute elder sister, "sits at home and frightens himself so much that he will not suffer any of his children to go to school." To Nelson's disgust, early in April the *Swift* cutter, bringing him Admiralty despatches and a home mail, was captured by an enemy privateer after her Captain had been killed in action. He sent Dr. Scott down to Barcelona to try to buy back the private letters, but they had, it appeared, already been forwarded to Paris, for Buonaparte's delectation ; and the Swedish and American Consuls told Lord Nelson's emissary on his arrival that their French *confrère* admired three portraits of Lady Hamilton too much to part with them, even to Buonaparte. Dr. Scott gathered that her ladyship's letters had been exhibited to at least one of these gentlemen. As far as the despatches went, Nelson could only hope that they had contained nothing which could embitter relations with other European Powers. "From us", he told Lady Hamilton, "what can they find out? That I love you most dearly and hate the French most damnably." After this incident, for eighty-odd days he heard nothing from home. His only sources of information were foreign newspapers. Those which were published outside France gave him fanciful details of an illness of George III and the composition of a new Ministry, and told him that an invasion had been tried and failed. In the French prints he read mostly of Buonaparte's tremendous camp on the Boulogne heights. The *Grande Armée* for the Invasion of England was vaunted as numbering above a hundred and seventy-five thousand, and included a corps of guide-interpreters, ready to take up their duties directly the force landed. Two thousand transports were awaiting orders to sail.

On the night of June 3 the French fleet in Toulon fired a *feu de joie* in celebration of Buonaparte's assumption of the Imperial purple ; next morning the British fleet exercised its great guns on the sixty-sixth anniversary of the birth of George III. Nelson meditated a lurid Naples rumour that the new Emperor was "to be divorced from Madame B. and married to a Blood Royal of Germany. Bravo ! Corsican." English visitors to Paris during the Experimental Peace had learnt that Buonaparte kept a bust of Nelson on his dressing-room mantelpiece ; but the admiration was unreciprocated. By Hugh Elliot's account, Acton was about to get his *congé* in order to satisfy " Napoleon ". The gossip of Neapolitans on the subject of their Queen far surpassed any hints discreetly dropped, years past, by that perspicacious connoisseur, Sir William Hamilton. Maria Carolina was now credited with three lovers, all French *émigrés*. One was military (Lieut.-Col. St. Clair), another naval (Capitaine La Tour). " However, I never touch on these matters, for I care not how much she amuses herself." Lord Nelson's interest in a royal lady whose conduct seemed to provide a perfect illustration of the text " Put not your trust in Princes " was dying a lingering death. He could no longer doubt that her failure to respond to his repeated mentions of " your Emma " was deliberate. He had finally asked outright that Her Majesty should write to Addington, representing, from her personal experience, that a pension had indeed been earned by the widow of Sir William Hamilton. " Your Majesty well knows that it was her capacity and conduct which sustained his diplomatic character during the last years in which he was at Naples. It is unnecessary for me to speak more of it." Maria Carolina triumphantly replied, after a long pause, that Mr. Addington was now out of office.

Seventeen days of blowing weather in July decided him that he had better not attempt another winter at sea. He said that he was ready to die for his country, but could not see that allowing himself to degenerate into a helpless invalid would benefit anybody. " I can every month perceive a visible (if I may be allowed the expression) loss of sight." He observed his physician's injunctions to wear a green shade, but Mr. Beatty feared that such precautions were of little value while the Admiral persisted in spending most of his days on deck, in Mediterranean glare, staring through a telescope at a fleet which refused to be tempted out to an engagement. And as the summer began to wane, without bringing the Invasion, Nelson began to wonder whether the new Emperor might not, after all, be considering peace negotiations with a Ministry which he had heard—incorrectly—included Mr. Fox. In late August he ordered fires in his cabin (" The Mediterranean seems to have altered "), and wrote to the new First Lord, Viscount Melville, and to Mr. William Marsden, who had succeeded Sir Evan Nepean, asking for leave of absence for the re-establishment of his health. He told Lady Hamilton that he hoped to eat his Christmas dinner at Merton, and that " the moment I get home, I shall put it out of your power to spend dear Horatia's money. I shall settle it in trustees' hands and leave nothing to chance." Dr. Scott had succeeded in extracting one ³⁰ portrait from the French Consul at Barcelona, who had already had it framed. A cup bearing another likeness of Admiral Nelson's Famous Woman ("your dear phiz—but not the least like you") was never used except for ornamental purposes. Notwithstanding ³¹ his disbelief that the invasion could succeed, he had been on tenterhooks since he had heard that she was fulfilling her usual summer programme. She was taking Horatia with her to Ramsgate, and to stay with the William Nelsons, now established in an official residence at Canterbury. "I am very uneasy at your and Horatia's being on the coast, for you cannot move if the French make the attempt. . . . Your trip to Canterbury I should suppose the very worst you could take, for on any alarm you must stay there, and in a town filled with soldiers."

His "letters relative to my health" were no sooner irretrievably gone than he began to regret them. He considered who would be his successor, and decided upon Lord Keith as the most probable man. A few months' sick leave was all that he had asked, and he had mentioned that Bickerton was capable, under present conditions, of taking his place; but he was well aware that "there will be so many desirous of the Mediterranean Command that I cannot expect they will allow me to return to it. I may, very possibly, be laid on the shelf." And as he waited philosophically to hear his fate—telling himself, "Whatever arrangements are made about me by the Ministers, it is all settled by this time"; hoping against hope, "They will do the thing handsomely"; reflecting, "Once it is gone from me, I stand no chance of getting it back again"—he realised, as never before, how dear "my favourite Command" had become to him.

He sometimes fancifully pictured his battered fleet as a fine time-piece, ticking over gently in the worn palm of his single hand. The names, state and whereabouts of his ships, little and great, were engraved upon his memory, night and day—

> H.M.S. *Bittern, Arrow, Halcyon, Sophie*—Gibraltar.
> ,, *Morgiana, Termagant*—going to heave down.
> ,, *Seahorse, Childers*—between the fleet and Spain.
> ,, *Spider, Hirondelle, Cameleon*—gone to the Adriatic.

Their admired clockwork movement, however, was the result of infinite toil and deep forethought.

> "If the *Maidstone* takes the Convoy, and when *Agincourt* arrives there is none for her and *Thisbe*, it puzzles me to know what orders to give them. If they chace the convoy to Gibraltar, the *Maidstone* may

have gone on with it to England, and in that case, two ships, unless I begin to give a new arrangement, will either go home without convoy, or they must return, in contradiction to the Admiralty's orders to send them home."

32

And sometimes the Admiralty, diverting a ship without his knowledge, would temporarily stop the whole machine. Lord Elgin, from his French prison, was begging that a transport should call at Cerigo to remove to safety "some marble antiquities" collected during his happy years as Ambassador to the Porte. An Admiral "pulled to pieces" by the demands of merchants for convoy had written to beg for more frigates, "the Eyes of the Fleet", until he was tired, and noticed that their Lordships had given up answering those parts of his letters. On October 13 he received a piece of news which increased his growing unwillingness to go home. The *John Bull* cutter arrived with secret instructions which had been sent in duplicate to Cornwallis, blockading Brest, to detach two frigates to intercept the Monte Video treasure fleet, expected off Cadiz, bound for Ferrol. These orders could only mean that war with Spain was imminent. She had long been paying France an annual subsidy, and a French 74 had not been turned out of Cadiz. In order that the Spanish commander should need no justification for bloodless surrender, Nelson instantly sent an 80-gun ship, together with four further frigates, to the spot. But the *Donegal* and her consorts arrived too late to avert disaster. Don Joseph Bustamente, finding himself detained by a force equal to his own, offered resistance. Within ten minutes one of his ships took fire and blew up, carrying with her to destruction thirteen ladies, passengers from South America. The other three ships soon surrendered. Spain issued orders for reprisals on British property, and Hookham Frere asked for his passport on November 5; but Spain did not formally declare war until December 12.

One of the Rev. Dr. Este's promising sons was at this time the Admiral's guest in the *Victory*. Lambton Este's foreign appointment had literally died upon him. He had come out as Secretary-Physician to Mr. Charles Lock's mission to the Levant, and having correctly diagnosed the dreadful malady with which his employer and two of the *suite* were presently stricken, he had resolutely immured himself with them in the *lazaretto* at Valetta until they had all died of the plague. He was now waiting a passage home in the *Superb*, in company with Lord Nelson. But on November 1 he was suddenly sent for to the Admiral's

cabin, after breakfast, to be told a change of plans. " Oh ! my
good fellow ! I have abandoned the idea of going to England
for the present. I shall not go yet, and when I may go is quite
uncertain—must depend on events, and upon my own precarious
health. At the same time, I am doing you an evident injustice
in detaining you here so long in uncertainty." The young
doctor began to say that if he could be of any service, his wish
would be to stay with Lord Nelson, but found himself somewhat
terrifyingly cut short, and told that he was going to Lisbon
without much delay, in the *Termagant* sloop, with Captain Pettet,
an officer of humble origin but much merit, whom he would
find a very worthy, agreeable companion. A signal was made   33
for the sloop to move up to the *Victory* : Captain Pettet came on
board to dine, and Lambton, entrusted with " the papers and
state of the Fleet, which had been accumulating for some time,
and the Admiral's despatches and letters ", sailed forthwith.
Off Cape St. Vincent the *Termagant* fell in with the *Swiftsure*,
from England, flying the flag of Sir John Orde, and a young man
who had become a confirmed " Nelsonite " during his weeks in
the *Victory* noted gloomily that the Admiral sent out to take
over the most lucrative portion of Lord Nelson's command was
such a martyr to the gout that he had not quitted his cabin since
leaving Portsmouth, and being at present absolutely confined to
bed, could not receive either him or Pettet.

Nelson heard of Sir John Orde's appearance on his station on
December 2, and supposing that his successor had come, sent
some of his effects on board the *Superb*, and warned Captain
Keats, " that treasure to the Service ", to expect him at any
moment. A fortnight passed before he received a notification
from Orde himself of his appointment to the chief command of
a squadron of five of the line to blockade Cadiz—obviously,
in view of a Spanish war, the station for prize-money. " He
is sent off Cadiz to reap the golden harvest, as Campbell was . . .
to reap my sugar harvest. It's very odd, two Admiralties to
treat me so : surely I have dreamt that I have ' done the State
some service '. But never mind. . . ." For another ten days
he was left " in most total darkness ". He did not even know
whether his country was at war with Spain. He issued a
General Order to his officers to detain all Spanish ships and
vessels of war, as well as of trade, and, in his own words, " set the
whole Mediterranean to work ". Meanwhile, George Campbell,
now one of his junior Admirals, had suddenly developed such

unmistakable symptoms of nervous breakdown that there was no question but that he must be sent home immediately, and Capel was reporting from the *rendezvous* off Toulon that the French fleet was embarking troops, and seemed to be on the eve of coming out. At last, after dark on Christmas Day, the *Swiftsure* joined Nelson's fleet off Cape San Sebastian, bringing him letters from the Admiralty and Downing Street.

His permission to go home was come, and his suggestion that Bickerton should fill his place during his absence had been accepted; but, under the impression that he was about to quit it, his command had been reduced, as Orde had notified him. He kept the news of his leave having been granted a complete secret, and took the fleet to reconnoitre Toulon. The enemy force there, which now appeared to have increased to eleven of the line and eighteen frigates, was still in port, amusing itself with night signals, composed of " a quantity of rockets and blue lights ", so after a week he went to Maddalena.

It was in Agincourt Sound, during the afternoon of January 19, 1805, a short winter's day of heavy gales from the north-west, that his look-out frigates H.M.S. *Active* and *Seahorse* came in sight, under a press of sail, flying the long-expected signal, " The Enemy is at sea."

CHAPTER XVII

1805
(*ætat* 46)

THE LONG CHASE

I

ON the same morning that Lord Nelson was sending his wine to Captain Keats's battered old ship, off Toulon, in preparation for a passage home, Napoleon I was passing to his coronation in Notre-Dame. December 2, 1804, was fine but bitterly cold in Paris, and the ladies in high-waisted, low-necked gowns, attended by gentlemen of the Imperial Court blazing in frogged and furred uniforms, who had to desert their carriages, owing to traffic difficulties, at some distance from the cathedral, suffered as they completed their journey on foot over frozen cobbles. Their sufferings, however, had only begun. Although carpenters had been at work throughout the night, by torchlight, for weeks past, in and around Notre-Dame, only a small percentage of ticket-holders were able to obtain a good view of the principal figures at a ceremony for which they were obliged to take their seats at 6 a.m. without hope of release till dusk. London, enduring an historic bout of fog, got newspaper reports of what even English editors called simply " The Coronation " on December 7, by which time Lord Nelson was calculating that it was seventy-eight days since he had heard from the Admiralty.

Buonaparte's second attempt at pageantry on a great scale sounded very typical. His first—the Review of his Army for the Invasion of England, in his camp overlooking the Channel, on his birthday—had been marred by the persistent presence of English ships in the middle distance and an accident to a French squadron detailed to make an effective appearance towards the close of his distribution of Crosses of the Legion of Honour. Londoners read with mingled wrath and pity that the aged Pope, rudely summoned from Rome, had decked the conqueror's latest triumph, though only as a spectator. Buonaparte had, in the end, bestowed the Imperial wreath upon himself with his own hands. The royal procession of a new dynasty had taken an hour to pass from the Carrousel to the cathedral, and the salutes had been audible on the English coast. But the inven-

tories of how many ells of purple velvet, powdered with bullion
Bees, had been supplied, and how many fountains had spouted
wine in the illuminated streets of the French capital, were quickly
cloying.   Even ladies devoted to the fashions were soon convinced
that Buonaparte had employed any quantity of white satin.
What the intelligent English reader wished to know was his
underlying intention in ordering such gorgeous mummery.   A
large number of people believed him to set no store on the religious
ceremony, but much on his claim to rank as the first crowned
head of Europe.   It might be that he was at work to distract
the attention of his people from the fact that after all what
Nelson called his " blustering and parading " at Boulogne, the
invasion of England had not yet taken place.   Nobody in London,
or in the British Navy, knew for several months that the conquest
of their country had indeed been prominent in his thoughts on
that crowded day, and that, far from having abandoned hope of
transporting his immense and fully equipped army across " the
ruffled strip of salt ", he was, at the moment, almost ready with
a new stratagem to gain, for the few necessary days, naval
control of the Straits of Dover.

Buonaparte's scheme, which received later modifications, was
masterly in its simplicity.   He had twenty ships in Brest, ten in
Toulon, and five in Rochefort, to which he was soon to add the fleet
of Spain, amounting to fifteen serviceable ships.   All were under
orders to evade the blockading British squadrons and, avoiding
action, hasten to a *rendezvous* at the great French arsenal,
Martinique.   Having arrived, they were to proceed independently
to deal havoc to the British possessions in that quarter, and then
unite for an equally swift recrossing of the Atlantic and unexpected appearance in the English Channel.   England would,
he thought, send at least thirty ships-of-the-line in search of them.
The Channel Fleet would be easily overpowered, or at least held
in check, while an army corps was landed in Ireland and the main
body disembarked on the English coast.

2

Dr. Scott had, upon one of his visits to Barcelona, been told
by his employer to make a bid for a large store of church plate
and vestments advertised in a Spanish newspaper.   When the
Mediterranean fleet quitted the Sardinian roadstead which had so
often offered it friendly shelter, on the afternoon of January 19,
1805, the churches of many little towns along the coast were in

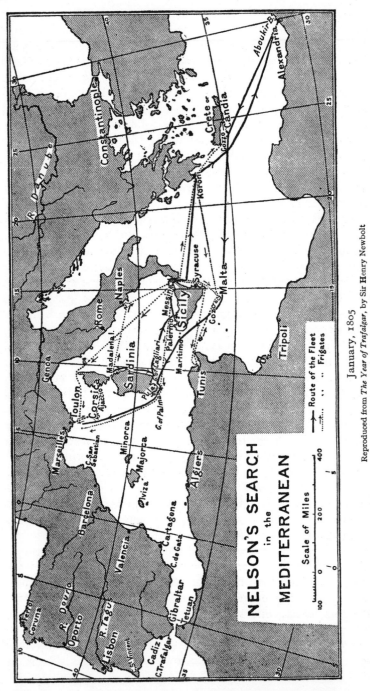

NELSON'S SEARCH
in the
MEDITERRANEAN

Scale of Miles

Route of the Fleet
.... " Frigates

January, 1805

Reproduced from *The Year of Trafalgar*, by Sir Henry Newbolt
By kind permission of Messrs. John Murray

possession of autograph letters and relics testifying to Admiral Nelson's gratitude. He left Agincourt Sound for the last time within three hours of hearing that the enemy were out. Darkness was falling and a fresh breeze was blowing from the W.N.W. It was impossible to leave the roadstead through the Straits of Bonifaccio. The *Victory* led, with a light at her stern, through the narrow passage between the Biocian and Sardinian rocks. At 6.35 she burnt a blue light, followed after ten minutes by another. The whole fleet was clear of the Straits a quarter of an hour later. Nelson was about to attempt a feat as remarkable as his successful Actions—to summon a fleet of " crazy " ships, which had not been into port for twenty-two months, to follow him on a chase of 4,000 miles.

The enemy were reported as steering for the southern end of Sardinia, after which the wind was fair for Naples, Sicily, the Morea or Egypt. The *Seahorse* was sent ahead to the islands of San Pietro to look for them. The night was squally, and during the next afternoon, as the fleet drew out from under the lee of Sardinia, it encountered a gale from the S.S.W. At 9.25 on the morning of Sunday the 20th the *Victory* made the general signal " Prepare for Battle ", and two hours later those for " Form the established Order of Sailing in two columns " and " Keep in close order ". Throughout that night and next day there were very hard gales, and for most of the time the fleet was under storm staysails. Early on the morning of the 22nd the *Seahorse* came in sight. She made the signal that she had intelligence to communicate, and Captain Boyle came on board the Admiral to say that yesterday afternoon he had seen an enemy frigate off Pula. The weather had been so thick, giving an horizon of only three miles, that he had not been able to discover anything further. Nelson prayed for a fair wind, and that the Sardes might defend their capital, in which case he would be in time to save them. (The storm which had prevented him from getting farther to the southward had, in fact, scattered Villeneuve's squadron, which was already limping back to Toulon, moderately damaged and much dispirited; but he was not to learn this for a month.) Satisfied that he lay in the path of any attempt upon Naples, he sent Boyle with an account of the situation to Acton, at Palermo, asking him to warn Naples. He also wrote to Ball at Malta, adding details of a dead foul wind and heavy sea; but the *Seahorse* had been his last frigate, so he had to keep this letter.

o o

On the 25th the gale abated, and he stood into the Gulf of Cagliari, having " neither ate, drank or slept with any comfort " for five days. " I am in a fever ! God send I may find them ! " No enemy landing had been attempted there, but next morning information that an 80-gun ship, dismasted and crippled, had anchored in Ajaccio led him to guess at the truth. Still, in spite of westerly gales, Villeneuve might have got round Sicily to the eastward.

> " I considered the character of Buonaparte; and that the orders given by him, on the banks of the Seine, would not take into consideration winds or weather; nor indeed could the accident of three or four ships alter, in my opinion, the destination of importance; therefore such an accident did not weigh in my mind, and I went first to the Morea and then to Egypt."

His estimate of Buonaparte's mentality was perfectly accurate, for on hearing of Villeneuve's resultless *sortie*, the Emperor had burst forth, " What is to be done with Admirals who allow their spirits to sink, and hasten home at the first damage they receive ? " The opinion of the Military Dictator had been :

> " The damages should have been repaired *en route*. If any Ship leaked dangerously, she should have been left at Cadiz, her crew and troops being transferred to *L'Aigle*, which is in that Port and ready to sail. A few topmasts carried away, some casualties in a gale, are every day occurrences. Two days of fine weather ought to have cheered up the crews and put everything to rights. But the great evil of our Navy is, that the men who command it are unused to all the risks of command."

1

Stromboli was burning very strongly as Nelson's fleet beat through the Straits of Messina, on the last day of January—" a thing unprecedented in nautical history; but although the danger from the rapidity of the current was great, yet so was the object of my pursuit; and I relied with confidence on the zeal and ability of the Fleet ". Seven frigates were now at his disposal, and he sent off half a dozen " in all directions, from Tunis to Toulon ", following the seventh to Koroni, where, receiving no news, he went on to Alexandria. " Celerity in my movements may catch these fellows yet." The *Phœbe* rejoined without any tale of a French invasion but equally certain reports that Egypt was practically defenceless. Cleopatra's Needle and Pompey's Pillar faded from view as the fleet instantly made sail with a fair wind for Candia. " This ", noted the Chaplain of the *Victory*, " is, I believe the true *Sirocco*, and occasions a peculiar sensation ; feel parched." The imperturbable Dr. Scott had devoured

The Art of Tormenting by a Miss Collier and the whole of D'Anquetil's *Memoirs of Louis XIV* by the time that the Admiral anchored in Valetta Bay, on the evening of February 18. At Malta Nelson learnt, at last, that the enemy were back in Toulon. He trusted that their Lordships would approve of his having gone to Egypt in search of them. " I have consulted no man, therefore the whole blame of ignorance in forming my judgment must rest with me. I would allow no man to take from me an atom of my glory, had I fallen in with the French Fleet, nor do I desire any man to partake of any of the responsibility—all is mine, right or wrong." He prepared to regain his station as soon as possible, and to complete the victualling which had been cut short by the departure from Maddalena; for he did not neglect the possibility that Villeneuve, goaded by orders from the banks of the Seine, might, with the first favourable opportunity, put to sea again; and next time he was determined upon a battle. Reports of the flying artillery and number of saddles embarked, combined with the recently ascertained defencelessness of Alexandria, still led him to believe that Egypt had been the destination.

Plenty of news, all disagreeable, gradually dropped in to him in Palmas Bay, which he reached, after a weary struggle, on March 8; and even Lady Hamilton received her first, and only recorded, specimen of firm treatment. " When I see you are hurt at my non-arrival, I only wish that you would, for one moment, call your *good* sense before you, and see if it was possible. You know I never say a thing which I do not mean, and everybody knows that all my things are on board the *Superb*, and there they remain." Not a bulkhead had been up in his fleet since January 21. During his absence the *Raven* sloop, bringing despatches for Sir John Orde at Gibraltar and a mail for the Mediterranean, had been wrecked off Cadiz and fallen into Spanish hands. The *Arthur* cutter, with despatches for him and for Ball, had been intercepted by the French fleet returning to Toulon. Finally, a convoy homeward bound from Malta had been waylaid, and its escort, a sloop and bomb-ketch, captured. The convoy had scattered during a gallant little action; seventeen sail had reached Gibraltar, and he hoped some more might have got into Algiers; three, he knew, had been sunk. He unhesitatingly attributed this last of his mishaps (" I must not call them misfortunes ") to the division of the command. " That would not have happened could I have ordered the Officer off

Cadiz to send Ships to protect them." At such a moment it was additionally galling to be told by everyone that Sir John Orde, owing to the capture of the Spanish galleons within the limits of his station, was likely to become the richest Admiral that ever England saw. Lord Nelson, worse off than on the day he left Portsmouth, nearly two years past ("What a time!"), commented "Bravo!" and "Never mind!" But he still longed to settle a sufficient sum upon Horatia to protect her in case of his death, " or even anything foolish that I may do in my old age ". Since, in every letter, he had pressed Lady Hamilton to have the child at Merton " *fixed*. Why not ? ", she had at last consented to do so, in spite of the comment that might result, and he had provided her with a not very convincing letter, suitable   3
to be shown to inquiring neighbours, in which he explained " the extraordinary circumstances of a child being left to my care ", and begged her to be its Guardian. Now he was told that the child's nurse was making difficulties. He sent instructions to Haslewood to pay a pension of £20 per annum to Miss Thompson's nurse on the clear understanding that she made no further attempt to keep or communicate with the child. Horatia, now old enough for a governess, should be entrusted to a Miss Connor, Lady Hamilton's cousin.   4

His young relative, Bolton, perhaps too easily and early promoted, knighted, married and " called Papa ", was not giving satisfaction. Twice, when he had sent the *Childers* on a   5
cruise which might have put her Captain in the way of prize-money, her long absence had made the Chief anxious. On both occasions the delay had been caused by nothing but lethargy. He set Hardy, " as good as ever ", to talk to " Sir Billy ", but feared that unless " that goose " mended his ways, their Lordships would be wishing Lord Nelson's recommendation at the devil.

Two other of his officers, to both of whom he was much attached, needed personal attention. Murray and Keats were having a nerve-racked altercation about the supply of hammocks to the *Superb*. The truth was that Captain Keats felt marital pangs, as his old ship was, he fancied, stinted, and Murray was dispersing a scanty store as equitably as possible. In the tactful but stately note which settled this misunderstanding, Lord Nelson remembered, " The situation of First Captain is certainly a very unthankful office."

Having heard that Sir John Orde had written to complain

that ships under Lord Nelson's command had been frequently out of the Mediterranean, he had sent their Lordships a plain statement of fact which he trusted would produce a " trimmer ". " I shall never enter into a paper war with him, or anyone else."

The loss of his private letters was painful, for he had heard nothing from home since November 2. The possibility that despatches might have fallen into enemy hands caused him greater uneasiness. Captain Layman swore that all had gone to the bottom, never to rise again, but as they had not been thrown overboard until the *Raven* struck the rocks, he kept on picturing them washing ashore. As usual in the case of a wreck, a court-martial was to be held. He had every confidence in Layman, who had never asked him for anything except to be detached on services of most danger and difficulty, and whose only outstanding fault was a tendency to talk and write too fast and too much. After seeing the narrative which the young man had prepared for the court he felt that his cup of misery was full. He read the Captain's " Orders for the Night ", compared them with the result, and exclaimed, " If this is laid before the court they will hang the Officer of the Watch!" Layman willingly deleted his " severe reflections " upon this officer, and next day, to Nelson's dismay, the court severely reprimanded the Captain of the *Raven* for lack of caution in approaching the coast, and ordered his name to be put at the bottom of the list of Commanders. The surprise was the greater to Nelson as the exertions of all officers and men to get the sloop into Cadiz had, by all accounts, been remarkable. Yesterday he had felt that his luck must change. " Much unhinged ", he set himself to write to every possible person who might assist a young officer, very severely sentenced, of whose professional ability and generosity of heart he was convinced. He wrote at once to the First Lord :

> " To Viscount Melville.
> *Victory* at Sea,
> 10th March, 1805.

" My dear Lord,
" I inclose some remarks made by Captain Layman whilst he was in Spain, after the very unfortunate loss of that fine Sloop, which your Lordship was so good as to give him the command of. Your Lordship will find the remarks flow from a most intelligent and active mind, and may be useful should any expedition take place against Cadiz; and, my dear Lord, give me leave to recommend Captain Layman to your kind protection; for, notwithstanding the Court-Martial has thought him

deserving of censure for running in with the land, yet, my Lord, allow me to say, that Captain Layman's misfortune was, perhaps, conceiving that other people's abilities were equal to his own, which, indeed, very few people's are.

" I own myself one of those who do not fear the shore, for hardly any great things are done in a small Ship by a man that does; therefore, I make very great allowances for him. Indeed, his station was intended never to be from the shore in the Straits; and if he did not every day risk his Sloop, he would be useless upon that station. Captain Layman has served with me in three Ships, and I am well acquainted with his bravery, zeal, judgment, and activity; nor do I regret the loss of the *Raven* compared to the value of Captain Layman's services, which are a National loss.

" You must, my dear Lord, forgive the warmth which I express for Captain Layman; but he is in adversity, and therefore, has the more claim to my attention and regard. If I had been censured every time I have run my Ship, or Fleets under my command, into great danger, I should long ago have been *out* of the Service, and never *in* the House of Peers.

" I am, my dear Lord, most faithfully,
your obedient servant,
Nelson and Brontë."

6

The result of all his efforts on behalf of " poor Captain Layman " was disappointing. That officer never recovered his place on the Commander's List, and is dryly stated to have terminated his existence with his own hand in the year 1826. Nearly a quarter of a century later, however, upon " the perusal of this generous and characteristic letter ", Sir Nicholas Harris Nicolas, G.C.M.G., conceived his *magnum opus*, and commenced editing the seven annotated, cross-referenced, conscientiously indexed volumes of Lord Viscount Nelson's Letters and Despatches, which remain to the present day the Bible of biographers of Nelson.

3

As soon as the wind served, Nelson left the Gulf of Palmas, and made a round, showing himself first off Toulon, and next at Barcelona, " in order to induce the enemy to believe I am fixed upon the Coast of Spain ". The Rochefort squadron, which had sailed on the same day as that from Toulon, had not been seen since. Anchoring again at Palmas on March 26, he was still clearing his transports when he received his first pleasant surprise for many months. A frigate which saluted the *Victory* with thirteen guns during the dinner-hour proved to be H.M.S. *Ambuscade*, from Portsmouth, bringing him as replacement for

Campbell, an old friend, an old " Crocodile ". " The arrival of Admiral Louis will enable me to get a little rest, which I shall take as soon as I am satisfied in my own mind that the French will not put to sea."

About 10 a.m. five days after he wrote these comfortable lines, history repeated itself. The *Phœbe* was discovered in the offing as he beat against a head wind on the second day of a passage from Pula Bay to his *rendezvous* west of Toulon, and she was again flying the signal that the enemy was out. The *Victory* signalled the fleet to prepare for battle at 10.23. Capel, and Moubray of the *Active*, who joined four hours later, had first seen a French fleet of eleven of the line, seven frigates and two brigs at 8 a.m. on the morning of March 31, steering S.S.W. with a light breeze at N.E. and all sail set. They had kept company with the slow-moving flotilla all that day. The *Phœbe* had seen her last of it with sunset, when she had been detached to warn the Commander-in-Chief. The *Active* had stood upon a wind to the southward that night, but with dawn found herself alone.

Nelson heard nothing further for twelve days, when he got a second-hand report that the French fleet, or at least a fleet, had been seen on the 7th off Cap de Gatte, steering to the westward with a fresh easterly wind.

Villeneuve, much luckier, had on April 1 spoken a neutral who told him that Nelson was not (as he had supposed) off the Spanish coast, but nearing the southern tip of Sardinia. He had therefore kept away, at once, to the westward. The Spanish ships at Cartagena had declared themselves unready, so he had pressed on, and gone by the Rock on the 8th. Next day, off Cadiz, Orde had seen him, but believing him to be bound for Brest, had hurried north with his small squadron to join Lord Gardner's fleet. *L'Aigle* and six Spanish ships under the command of Admiral Gravina had joined Villeneuve the same night, and a Combined Fleet amounting to eighteen sail of the line had sailed for Martinique, where it had arrived on May 14.

Nelson's sufferings during the twelve days while he was " entirely adrift, by my Frigates losing sight of the French Fleet so soon after their coming out of Port ", were so acute that he told Davison, " It cannot last long, what I feel." As in January, he had to weigh all the possibilities of Naples, Sicily, Sardinia, the Morea, or Egypt. He covered the channel from Barbary to Tunis with frigates and his fleet, and did what was most difficult for him, waited for information. He first took up a stationary position, between Sardinia and Galita. " I shall neither go to the eastward of Sicily or to the westward of Sardinia, until I know something positive." His fleet consisted of eleven of the line, four frigates and two corvettes. The *Amazon, Bittern, Phœbe, Moucheron* and *Ambuscade* had rejoined by the 6th, with nothing to tell him. He sent the *Moucheron* off again, to cruise between Galita and the shore and then go on to Tunis, the *Phœbe* to speak his look-out ship off Cape San Sebastian, and himself stretched across to Palermo. Three supply ships which had joined him on the preceding day transferred their stores at sea. On the 9th he started back from Palermo for Toulon. He had beaten against a head wind for a week, when he got an alarming rumour that the French fleet had passed the Rock. " If this account is true, much mischief may have happened." By the 18th he had made the momentous decision to follow them. " I am going out of the Mediterranean." But his good fortune seemed flown away. " I cannot ", he mourned to Ball, " get a fair wind, or even a side-wind. Dead foul !—dead foul ! " He guessed, from the fact that the Spanish ships from Cadiz had joined Villeneuve, that their destination was probably not the West Indies, but Brest, or even Ireland, and he therefore warned both quarters, adding that should the assistance of his fleet be needed, " I have the pleasure to say that I shall bring with me, eleven as fine Ships of War, as ably commanded, and in as perfect order and health, as ever went to sea." Still, his progress was so slow that he began to believe that easterly winds had left the Mediterranean. " From March 26th, we have had nothing like a Levanter, except for the French fleet. . . . I never have been one week without one, until this very unfortunate moment. It has half killed me, but fretting is no use." Since fretting was no use, as he struggled down the Mediterranean he composed letters home, confidential and business, foreshadowing a long absence, and pleasant notes of invitation to Captains to come on board the *Victory* severally " for some conversation ". In front of him as he wrote lay a letter from the Physician to the Fleet, " enforcing my return to England before the hot months ", and all his heavy luggage was still in the *Superb* : but he had entirely put behind him the dream of Merton, and fixed his course to follow the enemy " to the East or West Indies ". " What man can do shall be done. I have marked out for myself a decided line of conduct, and I shall follow it well up."

It was not until May 4 that he reached Mazari Bay, on the African coast, and as the wind was so adverse that he could not pass the Gut, he anchored to water his fleet and clear another transport. Here he was joined by the frigate *Decade*, from Gibraltar, and after hearing the latest rumours of the Rock, confided in Keats, " I am like to have a West India Trip." He still hoped that Orde had left behind him some small craft, with orders to dog the enemy and return to the mouth of the Straits with information.

" For I cannot very properly run to the West Indies, without something beyond mere surmise; and if I defer my departure, Jamaica may be lost. Indeed, as they have a month's start of me, I see no prospect of getting out time enough to prevent much mischief from being done. However, I shall take all matters into my most serious consideration, and shall do that which seemeth best under all circumstances."

Next day a breeze from the eastward enabled him to reach Gibraltar, and he went into Rosia Bay to provision. The wind was foul for beating out of the Straits, and many officers and men gladly hastened ashore. The linen of the fleet was landed, to be washed. Dr. Scott treasured the memory of an amusing incident of this evening:

" Lord Nelson, however, observing and weatherwise as he was perceived an indication of a probable change of wind. Off went a gun from the *Victory*, and up went the Blue Peter, whilst the Admiral paced the deck in a hurry, with anxious steps and impatient of a moment's delay. The officers said, ' Here is one of Nelson's mad pranks.' But he was nevertheless right, the wind did become favourable, the linen was left on shore, the fleet cleared the Gut, and away they steered for the West Indies. This course Nelson pursued solely on his own responsibility, there being a variety of opinions as to the route the enemy had taken; some saying, ' They had gone to Ireland ', some to this quarter, some to that."

Nelson told Scott, " If they are not gone to the West Indies, I shall be blamed. To be burnt in effigy, or Westminster Abbey is my alternative ", and he had already drawn up instructions for Bickerton to assume the command in the Mediterranean with a small squadron; but as far as certain confirmation went, he was " as much in the dark as ever ". He sadly pictured frigates sent by Orde, all captured. Three nights later, as he completed, in Lagos Bay, the victualling of his fleet for a five months' cruise, an unexpected old friend of Naples and Palermo days came alongside. That his decision had hardened after a private conversation with Rear-Admiral Donald Campbell of the Portuguese

Navy was never mentioned by him, but the fact of this officer's call could not remain a secret, and within four months, at the instigation of the French Ambassador at Lisbon, Campbell lost his command, one of the two reasons given for his dismissal being his having gone on board H.M.S. *Victory* to give the English Admiral the destination of the Combined Fleets.

9

On the morning after the friendly entertainment so expensive to Admiral Campbell, Nelson wrote in farewell to Ball, " My lot is cast, and I am going to the West Indies, where, although I am late, yet chance may have given them a bad passage, and me a good one : I must hope the best." He despatched the *Martin* sloop to Barbados, to announce his approach and request that an embargo be laid on all vessels in port, to prevent the news reaching the enemy at Martinique, or elsewhere. By 7 p.m. on the night of May 11 he was under full sail for the West Indies.

4

Villeneuve had crossed the Atlantic in thirty-four days. Nelson's fleet had a twenty-four days' passage. He hoped, " by exertions ", to gain a fortnight on an enemy whom he now believed to be under orders to capture the Jamaicas. The prospect of coming to the rescue of islands so well known to him fired him. " I was bred, as you know, in the good old school, and taught to appreciate the value of our West India possessions, and neither in the Field, nor in the Senate, shall their just rights be infringed whilst I have an arm to fight in their defence or a tongue to launch my voice."

10

The *Superb*, overdue for repairs at home, was still with him. " My dear Keats, I am very much pleased with the cheerfulness with which you are determined to share the fate of the fleet. Perhaps none of us would wish for exactly a West India trip; but the call of our Country is far superior to any consideration of self." Keats asked for permission not to stop when the other ships did, and lashed his studding-sail booms to his yards. Still, the old *Superb* set the pace, slower than desire. The Admiral sent her Captain a considerate line. " I am fearful that you may think that the *Superb* does not go so fast as I could wish. However that may be, (For if we all went ten knots, I should not think it fast enough,) yet I would have you be assured that I know and feel that the *Superb* does all which is possible for a Ship to accomplish; and I desire that you will not fret upon the occasion."

The " severe affliction " which he had felt at the enemy's escape out of the Mediterranean faded, together with home thoughts, as he made what haste he could to a decisive action in the Antilles, if not before.   He knew that all his home mail had gone up the Mediterranean in the *Nile* and *Avenger*, " and will never be received by me " . . . " but salt beef and the French Fleet, is far preferable to roast beef and champagne without them ".   The phrase " Self is out of the question " first began to appear in his letters written during these uneventful weeks of the Long Chase.

Blue days at sea succeeded one another, with hypnotic effect upon Dr. Scott.   " I know not what to write—it is the old story. Nothing new—we must take it as it comes."   On May 12, " Fourth Sunday after Easter ", noted Dr. Scott, " Performed the Church service to the people."   What the Admiral took to be an enemy privateer watched his fleet for two days, then disappeared.   On the 15th the Chaplain beheld with interest the uninhabited islets heralding Madeira, and on the 17th the *Victory* spoke a Portuguese vessel.   The friendly neutral had no news. She was bound for China, carrying a single priest " to convert the people there ".   Dr. Scott noticed that the weather was very fine and that he felt too lazy to read German.   " We are going with a soft wind."   The fleet was standing into the Trades, and during those days of slowest progress before reaching them Nelson transmitted to his officers his provisional plans for attack, in case he found the enemy at sea.   He guessed them to be bound for Martinique, so he did not intend to anchor at Barbados, where he hoped to pick up some reinforcements.   On May 22 " the usual Ceremonies on Crossing the Line were performed ".   On the 27th he calculated, " We shall be at Barbados the 3rd, or 4th, June. . . . Our passage, although not very quick, has been far from a bad one."   On the morning of June 3 the *Amphion* spoke two English merchant vessels who declared that the French fleet was in the West Indies.   Nelson arrived off Barbados with dawn of the following day (His Majesty's birthday), and Admiral Cochrane, whose flagship, the *Northumberland*, was lying in Carlisle Bay, came on board the *Victory* betimes attended by Sir William Myers, the Commander-in-Chief of the military at Barbados, and Governor of the Leeward Isles.   What these gentlemen had to tell, disturbed and puzzled Nelson.   On the previous night Sir William had received a letter from General Brereton, commanding the troops at Santa Lucia, which told him

that an allied fleet, of twenty-eight sail, had passed Gros Islet
going south, during the night of May 28–29. "Their destination,
I should suppose, must be either Barbados or Trinidad."
Brereton was an old acquaintance of Nelson. He had served as a
Major at the sieges of Bastia and Calvi. Cochrane and Myers
were unanimous that his information might be relied upon.
Against his inclination, Nelson changed his plans. "There is
not a doubt in the Admiral's or General's minds but that Tobago
and Trinidad are the enemy's objects, and, although I am anxious
in the extreme to get at their eighteen Sail-of-the-Line, yet, as
Sir William Myers has offered to embark himself with 2,000
Troops, I cannot refuse such a handsome offer." Reviewing the
situation seven weeks later, he explained, " I resisted the opinion
of General Brereton's information till it would have been the
height of presumption to have carried my disbelief further. I
could not, in the face of Generals and Admirals, go N.W. when it
was *apparently* clear that the enemy had gone South." He   11
worked his fleet up to Carlisle Bay, and at 9.30 next morning
weighed and made sail to the southward, having embarked the
martial Myers and his troops. The *Victory* threw out the general
signal " Prepare for Battle " at 2.15. Captain Bettesworth
had been detached with the *Curieux* brig to look into Tobago ;
word had been sent to the Governor of Dominica ; Colonel Shipley
of the Engineers had been directed to communicate with the
nearest post on Trinidad. The fleet arrived off Great Courland
Bay with sunset on the 6th. Its salute was duly returned by
Mud Fort, Tobago, and a schooner gave an even more welcome
greeting. A deeply interested merchant of the island had sent
off his head clerk in this vessel, with orders to stand towards the
approaching fleet and let him know whether it was friend or
enemy. By the most extraordinary coincidence of these days of
misinformation, the clerk's signal for a friendly fleet was the
same as that agreed upon between Admiral Cochrane and Colonel
Shipley for the enemy being in Trinidad. There seemed no
further reason to doubt the story of an American merchant
captain, spoken earlier in the day by the *Curieux*, that he had
been boarded by the French off Grenada ; and next morning the
distant view of troops abandoning Fort Abercrombie in flames
seemed to settle the matter. A second Aboukir was confidently
expected that evening in the Bay of Paria. Officers of the
squadron could hardly believe their senses when, on entering the
gulf, they found it calm and empty as a mountain tarn. No

enemy was to be seen, and it was soon evident that none had ever been seen by the inhabitants of Trinidad.

Nelson received more certain news of a French fleet being in the West Indies next morning, as he came out of the gulf. Captain Maurice, her late commander, had to report with regret from Barbados the loss of H.M. sloop *Diamond Rock*. (The pinnacled islet, so christened, standing out into the sea near the entrance to Fort Royal, had been a thorn in the side of the French of Martinique since it had been captured by a handful of blue-jackets in February 1804.) Maurice believed that the enemy, who had still been in Martinique on June 2, intended to sail on the 4th for an attack on Grenada and Dominica, and a French Commodore had told him that the Ferrol squadron, consisting of six French and eight Spanish sail-of-the-line, had arrived safely. Nelson doubted the Ferrol story, since its source was tainted and it was unconfirmed from Fort Royal, but welcomed the possibility of matching his compact fleet against one so un-wieldy, " and although a very pretty fiddle, I don't believe that either Gravina or Villeneuve know how to play upon it ".

Next noon, having arrived in St. George's Bay with great expedition, he heard from the Governor of Dominica that all were safe at Grenada, St. Vincent and Santa Lucia, and that the enemy had not moved from Martinique on the 4th, " proving all our former information to be false ". An hour later a letter from General Prevost was brought by Captain Champain of the *Jason*, who together with the General had been an eyewitness as an enemy fleet of eighteen of the line, six frigates and three brigs and schooners had passed Prince Rupert's Head on June 6. " In the evening, they were under the Saints, standing to the Northward." These authorities could not be doubted, and the last date and place mentioned enhanced Nelson's bitter disappoint-ment.

> " But for that false information, I should have been off Port Royal, as they were putting to sea; and our Battle, most probably, would have been fought on the spot where the brave Rodney beat De Grasse. I am rather inclined to believe that they are pushing for Europe, to get out of our way."

He had been " in a thousand fears for Jamaica ", " for that is a blow which Buonaparte would be happy to give us ". Now, he could only conclude that Villeneuve was on his return journey; but first he must satisfy himself that no attempt was being made upon Antigua or St. Kitts.

On June 12, in St. John Bay, Antigua, while the *Victory* echoed to the sound of the departure of Sir William Myers and staff, and all boats were employed transferring artillerymen to the *Northumberland*, Nelson began to piece together the available history of the enemy's operations in the West Indies. Villeneuve's unpractised fleet, carrying 3,000 French and 1,500 Spanish troops, had arrived at Martinique with three weeks' start of him, in very poor shape. The French had, on arrival, landed 1,000 sick, and had buried full that number during their stay. A frigate had certainly arrived from France on the 31st; "from that moment all was hurry". Nelson guessed that this ship was the mysterious stranger noticed by his squadron 200 leagues west of Madeira, and that she had given news of his approach to Gravina, "and probably hastened his movements".

Lord Nelson took his farewell with urbanity of a General to whose activity he would bear witness, and Sir William Myers left a famous man and ship happy in the knowledge that a letter was being sent to the Right Honourable Earl Camden recommending the very spirited, zealous and cheerful conduct of the Governor, the Leeward Isles, and the troops under his command. After the military were gone the *Victory* weighed promptly. All his former "affliction" at losing the French fleet in the Mediterranean returned as Nelson prepared to recross the Atlantic, again in haste.

> "If either General Brereton could not have wrote, or his look-out man had been blind, nothing could have prevented my fighting them on June 6th. . . . So far from being infallible, like the Pope, I believe my opinions to be very fallible, and therefore I may be mistaken that the Enemy's fleet is gone to Europe, but I cannot bring myself to think otherwise."

He considered, "I flew to the West Indies without any orders, but I think the Ministry cannot be displeased." He had saved the Colonies and upwards of two hundred sugar-laden ships. He mournfully decided that if he failed to come up with Villeneuve before the mouth of the Straits, he would there leave the command with Bickerton "and take their Lordships' permission to go to England, to try and repair a very shattered constitution". General Brereton and "his damned intelligence" obsessed his thoughts as his fleet pursued its long return journey; but as he still did not despair of getting up with the enemy before they reached Cadiz or Toulon, and matching his eleven ships against twenty, he summoned his Captains on board the *Victory* whenever it was calm enough for boats to pass, to dine, and for consultation. Villeneuve had only five days' start of him this time, and he would carry every rag, night and day.

> " I am thankful that the enemy has been driven from the West India islands with so little losses to our Country. I had made up my mind to great sacrifices; for I had determined, notwithstanding his vast superiority, to stop his career, and to put it out of his power to do further mischief. Yet, do not imagine I am one of those hot-brained people who fight at immense disadvantage without an adequate object. My object is partly gained. If we meet them we shall find them no less than eighteen, I rather think twenty Sail-of-the-Line, and therefore do not be surprised if I should not fall on them immediately : *we won't part without a battle.*"

13

He discussed, in view of their actions, every possible order that could have been given to the Combined Fleets. He ruled out attacks on Barbados, St. Lucia, Grenada, Trinidad or Tobago. If Jamaica had been their object (with some 4,000 to 5,000 men) they should have steered direct from Martinique. The theory that they had been waiting to go to Puerto Rico, when reinforced, would not hold water. The season was past; nor, if they had been expecting a reinforcement of fifteen of the line, had they any reason to hide. " My opinion is firm as a rock, that some cause, *orders*, or *inability* to perform any service in these seas, has made them resolve to proceed direct for Europe."

He did not yet guess the truth : that they had fled, not from the face, but from the very name of Nelson. The Rochefort squadron, having waited the prescribed forty-five days at its Martinique *rendezvous*, had returned without mishap. Villeneuve, whose original instructions had been to wait forty days for the Brest squadron, had, after a fortnight, received further Imperial demands, to occupy his time, while waiting, in making some attempts upon British possessions. He had taken under his command two sail-of-the-line which he had found at Martinique, raising his force to twenty. He had captured the *Diamond Rock* and some sugar-laden vessels, which had most imprudently ventured out from St. John. But from them he had heard of Nelson's arrival, with fourteen of the line. He believed Cochrane at Barbados to have five more. He had landed a number of his military as garrisons for the French islands (where they remained until after Trafalgar, when they became prisoners of war) and had made off in haste for the safety of Ferrol. His orders to await

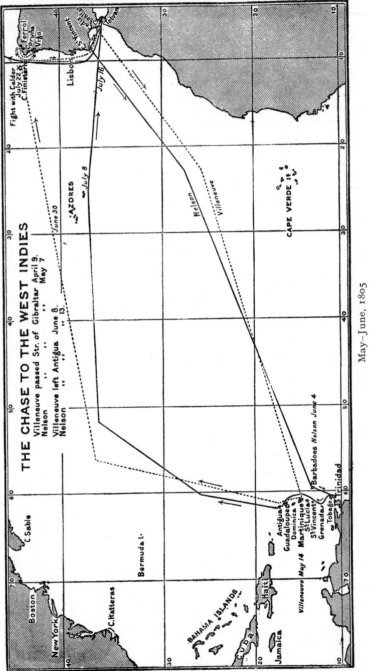

THE CHASE TO THE WEST INDIES

Villeneuve passed Str. of Gibraltar April 9.
Nelson   "   "   "   May 7
Villeneuve left Antigua June 8.
Nelson   "   "   "   13.

May–June, 1805

Reproduced from *The Year of Trafalgar*, by Sir Henry Newbolt
By kind permission of Messrs. John Murray

Ganteaume for forty days had been reduced to thirty-five; but only twenty-six had elapsed.

Nelson had sailed for Europe on June 13. On the 17th a report from the *Sally*, of North Carolina, bound for Antigua, made him hope that he was hard upon the heels of the enemy, and on the 19th he sent off the *Decade* and *Martin*, one to the Mediterranean by Gibraltar, and the other to Lisbon and Ferrol. Three nights later he retired from his quarter-deck to write down in his private diary : " Midnight, nearly calm. Saw three planks which I think came from the French fleet. Very miserable, which is very foolish." He encouraged Keats : " I think the *Superb* has improved in her sailing." Another of his Captains was writing home, " We are all half-starved, and otherwise inconvenienced by being so long away from a port, but our full recompense is that we are with Nelson." On the last day of June, Sutton was detached with the *Amphion* to Tangier Bay, to discover if the enemy had entered the Mediterranean. He was given a *rendezvous* west of Cape Spartel and told to keep the approach of Nelson's fleet as secret as possible. " Should you hear that I am gone to any other place after the Enemy, you will follow me, as I have not a single frigate with me." Sutton was also to rouse about the British Consul at Tangier, so that bullocks, onions, lemons and oranges in large numbers might be awaiting the fleet's arrival. Scurvy was beginning to enter the Admiral's thoughts, for, as he explained in an elegant letter destined for Her Majesty the Queen of Naples, in his nine days' tour he had not been able to get any of the famous delicacies of Great Britain's West India possessions save a few tamarinds and a little preserved ginger which he hoped might be acceptable to Madame, " the Fleet having received not the smallest refreshment, or even a cup of water " in the West Indies.

On July 8 he chronicled in sombre mood, " Crawled 33 miles the last twenty-four hours. My only hope is that the Enemy's Fleet are near us, and in the same situation." On the 17th the story read more hopefully :

> " Our whole run from Barbuda, day by day, was 3,459 miles; our run from Cape St. Vincent to Barbados was 3,227 miles; so that our run back was only 232 miles more than our run out. Allowance being made for the latitudes and longitudes of Barbados and Barbuda—average per day, thirty-four leagues, wanting nine miles."

With noon next day Cape Spartel was sighted, but no French fleet, nor any vessel bringing home news. He wrote to Collingwood,

P P

who had taken up his station off Cadiz, " I am, as you may
suppose, miserable at not having fallen in with the Enemy's Fleet ",
and after telling his tale, which included fears that the enemy might
have doubled back to Jamaica, he promised, the moment his ships
were watered and provisioned, to pay his old messmate a visit,
" Not, my dear friend, to take your Command from you, (for I
may probably add mine to you,) but to consult how we can best
serve our Country, by detaching a part of this large force ".

He anchored in Rosia Bay next evening, and acquainted the
Secretary to the Admiralty that when he had provisioned his
fleet for four months, and heard from Collingwood and Bickerton,
he would, unless he heard that the enemy had gone for any ports
in the Bay, join the squadrons off Ferrol or Ushant.   That night
he wrote in his diary, " I went on shore for the first time since
the 16th of June, 1803; and from having my foot out of the
Victory, two years, wanting ten days."   17

He went across to Tetuan again next morning, to receive the
" refreshment " necessary to banish scurvy from a fleet which
had, he thanked God, not lost an officer or man by sickness since
he had left the Mediterranean.

In the small hours of July 25, as he was passing the Straits
with a fine easterly wind, he read in a Lisbon paper, brought from
the Rock, of the arrival of Bettesworth in England, of the story
brought by the *Curieux*, and the result.   " I know it's true,"
he exclaimed, " from my words being repeated, therefore, I shall
not lose a moment, after I have communicated with Admiral
Collingwood, in getting to the northward."   He scribbled a line
to Parker of the *Amazon* to make haste to join him from Gibraltar,
and the sloop which had brought the newspaper sailed instantly,
carrying back to the Rock all his clean washing, " even to my
last shirt ".   He had thought her from Lisbon.

As he pressed again into the Atlantic, Collingwood's division
was sighted, some way to the leeward.   " My dear Collingwood,"
he explained, " we are in a fresh Levanter; you have an easterly
wind : therefore I must forgo the pleasure of taking you by the
hand until October next, when, if I am well enough, I shall (if
the Admiralty please,) resume the Command."

5

The *Curieux*, despatched home on June 12, had fallen in
with Villeneuve 900 miles N.N.E. of St. John, Antigua, and kept
company long enough to ascertain enemy numbers and course.

Her Captain was in the presence of the First Lord before that personage had got his shaving-water or his breakfast on July 9, and the early midsummer interview in Whitehall was picturesque, for Captain Bettesworth, aged five-and-twenty, and the recipient of twenty-four wounds in action, was the most personable of "Nelsonian" officers, and Lord Barham, whose silver hair was thin but whose eye was still bright, had been a frigate Captain in the West Indies when Nelson was three years old. The new First Lord was in his eightieth year, but he had long experience as Comptroller of the Navy. Within a few hours despatch vessels were under sail, with orders for the blockading squadrons off Rochefort and Ferrol to unite and take up a position 100 miles west of Cape Finisterre.

Sir Robert Calder's squadron of fifteen of the line met Villeneuve there on the cloudy morning of July 22. The action, which took place at long range, was indecisive. Two Spanish ships were captured. After four days Calder lost sight of the enemy, who first put in to Vigo, and, leaving three ships there, reached Ferrol on August 1. Calder, having sent five of his squadron to resume the Rochefort blockade, joined Cornwallis, twenty-five miles west of Ushant, a day before Nelson, who, delayed by northerly winds, had been three weeks making his passage from the Rock to the Channel Fleet. A frigate spoken on August 12 had told Nelson that, up to the 9th, there had been no tale of the enemy's arrival in the Bay of Biscay, or on the Irish coast. The *Victory* saluted the *Ville de Paris* at 6 p.m., and hove to, but was under sail again before 8. Cornwallis had excused him even the customary personal visit, and authorised him to go on to Portsmouth. He took with him only the *Superb*, and as there was little wind, Keats dined with him, on the last night of their long passage, and they discussed the large packet of English newspapers thoughtfully sent on board by Fremantle. From these they gathered that John Bull was howling for the recall and court-martial of Calder, and saying—quite unjustly so far as Nelson could judge—that Lord Nelson would have done better.

His last approaches towards home were tantalisingly leisurely. With daylight of the 17th he was abreast of Portland; at noon he saw the Isle of Wight, and at 1 that night the *Victory* and *Superb* anchored off the Princesses' Shoal. Having weighed with dawn, they worked up to the Motherbank, and anchored again. Yellow fever had been devastating the ports of Spain and Portugal, and as his fleet had touched at Gibraltar, Nelson found himself, " for the first time in my life ", in quarantine.   He hastened to assure the Admiralty, the Port Admiral and the Collector of Customs that there had been no fever in the garrison at the Rock, that he was twenty-eight days out and that he had not " even an object for the hospital " in either his flagship or the *Superb*.   Throughout his three weeks' struggle to join the Channel Fleet he had scarcely written a private letter.   He had been entirely occupied with preparations for the battle which had, in the end, fallen to Calder.   While he waited for permission to come ashore, on a wet Sunday, he sent short lines to Brother William and Davison, and a long screed (the third on the subject) to their Lordships, asking urgently that a volunteer pilot, whom he had in his haste borne away from Antigua, might be put in the way of a speedy and remunerative passage to his native Barbados. For the problem of the patriotic and ebullient Mr. James Marguette (a man of colour), alone in London, weighed upon his conscience.   18

He told his brother :

" I am but so-so, yet, what is very odd, the better for going to the West Indies, even with the anxiety.   We must not talk of Sir Robert Calder's battle: I might not have done so much with my small force.   If I had fallen in with them, you would probably have been a Lord before I wished; for I know they meant to make a dead set at the *Victory*."

To Lady Hamilton he sent two expresses, at twenty-four-hour intervals.   He had not heard from her since April.

" I have brought home no honour for my Country, only a most faithful servant; nor any riches—that the Administration took care to give to others—but I have brought home a most faithful and honourable heart. . . . God send us a happy meeting as our parting   19 was sorrowful."

His order of release came at 7 p.m. on the night of the 19th, and his welcome was the most enthusiastic that he had ever received.   From the moment that his flag had been descried at Spithead, the ramparts, and every place that could command a view of the entrance to Portsmouth harbour, had been thronged, despite heavy showers, and as his barge pulled to the shore it was greeted with loud and reiterated huzzas.   Taking Murray with him, he went first to make his bow to the Commander-in-Chief and the Commissioner.   His intention had been not to stay ten minutes, but he was obliged to drink tea with them.   He ordered tea again as he sat waiting for a post-chaise at the " George ",

Portsmouth High Street, while rain dripped down. Nine o'clock of a very wet night saw him on the road for London. "His Lordship's movements here were in unison with his pursuit after the Combined Squadron, for he was not an hour in the town." He reached Merton at 6 a.m. on the morning of August 20, 1805.

CHAPTER XVIII

1805
(*ætat* 46)

THE TWENTY-FIVE DAYS

I

INCREDIBLE though it may sound, a strange foreigner gained an interview with the great man, who had travelled throughout the night to his country retreat, on the very day of his arrival. The lucky intruder, who brought to his descriptions a quality of early-morning freshness, was a Mr. J. A. Andersen. He had sent several of his writings to Lord Nelson, and was now projecting a history of his native Denmark. In his *Excursions in England*, published two years later, he is quite distinct that his gracious reception took place on August 20, 1805. The visitor from London was

> "charmed with the situation of Merton. Merton Place is not a large, but a very elegant structure. In the balconies I observed a number of ladies, who, I understood to be Lord Nelson's relations. Entering the house, I passed through a lobby which contained amongst a variety of paintings and other *objets d'art*, an excellent marble bust of the illustrious Admiral. Here I met the Rev. Dr. Nelson, the present Earl. I was then ushered into a magnificent apartment where Lady Hamilton sat at a window. I at first scarcely observed his Lordship, he having placed himself immediately at the entrance. The Admiral wore a uniform emblazoned with different Orders of Knighthood. He received me with the utmost condescension. Chairs being provided, he sat down between Lady Hamilton and myself, and having laid my account of the Battle of Copenhagen on his knee, a conversation ensued."

Nelson stated that "labour deserves reward", and expressed a suspicion that authors were generally ill-paid. He asked to have his name put down as a subscriber for the author's forthcoming volume, and led him to see a portrait of the Crown Prince of Denmark in an upstairs drawing-room. On their way down he paused to point out a print of the Battle of Copenhagen; and as the hero stood, in the strong light of the stair-head, wrapped in thought, backed by engravings of his naval engagements, the guest was able to observe him better than good manners had previously permitted. On his last birthday Nelson had recorded, "Forty-six years of toil and trouble". He had noticed vaguely that he seemed

582

to be growing very thin. When animated, as his figure was light and he moved briskly, he did not look his age; but in repose he now looked more. Mr. Andersen found the lines of his face hard,

"but the penetration of his eye threw a kind of light upon his countenance, which tempered its severity, and rendered his harsh features in some measure agreeable. . . . His aspect commanded the utmost veneration, especially when he looked upwards. Lord Nelson had not the least pride of rank; he combined with that degree of dignity which a man of quality should have, the most engaging address in his air and appearance."

That afternoon Nelson sat down at 3.30 to a scene upon which his pen had dwelt often during upwards of two years, " shut up in the *Victory's* cabin ". Indeed, the dream of a lifetime was realised. He dined in his own country house, and offered hospitality to his own family—" people that do care for us ". Looking down his table, he saw, in fact, at last, the rich gleam of Worcester china, decorated with oak-leaves and laurel and the coat-of-arms of Viscount Nelson, Duke of Brontë, the glitter of plate bearing his own monogram, the profiles of a brother and sister and their spouses, of Mrs. Cadogan and Miss Sarah Connor, a full-face view of Lady Hamilton, in her element, and the bright hair and rosy cheeks of four healthy young people, attacking festal fare. Horatia was four and a half now, and " uncommonly quick ". She could write a letter, and was learning French and Italian and the piano, but had been frightened when told " how her dear, dear god-papa kill'd all the people ".

¹ Outside, as well as within, transformation had been wrought at Merton during the owner's long absence. The entrance had been successfully removed to the north front; the new drawing-room, bedrooms and kitchen were being employed, and he was lord of additional acres, on the opposite side of Merton High Road, in the parish of Wimbledon. The Merton Place coachman's cottage and stables had been across the road, and rented from a Mr. Bennett, an inconvenient arrangement. A spacious bricked tunnel now led under the road to his stables and new kitchen gardens, and Lady Hamilton had given orders for the construction of a walk, on which he might feel himself on his own quarter-deck, leading up to a rotund white summer-house, in fashionable classic

² style, christened " the Poop ". There had been an artificial mound and view-point here as long as man could remember. Villagers said that the Romans had made it. A footpath from the village wishing-well, near Spring House, undoubtedly led

direct to a Roman road known as the Ridgeway, in Wimbledon. It was boasted that a specimen of practically every tree peculiar to his native isle adorned Admiral Nelson's grounds, and there is contemporary evidence that many well-grown exotics were also to be seen, for when Mr. Thomas Baxter of the Worcester porcelain factories came to Merton with his sketch-book, he made studies of cedars of Lebanon and deodars, *Salix Babylonica*, tendrils of Virginia creeper overhanging a trellissed porch, and a shadowy arbour occupied by a drooping, white-gowned female figure.

3

Cribb, who had been provided with twenty underlings to assist him in his delving and planting, certainly merited congratulation. With regard to the rebuilding, although he approved the result, the Admiral was not so happy. He had written painfully, when the new drawing-room was mooted, " I hardly know how to find the money; but if it is to be done this year it is begun before this time; it is too late to say a word." He was now brought to realise that the dining-room needed enlargement, and a Mr. Chawner, who had completed the work begun by a Mr. Sprinks, had not been paid. The sums of £200 which he had sent home more than once to cover Lady Hamilton's structural improvements had long since been swallowed up by Sprinks, a drunken fellow. At some early hour after his arrival he resolved to raise the money to pay Chawner by selling some of his presentation plate, and there is no reason to believe that the close of a showery day at Merton was anything but unclouded.

In the village itself, where the return of the hero was again being celebrated with home-made decorations, two years and three months could not be expected to have made much difference. Life in Merton village flowed slow and steady as the Wandle, whose waters had for seven centuries driven a flour mill behind Mr. Perry's house, and now (since the place was so convenient for London) also provided the power for the factories producing snuff and printed calicoes, whose chimneys, sprouting amongst the Abbey meadows, perhaps detracted somewhat from the rural aspect of the neighbourhood. Residents comforted themselves with the assertion that qualities specially suitable for chintz and madder dyeing were found in the waters of the Wandle. These embellished the grounds of every adjacent mansion, and ran faithfully beside the straggling main street of gabled houses and wooden cottages, which they flooded regularly in stormy weather.

Merton Place, Surrey (side of the House and the River.) (7″ × 4½″.)

Water-colour sketch by Thomas Baxter (1782–1821), china painter.

Baxter designed the dessert service ordered by Nelson at Worcester in August 1802, and subsequently visited Merton. This sketch, which has never before been reproduced, shows the river Wandle (" Nile ") and west side of the house, including, on the ground floor, Lord Nelson's library.

Reproduced by kind permission of the Trustees, The National Maritime Museum, Greenwich.

Merton possessed two inns, overlooking the river. The carrier, whose cottage stood at the side of Lord Nelson's orchard, collected and delivered at the " Six Bells ". The " King's Head ", dating from the days of Edward VI, was the place from which the daily service of coaches ran to London, and a message to this house from Merton Place would always produce a post-chaise. The turnpike was exactly opposite the entrance to the Admiral's drive, and small payments to an Italian servant, Francatello, for turnpike charges, appear repeatedly in his accounts.

He set out for London early on the morning after his happy return, and was dropped at the Admiralty by Lady Hamilton, who went on to her little house in Clarges Street, to await the arrival of the Misses Bolton from Norfolk, and write to summon the Matchams from Bath. (" What a day of rejoicing was yesterday at Merton ! How happy he is to see us all ! ")

He was at the Admiralty by 9.45. " The public appearance in the streets of Lord Nelson, who in the short space of five weeks has viewed the four quarters of the Globe, attracted a concourse ", and his movements of this day were chronicled in detail in next morning's gossip columns. After leaving Lord Barham he took a hackney down to Messrs. Marsh, Page and Creed, Navy Agents, of Norfolk Street, Strand, and on to the Navy Office, Somerset House, where he saw Sir Andrew Snape Hammond, Comptroller. By noon he was back in Whitehall, having made an expedition to Messrs. Salters, silversmiths, where he had chosen a child's set of knife, fork and spoon to be engraved with the name " Horatia ", and a silver-gilt cup for which the inscription ordered was : " To my much-loved Horatia ". He was wearing " plain uniform and a green shade over his left eye ". A long interview with Mr. Pitt was his last engagement. He left town at four, having collected two nieces at what reporters called " his house in Clarges Street ".

His day had been surprisingly easy. Everywhere the name of Lord Nelson had acted as an open sesame to jealously guarded penetralia. Ministers now came treading rapidly down their soft carpets with outstretched hand and concerned inquiries for his health. Mr. Pitt had even spoken to Mr. Rose of riding over to Merton Place from Bowling Green House, Wimbledon. The moment seemed auspicious for the Admiral to mention to Rose that the widow of Sir William Hamilton had not yet received any acknowledgment of her patriotic services at the Court of the Two Sicilies, and he took the opportunity. At the Admiralty, Lord

Barham, " an almost entire stranger ", could not have been more forthcoming. The new Secretary of State wanted to see Lord Nelson without delay. . . . As he had worked his way up to Spithead, he had gathered from the newspapers sent on board by Fremantle, off Ushant, that far from being blamed for having missed the Combined Fleet, his dramatic dash " to save the West Indies only by a few days " had enhanced his reputation. Nevertheless, his agonies on that long passage had not been without reason. Lord Radstock, a stout admirer, who had a son in the *Victory*, had believed that " the loss of Jamaica would at once sink all his past services into oblivion ", and miserably doubted whether, should any serious misfortune have overtaken him, their Lordships would do much for him. The Admiralty, perplexed and harassed by his long silence, had indeed been " out of humour with him ". The alarm in the City upon the news of Villeneuve's escape out of the Mediterranean, and junction with Gravina, had been enormous. The alarm had been warm, and the relief at his reappearance, having banished Villeneuve from the West Indies, corresponded. Still, he had not been quite prepared for the extreme civility of his official welcome. " Thank God, he is safe and well ", wrote Miss Cecilia Connor, in a letter received by Lady Hamilton that morning.

> " Cold water has been trickling down my back ever since I heard he was arrived. Oh ! say, how he looks, and talks, and eats, and sleeps. Never was a man come back so enthusiastically revered. Look at the ideas that pervade the minds of his fellow citizens in this morning's *Post*. Timid widows and spinsters are terrified at his foot being on shore; yet this is the man that is to have a Sir R. Calder and a Sir J. Orde sent to intercept his well-earned advantages. I hope he may never quit his own house again."
>
> 5

That hope was quickly dissipated, and within two days he fully appreciated the reason for the extraordinary availability of Ministers. They were " full of the Enemy's Fleet ". On the day of his first call at the Admiralty, the frigate *Iris* had brought the unwelcome tidings that Villeneuve had put to sea again on the evening of the 13th from Ferrol, with twenty-eight or nine of the line. Cornwallis had kept seventeen ships to confront the Brest squadron of twenty-one, and sent eighteen, under Calder, to look for Villeneuve.

A very poor Admiral, who wondered if his interest was yet sufficient to get a small post in the Customs Office for his brother-in-law, but was still so bad at asking favours that he preferred to send his request through his friend Rose to a Prime Minister whom he was seeing almost daily, was more amused than flattered at his situation. "I am now", he explained to Captain Keats, "set up for a *Conjuror*, and God knows they will soon find out I am far from one. I was asked my opinion, against my inclination, for if I make one wrong guess, the charm will be broken. But this I ventured without any fear—that if Calder got fairly alongside their twenty-seven or twenty-eight Sail, that by the time the Enemy had beat our Fleet soundly, they would do us no harm this year."

Ministers very new to office, however, had looked funereal when assured that Buonaparte's career might be checked at a cost which would be highly unpopular at home. Already the news from India was making a strong and unfavourable impression. It was whispered in the City that if the Combined Fleet fell in with the homeward-bound convoy daily expected, the India Company would be bankrupt. They could not at such a moment lend an attentive ear to Admiral Nelson's opinions on the importance of Sardinia to their nation. Lord Castlereagh, privately written down by the Admiral as "a man who has only sat one solitary day in his Office, and of course knows but little of what is passed", hesitantly believed that he had not seen the despatches alluded to, addressed to his predecessors. But there was no escape. Lord Nelson offered, if they could not be found, to provide the whole series immediately. He had kept duplicates, with an index.

2

The accepted picture of Nelson, settled in peace during his last weeks at home, in a rustic retreat, alone with Lady Hamilton, is mistaken. He was in conference in London for at least part of fourteen of those twenty-five days, and within nine he had learnt beyond doubt from Pitt that "my services may be wanted". Nor even at Merton was there much peace to be had. A house with not more than fifteen bedrooms was accommodating never less than nine adults and seven children, in addition to a staff containing several foreigners. All the neighbours paid their respects, including royalty (in the large shape of the Duke of Clarence from Bushey), and most days guests from London stayed to dinner. Even the house-party itself was, as Sir William had complained in his senescence, so continually changing that a host knew not who was under his roof. Sea-friends were headed by Admiral Parker and Captain Keats. Captain Langford's

ship was back at Portsmouth from the West Coast of Africa, and
he had brought (hopefully recorded as "animals that will not
require much care") a crown-bird and a civet-cat to add to the
Merton *ménagerie*. Mr. Whichelo came to take a sketch of
Admiral Nelson for Admiral Parker. Mr. Rose wanted one from
the pencil of Mr. Edridge, who had recently achieved " a remarkably strong likeness " of the Prime Minister. Mr. Bolton, senior,
tore himself away, but Mr. John Scott came to fill his bed. Still
Lady Hamilton sounded trumpet-calls to the last of the Nelson
family. " We have Room for you all, so Come as soon as you can.
We shall be happy, most happy. Here are Sir Peter Parker,
and God knows who, so Nelson has not time to say more than
that he loves you, and shall rejoice to see you." Tragedy had
halted the Matchams. Their last-born, William Alexander
(named after Dr. Nelson and Mr. Davison, " a well formed child
with fair complexion and fine blue eyes "), had died suddenly.
But on hearing that their dear relative's length of stay was very
uncertain, the bereaved parents bravely made the effort.

Captain Keats paced the quarter-deck at Merton together with
his host, and the Admiral explained his Plan for Attack. " No
day can be long enough to arrange a couple of Fleets, and fight a
decisive Battle, according to the old system. When *we* meet
them, (for meet them we shall,) I'll tell you how I shall fight them.

" I shall form the Fleet into three Divisions in three Lines.
One Division shall be composed of twelve or fourteen of the
fastest two-decked Ships, which I shall always keep to windward,
or in a situation of advantage; and I shall put them under an
Officer who, I am sure, will employ them in the manner I wish,
if possible. I consider it will always be in my power to throw
them into Battle in any part I may choose; but if circumstances
prevent their being carried against the Enemy where I desire,
I shall feel certain he will employ them effectually, and, perhaps,
in a more advantageous manner than if he could have followed
my orders."

He paused, and Keats, who hoped to be with him when the
promised day came, wondered who was the officer intended for
this distinguished service. But Nelson swept on :

" With the remaining part of the Fleet formed in two Lines, I
shall go at them at once, if I can, about one-third of their Line
from their leading Ship."

He broke off again, and then asked, " What do you think of
it ? "

While Keats considered, in silence, something so novel, he proceeded with vigour :

" I'll tell you what I think of it. I think it will surprise and confound the Enemy. They won't know what I am about. It will bring forward a pell-mell Battle, and that is what I want."

Lord Minto was detained by affairs in a capital which he found very empty, except of disagreeable rumour. (He was going to be offered the St. Petersburg Embassy, and was going to refuse.) On the first Saturday after his distinguished friend's return, he took his chance at Merton,

" and found Nelson just sitting down to dinner, surrounded by a family party, of his brother, the Dean, Mrs. Nelson, their children, and the children of a sister, Lady Hamilton at the head of the table and Mother Cadogan at the bottom. I had a hearty welcome. He looks remarkably well and full of spirits. His conversation is a cordial in these low times. Lady Hamilton has improved and added to the house and the place extremely well and without his knowing she was about it. She is a clever being after all : the passion is as hot as ever."

The conventions, however, were being as strictly observed as ever. " Nelson ", wrote Lady Hamilton to his sister, " when he is in Town goes to a hotel." He never spent a night under the roof of 11, Clarges Street, which was her house. He booked rooms at Gordon's Hotel, 44, Albemarle Street, and it was there that he was at last tracked down by old Lord Hood, who had been trying to get in touch with him from the moment he had landed. The interview cannot have been satisfying, for the venerable patron called, according to reporters, at 12 noon, on the morning of August 28, followed closely by Lord Braybrooke and the Rev. Dr. Nelson, and at 12.30 appeared a deputation of many Directors, representing the West India Merchants and Planters come to offer their unfeigned thanks to Lord Nelson—" For his sagacity in ascertaining the course of, and bold and unwearied pursuit of, the Combined Squadron, to the West Indies and back again ". The hero had ready one of his modest replies, in which he assured them that from the state of defence in which he had found " our large Islands " he was confident that no troops landed by the enemy could have made any impression before relief could be summoned. He invited the company to a breakfast (at which tea, coffee, chocolate, rolls, cold hams, tongues and poultry were followed by choice wines and a dessert of the first quality), and, his duty done, hastened round to dine at Clarges Street, with " a family party " which included Lord Minto and Mr. Charles Greville. Lord Minto had been startled that morning to find the Victor of the Nile by his bedside before he was up, expatiating at top speed on his hopes " to see me Secretary of State, and so forth ". Nelson, who could not sleep late, and bleakly headed letters from Gordon's Hotel " 6 a.m.", had brought with him some papers concerning the Mediterranean, over which the ex-Viceroy of Corsica was begged to run his eye as he travelled to Merton to-morrow, where a further consignment would be awaiting him. Lord Minto obediently hunted out some of his ten-years-old despatches about Sardinia, " which is Lord Nelson's great hobby ", and when he departed for London again, his host personally superintended the packing of a post-chaise with many volumes of his own correspondence, " to show how his opinion had concurred with mine ". " To-day ", announced Lord Minto, on August 31, " he has sent me another load." 12

Sunday was a day of comparative peace at Merton Place, but the Admiral, although a clergyman's son, had no objection to Sunday travelling. When he called on Mr. Addington, now Lord Sidmouth, on his second day in town, he took that gentle-man at an awkward moment. The ex-Prime Minister was without his coat, having just been bled. The caller, fresh from Downing Street, looked to a dejected statesman very well, and after an hour of comfortable conversation, offered to renew it next day, but stipulated that he must first attend morning service at Merton. 13 The engagement was eventually transferred to a later date and country scene.

The summer of 1805 had been most disappointing; there had been much rain and wind, many deferred junketings and little call for muslins. A burst of seasonable heat coincided perversely with Nelson's mid-week stay at Gordon's Hotel, but opened in time for his first Sunday at home, when the whole Merton Place party attended the parish church of what he liked to call " our village ". It certainly lay in the most unspoilt quarter of the district, where no London whispers penetrated, where tall brick walls on which fruit had warmed for two hundred years enclosed an antique mansion with an air of shattered dignity (now a boarding-school), and dusty yellow lanes meandered towards water-meadows between cottages presenting four tightly closed windows and utilitarian front gardens. The relations of Merton Place with the Vicar had been cordial from the first. The Rev. Thomas Lancaster kept an academy, and had a younger son whom he hoped to send to sea, under the auspices of his most influential parishioner. 14

On an unascertained morning of this week, Lady Hamilton fulfilled a promise. An open chariot breasted Wimbledon Hill, and drew up outside a handsome house in the Dutch-Jacobean style, to be renamed in honour of this day's occasion " Nelson House ". Here some favoured young gentlemen in blue coats with brass buttons were summoned to the front parlour and ordered by their clerical pedagogue to recite to the Victor of the Nile, an ordeal which ended happily for all with a request from the chief guest for a half-holiday for the school, and with three hearty cheers for Lord Nelson and Lady Hamilton.

A daughter of Merton Vicarage, many years later, when she was a Victorian matron, tacitly supported her father's attitude towards Merton Place, and volunteered to the editor of *Lord Nelson's Despatches* :

" In revered affection for the memory of that dear man, I cannot refrain from informing you of his unlimited charity and goodness during his residence at Merton. His frequently expressed desire was, that none in that place should want, or suffer affliction that he could alleviate, and this I know he did with a most liberal hand; always desiring that it should not be known from whence it came. His residence at Merton was a continued course of charity and goodness, setting such an example of propriety and regularity that there are few would not be benefited by following it."

Nelson missed church on his second Sunday morning at home. For two days he had been in anxious expectation of news from Calder of a victory. Otherwise he had no doubt that he would himself " be ordered to sea, *very very* soon ". The *Victory* had received a signal not to go into port to undergo the very slight repairs necessary after the Long Chase. Hardy, who was on sick leave, was returning to her. On Saturday night, August 31, his brother-in-law seemed to Mr. Matcham unusually pensive, and he finally murmured, " They are mistaken ! I will go myself and talk with Mr. Pitt." The fruit of his country musings, which he so urgently wished to communicate to the Minister, was that the missing Combined Fleet was probably destined, not for the West Indies again, as had been decided in Cabinet conclave, but for Cadiz and Toulon. " They will then have collected sixty or seventy sail-of-the-line, and then there will be a difficulty in overcoming them." Matcham, who saw him on his return from his flying Sunday afternoon visit to the capital, treasured the report of that interview. After long discussion, the Prime Minister became a convert to the Admiral's view, and they agreed upon the number of ships which must be sent to attack such a combination. Pitt's next question was abrupt : " Now, who is to take command ? " " You cannot have a better man than the present one—Collingwood ", replied a good friend, but this suggestion was brushed aside. " No. That won't do. You must take the command." Nelson's objections were overruled, and Pitt asked him to be ready to sail in three days, to which the answer was, " I am ready now." [17]

When a post-chaise disturbed the drive of Merton Place at 5 a.m. on the following morning, Captain the Hon. Henry Blackwood of H.M.S. *Euryalus*, with despatches from Admiral Collingwood for the Admiralty, found the master of the house, according to his custom, already up and dressed. Nelson exclaimed, " I am sure that you bring me news of the French and Spanish Fleets, and that I shall have to beat them yet." A [18] young officer, with bronzed aquiline features, tersely expressed his hope of being present at the intended " drubbing ", and then explained that, finding himself so near his Lordship's villa so early, on his road from Portsmouth to the Admiralty, he had seized the chance to inform him that the Combined Fleet had been traced to Cadiz harbour.

The early visitor was welcome apart from his news. Captain Blackwood (who was the fourth son of an Irish peeress and baronet) had gone to sea, and, what was more, had been in action (at the Battle of the Dogger Bank), at the age of eleven. He was one of those younger officers to whom Nelson had been attracted by reputation before ever meeting him. When a Lieutenant, and just of age, he had been obliged to fly for his life from Revolutionary Paris, having been denounced as a spy. As a frigate Captain, he had been distinguished by brilliant seamanship, promptitude and daring. The incident which had first brought him a letter from Nelson had been his assistance at the capture of *Le Guillaume Tell*, one of the two 80-gun ships to escape from the Nile. (The little *Penelope*, of 36 guns, had sighted, chased, engaged and held on to the enemy second-rate until two of the line had been able to come up.) During the past two years Blackwood had been employed on the coast of Ireland and in the Channel; for the past eight weeks he had been watching the movements of Villeneuve. He set off for Whitehall as soon as he had delivered himself of his dramatic news, and Nelson followed. Harrison's romantic story that the Admiral was [19] discovered by Lady Hamilton later in the day pacing the

Lady Hamilton at Merton.

By Thomas Baxter. (7" × 5".)

This pencil sketch, which has never before been reproduced, represents Lady Hamilton in her later thirties, as Nelson knew her, at Merton. Only one of the famous Romney portraits was painted after her marriage, in 1791. all the remainder before she was twenty-one

" quarter-deck " in his garden, in low spirits, and was persuaded by her to go to London and offer his services, must be discounted. He had known from the morning of his first call at the Admiralty that his services might be needed very soon ; he had told George Matcham of the certainty of his speedy departure on the preceding evening.   Mrs. Bolton had written from Merton to the Matchams, a week earlier, urging them not to delay their journey, as his length of stay was very uncertain, and he had himself repeated the phrase in a letter to Beckford, refusing an invitation to Fonthill.   That Nelson, after revealing to Lady Hamilton the news brought by Blackwood, with all its implications, did utter the popular, " Brave Emma ! good Emma ! If there were more Emmas there would be more Nelsons ", need not fall under the same suspicion.   He had said very much the same, in other words, on several previous occasions, and it is clear from a note written by her, within two days, that she did accept the inevitable in heroic vein.   " My dear Friend," she told Lady Bolton, " I am again broken hearted, as our dear Nelson is immediately going.   It seems as though I have had a fortnight's dream, and am awoke to all the misery of this cruel separation.   But what can I do?   His powerful arm is of so much consequence to his

20 Country."   Nelson had always intended to go to town on the day of Blackwood's call, and had made an appointment with Lord Minto, which he kept.   Their main topic, however, was not, as had been threatened, Sardinia.   During the week-end the Ministry had decided " to give its best hope a *carte blanche* ". He told Minto, that morning, that there seemed no doubt that he would be going immediately to take command of Calder's fleet ; and next morning, that he was going to resume the Mediterranean Command as soon as the *Victory* could be got ready, which would be within the week.   When he had presented himself at the Admiralty, following Blackwood, Lord Barham had given into his hands the current list of the Royal Navy and begged him to choose his own officers.   He had replied, " Choose yourself, my Lord, the same spirit actuates the whole profession ; you cannot choose wrong ", but the elderly First Lord, pottering out of the room, had insisted, " This is my Secretary ; give your orders to

21 him."   Everything was now being done on the same handsome scale, and by September 6 the Press knew it.   " Lord Nelson's new appointment is very extensive, and in some degrees unlimited. Lord Nelson's new command comprehends not only the whole of the Mediterranean, but extends also to Cadiz.   His Lordship has

Q Q

the selection of his own favourite officers." The announcement was very popular, but could hardly increase public affection for a character whose every movement had been eagerly watched from the moment he had set foot on shore. A week earlier, Lord Minto, who possessed historic sense, had written to his wife :

> " I met Nelson to-day in a mob in Piccadilly, and got hold of his arm, so that I was mobbed too. It is really quite affecting to see the wonder and admiration, and love and respect, of the whole world ; and the genuine expression of all these sentiments at once, from gentle and simple, the moment he is seen. It is beyond anything represented in a play or a poem of fame." 22

Meanwhile, at Merton, over which the shadow of what was now inevitable had brooded heavily almost from the first, the *tempo* of daily existence, always confused and rapid, quickened. There was no cessation, rather the contrary, of large dinner-parties and sudden London journeys. It is possible to learn exactly what happened at Lord Nelson's villa, as observed by an ingenuous guest, from the very day of Blackwood's call. George Matcham, junior, was due to arrive that night from Somerset. He was nearly sixteen, but had never been to boarding-school, and would be set down by the Bath coach at the White Horse cellars, Piccadilly, at 10 p.m. His uncle, after a heavy day in London, had returned home to dine, with the ladies of the party, who had received at Clarges Street during the morning a hasty note warning them that his heavy luggage must be put on the road for Portsmouth within forty-eight hours. The invaluable Cribb was called to the rescue. George Matcham, junior, kept a diary. 23

3

George's first journey alone was very interesting. He took his seat in the coach at 4.30 a.m., and found the other passengers " an Elderly gentleman, an Old Gentleman and a Young Lady, who began the Conversation ". At Devizes, where they break-fasted at 9, their only outside passenger joined them, a young Lieutenant, come home with the West India Fleet. One more inside passenger, an Old Lady, at once covered her face with a coloured silk handkerchief and composed herself to sleep, so " the rest of us entertained ourselves with commonplace conversation ". George saw the White Horse on the Downs, and at Marlborough gladly exchanged seats with the Lieutenant and took his station on the coach-box. He opened conversation with the driver by the observation that one of the inside passengers had been taken ill, but Jehu only said that if the party had taken his rum neat at breakfast, instead of spoiling it with milk, he would have been the better for it. The coachman proceeded to praise strong liquors, and rain began to come down so steadily that by the time George had the opportunity of alighting at Newbury, to dine, he was " pretty well drench'd ". Four gentlemen who were not quite gentlemen now took their seats, having made an attempt to impress the company at dinner by cursing the waiter and complaining of the food. George wisely attached himself to the Old Gentleman, who quietly pointed out the various noblemen's mansions on either side of their road, and was met at Salthill by a footman in livery. After he had gone, someone believed that he was a Baronet. At Slough the Guard came on board, and at Brentford a Fat Farmer, who soon fell into a sound sleep. George, too, was beginning to feel the effects of having risen before dawn, but was stirred into quickened apprehension by the lights of London. " London look'd brilliant on approaching it." At last the Bath coach thundered into the courtyard of the Piccadilly hostelry, and he was almost at once accosted by a strange man, who tried to relieve him of his trunk. " Refused, thinking him some thief." The strange man, however, explained that he was Lord Nelson's gardener, waiting with a post-chaise to carry his lordship's nephew to Merton Place. George, who had been well brought up, saw to it that the Young Lady got a hackney to take her to her London destination, before going round the corner to 11, Clarges Street, where he waited while Cribb ran to fetch their equipage. The chaise was an open one, and all the way down to Merton it rained. When the young traveller arrived at last in his noble uncle's Surrey villa, he found it utterly quiet and dark. Every soul in that overcrowded, tragic house, surrounded by sighing, weeping trees and shining waters, had gone to bed early, after a day which had opened with a summons at 5 a.m. But soon a door clicked, and a light of welcome appeared above. " Lady H. came out *en chemise*, and directed me to my cousin Tom's room, where I was to sleep. Had not seen him for ten years, soon made acquaintance."

Not a suspicion of the sword of Damocles troubled young George's receptive brain, as he proceeded, daily from September 4 to 11, 1805, to enter in telegraphic form, in his compulsory journal, his impressions of the principal events and characters encountered on his historic " visit to see Lord N. my Uncle, before his departure ".

He paid his respects to his uncle early on the morning of September 4, and, as he was sent out shooting with his sophisticated Etonian cousin, failed to notice that a host who appeared at breakfast and at a dinner-party had in the interval been to London. Lord Nelson appeared to George " of middle height, and of a frame adapted to activity and exertion ". At his own table he was the least heard of the company, but could suddenly be witty. Far from being " the rude and boisterous captain of the sea ", he looked, in the plain suit of black which was his invariable wear in his own house, simply a gentleman. He never swore (in George's hearing at any rate), and always cut short the gentlemen's hour alone with their wine, after the ladies had retired for tea to the drawing-room. After dinner on his first night at Merton George lost 11s. 6d. " at Cards ". Lady Hamilton was ready with " £2 0s. 0d. from Lord Nelson ", and there is no further mention of George at cards. On the 5th Chevalier and Gaetano left for Portsmouth with their master's heavy luggage, but George did not note this. The house was being turned upside down in preparation for the entertainment of royalty on the morrow.

The weather was foul on the morning appointed for the visit of the Duke of Clarence and a christening party. At 6 a.m., as the Admiral sat at his desk in his country study, a tremendous storm broke over southern England. It was still in progress when he set off for a council at Mr. Pitt's house, and another disagreeable circumstance disturbed his departure. A Mr. Brand who appeared asking to see him, and succeeded in doing so, turned out to be the apothecary who had attended the late Mr. Maurice Nelson. The intruder said that Lord Nelson's brother had died owing him £133 2s. 6d. Maurice's grave had settled sufficiently for a headstone to be set up three years past. All that a distressed man could do was to drop the bill at Davison's house in St. James's Square, on his way to Downing Street, with a line, asking his agent, on his return to London, to look into the claim, and if he found it just, give Mr. Brand his due.

That morning's session in Downing Street did not leave him entirely satisfied. Government had decided that the Combined Fleets must be held in Cadiz, or forced to fight if they attempted to leave. If the blockade could be made sufficiently strict, they would probably be obliged to put out very soon, for Cadiz was already short of food. As it was not known that Villeneuve's course had been taken contrary to orders from Paris, the Mediterranean was naturally suspected to be his object. It had been settled that Nelson was to go out at once, in the *Victory*, and that other ships should be sent to him as soon as they were ready. He wanted to do what he called " the job " well. Half a victory would not content him or the nation; but he did not believe that the Admiralty could, at the moment, with the best will in the world, give him a force within two-thirds of that likely to be encountered. " And therefore, if every Ship took her opponent, we should have to contend with a fresh Fleet of fifteen or sixteen Sail-of-the-line." As the storm receded and the sunlight of a thunderous day broadened across a table in Downing Street, an expert who had come amongst them like a thunderbolt, and whose speech had a tumbling, boyish eagerness, explained to statesmen of very grave countenance that " annihilation " should be their object. " It is, as Mr. Pitt knows, annihilation that the Country wants, and not merely a splendid victory of twenty-three to thirty-six—honourable to the parties concerned, but absolutely useless in the extended scale, to bring Buonaparte to his marrow-bones. . . ."

He had not been much impressed by the new Secretary of State for War, though Lord Castlereagh was lending an unexpectedly sympathetic ear to his suggestion that neutrals likely to victual the enemy in Cadiz should be seized and sent into Gibraltar. He thought Mr. Canning, another stranger, attractively able, " a very clever, deep-headed man ", but something in Canning seemed to arouse the baser competitive instincts. He believed that he had long out-grown his youthful hero-worship of Pitt, a great man who had never been of any use to him. A chance to dine at Walmer had been neglected, four years past. Yet, when it came to deciding, in a dark hour, in an uneasy capital, what it was that the nation needed, Mr. Pitt, ah! Pitt, was, after all, the only man. George Matcham, junior, sharply noticed that when his uncle recounted to a family party in the drawing-room at Merton the incidents of his last interviews in London, he seemed to take particular pleasure in the fact that " the Minister ", upon his rising, had himself escorted him out of the room and to his carriage. " I do not think he would have done so much for a Prince of the Blood."

George Rose, who was as close a friend as either man had, and combined that feat with complete avoidance of publicity, sometimes bewildered listeners by declaring that he had found Pitt and Nelson so much alike. They differed only, he would mournfully say, in one having been as highly educated as a man could be, and the other having been sent, like Mr. Rose himself, early to sea. In vain the burly, inexpressive President of the Board of Trade tried to explain, " These two great men died as they lived, for their Country." The phrase " Self is out of the question ", 28 which had begun to appear in Nelson's private letters during the " Long Chase ", recurred noticeably, with the addition of the word " entirely ", towards the end of the twenty-five days, when he was living at fever-heat, happier than ever before ; and a sensitive, sickly young literary aspirant was touched by the flame which Rose could not communicate. Charles Lamb, who had been much prejudiced against Lord Nelson, saw him on an early September morning, after his new command had been announced, walking in Pall Mall, " looking just as a Hero should look ", and confessed to having " followed him in fancy, ever since ". 29

Rose's regrets that one sent early to sea could not enjoy cultural advantages were echoed by Nelson this week. " But ", he said politely to the President of the Royal Academy, " there is one picture whose power I do feel. I never pass a print-shop where your ' Death of Wolfe ' is in the window, without being stopped by it." He also asked the Rev. Mr. Este, who was what he called " a clever literary man ", to supply some " old books " for his improvement during the forthcoming cruise. Mr. Este, apparently, complied tactfully, for a year later he wrote sadly to Charlotte Nelson, asking if just Boswell's *Life of Johnson* and the *Little Comedies of Foote* could be recovered from H.M.S. *Victory*. 30

George Matcham's entry for the 6th of September opened heavily : " Fished in the Pond. Caught nothing. Sauntered about ye Grounds." With his uncle's return from Downing Street the scene sprang into life : " H.R.H. the Duke of C(larence) din'd here. Like the King. Col. and Mrs. Suckling came here with their Child to be Christen'd. . . . Christening by Mr. Lancaster, H(orace) and Ld. N. Godfathers. Lady H. God Mother. Introduc'd to´ ye Duke of C(larence). Talked much. His deference to Ld. N.'s opinion. Violent against Mr. P(itt) ; found out the reason. Seem'd estrang'd from ye K(ing). Lord Errol with him. Heavy." Colonel and Mrs. Suckling's Child was indeed a child, for his public baptism had been postponed for two years, so that the principal sponsor could be present in person.

The young people of the family, according to another account,

had their meal at a separate table from royalty, and Lord Nelson
presented his nephews to the Duke with the words, " My three
props ! "   The Colonel was that son of Uncle Suckling of Hampstead who had received a loan of £300 from his hard-pressed
cousin in the dark winter of 1800, and a letter of recommendation
to the brother of the First Lord six months later. He was now
happy with a post in the Royal Household at Windsor and a
young *belle*, whose influential parents had violently objected to
the match, but had come round : and there was evidently full-
blooded merriment in the approaching Regency taste at the
christening feast, for in February 1806 Colonel Suckling (late of
the 3rd Dragoon Guards) wrote to inform the Duke of Clarence
that, agreeably to His Royal Highness's command of the 6th
of September last, at Merton, another boy had been born, upon
which the Duke replied that he could not face the repetition of a
scene which would arouse so many memories, but hoped " our
little friend ", his godson, would be given the names " William "
and " Nelson ".

On the following morning, from the Admiralty, Nelson
scratched a few lines to be sent off in a brig to the squadron
blockading Cadiz. " My dear Coll., I shall be with you in a very
few days, and I hope you will remain Second-in-Command. You
will change the *Dreadnought* for the *Royal Sovereign*, which I
hope you will like. . . ."

Next day, being Sunday, the whole Merton Place party went
again to church ; later Admiral Sir Sidney Smith called. He did
not neglect to refer to his famous defence of Acre, and young
George thought him handsome. Time and chance had elected
that Sidney Smith was to be constantly in Nelson's company at
the present crisis, for they met at the Admiralty next morning,
and dined, with a company described as "rich and fashionable ",
at the " Ship ", Greenwich.

The benevolent Abraham Goldsmid had kindly asked the
young people from Merton Place to spend the day at Morden
Hall while their elders were absent ; but young George was
ungrateful. " Went with Horace, Charlotte and Anne to Mr.
Goldsmids. . . . Fine house. Reminded me of the ' Citz Country
House '. Saw his sons. . . . After breakfast row'd in the Boat.
Horace show'd his Skill. Grounds poor. Very polite. Did
not like their dinner ; jewish. The Hall the height of the house,
very gaudy ; as are all the rooms, but tasteless. H(orace) cut his
jokes on me ; let him go on."

"His Lordship and the rest" returned late from London, and George's still pretty mother told him with pardonable pride that the Duke of Devonshire had complimented her on her youthful appearance.

On the forenoon of the 10th Nelson drove over to Richmond Park alone, in a shower, and Lord Sidmouth thereafter preserved "a little round study table" upon which his friend had shown him how he meant to attack the Combined Fleets if he should be so fortunate as to bring them to action. At dinner that day, at *33* the London house of the wealthy Mr. James Crawford, the hero checked Lady Hamilton when she wished him to tell the company of his having been "mobbed and huzza'd in the City". "Why," said she, "you like to be applauded—you cannot deny it." His reply was, "I own it", but he went on to say that no man ought to be too much elated by popular applause. "It may be my turn to feel the tide set against me." He said that he hoped to be home for Christmas, and that nothing short of annihilation of the enemy's fleet would do any good. He reckoned that France and Spain together had a hundred ships-of-the-line at their disposal. Someone asked, "How many have we in all?" but the baffling reply of an Admiral in great good humour was, "Oh! I do not count our Ships." *34*

Next morning the late Sir William Hamilton's connection, Mr. Beckford, presented himself at Merton. His invitations to stay at Fonthill having been refused, he had rushed up to London and taken rooms at a hotel, sooner than miss Lord Nelson. Young George was unimpressed. "Mr. Beckford din'd here. Talkative. Praised his own composition. Play'd extempore on the Harpsichord. Sung. I thought it a very horrible noise." Wednesday, September the 11th, was altogether an awkward day, for George's last entry noted, "H(orace) got into a Scrape."

The Boltons, taking with them all the nieces and nephews, were leaving for London the next morning. Nelson had asked his neighbours, the Perrys, and Lord Minto from town to dine, mentioning that he expected to be at home all day. He had already been obliged to give up this hope, in deference to a request from Lords Castlereagh and Mulgrave. At a late hour a special messenger brought a letter, couched in most flowery terms, from a Colonel Macmahon, summoning him to Carlton House. "H.R.H. the Prince of Wales who had come up from Weymouth specially, would feel miserable etc." The command was un- *35* welcome, but H.R.H. had graciously entreated Lord Nelson

Entrance gates onto Merton high-road, Merton Place, Surrey.

Sketch by Thomas Baxter. $(7\frac{1}{2}'' \times 5\frac{1}{4}''.)$

This water-colour sketch, which has never before been reproduced, shows the gates through which Nelson drove for the last time at half-past ten on the night of Friday, September 13, 1805.

Reproduced by kind permission of the Trustees, The National Maritime Museum, Greenwich.

to name his own hour, however early. The Duke of Queensberry offered the loan of a carriage, and next morning Lady Hamilton accompanied the guest of royalty, though not to Carlton House. She waited at Clarges Street while Nelson was wished God-speed by a Prince whose (indiscreetly repeated) careless mention, "how Lady Hamilton had struck his fancy", had driven a jealous lover nearly crazy in the winter of 1800. No record exists of the farewell extended by an Heir to the Throne who could assume a fascinating grand manner, to an officer whose attachment to the royal family was deeply rooted. The reason why the Admiral was late for dinner at Merton that day, however, is well documented.

As Lord Castlereagh was Secretary for War and the Colonies, the Colonial Office, Downing Street, was the *rendezvous* appointed by him, and on Nelson's arrival he was shown into a little waiting-room on the right of the hall, into which, presently, was ushered another gentleman. General the Hon. Sir Arthur Wellesley at once recognised Nelson, "from his likeness to his pictures, and the loss of an arm", but the Admiral saw in a high-nosed, haughty, curt military officer nothing but the embodiment of all he found unsympathetic in a Service of which he was critical. The officer of the Senior Service mentioned that the Cabinet had been sitting since 1 o'clock, discussing the instructions to be issued to him and to Sir Sidney Smith. "He entered at once into conversation with me", reported the General long afterwards. "If I can call it conversation, for it was almost all on his side, and all about himself, and in, really, a style so vain and silly as to surprise, and almost disgust me." Disgusted though Sir Arthur may have been, he took occasion to remark, with reference to Sir Robert Calder's recent action, "This measure of success won't do nowadays, for your Lordship has taught the public to expect something more brilliant." Nelson almost immediately left the room, evidently guessing " that I *was somebody* " and gone to inquire who, decided the General, whose story continues : " When he came back, he was altogether a different man, both in manner and matter." Having discovered that he was, by a lucky chance, alone with the Victor of Assaye, the Admiral lost no time in proposing to a brilliant young General that he should lead the troops for an investment of Sardinia. Sir Arthur replied that he " would rather not ", as he was only two days back from the East Indies, but during the long *tête-à-tête* which followed, entirely revised his opinion of Lord Nelson. " He talked like an officer and a statesman. The Secretary of State kept us long waiting, and certainly, for the last half or three quarters of an hour, I don't know that I ever had a conversation that interested me more. . . . He really was a very superior man."

At Merton, while an historic interview was taking place in a London waiting-room, Lord Nelson's guests also waited, but less enjoyably. The Perrys and Lord Minto, lacking a host and hostess, sat unintroduced. At length the welcome sound of wheels was heard, but their hopes were dashed by the entry of another lost soul, this time a large, odd clergyman. The Chaplain of the *Victory*, in good spirits, was able to tell them that he had just seen the Admiral, for a moment, after the council in Lord Mulgrave's office had broken up, and had been told by him to collect his luggage and get down to Merton. To young Dr. Lambton Este (who was going as one of the six secretaries with commissions from the Foreign Office to be carried in the *Victory*) his lordship had mentioned, " I have just settled your business with Lord Liverpool. I am now going to the Admiralty."

This sounded hopeless, but at last, two hours late, the master of the house walked into his drawing-room, and introduced his guests to one another, whereupon Lord Minto, in a flash, recollected, " Mr. Perry ! Editor of *The Morning Chronicle*, whom I formerly sent to the King's Bench, or Newgate, I think for six months, for a libel on the House of Lords." A gentleman of the robe, a man of the world, hastened to say how glad he was " to have the opportunity of shaking hands on our old warfare ", and an evening trembling on the brink of social disaster seemed about to recover, when tragedy re-entered in the person of Lady Hamilton. From her appearance it was at once clear that the last drive together had taken place. All Lord Minto's old aversion returned as he occupied the seat of honour next to a hostess who could not restrain large tears, " could not eat, and hardly drink, and near swooning, and all at table ". He stayed, however, until 10 o'clock before taking his final leave of a very old friend whose attachment to him was, he flattered himself, " little short of the other . . . and is quite sincere ".

Nelson's hours at Merton were now numbered. The last of the dramatic high-tensioned twenty-five days was come. The summer was waning. There was early mist, driven away by hot sun at midday, and in the kitchens of Merton talk of mushroom ketchup. On the morning of the 13th, when he presented himself for his accustomed before-breakfast tour of his property, Thomas

Cribb made so bold as to impart, " some private family news ".
The Admiral congratulated an anxious dependant, and gave him
an extra tip, " to buy a Christening frock ", adding his favourite,
" If it's a boy, call him Horatio, if a girl, Emma." Cribb's
future son-in-law, Hudson, with some of the garden lads, watched,
with the realisation that he was witnessing something he would
remember all his life, a post-chaise summoned from the " King's
Head " dash up to the front door, and the master embark, " To
get his final sailing orders from the Admiralty ", the boy believed.

Nelson returned to dine with Lady Hamilton, and with the
Matchams, who had stayed to the last in a house suddenly and
noticeably quiet. Seated in the drawing-room, his relatives
listened to the arrival of the vehicle which was to carry the
Admiral through the night to Portsmouth. When they heard
him coming downstairs alone, George Matcham arose, and prepared to attend him, in dreadful silence, to the front door. The
heart of the accomplished civilian was too full for words, but
Nelson, up to the moment that they grasped hands, was speaking
cheerfully, only regretting that he had not, so far, been able to
repay the £4,000 which he had borrowed from his brother-in-law,
to buy Axe's field. George Matcham found his voice, to reply,
" My dear Lord, I have no other wish than to see you return
home in safety. As to myself, I am not in want of anything."

One of Nelson's last acts before this scene had been a visit
of farewell to the bedside of Horatia. The country September
night was advanced; a child in its fifth year had been deeply
asleep for hours. Touched by a sight always awe-inspiring,
even to a happy parent, he fell upon his knees, and prayed that
the life of Horatia might be happy. A prayer which he entered
in his private diary, later that night, while horses were being
changed, probably at Guildford, was copied by Dr. Scott:

" Friday night, at half-past ten, drove from dear, dear Merton, where
I left all which I hold dear in this world, to go to serve my king and
country. May the great God whom I adore, enable me to fulfill the
expectations of my country; and if it is His good pleasure that I should
return, my thanks will never cease being offered up to the throne of His
mercy. If it is His good Providence to cut short my days upon earth,
I bow with the greatest submission, relying that He will protect those so
dear to me, that I may leave behind. His will be done. Amen. Amen.
Amen."

CHAPTER XIX

1805
(*ætat* 47)

TRAFALGAR

" I can never hear the name of Nelson without tears coming into my eyes—such genius, such courage, so transcendent a fate " (A. L. Rowse, *A Cornish Childhood*).

I

He drank tea, by candlelight, at the " Anchor ", Liphook, and arrived at the familiar " George ", Portsmouth, at 6 a.m. on the morning of September 14. Outside its doors he saw the carriage of the Vicar of Merton, who had just parted with a fourteen-year-old son, going as a volunteer, first-class, to the *Victory*, and Mr. Lancaster waited while the Admiral dashed off four lines, opening, " My dearest most beloved of Women, Nelson's Emma ! " Within the hostelry he found visitors from London, come to see the last of him. George Rose was attended by Mr. Canning, almost a stranger, but newly appointed Treasurer to the Navy. George Murray, detained by business cares upon the death of a parent, had sent him a letter of deep regret, and a haunch of venison. After breakfasting, he went to the Dockyard, to pay his formal call upon jolly old Commissioner Saxton. He learnt from the Captains of the *Royal Sovereign*, *Defiance* and *Agamemnon* that their ships were at Spithead, but not yet ready for sea, and as he hoped to sail with a fair wind that evening, he gave instructions that they were to follow him, with the greatest expedition possible, to a secret *rendezvous*. The Captains of two further ships-of-the-line, refitting at Plymouth, were sent orders to put to sea as soon as they were provisioned for six months. A frigate stationed off Cape St. Vincent should tell them where he was to be found. If after cruising twenty-four hours they failed to find her, they must call at Cape St. Mary's and Cadiz, approaching these places with the utmost caution.

Sir Isaac Coffin and Captain Conn accompanied him back to the inn in the High Street. Towards noon he had despatched all necessary business on shore. The day was a Saturday, and the streets, already full, were likely to become much fuller; indeed, since his arrival had become known, an expectant crowd had swelled outside the "George". He decided to embark from the beach at Southsea, at the place where the bathing-machines were drawn up, immediately behind the Assembly Rooms, and quitted the "George" inconspicuously by its narrow, stone-flagged back entrance. Even so, he was quickly recognised, and enthusiasts, running ahead, spread the news of his altered route and approach by Penny Street and Green Row. He pushed his way through a pressing multitude, in good vein, explaining that he was sorry he had not two arms, so that he could shake hands with more friends, and it was soon evident that his Portsmouth following felt more poignantly than the admirers who had mobbed him daily in London. As his figure came in sight, some people dropped to their knees in silence, uncovered and called out a blessing on him; tears ran down many faces. The crowd, encroaching upon the parapet to watch him embark, pushed aside the sentries and threatened to get out of hand: a military officer who gave orders for its repulse with bayonets was himself obliged to beat a retreat. After the Admiral's barge had pushed off, many persons swarmed into the water, and he acknowledged greetings by waving his hat. He turned to Hardy, as the regular dip of oars gained pre-eminence over Portsmouth cheers on an afternoon of flat calm, and said, "I had their huzzas before. I have their hearts now."

The *Victory*, lying at single anchor at St. Helens, was the scene of much picturesque activity. As the wind had died, the politicians from London were invited to dine. George Rose, impressed by the ceremonious elegance of his entertainment, was surprised to hear that Lord Nelson was not a rich man, and departed muttering that "he would tell the whole". He had deemed the moment unsuitable for asking if his friend had found time to sit for a portrait by Edridge. He had been disconcerted by the almost testamentary urgence with which Nelson had recommended to his protection the cases of a brother-in-law, Mr. Bolton, and the Rev. Mr. Scott. Taking his statesman friend aside after the meal, Nelson had also entreated him again, with great earnestness, to approach the Prime Minister on the subject of Lady Hamilton's pension, and this Rose, having promised to do, did attempt within the next few days, though without conclusive result.

Next morning at 8 a.m. the *Victory* weighed, with light airs, and made sail to the S.S.E., having only Blackwood's frigate in company. There had been time for a boat to come off to the flagship and an express from Merton to be brought on board. Nelson replied :

> "Off Dunnose, Sept. 16th.
> 1805. 11 a.m.

" My beloved Emma,
" I cannot even read your letter. We have fair wind, and God will, I hope, soon grant us a happy meeting. The wind is quite fair and fresh. We go too swift for the boat. May Heaven bless you, and Horatia, with all those who hold us dear to them, for a short time, farewell,

> "Ever yours,
> "Nelson and Brontë."   𝟜

2

The almost solitary progress of the *Victory* towards Cape Trafalgar was stately in pace. The Dorset and Devon coastline, in September weather, slowly altered. Such fashionable watering-places as Lyme and Torquay had suddenly filled. For some weeks there had been rumours that the army for the Invasion of England was going to be used against Austria. Already a great part of it had been set on the march to the Rhine. Buonaparte had broken up his camp at Boulogne.

Shortly after Nelson had scribbled his first note of the 16th, the wind came foul, and for an anxious hour he found himself likely to be blown into Weymouth, " the place of all others I should wish to avoid ". Their Majesties and the Princesses were established at Gloucester Lodge, Weymouth, on their annual sea-bathing holiday, and he had no desire to present himself at a Court which had spurned Lady Hamilton, and since he had become her champion, so markedly ceased to show favour or bestow honours, that his neighbour, Perry, had been with difficulty restrained from a typically imprudent article in *The Morning Chronicle* on that subject. " I hope to escape without anchoring," he wrote in disquiet, " but should I be forced, I shall act as a man, and your Nelson, neither courting or ashamed to hold up my head before the greatest monarch in the world. I have, thank God," he ended unhappily, " nothing to be ashamed of."   5

By dint of perseverance, Weymouth was avoided, and he was able to inform Davison, in a further private letter of that after-noon, dated " Off Portland ", " My fate is fixed, and I am gone, and beating down Channel with a foul wind." (He had not been able, during the twenty-five days, to fulfil his often-made promise of taking Davison by the hand in St. James's Square.

On his release from his year of detention, a temporarily extinguished man had fled to the solitudes of his Northumberland
property, and there stayed; but up to a few days before
Trafalgar, Nelson continued to send long confidential screeds to
Swarland Hall.) A Torbay boat got alongside during the nasty
blowing night of the 16th and received a letter addressed to
Lady Hamilton, and the lordly tip of half a guinea for putting it
in the post. " I intreat, my dear Emma, that you will cheer up;
and we will look forward to many, many happy years, and be
surrounded by our children's children. God Almighty can, when
He pleases, remove the impediment." At Plymouth, in very
dirty weather, he signalled the two 74's waiting there to join him.
He doubted their ability to obey, but they succeeded in doing
so, off the Lizard, when it had fallen nearly calm. Two mornings
later, thirty leagues S.W. of the Scillies, his glass showed him a
frigate coming down to his little squadron. She was guessed to
be the *Decade*, from the fleet off Cadiz, bringing home, sick, his
old Second in the Mediterranean, and at 1.30 p.m. the *Victory*
hove to, and Sir Richard Bickerton came on board, very unwell,
but with the reassuring news that no battle had as yet been
fought by Admiral Collingwood. After forty minutes the *Victory*
made sail again, the *Decade* resumed her swift passage home, and
the *Euryalus* was sent on ahead with letters to the British Consul
at Lisbon, to Admiral Collingwood and to Captain Sutton, urging
them to secure every man possible, in every way, for the fleet,
and on no account to mention Lord Nelson's approach or acknowledge his arrival. " I would not have you salute even if you are
out of sight of land."

On the 25th, with sunset, the Captain of the *Constance*, steering
for the mouth of the Tagus, took charge of a letter opening, " My
dearest Emma,—We are now in sight of the Rock of Lisbon, and
although we have very little wind, I hope to get round Cape St.
Vincent to-morrow. We have had only one day's real fair wind,
but by perseverance we have done much. I am anxious to join
the fleet, for it would add to my grief if any other man was to give
them the Nelson touch, which WE say is warranted never to fail."

His anxieties were brought to an end on the 28th. Dawn of
that morning displayed a British bomb-ketch cruising. By noon
the prospect included eighteen of the line. In a warmer dusk
than he had recently experienced, with a breeze that carried the
scent of orange-groves to sea, he " got fairly into the fleet ", and
could make out, in Cadiz harbour, thirty-six enemy men-of-war

"looking me in the face; unfortunately there is a strip of land between us, but it is believed they will come to sea in a few days. The sooner the better." He could not communicate with Collingwood until the next morning. It was his birthday. He was forty-seven. He had been enthusiastically greeted before, when taking over a command, but on this occasion, in obedience to his orders, in silence; and the omission of customary salutes and hoisting of colours, at a moment when a fleet action was hourly expected, was recognised by all who took part as dramatic.

The rule of Collingwood had not been inspiring. Facing thirty enemy ships with twenty-two, he had imposed all the most disagreeable features of St. Vincent's iron *régime*. No visiting had been allowed, except on strict duty. Though country vessels from the North African coast came into his fleet often, the order was that no boats could be hoisted out, so no fresh food could be bought. "For Charity's sake", prayed Captain Edward Codrington of the *Orion*, who had never seen the hero, "send us Lord Nelson, ye men of power!" His first interview with the new Chief sealed the allegiance of this officer, for a much hoped-for letter from Mrs. Codrington was produced with the courtly comment that as this had been entrusted by a lady, the messenger was making a point of delivering it personally. "The signal has been made this morning", wrote a correct young man whose domestic affairs were in good order, "for all of us who did not dine on board the *Victory* yesterday, to go there to-day. What our late Chief will think of this I do not know; but I well know what the Fleet will think of the difference; and even you, our good wives, who have some causes of disapprobation, will allow the superiority of Nelson in all these social arrangements which bind his captains to their Admiral. The signal is made that boats may be hoisted out to buy fruit, stock, or anything. This, I trust, will be a common signal hereafter, but it is the first day I have seen it made." Captain Pulteney Malcolm of the *Donegal*, who knew both Wellington and Nelson intimately, afterwards assured inquirers that "Nelson was the man to *love*". Captain George Duff of the *Mars*, also writing to a good wife, reported on October 1, "Dined with his Lordship yesterday, and had a very merry dinner. He certainly is the pleasantest Admiral I ever served under", and three days before Trafalgar, "You ask me about Nelson, and how I like him. I have already answered that question as every person must do that ever served under him."

Fifteen commanding officers dined on board the *Victory* on the

Admiral's birthday, and as many on the succeeding day. On the third night after his arrival, " my dear Coll.", now his second-in-command of a fleet " as perfect as could be expected ", and Fremantle, another close personal friend, were tactfully entertained as sole guests. With Collingwood his line was, " Telegraph on all occasions, without ceremony. We are one, and I hope ever shall be. . . . Everybody in England admired your adroitness in not being forced unnecessarily into the Straits." To Fremantle he delivered a letter, asking first, " Would you have a Girl or a Boy? " The Captain of the *Neptune*, who already had two offspring of each sex, replied, " A girl ", and was smilingly told to " be satisfied ". The note from Mrs. Fremantle's sister announced the safe arrival of " Louisa ". The dinner-party broke up at 8 o'clock, after which the guests were carried to witness a theatrical performance in the flagship, in which the seaman taking the chief female part (much dressed) was somewhat cruelly convincing. The night was very warm, and Fremantle retired to sleep with all windows and doors open, happy that he had been promised " my old place in the Line of Battle, which is *his second* ". Nelson slept well until 4 a.m., when, to his disgust, he was woken by " one of my dreadful spasms ". In vain he had recounted his symptoms to physicians of repute. Mr. Beatty, no courtier, diagnosed them as characteristic of nothing worse than indigestion, and the sufferer had to admit, " I had been writing seven hours, yesterday." His own impressions of an arrival described by Codrington as " causing a general joy in the Fleet " are available from two sources. Lady Hamilton was told on October 1 :

" I believe my arrival was most welcome, not only to the Commander of the Fleet, but almost to every individual in it ; and, when I came to explain to them the ' *Nelson touch* ', it was like an electric shock. Some shed tears, all approved—' It was new—it was singular—it was simple ! ' and, from Admirals downwards, it was repeated—' It must succeed, if ever they will allow us to get at them ! You are, my Lord, surrounded by friends, whom you inspire with confidence.' Some may be Judas's ; but the majority are certainly much pleased with my commanding them."

A modestly anonymous officer afterwards communicated to *The Naval Chronicle* an historic note to him, dated October 3 :

" The reception I met with on joining the Fleet caused the sweetest sensation of my life. The Officers who came on board to welcome my return, forgot my rank as Commander-in-Chief in the enthusiasm with

R R

which they greeted me. As soon as these emotions were past, I laid
before them the Plan I had previously arranged for attacking the
Enemy; and it was not only my pleasure to find it generally approved,
but clearly perceived and understood."   10

The Plan of Attack expounded to his Captains at once on his
arrival was formally issued to them in a secret memorandum on
October 9, and in it are to be found the essential ideas eventually
adapted to suit the conditions at Trafalgar.   11

3

" The whole system here is so completely changed ", wrote
Fremantle on October 6, " that it wears quite a different aspect.
We are continually with something to change the scene, and know
precisely how far we may go, which is very pleasant."

Nelson had found the fleet stationed some fifteen to twenty
miles from Cadiz, and getting very short of water and provisions.
As soon as possible he moved it to fifty miles west of the port, in
order to give the enemy encouragement to come out (while
remaining in ignorance how far he was being silently reinforced),
and he ordered Admiral Louis, with six of the line, to Gibraltar
and Tetuan. An old Crocodile departed reproachfully. " You
are sending us away, my Lord—the Enemy will come out, and
we shall have no share in the Battle." Nelson readily explained
that he had no choice but to send his ships to water and provision
in detachments, and, " I send you first, to insure your being here
to help to beat them." But Louis had prophesied correctly.

An advanced squadron of fast-sailing 74's was thrown out, ten
to twelve miles east of the fleet, and a squadron of frigates, under
Blackwood, cruised indefatigably close to the harbour's mouth.
Still the Chief was beset with fears that the enemy might slip out,
in thick weather, and get into the Mediterranean. He dictated
letters to the Secretary to the Admiralty, to Lord Barham and to
Lord Castlereagh asking for " more *eyes*. . . . The last Fleet was
lost to me for want of Frigates : God forbid this should." He
wrote confidentially to Rose, to ask if Mr. Pitt could be prevailed
upon to drop a hint to the First Lord that the Prime Minister
would be very uneasy until the necessary forces reached Lord
Nelson. Meanwhile, he warned Blackwood : " Let me know
every movement. I rely on you that we can't miss getting hold
of them. Watch all points, and all winds and weather, for I
shall depend upon you."

On the 5th he learnt that the enemy in Cadiz were getting

their troops on board, and that the Spanish squadron of seven of the line at Cartagena had their topsails up, all of which sounded as if a junction was intended. Four days later all the Cadiz fleet but one had moved out of the Puerto Real and had bent their top-gallant sails. Nelson believed that Decrès, the Minister of Marine, was to take the command, but actually the tragic Villeneuve had received orders from Buonaparte, on September 28, to return to Toulon (after ranging along the Italian coast), and goaded by threats that he would be superseded if he did not put to sea, was preparing to do so. A report of the arrival of Louis's squadron at Gibraltar encouraged, and the news, on October 18, that his successor had reached Madrid, decided him. The Combined Fleet under his command consisted of fifteen Spaniards of the line, four of them three-deckers mounting 100 to 130 guns, four French 80-gun ships and fourteen 74's, five frigates and two gun brigs, all French. Of Nelson's twenty-seven ships, seven were three-deckers, of 98 to 100 guns, one was an 80-gun ship, sixteen were 74's and three 64's. But at a council of war called by Villeneuve, a unanimous resolution had been passed to avoid an action if possible.

A delicate and unpleasant task entrusted to Nelson by the First Lord in London was tackled without delay. Rear-Admiral Sir Robert Calder had gone afloat when his present Chief was one year old, and was very generally believed to have been inimical to a brilliant junior since the Battle of St. Vincent. At an early stage during his first interview with Sir Robert, to whom he was empowered to communicate the deep dissatisfaction of H.M. Government with his conduct in the engagement with the Allied Fleets in July, Nelson found that Calder had already written home, in complete confidence, to ask for an inquiry which must in any case be ordered. When Sir Robert discovered that he was, by their Lordships' instructions, to be sent home in a fast frigate— "turned out of my Ship . . . in the face of the Fleet"—the scene became distressing. A highly indignant man, entirely ignorant of the popular clamour which had forced the hand of a Government new in office, broke down so pitiably that Nelson decided to depart from the letter of his instructions, and as soon as the *Royal Sovereign* (another three-decker) joined, allow Sir Robert to go home in his own ship. " He is in adversity, and if he has ever been my enemy, he now feels the pang of it, and finds me one of his best friends." A fortnight's inevitable harassing delay followed, and when the expected reinforcement did arrive,

Nelson, sobered by the prospect of depriving his fleet of a 90-gun
ship which might be essential in an action, reconsidered an offer
made under the stress of emotion.   But four letters marked   *13*
" Private " from an afflicted brother-officer, all delivered within
twenty-four hours, held him to his original resolution, and Sir
Robert departed, a week before Trafalgar, taking with him
H.M.S. *Prince of Wales* and the Captains of two other ships-of-
the-line to give evidence on his behalf.   A third officer, having
discovered that the Admiralty order said that Captains were to
go home only " if willing ", was not willing, was wounded at
Trafalgar, and as eventually the court-martial did not sit until
Christmas week, 1805, was present to witness Sir Robert found
guilty of an error of judgment and severely reprimanded.

Amongst other cares during the first days of October, a
Levanter was hindering Nelson from clearing his transports.
" I am ", he explained in a letter to Ball, " not come forth to
find difficulties, but to remove them."   At the head of his list of
difficulties awaiting removal were the facts that his second-in-
command did not fancy his new ship or his Flag-Captain.
Collingwood had been promised that he would find the *Royal
Sovereign* better than the *Victory*, but he knew that she was
noted for her dull-sailing qualities, and had been christened by
the Channel Fleet " the West Country Waggon ".   Upon making
her acquaintance, however, he discovered that, as she had just
been re-coppered, the nickname was now a libel.   With regard
to Captain Rotherham, he was simply reminded that " in the
presence of the enemy, all Englishmen should be as brothers ",
and told " of course " to bring his Flag-Captain with him when
asked to dine quietly with the Chief.   To the officer commanding
the look-out frigates, who was becoming touchy upon this wearing
duty, Nelson sent two up-to-date newspapers (" I stole them
for you ") and the suggestion, " Do not, my dear Blackwood,
be angry with anyone.   It was only a laudable anxiety in Admiral
Louis, and nothing like complaining."   Admiral Knight, who
(as grave witnesses were eager to attest) had " almost made us
quarrel with the Moors of Barbary " at a most unsuitable moment,
received a comradely reminder, " In our several stations, my
dear Admiral, we must all put our shoulders to the wheel, and
make the great machine of the Fleet intrusted to our charge, go
on smoothly."   By ill chance, the Agent-Victualler at Gibraltar,
inured to dealing with crafty Tetuan, was ill.   The resourceful
Mr. Ford, Agent-Victualler Afloat, was speedily despatched to a

troublesome quarter towards which Louis's hungry squadron was
fast approaching, and was amply provided " with money to put
us right again " and private instructions " not to be *penny*
wise and *pounds* foolish ".

A strong letter must be sent to Lord Strangford, Minister
at Lisbon, complaining of the hostile attitude of the Portuguese
Government to H.M. ships. . . . The Sick and Hurt Department
had forwarded returns which were clearly ridiculous; the Dis-
penser was asking for a survey, and the Surgeon had sent what
Admiral Collingwood found " a very improper letter ". . . .
The troubles bred by young blood were also not absent, and a
particularly painful case needed instant attention. The First
Lieutenant of the *Hydra* was adrift in Italy, most probably in
prison by now. He had bolted with a ballet-dancer from Valetta.
The boy's father, an excellent officer, had offered to pay a
trail of debts, supposed to be about £200 or £300. If a few more
pounds were necessary, Lord Nelson would be answerable. " All
we want is to save him from perdition. . . ." The Chief had
just sat down to dinner on the 17th when a good digestive in the
shape of a weighty packet from his second-in-command was
delivered. The Consul at Lisbon and a Captain Dunbar had
apparently long been conducting a violent correspondence on the
subject of supplies to the fleet. Picking his way through the
papers that night, it appeared to Lord Nelson that the Captain of
the *Poulette* had acted very incorrectly throughout and should be
censured, and Mr. Gambier perfectly, until the moment that he
lost his temper.

All the routine business of the Mediterranean Command
remained to be dealt with by a man expecting a fleet action
" every day, hour and moment ". He sent a silky intimation
of his appointment to his old antagonist, the Dey of Algiers
(" I think your Highness will be glad to hear of my return to the
command of His Majesty's Fleets in the Mediterranean "), and
commiserated with her distressed Majesty of Naples, her now
inveterate foe, Sir John Acton, and H.E. Hugh Elliot, whose
recall was likely.

On the night of the 10th, as he concluded the dictation of
the last of two dozen essential letters, heavy rain began to fall,
to the irritation of many officers who had been engaged for the
past week scraping their ships and repainting them *à la Nelson*,
that is to say, in imitation of H.M.S. *Victory*, with black bands
between the varnish-yellow of the gun decks, and black ports,

so that, with closed ports, the ship presented a chequered appearance. Five ships-of-the-line had now joined him from home,   ¹⁴
and one from Gibraltar. On the morning of the 13th, when
H.M.S. *Agamemnon* and the frigate *Amiable* were signalled, he
was noticed to rub his " fin " and exclaim : " Here comes Berry !
Now we shall have a battle."   Young Sir Edward, the stormy
petrel of the Service, who had already seen seven general actions,
had a tale to unfold. He had been chased, and all but taken, by
the Rochefort squadron, when eight days out from Plymouth.
He brought English newspapers, in one of which Lord Nelson
found that General Mack was to be given the command of the
Austrian forces in Germany. After reading this, he prophesied,
" I know General Mack too well. He sold the King of Naples.
If he is now intrusted with an important command, he will
certainly betray the Austrian monarchy."   His warning to the
Duke of Clarence on the subject of this character, before he left
England, had been in terms which would be appreciated by
that blunt brother-officer.   " If your Royal Highness has any
communication with Government, let not General Mack be
employed.   For I knew him at Naples to be a rascal, a scoundrel
and a coward."

That night he drew his Chief Surgeon apart and asked him
" how long he thought it would be before Captain Hardy was
perfectly recovered ".   Upon Mr. Beatty's reply " he hoped not
more than a fortnight ", " Ah ! " smiled his lordship, " before
a fortnight, the Enemy will be at sea ; the business will be done,
and we shall be looking out for England."   Actually, only six
further days of waiting remained.

On the night of the 18th he noted in his private memorandum
book, " Fine weather, wind easterly. The Combined Fleets
cannot have finer weather to put to sea."   Next morning he
wrote to Collingwood, " What a beautiful day ! Will you be
tempted out of your Ship ? If so, hoist the assent, and *Victory's*
pendants."   On the back of this sheet Collingwood afterwards
added, " Before the answer to this letter had got to the *Victory*,
the signal was made that the Enemy's Fleet was coming out of
Cadiz, and we chased immediately."

The Combined Fleets of France and Spain had begun to get
under way at 7 a.m., but, from want of wind, only twelve ships
effected their exit that day. A breeze from the W.N.W. sprang
up during the afternoon, and they stood on the larboard tack to
the northward, dogged by two British frigates. During the

interval before the news raced from masthead to masthead, "The Enemy's Fleet is at sea", Nelson retired to his cabin to begin a letter.

"My Dearest beloved Emma, the dear friend of my bosom,
"The Signal has been made that the Enemy's Combined fleet are coming out of Port. We have very little Wind, so that I have no hopes of seeing them before to-morrow. May the God of Battles crown my endeavours with success, at all events I will take care that my name shall ever be most dear to you and Horatia, both of whom I love as much as my own life, and as my last writing before the Battle will be to you, so I hope in God that I shall live to finish my letter after the Battle. May Heaven bless you prays your
15   "Nelson and Bronte."

A letter to Horatia, opening "My dearest Angel", and signed "your Father", was dated the same day. Other officers who had given hostages to fortune seized a last chance to set down home-thoughts. In the *Euryalus*, Blackwood was writing to his lady:

"What think you, my dearest love? At this moment the Enemy are coming out, and as if determined to have a fair fight. All night they have been making signals, and the morning showed them to us getting under sail. They have 34 Sail-of-the-Line, and five Frigates. Lord Nelson, I am sorry to say, has but 27 Sail-of-the-Line with him; the rest are at Gibraltar, getting water. . . . Within two hours, though our Fleet was at sixteen leagues off, I have let Lord N. know of their coming out. . . . At this moment we are within four miles of the Enemy, and
16   talking to Lord Nelson by means of Sir H. Popham's signals. You see also, my Harriet, I have time to write to you and to assure you that to the last moment of my breath, I shall be as much attached to you as man can be. . . . It is very odd how I have been dreaming all night of my carrying home dispatches. God send so much good luck! The day is
17   fine, the sight of course beautiful, though so distant."

Captain Duff, of the *Mars*, who had taken his thirteen-year-old son, Norwich, to sea, wrote:

"My dearest Sophia,
"I have just time to tell you we are going into Action with the Combined Fleet. I hope and trust in God that we shall all behave as become us, and that I may yet have the happiness of taking my beloved wife and children in my arms. Norwich is quite well and happy, I have, however, ordered him off the quarter-deck.
18   "Yours ever, and most truly."

Blackwood's dream was to come true, but Duff, like his Chief, had written his last letter.

4

Daylight of October 20 found the British fleet close to the mouth of the Straits, in heavy rain and thick weather. These were the waters in which Howe, homeward bound after succouring the Rock, had encountered the fleet of Spain, in 1782, and nine years past Nelson had rescued Hardy. Through the sea-mist, at intervals, could be seen, upon the eastern horizon, the towering cliffs of Cape Trafalgar (which the learned and reverend Mr. Scott afterwards insisted should be pronounced with the accent on the third syllable, and when sharp Mr. Canning asked whether the same applied to Gibraltar, answered simply, " Yes ").   *19*

There was no sign of the Combined Fleet on this Sunday morning of 1805, so the fleet made sail to the N.W., and presently a signal from the *Phœbe* told that the enemy still lay to the north. The *Victory* hove to, and Collingwood, with Captains Duff, Hope and Morris (all commanding swift-sailing 74's), came on board for an hour, after which the fleet made all sail to the N.W., and Nelson added a paragraph to his sheet of yesterday, saying that the wind had not come far enough to the westward to allow the enemy to weather the shoals of Cape Trafalgar, and he feared that they might return into Cadiz harbour. During the morning, however, the horizon cleared, the wind shifted, and Blackwood telegraphed that nineteen, twenty-five and at length thirty-four enemy sail were out of port. " The enemy appear determined to push to the westward." " That ", wrote Nelson in his diary, " they shall not do, if in the power of Nelson and Brontë to prevent them ", and he replied, " I rely on your keeping sight of the enemy."

He was continually on the *Victory's* poop while Blackwood was communicating, and mentioned to a group of midshipmen there assembled, " This day, or to-morrow, will be a fortunate one for you young gentlemen." At dinner he stated that he expected to capture twenty to twenty-two of the hostile fleet, and Dr. Scott heard him say, more than once, " The 21st will be our day ", adding that it was the anniversary of a festival in his family.

It gradually became evident that October 20 was not to be the day. During the afternoon Nelson signalled two ships which had recently joined him from England to paint the hoops of their masts yellow. All his other ships were so painted, and black was, he knew, the colour used by the enemy. He issued his orders for signals during the hours of darkness. " If the

Enemy are standing to the Southward, or towards the Straits, burn two blue lights together, every hour, in order to make the greater blaze. If the Enemy are standing to the Westward, three guns, quick, every hour." Blackwood, according to his instructions, was keeping two frigates in sight of the enemy, and a further couple between them and Hope's 74-gun ship. From the *Defence*, signals were repeated to the *Colossus*, stationed between the *Defence* and *Mars*, whence Duff communicated with the *Victory*. At 8 p.m. the British fleet wore, and stood to the S.W. At midnight the frigates closest to the enemy could see, upon one side, the glow of lamps from the stern-cabin windows of thirty-three men-of-war, on the other only scattered lights.

The date October 21 was written down, and a little before dawn the English fleet, hitherto sailing almost parallel to the enemy, though out of sight, again altered course. Nelson, considering that he had drawn his prey far enough out of Cadiz, had turned to the N.E. as a preliminary to attack.

Since the beautiful morning of the 19th the weather had broken. Throughout the night of the 20th there had been but light breezes, inclining to calm, and the same conditions, prevailing at daybreak, were to last the day; but there was also a heavy swell from the westward, which might herald a storm. At a chilly hour, Collingwood's steward, entering his master's cabin with a light, found him already up and dressing. The Admiral asked, in greeting, whether his servant had seen the enemy, and upon receiving a startled reply, advised him to take a look out. The man obeyed, and beheld with awe, through puffing mist, " a crowd of great ships " some ten miles to the leeward. But upon glancing from this array to Nelson's second-in-command, calmly continuing to shave his regular features, in mixed poor light, while murmuring that " In a short time we shall see a great deal more of them ", he loyally decided that the spectacle in a British first-rate was the more inspiring. Alone of Collingwood's personal servants he was to survive this day. Collingwood, on the morning of a day when he was " to fight like an Angel ", was distinguished by composure and terse speech. Upon the arrival of his First Lieutenant, he advised Mr. Clavell to follow his example, and change his boots for shoes and silk stockings— " so much more manageable for the surgeon ". His Flag-Captain, north-country Captain Rotherham, who accompanied him as he visited the decks of the *Royal Sovereign*, was a dazzling sight in full-dress uniform. Rotherham said that he had always fought in his cocked hat, and always would.

Lord Nelson was observed upon the quarter-deck of the *Victory* with first daylight. He was wearing the same undress uniform coat which he had commonly worn since he left Portsmouth, and shoes and stockings as usual, but for the first time when expecting an action, no sword. His sword had been taken from its rack in his cabin, but left lying on a table. The coat was far from new, and its skirts were lined with white shalloon, not silk; but upon its left breast were embroidered the stars of the four Orders of Knighthood to which he was entitled. Mr. Beatty, representing several officers, expressed to the two Scotts the wish that someone might suggest to his lordship to cover his decorations with a handkerchief. The enemy were believed to have Tyrolean riflemen dispersed amongst their ships and were likely to have sharpshooters in their tops. Both the public and private secretary were certain that their employer would be highly displeased if anyone took the liberty of suggesting to him that he should make any alteration in his uniform on such an account, so Beatty took what he felt to be a duty upon himself, saying that he would make an opportunity when presenting his Sick Report for the day. He hung about, but the Admiral was at first closely engaged, giving instructions to his frigate Captains, and a few minutes before the enemy opened fire, ordered all persons not stationed on the quarter-deck or poop to get to their proper quarters. Hardy had been approached, however, and after the firing had begun, as he paced by Nelson's side, he mentioned that conspicuous decorations might draw enemy attention to the figure of the British Chief, and Nelson agreed that they might, but said, " it was now too late to be shifting a coat ".

22

The signal guns, rockets and Bengal fires of the British fleet had made Villeneuve aware, overnight, of their immediate neighbourhood, and before daylight his five squadrons had received the order to form in close line of battle on the starboard tack. As the British advanced, in greater numbers than he had expected, and he saw that, in very light westerly breeze prevailing, it was impossible to avoid an action, he decided to lay his ships' heads in the direction of Cadiz, and at a little after 6 a.m. made the signals to wear all together and form line of battle on the port tack. This manœuvre was not accomplished until about 10 a.m., and then most irregularly, the ships, in some cases three abreast, drifting rather than sailing into a curve about five miles long, stretching from north to south.

The *Victory's* first general signal of the day, made at 6.40, to form the order of sailing in two columns, each ship to engage her opponent, was followed after ten minutes by " Bear up, and steer east ". The Commander-in-Chief, leading the twelve ships of the northern or weather column, at once set the example, and Collingwood's southern or leeward division of fifteen ships fell into the wake of the *Royal Sovereign*. At 8 a.m. three junior frigate Captains came on board the *Victory*. Dr. Scott and Mr. Beatty at dawn had noticed that " his Lordship displayed excellent spirits ". Blackwood, who as senior frigate Captain had been summoned before 6, found him " in calm but very good spirits ". There is evidence from every eyewitness that he was in the taut, omniscient state common to him on such occasions. After receiving Blackwood's compliments on the approach of a long-looked-for hour, he briskly explained, " I mean to-day to bleed the captains of the Frigates, as I shall keep you on board until the very last minute."

Five months previously, writing to Lady Hamilton on his homeward passage from the West Indies, he had told her : " I have sent two Codicils, in which you are deeply interested, to Mr. Haslewood, to be placed with my Will and other Codicils, for if I kept them on board ship they might be lost, and then you and Horatia would not get what I intend, which would embitter my last moments." After a few minutes' professional conversation with Blackwood, he now asked him, together with Hardy, to witness his signature. The long document in his own hand, which he had achieved after his view of the enemy with dawn, has always been styled his " last Codicil ", though that word nowhere occurs in it.

" October the twenty-first, one thousand eight hundred and five, then in sight of the Combined Fleets of France and Spain, distant about ten miles.

" Whereas the eminent services of Emma Hamilton, widow of the Right Honourable Sir William Hamilton, have been of the very greatest service to our King and Country, to my knowledge, without her receiving any reward from either our King or Country ;—first, that she obtained the King of Spain's letter, in 1796, to his brother, the King of Naples, acquainting him of his intention to declare War against England ; from which letter the Ministry sent out orders to then Sir John Jervis, to strike a stroke, if opportunity offered, against either the Arsenals of Spain, or her Fleets. That neither of these was done is not the fault of

Lady Hamilton. The opportunity might have been offered. Secondly,
the British Fleet under my command, could never have returned the
second time to Egypt, had not Lady Hamilton's influence with the
Queen of Naples caused letters to be wrote to the Governor of Syracuse,
that he was to encourage the Fleet being supplied with everything,
should they put into any Port in Sicily. We put into Syracuse, and
received every supply, went to Egypt, and destroyed the French Fleet.

" Could I have rewarded these services, I would not now call upon
my Country; but as that has not been in my power, I leave Emma
Lady Hamilton, therefore, a Legacy to my King and Country, that they
will give her an ample provision to maintain her rank in life. I also
leave to the beneficence of my Country my adopted daughter, Horatia
Nelson Thompson; and I desire she will use in future the name of
Nelson only.

" These are the only favours I ask of my King and Country at this
moment when I am going to fight their Battle. May God Bless my
King and Country, and all those who I hold dear. My relations it is
needless to mention; they will of course be amply provided for.

" Nelson and Brontë."   25

The Captains signed their names, and Blackwood seized the
chance, before his juniors arrived, to suggest that the Chief
should shift his flag to the *Euryalus*, and conduct the battle from
her; but " he would not hear of it, and gave as his reason the
force of example ". The only visible result of the suggestion
was an order for more sail to be made upon the *Victory*. After
receiving their instructions, the four frigate Captains stalked
behind the Chief and his Flag Captain as he went the rounds of the
ship. The Admiral praised the manner in which the hawse holes
had been barricaded, and reminded gun crews not to waste a shot.
The word " Victory " was continually on his lips, and he appealed
to Blackwood several times for an opinion as to the number of
prizes they would take to-day, always adding that personally
he would not be satisfied by anything less than twenty. Blackwood, in reply, was " careful not to hold the enemy light ", and
suggested that the capture of fourteen ships would be " a glorious
result ". A feature of the picture which did not surprise any
contemporary was that the ship's company thus invoked included
Frenchmen, Spaniards, Scandinavians, Hindus, Germans, Italians,
Portuguese, Swiss, Dutch, Kanakas and Americans, and in spite
of the efforts of press-gangs, the *Victory* was undermanned. On
the other hand, the name of Nelson had brought to his flagship
nearly two hundred volunteers.

At about 9.30, Blackwood, having failed to get Nelson to
shift his flag to the *Euryalus*, suggested that one or two other

ships might precede the *Victory* into action. "I ventured to give it as the joint opinion of Captain Hardy and myself how advantageous it would be for the Fleet for his Lordship to keep as long as possible out of the Battle." Nelson answered briefly, "Let them go", and Blackwood departed, allowed to hail the *Temeraire* to go ahead. "On returning to the *Victory*, I found him doing all he could to increase rather than diminish sail." Blackwood got the ear of Hardy, and pointed out that unless the swift-sailing *Victory* gave way, the labouring *Temeraire* could not pass, but Hardy would take no action, and when, half an hour before the *Victory* opened fire, the *Temeraire*, having been signalled at 12.15 to take her place astern, ranged up on the *Victory's* quarter, Nelson ("speaking as he always did, with a slight nasal intonation") said, "I'll thank you, Captain Harvey, to keep in your proper station, which is astern of the *Victory*."

The approach to action was at a rate which promised a heavy casualty list for the leading ships when the enemy opened fire. The advance of the British fleet, though all possible sail was set, fell from three knots to a mile and a half an hour. "About 10 o'clock, Lord Nelson's anxiety to close with the enemy became very apparent." He remarked again and again, "They put a good face upon it", always adding quickly, "I'll give them such a dressing as they never had before." A little before 11 he went below to his cabin for the last time.

Bulkheads throughout the fleet were down, and the Admiral's quarters were scarcely recognisable, having been cleared of all fixtures. Nearly all the furniture had gone into the hold, and Dr. Scott, while upon the poop, had heard him giving particular instructions to the men engaged in unhanging his pictures, using the words, "Take care of my Guardian Angel." His desk had been left with his pocket-book lying upon it, and he now added a paragraph to the few professional notes which he had entered earlier, under date "Monday, October 21st, 1805". His last writing was a prayer:

"May the Great God, whom I worship, grant to my Country, and for the benefit of Europe in general, a great and glorious Victory; and may no misconduct in anyone tarnish it; and may humanity after Victory be the predominant feature in the British Fleet. For myself, individually, I commit my life to Him who made me, and may His blessing light upon my endeavours for serving my Country faithfully. To Him I resign myself and the just cause which is entrusted to me to defend. Amen. Amen. Amen."

27

John Pasco, Signal Lieutenant, entering the cabin with a report, and finding the Admiral upon his knees, waited until he rose to deliver his message, and forbore from proceeding to a personal request. " I could not, at such a moment, disturb his mind with any grievances of mine." Nelson soon followed him to the poop. The distance between the contending fleets was still about three miles. Having telegraphed Collingwood, " I intend to pass through the van of the enemy's line, to prevent him getting into Cadiz ", and changed the course of the *Victory* a little to the northward, Nelson could, for the moment, do nothing more. The sea was smooth, with a great ground-swell setting from the westward, and since the sky was now clear of cloud, the waters were richly dark blue in colour. With the approach of noon, bands struck up on board the ships of the two British columns, rolling gently towards the enemy, and the first sunlight of the day broke through, picking up, according to eyewitnesses, " in a beautiful manner ", a forest of masts with black hoops, and the freshly painted sides of a crescent-shaped formation of scarlet, black and yellow French and Spanish ships-of-the-line, which seemed to include a formidable number of three-deckers, amongst which Nelson's " old acquaintance ", the *Santissima Trinidad*, glowing in vermilion and white, with a dazzlingly white figurehead, was prominent. A Second Lieutenant of Marines, sent below with orders in the *Ajax*, was surprised by the *sangfroid* of the bluejackets. Nearly all had stripped to the waist and bound their handkerchiefs round their heads. A number were performing an elaborate horn-pipe to the strains of the martial music which had just struck up. Veterans, engaged in sharpening their cutlasses or polishing the guns, as if an inspection instead of an action was momentarily expected, broke off occasionally to take a look out of the yawning gun-ports and differ as to the identity and previous records of the ships which they were about to engage. Someone remarked that this lot would make a fine sight as prizes at Spithead.

On the poop of the *Victory*, as the National Anthem was followed by " Rule Britannia " and " Britons Strike Home ", Nelson had asked Blackwood whether he did not think there was one more general signal wanting, adding : " I'll now amuse the Fleet ". His conversation with his Signal Lieutenant had been, " Mr. Pasco, I wish to say to the Fleet, ENGLAND CONFIDES THAT EVERY MAN WILL DO HIS DUTY. You must be quick, for I have one more signal to make, which is

for close action." Pasco begged leave to suggest the sub-
stitution of " expects " for " confides ", as the first word was in
the Signal Book and would save seven hoists, and to this the
Admiral agreed. (" That will do; make it directly.") The
response throughout the fleet, as the message passed down both
lines, was, according to Blackwood, " truly sublime "; another
witness says that " it was received with three cheers in every
ship ". " Number 16 ", the signal for close action, followed,
and remained at the top-gallant masthead of the *Victory* until
it was shot away. The log of Blackwood's frigate shows that it
was preceded, by four minutes, by an order to be prepared to
anchor after the close of the action. Nelson had foreseen the
probability of a storm, and was anxious for the safety of his
ships on a lee shore.

The *Royal Sovereign*, sailing well with her new copper, was in
advance of her line, and rapidly closing with the enemy. Nelson
struck his thigh and exclaimed, " See how that noble fellow
Collingwood carries his ship into action ! " and these were the
last recorded words spoken by him without the background of
gun-fire, for by 11.40 Collingwood was under the direct fire of the
huge, swarthy *Santa Ana* and the French *Fougueux*, and partially
under that of four or five other ships. Collingwood broke the
enemy line astern of the Spanish three-decker bearing the flag
of Vice-Admiral de Álava. The *Belleisle* came into action next,
and relieved the pressure on the *Royal Sovereign*. Within ten
minutes the *Revenge*, ninth ship of the British lee division, was
going through, between the fifth and sixth 74 of the enemy rear.
A cloud of smoke closed over the division of the British second-in-
command. Lieutenant Pasco, looking through his glass, exclaimed. " There is a top-gallant yard gone ! " " Whose top-
gallant yard is that gone ? " asked the Commander-in-Chief
sharply. " Is it the *Royal Sovereign*? " " No, my Lord, an
enemy's." Lord Nelson smiled. " Collingwood is doing well."
He pulled out his watch, and called to the officers about him to
synchronise theirs by it.

The first shot at the *Victory* fell short of her. She was an
almost stationary target, carried along by the long Atlantic swell
and the remains of her own impetus. A second shot, fired after
two or three minutes, fell alongside; a third passed over her.
The last moment mentioned by Nelson had come, and he bade
Blackwood and Captain Prowse of the *Sirius* hurry on board
their frigates, and on their way along the column tell the Captains

28

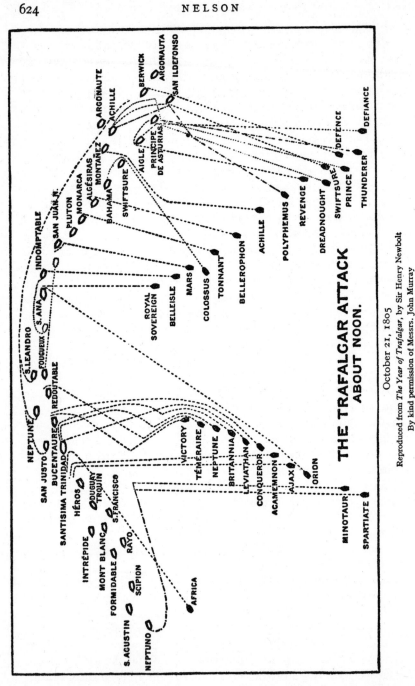

THE TRAFALGAR ATTACK
ABOUT NOON.

October 21, 1805

of all line-of-battle ships to get into action immediately. " They might adopt whatever they thought best, provided it led them quickly and closely alongside an enemy." He ended his instructions with an urgent repetition of their dismissal, and Blackwood, as they shook hands in farewell, uttered a cheerful sentence expressive of his hopes, on a speedy return, of finding his lordship well and in possession of twenty prizes. But the young officer went over the *Victory's* side " with a heart very sad ", shocked by the words, clearly heard, " God bless you, Blackwood; I shall never speak to you again."

The enemy found the range of the *Victory* with their sixth shot, which went through her main top-gallant sail. After a short silence, as concertedly as if by signal, seven or eight ships of the enemy van then poured in their broadsides. A round-shot, flying across the quarter-deck of the *Victory*, almost tore in two a figure engaged in conversation with Hardy. Captain Adair of the Marines called up a seaman to cast overboard, without delay, the fragmented corpse of the Admiral's official secretary, but Nelson had noticed. " Is that poor Scott? " Mr. Whipple, Captain's clerk, who undertook the secretary's duties, was killed by blast a few moments later.

As firing became general, and clouds of smoke enveloped the scene, the wind died to a mere breath. Still the *Victory*, sustaining " such a fire as had scarcely before been directed at a single ship ", without being able to bring her own guns to bear in reply, held steadily on her course. Her mizzen-topmast was shot away about two-thirds up; her sails were soon riddled. As usual, the French were aiming at masts and rigging. Seeing that a group of marines drawn up on the poop were suffering, Nelson ordered Adair to disperse his men around the ship. The next and most serious loss yet was that the *Victory's* wheel was knocked to pieces. But the tiller was quickly manned, and she was thereafter steered from the gun-room, " the First Lieutenant, John Quilliam, and Master, Thomas Atkinson, relieving each other at this duty ". A shot, penetrating the thickness of four hammocks in the nettings, hit the forebrace bitts on the quarter-deck. The pacing Admiral and his Flag-Captain halted, and were observed to look one another up and down with a question in the eye. But the only casualty was the buckle of Hardy's left shoe. Nelson smilingly commented, " This is too warm work to last long ", and as he resumed his march, said that never had he witnessed anything cooler than

S S

the conduct of the *Victory's* ship's company. The period of waiting, inactive, while advancing slowly under a raking fire, lasted probably about twenty minutes: then he gave the order to port the helm. His feint of attacking the van, so that Collingwood should be " as little interrupted as is possible ", had served its purpose. The *Victory* opened fire with her larboard guns, " in a determined, cool and steady manner ", as she hauled to starboard. She passed under the stern of a French three-decker, and fired into the cabin windows of the *Bucentaure*, first her forecastle carronade, and then, as she moved slowly ahead, a double-shotted broadside. Acrid smoke puffed back into the *Victory's* gun-ports, filling her lower decks, and a cloud of black dust and a shower of splinters descended upon her quarter-deck. Every glass there had long been scanning the enemy line in the fruitless attempt to discover the flag of the French Commander-in-Chief. The ship into which she had delivered her first fatally-disabling counterstroke had, in fact, been Villeneuve's flagship, but close behind the *Bucentaure* lay the French 80-gun *Neptune*, and astern of her a French 74 in the act of ranging up. Hardy had gravely reported his regret that it would not be possible to cut through this line, " closed like a forest ", without running on board one ship or the other. " I can't help it ", had been Nelson's reply. " It does not signify which we run on board of—take your choice ", whereupon Hardy had chosen the *Redoutable*. After the collision the *Victory* fell away at the rebound, but her yard-arm caught in the *Redoutable's* rigging, and the two ships hung together and so remained, locked in a death-grip, moving slowly before the wind to the S.S.E. While the *Victory's* starboard guns smashed in the *Redoutable's* sides, and her port guns continued to attack the *Santissima Trinidad*, lying ahead of the *Bucentaure*, men from the *Redoutable's* three tops attempted, with a deluge of langridge, musket-balls and hand-grenades, to clear the *Victory's* upper decks, and, under cover, a French boarding-party made ready.

Nelson had always been averse from the employment of small arms, or accumulation of explosives aloft, believing the danger of setting light to the sails to be greater than any possible gain, and the *Victory* had no guns mounted in her poop. The mizzenmast of the *Redoutable*, a much smaller ship, rose midway between the *Victory's* mizzen and main, and the crouching Frenchmen, rising breast-high to fire, had the English Commander-in-Chief's quarter-deck not forty-five feet distant and immediately below them, though the lurching of both ships in the swell made accurate aim very difficult. At the *Victory's* last refit Nelson had ordered a large skylight above his cabin to be removed and the space planked over, so as to give him more room amidships. Here, clear of the ropes and guns, in the centre of his quarter-deck, he had a walk twenty-one feet long, from the wheel to the hatch-ladder leading to his cabin. At about 1.35, Hardy, who had turned at the wheel, and was advancing towards the hatch-way, realised that he had taken the last step in that direction alone. Facing about, he saw the Admiral on his knees, with the finger-tips of his left hand just touching the deck. The single arm gave way, and Nelson fell on his left side, exactly on the spot where his secretary had been killed an hour earlier. Sergeant-major Secker of the Marines and two seamen were there in a moment, raising him. As Hardy bent, he saw a smile, and heard the words, " Hardy, I believe they have done it at last ", or " They have done for me at last." The large, consternated man muttered, " I hope not ", but the reply was, " Yes, my backbone is shot through."

29

5

The shuffling party carrying an officer with a fractured spine descended as quickly and quietly as possible from the light of day. A background of white and gold paint, and buff and blue, gave place to the half-lit glare of the universal red, chosen, it was said, by Admiral Robert Blake for his middle and lower decks so that seamen, accustomed to that colour, might not be distracted by additions to it in the carnage of action. As the party prepared to negotiate the last ladder leading to the cockpit, already thickly bloodstained and very slippery, they encountered a panting clergyman. The Chaplain of the *Victory* had been so overcome by horror and nausea as to be unable to continue his ministrations to the dying. The incident of Lieutenant Ram, mortally wounded, defiantly tearing off his bandages after the surgeon's mate had done with him, had temporarily defeated Dr. Scott. He was hastening blindly towards fresh air. Some hand, it was believed his own, had drawn a handkerchief over the features and orders of the Commander-in-Chief, so that the news of his fall might not spread and cause discouragement. Scott either recognised garments, or learnt from the bearers whom they were carrying. His love cast out fear, and he turned and followed the procession towards a scene which he soon afterwards shudderingly described, in answer to the direct question, " It was like a butcher's shambles." He never from that moment quitted his master, but as he never could be prevailed upon to write down or enlarge upon his experiences, the account of Mr. Beatty, Chief Surgeon, who had a record of twelve years in the Service, but who was often called away during the next three hours to attend other patients, is the principal source of information. Inquiries from Rose, begging to know what exactly had been the Admiral's last message to him, drew from Dr. Scott a letter, long and pains-taking, but so obviously brought forth after mortal labour, and so rambling and repetitive, that it is to be doubted whether, could he have nerved himself to attempt anything fuller, he would have been able to produce much more. It is clear that **30** throughout his hours of anguished constant attendance he scarcely thought; he could only feel. His description adds nothing to those of other eyewitnesses, except that, at first, Nelson, believing that he had only a few minutes to live, repeated in agitation that Rose must be told he had made a Will and left Lady Hamilton " to my Country ". No regular prayers were said, although between bouts of pain Nelson rather led than followed short prayers with his Chaplain : and the last words heard by Scott were, " God and my Country ! "

Beatty, a St. Andrew's man, published two years later a detailed narrative, a model of clarity, expressed in terms worthy of the occasion. **31**

On the arrival of yet another party, bringing down a silent figure with shrouded features, he directed the bearers to go far forward on the port side. He had already been presented with the dead bodies of two officers whom he believed to have drawn their last breaths during unskilful carriage below. He had over forty patients awaiting him. He gradually became aware that several of them were calling out, " Mr. Beatty ! Lord Nelson is here ! " " Mr. Beatty ! the Admiral is wounded ! " and turning, he saw a handkerchief falling from a pale but familiar countenance, and a coat with stars upon its breast. According to his custom, Lord Nelson had forbidden his attendants to distract the attention of surgeons from wounded of lesser rank.

Mr. Walter Burke, purser (a kinsman of the statesman), came running, and helped Beatty to remove the Admiral from the arms of seamen. On carrying him to one of the midshipmen's berths, they stumbled and almost fell. Beatty repeated his own name and that of the purser when the Admiral asked to whose arms he had been transferred. The easy business of stripping a one-armed man was quickly performed. Next to his skin, Lord Nelson had been wearing a large miniature set as a locket. Its picture was of Lady Hamilton as a Bacchante. He opened his eyes, and perceived the drooping figure of his Chaplain-Secretary, wringing his hands, and exclaiming, " Alas ! Beatty, how prophetic you were ! " He spoke to Scott, while Beatty was undressing him, saying, " Doctor, I told you so. Doctor, I am gone ! " and after a short pause, in a lower voice, " I have to leave Lady Hamilton, and my adopted daughter, Horatia, as a legacy to my Country."

Another officer was at this moment brought in and laid by the Admiral's side, and a zealous assistant, seizing upon the first object to hand, rolled up the emblazoned coat deplored by Beatty and slipped it beneath the neck of Mr. Midshipman Westphal, who was suffering severe hæmorrhage from a head wound. Beatty relinquished the Admiral's wrist, and turning down the sheet by which he had been covered, proceeded to an examination, keeping up a soothing monologue, in which it is noticeable that he already alluded with confidence to " a glorious victory ". He satisfied himself that the musket ball mentioned had gone deep into the chest, and probably lodged in the spine. He could perceive no external injuries to the back. He replaced the sheet, and asked if the patient would give him a full history of the occurrence, with all his sensations. Nelson answered that he had no sensation in the lower part of his body, and (which together with his pulse rate confirmed the surgeon's worst expectations) that he felt " a gush of blood every minute within his breast ". Respiration was short and difficult, and he felt very acute pain about that part of the spine where he had been struck by the ball. " I felt it break my back."

Beatty, who had promised that he would not put his lordship to much pain, and had been quietly told, " You can do nothing for me ", attempted nothing further. To the Chaplain, who was burning for employment, he suggested the administration of lemonade, which was in plentiful supply, and the construction of a paper fan. The cockpit, where three surgeons and their assistants were working with upturned sleeves and reddened forearms, by the light of candles in swaying horn lanterns, was below the water-line. The atmosphere during these hours of waiting was breathless. Burke and Scott spoke in turn, attempting to rouse the patient by hopes that he would live to carry the

joyful news of his victory to his country. The purser was told,
" It is nonsense, Mr. Burke, to suppose I can live : my sufferings are great but they will soon be over." To Scott, whose
meaning phrase had been, " Your dear Country and Friends ",
his sadder reply was, " Ah ! Doctor, it is all over—it is all
over."

Once, as the minutes dragged past, the dreadful cry of " Fire ! "
penetrated, but died unexplained.   From time to time the sound
of cheers swelled.   On one of these occasions the Admiral
anxiously asked the cause, and Lieut. Pasco, lying at some
distance, wounded in the right arm and thigh, raised himself on
his left elbow to assure him that it meant another enemy ship had
struck.   The Chief's strongly expressed wish to see his Flag-
Captain impelled the Principal Surgeon to send a succession of
messengers to Captain Hardy, and after a long wait, during which
the Admiral sighed, " Will no one bring Hardy to me ?   He must
be killed ", a bright-faced boy with a flesh-wound appeared, to
state with due formality that, " Circumstances respecting the
Fleet required Captain Hardy's presence on deck, but that he
would avail himself of the first favourable moment to visit his
Lordship."   The Admiral asked who had brought the message,
and was told by the purser, " It is Mr. Bulkeley, my Lord."
The name recalled to the dying man the visit of an old shipmate,
the proud father of sons, to an invalid languishing in Bond Street
lodgings, and the exhibition of a sea-officer's sword to a sea-
struck boy.   Dick Bulkeley heard and treasured the words,
" It is his voice ", and " Remember me to your father."

It was nearly three o'clock when the comfortable figure of
Hardy came stooping into the cockpit, bringing reliable news.
The *Victory* had been one of a group of four interlocked ships, of
which the French *Fougueux* and *Redoutable* had now been beaten
into silence.   Adair of the Marines had been killed while leading
a small force to repel a French boarding-party.   The fighting
Temeraire, with a prize to either side, was still attacking the
Santissima Trinidad.   Half an hour before, a tremor, quite
different from those caused by her guns in action, had passed
through the *Victory*.   She had worked herself free of the
Redoutable, but to find herself threatened by five ships of
Villeneuve's dismembered van.   Not until he had signalled the
Spartiate and *Minotaur* (also hitherto unengaged) had Hardy felt
himself at liberty to quit the deck.   The dialogue recorded by
Beatty sounds the unmistakable note of high tragedy.

" Well, Hardy, how goes the battle ?   How goes the day with us ? "

" Very well, my Lord.   We have got twelve or fourteen of the enemy's Ships in our possession, but five of their van have tacked, and show an intention of bearing down upon the *Victory*.   I have, therefore, called two or three of our fresh ships round us, and have no doubt of giving them a drubbing."

" I hope none of *our* ships have struck, Hardy ? "

" No, my Lord.   There is no fear of that."

" I am a dead man, Hardy.   I am going fast; it will be all over with me soon.   Come nearer to me. . . ."

Mr. Burke, perceiving that something very intimate was to be disclosed, stirred.   Together with Dr. Scott, he was supporting the Admiral in the semi-recumbent position which seemed the only one to bring him any relief.   Burke's arm was behind the pillow.   But he was desired not to move, and so, unwillingly, overheard the painfully achieved, low-spoken message.   " Pray let dear Lady Hamilton have my hair, and all other things belonging to me."

Beatty, who had successfully concluded the amputation of a midshipman's leg, now returned to the bedside, and the Flag-Captain, greeting him, voiced hearty hopes that the Chief Surgeon might yet hold out some prospect of life.   " Oh, no ", murmured the patient.   " It is impossible.   My back is shot through. Beatty will tell you."   Hardy shook hands, as he had done upon arrival, and departed in silence to send a warning message of the impending tragedy to Collingwood.

Beatty, on being begged not to waste his time on a hopeless case, explained that at present his assistants were doing all that was possible for the other wounded, but as the Admiral would not be gainsaid, he bowed and withdrew, the easier in his mind that two of his lordship's personal servants had now joined him. A few minutes later he was recalled to be told, " Ah ! Mr. Beatty, I have sent for you to say, what I forgot to tell you before—that all power of motion and feeling below my breast are gone." Realising that he was being called upon to confirm the sentence pronounced upon himself by his patient from the first, the Surgeon began confusedly, " My Lord, you told me so before ", and would have gone on to a futile examination of extremities, but was interrupted by the reminder that, " Scott and Burke have tried that already ", and, " You know that I am gone."   Thus pressed, he summoned resolution to state heavily, " My Lord, unhappily for our Country, nothing further can be done for you ", after which he found himself obliged to step aside to conceal his emotion. Nelson's voice followed him, saying, "I know. I feel something rising in my breast which tells me that I am gone", and softly, again and again, "God be praised I have done my duty."

Turning over in his mind the possibilities of palliatives, the Surgeon turned back again to inquire "if the pain was still very great", and was told, "it continued so very severe that he wished he was dead", with the yearning addition, scarcely audible, "Yet, one would like to live a little longer, too", and presently and feebler, "What would become of poor Lady Hamilton if she knew my situation? . . ." As his wounded flagship roared her last broadside at the flying enemy van, causing violent concussion in the heated and dusky cavern in which he lay, he addressed her by name, "Oh! *Victory*! *Victory*! how you distract my poor brain!" He reflected, "How dear is life to all men!"

Three midshipmen, walking cases, and some more seamen were occupying the Chief Surgeon's attention when Hardy made his second entry.

The scene had now assumed the appearance made familiar to succeeding generations by the artist Devis, who came out to meet the *Victory* on her homeward passage, and stayed three weeks in her, making his sketches from life and upon the spot. On the left of the picture stood Lieutenant Yule and Mr. Midshipman Collingwood, their British bulk and complexions contrasting with those of the Admiral's wizened, whiskered Neapolitan *valet*. Dr. Scott, his hanging features fixed in a tragic mask, continued his office of "most tender nurse", gently rubbing any part of his master's body in which he admitted of pain. The arm of Burke (a man in his sixty-seventh year, who had been thirty years afloat) still propped the pillows. Hardy loomed above the group, looking down. The efficient steward, Chevalier, recommended by Davison, put a question to the kneeling Chief Surgeon. Beyond them crouched Lieutenant Bligh, dazed by a head wound, and Neil Smith, Assistant Surgeon, at work. At a respectful distance, in the deepest shadow, hat in hand, lingered a bowed, homely, elderly figure, Mr. Bunce, carpenter of the *Victory*, acclaimed by her master "an invaluable man".

Hardy's last interview with Nelson was noted by Beatty as occupying not more than eight minutes. As before, a formal handshake opened the dialogue, but this time a man of few words and no graces kept hold of the hand of a hero while he announced that he was come to congratulate him, even in the arms of death,

" on a brilliant victory, which is complete ". Hardy could not say for certain how many of the enemy were captured, as it was not yet possible for anyone to make out every ship distinctly. He could answer for fourteen or fifteen.

The reply was, " That is well, but I bargained for twenty ", and then, with an access of energy, the order was given, " *Anchor*, Hardy, *anchor*." The Flag-Captain of a dying Commander-in-Chief hesitantly supposed that his Second would now take upon himself the direction of affairs, but such a suggestion brought Nelson almost upright in the arms of his attendants. " Not while I live, I hope ! " Dropping back, he ordered, " No, do *you* anchor, Hardy."

" Shall we make the signal, sir ? " asked the Flag-Captain, and was told, " Yes, for if I live, I'll anchor."

But he believed that he had only a few minutes more left, and his gaze pitifully outrunning his speech, he mentioned next :

" Don't throw me overboard, Hardy."

" Oh, no, certainly not ", was the wretched answer.

The Scottish Chief Surgeon was amongst them, taking notes, and his decorous record approached a Biblical cadence :

> " Then ", replied his Lordship, " you know what to do. And take care of my dear Lady Hamilton, Hardy. Take care of poor Lady Hamilton. Kiss me, Hardy."
> The Captain now knelt down and kissed his cheek, when his Lordship said : " Now I am satisfied; thank God I have done my duty."
> Captain Hardy stood a minute or two, in silent contemplation. He knelt down again, and kissed his Lordship's forehead.
> His Lordship said, " Who is that ? "
> The Captain answered : " It is Hardy ", to which his Lordship replied, " God bless you, Hardy ! "

He spoke very little more after Hardy's second withdrawal, and articulated with difficulty the orders for, " Fan—fan " or " Rub—rub ". The *Victory* had ceased to fire some time past, and within the next few minutes even distant gunfire died away. When his *valet* turned him, at his request, upon his right side, he whispered breathlessly, " I wish I had not left the deck ", and presently, to Scott, " I have not been a great sinner, doctor ", followed by " *Remember* that I leave Lady Hamilton and my Daughter as a legacy to my Country—never forget Horatia."

Beatty, returning at increasingly short intervals, found him, upon a first inspection, whispering with evidently failing strength, " Thank God, I have done my duty ", and upon the next, speech-

less, and with no discernible pulse at the wrist. At 4.30, about
three hours after the Admiral had been hit, his steward tiptoeing
in search of the Chief Surgeon with the noiseless speed and
speaking gesture of his calling, indicated something which brought
that officer back with him quickly. They had to touch the
shoulder of his lordship's private secretary, who was still
mechanically chafing a cold breast.   34

6

With sunset, as the obsessing battle-noises ceased and a
comparative hush fell upon the scene, two junior officers in the
dismasted *Belleisle* seized the chance to look about them, and,
unknown to one another, recorded impressions of the aftermath
of the greatest naval victory in history. Lieutenant Nicolas of
the Marines, who could draw, jotted down colour notes of bottle-
end green waters, amongst which appeared and reappeared
fragments of timber surrounded by bent wet heads and clutching
forearms. He saw, with the artist's eye, a central group which
included a couple of boats putting off smartly, in indigo shadow,
from the black and acid-yellow sides of the majestic *Royal
Sovereign*, lying in an unmeant attitude of heroic exhaustion,
with her sails as full of holes as if they had been powdered with
confetti. His companion, who could only describe, but felt   35
strongly that the " view of the Fleet at this period was highly
interesting, and would have formed a beautiful subject for a
painter ", saw, " just under the setting rays ", a dramatic huddle
of five or six elaborately decorated enemy prizes, trailing severed
rigging as they rose and fell helplessly on the Atlantic swell. A
bank of lavender fog, produced by gun-fire, drifted slowly towards
the land, and a heavy scent, unmistakable to anyone who had
taken part in a fleet action, burdened the air, and set hot men
coughing. To the northward could be seen the full canvas of the
enemy squadron flying for the security of Cadiz or Rota. About
a mile distant, the *Achille*, with the tricolour upon her ensign
staff still fluttering, was beginning to emit volumes of black
smoke from her hull. " Our tenders and boats were using every
effort to save the brave fellows who had so gloriously defended
her; but only two hundred and fifty were rescued." This
service was of no little difficulty or danger, as the *Achille's* guns
began to go off, one by one. About five o'clock the flames
reached her magazine, and she blew up with a tremendous explosion, sounding the last note of " the rout in Trafalgar's Bay ".

Communication between the victorious ships was difficult, but the result of the day was obvious and appreciated. Not until darkness fell did a chilly whisper steal through the loudly triumphant fleet : " No Admiral's lights on board the *Victory*." Many contemporaries attest that when London newspapers appeared on November 6, with the heading " Glorious Victory over the Combined Fleets. Death of Lord Nelson ", the instinctive comment of the British public was : " We have lost Nelson ! " and strangers stopped one another in the street to repeat the news and shake hands to an accompaniment of tears. In the British fleet on the night of Trafalgar the feeling was the same. Officers of all ranks, writing home against time, gave their opening sentence to the victory, but the remainder of a long paragraph to a loss which was unanimously felt to be personal as well as national. From the lower deck arose the same note. " I never set eyes on him," explained a humble writer to a humble home, " for which I am both sorry and glad; for to be sure I should like to have seen him, but then, all the men in our ship who have seen him are such soft toads, they have done nothing but Blast their Eyes and cry ever since he was killed. God bless you ! chaps that fought like the Devil, sit down and cry like a wench."

Nelson had spoken of " annihilation ", and been disappointed to hear on his death-bed that only fourteen or fifteen of the thirty-three ships opposed to him had struck. But eighteen were accounted for on the day of battle, and eventually annihilation was the result of Trafalgar, though only four of the " beauties " watched by the men of the *Victory* as she drew slowly towards action were carried into Spithead as prizes. Dumanoir's squadron of four van ships was met and captured off Ortegal by Sir Richard Strachan, on November 4, and of the eleven which succeeded in reaching Cadiz none ever put to sea again, and those under the flag of Admiral Rosily surrendered to Spain in 1808.

Collingwood's list of the enemy flag-officers engaged, forwarded to England with his despatches, spoke for itself :

" Admiral Villeneuve, Commander-in-Chief. *Bucentaure.* Taken. Admiral Don Frederico Gravina. *Principe de Asturias.* Escaped; in Cadiz; wounded in the arm.

" Vice-Admiral Don Ignatio Maria D'Álava. *Santa Ana.* Wounded severely in the head; taken, but was driven back into Cadiz in the *Santa Ana.* Rear-Admiral Don Baltazar Hidalgo Cisneros. *Santissima Trinidad.* Taken.

" Rear-Admiral Magon. *Algeziras.* Killed.

" Rear-Admiral Dumanoir. *Formidable.* Escaped."

Of these, Gravina died of his wounds, with the words, " I am going, I hope and trust, to join Nelson ", but Álava recovered, 36 and lived to see his nephew Miguel, who had been a Lieutenant of Marines in his flagship at Trafalgar, a Knight Commander of the Bath and a distinguished officer under the command of Lord Wellington, in the Peninsula and at Waterloo. Dumanoir was court-martialled. Villeneuve's end was more sinister. Although exchanged, after a few months' captivity, he did not reach Paris. On the morning of April 22, 1806, his *valet* tapped and listened repeatedly at the door of an hotel bedroom in the bustling town of Rennes, before summoning assistance to force the lock. The figure found lying on the bed had a knife in its heart, and at the inquest the servant deposed that his master's manner had for some days been so strange that he had taken the liberty of un-loading the Admiral's pistols. In circles opposed to Buonaparte it was whispered that a Tyrant's secret agents had disposed of an unsuccessful officer. In England some sympathy was felt for the melancholy French Commander-in-Chief, who had been observed as " a tallish, thin, English-looking Frenchman ". Even Collingwood, who had him as guest under adverse conditions, thought that a person who had admitted that his nation could not contend with Britain at sea had seemed a good officer and a well-bred man.

British casualties were reported as 1,690 killed and wounded; those in the Combined Fleet as 5,860; moreover, Collingwood reckoned the monetary loss of the enemy at £4,000,000, " most of it gone to the bottom ", and his prisoners as numbering 20,000. The survivors were taken to England, and during the next ten years a foreign officer, on parole, murmuring hopefully of exchange, was a familiar adjunct at the dinner-table of an English country gentleman. Amongst captives of lesser rank few exchanges were made, and the unfortunate remnant of the extinguished fleet which had been driven out by threats from Buonaparte to en-counter Nelson lingered, and sickened, interned in hulks, locked up in local gaols, or, if lucky, in mediæval keeps, of picturesque appearance, to provide the excuse for expeditions by British family parties, ready to purchase model ships, or sets of chessmen ingeniously carved from prisoners' dinner bones.

Collingwood did not anchor on the night of October 21, and during the following afternoon the gale foreseen by Nelson came on from the S.W., accompanied by torrential rain. Codrington of the *Orion* remarked, years later, that never had he been so glad to see the stars as after Trafalgar, as for four days following the death of the Chief no man in his fleet saw sun, moon or constellations.   During the storm the *Redoutable*, in tow of the English *Swiftsure*, went down, and the *Neptune* and *Aigle* ran ashore. At noon jolly-boats had still been plying from ship to ship, delivering wounded and prisoners; by 6 p.m. the victorious fleet was much scattered, and several prizes, with only a handful of men on board to navigate them, were no longer in tow.   Collingwood, who had shifted his flag to Blackwood's frigate, gave remorseless orders for the scuttling of that " Spanish perfection ", the *Santissima Trinidad* (which had towered over his flagship like a castle, as he advanced to the attack), and for the sinking or burning of other unmanageable prizes.

While the shoals of Cape Trafalgar roared under the *Victory's* lee, her over-driven Chief Surgeon and his assistants did what they could for those departed this life.   The body of Lord Nelson was stripped of the clothes in which it had been attired after death, with the exception of a shirt.   The hair, for which Captain Hardy was asking, in accordance with his instructions, as a memento for Lady Hamilton, was secured.   Beatty traced, with a probe, the course of the musket ball from the spine, but stopped there for the present.   There was not lead in the *Victory* sufficient to make a coffin.   A cask of the largest size used on shipboard, known as a leaguer, was brought forth, and a quantity of spirits, brandy being used in preference to rum.   At Gibraltar, Beatty counted upon obtaining spirits of wine.   The cask, which had a closed aperture at both top and bottom, was up-ended and placed in the charge of a sentinel on the middle deck.   A little before noon on the 24th the wounded ship, labouring deeply in the heavy seas, was taken in tow by the old *Polyphemus*, and managed to rig up jury topmasts and a mizzen.   But during the dark hours of that wild night the marine on duty perceived the lid of the cask in which the Admiral's body had been bestowed slowly rising.   The man's hair also rose upon his scalp, and he did not hesitate to fetch expert assistance.   The Chief Surgeon spoke undisturbedly of a disengagement of air, and the brandy was drawn off from the lower aperture, and the cask refilled from the top.   Next evening the *Polyphemus* was obliged to cut the towing hawser to prevent the *Victory* coming on board her, and in spite of burning blue lights and searching to the best of her ability, she lost sight of the flagship for forty-eight hours.   On the 26th the storm at last showed signs of abating, and Captain

Fremantle, with H.M.S. *Neptune,* came to the aid of his old Chief. Next morning, although strong gales with thunder, lightning and downpour still prevailed, Dr. Scott was able to approach his first letter since the action. It was with a trembling pen that he addressed his sheet " *Mrs. Cadogan, Merton Place, Surrey* ", and began to trace the words :

> " Hasten the very moment you receive this, to dear Lady Hamilton, and prepare her for the greatest of misfortunes."

37

CHAPTER XX

AFTERWARDS

I

TUESDAY, November 5, 1805, found London overwhelmed by the thickest fog known in the capital for many years. It extended for several miles outside town, blotting out hedgerows and cottages. In the City, shopkeepers, hopeless of doing any business, put up their shutters, to the distress of persons accustomed to certain lighted windows as landmarks on their homeward journey. In the streets carriages proceeded at a footpace, and pedestrians, afraid of being run over, were halloing before they attempted crossings. Stage-coaches were hours late. By midnight Whitehall was almost deserted; but two post-chaises, which had been crawling up from the west, turned in at the Admiralty gates at the same moment, and two weary and crumpled officers who had last met in the Atlantic, in dirty weather, recognised one another with astonishment.

On October 26 Admiral Collingwood had taken advantage of the first abatement of the great storm following Trafalgar to send away the *Pickle* schooner with his despatches. Lieutenant Lapenotière, falling in with the *Nautilus* lugger, in the mouth of the Tagus, had communicated the news to Captain Sykes, who had hastened with it to Lisbon, where Mr. Gambier, British Consul, had only detained him while he wrote to London. Sykes had made the port of Plymouth a few hours later than Lapenotière, who had the longer land journey from Falmouth. The words " Despatches from Admiral Collingwood " brought the First Lord out of bed, to sit at his desk doing business with his staff till 5 a.m., by which time expresses had been sent off to His Majesty and all his ministers, and compositors were setting up the type for a *Gazette Extraordinary*. The Prime Minister, who was in residence at 10, Downing Street, confided in Lord Malmesbury next day that during an eventful career he had become accustomed to being knocked up at all hours by messengers bringing news of every description, but hitherto, be it good or bad, he had always been able to lay his head on his pillow and sink into a sound sleep

639

again. On this occasion only had Mr. Pitt been unable to recover
repose, and at length got up and dressed, although it was three
in the morning. The image of Nelson in this quarter was too
vivid, too recent.

1

Despite the fog, a rumour that intelligence of the utmost
importance had been received at the Admiralty spread with
uncanny speed, and at an early hour anxious inquirers were
besieging an office which was, however, ready for them with a
bulletin dated 1 a.m. Lord Barham's message reached Windsor
Castle about seven o'clock, and it was noticed that His Majesty
remained utterly silent for about five minutes after learning the
news. It was asserted in Court circles that pure affliction for
the loss of his Admiral had dammed up the speech of a patriotic
monarch, notably loquacious. Whatever reflections visited the
troubled brain of George III, the only royal comment was
provided by his realistic consort. Having summoned the
Princesses, Her Majesty read aloud Vice-Admiral Collingwood's
despatch ("so elegant and so ample"), reducing herself and her
audience to tears. The Duke of York arrived from Oatlands
Park within the hour, to congratulate and condole, and the
whole party repaired to St. George's Chapel to return thanks to
Almighty God for the success of His Majesty's Arms at Sea.

A typical leading article of a daily paper published that
morning opened with the words, " It is with mixed sensations of
transport and anguish ", and though the Park and Tower guns
duly thundered, illuminations in London that night were described
as " partial ". Some days passed before officials, tradesmen and
private residents had decided how best to express joy for a signal
victory combined with a national loss. In St. James's Square,
the mansion of the fabulously wealthy Mr. Goldsmid, a personal
friend of Lord Nelson, exhibited but two small rows of plain lamps.
Drury Lane blazed with an anchor and immense " L.N." wreathed
with bays. " Nelson and Victory " was a popular form, and
crowds paused appreciatively outside a well-known shop saying
simply " Alas ! Poor Nelson ! "

Lord Mayor's Day was at hand, bringing poignant memories
of an ardent and eloquent chief guest. His portrait was brought
from the Council Chamber and hung above the Lord Mayor's seat
in the Guildhall ; his bust, garlanded with oak and laurel, presided
over the Sheriff's table. On November 9 the *London Gazette*
announced the first Trafalgar honours, and Vice-Admiral
Collingwood (blockading Cadiz) was not much pleased when he

discovered that his barony might not descend to his daughters, but the Rev. William Nelson was well satisfied to find that royal gratitude for the hitherto meagrely acknowledged services of Vice-Admiral Nelson had taken the extraordinary form of creating his elder brother an Earl. On the same day that the earldom was gazetted, a note in a strange hand was set on its way to Mr. Rose's country house :

> "Lady Hamilton's most wretched state of mind prevents her imploring her dear good Mr. Rose to solicit Mr. Pitt to consider the family of our great and glorious Nelson, who so gallantly died for his country, leaving behind a favourite sister, with a large family unprovided for. Her Ladyship is confident you will exert every nerve for these good people as a mark of your true and real attachment to our lamented hero. Mr. Bolton was ever much esteemed by his brother-in-law; and had it pleased the Admiralty to have spared Lord Nelson to his family, he meant to have made them independent. They at this moment surround her ladyship's bed, bewailing their sad loss and miserable state. Lady Hamilton, whose situation is beyond description, only prays that you, good sir, will do all you can for this worthy family; it will be the greatest relief to her mind. This is written by the mother of the most to be pitied Lady Hamilton, who begs leave to subscribe herself Mr. Rose's
>
> > "Most obedient and very humble servant,
> > "Mary Cadogan."
>
> "P.S.—If Mr. Rose would condescend to acknowledge this it would be a comfort to her just now."

The Matchams reached Merton on the following day. ("How is my Mother, and how did she bear the journey?" asked young George, left behind in Bath. "I trust now my Mother will get a little more composed.") The Matcham family had learnt the news from the *Gazette Extraordinary* of November 6, followed on the 7th by an intimation from the Admiralty and a message from Merton that Lady Hamilton was very ill. They stayed for a fortnight, miserably unoccupied, in a house which reminded them of its owner at every turn, detained by hopes of the arrival of a promised frigate from Lord Collingwood's fleet, and the consideration "it really is cruel to mention our going to my Lady at present". The character described by his critical nephew as "William, now Lord Nelson" came down from town with his co-executor, Mr. Haslewood, to read the Admiral's Will (dated May 1803) and seven codicils, to the assembled family in Lady Hamilton's bedchamber. The new peer exercised his privilege of franking letters for his relatives; his handsome Horace was now Viscount Merton. During the night of the 26th Captain Blackwood

T T

arrived at the Admiralty bringing more despatches, but no private letters from the *Victory*. The body of Lord Nelson was being brought home in his own flagship, and it gradually became evident that "the last sad scene" pictured by the Matchams was to be much longer delayed and on a scale undreamt-of by them when they had spoken of staying at Merton "till all is over". Lady Charlotte Nelson wrote to tell her aunt that her father, who was in daily touch with the Herald's Office, said that whether brothers-in-law attended or not, "the Nephews must be at the Funeral", and George received his mourning ring, which was very handsome, being of heavy gold, with a duke's and viscount's coronets in coloured enamel surmounting the initials "N" and "B" and, within, the inscription, "Lost to his Country, Oct. 21, 1805".

Newspaper paragraphs announced that Lord Hood had called at Lord Hawkesbury's office to discuss arrangements for a lying in state in the Painted Chamber, Greenwich, and Lord Hawkesbury had been with the Master of Works to St. Paul's. Towards the end of the month a rumour that Lady Hamilton was about to publish interesting correspondence from Lord Nelson got her out of her bed and up to London. At Clarges Street she took to her bed again, but sent Rose, who had apparently dreaded that there might be some ground for the notice, a letter calculated to allay his fears on this point.

On December 3, at a Special General Meeting of the Committee of the Patriotic Fund, held at Lloyd's Coffee House, a magnificent list of proposed gifts was headed by resolutions to present silver-gilt vases of the value of five hundred guineas to the widow of Lord Nelson, to the present Lord Nelson and to Lord Collingwood. Daily, on the front pages of journals, the names of subscribers towards the Fund for the Relief of Widows and Orphans of Trafalgar occupied more columns. The attention of the public was drawn to the fact that in France the officially inspired *Moniteur* had not as yet mentioned the action of October 21. The news of Trafalgar had indeed come in good time to raise spirits in England, depressed by the Surrender of Ulm, and, on the last day of 1805, by confirmation of what had befallen at Austerlitz. Nelson had given to England, finally, the dominion of the sea, but Buonaparte was now unmistakably master of the Continent, and Pitt had rolled up the map of Europe for ten years.

The funeral of Nelson was planned on lines comparable only with that of another national hero whose death on active service had touched the public imagination, and like Sir Philip Sidney he was to be borne with pageantry through the streets of the capital to rest in St. Paul's.

Hardy's report of the *Victory's* damages had been long, but within a week of reaching Gibraltar a ship which had been making, in bad weather, twelve inches water an hour, was ready to undertake a midwinter passage to England. She got through the Straits on the night of November 4, joined Collingwood's squadron, cruising off Cadiz, next morning, and parted company the same evening. After that, for a month, the English Press, waiting for news of her, published well-founded surmises of storm and tempest. At last, early on December 5, the day appointed for a National Thanksgiving, warning of the approach, from St. Helens, of a large ship under low jury masts, which had been towed through the cheering Channel Fleet, drew to the Sally port at Portsmouth, and the Blockhouse Fort opposite, crowds far exceeding in number those which had gathered on the same spot on a September day to watch Admiral Nelson wave farewell. The *Victory*, with his flag half mast, anchored at Spithead, but the *Revenge* came into the harbour to be docked for repairs. " She bore marks of her bravery in the action, and the acclamations had a very pleasing effect."

Next morning, betimes, Hardy set off in an open boat for Lymington, whence he posted to Cuffnell's Park, near Lyndhurst. John Scott, official secretary, who had been named in a codicil together with him as custodian of all Lord Nelson's papers and effects for executors, had been blown to pieces by one of the first shots to reach the *Victory*; but at Portsmouth Nelson's Flag-Captain had found the Captain of the *Euryalus*, and held consultation. Two sea-officers, impressed with a great sense of urgency, had decided that the statement of Lord Nelson's last wishes witnessed by them on October 21 must be mentioned without delay to his Lordship's Privy Councillor friend, whose name had been so often on his lips during the death scene (" Mr. Rose will remember "), and Blackwood saw to it that his lady sent to Lady Hamilton, the same night, an assurance that Hardy " has in his possession papers, and the last *will* of his ever to be regretted Commander, which will prove highly gratifying to you ". Blackwood's postscript on the back sheet stated bluntly, " Hardy may have spoken his mind on former occasions more freely than you could have wished; but depend upon it that the last words of our lamented friend will influence his conduct."

Hardy's dramatic arrival at Cuffnell's Park was followed by an anticlimax. Mr. Rose was no stranger to applications by Lady Hamilton for a Government pension in recognition of her services at Naples. He had first heard of them in 1801, and his heroic friend had more than once spoken to him on the subject. Lady Hamilton herself had written to him as lately as November 4, when pressing him to " put in a good word " to Mr. Pitt for a post for Mr. Bolton. " I promise not to bore you with my own claims, for if those in power will not do me justice I must be quiet." However, Mr. Rose said that he would take the first opportunity of speaking to Mr. Pitt, and he was sure that now, considering when, and by whom, Lady Hamilton's claims were supported, the Prime Minister would give ear, he hoped favourably.

On his return to his ship, Hardy found, to his annoyance, that the steward Chevalier, whom he had allowed to hasten to Clarges Street bearing a simple letter of condolence, had fled back in a flutter, having caused a storm by asking Lady Hamilton, quite unnecessarily, not to mention Captain Hardy's communication to Earl Nelson. Next morning the Chief Surgeon of the *Victory* came to Hardy, and suggested that as, according to Portsmouth rumours, the body of Lord Nelson was to be literally exposed to the public view at a lying in state ceremony when they got to Greenwich, its condition should be examined. During the week that the flagship lay at anchor at Spithead, the object of unceasing reverential attention, it was not possible to do anything, but directly she sailed for the Downs, Beatty, with his assistants, began an autopsy. To his relief, the body was in a perfect state of preservation, and death-masks (obtained either then or ten days later) represented features unchanged, except by an expression of profound repose. He was able, at last, to extract the fatal musket ball, which he found lodged in the muscles of the back, a little below the right shoulder-blade, together with some gold lace and silk lining from an epaulette and a shred of navy blue cloth. The ball, after entering the left shoulder and breaking two ribs, had penetrated to the left lobe of the lungs and divided a large branch of the pulmonary artery, so the immediate cause of death, although on its further passage the ball had fractured the spine, had been, as he had expected, hæmorrhage from a vessel near the heart. He took the opportunity of examining the vital organs, and found that all were so healthy that they rather resembled those of a youth than a man in his forty-eighth year. These facts, taken together with his observations of his lordship's habits, led the Chief Surgeon of the *Victory* to suppose that Admiral Nelson might have survived to a great age, though, had he remained for longer than a few more years at sea, and overtaxing his remaining eye, he must almost certainly have become totally blind.

2

" He is to be buried in St. Paul's," wrote Mrs. Codrington to her Trafalgar Captain, " directly under the Cupola, which will be his *monument*, and may at the same moment, remind *thousands* of spectators of his merits and his loss; and animate, in a last look at London, the departing midshipman, lieutenant, captain and admiral to imitate his example."

Throughout the raw night of January 8–9 London could hardly be said to have slept. Thirty-one Admirals and a hundred Captains were up with their full-dress uniform. For days past country parties had been arriving to lodgings in the City and suburbs. " Town was never so full." A sudden hailstorm had drenched the capital as the coffin, brought in procession by water from Greenwich (on a day of brilliant sunshine, but impeded by a strong south-westerly wind), had been landed at Whitehall stairs.

At midnight an army of men detailed to cast gravel upon the route came on duty, and all wheeled traffic ceased by order. The crowd which had gathered outside the Admiralty to watch the coffin carried into the Captains' Room at 4 p.m. had not dwindled, although no hopes of admittance were held out, and by 3 a.m. thousands of people were in motion in the dim streets, hurrying to take up the positions at which they had arranged—in some cases at large cost—to watch the *cortège* passing to St. Paul's.

At Greenwich on the Sunday and Monday mornings there had been serious accidents, and seamen with boarding-pikes had been required to restrain the multitude determined to witness the lying in state. On the Tuesday the provision of more and stronger wickets, and Life Guards instructed to keep the queue on the move, had prevented further disaster, and it was reckoned that about 30,000 people had received an impression of the Painted Hall glowing with wax lights in plated sconces, and a crescent-shaped *daïs* protected by a rail, enclosing an intricately ornamented black-and-gold canopy towering above a coffin with a viscount's coronet lying upon it, guarded by ten officials of the Lord Chamberlain's Department, in deep mourning and bag wigs, and a single clergyman, dressed in a cassock and without powder, drooping in an armchair. The *London Gazette* and *The Courier* were certain that " Lord Nelson's favourite Chaplain ", who sat hour after hour with his eyes sunk upon the ground and a hand shielding his brow, " had been earnestly requested by the Admiral to pay particular attention to his remains from the moment of his death till they were interred ". It may have been that at some time during the death scene a mortally wounded patient had uttered the very usual words, " Don't leave me ". Scott's letter to Rose contained the jealously secretive phrase, " I do not mean to tell you all that he said ", and in several of his bulletins to Lady Hamilton, from Portsmouth and Greenwich, he had repeated that he was unable to come to her as he was still on duty. Whatever his reason, Dr. Scott, a spiritually minded man, never left the body of Nelson unattended. When it was landed at Greenwich at dusk on Christmas Eve he took lodgings at Park Row— " Number 21, near the East Gate of the Hospital ", but did not occupy them at nights. For a fortnight he kept vigil, first in the Record Room, then in the Painted Hall. His appearance as the date of the State Funeral dawned was so ghastly that it was remarked " he looked like the Chief Mourner ", and when the coffin was brought out of the Admiralty at noon, in dead silence, a coachload of nearest relatives, pompously attired in black velvet mourning cloaks and mourning swords, were surprised to find an emaciated figure in clergyman's dress clawing at the windows of their stationary carriage, to the embarrassment of the Heralds. Lord Nelson's brother-in-law, recognising Dr. Scott, hastily expressed himself happy to meet him, and the distracted Chaplain-Secretary, having shaken all in the coach by the hand, embarked to follow his employer on the last stage of his long journey with the wild words, " Ah ! poor fellow ; I remained with him as long as I could, and then they turned me away." A note to Lady Hamilton, dated the night before, " Admiralty— half past 12 o'clock ", had ended—" When I think, setting aside his heroism, what an affectionate, fascinating little fellow he was, how dignified and pure his mind, how kind and condescending his manners, I become stupid with grief for what I have lost." 7

3

The ·drums of the volunteer corps who were to line the streets beat to arms an hour before dawn on January 9. Young George Matcham's long day began at 6 a.m., when he rose at the

Gloucester Coffee House to put on full dress by candlelight. He drove first with his father to pick up the Boltons at Clarges Street. (On their arrival in London on the 6th, the Matchams had found Lady Hamilton " in bed, and very low ", but on the 8th she had undertaken an expedition " to Brumton ", to visit another detachment of the Boltons lodging in that pleasant suburb.) From Clarges Street the Matchams and Boltons proceeded, still in darkness, " to the Earl's where breakfast was laid out ". There were two young Honourable Walpoles already there, gentlemanly looking lads, but nobody to introduce the strange cousins. The Earl was understood to be in a passion, firstly on account of the position allotted to him in the procession, and secondly because he had not been allowed any tickets to bestow upon acquaintances. Mr. Suckling had sent in his name but been refused. Sir Charles Malet of Wilbury had been refused. The Prince of Wales, after a severe tussle with Authority, was attending as a private person. Sir Peter Parker, Senior Admiral of the Fleet, was to be Chief Mourner at a State Funeral for which tickets could be obtained only by application to the Bishop of London, the Bishop of Lincoln (Dean of St. Paul's) and his Chapter, and the Surveyor-General.

While the Matchams, Boltons and Walpoles discussed the funeral meats so coldly furnished forth, three coaches provided for the nearest relatives drew up outside their windows, and bulky Earl Nelson, attended only by slim Viscount Merton, appeared to mount into the leading equipage, which was drawn by six caparisoned horses. St. James's Park, where the family joined the tail of the procession mustering to pass to Whitehall, was their first halt, and while they waited a weary while, young George saw the Duke of York talking much to his *aides-de-camp*, and many Admirals and Captains, in full-dress uniform (but with black waistcoats), jangling with medals, and highly confused at not being able to find their carriages. He thought that Mr. Naylor, York Herald, in a surcoat of armorial bearings, looked ridiculous amongst so much black. In a coach well to the fore, ranked to precede those of the younger sons of Barons, sat a solemn trio bearing white staves : the Treasurer, Comptroller and Steward of the Household of the deceased. All had indeed known Nelson well : Alexander Davison, Esq., of St. James's Square and Swarland Hall, William Haslewood, Esq., Senior Partner of Messrs. Booth & Haslewood, Attorneys, of Craven Street, Strand, and William Marsh, Esq., Senior Partner of

Messrs. Marsh, Page & Creed, Navy Agents, of Norfolk Street, Strand.

Daylight broadened, and it became clear that Nelson's funeral was to be vouchsafed as dazzling a day as could be remembered in January London. Early sunlight beamed upon Portland stone and urban grass, from which the frost was passing. In the City the dome of St. Paul's rose against cloudless pale blue skies as if it had been cut out of pasteboard. The great bell of the cathedral began to toll at 8.30, by which time most ticket-holders were in their seats, and every window on the route from the Admiralty was filled; but the last part of the procession did not reach the Horse Guards, where it was to fall in behind the troops, until nearly noon. The military, under the command of the veteran Sir David Dundas, had been chosen chiefly from regiments which had served in the glorious campaigns amongst the sands of Egypt, after the Battle of the Nile (and were to serve under Wellington in the *sierras* of the Peninsula and the wet woods of Belgium). Afterwards, it was objected that ten thousand regular soldiers were far more than was necessary upon a naval occasion, and the appropriateness of flying artillery with twelve field pieces and ammunition tumbrils was questioned; but within the cathedral, by general consent, nothing could have been more effective than the solitary splash of colour produced by the jackets and kilts of the statuesque Highlanders, who stood throughout the ceremony resting on their arms reversed.

In the cathedral, Mrs. Codrington, hoping not to faint, packed tight amongst tier upon tier of spectators (many of whom were ladies attired in very large black poke bonnets and carrying large flat black muffs), found the moment when " the sailors of the *Victory* brought in Nelson's colours " the only thing about the pageant " that was *Nelson*—the rest was so much the *Herald's Office* ". Lady Elizabeth Foster, watching with a Devonshire House party from a window commanding Temple Bar, noticed that when " the dear forty-eight *Victory* men " and forty-eight Greenwich pensioners came in sight, an English crowd, growing restive, muttered, " We had rather see them than all the show."

At last the sound of fifes and muffled drums playing the Dead March in Saul gave notice that the procession was in motion. Minute guns boomed. At the Admiralty the coffin was borne out to the funeral car, which was fashioned to represent, in some sort, the Admiral's flagship, having a winged figure of Fame bearing a laurel wreath inclining from the prow, and upon the great lantern, above the stern windows, the inscription *H.M.S. Victory* in yellow block capitals. (A last-minute check of measurements had demonstrated that the car, which had pillars in the form of palm trees, was too high to pass under Temple Bar, where it was to be met by the Lord Mayor, on horseback, with a drawn sword, and too wide to enter the Admiralty gates.) The Portsmouth rumours that the body of Lord Nelson was to be literally exposed during the lying in state had been quite without foundation. While the *Victory* lay at anchor in the Swin, on her difficult passage to the Nore, the coffin made of part of the main-mast of *L'Orient*, sent to the Victor of the Nile by Captain Hallowell, had been brought on board. It was said that during his last leave the Admiral had visited Mr. Peddeson of Brewer Street and inspected the relic, saying that he thought he might have need of it on his return. On the afternoon of December 22, certain of his officers beheld the body of Nelson transferred to this historic shell, and encased in others of lead and elm. It had then waited for a fortnight until an outermost coffin, des-cribed as " the most elegant and superb ever seen in Europe ", had been delivered at Greenwich. Mr. Ackerman, of the Strand, whose thirteen plates of emblematical devices crowded a covering of black velvet, had forgotten nothing, from the British Lion, with the Union Flag, and Britannia and Neptune, to the Sphinx, the Eagle, the Crocodile, the Sea-Horse and the Dolphin, " noblest fish of the Sea ".

The procession was so long that the Scots Greys, leading it, had reached the cathedral before the officers of both services, bringing up the rear, had left the Admiralty, but it was remarked that the only general sound made by an unusually orderly mob was one resembling a murmur of the sea, caused by a spontaneous movement to uncover as the funeral car came in sight. There was an awkward pause of thirty-five minutes after the Prince of Wales made his appearance, attended by his brother Clarence and Lord Moira. The hearse had been brought to an unexplained standstill exactly opposite the statue of King Charles at Charing Cross. Two o'clock had sounded before the expectant silence was broken by words of command, the troops manœuvred to line and guard the entrance to the cathedral, and the coffin was taken from the car by twelve men of the *Victory*, to be met at the rails by six Admirals bearing a canopy.

The youngest relative, following his father, with bent head, up tremendous steps into darkness, thought the scene " the most aweful sight I ever saw. All the bands played." Sunlight and military music gave place to torchlight and the soaring voices of choristers. Simple words, very well known to a clergyman's son, swelled in the great dome. The first three anthems of a service which lasted four hours were, " I am the Resurrection and the Life ", " I know that my Redeemer liveth " and " We brought nothing into this world ". The Bishop of Chichester read the First Lesson. Young George found the Dean's voice heavy and monotonous. As the coffin was moved from the choir to the space beneath the dome, for interment, the Duke of Clarence, close behind his Royal kin, lumbered out of line to shake hands with Lord Nelson's brother-in-law and say in a stage whisper, " I am come to pay my last Duties here, and I hope you and I shall never meet on such a like occasion."

It had been foreseen that darkness must fall outside before the service ended. Within, the choir appeared but dimly lit, although many torches had been employed, but an effect of extraordinary brilliance had been achieved beneath the dome, and exactly above the bier, by the introduction of a temporary chandelier of a hundred and thirty lamps. The last stages of a State Funeral designed by the College of Arms arrived. Garter King at Arms lifted up his voice to proclaim the styles and titles of the departed. The officers of Lord Nelson's Household broke their white staves and handed them to Garter to be cast upon the coffin, about to be lowered by machinery into the crypt. The black and white marble sarcophagus awaiting the body of England's greatest naval hero was entirely unrelated to his story. It was a relic of royal disfavour—ordered in his heyday by Cardinal Wolsey, of the sculptor Benedetto de Rovezzano, and left neglected in a chapel at St. George's, Windsor, until a question of reconstruction happened to coincide with the call for a monument of distinction.

The final incident of Lord Nelson's funeral, found by many spectators the most impressive, was undisciplined and unrehearsed. It had been set down that the men of the *Victory* were to furl the shot-rent colours which they had borne in the procession, and lay them upon the coffin; but when the moment came, they seized upon the ensign, largest of the *Victory's* three flags, and tearing a great piece off it, quickly managed so that every man transferred to his bosom a memorial of his great and favourite commander.

Some of the congregation did not manage to leave St. Paul's

until past nine that night. The Matchams, after a long search for their carriage, got to Clarges Street about eight. They called there every day until January 12, when, taking young Tom Bolton with them, they mounted the Bath coach, quite unnoticed, and found a strange foreign gentleman their only fellow-traveller. As the Bath coach rattled out of a London in which high and low were still sporting a black cockade with the word " Nelson " upon it, the foreigner praised English travelling. Darkness closed in upon Lord Nelson's nearest relatives. " The night was very cold and dark, and the roads so bad that we did not arrive at Newbury before four o'clock in the morning. It then began to snow heavily. . . ."[8]

4

Most of the major characters of the Nelson drama lingered upon the stage long after his abrupt exit. He had been barely forty-seven. More than thirty years passed before the last of those who had known him best were quietly swept into the property box, all passion spent.

When his officers mourned the Nation's loss after Trafalgar, several added in despair that they had also lost their Patron. Codrington deemed the future of Hardy sunk in the grave together with his illustrious Chief. The voice was that of the eighteenth century, and they had under-estimated, amongst other things, the regard which immediately, and for all time, attached itself in the national mind to everyone and everything connected with the name of Nelson. Hardy was not forgotten, and his professional rise was regular. He was created a baronet in February 1806, and for five years was a successful and applauded figure as Commander-in-Chief on the South American station. He became a Rear-Admiral in 1825, and struck his flag on the anniversary of Trafalgar, two years later. He joined the Board of Admiralty as First Sea Lord, and upon the accession of William IV received the G.C.B. He accepted a congenial appointment as Governor of Greenwich Hospital on the understanding that in the event of a war he should return to active service, and he died with the rank of Vice-Admiral of the Blue, aged seventy. With him died his baronetcy.

Two of Nelson's favourite officers made matches which were in some degree the result of finding themselves the lions of the drawing-room. Lady Harriet Walpole, daughter of the Earl of Orford, idolised her frigate Captain (an equally dashing figure in the hunting-field), and edited cherished memoirs and letters for the benefit of the six children of Sir William Hoste.

Lady Hardy, daughter of Admiral the Hon. George Berkeley, and granddaughter of the Duke of Richmond, noted in her diary on March 20, 1840, " Six months from the day of Sir Thomas's death "; two days later, " I left off my Widow's Cap ", and on the 25th, " I told my daughters of my engagement to Lord Seaford." One of the least resentful of her comments on Nelson's Hardy was, " His whole object of interest was his Ship." Her opinion of Nelson's wife was, " a good woman, surpassingly tiresome and prejudiced . . . who, however, retained to the last the most extraordinary devotion to his Memory ". 9

In 1810, when Lady Charlotte Nelson married Lord Hood's grandson and namesake, Nelson's widow, flattered by a call from the bridal couple, wrote of, " A Union of Names that will not easily be forgotten ". Lady Nelson, never strong and always on the move, lived to be seventy-three. There is a shadowy glimpse of her " rather prosy " in an hotel at Lyons, and a surprising one upon a boating expedition on the Lake of Geneva, in company with her daughter-in-law, an infant grandchild and nurse, and Lord Byron. 10

Within three years of Nelson's death, his sisters, who took great interest in a person with whom they had lost touch, heard but did not believe a story that " *the* Viscountess is going to be married to a Lynn gentleman—one of the merchants there ". They thought it more likely that she was courting such circles in quest of a rich wife for her son—" a large fortune to be given for the honour of her connection. . . . She would never lower her dignity to marry a tradesman." To see " my Josiah " settled was indeed his 11 mother's chief concern for many years; for the " few months with Lady Nelson " prescribed for an unsatisfactory young officer by an exasperated senior in 1800 proved a life-sentence. Captain Nisbet was never employed again at sea in the Royal Service, and did not marry until he was forty. Some streak of the Herbert capacity for business, however, appears to have descended to him. Although he was never a member he operated largely upon the Stock Exchange both in London and Paris; he became a man of means. The first hint of wider interests for Lady Nelson was given in the parlour of 8, The Beacon, Exmouth, on an April evening of 1819, when Captain Nisbet startled two ladies seated side by side on a sofa with the announcement: " Madam, your commands are obeyed ! Lady Nelson, there is

12 Mrs. Nisbet. Fanny, my love, kiss your mother!" The bride of twenty-eight with whom he had stolen a love match was blightingly described by Lord St. Vincent's heiress as having
13 been "a kind of companion" to Lady Nelson. She was also a Herbert connection, a god-child and namesake. Seven children were born of the marriage, of whom three survived and left issue, and it is a curious fact that both a son and a grandson of Josiah Nisbet were christened "Horatio". The family occupied a house on the Quai Voltaire, where they lived in some state, and when the Matchams appeared in Paris a reconciliation took place, and her pretty nieces drank tea repeatedly with "the old Viscountess", who, according to a miniature in a massive frame surmounted by a coronet on a cushion, wore the latest Paris fashions with effect in spite of considerable *embonpoint*.

Josiah Nisbet died suddenly of pleurisy at the age of fifty, successful proprietor of a yacht in which he undertook long cruises, a full nursery and a solid fortune, but perhaps never quite so proud a man as when he had commanded H.M.S. *Thalia*, aged nineteen, according to Nelson, "a seaman every inch of him". His mother, with his widow and children, returned to England, and almost the last vision of Lady Nelson is much in character— proceeding from the Sea House Hotel, Brighton, to the Royal Pavilion, in order to pay her Christmas respects to the Sailor King who had given her away as a bride, upon her marriage to the Captain of the *Boreas*. Admiral Sir William Hotham (who had called at her London lodgings, in Upper Harley Street, a few days before) was not surprised to hear of her death, on May 6, 1831, "for she had long been complaining and was in great dejection of spirits when I saw her. She said to me that her son was gone, that three or five of his children were also dead, and that her daughter-in-law lay, at that time, dangerously ill up- stairs of inflammation of the lungs. She appeared the very
14 picture of illness and despondency." The carriages of Earl Nelson and Sir Thomas Hardy were amongst those to follow her coffin to the parish church of Littleham, Devon, where an inscription composed by Mrs. Josiah Nisbet commemorates "grateful remembrance of those virtues which adorned a kind mother-in-law and a good husband".

Lord St. Vincent's standpoint had always been, "I love Lady Nelson, and admire her dignified pride and spirit." He was amongst the influential people from whom Lady Hamilton implored assistance to support her claims to a pension in 1808.

She was careful to address him as a person with a feeling breast, a patriot, and particularly a naval patriot, a statesman (the *rôle* in which he had come to grief), an old friend of her eminent husband, and the character whom Nelson had desired to see " always at the head of the Admiralty ". She enclosed a copy of " the noble and confiding " Nelson's last prayer and dying request, and boldly suggested that his infant daughter was surely not less worthy of the attention of her King and Country than Miss Willoughby, natural daughter of Mr. Fox. Lord St. Vincent responded, though not warmly. He had not yet forgiven an " infernal " influence superior to his own.

He had announced in 1799, " It is of no consequence to me whether I die afloat or ashore ", but he outlived Nelson by nearly eighteen years. He never again held office, after the failure of his characteristically unsparing attempt to point out and root out the abuses which were sapping the strength of the Navy, though at Grenville's request, after the death of Pitt, he accepted the rank of Admiral of the Fleet and went to sea for twelve months. Until 1810 he attended occasionally in the Lords when naval questions were under discussion, but for the last thirteen years of his life he was little seen except in his Essex country house, by friends to whom he would sometimes confide such musings as : " I did what I could to keep them in order, but a Fleet is a difficult thing to manage." Towards the end his memory failed, and his anecdotes became only approximate in date and place.

There was an awkward moment at a Review held to impress the Allied Sovereigns visiting London after the Congress of Vienna, when the Czar of Russia asked if Earl St. Vincent was dead. When George IV embarked in state in the *Royal George* yacht, from Greenwich for Scotland, an invitation to his " Old Oak " was not forgotten. Earl St. Vincent stayed with the Governor, and was observed (a caricature of himself) on the terrace fronting the Hospital at 5 a.m. with four old shipmates hobbling to the leeward of him—two from the *Ville de Paris* and two from the *Victory*. He gruffly commented, " We all, in our day, were smart fellows." This was his last public appearance.

The taste of the day was turning towards the spectacle of the grand old warrior the favourite of a nursery party, and Lord St. Vincent was a notoriously indulgent great-uncle to the " two dear little girls " of his heir, drowned off Brest in 1805. But the infant who appears in the final picture of him, on his knee at a crowded dinner-table, pawing a Star of the Bath, and asking shrilly of a terrible countenance, deep-sunk in Georgian neck-cloth and collar, " Where did you find it ? " was surely a boy, for the unexpectedly romantic and gently spoken response was : " I found it upon the sea, and if you become a sailor, and search diligently, perhaps you may find just such another."

Intimates of Admiralty days said that he had never been quite the same since he lost Troubridge. He confessed that he could not banish a certain winter storm scene from his mind, sleeping or waking. He was noticed to fidget while the post-bag was unlocked. " What news of the *Blenheim*? "

Sir Thomas Troubridge, when appointed to the chief command in East India seas to the eastward of Point de Galle, in Ceylon, had gone out with his flag in the old *Blenheim*. After an adventurous passage he had joined Sir Edward Pellew, who was not surprised to see a successor, but startled at the division of his station at a moment when he expected concerted action by the French. Pellew sent a very strong remonstrance to the Admiralty, and after the necessary long pause, orders came for Troubridge to take the chief command at the Cape of Good Hope. Mean-while, the *Blenheim*, formerly a three-decker, but cut down to carry only 74 guns, had been ashore in the Straits of Malacca. When she arrived at Madras, her Captain reported that there would be great danger in attempting to take her to the Cape at such a season. There had been no quarrel between him and Pellew, but Troubridge was in haste to be gone. Such was his confidence and prestige that many wealthy passengers embarked at Madras in a ship which was, in the opinion of several of her officers, no longer seaworthy. The *Blenheim* sailed in mid-January 1807, in company with a Dutch prize frigate and the *Harrier* brig. The brig alone emerged from a cyclone near the south-east end of Madagascar. A year later news reached the Admiralty that two vessels had put in for wonderfully rapid repairs at an islet off Madagascar and sailed again. The deposi-tions of humble native witnesses drew the life-size portrait of the burly authoritative principal British officer recognisably. Inhabitants of Bourbon Island supplied, after another twelve months, a tiny, bird's-eye picture of a line-of-battle ship in distress, with an Admiral's flag flying.

5

On the last Friday evening of January in the year of Waterloo George Matcham, junior, entered in his diary : " The Squire arrived with Horatia from Dover." This entry was the sequel to an equally curt announcement in the *Morning Post* of the preceding Friday, copied from the *Gazette de France*: "Calais, 17 Janvier: The celebrated Emma, widow of Sir William Hamilton, died here yesterday." Colonel the Hon. R. F. Greville at once wrote to the Prefect of the Department of Calais, but his man of business had forestalled him and was able to assure him next morning: "Lady Hamilton is certainly dead, and was buried on Friday last. I understand that she died in extreme poverty." **16** The records of the Calais municipality stated that death had taken place at one hour before noon on the 15th, not the 16th, in the house of the Sieur Damy, Rue Française, and that Dame Emma Lyons, a native of Lancashire in England, daughter of Henri Lyons and Marie Kidd, and widow of William Hamilton, had been fifty-one years old. The news was a relief to Sir William Hamilton's heir, for he had been receiving letters from persons who claimed that Lady Hamilton had made over to them, for ready money, the greater part of the annuity chargeable upon his estate, and until he had discovered the truth he had been withholding payment. It gradually became known that funeral expenses, amounting to £28 10s., had been met by Henry Cadogan, Esq., Lloyd's agent at Calais, that the Captains of all **17** the English vessels then in port had attended the ceremony, and that Mr. Cadogan, finding that a *procès* had been commenced to detain the person of Miss Horatia Nelson for Lady Hamilton's debts, had conveyed her in a vessel for England, and not quitted her until she was delivered to Lord Nelson's brother-in-law. Mr. Cadogan's lady visited pawnbrokers' and jewellers' shops, and the scattered property of a schoolgirl of Empire days followed her to Sussex in a basket—three gowns, one of silk, a number of shawls (one Indian), two necklaces and watches, several trinkets and a gold pin. . . . Lady Hamilton's ward, docile, elegant and highly accomplished, did her late guardian great credit. William Haslewood, who saw her in his London office soon after her arrival, found Miss Nelson little and pale for her fourteen years. He trusted that the invigorating breezes of a country home only seventeen miles from Brighthelmstone might soon restore her bloom and increase her strength. "The kind of life she had passed during the last two years must have given a shock to her constitution."

Ashfold Lodge, in the picturesque village of Slaughan, was not unknown to her. Nelson's sisters had never lost touch with

Lady Hamilton, whose regular annual appearances in Sussex and Norfolk, until 1808, bringing a large party from Merton and gorgeous gifts for all, were remembered by their children and grandchildren as gala days. " My dear Horatia," wrote Mrs. Bolton, " give my kindest love to her. The more I *think*, the dearer she is to me." Mrs. Bolton looked forward to her rubbers of whist with her ladyship, her husband sent thanks for tobacco, and the younger ladies for brooches, gowns, bonnets, material for patchwork, books, Twelfth Night cakes, and Valentines so exquisite they could only have come from Clarges Street. Emma Bolton, aged three, christened a splendid wax doll " Emma Hamilton ", " entirely her own idea ", and when her uncle Tom went up to Cambridge, he sent her ladyship an amusing account of his rooms, and felt low that he could not come to Merton as usual every week-end. He had nailed up two portraits of her in his Cranswick study. As late as 1811, she stood sponsor to " Nelson ", youngest son of Mrs. Matcham. But as years passed, both Boltons and Matchams came to realise with disquiet that when they had heard nothing from Lady Hamilton for a long spell, it was a sign that things were not going well with her, and that something in the nature of a bombshell might be expected. They had at first no suspicion that the news of Trafalgar had found her already heavily involved, with debts dating from before her husband's death. She continued to entertain on her old lavish, undiscriminating scale. Horatia's early memories included three personal maids attendant upon her guardian, one Black, one French and one Italian. Nelson's relatives heard with concern that when two sons of their Sovereign were her guests, such was Lady Hamilton's kindness of heart that she had made no suggestion that " Poor Blindy ", their brother Maurice's old *protégée*, entirely sightless and crippled, but by no means deaf or incurious, should " keep her room the time they were there—at least the Prince ". High hopes were built by them on reports of this festivity—the gracious notice taken of Horatia —a royal scheme that Nelson's adopted child should be taken to Windsor, to win the heart of " George our King ". " He ought to have a fellow-feeling, for, like her, he has lost a *great* supporter." When they heard that Lady Hamilton was thinking of selling Merton they were neither surprised nor sorry. The " Paradise " from which Nelson had torn himself away at the call of duty, promising a speedy and victorious return, seemed to all of them permanently shadowed by some ineffable melancholy.

U U

George Matcham and his eldest son, halting there after a business call upon Goldsmid at Morden on a day of high summer, when Lady Hamilton was absent, felt themselves strangely indisposed to linger. The " vast improvements " sanctioned but never seen by the master had been effected. The grounds, under the care of Cribb, were ready for his eye, his beasts gathered in the shade, a still-life in strong sun. . . . So vividly were his last sayings at Merton remembered that when her sailor son-in-law thanked Mrs. Bolton for a pleasant leave, using the words, " never spent such a happy time before ", the heart of Nelson's sister sank within her.

Young George, dashing over Westminster Bridge in a phaeton and four on his way home from Oxford in June 1808, met Lady Hamilton, " low on account of ye house at Merton not being sold ". This was the first intimation received by the family that her situation was desperate.

6

Within seven months of Nelson's death she had quarrelled fatally with his brother and heir, and consequently with Davison, who was, she thought, quick to transfer his allegiance to the quarter likely to be most influential.

On May 12–14 in the year following Trafalgar, Parliament debated and finally voted a pension of £5,000 per annum to be attached to the new Nelson peerage, £10,000 to enable the present Earl to buy an estate, and £10,000 apiece to his sisters. A pension of £2,000 per annum had already been granted to Viscountess Nelson in February. There had been no mention of the woman and child confidently entrusted by the Admiral to his King and Country, " now I am going to fight their Battles ".

Earl Nelson was still staying in Clarges Street with his wife and daughter, and according to Lady Hamilton, on hearing at her dinner-table of the splendid grant to his name and house, he produced the famous pocket-book containing the memorandum of his brother's last wishes—" threw it to me, and said, with a very coarse expression, that ' I might now do as I pleased with it ' ". A violent scene between two very hot-tempered persons [22] followed, and though they were afterwards persuaded by well-wishers to exchange conciliatory notes, and even visit one another, happy relations were never resumed.

Lady Hamilton did her guest injustice in concluding that he had deliberately suppressed the document explaining her claims until his own future was assured, but there seems no doubt that he had left her in ignorance of its persistently unlucky fate since it had passed into his hands as executor. In fact, he had taken considerable action, and it had not been in his power to suppress it even had he so wished, for Rose had already seen it and undertaken to show it to Pitt. Blackwood and Hardy were well acquainted with its contents, and as early as December 11 Davison had forwarded a copy to Brighton, which had evoked from the Prince of Wales a letter in the best style of the First Gentleman in Europe.

23   Earl Nelson had taken the original to Doctors' Commons on December 23, together with his brother's Will and seven codicils. Here, however, Sir William Scott, the future Lord Stowell, a person who remembered having met him with his brother and Lady Hamilton at Oxford, and who was well disposed towards her, advised him that it did not relate to any property possessed by the deceased, and therefore did not affect his power as executor to deal immediately with the estate. Earl Nelson registered the other documents, and left the pocket-book with Sir William, to be shown to the Prime Minister privately by Rose. Moreover, many persons, described by him as " of consequence ", were of opinion that as the Admiral's recommendation spoke freely of the Queen of Naples secretly assisting the British Fleet before the Battle of the Nile, its publication should be avoided, for diplomatic reasons. Sir William Scott took a copy, but Rose was never able to perform his part, as by the next time he saw Pitt, the Prime Minister was on his death-bed and the doctors forbade all talk of business. On February 15 the luckless relic was taken on by the Earl to the new Prime Minister. This character was the " cold-hearted Grenville ", whom Nelson had always prophesied would do nothing to help Lady Hamilton, and it is clear that on this occasion, and whenever afterwards approached on the same subject, his chilliness was remarkable. The Earl read the document aloud to him, " and strongly pointed out to him the *parts* relative to Lady Hamilton and the child ". The Earl observed to Lord Grenville that in doing this " he thought he was most effectually promoting the interests of Lady Hamilton and doing his duty, in which Lord Grenville acquiesced ". But the Prime Minister saw to it that the Earl departed from a most uncomfortable interview with the essential document still in his pocket, and there it remained until the awkward moment when the complacent legatee returned it to the wondering and chagrined Lady Hamilton. According to her own account, she

" had it registered the next day at Doctors' Commons, where it rests for the national redemption ". It was certainly brought in and proved by Earl Nelson and Haslewood on September 11, 1806, and on the 30th of that month came a result in the shape of a copy of a document recorded in the College of Arms, signed at His Majesty's command by Lord Spencer, and countersigned by the Earl Marshal and Clarencieux. His Majesty had granted the petition made on behalf of Horatia Nelson Thompson, an infant, by William, Earl Nelson and William Haslewood (executors) and Dame Emma Hamilton (sole guardian), that the infant should comply with the injunction contained in the last codicil of the late Lord Nelson—" I do leave to the beneficence of my Country my adopted daughter, Horatia Nelson Thompson ; and I desire she will use in future the name of Nelson only." Horatia Nelson Thompson had received royal licence and authority to assume and use the name of Nelson only, but nothing further ever resulted except miserable family dissension, nervous quibbling in Government Departments and an ineffaceable impression upon the public mind that the last wishes of England's greatest naval hero were neglected.

" The desk ", explained an admiring brother-officer of Hardy, " was not his *forte* ", but Hardy, a man of his word, although irritated by receiving no reply to several letters, wrote once more to Lady Hamilton before he sailed for the North Atlantic station, offering to take any boy recommended by her, and from Chesapeake Bay to Scott, inquiring as to her well-being. In 1812 he was still at work for her, though without, he regretted, the faintest " influence ".

Rose, with fainter hopes after the rebuff to Earl Nelson by Grenville, proceeded to tackle Canning relentlessly. The Prime Minister, who had been Foreign Secretary when Lady Hamilton had been Ambassadress at Naples, had not denied that her services deserved reward. But Canning, now Foreign Secretary, thought that Lord Grenville's letter, forwarded by Rose, " worded with the coldest caution ", gave the Prime Minister the opportunity, as he evidently had the intention, of saying that the Foreign Secret Service Fund was not the appropriate source. Three Administrations had succeeded one another since the services mentioned by Lord Nelson as Lady Hamilton's sole claim for recognition had been performed, they had been performed by a lady at a foreign Court at which her husband was Ambassador, and far from having been kept secret, they had been made known to every person whom she had solicited, " and printed in extracts of a will registered in Doctors' Commons and accessible to all mankind ". If any " unexceptionable mode " could be devised of giving Lady Hamilton the compensation she richly deserved, Canning would be happy; meanwhile the only contribution he could make towards solving the puzzle was an offer that he should, at a propitious moment, ask the Duke of Portland to ascertain if His Majesty would be pleased to 24 recommend " a small pension to the child ".

In June 1806 both the Boltons and Matchams feared that their brother William had acted shabbily to Lady Hamilton and to Dr. Scott. In spite of strong hints, and even squibs in the newspapers on the subject, the Earl had not resigned the prebendal stall at Canterbury which the Admiral had got for him and had frequently mentioned to the penurious Scott. (" Only you remain quiet; let me get my brother a step; that is all, and you shall have his.") The Earl's justification was that no step in 25 clerical rank had come to him. Before long, his sisters had other and personal reasons for complaint. They had already noticed a certain distance and pomposity in his attitude. They heard of, but did not see, his heir, " our young peer, flying about " at Norfolk balls and public occasions. On the day after Christmas in the following year the young Horatio took to bed with a cold. Canterbury physicians diagnosed a consumption of the lungs contracted from his having exposed a delicate frame unduly in the pursuit of field sports. His distracted parents hurried him to London for further advice. He died, on January 17, 1808, at Warne's Hotel, Conduit Street, of typhus fever. He was nineteen, and generally thought to have resembled his famous uncle, both in sweetness of disposition and activity. Their cousin, John Fisher, Bishop of Salisbury, calling at the hotel to offer the family spiritual consolation, found little Lady Charlotte sitting like a marble statue, so overcome by grief as to be incapable 26 of motion.

The Countess was long past the age for child-bearing. Tom Bolton, small and studious, Mrs. Cadogan's favourite amongst the young gentlemen, was now heir presumptive to the Nelson title and the estate, yet to be chosen. But Earl Nelson loved the thought of an heir presumptive no more than Queen Elizabeth and other potentates. A proposal forwarded by Haslewood that the families of Nelson's sisters should now take his surname aroused exhibitions of such " shocking rancour " against them, one and all, that George Matcham decided in despair, " It is evident he is as great an enemy to us as our dear lost friend was our patron." 27

Time softened the blow which had suddenly made great possessions and an hereditary title a fruitful source of mortification to a somewhat material-minded man. He was solaced by the match of his daughter with Lord Bridport's heir (by which he became the grandfather of six children), and determined that his brother's Sicilian duchy, at least, should descend in this line. When at last, in 1816, he had pleased his fancy in the choice of an estate, and completed its embellishments, he summoned Tom Bolton to stay for a month, and constant entertainment of the younger members of his sisters' families followed, though, with the customary perversity of important connections, he always showed most favour to young George Matcham, who took least trouble to be attentive to him and was openly appreciative of the ridiculous in his character and appearance.

Standlynch, rising four-square on a steep beech-crowned bluff, above the dark clear waters of the Avon, five miles below Salisbury, was a red-brick Georgian country house, with stone facings, conceived in the grand manner some eighty years past, with classic improvements by Nicholas Revett and flanking wings by the younger Wood of Bath. Its name was changed to Trafalgar House, and to-day the portrait of a light-haired boy, in blue-and-white uniform, with both hands on his sword-hilt, occupies the place of honour in the light and lofty saloon of a house with a dramatic view, through Doric pillars, of a landscape typical of the country for which he fought and died.

Both Tom Bolton and George Matcham married local young ladies of the name of Eyre, whom they met under their uncle's roof, lineal descendants of the lords of the manor of Standlynch; so, with the succession of the third earl, the property devolved to the blood of its original owners. But when Tom Bolton's " Horatio " was five years old, his prospects were unexpectedly threatened.

In April 1828 old Countess Nelson died, and within a few months Wessex was afforded the extraordinary spectacle of a very stout gentleman in his seventy-second year, with a nut-cracker profile, wearing an unusually large shovel hat and a tightly buttoned black frock-coat, which swept the tops of his Hessian boots, presenting himself as Cupid's messenger to the astonished gaze of a young lady with a shower of blonde ringlets, whose appearance was vocal of old family and reduced fortunes. But Earl Nelson, who was pronounced by the Bishop of Salisbury to possess a good plain understanding, uncommon application and a sound kernel within a rough husk, had made no mistake. Hilare, third daughter of Admiral Sir Robert Barlow, had been married before, at sixteen, to a cousin, who had died in India. She was twenty-eight, and had been a widow four seasons. After refusing the offer several times, she accepted Admiral Nelson's brother, a settlement of £4,000 per annum, the gift of a house in Portman Square and the position of mistress of Trafalgar House.

The Earl, who had startled his family soon after the death of his son by rebellious growlings that he would have an heir yet, died after six years of remarriage unsatisfied, and the Dowager Countess Nelson passed on to become a popular figure in yet another Georgian Great House. Godmersham Park, Kent, has often been identified as the prototype of Mansfield Park, and her third husband was George Knight, nephew of Jane Austen.

7

"Only let me spend my winter without the thought of a prison", wrote Lady Hamilton to the old Duke of Queensberry, in September 1808. "'Tis true my imprudence has brought it on me." The Duke did not, as she had suggested, buy Merton, but he added a codicil to his Will leaving her £500 a year, which she never got, as the Will was still being contested in 1815.

She had left Merton for a small river-side house at Richmond, "upon a plan of economy most laudably laid down", but young George Matcham, calling at dinner-time, "could almost have wept at the change", for although she had parted with her carriage and all her staff except two maids and a foot-boy, the only difference in her situation seemed that the quality of her guests was worse than it had been at Merton. She had been ill, and was still "low". On hearing the news of Trafalgar she had told Rose, "My heart and head are gone." A year later, a letter from William Hayley, who had known her in her spring-time in Romney's studio, had found her sitting in a stupor, in London, on a midsummer day, "leaning my cheek upon my hand, and very unhappy". "All seems gone like a dream." The old philosopher had told her that England would expect a heroic and serene bearing in the confidential friend of the immortal Nelson, and she had tried to assume it. " I did try and get a victory over myself and seem to be happy, alltho' miserable." Unfortunately, her efforts at seeming to be happy repelled some of her best friends. An acquaintance of Dr. Scott, hailed from a carriage window in London by the voice of a lady whom he recognised as Lady Hamilton, did not escape without a promise to come down to Merton next day to cheer her in her desolation. To his disgust, he found her entertaining sumptuously a mob of noisy parasites —" Signor Rovedino and Madame Bianchi, with other birds of the same feather ". Early next morning, in the garden, she attempted to justify herself by explaining that having such people to live with her was " a less expensive plan than taking Horatia to town for singing and Italian lessons "; but upon being pressed, the large and tearful lady admitted that she was already terri-fyingly in debt.

29

She might have pleaded that not all her debts had been selfishly incurred. She supported many poor relations, who requited her ill. The annuity of £500 left her by Nelson, charged upon his Brontë estate, produced nothing for three years, and after that was remitted irregularly. Cynics, who noticed that she went repeatedly to the theatre for the purpose of swooning when Braham sang " The Death of Nelson ", would have been quick to record that Lady Hamilton was gambling again, and there is no such record. She did at a later date admit having been " dreadfully imposed upon for my good nature, in being bail for a person I thought honourable ", but " my imprudence ", stormy references to the machinations of " artful mercenary wretches ", and Earl Nelson's meanness in throwing upon her the bills for the last improvements made at Merton were the only excuses ever offered by her for cumulative embarrassment. A meeting of what she called " my City friends " took place in London in November 1808, and her spirits soared. " They have rescued me from Destruction. . . . They are paying my debts. I live in retirement, and the City are going to put forward my claims. . . . *No power on earth* shall make me deviate from my present system." She had not been upon good terms with Davison since 1805, but he came forward now as one of her friends, and within the month, when the second and much more serious crash in his career took place, she too remembered nothing but that someone Nelson had loved was in distress. She wrote at once, offering any assistance Nelson would have given had " his powerful arm " been there. She wrote to the long-suffering Rose

30

and sent her secretary, Harrison, to see Davison in Newgate, and inquire what he wanted her to do on his behalf.

Next summer she performed her usual summer tour, to Ashfold and the coast for sea-bathing. The Boltons heard with pleasure that she had been going to " great Parties ". Abraham Goldsmid had given nearly £13,000 for Merton. She took lodgings in Bond Street. " The harp and viol were soon resounding from her lighted apartments, wilder extravagances than ever were committed." One by one she parted with her Nelson relics. Messrs. Salter received back the inscribed gift presented to Horatia during the twenty-five days, accompanied by an incoherent note that the child was " the daughter, the true and beloved daughter of Viscount Nelson. . . . Her mother was too great to be mentioned"—a reference thought to point at the Queen of Naples. The death of shrewd old Mrs. Cadogan in January 1810 removed from her " the best of Mothers ", and the last brake upon her irresponsibility. She left 136, Bond Street, for 76, Piccadilly, for 16, Dover Street, for 150, Bond Street. . . . The last reports of her in England are wholly pathetic. Major Pryse Lockhart Gordon, encountering a group of two sombrely clad women and half a dozen school-children in Greenwich Park on an April afternoon of 1811, would scarcely have recognised in a tall, voluminously shawled figure the once-admired Lady Hamilton—all her hair pushed out of sight under a huge shabby cap. Ready tears sprang to her eyes when he recalled to her their last meeting—at a ball given in honour of her birthday, by Admiral Nelson, on board the *Vanguard*, in Palermo Mole. She explained that as to-day was again her birthday, she was giving a little *fête* for dear little Horatia Thompson Nelson, her *gouvernante*, and some young companions, at the " Ship " hotel. She beckoned one of the nursery party, and introduced to him " the child who would have had a father if he had not gone forth to fight his Country's battles ".

Not all her stage friends were ungrateful. When she became, in the reserved words of her daughter, " too involved to remain at large ", Mrs. Billington harboured her in dramatic secrecy for several weeks at Fulham. But at last the inevitable happened. The squalid and alarming scene of arrest for debt took place. The New Year of 1813 found her, with " a fine snow scene " outside, huddled in ugly obscure rooms in the purlieus of the Temple, permitted to reside " within the rules of the King's Bench " on the condition that she made no attempt at escape.

The Matchams, to whom the news came as a shock after one of her ominous silences, wrote at once offering to take the child, sent gifts of game and a store of potatoes sufficient to last the winter, and volunteered to make an expedition to London to call upon her. They had been chilled, but had promptly responded to her last communication—a sudden request for the loan of £100. They were thinking of letting Ashfold and taking their large family abroad for reasons of economy. They suggested "a joint wish that we may all settle abroad in some city, town, or village". 35

All her effects left at her Bond Street lodgings had been seized and sold. She suffered a recurrence of jaundice, attended by the mental depression characteristic of the disease, and lay abed for weeks. Still she kept up a gallant pretence that her difficulties would soon be solved, and for a few months she did enjoy liberty again. She was re-arrested and back in " that vile Banco Regio " by July. With the approach of the thirteenth anniversary of the Battle of the Nile, she had regained enough of her old spirit to invite company to 12, Temple Place.

" Do come " [she wrote to a Mr. Thomas Lewis]. " It is a day to me glorious, for I largely contributed to its success, and at the same time it gives me great pain and grief thinking on the Dear Lamented Chief who so bravely won the day, and if you come we will drink to his immortal memory. He cou'd never have thought that his Child and myself shou'd pass the anniversary of that victorious day were [sic] we shall pass it, but I shall be with a few sincere and valuable friends, all Hearts of Gold, not Pinchbeck, and that will be consoling to the afflicted heart of

" your faithful friend
" Emma Hamilton." 36

In the spring of the following year, her hopes that the Prince of Wales, now Regent, would give a favourable answer to a long memorial of her claims to a pension were shattered by the publication of Nelson's private letters to her, stolen by James Harrison, the hack author, whom she had sheltered, together with his wife and family, since 1806. The Prince who was to live to believe 37 that he had led a charge at Waterloo had begun, directly after Trafalgar, to find that he had lost a great personal friend, and as the event had receded, his allusions to intimacy with a national hero had increased in pathos. The world now learnt what Nelson had thought of him.

Harrison's act shattered something further, and nearest of all to the heart of Lady Hamilton—almost the last of her

" regained reputation ", in defence of which she had fought at all costs for sixteen years.   Still, a few people believed the letters to be forgeries. . . .

A City friend who had known Nelson since Jamaica days rescued her after she had endured a second bout of detention lasting nearly nine months.   Alderman Joshua Jonathan Smith, senior partner of Messrs. Smith and Seiffe, sugar refiners, obtained her discharge from Lord Ellenborough in the first week of July 1814, and then she sailed from Tower Wharf for France in a vessel called *The Little Tom*, with Horatia, and less than £50 in her pocket.   Her few letters from the Calais district have the fragile charm of a contemporary water-colour.

She settled in a farmhouse on the common of a village called St. Pierre, two miles outside the town.   Every morning she took Horatia to a select day-school, kept by an old English resident. " I have an ass, for Horatia, as she wants, now she is 14, exercise. I go in a cart for my health."   At one o'clock she fetched her " ward ".   " She already reads, writes, and speaks Italian, French and English, and I am teaching her German and Spanish. . . . We read English, Roman and Grecian History." They dined early in their peaceful abode, which had large rooms and a fine garden, and the excellence and cheapness of their fare delighted her.   With child-like solemnity, she detailed to Colonel Greville, Alexander Davison and Sir William Scott that the best meat at St. Pierre was 5d. a pound, and a turbot, fresh from the sea, half-a-crown.   The milk from the cows on the common was like cream, and only two *sous* a quart.   Chickens and ducks cost 1s. 1d. the pair, turkeys 4s., partridges 5d. the couple, and good Bordeaux wine, red and white, fifteen pence the bottle. The exiles took part in all the mild local gaieties, walking two miles to assist at a *fête champêtre pour les bourgeois*, and one mile every Wednesday to a dance attended by all " persons of Rank " in the neighbourhood.   " We pay 3d. to go in."   Horatia, who danced all the country dances, and spoke French like a French girl, was " adored " and everyone was very kind to them both, " but our little world of happiness is in ourselves ".   On Sundays they went to the village church, " and read our prayers in French, for they are exactly like ours ".   Her health was mended by the simple regular round, the country air, the gentle exercise, the sensation of liberty, and above all the success of her last appearance in her favourite " Attitude ", that of the English lady.   " The Jaundice is leaving me, but my Broken

Heart does not leave me." Horatia was taken to the Comedy by the Governor's lady, in a party which included Prince Henry of Prussia. If her guardian could live to see Lord Nelson's child " well settled " she would " dye happy ".

They had arrived in Picardy in July. By early October signs of autumn were visible. They moved into the town, and took part of a house in a street running parallel with the southern rampart and *fosse*. Number III, Rue Française, was a choice dictated by the purse, not the eye, for its aspect in a city of sea-fogs was due north. Lady Hamilton's regular round, while her charge learnt " the harp, geography, arithmetic and five languages grammatically ", began to include visits to a *Mont de Piété* which was to attract Victorian tourists by a placard recording her patronage. She called and called at " Dessins ", the best hotel in the town, which she had given to English correspondents as her permanent address for letters. She was not yet experiencing actual want, but she was in debt again. From the time that she realised that her last fresh start in life had failed, she fell silent. Horatia takes up the story of the last four months, which is all darkness :

" At the time of her death she was in great distress, and had I not, unknown to her, written to Lord Nelson to ask the loan of £10, and to another kind friend of hers, who immediately sent her £20, she would not literally have had one shilling till her next allowance became due. Latterly she was scarcely sensible. I imagine that her illness originally began by being bled whilst labouring under an attack of jaundice whilst she lived at Richmond. From that time she was never well, and added to this, the baneful habit she had of taking wine and spirits to a fearful degree, brought on water on the chest. She died in January, 1815, and was buried in the burying ground attached to the town. That was a sad miserable time to me.

" The service was read over the body by a Roman Catholic priest who had attended her at her request during her illness. Lady H. had, ever since she had been in Calais, professed herself a Catholic.

" Latterly her mind became so irritable by drinking that I had written to Mr. Matcham, and he had desired that I would lose no time in getting some respectable person to take me over and that I was to come to them, where I should always find a home. After her death, as soon as he heard of it, he came to Dover to fetch me.

" With all Lady H.'s faults,—and she had *many*,—she had many fine qualities, which, had [she] been placed early in better hands, would have made her a very superior woman. It is but justice on my part to say that through *all her* difficulties, she *invariably* till the last few months, expended on my education etc., the whole of the *interest* of the sum left me by Lord Nelson, and which was left entirely at her control."

8

The pleasures of Ashfold were described by Squire Matcham as including " a fine extent of pasture and grain enclosed by a thick wood of oaks. A small valley belonging to the estate to the left runs down to the water, which forms the boundary. Above, the Downs present, literally, their misty mountain tops ".

Horatia spent two years in this setting, growing tall and fair, slight and lively. When the Matchams fulfilled their long-meditated plan of taking their family abroad, she passed on to the Boltons in Norfolk. She was sixteen, and engaged to be married. She wrote to her self-appointed guardian, George Rose, explaining that Mr. Blake's friends refused their consent unless some modest preferment could be found for him, and Rose, who was dying, but had never forgotten that she had been " recommended to my best attention by the Hero in parting from him, when he last sailed from Spithead, and strongly recommended to his Country in his last moments ", did what he could. He enclosed her note in one to the Prime Minister, asking if either the Chancellor might be approached on behalf of Mr. Blake (" He is now a Curate "), or, preferably, a pension of £200 per annum be granted to Miss Nelson. Eighteen months later the Matchams heard, in Paris, that the engagement was broken off. Horatia, having discovered in time that her future partner lacked one quality which she considered essential, had wisely given him his *congé*, " with full concurrence of all her friends ". Her aunt was relieved to hear presently that she was " never so happy ", which made the travellers wonder whether the appearance of a rival might not have been partially responsible for Mr. Blake's fatal " bad temper ", but two years elapsed before *The Times* recorded the marriage, at Burnham, on February 19, 1822, of Miss Nelson Nelson to the Rev. Philip Ward, M.A.

This time all promised well. At a date when a handsome and serious-minded young divine was the ideal of every novel-reading maiden, Mr. Ward fulfilled every requirement. He possessed as background a house at Bircham Newton, a military brother, and sisters of such beauty and amiability that they were known as " the Norfolk Graces ". Nelson's prayer by the bedside of a sleeping infant at Merton was answered. The life of Horatia was happy, full and long. She settled to Victorian matronhood, bearing an annual child in rural peace, her only causes for anxiety, nursery epidemics (which included cholera) and, as the years slipped by, the number of fine boys for whom employment must be found. She never learnt her parentage. At fourteen she had been old enough to besiege her guardian with questions. " On her death-bed at Calais I earnestly prayed her to tell me who my mother was but she would not, influenced then, I think, by the fear that I might leave her."

On her arrival at Ashfold, Squire Matcham had made inquiries on her behalf, through Haslewood, of Alderman Smith, who had spoken of " sacred deposits " left with him by the lady whom he had rescued from prison; but the result was disappointing. Lady Hamilton had spoken to Smith of " documents which prove Horatia's parentage " being in the care of Haslewood, and to Haslewood of sending him " a packet concerning that dear child ". She had never fulfilled her declared intention, and when her Will and other effects arrived from France, no such information was amongst them. The only packet relating to Horatia to come to light was produced out of the vaults of Coutts, bankers to the Cavendish family, to whom they had been entrusted by an intimate friend of Lady Hamilton, Elizabeth, mistress, and eventually second wife, of the seventh Duke of Devonshire. It contained nothing new—" two letters from the late Lord N: the last dated October 20th, 1805, to Horatia, to whom he calls himself Father ".

Mr. Ward, when his turn came to be interested, sought out and interviewed Tom Allen, the Admiral's old body-servant, and Tom was very ready with a winter's tale, inaccurate in every detail that could be checked. An agitated female, whom he had recognised as the sister of a Genoese merchant, and a Lieutenant in the Navy had arrived at his master's lodgings in Half Moon Street on a late January evening of 1801, when the Admiral was dressing for dinner. She had come over in the *Seahorse*, commanded by Sir " William " Fremantle, " who was acquainted with the whole story ". On Allen's telling the Admiral of her appearance, " he immediately desired me to call a hackney-coach, and say nothing concerning it to the servants. He got into the coach and drove off, not returning for a couple of hours." Allen added that he afterwards heard that the female, " who appeared to be very near her confinement ", had died in child-bed.

Horatia's comment was, " Tom probably wished to make himself of consequence, but had not imagination sufficient to concoct such a tale." Researches proved that Nelson was not in London at the date mentioned, that Captain (later Sir Thomas) Fremantle had relinquished the command of the *Seahorse* more than three years previously, and that the ship had not arrived from the Mediterranean in January 1801. Therefore, though some such incident might have occurred, it could have no reference to the birth of Horatia. Two years passed before another clue offered.

When Captain Ward of the 81st Regiment happened to be staying at Bircham Newton in 1828, his sister-in-law received a letter from the daughter of her old nurse, with whom she had long lost touch. The captain, when next in London, called upon Mary Johnstone, *née* Gibson, who was eager to help, but the only tangible evidence in her possession was a carefully preserved bundle of thirty-eight notes from Lady Hamilton to the deceased Mrs. Gibson, making appointments for " dear little Miss Horatia " to be brought to visit her, a likeness of the child given by Lord Nelson to her attendant, and one line from the Admiral himself, post-marked November 19, 1802: " Mrs. Gibson is desired on no consideration to answer any questions about Miss Thompson, or who placed her with Mrs. G., as ill-tempered persons have talked lies about the child." Her reminiscences were that Lady Hamilton had brought the infant, then no more than eight days old, to 9, Little Titchfield Street, in a hackney-coach, unattended, in either January or February 1801 (Captain Ward could not remember which). No information had been offered to Mrs. Gibson except of handsome recompense. " Lady Hamilton constantly visited her : Lord Nelson was frequently her companion, and often came alone, and played for hours with the infant on the floor, calling her his own child."

Horatia put " implicit confidence " in Mary Johnstone's statement, and recollected her and her mother kindly. " Mrs. Gibson wished Lady H. to take her to Merton as resident nurse, but it being supposed she spoiled me, the old woman was not allowed to remain, tho' she tried hard to do so."

The investigation then languished, perforce, for sixteen years, until October 2, 1844, when Sir Harris Nicolas, author and antiquary, who had, in his youth, captured French frigates off the Calabrian coast, happened to be taking a stroll in the Strand. His seventh and final volume of *Lord Nelson's Letters and Despatches* was almost ready to go to press, and he still had not satisfied himself as to the authenticity of the mutilated letters anonymously published in 1814, and consequently the relations between his hero and Lady Hamilton. Upon their encountering the Vicar of Tenterden, Kent, in town, with his lady upon his arm, a mutual acquaintance performed introductions, and Sir Harris realised in Mrs. Ward the Admiral's "only child", "the mysterious Horatia" of the famous "last codicil". A couple who evidently shared his leading enthusiasm accompanied the eager editor forthwith to 55, Torrington Square, where Mrs. Ward saw in his study a safe, entirely filled with Nelson manuscripts, as large as that which she remembered Lady Hamilton sending from Richmond to Harrison. Conversation turned naturally to Harrison's "horrid book", which the lady believed to be a forgery. A month later she sent Sir Harris eight pages of neat notes on the Harrison volume, and soon two persons long and deeply interested in the same subject were in regular correspondence. They gladly pooled the results of their previous inquiries, and set to work in partnership with renewed hope. Both had been approached by persons called Evans, dealers in Nelsoniana. Sir Harris brought to the fray a letter to one of Locker's sons from the late Sir Thomas Hardy, enclosing a statement from Lady Hamilton dated November 7, 1812: "Horatia is our dear Nelson's daughter." Sir Thomas, it is true, had discounted this, and died in the belief that the child adopted by Nelson had been born during the action at Copenhagen to a sailmaker's wife of the name of Thompson, in the *Elephant*, but Sir Harris had satisfied himself that neither the sail-maker nor the sail-maker's mate in that ship, at that date, had borne the name of Thompson; in any case, the child left with Mrs. Gibson by Lady Hamilton had been seen by Nelson before he left London for the Baltic.

Mrs. Ward, much richer in material, had news of a clerk called Thomson, or Thompson, who had served twenty-nine or thirty years ago in the Admiralty, and might be the widower of Allen's agitated female, and certificates and letters showing that Lady Hamilton had stood sponsor to an infant at the Foundling Hospital, a thing she thought very probable, for "Lady H. was always remarkably fond of visiting these kind of places. Hardly a month passed but we used to drive to the Magdalens, or the Blind School, or many other places of this kind."

A merchant of Lisbon, called John James Stephens, who had left "Lord Nelson's daughter" a legacy of £500, might have had some private reason for doing so. Mrs. Ward wished now that when she had been in Portugal with her husband, they had tried

Horatia kneeling at her father's tomb.

By W. Owen, R.A. (1769–1825).   (50″ × 40″.)

Presented by the Rev. Hugh Nelson-Ward, grandson of Horatia,
to the National Maritime Museum, Greenwich.

*Reproduced by kind permission of the Trustees, the National
Maritime Museum, Greenwich.*

to discover if the man still existed. . . . It had already become obvious to her that " a long confabulation " would be more rewarding than covering many sheets with fine Italian script to a correspondent who was a stern critic (" 'Tis a sad habit not to date one's letters, I grant "), and a wearer of bonnet and shawl who was proposing to " run up to Town on Monday " from " our old Vicarage ", gave 30, Cambridge Street, Connaught Square, as her direction, and since she did not know much of London localities, asked if that address was far from Torrington Square.

After his second interview with Mrs. Ward, the figure of Haslewood appeared to Sir Harris to grow in significance, and he began to plan a trip to Brighton, where Lord Nelson's attorney, well stricken in years, resided in retirement. Mrs. Ward had at first very little faith that Haslewood would be helpful; he had told Mrs. Matcham long ago that he " really knew nothing ". Besides, as a lady of 1844, with a sense of social values, pointed out, " You must remember that Mr. Haslewood's connexion with Lord Nelson was not that of a friend, but that of lawyer and client. . . . I cannot credit that Lord Nelson would have confided in Mr. Haslewood that which he never revealed to his own family, or even Mr. Davison, a man he esteemed very highly." Unfortunately, Alexander Davison was not available. He had died in Regency Square, Brighton, an octagenarian, fifteen years previously. She expected that " Wm. Haslewood Esq., of Kemp Town will look very wise and tell you nothing ". Nevertheless as the date of Sir Harris's expedition drew near she became infected by his belief that he was upon the eve of solving the mystery. " Do, my dear sir, let me hear from you after the interview. You may easily imagine how very anxious I am to hear your account."

The interview was not entirely unfruitful. Sir Harris left it clearly understanding that he was at liberty to deny that Lady Hamilton had been the mother of Lord Nelson's child.

" I have always said ", pronounced Mrs. Ward triumphantly, " that Lady Hamilton was not, and could not have been my mother." But Sir Harris had to confess that all his powers of persuasion had failed to woo the aged attorney to offer proof of his decided announcement. " 'Tis singular ", mourned Mrs. Ward, " that whenever we fancy that we see a glimmering of light in the distance, how short a time it is before it is extinguished." She had been following her fifth false trail—a Mr. Russell, a small lawyer of Cowes, who had helped Lady Hamilton

X X

to draw up one of her memorials of her claim to a pension. " Do you think that Wm. Haslewood will die and make no sign ? " After five months' consideration of this imminent possibility, she decided to take the step of writing to him personally, without mentioning Sir Harris, asking whether he would, under promise of inviolable secrecy, divulge the name of her mother. She got a prompt reply, but it was characteristic of a person whom she had warned Sir Harris had " more of the fox about him than you would give him credit for ". " Your mother ", wrote Haslewood, after a pompous preamble as to professional secrecy, " was well acquainted with Lady Hamilton, and saw you often during your infancy; but soon after her marriage she went to reside a considerable distance from London, which or [sic] never visited afterwards." He lamented that he could say no more. He had indeed already said more than he could support.

Sir Harris, in the following spring, published in his final volume an article headed " Miss Horatia Nelson Thompson (now Mrs. Ward) ", which left the problem of her mother's identity unsolved, but drew attention to the fact that all Lord Nelson's conduct displayed beyond doubt that he believed her to be his child. " By the bye, *candidly*," asked Mrs. Ward, " *do you* think there is *any*? It is a singular fact that my children are reckoned strikingly like Mrs. Henry Girdlestone's (she was a niece of Mrs. Bolton) and other branches of the family, not one, but several in each family, have the resemblance." She was on the track of another Mrs. Thompson, a Frenchwoman, wife of Richard Thompson, Esq., of Denham Court, near Uxbridge, a great sportsman and frequenter of White's, host to Beau Brummel. " To the first and last they were both very kind to Lady H." Sir Harris, equally persistent, had heard of another christening, at Merton parish church this time, at which both Lord Nelson and Lady Hamilton had been godparents. He had written to the present incumbent. This effort brought forth a copy of the baptismal register of " Fatima ", the twenty-year-old negro maid whom Horatia perfectly remembered, and a suggestion by the Rev. Mr. Bond that Cribb, Lord Nelson's head gardener, a highly respectable man, though very old, had a retentive memory and delighted in anecdote.

The Evanses, with whom both Sir Harris and Mrs. Ward had exchanged letters and visits, had turned out to have nothing in common except unsatisfactory character. ("Two of the name bad men.") Mrs. Ward threw cold water on the vicar of

Merton's suggestion. "Mr. Cribb *can* know *nothing.*" Her despairing conclusion was : "I have always, if you remember, told you that I never for an instant gave credence to the story of the Queen of Naples, and, of course, to a certainty, none of her daughters. . . . My opinion has always been that either a foreign person, or at any rate one from abroad, was the person."

Sir Harris retired from the struggle after two years, baffled, but satisfied that he had shirked no possible inquiry. It would appear that he had also a daily companion to remind him of an interesting quest in partnership with an accomplished and quick-witted lady. Not all his confabulations with Mrs. Ward had been restricted to the clan of Thompson.

"When I got home, I found that my son had given away two of the puppies, leaving only a black one, who is not so pretty as I should have liked to send you." Young Mr. Ward, however, had been instructed to get back the pick of the litter, and it was to be dropped at Torrington Square " *en route* for Cambridge ".

As far as can be judged, Lord Nelson's Horatia inherited nothing from her mother except aptitude for languages and love of animals, and nothing from her father except his favourite " activity ". But Nature had performed one of her celebrated tricks. Lady Hamilton's pupil was a perfect " throw-back " to the long-lived, country-rooted clerical Nelson stock of preceding generations. The child born on a winter's day in the year of Copenhagen, with whom Nelson had played on the carpet in Sloane Street lodgings (taken so that " I might be in an airy situation " after severe cow-pox following vaccination), lived to be eighty-one.

Six years after Mrs. Nelson-Ward had been laid to rest in Pinner churchyard under a tombstone inscribed, " the adopted daughter of Vice-Admiral Lord Nelson ", a load of manuscripts rumbled up to the doors of the Pavilion, Fonthill, the old laundry quarters of the bizarre Wiltshire country seat in which Lord Nelson and Sir William and Lady Hamilton had spent the Christmas before her birth as guests of Beckford. The latest collection of holograph correspondence for which Mr. Alfred Morrison, the then owner of the Fonthill estate, had bid at Sotheby's had been put up to auction by a Mr. Joseph Mayer of Liverpool. It included hundreds of letters in the handwriting of Lord Nelson, addressed to Lady Hamilton, some of which, as they had been entrusted to private messengers, were completely unguarded. The correspondence was almost one-sided, as Lord Nelson had always burnt Lady

Hamilton's replies, but Admiral Keats had returned to her, with the seals unbroken, two letters dated October 1805, beginning "My most dear" and "My dearest life", addressed to a Commander-in-Chief who had already fallen in action.

Parts of Mr. Morrison's purchase had already been quoted by Dr. Pettigrew, in his *Life of Nelson*, published in 1849, but as he had given no references, their authenticity had been questioned, and his taste censured. Sixteen months before he had chanced upon this tremendous *cache*, Mr. Morrison had secured, also at Sotheby's, from the executors of Mr. Finch-Hatton, grandson of Colonel Robert Greville, the private papers of Sir William Hamilton.

He caused the two complementary collections to be privately printed, in 1893–4, and any doubts as to Horatia being the child of Lord Nelson and Lady Hamilton were settled.   *42*

9

Less than three weeks after Sir Harris Nicolas met Mr. and Mrs. Ward in the Strand, Queen Victoria was on her way from Osborne House in the Isle of Wight to London, to open the new Royal Exchange. Her eye was attracted by a Georgian ship-of-the-line decorated with flags and laurels. She inquired the cause, and was told that the date was the anniversary of the Battle of Trafalgar. The *Victory* was immediately signalled that Her Majesty, attended by the Prince Consort and *suite*, was coming on board, and Captain George Moubray, aged seventy-one, who had been First of the *Polyphemus* at Trafalgar, braced himself to escort a young ruler of Great Britain upon a tour of Nelson's flagship. On the quarter-deck Her Majesty read aloud in clear accents the inscription "Here Nelson fell", and plucked two leaves from the wreath in which it was enshrined. She then turned her gaze to the break of the poop, where, over the steering wheel, were inscribed the words, "England expects that every man will do his duty", and repeated the famous signal with much emphasis. While the Prince was surveying Portsmouth harbour from the poop, Her Majesty, who remembered her history lesson, expressed the desire to be shown the spot where the hero had drawn his last breath. The indomitable royal crinoline was manœuvred on the difficult journey down to the close dimness of the cockpit, and there Her Majesty stood several moments in silence, "much affected by the reflections which such a scene awakened".

She was twenty-five, and had been married four years, and was the happiest woman in the world. In those four years the succession had been amply secured—a girl, a boy, a girl, a boy. " They say no sovereign *was more* loved, and that for our *happy domestic* home, which gives such a good example." Prince Alfred, born nine weeks past, was to be the sailor of the family, and had been named after the founder of Britain's Navy. The Prince Consort was alive to the importance of naval heroes to an island race.

The story of the *Victory* since Trafalgar was a surprising one. She had been recommissioned in 1808, after a thorough refit, and for nearly six years had carried the flag of Saumarez, commanding the Baltic Fleet. She had been out to the Peninsular War twice, and when it had been proposed to send her to sea again in the year of Waterloo, six Admirals had put in a claim for her. But the end of the war against Buonaparte had meant the close of her fighting career. Three years before Queen Victoria's visit, public opinion had been suddenly and strongly excited by a report that " this sacred ship " was to share the fate which had already overtaken the *Temeraire*. The roar of John Bull, especially in the newspapers of the outports, was loud until an announcement was made that H.M.S. *Victory* was to remain, as she had been since 1825, flagship of the Admiral Commanding-in-Chief at Portsmouth, whereupon it dropped to mollified mutterings that " it must be the wish of every Englishman's heart that she may be preserved as long as one plank of her will hold to another ", and criticism returned to Trafalgar Square.

As early as 1827, the demolition of the " filthy and disreputable hovels " which covered an area west of the St. Martin's in the Fields had been ordered with the object of providing London with a worthy memorial to Nelson. " Trafalgar balconies " abounded in domestic architecture, and innumerable streets and licensed premises bore his name. The Guildhall and St. Paul's had long possessed monuments which included approved likenesses ; an arch in the park of Castle Townsend, near Cork, displayed an inscription that it had been built by twelve hundred Sea Fencibles, in five hours, on November 10, 1805. Portsdown Hill, and Sackville Street, Dublin, were dominated by graceful columns, and the Calton Hill, Edinburgh, by a stalwart Gothic tower. Liverpool, Birmingham, Glasgow, Norwich and Yarmouth had all produced something massive, but throughout the remainder of the reign of George IV and all that of his successor, work on

" the manifestation of National gratitude in the English Capital "
had proceeded slowly or not at all. The donation of a Czar who
was preparing to improve relations with England by a personal
appearance settled the question of completion, and in the year
preceding Queen Victoria's inspection of the *Victory*, Trafalgar
Square was open to traffic and to adverse comment. For although
everything had been planned on the grand scale, Nelson's countrymen did not at first sight take kindly to the result. A measure-
ment of 170 ft. 6 in. was mentioned for the fluted granite column
surmounted by a 17-feet figure wearing a cocked hat 3 ft. 9 in.
across. The pedestal had been adorned in *basso relievo* by four
separate leading artists with representations of the actions at
St. Vincent, the Nile, Copenhagen and the scene in the cockpit.
The open space surrounding the monument was soon adopted as
a rallying ground for John Bull in contentious mood, but generations succeeded one another before a poet saw romance in the
figure of the Admiral, " riding the sky, with one arm and one
eye ".

     Sir Harris Nicolas felt himself obliged to mention the affair
in his final volume, but thought everything about it so bad that
he had better spare himself the pain of adding one word to what
had already been said. Mrs. Ward had told him at their first
interview that the coat and waistcoat worn by Nelson at Trafalgar
should still be in the possession of the widow of Alderman
Smith, to whom Lady Hamilton had parted with them in return
for monetary assistance. He had been down to Twickenham,
where an old lady had babbled as he sat staring at garments,
crumpled, faded and stained but " authentic beyond the possibility of doubt ". She was asking £150. The Prince Consort
had graciously accepted the dedication of Sir Harris's edition of
Lord Nelson's Letters and Despatches. He forwarded to H.R.H. a
proof of an Appeal to the Nation to buy the relics. Within a few
hours came a reply from Buckingham Palace that H.R.H.
commanded the purchase without delay on his own account.
" It will be a pleasure and pride to him to present them to Greenwich Hospital." A new and powerful influence was arising
in the vicinity of the Throne. A long story was drawing to its
close. In September 1854, when the Prime Minister, with his
humble duty, begged leave to lay before Her Majesty certain
proposals for the Civil List, he approached his conclusion with some
diffidence. A numerous party in the Commons had wished that
the Government should propose a special vote for these funds,

but the Cabinet's recommendation seemed to Lord Aberdeen preferable, as it would avoid a Parliamentary Debate on the subject. " There seems little doubt that the person referred to was really Lord Nelson's daughter, according to evidence recently produced, and was recommended by him to the Country just before the Battle of Trafalgar." Amongst the results were pensions from Her Majesty to three grand-daughters of Lord Nelson, and for the fifth surviving grandson, from the Prince Consort, an Indian cadetship.

10

When Abraham Goldsmid bought Merton Place it seemed that the traditional silver lining had appeared in the noticeable cloud brooding over the house. The Dutch-Jewish financier who owned adjoining property announced his tactful intention of preserving some of the rooms as the Admiral had used and left them. Mrs. Bolton comforted herself and Lady Hamilton with prospects of driving down from London to take " a *melancholy pleasure* in tracing former times in those walks ". For eighteen months the house became in effect what it had always unconsciously been, a Nelson museum. But on September 17, 1810, Sarah Connor, an uneducated but graphic correspondent, told Lady Hamilton that she had again waited in all day for a promised call from the banker. A trip to his business house had drawn from a clerk the disquieting intelligence that Mr. Goldsmid's attendances recently had been irregular. " It was feared he should lose a large sum of money. It would not ruin him, as he was so rich, but the sum was large." Eleven days later, Abraham Goldsmid wandered out alone into a part of the grounds called " The Wilderness ", and there took his life. The house was never again a private residence, and the malediction upon it seemed to grow. Horatia well remembered hearing that Mr. Cribb, head gardener, had been assigned the dreadful duty of removing " Fatima, the black maid taken out of a slave ship, of whom Lady Hamilton was very fond, from Bear Lane Workhouse, where 10s. a week was being paid for her, to St. Luke's madhouse, where she died ".

On Christmas Eve, 1863, James Hudson, son-in-law of Cribb, wrote to his son from Merton :

" When first we came to live here there were but three cottages on the Estate, and only eleven persons, three men, three women and five children. Now there are over two hundred houses, and nearly a thousand people.   For nearly seven years after we came here, Nelson's beautiful mansion stood entire and furnished, as when he had left it to take command of the Channel Fleet, never to return.   During that time we could at our pleasure take a stroll through the deserted rooms and admire the beautiful furniture, and indulge in those melancholy reflections that such a scene was calculated to inspire; and when tired of that, we could take a turn in the gardens, or ramble in the walks and beautiful pleasure grounds by which it was surrounded, and listen to the feathered songsters that filled the place with melody.   But now, what a change has come over it !   Of that mansion not so much as a stick or stone remains to mark the spot on which it stood.   Those beautiful pleasure grounds and gardens all destroyed, the trees and shrubs all cut down, the birds have hied themselves to some more quiet and secluded spot, and nearly all the ground covered with unsightly bricks and mortar; and if this is not sufficient to disfigure and transform the place, they are going to make a railroad right through the centre of it.   I was served last week with a notice my premises *is*, or may be, required for the purpose.   Even the consecrated ground of the venerable Abbey, that has lain undisturbed for more than seven hundred years, is to be desecrated by the pick axe and spade of the navvy.   I think the people of this country are going railway mad."   43

The evidence of Hudson that nothing remarkable was left of Merton Place within sixty years of Trafalgar is confirmed, with additions in the Ichabod vein, by every succeeding biographer of Nelson who made the due pilgrimage, but even the site of a hero's home holds attraction, and such pilgrimages, always touching, are seldom entirely unrewarding.

The extent of the estate can be judged with comparative accuracy from the advertisements preceding its sale, in 1808 and 1815.   Large-scale maps of the district, published as late as 1817,   44 show Morden Grove as the property of A. Goldsmid, Mr. Halfhide's smaller house, and Merton Place, still under the name of " — Greaves, Esq.," from whom Nelson bought it.   A vicar of Merton has printed locally a booklet dealing with the environs, residence and circle of the most famous parishioner.   In 1946, sign-   45 posts on a by-pass, curving through Surrey water-meadows to avoid Kingston, talk promisingly and musically of Merton and Morden, recalling the well-known picture of the arrival of a frigate Captain, very early on an autumn morning, to the house where Lady Hamilton played at being a *châtelaine* and a *bergère*, and Nelson was never so happy.   The railway anathematised by old Hudson, and in a form undreamt of by him—underground—carries the traveller from London to either of two stations convenient for Merton Place in half the time proudly mentioned by the purchaser in 1802.   In the vicinity of the stations crowds and noise and, what is worse than the "modern development" deplored by earlier biographers, mid-Victorian minor commercial architecture in decay, distract the imagination, but still a wider air than that of the City is noticeable at Merton—figures mostly walking and talking slower than in the Strand, and during the working-hours of the day, as in 1802, a preponderance of women and children, and dogs. The waters of the Wandle still run by the side of the High Street. "Hamilton", "Hardy", "Nelson" and "Victory" roads, filled with identical small dwellings, stretch, only slightly uphill, towards what was once "the Poop". In the vicinity of the church something of the old magic still lingers. There are chestnuts and hawthorns and lilacs and laburnums, fragments of warm red-brick wall and buff lanes vanishing towards stiles. On a May day it is clear where Hudson's birds have betaken themselves. Within the church, high over the chancel arch, in very poor light, hang six heraldic paintings. One is the hatchment noticeable over the front door of Merton Place in engravings published in 1806, flowingly inscribed, " The Seat of the gallant Admiral Lord Nelson, who died in battle, Oct. 21, 1805 ". Time has struck a blow at the gold and silver paint and primitive oil colours, but the shapes can still be discerned of a palm tree *issuant* between a disabled first-rate and a battery in ruins, and a sailor, armed with a cutlass and a pair of pistols in his belt.

AUTHORITIES

CHAPTER I

"Nephew to Captain Suckling"

1. *The Nelsons of Burnham Thorpe*, M. Eyre Matcham, 1911, 87.
2. The name Horatio came to Horatio Nelson *via* the families of de Vere, Townshend and Walpole. Mary, daughter and co-heiress of Horatio de Vere, Baron Vere of Tilbury (1565–1635), married Sir Roger Townshend of Raynham, and had issue, Horatio, first Viscount Townshend (1630–87), who had issue, Charles, second Viscount Townshend, ward of Robert Walpole, and husband of Robert Walpole's sixth daughter, Dorothy. Robert Walpole's fifth son, Horatio, first Baron Walpole of Wolterton (1678–1757), was godson of Horatio, first Viscount Townshend, and father of the second Baron Walpole of Wolterton (1723–1809), god-father of Horatio Nelson.
3. Nelson's godmother, Joyce Pyle, was a spinster lady aged 51, daughter of Mary Rolfe of Heacham and the Rev. Thomas Pyle of Lynn, and sister of the Rev. Edmund Rolfe, Chaplain to George II. (*Rolfe Family Records*, R. and A. Gunther. Privately printed, Hazel, Watson and Viney, Ltd., London and Aylesbury, 1914, pp. 46 and 65.)
4. *The Life and Services of Horatio, Viscount Nelson, from his lordship's manuscripts*, Rev. James Clarke, Librarian and Chaplain to George, Prince of Wales, and John M'Arthur, Secretary to Admiral Lord Hood. The first edition, published 1809, is in two volumes. The edition quoted in the present work is that of 1840 in three volumes: I, 159.
5. Matcham: 58–9.
6. By J. T. Heins, in the collection of Earl Nelson at Trafalgar House.
7. *The collection of autograph letters and historical documents formed by Alfred Morrison. The Hamilton and Nelson Papers*. Printed for private circulation, 1894. Two vols. Hereafter cited as "Morrison MS.": 936.
8. *Despatches and Letters of Vice-Admiral Lord Viscount Nelson*, with notes, Sir N. H. Nicolas, 1844. Seven vols. V, 238.
9. *A Family Historical Register*, by Edmund Nelson, Rector of Burnham Thorpe, 1781, with notes by Horatia Nelson-Ward, Nelson-Ward MS., National Maritime Museum, Greenwich. The Fowles were connections. Elizabeth Turner, sister of Nelson's grandmother, Anne Suckling, *née* Turner, married John Fowle.
10. Clarke and M'Arthur: I, 15.
11. *Nelson in England*, E. H. Moorhouse, 1913: 12. *A History of Burnham Thorpe, Lord Nelson's birthplace*, Anon., Norwich, 1937, 25. The garden which Nelson knew still flourishes, and a Rector of Burnham Thorpe still looks upon it from his study window. An old brick wall, running up the slope of the hill towards the new Rectory, shelters venerable mulberry, quince, medlar and pear trees. The Rev. Edmund Nelson's successor (Daniel Evererd, Rector 1802–53) built a coach-house and stabling on the site of the old house, and cottages near by for grooms and

gardeners. His nephew and successor (1853–75) pulled down more than a third of his work : all that remains of the Old Parsonage to-day is a small portion of wall, built into a coach-house.

12. *Memoirs of the Life of Vice-Admiral Lord Viscount Nelson*, Thomas Pettigrew, 1849. Two vols : II, 263. The unillustrious old school-friend was called Levett Hanson.

13. " Sea-officer " has been employed in the present work in preference to " Naval officer ", as the latter, in Nelson's day, and invariably when used by Nelson, denoted an Admiralty official in charge of an oversea dockyard or establishment.

14. *Nelsonian Reminiscences, Leaves from Memory's Log*, G. S. Parsons, R.N. Ed. W. H. Long, 1905, 199.

15. Nicolas : I, 4.

16. *Naval Chronicle*, XIII, 170–1, " Memoir of Captain D'Auvergne ".

17. MS. journal of Thomas Floyd, R.N.

18. Clarke and M'Arthur : I, 18–22 ; Nicolas : I, 4–6 ; Matcham : 283 ; Floyd MS.

19. Walden's Island was named after Frederick Walden, midshipman of the *Racehorse*, who was directed by Captain Phipps to land there on August 5, 1773, to discover if open water was visible from it.

20. Cornwallis Wykeham-Martin Manuscript, Historical Manuscripts Commission, VI, 341–2. *Autobiography of Miss Cornelia Knight*, 1861, two vols. : II, 286.

21. Malaria seems to cover his symptoms on this occasion. Although it had been long known (and had carried off Alexander the Great, Oliver Cromwell and James I), it was not until 1800 that Laveran found the micro-organism called the plasmodium; and the disease was very little understood until the closing years of the nineteenth century. Alkaloids, including " Jesuit's Bark " (quinine), were employed in Nelson's time, but not in sufficient quantities or over a sufficiently long period. In various countries the mosquito was connected with the disease, in popular belief, but medical men still talked vaguely of avoiding " night air ".

22. Clarke and M'Arthur : I, 23–4.

23. *Ibid.*: 24–5.

24. The mothers of Horace Hammond and Horatio Nelson were first cousins; moreover, Mrs. Hammond had married a cousin, the son of Susan Walpole, Mrs. Nelson's great-aunt, and Horace's father was god-parent to Horatio.

25. Add. MS., British Museum, 34,988, " Nelson Papers ", LXXXVII, ff. 1, 2.

26. Nicolas : I, 7 and 23–4 ; Clarke and M'Arthur : I, 26–8.

27. *East Anglian Heroes*, T. Foley, Norwich, 1905, 19, 23.

CHAPTER II

POST-CAPTAIN

1. Margaret, wife of Admiral of the Fleet Sir Peter Parker, was daughter of Walter Nugent, Esq., mother of Vice-Admiral Sir Christopher Parker, and grandmother of Captain Sir Peter Parker (killed in action 1814) and Admiral Sir Charles Parker.

2. Captain Everitt, of the *Hinchingbrooke*, who had been killed by a random ball, had been at the moment commanding the *Ruby* in place of Captain Deane, absent sick.

3. The caddies are now an exhibit of the Nelson-Ward Collection, National Maritime Museum.

4. Benjamin Moseley, M.D. (1742–1819), studied medicine in London, Paris and Leyden, before settling to practise in Jamaica, in 1768, where he was appointed Surgeon-General. He made a considerable fortune in the West Indies and Newfoundland, and died Physician to the Royal Hospital, Chelsea.

5. Thomas Dancer, M.D. (1755?–1811), settled in practice in Bath on his retirement from Jamaica, corresponded with Sir Joseph Banks on botanical topics, and published several treatises.

6. Matcham : 284.

7. Two Despards went on this expedition. The younger, afterwards Colonel Edward Despard, of the 79th Regiment, was executed for high treason in 1803.

8. The " fever " described by Nelson as " destroying the Army and Navy " on this expedition was undoubtedly the mosquito-borne yellow fever of the Caribbean, nicknamed " Yellow Jack ". Dalling's plan of the operations, " Capt. Nelson being in command of the naval force ", is to be found in Add. MS. 34,990, " Nelson Papers ", LXXXIX, f. 32.

9. Morrison MS., 703.

10. Clarke and M'Arthur : I, 64, " from the Viscountess Nelson ".

11. Captain James Kirke, a Commissioner of the Victualling Office, died in 1787, leaving issue.

12. " The Grove ", Highgate, " Linden House ", and " The Hermitage ", Millfield Lane, have all been identified by various topographical authors as William Suckling's house, from which Nelson's letters are dated simply " Kentish Town ". It appears clear, however, that the house he knew has been demolished. Foley : 16.

13. Nelson-Ward MS., N.M.M.

14. Morrison MS., 700.

15. Clarke and M'Arthur (I, 76), who evidently got the story from Davison, though they do not acknowledge him in a footnote as their source, as they invariably do when the information comes from the Nelson family, Locker, Hardy, Bromwich, etc. The present author wishes to thank Mrs. C. G. Brocklebank, who has made inquiries in Quebec with the following result. Sir James Le Moine (author of many rare " Canadiana "), in *Picturesque Quebec* (Dawson Bros., Montreal, 1882, pp. 232–5, 254 and 532), and in an article in the *Revue Canadienne* of 1867 (subsequently incorporated in *Maple Leaves*, and amended in *Tourist's Note-Book to Quebec*, 1876, pp. 26 and 36) and his *Chronicles of the St. Lawrence* (Quebec, 1878, p. 198), published the results of exhaustive research into this early incident of Nelson's career. His authorities for the fact that Miss Simpson, not her cousin, Miss Prentice, was the object of Nelson's passion, were notes of conversations with Lieut.-Colonel John Sewell, of the 49th Regiment, a veteran whose birth was nearly contemporary with Nelson's visit to Quebec, and " several passages " in the family correspondence of Mrs. Matthews and Mr. James Thompson, senior, whose diaries and letters

were acquired by the Quebec Literary and Historical Society. Miss Simpson, afterwards Mrs. Matthews, was " cousin to Mr. James Thompson, one of Wolfe's officers, Overseer of Works in Quebec in 1782, father of the late Judge John Gwalor Thompson of Gaspé, and of the late Com. General James Thompson of Quebec ". The Hon. William Smith, historian of Canada, had told Colonel Sewell that, in his opinion, Matthew Lymburner of Quebec, not Alexander Davison, was the person to dissuade Nelson upon the quayside from his romantic pilgrimage to Bandon Lodge. Both may have been present.

Miss Simpson's husband was Colonel Matthews, Governor of the Chelsea Pensioners' Hospital; and according to family tradition, to the day of her death, " a stately London matron ", she spoke with tenderness of " her first love, the hero of Trafalgar ".

16. Nicolas: I, 294. Thirty letters from Prince William to Nelson are to be found in Add. MSS. (B.M.) 34,902–34,932, " Nelson Papers " I–XXI.

17. Clarke and M'Arthur: I, 78. " From minutes of a conversation with the Duke of Clarence at Bushey Park."

18. Matcham: 251.

19. Bromwich has to wait another ten years for this promotion. He died Warden of Portsmouth Dockyard, " a place which he obtained through the interest of his noble friend ".

20. Davison reported the incident to Clarke and M'Arthur.

CHAPTER III

"SENTIMENTAL JOURNEY"

1. Now an exhibit of the Nelson-Ward Collection, N.M.M.

2. The order for British sea-officers to wear *épaulettes* was not given out until June 1, 1795.

3. Nicolas: I, 88, 90, 92, 94.

4. Foley: 22.

5. Nicolas: II, 94.

6. *Ibid.*: I, 96–8.

7. Miss Andrews, whose Christian name is never mentioned by Nelson, married (1) Rev. Mr. Farror, (2) Col. Warne of the East India Service. She attained three-score years and ten, surviving Nelson by nearly forty years.

8. Nicolas: I, 102.

9. *Ibid.*: 107–8.

10. Add. MS. 34,990, " Nelson Papers ", LXXXIX, f. 26.

11. *Biographia Navalis*, J. Charnock, 1794–8, VI, 180.

12. Nicolas: I, 156. Nelson's expectation was not fulfilled. Sandys reached flag-rank and outlived him.

13. *Ibid.*: 124, 131.

14. *Ibid.*: 118–23.

15. *Ibid.*: 113 *et seq.*; Clarke and M'Arthur: I, 101–12.

16. Clarke and M'Arthur: I, 113.

17. This first letter of Nelson to his wife has never before been published. Llangattock MS., Nelson Museum, Monmouth, " Nelson Papers ", I, Letters of Lord Nelson to Lady Nelson, under date Aug. 19, 1785.

18. *Ibid.*, Sept. 11, 1785.

19. Nicolas : I, 144, 160.

20. Nicolas (I, 217) gives " about 1763 " as Frances Woolward's date of birth, and says that she died on May 4, 1831, aged sixty-eight, a statement followed by the *Gentleman's Magazine* for that date. The register of Nevis notes her baptism in May, 1761, but on the sarcophagus over her grave and the memorial tablet in the church of St. Mary and St. Andrew, Littleham, near Exmouth, erected by her son's wife, her age is given as seventy-three, and her date of death as May 6, 1831. This would make her at least four months older than Nelson, born Sept. 29, 1758, and is the age accepted by Admiral Mahan in his biography of Nelson. Clarke and M'Arthur absurdly describe her as seventeen, when she was a widow with a child of five.

21. *Nelson's Wife*, E. M. Keate, 1939, 4, 8–10.

22. Morrison MS., 472.

23. Nicolas : I, 255.

24. Keate : 68; Nicolas : I, 2, 8.

25. Nicolas : I, 151 *et seq.*

26. *Ibid.* : 178.

27. Morrison MS., Note to p. 79, Vol. II.

28. Nicolas : I, 78.

29. Llangattock MS., I, Letters of Lord Nelson to Lady Nelson, Sept. 23, 1786.

30. Nicolas : I, 208 *et seq.*

31. *Ibid.* : 224 *et seq.*; Clarke and M'Arthur : I, 138 *et seq.*

32. Llangattock MS., I, Letters of Lord Nelson to Lady Nelson, Jan. 1, 1787. Add. MS. 34,902, " Nelson Papers ", I, f. 1.

33. Llangattock MS., *ibid.*, Feb. 24, 25, 27, 28.

34. *Ibid.* : March 4.

35. The register of Nevis gives March 11 as the date, and this has been followed by Clarke and M'Arthur, but Lady Nelson herself gives March 12 (Nicolas : I, 217), as does Prince William. The certificate is in the British Museum, Add. MS. 28,333.

36. Both exhibits of the N.M.M. The frigate presented by H.M. Queen Mary.

37. After President Herbert went home, Montpelier almost shared the fate of Governor Parry's house, for which Nelson had searched attended by native guides. A tablet commemorating the wedding of Nelson was fixed in 1911 to a pillar of entrance gates leading to ruins overgrown by Caribbean greenery (*The British West Indies*, Sir A. Aspinall, 1912, 38).

38. *The Admirals Hood*, Hon. D. Hood, 1941, 94.

39. *Letters and Papers of Sir T. Byam Martin*, ed. Sir R. V. Hamilton, Navy Records Society, 1903, I, 67.

40. Clarke and M'Arthur : I, 136–8.

41. *Pages and Portraits from the Past, being the private papers of Sir William Hotham, G.C.B., Admiral of the Red*, A. M. W. Stirling, 1909, two vols. : I, 27; II, 217–18.

CHAPTER IV

FIVE YEARS ON THE BEACH

1. Josiah Webbe of New River, Nevis, was the grandfather of Dr. Josiah Nisbet and Mrs. James Tobin. Two Tobin sons, George, *b.* 1768, and John, *b.* 1770, became respectively a Rear-Admiral and a dramatist, and George and " his little Dasher " are frequently mentioned in Nelson's letters. Mrs. Nelson stayed with the Tobins of Bristol again in 1796.

2. Nicolas : I, 266.

3. Matcham : 45.

4. Nicolas : I, 252.

5. *Ibid.* : 281.

6. Nelson wrote to Prince William on May 7 (Nicolas : I, 233) from Nevis that Herbert was " near going ", and in the Nevis Register the marriage, on May 18, 1787, of Martha Williams Herbert to Andrew Hamilton is the next entry below that of Frances Herbert Nisbet to Horatio Nelson, Esq., Captain of H.M.S. *Boreas.*

7. Llangattock MS., " Nelson Papers ", III, Jan. 2, 1799. Lady Nelson's sister-in-law, Mrs. Walter Nisbet, born Parry, stayed in Berners Street, and Martha Hamilton, born Herbert, in Harley Street. Lady Nelson herself lodged in Upper Seymour Street and Somerset Street and died in Harley Street.

8. Nicolas : I, 273–4.

9. *Ibid.* : 276.

10. The Rector took " my suite, viz. Will " (his indoor servant) when he travelled. Fanny had, in Nevis, a male negro slave, Cato, left to her in the will of a neighbour. By 1798 she certainly had a personal maid, " Ryson ".

11. *A Family Historical Register,* by Edmund Nelson, Rector of Burnham Thorpe, 1781, Nelson-Ward MS., N.M.M. *See also* Matcham : 107.

12. Barton Hall, Neatishead, was recently sold to Captain Peel by Sir E. Preston, Bart., a descendant of the family from whom the Matchams took a lease in 1787, and at Beeston Hall Sir E. Preston possesses dining-room chairs, a sideboard and wine-coolers bearing a black strake in token of mourning for Nelson. Family tradition states that they were bought from the Matchams.

13. Foley : 28.

14. Cornwallis Wykeham-Martin MS., Historical Manuscripts Commission, VI, 341–2.

15. Llangattock MS., " Nelson Papers ", V. Account supplied to J. M'Arthur by Lady Nelson.

16. Matcham : 63. *A History of Burnham Thorpe,* Anon. Privately printed, 1936.

17. *Coke of Norfolk,* A. M. W. Stirling, 1912, 216. The Cokes called upon the Horatio Nelsons after the first visit of the Nelsons to Wolterton, in 1791. Matcham : 96.

18. Matcham : 63, 65, 69, 71.

19. Llangattock MS., " Nelson Papers ", V; Clarke and M'Arthur : I, 160; Nicolas : I, 287 (n.).

20. Nicolas : I, 287. For a description of such calls at the Admiralty, see *The Life of a Sailor*, Capt. F. Chamier, R.N., 1830, IV, 7.

21. Nicolas : I, 293, 294 (n.).

22. Matcham : 72–4.

23. Foley : 37.

24. *Ibid.* : 26.

25. Nicolas : I, 297.

26. Clarke and M'Arthur : I, 160; Matcham : 76.

27. Llangattock MS., " Nelson Papers ", I, Jan. 7, 1793.

28. Nicolas : I, 253–8; VI, 279. Joe King became in 1804 boatswain of Gibraltar Dockyard.

29. Llangattock MS., " Nelson Papers ", I, Aug. 4, 1793.

30. Matcham : 102.

31. Until other evidence appears, it seems reasonable to conclude that Nelson's wife was a one-child sterility case. Her record of joint-pains and hysteria supports this theory.

CHAPTER V

SHIP-OF-THE-LINE

1. Llangattock MS., " Nelson Papers ", I, June 23, 1793. Nelson's description of a bull-fight agrees in every detail with that of Lieut. Thomas Thorp, R.N. (Thorp MS., 1, 9).

2. Add. MS. 34,902, " Nelson Papers ", I, f. 42.

3. Llangattock MS., " Nelson Papers ", Sept. 11, 1793.

4. Morrison MS., 92, 118.

5. Sir William Hamilton was idolised by his first wife, who deplored " the dissipated life you lead, my dear Hamilton ", but recorded in the last year of her lingering existence, " My only regret in leaving this world is leaving you. . . . You have never known half the tender affection I have borne you. . . . You are absent from me. . . . I seek peace in company and there am still more uneasy. I return home, and there the very dog stares me in the face and seems to ask for its beloved master " (Morrison MS., 116, 120). Twenty-one years later Sir William fulfilled her dying request that his body should be buried beside hers.

6. Morrison MS., 52.

7. *Life of the Right Hon. Horatio, Lord Viscount Nelson*, by Mr. Harrison, 1806, two vols.: I, 108. James Harrison, the hack-writer employed by Lady Hamilton, was an untrustworthy character, and all evidence from this source is suspect, but he was certainly provided with much detail of no propaganda value, and several instances, which can be checked, prove that he cannot be entirely disregarded.

8. Llangattock MS., " Nelson Papers ", I, Sept. 14, 1793.

9. Palazzo Sessa, Vico Santa Maria a Capella Vecchia, was, owing to its situation beneath the St. Elmo battery, damaged in Nelson's bombardment of Naples in 1799, after having been plundered by Neapolitan revolutionaries. It was never again permanently used by a British diplomatic representative after the retirement of Sir William Hamilton (who lent it for the few months until his lease expired, to Mr. Lock, Consul-General), and in 1905 the British Consul-General had difficulty in identifying

it, although it was still the property of the Sessa family. (*Emma, Lady Hamilton*, W. Sichel, 1905, 88 (n).) A photograph of the exterior is reproduced in Vol. II facing p. 214 of *Nelson's Friendships*, H. Gamlin, 1899.

10. Morrison MS., 226.

11. *Memoirs and Letters of Sir William Hoste, Bart.*, edited by his widow, Lady H. Hoste, 1833, I, 18.

12. Clarke and M'Arthur : I, 200 (n.).

13. *Ibid.* : 140.

14. Llangattock MS., " Holog. Corresp.", Lord Nelson to Lord Hood, 22.2.'94 and 18.3.'94; " Nelson Papers ", I, Lord Nelson to Lady Nelson, 30.1.'94–30.5.'94, and V, " Journal of occurrences between April 4th and May 23rd, when the English got full possession of Bastia in the island of Corsica ". Add. MSS. 34,902, " Nelson Papers ", I, ff. 44–51 and 34,903, II, 218 *et seq.*

15. Sir William Hoste, then a midshipman, believed " the fever " to be water-borne. (*Service Afloat, or the Naval Career of Sir W. Hoste*, 1887, 17.)

16. Nicolas : I, 404–76. Llangattock MS., " Holog. Corresp.", Lord Nelson to Lord Hood, 7.6.'94 and 23.9.'94; " Nelson Papers ", I, Lord Nelson to Lady Nelson, 7.6.'94–24.9.'94.

17. The references for Nelson's own accounts of his loss of an eye are Llangattock MS., " Nelson Papers ", I, Lord Nelson to Lady Nelson, 1.8.'94 and 18.8.'94, and Nicolas : I, 432–3, 439, 464, 480, 487–9. The surgeons' certificates, and two of his own letters, mistakenly give the date of his injury as July 10, 1794 (Add. MS. 34,903, " Nelson Papers ", II, ff. 367, 369).

CHAPTER VI

" OLD MEDITERRANEAN MAN "

1. Llangattock MS., " Nelson Papers ", I, Lord Nelson to Lady Nelson, Sept. 12 and 20, 1794.

2. Add. MS. 34,988, " Nelson Papers ", LXXXIX, ff. 123–4.

3. Matcham : 119.

4. Llangattock MS., *ibid.*, June 27, 1794.

5. Foley : 30–2.

6. The *Tancredi* of seventy-four guns, commanded by Captain Caracciolo, of whom hereafter.

7. Llangattock MS., *ibid.*, II, March 10, 1795.

8. Nicolas : II, 18.

9. This miracle may be partially explained by the fact that the French, on this as on later occasions, concentrated their fire on enemy sail and rigging, with the object of damaging ships so severely aloft that they were unable to manoeuvre. The English chose the enemy hulls as their principal targets, and particularly the gun-ports, where the gun crews were inevitably exposed.

10. The red-hot shot and incendiary bombs employed by the French Navy at this date were generally regarded as contrary to the laws of civilised warfare.

11. Add. MS. 34,902, " Nelson Papers ", I, f. 54. Llangattock MS.,

Y Y

ibid., April 1, 1795. *The Life of Nelson, the Embodiment of the Sea-Power of Great Britain*, Admiral A. T. Mahan, 1897. Two vols., I, 163–83.

12. *Life and Letters of Sir Gilbert Elliot, first Earl of Minto*, edited by Nina, Countess of Minto. Three vols., 1874, I, 256.

13. *Ibid.* : 88.

14. *Ibid.* : 235.

15. Hotham : II, 43.

16. Nicolas : II, 42.

17. *The Nelson Memorial*, Sir J. K. Laughton, 1896, 39.

18. Nicolas : II, 50–2, 64 ; VII, xix–xxx.

19. For the dismissal of Lepée, Nicolas : I, 90.   For the career of Allen (who became something of a John Brown), *Nelsonian Reminiscences*, " Recollections of Tom Allen, the last of the Agamemnons ", G. S. Parsons, Lieut. R.N.; ed. W. Long, 1905, 276.   For Nelson's comments on Allen, Pettigrew : II, 150–1.

20. Hoste, *Memoirs*, I, 44.

21. De Vins had got his dates and spelling wrong.   Admiral Thomas Mathews resigned his command August 1744.

22. Llangattock MS., *ibid.*, July 24, Aug. 2 and 25, Sept. 15 and 21, Oct. 5, Nov. 2 and 13, Dec. 2.   Nicolas : II, 57–117.

23. Harrison : I, 140.

24. Hoste, *Memoirs*, I, 52.

CHAPTER VII

" Nelson's Patent Bridge "

1. Nicolas : II, 186–7.

2. Captain Ralph Willett Miller was killed in the explosion on board the *Theseus*, off Cæsarea, in May 1799.

3. *The Wynne Diaries*, edited by Anne Fremantle. Three vols., 1935–8.

4. Nicolas : II, 285 and n.

5. Llangattock MS., " Nelson Papers ", II, Lord Nelson to Lady Nelson—*Diadem*, Porto Ferrajo, Oct. 17, 1796.

6. Nicolas : II, 301.

7. Minto : II, 367–70

8. Hood : 172.

9. Nicolas : II, 224.

10. Llangattock MS., " Nelson Papers ", II, Dec. 9, 1796.

11. Nicolas : II, 312 *et seq.*

12. Harrison : I, 149.

13. Nelson's letter to his brother William describes the air struck up by the band as he entered as " one particular tune ".   Sir Harris Nicolas (II, 326) suggests that modesty led him to avoid mentioning its title. " See the Conquering Hero " was popular at the date, and was certainly the tune played by Jervis's order to welcome Captain Faulknor when the *Zebra* came out of action at Fort Royal of Martinique on March 20, 1794.

14. Nicolas : II, 363–6.

15. Minto : II, 363–6. Sir Gilbert's sister-in-law, Lady Malmesbury (Minto : I, 402–3), was more favourably impressed by Lady Hamilton. " She really behaves as well as possible, and quite wonderfully, considering her origin and education."   " Lady Hamilton behaves incomparably."

Georgiana, Duchess of Devonshire found in Naples, in 1793, that Lady Hamilton " is ador'd here, not only for her beauty and her talents but for her charity—they say she assists the poor to ye greatest degree ".

16. *A Narrative of the Battle of St. Vincent, with Anecdotes of Nelson before and after that Battle*, by Colonel John Drinkwater-Bethune, 1840, 14–15. Drinkwater, who afterwards took the additional surname Bethune, is the authority for " Westminster Abbey, or Glorious Victory ! " He produced two publications on this action. His first, *Narrative of the Proceedings of the British Fleet commanded by Admiral Sir John Jervis, in the late action with the Spanish Fleet, on the 14th February, 1797, off Cape St. Vincent, in a letter to a Friend, by an Officer of His Majesty's Land-forces, illustrated by eight plans*, published in the same year, had no sale and was pulped. Copies of it are very rare.

17. Nelson sent to Locker and to Prince William almost duplicate copies of his *Few Remarks relative to myself in the " Captain ", in which my Pendant was flying on the Most Glorious Valentine's Day, 1797*. Locker's copy, holograph throughout, he authorised the recipient to prune and publish. Prince William's copy was signed, in addition, by Berry and Miller. The copy in the Llangattock MS., " Nelson Papers ", IV, Nelson Family Correspondence, is probably that lent to Clarke and M'Arthur. The other two are in Add. MS. 34,902, " Nelson Papers ", I, 116, 119. See also, *The Naval History of Great Britain, from the Declaration of War by France in 1793, to the Accession of George IV*, William James, third ed., 1837, six vols, II, 37 *et seq.*; Mahan: I, 268–83; Nicolas: II, 331–59; *Correspondence and Memoirs of Vice-Admiral Lord Collingwood*, edited by G. N. Collingwood, 1829, 35–43; Clarke and M'Arthur : I, 503–6.

18. Nelson's topaz, and the sword, were preserved by the only child of the short-lived Miller, described by Nelson as " the only truly virtuous man I ever knew ".

19. Llangattock MS., " Nelson Papers ", III, Lord Nelson to Lady Nelson, Feb. 16, 1797. Nicolas : II, 346, 350, 351, 353, 382. " The pains I suffer in my inside " were still troubling Nelson on April 30.

20. Nicolas : II, 347–9.

21. Drinkwater-Bethune : 83–8.

22. Nicolas : II, 349–51.

23. *Ibid.* : 370.

24. Clarke and M'Arthur : I, 349; Matcham : 142; Foley : 34–7.

25. Llangattock MS., " Nelson Papers ", III, June 29–30, 1797.

26. *Ibid.* : V.

27. Nicolas : II, 377.

28. Add. MS. 34,988, " Nelson Papers ", LXXXIX, ff. 186–189.

CHAPTER VIII

In-shore Squadron, Cadiz Bay : Santa Cruz, Teneriffe

1. Nicolas : II, 378–81.

2. *Private Papers of George, second Earl Spencer, First Lord of the Admiralty, 1794–1801*, ed. Sir J. Corbett, Navy Records Society, 1914, XLVIII, II, 387–97.

3. *Ibid.* : 403.

4. The four main mutinies of 1797 were : (1) Channel Fleet at Spithead, April 3–17; (2) Channel Fleet at St. Helen's, April 24–May 7; (3) unattached ships at Sheerness and the Nore, May 12; (4) North Sea Fleet at Yarmouth, May 27. See *The Naval Mutinies of 1797*, C. Gill, 1913, and *Spencer Papers*, II, 103–74.

5. Nicolas : VII, cxliv.

6. *Ibid.* : cxli.

7. *Ibid.* : II, 394–5.

8. Llangattock MS., " Nelson Papers ", III, Lord Nelson to Lady Nelson, June 15, 1797.

9. Sykes survived, and St. Vincent rewarded him with a gunner's warrant. Towards the end of 1797 Miller was regretting that he could not prevail upon St. Vincent to make the man a lieutenant—" His manners and conduct are so entirely above his situation "—but Sykes, who had been in the service only since the *Agamemnon* was commissioned in February 1793, had not served the requisite six years. He died at the age of eighty, the proprietor of a fishmonger's shop in Church Passage, Greenwich.

10. His brother-in-law, Matcham, alludes to an early occasion, recorded nowhere else, when Nelson, as a Lieutenant, " by his personal exertions " was successful in quelling a mutiny (Matcham : 284).

11. Nicolas : II, 403–12.

12. *Spencer Papers*, II, 213.

13. Captain Sam. Hood, youngest brother of Alexander Hood, both cousins to the Lords Hood and Bridport.

14. " George Thorp, 1790–97 ", T. A. Thorp, *Blackwood's Magazine*, 1535, 190.

15. Clarke and M'Arthur : II, 52.

16. Nicolas : II, 421.

17. Add. MS. 34,906, " Nelson Papers ", I, ff. 219, 141; Llangattock MS., " Nelson Papers ", V; Nicolas : II, 423–43.

18. Clarke and M'Arthur : II, 51–9.

19. Fremantle : II, 184–90.

20. Hoste, *Memoirs*, I, 73.

21. Llangattock MS., " Nelson Papers ", V.

22. *Biographical Memoir of Lord Viscount Nelson*, J. Charnock, 1806, 103.

23. Llangattock MS., *ibid.*, Notes on a letter from Lord St. Vincent dated 31.1.1807, made by Lady Nelson. From Nelson's despatch and journal it may be deduced that he did set foot on the mole, together with Fremantle, and Bowen and Thorp, who had swum ashore after their boat sank.

24. Nicolas : IV, 245.

25. Harrison (I, 200, 225) repeats the story, evidently current, that " an ingenious French Surgeon ", " in taking up one of the arteries united it with a nerve ", and that the ligature used was " according to the customary practice of French surgeons " of silk, instead of waxed thread; Robert Southey (*Nelson*, edition published 1922, 115) follows him. It seems probable that Thomas Eshelby, Principal Medical Officer, operated, assisted by Ronicet, but it is, of course, possible that Eshelby (who is not mentioned by Mrs. Fremantle as the surgeon attending Nelson, until the *Seahorse* sailed

for home) had been left behind with the fleet off Cadiz, for some reason, and was picked up again there. Six years after Nelson's operation a favoured ship's surgeon ventured to ask him details as to his sensations during the ordeal, and was told that " the coldness of the knife " in making the first circular cut through the integuments and muscles had most impressed him, and Mr. (afterwards Sir George) Magrath received orders that whenever there was a prospect of the *Victory* coming to action, he was to have his instruments ready in a hanging stove, kept in the galley. Anæsthetics were unknown. Rum was generally administered before a major operation, and the patient was given a mouth-pad to bite upon. Nelson, at the time, was satisfied with his surgeon's work, but Magrath believed that the Admiral's subsequent neuralgic predisposition " was originally induced by the clumsy application of the ligature . . . to the humeral artery ". The ligatures used at this date to arrest the hæmorrhage from a divided blood-vessel were usually left long, and hanging out of the wound, and from day to day they were gently pulled, until they sloughed away. They certainly provided drainage, but were themselves a chief cause of the suppuration that requires drainage. Inflammation and suppuration were regarded as inevitable; gangrene and pyæmic abscesses as bad luck. Twelve weeks after his amputation Nelson wrote of " the ligature still fast to the nerve ", and " unlucky mismanagement ". Any nerve divided was also, at this date, ligatured, above the site of the section, a practice now obsolete, but believed by eighteenth-century surgeons to prevent the sepsis from running up. Eshelby, or Ronicet, evidently took off the limb " very high ", so as to have a clear field of operation, but took up a severed nerve together with the brachial artery.

26. Knight : I, 286.
27. Parsons : 268–9.
28. Bowen was described by a jubilant Spanish pamphlet as the originator of the Santa Cruz Expedition, " which he represented as very easy, having previously cut out of that bay the Spanish frigate *Prince Ferdinand*, from the Philippine Islands ". His chief pilot, a Chinese, taken out of this prize, was killed by his side. St. Vincent was " quite unmanned " by the news of Bowen's death.
29. Nicolas : VII, ccxxvi.
30. *Spencer Papers*, II, 413–4.
31. Llangattock MS., " Lord Nelson's Collection ", Portfolio I, Letter from Lord Nelson to William Suckling, Esq., Aug. 30, 1797.
32. Fremantle : II, 188–91.

CHAPTER IX
DOCTOR'S ORDERS

1. Llangattock MS., " Nelson Papers ", III, Aug. 13–16, 1797.
2. Clarke and M'Arthur : II, 62.
3. Matcham : 124.
4. *Gentleman's Magazine*, " State of the Weather in September, 1797 ", under date.
5. Matcham : 148. This story was told to the Hon. and Rev. J. H. Nelson, about 1851.

6. 141, Bond Street has been re-numbered and rebuilt.

7. *London, Past and Present*, H. B. Wheatley, 1891, III, 273.

8. Nicolas : VII, cxlviii.

9. Harrison (I, 229–30) and Southey (116) report this anecdote, but represent it as taking place when Nelson was applying for " smart-money " (two years' pay as wound gratuities).

10. Morrison MS., 466.

11. Later, when the patient became accustomed to the lack of an arm, and pushed his stump home without effort, the slash was abandoned. The four uniform coats belonging to Nelson exhibited at the National Maritime Museum all have complete sleeves.

12. Lady Berry confirmed this to Sir H. Nicolas (Nicolas : II, 448 (n.)).

13. Minto : III, 2–3.

14. *My Confidences*, F. Locker-Lampson, 1896, 39.

15. Drinkwater : 97.

16. Clarke and M'Arthur : II, 67.

17. Fremantle : II, 195–6.

18. Matcham : 151.

19. Two photographs of *The Roundwood* are reproduced in *Nelson in England*, E. Hallam Moorhouse, 1913.

20. Harrison : I, 228.

21. Nicolas : II, 456. Berry's wedding took place at Canterbury, on Dec. 26, 1797, according to the *Gentleman's Magazine*.

CHAPTER X

THE NILE

1. *Diary of Lady F. Shelley*, ed. R. Edgcumbe, 1912, 77–8.

2. *Memoirs of the Earl of St. Vincent*, J. S. Tucker, 1844, two vols., I, 348.

3. Nicolas : III, 25.

4. Llangattock MS., " Nelson Papers ", III, April 9, 1798; Add. MS. 34,988, " Nelson Papers ", LXXXVII; Nicolas : VII, cxlix–cl; Pettigrew : I, 114–15.

5. Morrison MS., 315.

6. Spencer : II, 448–9.

7. The reference for Lady Hamilton's two letters, endorsed " June 17, 1798 ", is Add. MS. 34,989, " Nelson Papers ", LXXXVII, ff. 1, 3, and for Nelson's reply, Egerton MS., 1614 (B.M.). Nelson's letter is mistakenly dated 6 p.m. May 17, without date of year, but Lady Hamilton's mention of Bowen proves that June 17, 1798, was the date, as Captain James Bowen of the *Transfer* sloop was at Naples from June 12 to August 2 of that year, and not in the Mediterranean in the following year. These letters are important evidence on the disputed question of Lady Hamilton's claim to a pension for public services. The credit for bringing these letters together belongs to Walter Sichel (*Emma, Lady Hamilton*, 1905), who goes into the matter in detail (pp. 202–22 and 486–8). Sir J. K. Laughton (" Nelson's Last Codicil ", *Colbourn's United Services Magazine*, May 1889, and *D.N.B.* article under " Emma Hamilton ") dismisses Lady Hamilton's

claims as fictitious, and supposes Nelson's letter written in the following year, but he had not seen Add. MS. 34,980. Harrison (244 and 252), employed by Lady Hamilton, at a date when she was memorialising the Government for a pension, offers a *farrago* about " a talismanic gift " procured by Lady Hamilton " from some being of a superior order, sylph, fairy, magician or other person skilled in the occult sciences, as many in Naples, as well as elsewhere, positively profess themselves to be ". This " small association of talismanic characters " had, according to him, such potency that any Sicilian governor became hypnotised, and bound to silence " by the dread of an assured death ". J. C. Jeaffreson (*Lady Hamilton and Lord Nelson*, two vols., 1888, 329–42) is chiefly concerned with the inaccuracies of Pettigrew (II, 611–13), who draws an imaginative picture of the actions of June 17, but had seen originals of letters quoted by him, without reference, and reproduces Nelson's letter from the Egerton MS., on the back of which Lady Hamilton had written, " This letter I received after I had sent the Queen's letter for receiving our ships into their ports—for the Queen had decided to act in opposition to the King, who woud not then break with france and our fleet must have gone down to Gibraltar to have watered, and the Battle of the Nile would not have been fought for the french fleet woud have got back to Toulon." Clarke and M'Arthur tersely attribute the watering at Syracuse to the exertions of Sir William and influence of Lady Hamilton (II, 102). Mahan (I, 130) inclines to the opinion that the Syracusan authorities, having offered a show of resistance, then helped Nelson, whose own orders were to exact supplies; but Mahan had not seen Sichel's discovery. One more letter which must be considered is quoted in note 16.

The facts from the evidence now available are that Lady Hamilton did approach the Queen, that the squadron was supplied, and that Nelson, in the last codicil to his Will, attributed this to Lady Hamilton's agency (Add. MS. 34,992, " Nelson Papers ", XCI, f. 3).

8. Morrison MS., 318, 322, 327. The words " under the rose " are used by Nelson to St. Vincent (Nicolas: III, 39).

9. Morrison MS., 320.

10. *Ibid.*: 321.

11. Spencer: II, 473.

12. *The Letters of Lord Nelson to Lady Hamilton, etc.*, anonymously published 1814, two vols., hereafter cited as *Nelson Letters*, II, 231–8.

13. Nicolas: III, 45.

14. *Ibid.*: VII, cliii.

15. *Nelson Letters*, I, 181–6.

16. Morrison MS., 325. The Secretary to the French Minister at Naples duly protested to de Gallo of the number of lemons, onions and bullocks supplied to the British fleet. The following letter, also dated July 22, rests on the authority of Harrison (I, 256). Sir H. Nicolas (III, 46–7) printed it, but doubted its authenticity on the grounds that " the classical allusion " was not in Nelson's style, and that the conclusion was repetitive of his letter of the 18th. But the Fountain of Arethusa was a topographical fact, familiar to anyone acquainted with the Mediterranean ports at this date, and Nelson frequently repeated phrases which hit his fancy. The " laurel or cypress " phrase was first used by him at Teneriffe, in a letter to St. Vincent (Nicolas: II, 421):

" My dear Friends,

" Thanks to your exertions, we have victualled and watered : and surely watering at the Fountain of Arethusa, we must have victory. We shall sail with the first breeze, and be assured I shall return either crowned with laurel, or covered with cypress."

An Order by Nelson to the Captains of his squadron, of the same date (Add. MS. 34,963, " Nelson Papers ", LXII, f. 10), is endorsed " The Queen's Letter, privately got by me, got him and his Fleet victuled and watered in a few days. Emma Hamilton." See also Morrison MS., 1045–6.

17. Narrative of Captain Berry (Nicolas : III, 49).

18. Mahan : I, 131.

19. Narratives of Captain Miller (H.M.S. *Theseus*) and Captain Berry (H.M.S. *Vanguard*) (Nicolas : VII, cliv and III, 49–50). Log of the *Vanguard* (ibid., 53).

20. He met the death he had smelt that night, on Dec. 3, 1799, as purser of *Le Franklin*, renamed H.M.S. *Canopus*.

21. These were the Casabiancas immortalised by the poetess Hemans.

22. The ornamental dress-sword, made by Messrs. Rundle and Bridge, with hilt in the shape of a crocodile's head, presented to Nelson by the Captains of his squadron, is now an exhibit in the National Maritime Museum, together with the following other trophies of the Battle of the Nile—the Sultan's gifts of the Chelengk, gold and cedar canteen, musket and sabre, the Neapolitan Order of St. Ferdinand; the undress uniform coat worn by Nelson on that occasion.

23. An account of Lieut. Duval's journey is to be found in James's *Naval History*, II, Appendix 14.

24. Contemporary accounts of the Battle of the Nile were written by Berry (*Authentic Narrative*, published with a plan, 1798) and Miller (Nicolas : VII, cliv–clx), by the Chaplain of the *Swiftsure* (*Voyage up the Mediterranean, illustrated by engravings from the author's drawings*, Rev. Cooper Willyams), and by Rear-Admiral Blanquet-Duchayla (Nicolas : III, 67–71). See also *Navy Records Society*, XVIII (ships' logs of the *Goliath, Zealous, Audacious, Orion, Theseus, Vanguard, Defence, Bellerophon, Majestic, Alexander, Swiftsure* and *Culloden*); *Spencer Papers*, II, Part vii; *Annual Register, Gentleman's Magazine*, and contemporary newspapers, under date; Clarke and M'Arthur : II, 109–27; James : II, 229–66; Mahan : I, 344–58.

25. *The Farington Diary*, by J. Farington, R.A., ed. 1923, J. Greig, under entry for Sept. 26, 1798.

CHAPTER XI

NAPLES

1. Nicolas : III, 127, 195; VII, clxii; Spencer : II, 474, 477.

2. Nicolas : II, 125 (n.).

3. Add. MS. 34,989, " Nelson Papers ", XXXVIII, f. 3.

4. Llangattock MS., " Nelson Papers ", III, Sept. 26, 1798. This

letter is quoted by Clarke and M'Arthur (II, 147), without date, and without the references to Lady Hamilton's reputation, which are now printed
for the first time.

5. Knight : I, 116.

6. Nelson commissioned the purchase of this picture in 1801, when
Sir William Hamilton proposed to put it up for sale at Christie's. He
obtained it for £300, and had it in his cabin in the *St. George*.   The portrait
in morning dress was bought by Alderman Smith, at the Merton sale in
1808, and sold by his daughter to Mr. A. de Rothschild.   It is reproduced
in Ward and Roberts' *Catalogue Raisonné, Works of Romney*.   Romney
produced several versions of the *Bacchante*.

7. Knight : II, 287.

8. Nicolas : III, 137.

9. Cf. *Nelson Letters*, I, 182, with Nicolas: III, 137; and Add. MS.
34,989, "Nelson Papers", LXXXVIII, f. 3, with Nicolas : III, 134, 137.

10. Nicolas : III, 138.

11. This story originates from doubtful sources—*Memoirs of Lady
Hamilton*, Anon., 1815, ed. W. Long, 1892, 156–7, and Harrison : I, 138.
In the *Memoirs*, Nisbet is said to have objected to Lady Hamilton usurping
his mother's place.   Both authors declare that the Hamiltons asked Nelson
to overlook Nisbet's outburst.

12. Nicolas : I, 15; *Nelson Letters*, I, 233 ; Matcham : 233.

13. Nicolas : III, 144.

14. *Ibid.* : 145.

15. *Nelson Letters*, I, 219.

16. Add. MS. 34,989, " Nelson Papers ", LXXXVIII, ff. 8–24.

17. Nicolas : III, 171.

18. Pettigrew : I, 169.

19. Add. MS. 34,989, " Nelson Papers ", LXXXVIII, f. 30.

20. Nicolas : III, 195.

21. The castle of St. Elmo also possessed " subterranean and concealed
ways ", so described in a letter from the Queen to Lady Hamilton
(Pettigrew : II, 275).

22. Nicolas : III, 206–7.

23. Egerton MS. 2640, f. 163.

24. The four principal eyewitnesses' accounts of the Royal escape
are: (1) the Queen's letter to her daughter, the Empress (*Fabrizio Ruffo,
Revolution und gegen-Revolution von Neapel, Nov. 1798–Aug.* 1799, Freiherr
von Helfert, Vienna, 1882, 387, 2); (2) Nelson's despatch to St. Vincent
(Nicolas : III, 212); and (3 and 4) letters of Sir William and Lady
Hamilton to Charles Greville (Morrison MS., 369, 370).   Lady Hamilton's
second account, written fourteen years later (Morrison, 1046), differs in
detail from her first, and says that she attended a farewell reception given
by Kelim Effendi, in company with her husband, mother and Nelson,
before she stole on foot to conduct the Royal party to Nelson's boats.
Clarke and M'Arthur (II, 195) add two anecdotes, one of which is mentioned
by Harrison (I, 383), and both of which are found in the anonymous
Memoirs of Lady Hamilton.   Nelson's letters to his wife at this date, in
the Llangattock MS., add no information.   Major Pryse Lockhart Gordon
(*Personal Memoirs*, two vols., 1830, I, 205–6) repeats what he heard from
the Hon. John Rushout, who had been present.

25. Mack, after spending two years in France, as a prisoner of war, took part in an unsuccessful campaign against Napoleon, after which he was court-martialled, deprived of his rank and orders, and imprisoned. He died at the age of seventy-six, having been reinstated as a Lieutenant-Field-Marshal.

26. The references for the passage of the *Vanguard* from Naples to Palermo, Dec. 23–6, 1798, are : article by Captain W. H. Smyth, *Royal United Service Magazine*, May–June 1895 ; Nicolas : III, 212–3 ; Morrison MS., 369, 370, and 470 ; and *Memories of General Pépé*, Lugano, 1847, 28 *et seq.*

CHAPTER XII

"Inactive at a Foreign Court"

1. Llangattock MS., " Nelson Papers ", III, Jan. 17, 1799.
2. *Nelson Letters*, I, 237 ; Morrison MS., 346.
3. Nicolas : III, 138.
4. Pettigrew : I, 220.
5. *Naples in 1799*, C. Giglioli, 1903, 208.
6. Nicolas : III, 333–4.
7. *Nelson Letters*, 9–10.
8. Master's Log of the *Foudroyant* under entry for June 26, 1799.
9. Nicolas : III, 387.
10. *Ibid.* : 389.
11. Foote, Captain E. J., *Vindication of his Conduct when Captain of H.M.S. Seahorse, etc.*, 1799, 1807, 189, and Add. MSS. 34,944, " Nelson Papers ", XLIII, f. 225, and 34,991, X, ff. 237 *et seq.* and 34,992, XI, ff. 84 *et seq.*
12. Nicolas : III, 478.
13. Morrison MS., 411.
14. Nicolas : III, 386.
15. Harrison : II, 100 ; Morrison MS., 405.
16. Nicolas : III, 388, 393.
17. Micheroux's *Compendium* and letter from Sir J. Acton ; Gutteridge : 116–17, 249 ; P. Sacchinelli, *Memorie storiche sulla vita del Cardinale F. Ruffo*, Naples, 1836, 225 ; Add. MSS. 34,963, " Nelson Papers ", LXII, f. 104, and 34,944, XLIII, ff. 238, 245, 247, 250, 254, 257, 275.
18. Add. MS. 34,944, " Nelson Papers ", XLIII, f. 250 ; Sacchinelli : 252.
19. Egerton MS., 2640, f. 309. A. Ricciardi, *Archivio Storico*, XIII, 36, states that some Russians at Castel Nuovo did render honours of war to the departing garrison, who, however, laid down their arms upon the quayside before embarking in the waiting polaccas.
20. Gutteridge : 279 ; Sacchinelli : 265.
21. Clarke and M'Arthur : II, 270.
22. Gutteridge : 279 ; Sacchinelli, 265.
23. Add. MS. 34,912, " Nelson Papers ", XI, ff. 134, 135.
24. Nicolas : III, 115.
25. Nelson's actions in the Bay of Naples in June 1799 have aroused

more controversy than any other incident in his professional career. *Nelson and the Neapolitan Jacobins*, ed. H. Gutteridge, Navy Records Society, XXV, containing many contemporary documents and a bibliography, and Nicolas : III, 477–523 are essential to a preliminary study of the subject. See also the propagandists, Andrea Cacciatore (1850), Pietro Cala Ulloa (1877), Francesco Lomonaco (1835), Vincenzo Coco (1800), and, particularly, P. Colletta, *Storia del Reame di Napoli dal 1734 sino al 1825*, two vols., Capolago, 1834. Pryse Lockhart Gordon (I, 162, 214–29; II, 339–67 and 429) is interesting only as showing the point of view of the pro-Jacobin Neapolitans, as appreciated by a British tourist. Some letters of Charles Lock are printed in *The Locks of Norbury*, Duchess of Sermoneta, 1940, chapters XIV–XVIII. Lock, who had been disappointed in hopes of making £4,000 by securing the privilege of victualling Nelson's Fleet, describes the Admiral as speaking ungrammatically (" Tyson has shown you that there paper." " I shan't say nothing to Hardy."), a suggestion confirmed by no contemporary, nor by Nelson's private letters.

26. *Parliamentary History*, XXIV, 1394. Sermoneta : 170, 179.

27. Foote, Capt. E. J., *Vindication*, London, 1807.

28. Add. MS. 34,991, " Nelson Papers ", XC.

29. Nicolas : III, 406.

30. Clarke and M'Arthur : II, 187.

31. Southey : 183–7.

32. Nicolas : III, 522.

33. Brenton, Capt. T. E., *Naval History*, 1837. Two vols., I, 481–4.

34. *Vindication of Lord Nelson's Proceedings in the Bay of Naples*, Commander Jeaffreson Miles, 1843.

35. Morrison MS., 403 and 408; Clarke and M'Arthur : II, 276.

36. Pettigrew : I, 260–77. Cornelia Knight (I, 140) declared that the Queen had been, to her certain knowledge, the cause of many pardons being granted.

37. Parsons : 5; Clarke and M'Arthur : II, 277–8; Colletta : II, 160.

38. Nicolas : III, 408, 414–19.

39. Egerton MS., 1623, 27 and 72. Parsons (14–20) misdates this *fête* by five months. Otherwise his description agrees with that of Clarke and M'Arthur (II, 316). Pettigrew (I, 291) following Harrison, Lock and Pryse Lockhart Gordon, says that the wreath was bestowed upon Nelson himself, who wore it for the remainder of the entertainment.

40. *Letters of Mary Nisbet of Dirleton, Countess of Elgin*, arranged by Lt.-Col. Nisbet Hamilton Grant, 1926, 17–28.

41. Nicolas : IV, 117.

42. Sermoneta : 191. Nicolas : IV, 127.

43. Fortescue MS., Historical Manuscripts Commission, VI, 224. Minto : III, 139; Morrison MS., 441; *Nelson Letters*, I, 269.

44. Pettigrew : I, 305.

45. Morrison MS., 456.

46. Parsons : 11–14. Parsons' recollections are hopelessly confused as to date, and his diction is suited to his Victorian audience, but he is clear as to individual incidents.

47. Nicolas : IV, 205–6.

48. Knight : I, 147.

49. Parsons : 34–6, 47–53.
50. Llangattock MS., " Nelson Papers ", III, June 26, 1800.
51. Nicolas : IV, 263.
52. *Ibid.* : 262.
53. *Ibid.* : 225, 242.

CHAPTER XIII

STORMY HOMECOMING

1. Nicolas : IV, 263–5 ; Knight : I, 250.
2. Minto : III, 114, 146, 150.
3. *Musical Times*, London, June 1939, " When Haydn Met Nelson ", article by D. M. Craig. *See also* Knight : I, 152, and R. P. Keigwin, *Mariner's Mirror*.
4. Llangattock MS., " Nelson Papers ", III, Sept. 20, 1800.
5. Morrison MS., 439, 442, 454, 472, 473 ; Foley : 48–57 ; Matcham : 169, 172, 175.
6. Nicolas : III, 229, 239, 375 and IV, 50 ; Morrison MS., 385 ; Pettigrew : I, 368.
7. *Remains of the late Mrs. Richard Trench*, ed. by her son, the Dean of Westminster, 1862, 104–12.
8. *Ibid.* : 291.
9. Llangattock MS., " Nelson Papers ", III, Nov. 6, 1800.
10. *Naval Miscellany*, Navy Records Society, ed. Sir J. K. Laughton, 1912, II, 329.
11. Llangattock MS., " Nelson Papers ", III, Sept. 26, 1799. Lady Nelson's annotations have been imperfectly erased. The only words in defence of her son clearly visible are " He did not like ", followed by an erasure, and a comment that personal reflections are impermissible.
12. *Recollections of the Life of the Rev. A. J. Scott, D.D. Lord Nelson's Chaplain*, by his daughter and son-in-law, Mrs. and Dr. Gatty, 1842, 192.
13. Matcham : 271.
14. Morrison MS., 516.
15. Pettigrew : I, 391.
16. Nicolas : VII, ccix.
17. Add. MS. 34,989, " Nelson Papers ", LXXXVIII, f. 35.
18. Harrison : II, 270.
19. Pettigrew : I, 411.
20. Collingwood : 83.
21. Shelley : 78–9.
22. *Letters of Lady H. Cavendish*, ed. G. Leveson-Gower and I. Palmer, 1940, 180, 192, 353.
23. Harrison : II, 278.
24. *Gentleman's Magazine*, 1801, 206–8, 297–9.
25. Nelson's hired home of this winter, 17 Dover Street, still occupies the same site, but only the exterior brickwork remains unchanged ; 23, later 99, Piccadilly, has been demolished, and the numbering has been again altered.
26. Nicolas : IV, 271 ; Pettigrew : II, 392.

27. Morrison MS., 442. The anecdote of the Rector was reported by Nelson's daughter to Sir H. Nicolas (Nelson-Ward MS., National Maritime Museum).

28. Nicolas : VII, 392. The house was in Dover Street, not Arlington Street, and Lady Nelson made several efforts at reconciliation.

29. Clarke and M'Arthur (II, 380) are the authorities for Nelson's last words to his wife. His letter from Southampton and the unfinished letter from Lady Nelson are in Llangattock MS., " Nelson Papers ", III. Lord Nelson's accounts (Morrison MS., II, 392) show that £420 was paid by Messrs. Marsh, Page and Creed to Lady Nelson, Jan. 13.

30. Lady Nelson sent him a packet of newspapers, received Jan. 31, and did write, but evidently not fully (Nicolas : VII, ccxxviii), for, on reading that Davison had been commanded to buy " a fine house " for him and his wife, Nelson applied to his friend for contradiction of the report. " I do not believe that Lady Nelson can have desired any such thing " (Nicolas : VII, cxcix).

31. The almost daily letters of Nelson to Lady Hamilton during these weeks must be brought together from four sources : Morrison MS., 502–49; *Nelson Letters*, I, 20–38; Add. MS. 34,989; and Pettigrew: I, 408–46, and II, 645–55. They overlap, but each has letters not to be found in others.

32. Pettigrew : II, 646.

33. Morrison MS., 504.

34. *Nelson Letters*, I, 24 ; Pettigrew : I, 422.

35. Morrison MS., 532.

36. *Ibid.*: 285.

37. *Ibid.*: 628. Mrs. Cadogan went to the Manchester district in April 1801 to see the younger Emma, who was established in a school kept by a family called Blackburn. The younger Emma went abroad, apparently still unmarried, in 1810 (Morrison MS., 1003), for although she passed as Emma " Connor " and " Carew ", these surnames were, respectively, that of Lady Hamilton's maternal aunt, and that adopted by her first cousin, Anne Connor. Emma " Carew " resented Lady Hamilton's refusal to acquaint her with her parentage. See also, Sichel : 518, 479.

38. Morrison MS., 528, 530. There are suggestions in the first of these letters, both that Horatia was a surviving twin, and that Nelson and Lady Hamilton had some London meeting-place outside Sir William's house, but Nelson's reference to " the dear thatched cottage " mentions no address.

39. Pettigrew : I, 421.

40. *Ibid.* : 452.

41. Morrison MS., 538.

42. Pettigrew : I, 446.

43. *Nelson Letters*, I, 36.

44. Three letters from Mrs. William Nelson to Lady Hamilton (Add. MS. 34,989, 38–43), three from Nelson to Lady Hamilton (Morrison MS., 529, 530) and *Nelson Letters* (I, 36) give details of this brief leave unnoticed by the Press or biographers. The paternity of Horatia is fully discussed by Nicolas (VII, 369–96), who had not seen the Morrison MS., and Pettigrew (II, 638–56). The author of the anonymous *Memoirs of Lady Hamilton* says (307) that Mrs. Cadogan attended her daughter in her confinement, and that Francis Oliver (" confidential steward ")

accompanied Lady Hamilton to deliver the infant, hidden in a large muff, at Little Titchfield Street. He evidently got many of his facts from Oliver, but Harrison is indicated by him as the thief of the stolen Nelson letters, published 1814. The fact that Lady Hamilton gave birth to a child in her husband's house, undetected by him or the world, is not incredible. Several contemporary instances are well documented. Jan. 29 has been agreed by biographers to have been the probable date of Horatia's birth, falsely registered by her parents, and always kept on Oct. 29 of the previous year. On the evidence available, any date between Jan. 27 and 30 is possible.

CHAPTER XIV

COPENHAGEN

1. In 1801, the 49th was the Hertfordshire Regiment; the 95th, always composed of riflemen, was, after Waterloo, taken out of the numerical score of corps and renamed the Rifle Brigade.

2. *Naval Chronicle*, XXXVII, 446.

3. Nicolas: IV, 288.

4. Pettigrew: I, 448.

5. Clarke and M'Arthur: II, 386–88.

6. *Ibid.*: 394. Ferguson, Surgeon of the *Elephant*, recounted his experiences to Nelson's brother-in-law, George Matcham, and Hardy transmitted them from Matcham to the Rev. J. S. Clarke. See also Nicolas: IV, 299–325; Mahan: II, 84–98; and Fremantle: II, 37–48.

7. Nicolas: IV, 304.

8. *Ibid.*: 308–9; Minto: III, 219.

9. Fremantle: III, 41.

10. Nicolas: IV, 310. The artist was Benjamin Haydon.

11. The Navy Records Society in 1900 (XVIII, 80–135) printed the logs of the ships engaged at Copenhagen, and personal letters descriptive of the action, from Rear-Admiral Graves, Sir T. B. Thompson, and Midshipman Daubeny. Southey (220–36) bases his description on part of the narrative of Colonel Stewart (printed in full by Nicolas) and Ferguson's account (communicated to Clarke), and attributes the story of the " blind eye ", incorrectly, to Ferguson. He had also another eyewitness available in his brother, Thomas Southey, in the *London*. Sir J. K. Laughton, in his biography of Nelson (1895), presents the theory that Nelson had a preconcerted understanding with Parker, and regarded signal 39 as giving him permission to retire if he wished. This theory is disproved by Graves's letter, printed by the Navy Records Society, but two contemporaries present at the action, but not in Nelson's ship or the naval profession, believed something of the kind. One was Sir Hyde's Secretary, the Rev. A. J. Scott, the other Colonel Hutchinson of the 49th Regiment (" Nelson at Copenhagen ", H. G. Hutchinson, *Blackwood's Magazine*, CLXVI, 1899). Hutchinson, who was in the *Monarch*, believed the signal to be discretionary—either to continue or discontinue the action. Nelson's personal letters for the date are to be found in Nicolas: IV, 294, 298, 332–42, 458, and VII, ccii–ccviii; Pettigrew: I, 442–52, and II, 17–36; Morrison

MS., 548, 551, 553–5; and Navy Records Society, XX, 414–29. The question raised by some contemporaries and many subsequent historians as to whether Nelson's use of a flag of truce was an unjustifiable *ruse de guerre* is fully dealt with by Mahan, by Sir G. Callender, in his notes to his edition of Southey's biography of Nelson, and succinctly by C. S. Forester in his life of Nelson (1929). Nelson's own views on the subject are to be found in Nicolas (see *ante*) and Morrison MS., 556, 566, 579. The total of British killed and wounded was reckoned at 254 killed and 689 wounded. Danish figures later showed 375 killed, 670 wounded and 1,770 prisoners.

12. Pettigrew : II, 17.

13. Letter from an officer of Lord Nelson's squadron, published in *The Courier*, 18.4.1801.

14. Nicolas : IV, 332 *et seq.*; Clarke and M'Arthur : II, 409; Fremantle : III, 44, 53–4.

15. Pettigrew : I, 445.

16. *Naval Chronicle*, V, 452.

17. Fremantle : III, 52.

18. Morrison MS., 557.

19. Nicolas : VII, ccix.

20. Llangattock MS., " Nelson Papers ", Nelson Family Correspondence, IV, Lord Nelson to William Marsh, Esq., March 11, 1801. The allowance to Lady Nelson was later increased to £450 quarterly.

21. *Ibid.*, March 8, 1801.

22. *Ibid.*, March 16, 1801.

23. Two copies of this letter exist. The one sent by Nelson to Lady Nelson, and superscribed by her, is in the British Museum, Add. MS. 28,333, f. 3. The opening passage, relating to Nelson's efforts on behalf of Josiah Nisbet, has been cut off from this copy. A second copy, probably sent by Nelson to Lady Hamilton, for her information, is in the Morrison MS., 536.

24. Morrison MS., 472.

25. Nicolas : IV, 351.

26. Morrison MS., 557.

27. Pettigrew : II, 63.

28. Morrison MS., 589, 605; Nicolas : IV, 378, 382, 391, 407; Pettigrew : II, 77–9.

29. Nicolas : IV, 403.

30. Pettigrew : II, 19, 60.

31. Morrison MS., 595.

32. Nicolas : IV, 401.

CHAPTER XV

"Squadron on a Particular Service" and "Experimental Peace"

1. Nicolas : V, 21.

2. Southey (259) mentions, " on the authority and by the desire of Sir Humphry Davy " (*Salmonia*, 1827, 6) that, having been a good fly-fisher, Nelson was now practising the art with his left hand.

3. Pettigrew : II, 103.

4. *Ibid.* : 119–22.

5. Matcham : 190.

6. Llangattock MS., " Nelson Papers ", III, Lady Nelson to Lord Nelson, no date or place.

7. Nicolas : IV, 425–8.

8. *Ibid.* : 250; Clarke and M'Arthur : II, 443.

9. Nicolas : IV, 460–9.

10. " Letters of William Cathcart ", *Naval Miscellany*, ed. Sir J. K. Laughton, Navy Records Society, 1902, I, 294.

11. The letters for this period are to be found in Morrison MS., 607–14, 621–2, 625–31, 634–6; *Nelson Letters*, I, 39–107; Pettigrew : II, 131–231; Nicolas : IV, 425–518.

12. An architect's ground-plan of Merton Place, and an engraving of the east front, before the principal entrance was transferred to the north, are to be found facing pp. 190 and 180 in *Nelson in England* (E. Hallam Moorhouse, 1913). The National Maritime Museum possesses a collection of views of Merton and sketches of Lady Hamilton and her circle by Thomas Baxter. The artist son of Captain Locker produced a painting of the house, engraved in 1804. Another engraving, published in 1805, shows a hatchment over the new north entrance. See also *Lord Nelson's Home Life at Merton*, 1926, and *Historical Notes on the Parish Church of St. Mary the Virgin, Merton*, both by the Rev. J. Jagger Vicar of Merton, printed and published by G. Kennard, Kingston Road, Merton Park; *Reminiscences of Old Merton*, W. Chamberlain, 1925; and *The Wimbledon and Merton Annual*, 1905.

13. Morrison MS., 199.

14. *Ibid.* : 625.

15. *Memoirs of Lady Hamilton*, 226.

16. George Matcham, writing to *The Times*, Nov. 6, 1861. The description of the *surtout* and hat come from the log of a midshipman of the *Monarch*, April 1, 1801.

17. National Maritime Museum MS., letters from Lady Hamilton to Mrs. Gibson, Oct. 24, 1801.

18. Pettigrew : II, 139.

19. Charnock (199), who got information from Nelson's old Captain, Locker, is the authority for the story that Nelson, when his addresses were rejected at Ipswich, prophesied " that the city might welcome him " some day.

20. *Nelson Letters*, I, 63.

21. Morrison MS., 632; Pettigrew : II, 211.

22. Matcham : 192–3.

23. Morrison MS., 806.

24. Llangattock MS., " Nelson Papers ", V, Lady Nelson to the Rev. E. Nelson, Oct. 1801.

25. Morrison MS., 812.

26. Matcham : 286.

27. National Maritime Museum, Nelson-Ward MS., letter from Mrs. Nelson-Ward to Sir H. Nicolas.

28. National Maritime Museum MS., letter of Lady Hamilton to Mrs. Gibson, Dec. 14, 1801.

29. Morrison MS., 540; Nicolas : IV, 485.

30. Llangattock MS., " Nelson Papers ", III, Lord Nelson to Lady Nelson, Dec. 18, 1801.

31. Minto : III, 242.

32. Morrison MS., Lord Nelson's Accounts, II, 398; *The Farington Diary*, J. Farington, R.A., ed. J. Greig, 1923, I, 342.

33. *The Courier*, April 22, 1803; Nicolas : V, 59. Nicolas makes one of his rare mistakes in identifying this Captain (afterwards Rear-Admiral) James Macnamara (1768–1826) with the older officer of the same name, the " Mac " who accompanied Nelson on his St. Omer tour of 1783.

34. Matcham : 201.

35. Morrison MS., 673–4.

36. Pettigrew : I, 438.

37. *Jackson's Journal*, Oxford, July 24, 1802.

38. The husband claimed that his lady had given birth to a daughter, by her lover, under his own roof, and he laid the damages at £20,000 but obtained only £100 (*Complete Peerage*, G. E. Cokayne, 1932, VIII, 501 (note c). The case is reported in the Press, 28.5.1801 and letters appear in issues of July 6 and 7, 1801).

39. Llangattock MS., " Lord Nelson's Collection ", Portfolio 2, MS. " Report on the Forest of Dean " (printed in Nicolas : V, 24).

40. Hallam Moorhouse : 210.

41. Clarke and M'Arthur : I, 23.

42. Matcham : 78.

43. Egerton MS. II, 240, 151.

44. Nelson's own accounts for the Tour are printed in Morrison MS., II, 401–5. The remaining facts come from contemporary newspapers under date, and it is worthy of note that Harrison's description (II, 379–403) is confirmed by the Press.

45. Minto : III, 258.

46. National Maritime Museum MS., correspondence of Lady Hamilton and Mrs. Gibson : (1) Letter from Mrs. Gibson, 115, High Street, Margate, Sept. 29, 1802, on the back of a note from Lady Hamilton, postmark Sept. 28, 1802; (2) Lady Hamilton to Mrs. Gibson, no date, postmark Ramsgate, 73; (3) *ibid.*, Oct. 2, 1802.

47. Morrison MS., 679–80, 84.

48. *Nelson Letters*, I, 159; Nelson-Ward MS., National Maritime Museum MS., letter from Captain Ward to Mrs. Nelson-Ward, Sept. 18, 1828.

49. Minto : III, 274–5; Nicolas : V, 42.

50. Nicolas : V, 47.

51. *Life and Correspondence of Addington, First Lord Sidmouth*, by his son-in-law, C. Pellew, 1847, II, 170.

52. Horatia told this fact to Sir Harris Nicolas, Nelson-Ward MS., National Maritime Museum.

53. Matcham : 206–7; Nicolas : V, 51–2, and VII, 377; Pettigrew : II, 295. The account of Harrison (II, 412–13) is crude propaganda.

54. No. 11, Clarges Street, still in existence, on the east side of the street.

55. Morrison MS., 710.

56. *Ibid.* : 418–24.

57. National Maritime Museum MS., letter of Lady Hamilton to Mrs. Gibson.

z z

58. Nicolas : V, 66; Pettigrew : II, 299; Morrison MS., 712; Matcham : 208.

59. *Adventures and Recollections of Colonel Landman*, 1852, II, 258–63.

CHAPTER XVI

MEDITERRANEAN COMMAND

1. Nelson-Ward Collection, National Maritime Museum.
2. Nicolas : V, 106–11.
3. *The Courier*, April 11 and 16, 1803.
4. Scott : 191–2.
5. Morrison MS., 720.
6. Earl Nelson possesses, at Trafalgar House, an ottoman, with a leather mattress, an armchair, with padded right arm, and a small circular table, all used by Nelson in the *Victory*. Another circular table, with an inscription by Lady Hamilton, an armchair with pockets and a folding bedstead are to be seen in the National Maritime Museum, and the dining-table, sideboard and dressing-table-washstand exhibited in H.M.S. *Victory* are lent by the National Maritime Museum.
7. Letter of Dr. Leonard Gillespie, R.N., *The Times*, 6.10.1894.
8. Nicolas : V, 154.
9. That Lady Hamilton bore a second child to Nelson, almost exactly three years after Horatia, has been questioned. The essential " Mrs. Thomson " letter of Aug. 26, 1803, published in the *Nelson Letters* (I, 135 and 175) in 1814, was made almost incomprehensible by deletions, and when the Rt. Hon. W. Croker bought, in 1817, the collections catalogued and sold by Messrs. Philips of Bond Street as " Lord Nelson's Papers ", the letters printed in 1814, although catalogued, were missing. Pettigrew printed an expurgated version of the letter in which that of Aug. 26 was said to be enclosed. Sir Harris Nicolas (VII, 377, 389) doubted its authenticity. The Morrison MS., containing several references to an illness of Lady Hamilton, and one to a " little Emma ", had (see notes 17–23) not yet come to light. Admiral Mahan (II, 210) accepts the evidence. Mrs. Gamlin (*Nelson's Friendships*, 1899) makes an elaborate attempt to prove that the infant referred to was an Emma born to Sir William and Lady Bolton, late in March 1804. But all her guesses are unlucky, being based on the conviction that Nelson's relations with Lady Hamilton were platonic.
10. Matcham : 209.
11. *Authentic Narrative of the Death of Lord Nelson, etc.*, by William Beatty, M.D., Surgeon to the *Victory*, 1807, 80–1.
12. Nicolas : V, 273.
13. Beatty : 82.
14. Morrison MS., 778.
15. Pettigrew : II, 332–5 ; Nicolas : V, 160.
16. *History of Antony and Dorothea Gibbs*, J. A. Gibbs, 1922, 248.
17. Pettigrew : II, 373 ; Morrison MS., 747.
18. *Nelson Letters*, II, 15.
19. Morrison MS., 749.

20. *Ibid.*: 750.
21. *Ibid.*: 746.
22. *Ibid.*: 745.
23. *Nelson Letters*, II, 21.
24. *Life of Admiral Sir Edward Codrington*, ed. Lady Bourchier, 1873, I, 126.
25. Nicolas : V, 298.
26. *Ibid.*: 475.
27. Morrison MS., 811.
28. Nicolas : VI, 72, 76, 131, 147–8, 150.
29. *Ibid.*: V, 143, 175, 218, and VI, 96, 148, 278, 307, 357, 390, 441 ; Pettigrew : II, 392, 406.
30. Pettigrew : II, 421.
31. *Nelson Letters*, II, 41.
32. Nicolas : VI, 51.
33. *Ibid.*: 257–8.

CHAPTER XVII

THE LONG CHASE

1. *Histoire du Consulat et de l'Empire*, L. A. Thiers, Paris, 1863, V, 159.
2. Pettigrew : II, 464.
3. Morrison MS., 779.
4. Nicolas : VI, 441.
5. Morrison MS., 813.
6. Nicolas : VI, 355.
7. *Ibid.*: 419.
8. Scott : 171.
9. Clarke and M'Arthur : III, 96.
10. Nicolas : VI, 450.
11. *Ibid.*: 494.
12. *Ibid.*: 455.
13. Clarke and M'Arthur : III, 106.
14. Nicolas : VI, 464.
15. Capt. the Hon. Sir R. Stopford, *Letters and Papers of Sir T. Byman Martin*, Navy Records Society, 1903, I, 75.
16. Nicolas : VI, 468.
17. *Ibid.*: 475.
18. *Ibid.*: 470, and VII, 10.
19. Add. MSS. 34,919–34,930 ("Nelson Papers", XVIII–XXIX) cover Nelson's official Mediterranean Command correspondence from May 1803 to Aug. 1805. He began, on July 24, 1803, to make private entries in octavo note-books, and these entries, alluded to by Clarke and M'Arthur as "Diary" and "Private Journal" (and incorrectly quoted by them), were copied by Sir H. Nicolas, who added (V, 273) that the original Private Journal was not to be found. It is to be found in Add. MSS. 34,966–34,968, "Nelson Papers", LXV–VII, and Add. MS. 35,191, "Bridport Papers", I (Diary for May 18, 1803 to July 23, 1803, having been "reported" missing "until discovered amongst the 'Bridport Papers'").

A volume from which Clarke and M'Arthur (followed by Nicolas and Scott) quote, covering dates from Aug. 18 to Oct. 21, 1805, printed in full by Dr. Beatty, is in Somerset House, together with Nelson's Will.

Nelson wrote to Lady Hamilton frequently during the Long Chase, but the originals of only two letters (Morrison MS., 813, 814) are forthcoming. One more is printed in the *Nelson Letters*. Pettigrew (II, 460–87) produces all of these, expurgated, and twelve more.

CHAPTER XVIII
THE TWENTY-FIVE DAYS

1. Morrison MS., 815.
2. *Nelson Letters*, II, 94.
3. Exhibited at the National Maritime Museum, Greenwich, Nelson-Ward Collection.
4. Exhibited at the Nelson Museum, Monmouth, Llangattock Collection.
5. Morrison MS., 828.
6. Nicolas : VII, 16.
7. *Ibid.* : 18.
8. Matcham : 226.
9. " Memorandum of a conversation between Lord Nelson and Admiral Sir Richard Keats, the last time he was in England before the Battle of Trafalgar, communicated to Edward Locker, Esq., and allowed by Sir Richard to be transcribed by him, 1st Oct., 1829 " (Nicolas : VII, 241).
10. Minto : III, 362.
11. Matcham : 226.
12. Minto : III, 367.
13. Pellew : II, 380.
14. Commander Henry Lancaster, youngest son of the Vicar of Merton, was, at the age of fourteen, a Volunteer, First Class, in the *Victory* at Trafalgar.
15. Mr. Brackenbury, who succeeded Mr. Lancaster as headmaster of " Nelson " (now " Eagle ") House, High Street and Lancaster Lane, Wimbledon, was told this anecdote by a pupil present on the occasion of Nelson's visit.
16. Nicolas : VII, ccxviii (n.).
17. Matcham : 234.
18. *Blackwood's Magazine*, XXXIV, 1 *et seq.*
19. Harrison : II, 458. Lady Hamilton repeats the " Brave Emma ! " sentence in a letter to Dr. Scott (Scott : 210).
20. Nicolas : VII, 28.
21. Clarke and M'Arthur : III, 119.
22. Minto : III, 363.
23. Matcham : 228 *et seq.*
24. Letter to *The Times* from G. Matcham, 6.11.1864.
25. Nicolas : VII, 80.
26. *Ibid.* : 62. Admiral Mahan (II, 329) has drawn attention to the fact that here may be noted the first germ of Castlereagh's famous " Orders in Council " of 1807.

27. Pettigrew : II, 497.

28. *Diaries and Correspondence of the Right Hon. George Rose*, ed. Rev. L. Vernon-Harcourt, 1860, 2 vols; I, 223.

29. Hallam Moorhouse : 241.

30. Morrison MS., 867.

31. Foley : 67.

32. Nicolas : VII, 32.

33. Pellew : 37.

34. *Private Correspondence of Lord G. Leveson-Gower*, ed. Castalia, Countess Granville, 1916, II, 112.

35. Morrison MS., 837.

36. Wellington's two records of this interview are to be found in *Correspondence and Diaries of W. Croker*, II, 233, and a review of Barrow's *Life of Earl Howe* in *The Edinburgh Review*, 1838, 331 *et seq.*

37. Scott : 180. Beatty (95–9) copied the complete entries for Sept. 14 to Oct. 21 from this small volume, the only one of the set of fifteen not to be found in the " Nelson Papers " or " Bridport Papers ", B.M. Add. MS. 34,992, " Nelson Papers ", XCI, however, contains a MS. copy. The original is in Somerset House.

CHAPTER XIX

TRAFALGAR

1. Llangattock MS., printed by Pettigrew (II, 495), with opening words altered.

2. Clarke and M'Arthur : III, 120.

3. Rose : I, 255, 268.

4. Pettigrew : II, 498.

5. *Ibid.* : 500.

6. *Nelson Letters*, II, 96.

7. Llangattock MS. (printed Pettigrew : II, 501).

8. Fremantle : III, 210–11.

9. Pettigrew (II, 506) prints the whole of this letter, mutilated in the *Nelson Letters* (II, 101).

10. *Naval Chronicle*, XV, 37.

11. Nicolas : VII, 89–92.

12. Morrison MS., 843.

13. Nicolas : VII, 119, 120.

14. Fremantle : III, 210 ; Nicolas : VII, 71 ; Codrington : I, 52.

15. This letter is now an exhibit at the British Museum, having been purchased in 1852 for £20 from the descendants of Alderman Smith, to whom it had passed from Lady Hamilton. A contemporary copy is in the Morrison MS., 847.

16. In 1803 Sir Hume Popham produced his *Telegraphic Marine Vocabulary*, which enabled an Admiral to signal communications which were not in the Signal Book proper, provided that he hoisted a preliminary signal known as " the Telegraph Flag ". Nelson's famous signal " England expects . . ." was made in twelve hoists, by the Popham system.

17. Nicolas : VII, 131.

18. *Ibid.* : 71.

19. Scott: 221.
20. Collingwood: 124.
21. Both Collingwood and Clavell were wounded at Trafalgar, Collingwood in the leg.
22. Beatty: 137; Nicolas: VII, 349–50. The coat is exhibited at the National Maritime Museum.
23. James gives 8.30 for this signal, but Nelson's Private Diary shows that he had begun to observe the result at 7.
24. Add. MS. 34,959, "Nelson Papers", LVIII, ff. 355–7. Nelson executed two testamentary deeds, one for England, and one for Sicily. The second was preserved at the Castello Maniàce and was brought home by a later Duke of Brontë. It is now in the National Maritime Museum.
25. Morrison MS., 848, and Add. MS. 34,992, "Nelson Papers", XCI, f. 16, present copies of this document.
26. *The Story of H.M.S. "Victory"*, Sir G. Callender, 1929, pp. 100–1.
27. Add. MS. 34,990, "Nelson Papers", LXXXIX, f. 16 (copy of the original in the fifteenth memorandum book, *see* note 19, Chap. XVII).
28. Beatty: 26.
29. Collingwood: 163; Beatty: 34.
30. Scott: 185–91.
31. Beatty: 36–51.
32. He may have been wearing more than one, as Hardy speaks of returning "lockets". Pettigrew: II, 550.
33. The original is at the National Maritime Museum, Greenwich. Contemporary "keys" to the crowd picture exist.
34. In May 1912 the Admiralty appointed a Commission to inquire into the tactics of Trafalgar. Its report was published in 1913 (Blue Book Cd. 7120) with a bibliography on p. v. Navy Records Society, XVIII (ed. Admiral T. Sturges-Jackson), prints the logs of all the ships engaged at Trafalgar, and private letters from several officers. *See also* Appendix B, Vol. III, *Sea Kings of Britain*, Sir G. Callender; *The Campaign of Trafalgar* (1910), Sir J. S. Corbett, Chapters 23 and 24; *The Year of Trafalgar*, Sir H. Newbolt (1905), Chapters 5–8; *Fighting Instructions, Nelson's Tactical Memoranda*, Sir J. S. Corbett, Navy Records Society, XXLX, 280–320; *Journal of the Royal United Service Institution*, Vol. LXXXII, 528, Nov. 1937 (article by Rear-Admiral A. H. Taylor); and *The Trafalgar Roll*, Col. R. H. Mackenzie, 1913.
35. A large oil-painting was made from Lieut. Paul Harris Nicolas's sketch by W. J. Huggins, marine painter to William IV.
36. *The Diaries and Correspondence of the First Earl of Malmesbury*, four vols., 1844, IV, 354.
37. Morrison MS., 849.

CHAPTER XX
AFTERWARDS

1. Malmesbury: IV, 311.
2. Rose: I, 242.
3. Lloyd's possesses a collection of presentation Nelson plate and

letters, and has published a catalogue, *The Nelson Collection at Lloyd's,* ed. W. R. Dawson, 1932.

4. Morrison MS., 854.
5. Rose : I, 241.
6. Codrington : I, 186.
7. Morrison MS., 860.
8. Matcham : 245–8; Leveson Gower : II, 154; Codrington : I, 97; *Naval Chronicle, London Gazette,* and newspapers under date. A series of aquatints of sketches of Nelson's funeral, by A. Pugin, C. Turner, G. Cruikshank, W. M. Craig, etc., and many contemporary publications, illustrate the ceremony in detail.
9. *Nelson's Hardy and his Wife,* J. Gore, 1935, 202, 149.
10. Keate : 284.
11. Morrison MS., 957.
12. Gamlen : II, 272.
13. *Historic Houses in Bath,* R. E. Peach, 1883, 137.
14. Hotham: II, 217.
15. Morrison MS., 949.
16. *Ibid.* : 1060.
17. Pettigrew's note (II, 636) that Mr. Cadogan was " a relative of my friend Mr. Rothery " is the only clue as to this gentleman's identity. It has been suggested that he was a connection of Lady Hamilton's mother, but Lady Hamilton, in her Will (Morrison MS., 959), calls her mother "Mary Doggin, or Cadogan ".
18. Morrison MS., 939, 902, 905, 936, 915, 928, 977.
19. MS. letters of Horatia Nelson-Ward to Sir H. Nicolas, Nelson-Ward MS., National Maritime Museum. E. S. P. Haynes, Esq., great-grandson of Sir H. Nicolas, published in 1908, in *Early Victorian and other Papers,* an article reprinted from *The Cornhill Magazine,* " Lady Hamilton and Horatia ", based upon the original correspondence in his possession.
20. Morrison MS., 931.
21. Matcham : 255, 266; Morrison MS., 881.
22. Morrison MS., 1046.
23. Nicolas : VII, 310; Pettigrew : II, 624.
24. The document authorising Horatia to bear the name of Nelson is to be found in the Morrison MS. 894. *See also* Add. MSS. 34,989, " Nelson Papers ", LXXXVIII, ff. 53–7, and 34,992, XCI, ff. 103–48; Egerton MS. 2240, f. 57; Pettigrew : II, 626; Rose : I, 250–73; Matcham : 282; Gamlin : II, 248.
25. Scott : 203.
26. Farington : V, 4, 7, and 8.
27. Morrison MS., 943.
28. *Ibid.* : 951.
29. Scott : 223.
30. Her cousin, Ann Connor, spread stories that she was an un-acknowledged daughter of Lady Hamilton. Money gifts to an uncle, William Kidd, who declared that he had " not been brought up to work ", had to be sent to a neighbour, who would see that they were doled out for meat, clothing and lodging, not taken straight to the ale-house (Morrison : 930).

31. The National Maritime Museum possesses a series of MS. letters from Lady Hamilton to Alexander Davison, dating from 1806 to 1814. Davison, who served as Treasurer of the Ordnance from 1806 to 1807, was prosecuted in the Court of King's Bench on Dec. 7, 1808, upon a charge " that having been employed by government as an agent on commission and receiving 2½ per cent as the price of his skill and knowledge, he had, by means of false vouchers and receipts, received as an agent for government a commission on the amount of goods, which he himself had supplied as a merchant from his own warehouse ". Many persons of distinction gave evidence as to Davison's probity and public spirit, but he was found guilty, and having paid into the Exchequer all the commission received by him, amounting to £8883 13s. 1d., was ordered further to be imprisoned in Newgate for twenty-one months (*Annual Register*, 1807, 100 *et seq.*, and 1808, 133–5; *Parl. Papers, Accts. and Papers*, 1806–7, 201–13, King's Bench, Trin. Term, 48 Geo. III, Crown Roll, 192).

In the grounds of Swarland Hall, visible from the Morpeth–Alnwick road, a Nelson Column, erected " not as a record of his public services (which is the duty of his Country), but as a commemoration of private friendship", still testifies characteristically to Davison's admiration for Nelson. The Nelson Museum, Monmouth (Llangattock Collection), includes a curious piece of mourning plate, representing Nelson's sarcophagus, (with a pyramidal roof, formed of the eighty-four guineas found in Nelson's purse after Trafalgar), and several pieces of flamboyant table silver, with inscriptions that they were gifts to the Admiral from " his affectionate A.D.". Davison died in Regency Square, Brighton, in December 1829, in his eightieth year. Major-General Hugh and Lieutenant-Colonel Sir William Davison supplied Sir Harris Nicolas with many letters from Nelson to their father.

32. Scott : 225.

33. Nicolas : VII, 388.

34. Pryse Lockhart Gordon : II, 388–90.

35. Morrison MS., 1021, 1053.

36. *Lady Hamilton and Lord Nelson*, J. C. Jeaffreson, 1888, 312. This letter failed to reach the addressee. The cover is marked " Gone away ", " Not known ".

37. Matcham : 277.

38. Morrison MS., 1055; Rose : I, 271; *Sotheby's Catalogue*, 8, 7, 1905; Additional MS. 34,992, f. 199; MS. correspondence of Lady Hamilton with Alexander Davison, National Maritime Museum.

39. Nelson-Ward MS., National Maritime Museum; *Blackwood's Magazine*, May 1888, 648 (letters of Mrs. Nelson-Ward to Mr. J. Paget, 1874). Mrs. Nelson-Ward disposes of the legend repeated by Pettigrew (II, 635) that Lady Hamilton was found starving by a Mrs. Hunter and buried in a deal box.

40. Gamlin : II, 244.

41. Matcham : 290.

42. Nelson-Ward MS., National Maritime Museum; Nicolas : VII, 369–96; Pettigrew : II, 638–56. It should be noted that when Commander Jeaffreson published, in 1888, his " Lady Hamilton and Lord Nelson, an historical biography based on letters and other documents in the possession

of Alfred Morrison, Esq., of Fonthill ", he had seen only the first collection of letters, bought by Mr. Morrison from Mr. Finch-Hatton's executors, not the second collection, used by Pettigrew; and that other authors, when speaking of having examined the Morrison MS., are referring to the first collection, not the second, bought in July 1887.

43. Jagger : 23.
44. Morrison MS., 398; *The Times*, 22.3.1815.
45. *See ante*, note 12, Chapter XV.

INDEX

3 A